THE O:

STRA͏ ͏E.S

ONE WEEK LOAN

N ͏ͰMENT

THE OXFORD HANDBOOK OF

STRATEGIC SALES AND SALES MANAGEMENT

Edited by

DAVID W. CRAVENS,
KENNETH LE MEUNIER-FITZHUGH,
and
NIGEL F. PIERCY

OXFORD
UNIVERSITY PRESS

OXFORD
UNIVERSITY PRESS

Great Clarendon Street, Oxford OX2 6DP

Oxford University Press is a department of the University of Oxford.
It furthers the University's objective of excellence in research, scholarship,
and education by publishing worldwide in

Oxford New York

Auckland Cape Town Dar es Salaam Hong Kong Karachi
Kuala Lumpur Madrid Melbourne Mexico City Nairobi
New Delhi Shanghai Taipei Toronto

With offices in

Argentina Austria Brazil Chile Czech Republic France Greece
Guatemala Hungary Italy Japan Poland Portugal Singapore
South Korea Switzerland Thailand Turkey Ukraine Vietnam

Oxford is a registered trade mark of Oxford University Press
in the UK and in certain other countries

Published in the United States
by Oxford University Press Inc., New York

© Oxford University Press 2011

The moral rights of the authors have been asserted
Database right Oxford University Press (maker)

First published 2011
First published in paperback in 2012

British Library Cataloguing in Publication Data

Data available

Library of Congress Cataloging in Publication Data

Data available

Typeset by SPI Publisher Services, Pondicherry, India
Printed in Great Britain
on acid-free paper by

Ashford Colour Press Ltd, Gosport, Hampshire

ISBN 978–0–19–956945–8
978–0–19–966461–0

1 3 5 7 9 10 8 6 4 2

Contents

PART I SALES STRATEGY AND ENVIRONMENT

PART II SALES MANAGEMENT

PART III THE SALES FORCE AND THE CUSTOMER

PART IV THE ORGANIZATION AND SALES RELATIONSHIPS

List of Figures

LIST OF TABLES

List of Contributors

Artur Baldauf, Doctor in Business Administration, University of Economics and Business Administration of Vienna, is a Professor of Management and Chair of the Management Department at the University of Bern, Switzerland. Before his appointment in Bern he was Associate Professor of Marketing at the University of Vienna. He has also been a Visiting Marketing Professor at Texas Christian University, USA, University of Economics and Business Administration of Vienna, Austria, and Bocconi University, Italy. He researches strategic management and sales force management, focusing on sales management control and effectiveness issues. His research has been published in international and national journals. In 2005 he was awarded the James M. Comer prize for the best contribution to selling and sales management theory/methodology of the *Journal of Personal Selling and Sales Management.*

Steven P. Brown is Bauer Professor of Marketing at the C. T. Bauer College of Business, University of Houston. His research interests focus on identifying ways of building and sustaining competitive advantage through effective sales and service organizations. His research has investigated how organizational climate and managerial leadership motivate and facilitate the efforts of front-line sales and service personnel, and how these, in turn, impact customer satisfaction and organizational performance. Other research interests include customer-perceived service quality and satisfaction, buyer-seller relationships, consumer information processing and decision-making, and methods of meta-analysis. His research has been published in leading marketing and psychology journals, such as the *Journal of Marketing, Journal of Marketing Research, Journal of Consumer Research, Psychological Bulletin, Journal of Applied Psychology,* and *Journal of the Academy of Marketing Science.* He serves on the editorial review boards of the *Journal of Marketing, Journal of Retailing, Journal of Service Research,* and *Journal of Personal Selling and Sales Management.*

Noel Capon is the R. C. Kopf Professor of International Marketing and past Chair of the Marketing Division, Columbia Business School. He received Ph.Ds from University College, London University, and Columbia University. Professor Capon also taught at UCLA, Harvard Business School, INSEAD, HKUST (Hong Kong), and CEIBS (Shanghai). He is Founder and Director of executive programs in Managing Strategic Accounts, Strategic Pricing, Advanced Marketing Management, and the Global Account Manager Certification Program; he also designs, directs, and teaches custom programs for major corporations globally. He has published over 80 refereed articles and book chapters, and 20 books, most recently *Managing Global Accounts, The Marketing Mavens, The Virgin Marketer* (marketing planning workbook), and three textbooks—*Managing Marketing in the 21st Century* (US, European, and Russian editions) and *Capon's Marketing Framework* (US and European editions), and *Marketing for China's Managers; Current and Future*.

Larry B. Chonko, Ph.D, is the Thomas McMahon Professor in Business Ethics at the University of Texas at Arlington. He is a recipient of the Southwestern Business Dean's Association Innovative Achievement Award and the American Marketing Association Sales Interest Group, Lifetime Achievement Award. His scholarly work has appeared in a variety of journals, nine of which have received "best paper" recognition, one nominated for "Best Sales Papers" of the 20th century and one selected as having the most impact on the discipline by the *Journal of Business Research*. Professor Chonko has authored or co-authored 15 books and served as Editor of the *Journal of Personal Selling and Sales Management*

David W. Cravens is Emeritus Professor of Marketing in the Neeley School of Business at Texas Christian University. He previously held the Eunice and James L. West Chair of American Enterprise Studies and was Professor of Marketing. Formerly, he was the Alcoa Foundation Professor at the University of Tennessee, where he chaired the Department of Marketing and Transportation and the Management Science Program. He has a Doctorate in Business Administration and MBA from Indiana University. He holds a Bachelor of Science in Civil Engineering from Massachusetts Institute of Technology. Before becoming an educator, he held various industry and government management positions. He is internationally recognized for his research on marketing strategy and sales management, and has contributed over 150 articles and 25 books. He is former editor of the *Journal of the Academy of Marketing Science*. He has held various positions in American Marketing Association and the Academy of Marketing Science.

William L. Cron is the J. Vaughn & Evelyn H. Wilson Professor of Marketing and Senior Associate Dean for Graduate Programs and Research at the M. J. Neeley School of Business, Texas Christian University, Fort Worth, Texas, USA. Professor Cron has published over 80 marketing and sales management articles and manuscripts. He has served as an adviser to the boards of numerous medical supply distributors in the US and currently sits on the board of Midmark Corporation. He also serves on the boards of the Education Foundation of the Health Industry Distributors Association and the American Marketing Association Foundation.

Thomas E. DeCarlo is the Ben S. Weil Endowed Chair of Industrial Distribution and Professor of Marketing and Industrial Distribution at the University of Alabama at Birmingham. His primary research interests deal with strategic issues in sales force management, customer relationship management, and marketing communications. Dr DeCarlo's research has been published in journals such as the *Journal of Marketing, Journal of Consumer Psychology, Journal of Personal Selling & Sales Management, Journal of International Business Studies, Journal of Service Research*, and *Industrial Marketing Management*. He is co-author of *Sales Management*, a top-selling sales management textbook. Dr. DeCarlo has had professional relationships with a number of Fortune 500 organizations in areas of market analysis and customer segmentation, sales force management, brand management, and new product development. He earned his Ph.D from the University of Georgia.

Andrea L. Dixon, Ph.D, Indiana University, is the Holloway Endowed Professor in Marketing and Executive Director, Center for Professional Selling and Keller Research Center at Baylor University. She has published in the *Journal of Marketing, Harvard Business Review, Organizational Science, Journal of the Academy of Marketing Science, Leadership Quarterly, Journal of Personal Selling and Sales Management*, and others. In 2002, her research in the *Journal of Marketing* was the award-winning research in sales. Previously UC's Executive Director, MS-Marketing, she developed and institutionalized an integrated Capstone experience. She has taught graduate and undergraduate courses resulting in several teaching awards (Academy of Marketing Science, Irwin Publishing, UC's Dornoff Teaching Fellow, and IU's Distinguished MBA Professor). Before her faculty appointment, she was GAMA International's Senior Director of Marketing. She is a member of Duke University's Global Learning Resource Network.

Kenneth R. Evans, Ph.D, is the Dean of the Price College of Business and Fred E. Brown Chair at the University of Oklahoma. Previously he served on the faculties of the University of Missouri and Arizona State University, where he was the marketing department chair, associate dean of both undergraduate and graduate studies, acting dean and chairperson of the campus-wide Council on International Initiatives. Dr Evans is a member of the editorial review boards for a variety of top class journals. He received his Ph.D from the University of Colorado. His research and teaching interests are in the areas of marketing management, sales/sales management, marketing theory, and services marketing. He has published in the *Journal of Marketing, Journal of the Academy of Marketing Science, Journal of Personal Selling and Sales Management, Journal of Business Research, Industrial Marketing Management*, and the *Journal of Advertising*, and has published over 100 articles, reviews, and chapters over his career.

Karen Flaherty is Associate Professor of Marketing at Oklahoma State University. She earned a Ph.D in Marketing from the University of Massachusetts at Amherst in 2000. Her research interests include the study of sales force leadership, control systems, motivation, and performance. Her work has been published in journals such as the *Journal of the Academy of Marketing Science, Journal of Retailing, Journal* *of Business Research, Journal of Personal Selling and Sales Management,* and *Industrial Marketing Management.* She serves on the editorial board of the *Journal of Marketing Theory and Practice* and the abstract review board of the *Journal of Personal Selling and Sales Management.*

Samuel Grossenbacher (Doctor in Business Administration, University of Bern) is a Marketing Vice President at AXA Winterthur. Before working in the insurance industry, he was a research assistant at the Department of Management at the University of Bern. He conducts research in the fields of sales force management and managerial cognition.

Gary K. Hunter is Assistant Professor of Marketing, the Weatherhead School of Management at Case Western Reserve University in Cleveland, Ohio. He earned a BS from West Point, an MBA from the University of Tennessee, and a Ph.D from the University of North Carolina at Chapel Hill. He has over 10 years of management experience with Procter & Gamble, PepsiCo, and the US Army. His research focuses on sales technology, customer relationship management, and buyer-seller relationships. His publications include award-winning articles in the *Journal of Marketing,* the *International Journal of Research in Marketing,* and the *Journal of Personal Selling and Sales Management.*

Thomas N. Ingram (Ph.D, Georgia State University) is Professor of Marketing and the FirstBank Professor of Business Administration at Colorado State University. Professor Ingram worked for Exxon and Mobil in sales, product management, and sales management prior to entering academia. He is the former editor of the *Journal of Personal Selling and Sales Management.* His sales research has appeared in the *Journal of Marketing, Journal of Marketing Research, Journal of Personal Selling and Sales Management,* and the *Journal of the Academy of Marketing Science,* among others.

Mark W. Johnston is the Alan and Sandra Gerry Professor of Marketing and Ethics at the Roy E. Crummer Graduate School of Business, Rollins College. He is co-author of *Sales Force Management,* 11th edn, *Contemporary Selling: Building Relationships, Creating Value,* 4th edn, *Marketing Management,* and *Essentials of Marketing Management.* His book *Sales Force Management* has been translated into Spanish, Russian, and Chinese. His research has resulted in over 50 articles in professional journals such as *Journal of Marketing Research, Journal of Applied Psychology,* and *Journal of Personal Selling and Sales Management,* and he was cited by the *Journal of Business Research* as one of the most important researchers in marketing. He has conducted seminars and consulted with companies around the world on a variety of topics including sales force motivation and improving sales performance.

Wesley J. Johnston is the CBIM Round Table Professor of Marketing and Director of the Center for Business and Industrial Marketing in the Robinson College of

Business at Georgia State University. His research interests include sales force management, buyer-seller relationships, and sales force automation, and he has published in the *Journal of Marketing, Journal of Consumer Research,* and *Decision Science.* He is currently the Editor of the *Journal of Business and Industrial Marketing.* His latest book is entitled *Managing Salespeople: A Relationship Approach.* He has taught in doctoral programs in the UK, Australia, Finland, Jamaica, and the US. He holds a BA, MBA, and Ph.D from the University of Pittsburgh and an honorary degree in Economics from Oulu University, Finland.

Eli Jones is the Dean of the Sam M. Walton College of Business, where he also holds the Sam M. Walton Leadership Chair in Business. Previously, he served as Dean of the E. J. Ourso College of Business and Ourso Distinguished Professor of Business at Louisiana State University. He was on the faculty at the University of Houston from 1997 to 2008 and received a B.S. in journalism, an M.B.A., and his Ph.D, all from Texas A&M University. Before becoming a professor, he worked for three Fortune 100 companies. His research and teaching interests are in marketing strategy, particularly sales and sales management. He has published in the *Journal of Marketing, Management Science, Journal of the Academy of Marketing Science, Journal of Applied Psychology,* and the *Journal of Personal Selling & Sales Management,* among others. Additionally, he has co-authored several books, and he serves on two editorial review boards, a corporate board, and numerous charitable boards.

Raymond W. (Buddy) LaForge is the Brown-Forman Professor of Marketing at the University of Louisville. His research is published in many journals, including the *Journal of Marketing, Journal of Marketing Research, Journal of the Academy of Marketing Science,* and *Journal of Personal Selling and Sales Management.* He has co-authored a number of books including *Sales Management: Analysis and Decision-Making* (7th edn), *Professional Selling: A Trust-Based Approach* (5th edn), and *Strategic Sales Leadership: BREAKthrough Thinking for BREAKthrough Results.* He has received a number of awards such as the Outstanding Sales Scholar Award, Distinguished Scholar Award, and the Distinguished Sales Educator Award.

Nikala Lane is Associate Professor in Marketing and Strategy at Warwick Business School, University of Warwick, and was previously Senior Research Associate at Cardiff Business School. She has published articles in major journals such as the *British Journal of Management, Journal of Management Studies, Journal of Business Research, Journal of Personal Selling and Sales Management,* the *Journal of Strategic Marketing,* and *Journal of the Academy of Marketing Science.* She has particular interests in strategic customer management issues, and recently co-authored a book on this subject with Nigel Piercy.

Nick Lee (Ph.D) is Professor of Marketing and Organizational Research at Aston Business School. His research interests include sales management, social psychology, research methodology, and ethics. He is the Co-Editor of the *European Journal* *of Marketing*, and serves on the editorial board or review panel of several other journals. His research has won multiple awards, and he is a regular speaker at international conferences on sales and methodological issues. Dr Lee lectures in marketing science and sales management at postgraduate and doctoral level. His work has appeared or is forthcoming in journals such as the *Journal of the Academy of Marketing Science, Journal of Business Ethics, Industrial Marketing Management, European Journal of Marketing, American Journal of Bioethics*, and the *International Journal of Psychophysiology*. His first book, *Doing Business Research*, was published by Sage in 2008.

Thomas W. Leigh (DBA, Indiana University) is Emily H. and Charles M. Tanner, Jr. Chair of Sales Management at the University of Georgia. He has served as: President of the AMA Academic Council and the Sales SIG; Visiting Professor at Ogilvy & Mather (NY); Board Chairman of the ARC East Georgia Chapter; and Director of the Coca Cola Center for Marketing Studies (1995–2001). Dr Leigh's research appears in the *Journal of Marketing Research, Journal of Marketing, Journal of Consumer Research, Journal of Applied Psychology, Journal of Advertising, Journal of Advertising Research, Journal of Personal Selling and Sales Management*, and *Journal of the Academy of Marketing Science*. He received the Lifetime Achievement Award from the AMA Sales Special Interest Group in 2006. His executive education experience includes roles for UGA, Penn State, Northwestern and Georgia State University, and Rollins College, as well as for Beatrice Foods, Marriott, CISCO, CIGNA, and Digital Equipment.

Kenneth Le Meunier-FitzHugh is a Senior Lecturer in Marketing at the University of East Anglia, UK, and obtained a Ph.D in Marketing and Strategic Management from Warwick Business School, University of Warwick. Before taking up his current post he was Lecturer in Marketing and Sales Management at Cranfield University. His research interests focus on exploring the interface between sales and marketing. He has a number of publications in academic journals including the *Industrial Marketing Management, European Journal of Marketing*, and *Journal of Marketing Management*, and he was awarded the Marvin Jolson award for the best contribution to sales management practice by the *Journal of Personal Selling and Sales Management* 2008. Prior to undertaking an academic career, he spent 20 years working in sales and marketing at senior levels for a range of organizations.

Sally E. Lorimer is a consultant and business writer. She was previously a principal at ZS Associates, where she consulted with numerous companies on sales force effectiveness. She holds a Master of Management degree from the Kellogg School of Management at Northwestern University. She is the co-author of four books on sales force management, including *Building a Winning Sales Management Team* (2012) *Building a Winning Sales Force* (2009), and *Sales Force Design for Strategic Advantage* (2004).

Graham R. Massey is a Senior Lecturer in Marketing at the University of Technology, Sydney, and a member of the UTS Centre for Management and Organization Studies. Graham was awarded his Ph.D in Marketing by the University of New South Wales, and has research interests in cross-functional working relationships between peer managers. He has worked in various sales and marketing roles in industry, in both consumer and business markets. In those roles he has been responsible for sales management and business development, new product development, advertising and promotion, and marketing research. His work has been published in various journals including the *European Journal of Marketing, Industrial Marketing Management, Journal of Business and Industrial Marketing*, and the *Journal of Product and Brand Management*. Graham and his co-author, Philip Dawes, were awarded Outstanding Paper of 2005 in the *European Journal of Marketing*, for "Antecedents of Conflict in Marketing's Cross-Functional Relationship with Sales."

C. Fred Miao is an Assistant Professor of Marketing at Clarkson University. Dr Miao received his Ph.D degree from University of Missouri-Columbia in Business Administration with an emphasis on marketing. Prior to his doctorate education, he worked for General Motors in production purchasing, and served as a consultant for a materials management company. His research interest includes sales management, marketing channels, and marketing strategy. His work has appeared the in the *Journal of the Academy of Marketing Science, Journal of Business Research, Journal of Personal Selling and Sales Management*, and *Industrial Marketing Management*.

Linda D. Peters is an Associate Professor in Marketing at Nottingham University Business School, and is currently conducting research in the areas of business network formation and management, and collective learning in networks. She is particularly interested in how networks learn, how learning relates to value creation, and issues regarding the use of electronic communications media by organizational teams. Her interests extend to relationship and internal marketing issues, organizational learning and knowledge management, value creation and SD logic, and organizational team working and communications. She received her doctorate from the University of East Anglia in 2002, has an MBA from Strathclyde Graduate Business School (1994), and is a Chartered Marketer. Her industrial experience includes work in the fields of market research and database management.

Nigel F. Piercy is Professor of Marketing and Strategy, and Associate Dean at Warwick Business School, University of Warwick. He holds a Ph.D from the University of Wales and a higher doctorate (D.Litt.) from Heriot-Watt University, Edinburgh. His current research interests focus on strategic sales and account management. His work has been published in many journals including the *Journal of Marketing, Journal of International Marketing*, and the *Journal of the Academy of*

Marketing Science. His most recent books are *Strategic Customer Management: Strategizing the Sales Organization* (with Nikala Lane, 2009), *Market-Led Strategic Change: Transforming the Process of Going to Market,* 4th edn (2009), and *Strategic Marketing,* 9th edn (with David W. Cravens, 2009).

Manoshi Samaraweera is an Assistant Professor of Marketing in the College of Business at University of Central Oklahoma. She obtained her Ph.D. in Marketing from the University of Houston. Her key research focus is in Sales and Sales force Management.

Charles H. Schwepker, Jr. (Ph.D, University of Memphis) is the Mike and Patti Davidson Distinguished Marketing Professor at the University of Central Missouri. He has experience in wholesale and retail sales, and conducts research in sales management and personal selling. His articles have appeared in the *Journal of the Academy of Marketing Science, Journal of Business Research, Journal of Public Policy and Marketing,* and *Journal of Personal Selling & Sales Management,* among others. Charlie has received both teaching and research awards. He is a member of six editorial review boards and has won several awards for outstanding reviewer. He is a co-author of *Sales Management: Analysis and Decision-Making,* 8th edn. (2012), *Professional Selling: A Trust-Based Approach,* 4th edn. (2008), and *SELL,* 3rd edn. (2013).

Prabhakant Sinha is a founder and co-chairman of ZS Associates, a global leader in sales and marketing consulting, outsourcing, software, and technology. He received his Ph.D from the University of Massachusetts and a B.Tech. from IIT Kharagpur. He teaches in executive education programs on sales force effectiveness at the Indian School of Business and the Gordon Institute of Business Science. He is the co-author of five books on sales force management, including *Building a Winning Sales Management Team* (2012), *Building a Winning Sales Force* (2009), and *The Complete Guide to Sales Force Incentive Compensation* (2006).

Harish Sujan is the Freeman Professor of Business at the Freeman School of Management at Tulane University, USA. He obtained his PhD from UCLA. His research has been in the area of sales management and consumer research. Within sales management his primary focus has been on how motivation can enhance selling smarter (intelligence). A 1986 paper with Bart Weitz and Mita Sujan was listed in the top ten papers in sales in the twentieth century. A 1994 paper on the effect of learning goals on working smarter has received considerable cites. The *Journal of Personal Selling and Sales Management* has recognized him on two occasions: by awarding him the best paper of the year in 1999 and the best reviewer of the year in 2012. His current work includes a study of doctors as salespeople— what they can say to improve their patients' self-care.

William Zahn is an Assistant Professor of Marketing at St. Edward's University's School of Management at Business. He received his Ph.D from the University of Houston. His primary research interests are sales force management and motivation. After receiving his BA in marketing from the University of Texas at Austin, he counselled the Texas Department of Health and Human Services on marketing Medicaid Services. He also served as a software design consultant for multiple companies in the oil and gas industry.

Andris A. Zoltners holds the Nemmers Professorship in Marketing at the Kellogg School of Management at Northwestern University. He received his Ph.D from Carnegie-Mellon University. He is a founder and co-chairman of ZS Associates, a global leader in sales and marketing consulting, outsourcing, software, and technology. For over 30 years he has served the business community as a professor, consultant, and speaker. He is the co-author of five books on sales force management, including *Building a Winning Sales Management Team* (2012), *Building a Winning Sales Force* (2009), and *The Complete Guide to Accelerating Sales Force Performance* (2001).

CHAPTER 1

OVERVIEW OF STRATEGIC SALES AND SALES MANAGEMENT

DAVID W. CRAVENS

KENNETH LE MEUNIER-FITZHUGH

NIGEL F. PIERCY

1.1 INTRODUCTION

The Oxford Handbook of Strategic Sales and Sales Management is a compendium of chapters by prominent academics addressing some of the most important issues in the field of sales management and sales strategy. It is produced in four parts. The contributors are practicing academics, mostly currently researching in the area in which they have written their chapters for the Handbook. The book is part of an important series of Handbooks that Oxford University Press is developing across the social sciences and humanities, including several in business and management. These Handbooks address key topics in their field and identify the evolution of debates and research on these topics. However, this is the first time that the Handbook series has addressed any marketing issues, and beginning with the critical element of sales and sales practices is appropriate, as one of the earliest business texts to gain popular appeal was on sales, Dale Carnegie's *How to Win Friends and Influence People* (1936).

The Oxford Handbook of Strategic Sales and Sales Management is targeted at academics, researchers, and graduate students, for whom it should be a useful resource, sitting between the specialist journal article or monograph and the extensive range of established textbooks in the field. It is intended to provide the graduate student, researcher, or lecturer with a well-informed and authoritative guide to the subject and to the current debates taking place in the field of sales management, and is a blend of mature thinking and cutting-edge speculation. Teachers of sales management and strategy will find much of the traditional material for their presentations contained in the Handbook, as well as illustrations of how to introduce the newer issues of debate in their teaching.

Operating in the very competitive and rapidly changing global business environment requires creating and delivering superior customer value. Many companies are pursuing strategic transformations to compete effectively in a challenging business environment. The success of these efforts is likely to require significant transformations within a firm's sales organization. Important changes may include (Piercy and Lane 2005):

- involvement in strategic decision making at the corporate and business strategy levels;
- market sensing and analysis;
- building cross-functional collaborative relationships;
- serving as the customer's advocate inside the organization.

Sales organizations need to strategically align their operations with the firm's business and marketing strategies to create a more customer-focused sales organization (Sheth and Sharma 2008). The number of people in sales and sales-related jobs totaled over 16 million in the United States in 2008, according to the U.S. Bureau of Labor Statistics estimates. Global sales jobs totals are far greater. The numbers of staff and the expenditure involved in the sales function highlight its importance and priority in the organization.

The *Handbook of Strategic Sales and Sales Management* provides an in-depth examination of sales organization strategy, sales management processes, the sales force and the customer, and organizational relationships. The interrelationships of these topics are shown in Figure 1.1. The various chapters offer an important state-of-the-art perspective concerning sales management and sales strategy. The chapter authors are recognized experts on the various topics in the Handbook. A brief overview of the chapters in each of the four parts follows.

Fig. 1.1. Sales Strategy and Management Processes

1.2 SALES STRATEGY AND ENVIRONMENT

Sales force strategy "consists of a set of strategic decisions that determine to whom the sales force will sell and the role of the sales force in creating customer value which is consistent with the overall strategy of the firm and/or business unit" (Cron and Cravens 2010: 21). Importantly, sales force strategy is linked to business units and marketing strategies in an interconnected set of relationships. In this section we overview several important aspects of sales force strategy which are examined in Part I of the Handbook. Also considered are the dynamic sales environment and a global perspective concerning selling and sales management.

1.2.1 The Evolution of the Strategic Sales Organization

An important change which has occurred during the last decade in many sales organizations is a shift away from a tactical focus to a strategic emphasis. Chapter 2 examines these imperatives and their implications. **Nigel F. Piercy and Nikala Lane** detail how sales organizations are becoming more involved in business and marketing strategies, and conclude that the emergence of the strategic sales organization can be explained by several factors: changing customer relationship requirements; the changing sales task; and, the importance of strategic sales capabilities to cope with complexity, growing customer sophistication, commoditization pressures, and the need for radically different selling approaches. The characteristics of the strategic sales organization are discussed in terms of the factors significant in developing a new sales domain and those exercising a broader shaping influence on how a strategic sales organization will function. The bottom line is that sales organizations are changing rapidly, and transformations are expected to continue in the future. Strategic transformation impacts salespeople and managers, requiring training and career development initiatives to meet new role expectations. These new challenges will require considerable thought about the capabilities and competencies required by sales executives.

1.2.2 Strategic Leadership in Sales

Chapter 3 examines the important relationship between the role of the salesperson and the role of sales managers. **Karen Flaherty** considers how these roles vary across organizations, noting a distinct trend toward the salesperson's role including involvement in shaping strategy. The result is that the salesperson's job has changed to meet new role expectations. Salesperson strategic roles can be characterized as competence deployment, competence modification, and competence definition. These roles call for different capabilities and perspectives concerning the sales force. Successful strategic sales leadership requires the utilization of management perspectives and processes that correspond best with the current environment, required salesperson roles, and the strategic direction of the organization. An integrative framework for sales leadership is proposed. Matching the salesperson's role in the sales organization with the appropriate leadership approach is critically important in delivering superior customer value and organizational performance. The framework examines three alternative leadership modes: command, coach, and sponsor.

1.2.3 Achieving Sales Organization Effectiveness

David W. Cravens writes with considerable authority on the sales organization and how sales is an important contributor to achieving business and marketing objectives. The organization's effectiveness can be measured based on sales, market position, customer satisfaction, and profits, relative to competition and internal objectives. Effectiveness is a summary assessment of the sales organization's outcomes, and may be determined for the entire organization or for smaller units such as regions and districts. Sales unit effectiveness is a composite assessment of the unit's performance. Importantly, effectiveness and salesperson performance are different although closely related constructs. The salesperson contributes to unit effectiveness along with other determinants including the sales manager, business competencies, and the market and competitive environment (Walker, Churchill, and Ford 1979).

In Chapter 4, a conceptual framework for analysis and decision-making concerning sales organization effectiveness is proposed and examined. Important determinants of effectiveness are discussed including sales management control, salesperson performance, and sales unit design. Sales management is a core determinant of effectiveness, including management processes, design of the organization, and manager performance. Each salesperson also contributes to effectiveness. Also considered are research findings concerning sales personnel gender.

1.2.4 The Changing Sales Environment

Nick Lee reviews the rapidly changing business environment, and highlights it as an important and challenging influence on sales organizations. Chapter 5 examines the dynamic environment impacting the sales organization. A core characteristic of the changing sales environment is its complexity. Dimensions of the environment include globalization, changes in channel delivery and information provision, customer co-production and de-massification of the marketplace, hyper-competition and buyer concentration, sales force automation, customer expectations, ethics expectations, and increased emphasis on wellbeing in the workplace. Each of these environmental forces interacts with the others, significantly compounding analysis of the effects on the sales organization.

A number of key changes in the contemporary business and social environment are examined and their implications regarding sales and sales management research and practice are discussed. A relevant and recognized implication is a move toward a more relationship-oriented focus for the sales force. Psychological levels of analysis are considered from the perspective of the individual salesperson or sales manager, possible dyads, teams, and stakeholder or wider society. An interesting perspective is developed regarding the potential for biological and neuroscientific insights into sales force performance and behavior.

1.3 SALES MANAGEMENT

In this section we overview several relevant sales management topics that are discussed in Part II of the Handbook. Sales management has changed out of all recognition over the past twenty years, partly due to the increasing competition and spiraling costs of running a sales team, but also due to rapid development of communication technologies that could not be envisaged twenty years ago. Therefore, a review of up-to-date techniques and developments is timely. The chapters examine sales organization designs, sales force market sensing, contracted sales forces, salesperson motivation and training, job stress, and sales force size and effort allocation.

1.3.1 Structuring the Sales Force for Customer and Company Success

Structure follows strategy, according to **Andris A. Zoltners, Prabhakant Sinha, and Sally E. Lorimer.** Chapter 6 provides a complete analysis of organizing the sales force for customer and company success. A framework is developed to guide the design and management of the sales organization that is consistent with company strategy and drives results. The sales force's requirements for generalists and/or specialists are guided by the firm's product offerings, markets served, and selling activities.

Sales force structure decisions impact customer and company results by directly influencing salespeople and their activities. Developing an effective sales force organization design requires:

- determining the mix of generalists and product, market, or activity specialists that creates the right balance of sales force effectiveness and efficiency;
- designing reporting relationships for salespeople and managers that enable coordination and control of sales activities and processes;
- pursuing initiatives such as training, incentives, coaching, performance management, and information support to reduce stress and encourage the accomplishment of business objectives.

Sales force structures need to change as business needs evolve. Directing careful attention to implementation helps ensure that sales force structure alterations are well received by customers, salespeople, and managers.

1.3.2 Sales Force-Generated Marketing Intelligence

Challenges abound for management to obtain the desired type, frequency, and quality of market information from the organization's sales force. In Chapter 7 **Kenneth R. Evans and C. Fred Miao** look at the role of the sales force in the marketing information system (MIS). Sales force-generated marketing intelligence is guided by important antecedents which are categorized according to factors associated with the firm and the individual level. Antecedents at the firm level include organizational culture, sales force control philosophy, training, job descriptions, compensation, and rewards. Relevant personal-level antecedents consist of role conflict and role ambiguity.

Key dimensions of sales force intelligence are new product planning and development, sales forecasting, competitive strategy, pricing strategy, and territorial customer knowledge. The challenge is to integrate the sales force into the MIS. Information generated by the sales force must be captured and disseminated across functional boundaries. The MIS contributes to important sales force strategic options such as customer relationship management. The process of obtaining the

Two aspects of organizational climate are particularly relevant in sales force contexts: climate for service and sales climate. The former is well established in the literature, whereas the latter is a construct developed in this chapter. Prior research has been focused on a single aspect of organizational climate (e.g. climate for service, climate for safety, climate for diversity). No research has considered the interrelationships between multiple aspects of climate or their individual and joint effects on disparate performance criteria. Given the need to perform well on multiple dimensions, it is important to understand how supportive control elements can be developed to foster multi-dimensional performance effectiveness.

1.4.4 Salespeople's Influence an Consumers' and Business Buyers' Goals and Wellbeing

It has been considered important to help salespeople acquire a clearer understanding of their customer's perceptions and views. However, research in social cognitive psychology suggests that behavior is only sometimes tactically motivated; instead, customers may be unaware of their own goals until they have acted. In Chapter 15, **Harish Sujan** evaluates the influence of persuasion tactics, separating out buyer behavior that is driven by conscious and non-conscious goals. Research relating to the explicit goals customers pursue is reviewed. Long-term and short-term goals are separated.

Important theoretical distinctions alluded to in motivational psychology are discussed. Theories that are examined include those relating to learning goals, implementation versus deliberation mindsets, action identification, goal shielding, and prevention versus promotion focus. This discussion is contrasted with the understanding that currently exists for when consumers learn of their goals from their actions. Some of the questions raised are: do customers' actions based on non-conscious goals occur more in familiar rather than unfamiliar situations; with simple rather than complex behaviors; with difficult, negative choices rather than with simpler or positive choices; or with goals that go against a social norm and so need to be suppressed, rather than socially acceptable goals?

1.4.5 Sales Technology

Gary K. Hunter views sales technology as an umbrella term which includes interrelationships among sales strategy, sales processes, salespeople, and information technology. Sales technology includes sales aspects of customer relationship management (CRM) and sales force automation (SFA) applications. Sales technology management involves much more than purchasing state-of-the-art innovations and installing them on salespeople's laptops. Increasingly, companies are developing sales technology departments which perform various functions for the sales organization. The sales technology portfolio includes all information technologies involved in implementing, evaluating, and controlling the organization's selling effort. The array of capabilities includes laptops, cellphones, PDA devices, word processing, spreadsheet, graphics, and database applications. Sales technology involves far more than automating tasks.

Managers face challenging decisions as to how best to use technology to improve the efficiency and effectiveness of their sales efforts. Sales managers need to customize their sales technology portfolios. Important factors associated with sales technology and its interrelationships with sales strategy, sales processes, and salespeople involving a range of sales contexts are discussed. Equipping, training, supporting, and motivating salespeople to adopt sales technology are examined in depth. Relationships between sales technology and performance for different types of use are considered. Finally, sales technology, productivity, and performance relationships are discussed.

1.5 The Organization and Sales Relationships

The last section of the Handbook examines the sales organization's relationships with other functions and the business. The sales organization is increasingly involved in strategy development and implementation with various components of the business. The chapters consider organizational commitment to sales; the strategic role of the sales organization; sales force agility, strategic thinking, and value propositions; marketing and sales relationships; and total integrated marketing.

1.5.1 Organizational Commitment to Sales

The sales force plays an important role in delivering superior value to customers, and the company has an important responsibility in addressing the changing needs of the market through organizational integration and transformation processes relative to sales activities. Important macro-trends impact organizational commitment to sales. Chapter 17, by **Wesley J. Johnston and Linda D. Peters**, examines organizational commitment to sales. The central role of marketing in enhancing organizational capabilities within business networks is first discussed. Marketing is a translator of value to and from the marketplace, linking the externalization of competitive advantage in the marketplace with value to the organization. The intent is the creation of value for the organization and the customer.

Important macro-trends are impacting organizational commitment to sales, changing the role of the sales function in the co-creation of value with customers. How the sales function may operate as a partner in value co-creation is discussed, and the role of the customer in this process is examined. Value needs to be defined by the customer. The sales organization also plays an important role in facilitating innovation and a learning organization. A perspective emerges which defines the commitment of both marketing and sales to building core competencies and positioning them as value propositions which create competitive advantage for the organization.

1.5.2 The Strategic Role of the Selling Function

There is growing agreement among sales force authorities that the strategic importance of the sales force may have reached an all-time high. **Thomas W. Leigh, William L. Cron, Artur Baldauf, and Samuel Grossenbacher** provide an insight into current thinking. There is strong support by scholars for the need to address the strategic role of the sales function as a resource which drives competitive advantage and organizational performance. The objective of Chapter 18 is to examine the strategic role of the selling function based on the resource-based view (RBV) perspective on the firm. The RBV provides a relevant foundation for developing a conceptual framework on the strategic role of the selling function. This approach is based on the logic that distinctions in resources and organizations' capabilities may offer potential competitive advantages that are linked to variations in returns.

The strategic sales function framework proposes a direct effect of sales organization resources and capabilities on sustainable competitive advantage (SCA) and an indirect effect through the mediation of SCA on the financial performance of the firm. Dynamic meta-capabilities and organizing processes and contexts are proposed as moderating influences on the core processes. The intent of the framework is to extend the current perspective concerning the strategic role of the sales force. The framework identifies relevant variables and interrelationships.

1.5.3 Sales Force Agility, Strategic Thinking, and Value Propositions

Agility involves being flexible and quick to respond, ready to consider and make changes in value propositions offered to customers. Agility requires salespeople to be willing to respond to new evidence and to initiate change based on new or anticipated marketplace developments. In Chapter 19, **Larry B. Chonko and Eli Jones** observe that customers are exposed to far more information, other buyer behaviors, and ideas than in the past. Accordingly, organizations and their sales-people continuously experience the compelling need for change, and often find it necessary to respond and change rapidly or risk the loss of sales and perhaps more. Following an unchanged long-term strategy may result in a form of inertia when experiencing marketplace disruptions, either for the entire business or with indi-vidual customers.

Conflicts may develop when a salesperson reaches an understanding of the strategic relationship with the customer, and then the ideas offered to the customer may be viewed as obsolete by the customer, on the basis of modified needs, wants, and preferences driven by real-time marketplace information. This chapter develops a conceptual framework which proposes how agile salespeople should make decisions and act on value propositions offered in sales encounters. The framework provides a process on how salespeople can couple the skills of thinking strategically with those of acting with agility. Salespeople need to be always willing to examine new evidence, and to make changes based on new developments which are occurring or anticipated.

1.5.4 The Importance of Effective Working Relationships between Sales and Marketing

Firms are typically composed of functionally specialized departments such as Finance, Manufacturing, R&D, Sales, and Marketing. These departments are often highly interdependent, and a key role of their managers is to forge effective ongoing "cross-functional relationships" (CFRs) with other managers. One of the most important of these CFRs, according to **Kenneth Le Meunier-FitzHugh and Graham W. Massey**, is the sales–marketing CFR. Managers of sales and marketing departments are expected to work together to deliver value to customers, yet they often operate as functional silos with different cultures, objectives, and values. Chapter 20 examines "The Importance of Effective Working Relationships between Sales and Marketing". It provides a framework for analysis and discussion concerning this important organizational relationship.

The chapter reviews current thinking on sales–marketing cross-functional rela-tionships, identifies gaps in academic literature, and discusses a range of controlla-ble and uncontrollable factors that may influence this interface. Many organizations are unsure how to manage the sales–marketing cross-functional relationship. The few empirical studies published to date examine the contextual conditions under which such relationships are enacted, e.g. the level of functional interdependence, power relations, and cultural differences. The main types of variable that influence the effectiveness of such relationships are discussed. These include organizational structure variables, the types of interaction and communi-cation prevalent in the cross-functional relationship, and key variables such as interpersonal trust.

1.5.5 Marketing. The Anchor for Sales

Noel Capon, one of the most respected academic writers in marketing, argues that a carefully formulated market-focused strategy will be ineffective unless the sales force executes it well. A hard-working, highly motivated sales force will not achieve its potential unless guided by a marketing strategy well tuned to environmental realities. Marketing is the architect and the sales force is the builder; their activities are closely linked and interdependent. Chapter 21 identifies and determines how to access the market and other relevant environments, and how to develop a strategy to succeed in the market. In addition to strategy implementation with customers, the sales organization must closely monitor marketing plans and actions to ensure that marketing is following a promising avenue.

Six marketing imperatives—the tasks that marketing must accomplish—and four marketing principles that act as guidelines for making marketing decisions are identified and examined. The market strategy is a key output from marketing's efforts, and the sales strategy must implement the market strategy. Accordingly, the sales force must understand how the firm develops a market strategy so that sales can creatively work within that framework to design and implement an effective sales strategy. Sales managers must know what marketing is trying to accomplish, since they have an important role in helping marketing to be successful. Moreover, successful marketing helps the sales force succeed. The chapter provides a comprehensive examination of what every sales manager needs to know about marketing.

1.6 SUMMARY

The Oxford Handbook of Strategic Sales and Sales Management provides a snapshot of the current thinking on the strategic role of sales and sales management, and identifies some the key challenges presented to senior managers. The importance of a sales organization continues to be critical in creating value, and profits for organizations. Escalating sales and selling costs require organizations to be more focused on results and highlight the shifting of resources from marketing to sales, and the growth in customer power now requires a strategic, not a tactical response.

The Oxford Handbook of Strategic Sales and Sales Management provides an unrivalled collection of articles by the leading academics in the field of sales and marketing management. Sales is experiencing a renaissance driven by a number of factors including building profitable relationships, creating/delivering value, strategic customer management, sales and marketing relationships, global selling, and the change from transactional to customer relationship selling. The role of sales in the delivery of strategic goals has never been more essential. We hope that you enjoy using the Handbook and find it to be a valuable resource.

REFERENCES

BROWN, S. P., E. JONES, and T. W. LEIGH (2005). "The Attenuating Effect of Role Overload on Relationships Linking Self-Efficacy and Goal Level to Work Performance," *Journal of Applied Psychology* 90.5, 972–9.

CARNEGIE, D. (1936). *How to Win Friends and Influence People*. New York: Simon & Schuster.

CRON, W. L., and D. W. CRAVENS (forthcoming). "Sales Force Strategy," in J. Sheth and N. K. Malhotra (eds.), *Wiley International Encyclopedia of Marketing*, Chichester, UK: Wiley.

PIERCY, N. F., and N. LANE (2005). "Strategic Imperatives for Transformation of the Sales Organization," *Journal of Change Management* 5, 249–66.

SCHNEIDER, B. (1990). "The Climate for Service: An Application of the Climate Construct," in B. Schneider (ed.), *Organizational Climate and Culture*, San Francisco: Jossey-Bass, 383–412.

——(2000). "The Psychological Life of Organizations," in N. M. Ashkanasy, C. P. M. Wilderom, and M. F. Peterson (eds.), *Handbook of Organizational Culture and Climate*, Newbury Park, CA: Sage, xvii–xxii.

SHETH, J. N., and A. SHARMA (2008). "The Impact of the Product to Service Shift in Industrial Markets and the Evolution of the Sales Organization," *Industrial Marketing Management* 37.3, 260–69.

WALKER, O. C., G. A. CHURCHILL, and N. M. FORD (1979). "Where Do We Go From Here? Selected Conceptual and Empirical Issues Concerning the Motivation and Performance of the Industrial Salesforce," in G. Albaum and G. A. Churchill (eds.), *Critical Issues in Sales Management: State-of-the-Art and Future Research Needs*, Eugene: University of Oregon, 10–75.

WOTRUBA, T. R. (1991). "The Evolution of Personal Selling," *Journal of Personal Selling & Sales Management* 11.3, 1–12.

PART I

SALES STRATEGY AND ENVIRONMENT

....

CHAPTER 2

THE EVOLUTION OF THE STRATEGIC SALES ORGANIZATION

....

NIGEL F. PIERCY

NIKALA LANE

2.1 INTRODUCTION

....

The goal of this chapter is to establish the case for radical review, by both scholars and company executives, of the ways in which sales organizations operate and the implications for how they are organized and positioned in the firm. We examine the current evidence and rationale for organizational change and introduce the concept of strategic customer management, as a way of describing the emerging role of the sales function, and the growth of the strategic sales organization as a way of implementing strategic customer management initiatives.

2.1.1 The Search for a New Type of Sales Organization

There is some consensus that the ability of a company to manage its relationships with its markets is probably a higher priority now than ever before, yet traditional marketing remains largely concerned with the tactics of advertising and promotion. A central problem is that many traditional marketing and sales approaches were not designed for complex, consultative and collaborative, technology-based customer relationships where, for example, the "product" is being created jointly by buyer and seller as it is being "sold". Indeed, this example underlines interesting parallels between new strategic sales approaches and the concept of "co-creation" which is central to the broader services dominant logic of marketing (Vargo and Lusch 2004).

The core capabilities for survival and performance have shifted decisively in many markets, and some firms are struggling to enhance these customer-related capabilities. The ability of companies to achieve competitive superiority and enhanced business performance through the way they manage customer relationships is a core capability, but one which has been largely neglected by conventional sales and marketing approaches.

The urgency of addressing this critical capabilities issue is underlined by escalating customer power and buyer concentration in many markets. The complex demands of powerful customers mean that the field sales force can no longer passively accept and execute plans produced by corporate marketing. The reality for many companies is that "As power shifted from the seller to the buyer, it also shifted from headquarters to the field" (Shapiro 2002: 2).

Accordingly, there is growing evidence of the expanding influence of sales functions over strategic marketing and business decisions. For example, research findings suggest that often the sales department has more influence than the marketing department over several "marketing" decisions (Krohmer, Homburg, and Workman 2002), and that "primary marketing coordinators increasingly reside in sales rather than the marketing organization" (Homburg, Workman, and Jensen 2000: 466). The sales organization is playing a growing role in formulating as well as executing marketing strategies (Cross, Hartley, Rudelius, and Vassey 2001). Indeed, it has been apparent for some time that the sales organization may have a decisive influence on the direction of new product innovation through its intelligence collection and interpretation activities (Lambert, Marmorstein, and Sharma 1990), and in assessing and accessing key market segments (Maier and Saunders 1990).

Accordingly, there is some agreement that "The shaping of the selling function has become a strategic corporate issue," requiring clarity about the new sales role, new structures, and new management approaches (Shapiro, Slywotsky, and Doyle 1998: 1). However, it should be recognized that the new types of processes and structures required to enhance and sustain value delivery to customers through the reinvented sales organization are likely to demand evaluation and appraisal that extends far beyond the domain traditionally associated with selling activities (Ogbuchi and Sharma 1999).

For many companies, the requirement is a form of sales organization that behaves differently, does different things in different ways, and delivers value in new ways. It involves a strategic responsibility for the management of the links between a company and its market, and for confronting the important choices and decisions that exist. The core responsibility of the strategic sales organization is strategic customer management—placing the management of the customer portfolio and its implied investment decisions at the center of business strategy.

It is now a decade since Neil Rackham concluded that "Sales functions everywhere are in the early stages of radical and profound changes comparable to those that began to transform manufacturing 20 years ago" (Rackham and DeVincentis 1999: 3). The impact of that change is becoming increasingly apparent, and characterizes the search for a new type of sales organization.

2.1.2 Structuring the Case for Strategic Sales Organization

We address the issues surrounding the strategic sales organization in the following way. First, we examine the underlying forces which are linked to sales organization change, and the emerging challenge of strategic customer management. This leads to a review of new organizational forms being developed in sales and, lastly, a model of the strategic sales organization as a basis for analysis and planning. We close with some remarks regarding the hallmarks of the sales organization of the future.

2.2 FORCES DRIVING SALES ORGANIZATION CHANGE

There is a compelling logic underpinning the concept of a new form of strategic sales organization which is capable of effectively addressing strategic customer issues. Indeed, evidence from the US suggests that currently many senior managers are dissatisfied with the productivity of their sales organizations, and many see sales force cost poorly aligned with their strategic goals (Deloitte Touche 2005). The forces driving and reshaping the sales organization include escalating demands from major customers for something new and better from their suppliers, and the impact of strategic sales capabilities on business performance.

2.2.1 Customer Relationship Requirements

A dramatic change in modern business-to-business marketing has been the rapid and disruptive escalation in the demands for enhanced service, new types of relationships, and greater added-value by business-to-business customers. The H. R. Chally consultancy's *World Class Sales Excellence Research Report* is illustrative (H. R. Chally 2006). This study investigates the views of corporate purchasers and their expectations for the relationship with the supplier's salesperson. Desired supplier relationship characteristics are summarized as: (1) *personal accountability for the buyer's desired results*—the sales contact with the supplier is expected to be committed to the customer and accountable for achievement; (2) *understanding the customer's business*—to be able to add value, the supplier must understand the customer's competencies, strategies, challenges and organizational culture; (3) *customer advocacy*—the salesperson must be the customer's advocate in his/her own organization, and operate through the policies and politics to focus on the customer's needs; (4) *designing the right applications*—the salesperson is expected to think beyond technical features and functions to the implementation of the product or service in the customer's environment, going beyond the transaction to the customer's end state; (5) *accessibility*—customers expect salespeople to be constantly connected and within reach; (6) *problem solving*—customers no longer perceive themselves to be buying products or services, but rather buying solutions to their business problems, and expect salespeople to diagnose, prescribe, and resolve these issues, not to sell them products; and (7) *creativity in responding to customer needs*—buyers expect salespeople to be innovators, who bring them new ideas to solve important business problems, making creativity a major source of added value.

These qualities characterize how world-class sales forces are distinguished in the eyes of their customers. They constitute a customer environment which is radically different from the transactional selling approaches of the past, and which poses substantially different management challenges in managing business-to-business customer relationships. The sales and service organizations which meet these customer demands and expectations and develop sustainable and attractive customer relationships are likely to look very different from those of the past, and to work very differently.

2.2.2 The Changing Sales Task

An important driver of sales organization change relates to the ways in which the sales task itself is evolving. For example, Oracle has adopted a sales model where salespeople do not place or process orders: after a software demonstration they leave customers to place their own orders on the Web (Clark and Callahan 2000). Cisco, for example, has a successful strategy of using personal selling resources only when a purchase is significant and complicated, and the buyer's decision is characterized by high uncertainty—typically the first sale to a customer or a new application—but leaving subsequent purchases to be made over the Internet (Royal 1999). Nonetheless, the challenge for management is to match sales force investment to competitive strategy, not to indulge in crude downsizing of sales operations (Olson, Cravens, and Slater 2001).

Shapiro, Slywotsky, and Doyle (1998) describe the evolution in the sales task as one which underlines a fundamental change in approach:

Old approach emphasizes:	Necessary new approach emphasizes:
1. Getting new accounts	1. Retaining existing accounts
2. Getting the order	2. Becoming the preferred supplier
3. Pressuring the company to cut prices	3. Pricing for profit
4. Giving service to get sales	4. Understanding cost implications and managing each account for long-term profitability
5. Managing all accounts in the same way	5. Managing each account for maximum long-term profitability
6. Selling to anyone	6. Concentrating on the high profit potential accounts

(Adapted from Shapiro, Slywotsky, and Doyle 1998: 8)

Their logic is that "most established sales forces are in deep trouble. They were designed for a simpler, more pleasant era" (Shapiro, Slywotsky, and Doyle 1998: 9). They suggest that incremental change in existing structures and systems will not meet the company's new needs, and that clear specification of the sales task is strategically the appropriate place for management attention to focus. Their key questions proposed are: (1) which accounts? (2) which products and services? (3) what specific activities are to be accomplished? and (4) what are the key interactions with other parts of the company? They conclude:

The fundamental changes reshaping the business landscape require that management view the sales function in a radically different way than has been prevalent (and productive) for the past three decades. The sales function has evolved from a tactical to a strategic boardroom issue. This transformation is driven by the changing nature and content of the sales task, which will force companies at a minimum to change their mix of selling capacity, and in most cases to redesign their sales force. (Shapiro, Slywotsky, and Doyle 1998: 16).

Shapiro, Slywotsky, and Doyle (1998) argue that as a result of these factors, the quality of the sales effort is growing relative to other capabilities as an influence on company financial performance.

2.2.3 Strategic Sales Capabilities

The growing importance of what can be called strategic sales capabilities is underlined by several further issues.

2.2.3.1 *The Complexity of Customer Relationships*

At one level, there are growing substitution effects taking place between traditional
sales force activities and newer alternatives. For many companies, channels development has included the establishment of direct channels, such as those based
around Internet websites. Even in consumer marketing, by 2007, 10 per cent of all
retail spending took place on the Internet (Rigby 2007), and this figure is much
higher for many business-to-business sellers. At the same time, there is a growing
trend in major companies towards the outsourcing to third parties of routine sales
operations (Anderson and Trinkle 2005). For example, while in the US Procter &
Gamble has a 200-person team wholly dedicated to Wal-Mart (the single customer
that constitutes 20 per cent of P&G's business), it is preferable for P&G to
outsource routine sales visits to stores to a third party sales organization. Similarly,
global corporate expenditure on customer relationship management (CRM) technology is measured each year in billions of dollars, and individual expenditure by
companies can be in tens of millions of dollars. CRM explicitly aims to automate
many of the customer-related functions traditionally associated with the sales
force.

However, these developments raise the question whether a company's most
important business-to-business customer relationships can be managed securely
and to full advantage through a website, a third party seller, or a CRM system.
Addressing this question is important to understanding the strategic role of sales,
rather than considering only the routine activities involved in taking and processing orders.

For instance, Dell Computers is an Internet-based company—the majority of
sales and service provisions are on the Web. Nonetheless, Dell maintains account
executives in the field as well as internal salespeople in branches, because their view
is that the technology exists to free salespeople to sell and develop customer
relationships, not to process orders (which the technology generally does better
and more cheaply). Indeed, part of Dell's fight-back against the decline of its direct
model in delivering sales growth is developing multiple, global sales channels.
There is a substantial business and competitive risk in underestimating the role
of the sales force in defending, sustaining, and rebuilding a company's competitive
position.

Writing in *Harvard Business Review*, Thomas Stewart summarizes the new and
emerging role for the sales organization facing increasingly complex customer
relational demands in the following terms:

Selling is changing fast and in such a way that sales teams have become strategic resources. When corporations strive to become customer focused, salespeople move to the foreground; engineers recede. As companies go to market with increasingly complex bundles of products and services, their representatives cease to be mere order takers (most orders are placed online, anyway) and become relationship managers. (Stewart 2006: 10)

Understanding and enhancing the ways in which sales resources add value and protect customer relationships is becoming of strategic importance in markets being driven towards commoditization. To the extent that a marketing strategy depends upon strong and sustained customer relationships, there is an implicit reliance on strategic sales capabilities. Moreover, to the extent that a sales force has built and sustains strong customer relationships by creating value for customers, then this provides a strategic resource for the company, which should impact favourably on its freedom to make significant strategic choices.

2.2.3.2 *Customer Sophistication*

Relatedly, the growing sophistication and aggressiveness of purchasers in business-to-business markets has driven up the strategic importance of effectively managing buyer–seller relationships (Jones, Brown, Zoltners, and Weitz 2005). The challenge to sellers is to implement effective marketing strategies in a dramatically changed world of sophisticated buyers (Shapiro, Slywotsky, and Doyle 1998).

Enhanced customer sophistication is underlined by the shift in the traditional role played by purchasing functions in customer organizations. Increasingly, purchasing has become a strategic function directly linked to the customer's strategic plans, with a major level of responsibility for profitability, cost control, and enhanced shareholder value (e.g. Janda and Seshandri 2001). Professional purchasing managers use complex sourcing metrics to select the "right" suppliers, and to dictate the terms on how they will be supplied, so more than ever before supplier profitability is determined at the point of sale, where the sales organization meets the customer (e.g. De Boer, Labro, and Morlacci 2001; Talluri and Narasimhan 2004). Not only has the sales task become much more complex, the stakes are much higher.

Sellers in business-to-business markets face much more complex decisions about their marketing and sales investments in customer relationships than in the past. Historically, seller profits were generally in line with account size, because prices tended to be cost-based, sales costs were relatively low, and the size of accounts did not vary dramatically. However, consolidation by merger and acquisition and the effects of market attrition have changed this situation in many markets. In industrial markets, sales situations are increasingly characterized by fewer, larger, and more complex purchasing organizations, and in consumer markets there has been a massive shift in power to retailers (Shapiro et al. 1998).

Unsurprisingly, very large customers are powerful and demand customized sales and account management, thereby posing challenges for the supplier in terms of profitability. Other customers also demand special treatment, but it is likely to be different. Small and medium-sized accounts require yet more different approaches, mainly because of the cost of serving them. The strategic challenge is to match sales efforts and approaches to different parts of a complex portfolio of customers, to balance revenue and profitability with business risk. These choices are likely to impact substantially on company performance.

Accordingly, in many sectors, traditional sales models may be obsolete as a result of growing customer sophistication. For example, in the pharmaceuticals business, high sales pressure placed on doctors to prescribe new drugs has resulted in formal training courses in medical schools to teach future doctors how to resist sales pitches. Firms in the pharmaceutical industry are searching for new and better ways to get to market. Companies like Pfizer, Wyeth, Novartis, and GlaxoSmith-Klein recognize that the era of "hard sell" is over in their sector, and are working to develop new sales models.

Such fundamental changes in the requirements of business customers mandate a strategic response from sellers that is more robust than simple acquiescence to demands for lower prices and higher service levels. The challenge is to reposition sales as a core part of a company's competitiveness, where the sales organization is closely integrated into a company's business strategy (e.g. Stephens 2003). These market trends have elevated the importance of the effective deployment of sales capabilities to a strategic issue. Many traditional approaches to marketing and sales neglect the implications of customer sophistication, complexity, and scale, and may provide a route to losses in profits and business performance.

2.2.3.3 *Commoditization*

Significantly, one impact of the parallel revolution which has taken place in operations management and supply chain design has been to reduce product and service differentiation in many sectors. Competing products are frequently built on near-identical modularized platforms, and supply chains are designed for maximum speed and lowest cost. Benchmarking systems encourage suppliers to achieve similar performance against each other on the same operations and supply chain metrics. It is unsurprising that the result is growth in product similarity rather than differentiation. Products as diverse as mid-market cars, personal computers, and financial services are difficult to distinguish one from the other, once the brands and badges are removed. Lack of product differentiation raises major questions about sources of competitive advantage.

Moreover, customer organizations have increasingly pursued aggressive and proactive commoditization strategies with their suppliers: from the purchaser perspective, if all competitive offerings can be made essentially similar, then differentiation is only achievable through price, which is a preferred situation for the purchaser. The chief purchasing officer's modern armoury includes: RFPs (Request for Proposal or an invitation to suppliers to bid for business on a specific product or service); Internet auctions; purchasing consultants; and buying consortia. These mechanisms all seek to reduce purchasing to a comparison of prices and technical product specifications. The challenge to sellers is to constantly expand the scope and value of the offering to the customer, and the impact of the offering on the customer's business performance. Achieving differentiation with strategic customers requires new types of buyer–seller relationships that assist customers in implementing their own strategies. This underlines the priority for a strategic sales role in developing and implementing business and marketing strategy.

Indeed, modularization and benchmarking in operations, and lean design in supply chains, may mean in some situations that the sales/customer interface is the *only* place remaining where competitive differentiation can be achieved. For example, research by the US consultancy H. R. Chally suggests that salesperson effectiveness accounts for as much as 40 per cent of business-to-business customer choice of supplier, simply because technology has made the products themselves increasingly substitutable (Stephens 2003).

Strategic sales capabilities may be a vital component of competitive advantage or even the only source of competitive differentiation that remains. For example, SKF is the world's largest maker of industrial bearings—a business highly susceptible to commoditization. SKF's fight to overcome commoditization threats relies on the company's 5,000 sales engineers developing close relationships with customers and liaising with technical experts deep inside their own business. The goal for sales engineers is to align customer needs with complex technical solutions, often involving customized products. In important ways, the sales engineer stands between the company and commoditization (Marsh 2007).

2.2.3.4 *Corporate Expenditure on Sales Organizations*

Notwithstanding the anticipated impact of the Internet, CRM, and contract selling on reducing sales costs, it is notable that corporate expenditure on sales operations continues to exceed that on higher-profile advertising and sales promotion activities. Only rough estimates exist, but in 2000 levels of expenditure on personal selling by British companies were estimated at £20 billion, compared to £13 billion on advertising and £14 billion on sales promotion (Doyle 2002). For many companies, sales activities are frequently among the largest expenses in the marketing budget. US survey data suggest that in 2006 the average salary for salespeople was approximately $150,000, while high performers averaged more than $160,000. Survey participants expected sales incomes to continue to increase (Kornik 2007). Research in the US also finds that while in some sectors companies spend as little as 1 percent of sales revenue on their sales force (e.g. banking, hotels), the average company spends 10 per cent of sales on its sales force, and some spend as much as 22 per cent (e.g. printing and publishing) (Dartnell Corporation 1999). In fact, it is not uncommon for sustained sales force costs to be as high as 50 per cent of sales in some companies (Zoltners, Sinha, and Lorimer 2004).

The outcome of these complex forces acting on the sales organization can be summarized in the following terms:

Today's competitive environment demands a radically different approach. Specifically, the ability of firms to exploit the true potential of the sales organization requires that company executives adopt a new mindset about the role of the selling function within the firm, how the sales force is managed, and what salespeople are expected to produce. The sales function must serve as a dynamic source of value creation and innovation within the firm. (The Sales Educators 2006: 1)

Fulfilling that potential and delivering value creation and innovation to a company will require more than the conventional and traditional sales department and mandates attention to the development of the strategic sales organization.

2.3 THE STRATEGIC CUSTOMER MANAGEMENT CHALLENGE

2.3.1 Antecedents to Strategic Customer Management

Several authorities have, at different times, attempted to capture the evolving challenges facing the traditional sales organization in meeting the demands of the strategic role it is increasingly required to fill.

Rackham and DeVincentis (1999), for example, make a distinction between customer types: intrinsic value customers (value is intrinsic in the product itself); extrinsic value customers (focused largely on the benefits of the extrinsic elements of the value equation); and strategic value customers (demand an extraordinary level of value creation). On the basis of these customer differences, they argue that transactional selling fits with the needs of the intrinsic value buyer, who treats suppliers as a commodity and buys largely on the basis of price and convenience. However, they associate the needs of the extrinsic value buyer with consultative selling—where salespeople have a grasp of the customer's business issues and the sales effort creates new value and provides additional benefits beyond the product itself. Lastly, they link strategic value buyers with the need for an enterprise selling approach. Enterprise selling is reserved for strategically important customers, and both the product and the sales force are secondary to leveraging the corporate assets of the supplier to contribute to the customer's business success.

Importantly, Rackham and DeVincentis underline the different value-based and relational demands made by different types of customer, the need to match supplier investments with the value of the customer, and the emergence of approaches to selling which are quite different to simple, transactional models. However, while Rackham and DeVincentis (1999) underline complex customer demands and customer value as critical shaping forces, they are less explicit regarding the implications for how the sales organization should evolve to meet these challenges.

More specifically focused on strategic sales leadership, more recently a leading group of academics, writing as The Sales Educators, have pursued the notion of the entrepreneurial sales organization to respond to changing market and company demands, arguing that the sales function is the natural home for entrepreneurship in a company (The Sales Educators 2006). Their prescription identifies six elements to the entrepreneurial sales organization; when combined, they suggest these elements will produce an entrepreneurial sales organization:

- The Creative Sales Force: the creativity required in new types of sales force means the abandonment of assumptions, the rejection of accepted precepts, and the elimination of established methods, bringing a fresh start and a freedom from the constraints of the past.
- The Expeditionary Sales Force: innovation becomes a core competency in sales, consisting of an ability to generate meaningful innovations and gain their adoption by senior management, other functions in the firm, and customers.
- The Empowered Sales Force: empowerment is key to the role of sales managers and salespeople as entrepreneurs, allowing them to be opportunity identifiers, creative problem-solvers, and organizational value creators. The challenge is finding a balance between tightness and looseness of control.
- The Strategic Sales Force: a strategic orientation in selling involves, first, connection between the sales force and the company as a whole, and second, connection between the overall role, direction, and priorities of the sales organization and the day-to-day operational decisions made by sales managers and salespeople. The strategic sales organization is closely aligned with the company's strategic intent.
- The Technological Sales Force: as technology transforms sales force capabilities, the integration of technology into selling and sales management has become mandatory as a way to enhance the firm's ability to compete (The Sales Educators 2006).

Usefully, The Sales Educators make explicit the shift from routine, tactical functions towards the creative; the empowerment of the new sales force, and the need for new organizational forms and intra-organizational collaboration and partnership. In this sense, they add additional dimensions to the earlier Rackham and DeVincentis (1999) formulation. In addition, they underline the strategic sales organization argument.

2.3.2 The Domain of Strategic Customer Management

In attempting to capture and integrate these various arguments, we introduce the term "strategic customer management". We use this phrase to attempt to describe the primary thrust of a strategic sales organization. Our view of the developing organizational domain for strategic customer management is shown in Figure 2.1. This indicates that strategic customer management includes making strategic choices about customer investments, for example, based on the customer portfolio (Figure 2.2), but also extends to managing relationships with strategic customers.

Importantly, there are two sides to strategic customer management. The first relates to the strategic management of the customer portfolio—making investment choices between different types of customer to deliver the goals of marketing strategy, but also playing a role in shaping that strategy. The second component relates to the management of strategic customers—building relationships with the potentially dominant customers in the company's portfolio, some of which may be

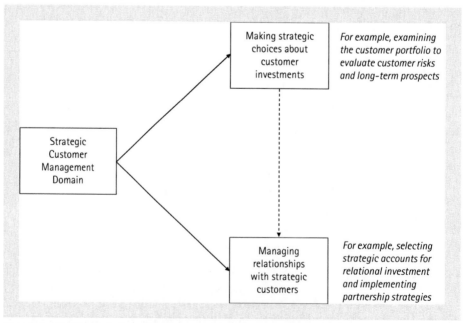

Fig. 2.1. The Evolving Strategic Customer Management Domain

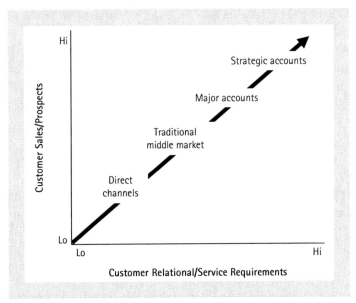

Fig. 2.2. Sales Relationships Across the Customer Portfolio

classified as strategic accounts and handled differently from the rest. These are important strategic decisions which impact directly on the profitability and risk profile of the company's business (Piercy and Lane 2009b). We will comment further on these roles shortly. Importantly, the challenges of strategic customer management underpin the development of new organizational models in sales and the development of the strategic sales organization.

2.4 NEW SALES ORGANIZATION MODELS

It is a normal part of organizational development that specific forms and structures evolve and change as the outside world changes, as demands on the company reconfigure, and as management priorities shift in line with new strategies, looking for the best ways to enhance performance.

The new demands on organizations emphasize: agility and nimbleness over bureaucracy; flat structures over pyramids; collaboration and partnership; knowledge-based work; internal and external networks; and innovative ways of motivating new types of employee over traditional approaches (see e.g. Cravens and Piercy 2009). The top-heavy bureaucracies of the past cannot survive because they are too slow, weak at achieving integration, and too costly. Nowhere is this more relevant than at the front end of the organization, where marketing and sales departments interface with the customer.

Indeed, there is a compelling rationale that innovation in management thinking may be far more important than simply innovation in technology and products. It is step-changes in management thinking which are directly connected to sustainable competitive advantage (Mol and Birkenshaw 2007). The emergence of strategic customer management and the strategic sales organization may be just such a "giant step."

2.4.1 Reshaping and Repositioning Traditional Functions

Organizational evolution suggests that traditional specialist functions change in how they operate and in the level and type of relative influence they exert in the company. In some cases they may disappear altogether, in others they reappear in different forms.

There are many precedents for organizational evolution. In the 1960s, transport and warehousing tended to be an important but tactical function, but it is one which has grown into responsibility for supply chain strategy as a key component of business strategy. In the same era, companies often had industrial relations and personnel departments, but they have tended to evolve into units with a broader perspective on recruiting and developing people in human resource strategy as a key part of how a company competes. Similarly, once the potential for strategic purchasing to impact positively on business performance became apparent, tactical/operational purchasing and supply departments took ownership of the critical strategic activity of supplier relationship management, with substantial shifts in the strategic significance and organizational positioning of these units.

By contrast, sales and marketing functions have not generally experienced this kind of strategic shift. Nonetheless, big changes have taken place in what companies need their "front-end" organizations to deliver. Accordingly, Sheth and Sharma (2008) argue that an evolution is taking place in sales processes and organizational structures, influenced by: the adoption of a service dominant logic of marketing; changes in supply chain practices; changes in customer purchasing goals, methods, and technologies; and the growth of the use of information technologies in customer relationship management practices. Their argument is that many sales organizations were established at a time when the product was the firm's focus, and salespeople served specific geographical areas or were product experts, confining the sales force to locational, product, and temporal limits, yet alignment with market characteristics strongly favors customer-focused sales organizations (Sheth and Sharma 2008).

2.4.2 New Organizational Models for Marketing and Sales

Lead players provide examples of the development of new organizational forms for marketing and sales.

In some cases organizational change is driven largely by economics—such as the cost of conventional selling activities compared to electronic alternatives. For example, it is some years since financial services companies like Prudential, Sun Life of Canada, Friends Provident, and Britannic recognized that it was no longer financially attractive to sell insurance and pensions to consumers on low and middle incomes through an on-the-road sales force. Widespread sales force downsizing followed that conclusion: in the UK, "the man from the Pru" was phased out after almost 150 years knocking on consumers' doors (English 2001).

However, organizational change in selling is also mandated by more complex factors of the type discussed earlier. Sheth and Sharma (2008) have, for example, linked a paradigmatic shift in selling—shifting focus from the exchange of goods to providing a service—in ways specified by the service-dominant logic of marketing (Vargo and Lusch 2004). Moreover, Sheth and Sharma (2008) describe the decline of the traditional product-oriented sales force. They suggest that the product-oriented sales organization will be reshaped by the impact of technology replacing some traditional sales functions (e.g. order taking), and by the need for improvements in the level of customer contact, leading to the growth in the number of customer-focused sales organizations.

However, in more fundamental organizational redesigns, some leading companies have already started to evolve new ways of reshaping the organizational interface with the market to meet new demands. One example is customer business development structures that focus on the opportunities provided by major customers and suppliers. Increasingly, innovative job titles like Director of Strategic Customer Management and Strategic Customer Manager indicate this type of change in the role of what was once a conventional sales function.

For example, Procter & Gamble, under the leadership of A. G. Lafley, transformed itself from the slow-moving, inward-looking bureaucracy it had become in the 1990s into a nimble, innovative, and aggressive competitor. Part of that transformation was the creation of Customer Business Development (CBD) organizations at the front of the business. The goal of CBD was to transform the old, narrow idea of buyer–seller relationships with customers into a multifunctional, collaborative approach designed to achieve mutual volume, profit, and market share objectives. CBD teams work with customers to develop the customer's plans and strategies to the advantage of both customer and P&G. CBD team members work collaboratively with experts from finance, management systems, customer service, and brand management to develop and implement business strategies that deliver sustainable competitive advantage for P&G brands (Piercy and Lane 2009b).

Other companies have moved beyond traditional functional departments to organize around the key processes that impact on customer value.

For example, it is more than a decade since consumer goods company Kraft Foods pioneered the move away from traditional product and brand management approaches in order to place greater emphasis on customer management. Kraft organizes its teams around three core processes: the *consumer management team* replaced the brand management function to focus on customer segments; *customer process teams* replaced the sales function to serve retail accounts, and the *supply management team* manages the logistics function. A *strategic integration team* develops effective overall strategies and coordinates the other teams. Some traditional functions remain, but their role is to coordinate activities across teams to ensure that shared learning takes place, to acquire and develop specialized skills, to deploy specialists to the cross-functional process teams, and to achieve scale economies (Day 1997).

It is likely that future developments will go yet further than customer business development and process-based organizations. Companies who prioritize strategic customer management initiatives are likely to need to develop what can be called a strategic sales organization to implement those initiatives effectively.

2.5 CHARACTERISTICS OF THE STRATEGIC SALES ORGANIZATION

The sales organization that fulfills a strategic role and aligns sales efforts with business strategy—the strategic sales organization—is embryonic for many companies and how it will evolve is to some extent a matter for speculation. We have attempted to identify and trace the characteristics most likely to be required in such organizational developments, and our conclusions are summarized in this section of the chapter, based on Piercy and Lane (2009b).

The framework we propose for analysis is shown in Figure 2.3. It identifies factors which impact on the definition of the sales domain, and those which have a broader impact on shaping the sales role in an organization.

2.5.1 Developing the Sales Domain

The following are factors to consider in examining how the domain of sales in a firm is changing, or can be enhanced, to facilitate the achievement of superior

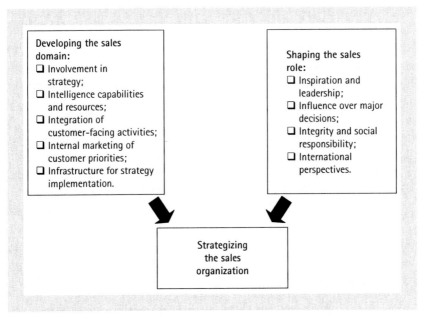

Fig. 2.3. The Strategic Evolution of the Sales Organization

customer value, to make customer strategy issues explicit, and to effectively implement strategic customer management initiatives.

2.5.1.1 *Involvement in Strategy*

A first set of concerns focuses on the placement of the sales organization at the center of the debate about business and marketing strategy decisions in companies, and aligning sales operations with strategic direction. Implicit is the elevation of the sales functions above the tactical role of managing transactions to address the revenue-building demanded by business strategy, and becoming a partner with other functions in making key business strategy decisions. One key point of focus is the customer portfolio and the evaluation of the prospects and risk characteristics of different customer types, as a basis for relational investment choices.

A strategy-building role is a critical test in our strategic sales model (Figure 2.3). This underlines the importance of sales involvement in the generation and evaluation of marketing and business strategy, rather than just being a tactical operation responsible for implementing or executing strategies created by others. The effect is putting sales back into the business strategy process (e.g. Stephens 2003).

Several compelling reasons exist for putting the sales voice back in the strategy debate. First, many of the most significant resource investment decisions firms make actually hinge on assumptions about the company's customer base—its customer portfolio (Figure 2.2). Second, the shape of the customer portfolio has a direct impact on the profit opportunities which are open to a company. Third, many of the most serious business risks companies face relate to the dependence they have on certain parts of the customer portfolio. Fourth, modern markets are increasingly characterized by fragmentation and granularity (Piercy 2009), so just looking at averages like market share and overall growth rates may provide little insight into to the most important emerging trends, opportunities, and threats. Putting sales back into the center of the debate about competitiveness and business strategy recognizes that some of the most important "unknowns" relate to customers, rather than to internal operations, systems, and processes, or to external sales promotional activities.

In fact, the involvement of the sales organization in strategy has two aspects. The *first* strategic sales issue is concerned with developing a perspective on sales relationships which does not focus simply on the tactical management of transactional selling processes, but examines the different relationships that may be formed with different types of customers as the basis for long-term business development (Olson, Cravens, and Slater 2001). This implies a new appraisal of the activities and processes required to enhance and sustain value delivery to customers through the sales organization. It is also increasingly the case that major customers require a highly specific value proposition built around "unique value" for the customer.

The *second* strategic sales issue is concerned with the role of sales and account management in interpreting the customer environment as a basis for strategic decisions. As the costs of dealing with major customers continue to increase, companies face major choices in where they choose to invest resources in developing a customer relationship and where they choose not to invest. With large customers in particular, the risks in investment or disinvestment are high, and it is likely that the intelligence-gathering and market sensing capabilities of the sales and account organization will play a growing role in influencing strategic decisions about resource allocation in the customer portfolio.

2.5.1.2 *Intelligence Capabilities and Resources.*

A further set of strategic questions surrounds the capability of the sales organization for building customer knowledge as a strategic resource critical both to strategy formulation and to building added-value strategies with major customers. Superior market sensing is becoming one of the most critical processes for building and enhancing strategic capabilities, reflecting how well managers understand their customers and markets. In an evolving service dominant logic of marketing (Vargo and Lusch 2004), the most successful organizations are likely to be those with a core competence in market sensing processes (Day 1999, Sheth and Sharma 2008). The critical sales role in market sensing is underlined by the service-centered view that communication processes are characterized by dialogue, and by asking and answering questions—salesperson knowledge of customers and solutions is a competitive advantage, leading ultimately to more customer-oriented and relational buyer–seller strategies that co-create value with the customer (Sheth and Sharma 2008).

In fact, one of the defining characteristics of agile, fast-moving businesses is that they show a high level of strategic sensitivity—they have a high level of awareness of what is happening around them and what is going to happen next. Fast, nimble companies are very good at scanning for information and insight (Doz and Kosonen 2007). There is a strong argument that one of the key attributes of leading companies is that they are fact-obsessed (Davenport and Harris 2007). Fact-based management and evidence-based management are approaches which allow managers to challenge corporate decision-making assumptions and stereotypes and look for new knowledge and its implications—breaking free of the "dangerous half-truths and total nonsense" to which managers all too often cling (Pfeffer and Sutton 2006: 2).

Indeed, it can be argued that companies can take risk out of the business only by paying closer attention to how customers are changing and how markets are developing. Adrian Slywotsky (2007: 10) summarizes the challenge of becoming a knowledge-intense organization:

The best countermeasure for defeating customer risk is creating and applying proprietary information about your customers ... It's answering the question: what do we know about customers that others don't? And then using that information to make and keep profitable customers for life.

However, effective market sensing and superior market knowledge goes much further than simply undertaking market research. The difference between market sensing and marketing research is that market sensing describes the processes in the organization which develop enhanced management understanding about the external world, while marketing research is mainly concerned with techniques of data collection and reporting—surveys, observation studies, market experiments, and so on. The difference is between process (understanding) and technology (collecting data through formal techniques).

Moreover, superior intelligence resources are also closely related to competitiveness as well as to strategy-building. For example, one clear and repeated demand by corporate buyers is that suppliers should demonstrate deep knowledge of the customer's business, such that they can identify needs and opportunities before the buyer does (H. R. Chally 2006). Customers are increasingly unwilling to spend time with suppliers who do not understand the business, and who see it as the customer's job to educate the seller's salespeople.

Even in the consumer goods sector, retailers continue to report that their suppliers perform inadequately in the key areas which help differentiate them (the retailers) to the consumer, such as consumer insight development. Major retailers emphasize that trade relationships are no longer based on buyer–seller roles, and characterize the best-in-class supplier as one that has a firm understanding of the retailer's position, strategy and ambitions in the marketplace—they require consumer market insight from their suppliers (IBM Institute for Business Value 2005).

In the buyer's eyes, the deployment of superior knowledge and expertise has become a defining characteristic of the world-class sales organization. The buyer logic is straightforward: if the seller cannot bring added value to the relationship by identifying new opportunities for the buyer to gain competitive advantage in the end-use marketplace, then the seller is no more than a commodity supplier, and can be treated as such (the product is likely to be bought only on price and technical specification).

In the many situations faced by sellers now, major customers demand that the seller displays not simply a superior understanding of the customer's own organization but detailed and insightful knowledge of the customer's end-use markets and the customer's strategies. The inability to offer the customer ways of becoming more efficient and more competitive in the end-use market has become critical. The strategic sales role is becoming one of deploying end-use market knowledge to enhance the customer's competitive position and cost efficiency.

Customers evaluate their suppliers on the seller's success in enhancing the customer's competitive position, and increasingly expect proof of this achievement. The challenge to suppliers from an increasing proportion of their customers is to understand the customer's business and the customer's end-use markets, and to leverage that knowledge to create competitive advantage for the customer. The alternative is to face growing commoditization and declining margins. Meeting this challenge is a central element of strategic sales choices. The corresponding challenge for the strategic sales organization is to develop, deploy, and sustain new skills and capabilities in market sensing.

2.5.1.3 *Integration of Customer-Facing Activities*

Important organizational dilemmas are associated with the need to establish the cross-functional relationships necessary to lead processes which define, develop, and deliver superior value propositions to customers, and to manage the interfaces between functions and business units impacting on service and value as it is perceived by customers. Total integration around customer value is a mandate which has proved elusive in the traditional functional organizations (Hulbert, Capon, and Piercy 2003). Sheth and Sharma (2008), for example, underline the growing mandate for the salesperson to take responsibility for marshalling internal and external resources to satisfy customer needs and wants.

The reality is that powerful customers increasingly demand that sellers provide problem-solving and creative thinking about their business. They require the commitment of, and access to, the supplier's total operation. Indeed, one European executive recently described this as "the convergence of strategic management, change management and process management, all critical elements of transforming the sales function to meet today's customer requirements" (Seidenschwartz 2005).

However, it is also apparent that, where suppliers have developed programmes of value creation around major customers, they have often been plagued by problems of "organizational drag"—the seller's organizational functions are not aligned around processes of creating and delivering customer value (Koerner 2005). Major retailers across the world emphasize supplier organizational structure and culture as key obstacles to improving customer management effectiveness (IBM Institute for Business Value 2005).

Success in the new marketplace increasingly demands the careful and systematic integration of a company's entire set of capabilities into a seamless system that delivers superior customer value—what we have called elsewhere "total integrated marketing" (Hulbert, Capon, and Piercy 2003). Our logic is based on the observation that superior performing companies seem to share one simple yet vital characteristic: they get their act together around the things that matter most to their customers, and they make a totally integrated offer of superior value in customer terms.

It is likely that one of the most critical roles of the strategic sales organization will be managing processes of customer value definition, development, and delivery that cut across functional interfaces and organizational boundaries to build real customer focus. Many of the barriers to developing and delivering superior customer value come from the characteristics of supplier organizations. The challenge of strategic customer management mandates effective approaches to cross-functional integration around value processes. Rather than managing only the interface with the customer, the strategic sales force must cope with a range of interfaces with internal functions and departments, and increasingly with partner organizations, to deliver value seamlessly to customers.

2.5.1.4 *Internal Marketing of Customer Priorities*

A related challenge is using sales resources to "sell" the customer across functional and divisional boundaries within the company and across organizational boundaries with partner companies, to achieve seamless value delivery for customers. Superior service and responsiveness to customer needs careful cultivation and management. Internal marketing is associated with the need for firms to market to employees. Satisfying the needs of internal customers should put an organization in a better position to deliver the service and quality necessary to satisfy external customers (Ahmed and Rafiq 2003). Sales organizations will need to become better at obtaining resources from their own firms—an issue examined rarely in marketing and very infrequently in the sales literature (Sheth and Sharma 2008). Internal marketing capabilities are seen as particularly important in global account management (Millman 1996)—involving the promotion of ideas and initiatives, and changing organizational focus towards issues like customer-centric marketing (Shi, Zou, White, McNally, and Cavusgil 2005).

Indeed, research at Northwestern University has found internal marketing to be one of the top three determinants of a company's financial performance: companies with better integration of internal and external market processes report better financial results (Chang 2005). Other studies suggest that many organizations are struggling to deliver their value propositions to external customers because of inadequate investment in the internal marketplace and a lack of internal marketing (*Marketing Week* 2003).

The risk of undermining the competitive position with a major customer as a result of such internal market factors is too serious to be ignored. One role of the strategic sales organization is likely to be "selling" the customer to employees and managers, as a basis for understanding customer priorities and the importance of meeting them, an activity that parallels conventional sales and marketing efforts. Sales organizations are familiar with the idea that what they are actually selling to customers is the company—its reputation, standing, capabilities, and so on—more than just products. The internal marketing parallel is selling the customer to the company—to the internal market of employees, managers, and partner organizations.

Like any other radical, change-oriented initiative, strategic customer management is likely to fail without careful attention to the internal marketplace. We can consider the importance of the internal market to successfully implementing strategic customer management in the light of the type of barriers which may be anticipated, and the need to plan around implementation barriers. Internal marketing programmes, at different levels, provide a way of operationalizing this, and provide a further strand to the emerging role of the strategic sales organization.

2.5.1.5 *Infrastructure for Strategy Implementation*

These factors lead to challenges in developing the structure and processes needed to manage sales and account management organizations in order to match customer relationship requirements and to build competitive advantage. Structures, compensation systems, evaluation systems, and training and development investments have to be designed to align with relationship and partnership, not the transactional focus of the past.

For example, LaForge, Ingram, and Cravens (2009) have recently described the importance of effective realignment of the sales organization with business strategies as a critical element of company transformation in order to deliver superior customer value. They examine key linkages between firm transformation strategy, sales organization strategy, and sales management practice. These authors provide an integrative model with which to address sales organization alignments issues, but further they identify the underlying organizational interfaces where strategic alignment is a priority.

These challenges are among the most immediate for executives in assessing how to build the sales organization as an effective strategic force in a company. However, there are also other broader drivers of change to which attention should be given.

2.5.2 Shaping the Sales Role

In addition to redefining the domain for the sales organization, a number of factors impact on how enhanced scope and responsibility should influence the way in which sales executives address issues.

2.5.2.1 *Inspiration and Leadership*

One outcome of focusing attention on the strategic role of the transformed sales organization should be to renew the ability of those who manage key external relationships with customers to inspire and provide leadership within the business.

Issues of leadership for the strategic sales organization are underlined by The Sales Educators (2006). Indeed, there is accumulating evidence that leadership questions are given more critical importance in many organizations, operating in the market environments they now face, than ever before.

In fact, for more than twenty years many of the world's top companies have been "academy companies" offering intensive leadership training to their executives, because their best young employees are hungry for leadership development. Prime examples are General Electric, Procter & Gamble, and Nokia. The "academy company" logic is that competitors can copy every advantage you have got, except one. So, the best companies have realized that their real business is building leaders (Colvin 2007).

However, less positively, a recent Roffey Park management agenda study reports that while the overwhelming majority of board directors in the UK (82 per cent) rated the leadership enjoyed by their organization as good or excellent, only half of middle managers (52 per cent) felt they could take such an optimistic view of leadership in their businesses. Even bigger gaps opened up regarding the related issues of morale and the values of the organization (Stern 2008). Leadership issues are likely to be critical in developing a strategic sales organization.

The leadership dilemmas for a strategic sales organization can be considered at several levels. First, leadership can be examined within the strategic sales organization: key questions are how senior and middle-ranking executives in the sales organization can implement the leadership and followership characteristics relevant to the strategic sales initiative. Second, leadership extends to the role of the strategic sales organization within the company and the "top team" responsibilities that come with higher profile—achieving cross-functional and high level influence to support the goals of strategic customer management. Thirdly, perspectives on leadership should include external relationships—playing a key role in the tangled web of relationships common in linking suppliers, collaborators, and customer value. Lastly, leadership includes the role played in the broader professional business community—winning a seat at the management "top table" to influence opinion, public policy and the professional futures of sales and account management.

2.5.2.2 *Influence over Major Decisions.*

The new sales role defines the new degree and extent to which the sales organization exerts influence over the company's strategic agenda and the key decisions which are made. Inspirational leadership is important, but leadership has to turn into influence if things are to be changed.

One of the most significant problems for marketing departments has been being ignored by key decision-makers and other functions. Research suggests that when marketers try to share insights and information with other departments, they are frequently ignored or misunderstood—so there is an increasingly difficult struggle to get the customer's voice heard in the company (Fazio Maruca 1998).

Part of the problem is insufficient or weak efforts at communicating with other departments. For example, in studying the integration of marketing and R&D, research findings suggest that it is inter-functional rivalry and political pressures that severely reduce R&D's use of information supplied by marketing and sales personnel (Maltz, Souder, and Kumar 2001). This speaks to declining influence and credibility in contributing to the important debates and decisions within the business, which is likely to undermine the ability to implement change. In the absence of formal authority and perhaps weak credibility in some companies, those looking to the strategic sales organization as a force for important change will rely on rebuilding influence within the organization to achieve these goals.

The landscape of power and influence inside a company is likely to be a powerful determinant of whether a strategic sales initiative succeeds or fails, and may involve active strategies of influence and change. Achieving the type of change implied by strategizing the sales organization will depend in part on the success of executives in engaging with the rest of the organization and confronting the realities of how it makes important decisions.

2.5.2.3 *Integrity and Social Responsibility*

For many companies there has probably never been a time when scrutiny of their ethical and responsible behavior was closer, and when the cost of being judged unethical or irresponsible was higher. Managing relationships with customers, partners, and suppliers with integrity is a huge challenge, but not one that can be ignored. Increasingly, major customers cannot do business with people whom they cannot trust, or whose corporate reputations carry a danger of contamination by association. This may be the highest priority in new types of buyer–seller relationship (Galea 2006).

For the strategic sales organization to fulfill its leadership commitments and to exert influence in a company also brings the responsibility for championing integrity—both in dealing with external customers and partner organizations and in working with others in the company. This responsibility brings some limitations on what actions can be taken but, more importantly, is also a source of competitive strength in the marketplace.

Certainly, the level of scrutiny of the ethical standards and corporate social responsibility initiatives undertaken by companies has never been so searching. The attention of pressure groups and the media given to company behavior is unprecedented, and frequently hostile. Damage to corporate reputation, however it is brought about, reduces the ability to compete and can undermine the value of a company.

Historically it has been easiest for critics and observers to focus on the selling behavior of suppliers, and much attention has been give to the "front-end" ethical standards of salespeople and sales management. This continues to be the case. However, the debate has moved on to a much broader ground concerning corporate social responsibility—initiatives to show "green" or environmental improvements, protecting the working conditions of employees at different stages of the supply chain, reducing the use of scarce resources in the value chain, and so on. This debate has now reached a level of maturity such that it has a substantial impact on buyer–seller relationships and the competitive position of selling organizations (Piercy and Lane 2009a).

Importantly, ethical standards and corporate social responsibility initiatives are concerned with more than corporate reputation or philanthropy. The pursuit of high standards and investment in social responsibility initiatives has a growing impact on customer value and the attractiveness or lack of attractiveness of a supplier to the customer. Increasingly, moral and social issues form part of the value proposition offered to the market, how a company is positioned compared to competitors, and its areas of greatest vulnerability to competitive attack (Piercy and Lane 2009a).

The centrality of moral and social issues to the strategic sales organization is reinforced by Ferrell and Ferrell (2009), who appraise sales ethics in an enterprise-wide stakeholder approach. The underlying logic of their approach is that strategic sales leadership built on an ethical organizational culture contributes to ethical decision-making and plays a strong role in building transparency and trust with stakeholders. Their framework seeks to provide a strategic approach to developing and sustaining an enterprise-wide perspective that includes sales ethics. The approach uses a stakeholder framework (including the needs of employees, suppliers, regulators, special interest groups, communities, and the media) to position sales in a strategic role, participating in the development and implementation of ethical marketing practice. Their strategic approach to ethics develops a process for addressing stakeholder issues, including: creating a strategic focus on stakeholders; risk tolerance and culture; developing guidelines and boundaries for acceptable practices; and creating mechanisms for continuous improvement. In this approach, the strategic sales organization needs to consider enterprise-wide stakeholders, to identify and prioritize their concerns, and to gather information to respond to significant individuals, groups, and communities.

Their concern is that frequently sales has operated in a situation where role and rewards are based on a single, financial criterion, so that incentives for performance obscure stakeholder perspectives. Instead, they look for a corporate culture that establishes appropriate norms and values to set boundaries for activities, including compliance, core practices, a commitment to excel, and voluntary contributions to integrity. Implementation of their approach is facilitated by a triple bottom-line concept, incorporating economic, environmental, and social factors.

Ferrell and Ferrell (2009) make the telling point that ethics is an enterprise-wide issue in which sales plays a critical role, rather than simply mandating compliance with codes of "fair practice" from those in selling roles.

2.5.2.4 *International Perspectives*

The globalization of markets, the emergence of global customers, and the spread of international competition mandates an international perspective on how customer relationships are managed in domestic and overseas markets.

International issues are critical to developing business models and new strategies, to managing the customer portfolio, and to developing the sales organization infrastructure. Aggressive globalization and the challenges of gaining a strong competitive edge underline the importance of sales management strategies in establishing a competitive advantage in international markets. Increasingly, top management in many global enterprises are developing their sales force capabilities, recognizing the importance of the sales force in core business processes like customer relationship management, supply chain management, and product development management. Multinational firms like Nestlé SA, Novartis, and Caterpillar Inc. have been widely recognized for their successful global sales management systems (Cravens, Piercy, and Low 2006).

Certainly, the growth in importance of global customers has led many suppliers to develop specialized organizational units and processes to manage their relationship. Global account management (GAM) is "an organizational form and process by which the worldwide activities serving a given multi-national customer are coordinated by one person or team within the supplying company" (Yip and Madsen 1996: 25).

In common with the strategic sales organization, global account management teams are multi-functional and can only operate effectively by addressing cross-functional coordination and communication around strategy development for global customers. Global account managers frequently report to very senior

levels of the organization. Effective organizational responses to the global customer are becoming extremely important in a wide range of companies. GAM is
in many ways similar to strategic account management, suffering from the same
vulnerabilities and involving the same choices (Yip and Bank 2007). However,
here there may be less choice involved for the seller. If the customer is a global
business with buying points across many countries, there may be no option
other than to respond on a global account management basis or to lose the
business.

Indeed, from a strategic sales perspective, part of the challenge of GAM is translating central decisions into the operations of decentralized sales organizations.
One of the issues then becomes the extent to which country-based sales management practices will have to be altered to allow this translation to happen. Importantly, market conditions and consequently customer priorities may be significantly
different in global markets. For example, some of the most attractive prospects are
in emerging markets, where local market conditions are substantially different
from those in developed countries. The importance of adapting customer strategy
to these local conditions is a critical factor for success.

Accordingly, assumptions about local market conditions should be challenged
and questioned in many cases. Those local conditions shape and define what
customers will need and require from suppliers, and those needs may be very
different. However, there are also important issues to consider about how well sales
management and account management practices and policies cross national
boundaries—or how well they cross cultural and economic divides.

While much marketing and sales thinking emphasizes differences between
international markets, when we come to consider strategic sales rather than
operational sales issues, that thinking may have exaggerated the importance of
international market differences (Cravens, Piercy, and Low 2006).

One important issue in understanding global trends in sales management
(rather than simply selling) is whether real differences exist between different
cultures and countries. In particular, this raises a crucial question: how important
are country differences when we make multi-country sales force decisions
on things like the level of management behavior-based control and incentive
compensation? The convergence of sales management practices across countries
in a flattening world may be a high priority in meeting the demands of global
accounts in particular. This may replace the individual country-based practices
developed in an earlier era of "think globally, act locally" to reflect country and
market differences.

Senior sales executives managing global sales strategies face complex dilemmas.
Global account management involves deciding how to identify and serve international accounts. But should one global sales force be used, or should account
responsibilities be delegated to country sales forces? How should salespeople be
allocated between direct and non-direct sales forces around the world? How

important are country differences in multi-country sales force decisions like sales management control and incentive compensation? These dilemmas underline the strategic issues in managing across national boundaries.

In fact, knowledge about global sales management practices outside the US and western Europe is limited. There are relatively few published studies on sales management in developing countries to guide management decisions. However, our research sheds some light on some of the relevant issues (Baldauf, Cravens, and Piercy 2001; Cravens, Piercy, and Low 2006; Piercy, Low, and Cravens 2004).

2.6 CONCLUDING REMARKS

The emerging agenda for executives and marketing and sales scholars is concerned with the role of strategic customer management, rather than traditional sales or selling. The goal is to position the management of the customer portfolio and the design of relationship strategies for major customers as key issues driving business strategy and performance. Strategic customer management focuses on the shift from sales as a tactical activity, concerned only with implementing business and marketing strategy, to a strategic process that aligns corporate resources with customer needs and confronts complex, important, and hard decisions about investment in customers and the risks in dependence on major customers.

2.6.1 A New Perspective on the Sales Organization

A new perspective on the strategic sales organization is likely to be distinguished by several characteristics:

- **The effective co-alignment of sales processes with business strategy**: the implementation of business strategy relies on the effective management of customer relationships—particularly with major customers—while the formulation of effective business strategy recognizes the resource provided by strategic sales capabilities.
- **A customer perspective in marketing and business strategy**: effective strategy increasingly relies on a profound understanding of customers and markets, yet the market sensing capability provided by the sales force is frequently ignored by decision-makers (Le Meunier-FitzHugh and Piercy 2006).
- **Management focus on the customer portfolio**: customers differ in their attractiveness, their prospects, and the risk they bring to the supplier business. The customer portfolio highlights the different relationship requirements and

business opportunities with different groups and types of customers. Some of the most important decisions about customers relate to investment in meeting requirements but also in making decisions not to invest.

- **Developing effective positioning with dominant customers:** it is characteristic of the customer portfolio that some customers are likely to be dominant in the market concerned. The dependence of a supplier on a dominant customer and the ways to survive in this situation are among the most critical issues companies face.

Strategic customer management makes explicit some of the most critical competitive and customer issues that companies face and which will shape their futures for better or worse.

REFERENCES

AHMED, P. K., and M. RAFIQ (2003). "Internal Marketing Issues and Challenges," *European Journal of Marketing* 63, 146–63.

ANDERSON, E., and B. TRINKLE (2005). *Outsourcing the Sales Function: The Real Costs of Field Sales*, Mason, OH: Thomson.

BALDAUF, A., D. W. CRAVENS, and N. F PIERCY (2001). "Examining the Consequences of Sales Management Control Strategies in European Field Sales Organizations," *International Marketing Review* 18.5, 474–508.

CHANG, J. (2005). "From the Inside Out," *Sales & Marketing Management* (August), 8.

CLARK, B., and S. CALLAHAN (2000). "Sales Staffs: Adapt or Die," *B to B* (April 10), 55.

COLVIN, G. (2007). "Leader Machines," *Fortune* (October 1), 60–72.

CRAVENS, D. W., and N. F. PIERCY (2009). *Strategic Marketing*, 9th edn, Burr Ridge, IL: Irwin/McGraw-Hill.

——––and G. S. Low (2006). "Globalization of the Sales Organization: Management Control and its Consequences," *Organizational Dynamics* 35.3, 291–303.

CROSS, J., S. W. HARTLEY, W. RUDELIUS, and M. J. VASSEY (2001). "Sales Force Activities and Marketing Strategies in Industrial Firms: Relationships and Implications," *Journal of Personal Selling & Sales Management* 21.3, 199–206.

DARTNELL CORPORATION (1999). *Dartnell's 30th Sales Force Compensation Survey: 1998–1999*, Chicago: Dartnell Corporation.

DAVENPORT, T. H., and J. G. HARRIS (2007). *Competing on Analytics: The New Science of Winning*, Boston, MA: Harvard Business School Press.

DAY, G. S. (1997). "Aligning the Organization to the Market," in D. R. Lehman and K. E. Jocz (eds.), *Reflections on the Futures of Marketing*, Cambridge, MA: Marketing Science Institute, 69–72.

——(1999). *The Market-Driven Organization: Understanding, Attracting, and Keeping Valuable Customers*, New York: Free Press.

DE BOER, L., E. LABRO, and O. MORLACCI (2001). "A Review of Methods Supporting Supplier Selection," *European Journal of Purchasing & Supply Management* 7.2, 75–89.

DELOITTE TOUCHE (2005). *Strategic Sales Compensation Survey*, New York: Deloitte Touche Development.

DOYLE, P. (2002). *Marketing Management and Strategy*, 3rd edn, London: Prentice Hall.

DOZ, Y., and M. KOSONEN (2007). *Fast Strategy: How Strategic Agility Will Help You Stay Ahead of the Game*, Philadelphia: Wharton School.

ENGLISH, S. (2001). "Britannic Will Close Door on Sales Team," *Daily Telegraph* (March 8), 6.

FAZIO MARUCA, R. (1998). "Getting Marketing's Voice Heard," *Harvard Business Review*, January–February, 10–11.

FERRELL, L., and O. C. FERRELL (2009). "An Enterprise-Wide Strategic Stakeholder Approach to Sales Ethics," *Journal of Strategic Marketing* 17.3–4, 257–70.

GALEA, C. (2006). "What Customers Really Want," *Sales & Marketing Management* (May), 11.

HOMBURG, C., J. P. WORKMAN, and O. JENSEN (2000). "Fundamental Changes in Marketing Organization: The Movement Toward a Customer-Focused Organizational Structure," *Journal of the Academy of Marketing Science* 28.4, 459–78.

H. R. CHALLY (2006). *The Chally World Class Sales Excellence Research Report*, Dayton, OH: H. R. Chally Group.

HULBERT, J. M., N. CAPON, and N. F. PIERCY (2003). *Total Integrated Marketing: Breaking the Bounds of the Function*, New York: Free Press.

IBM INSTITUTE FOR BUSINESS VALUE (2005). *The Strategic Agenda for Customer Management in the Consumer Products Industry*, New York: IBM Institute for Business Value.

JANDA, S., and S. SESHANDRI (2001). "The Influence of Purchasing Strategies on Performance," *Journal of Business & Industrial Marketing* 16.4, 294–306.

JONES, ELI, S. P. BROWN, A. A. ZOLTNERS, and B. A. WEITZ (2005). "The Changing Environment of Selling and Sales Management," *Journal of Personal Selling & Sales Management* 25.2, 105–11.

KOERNER, L. (2005). "Conducting An Organizational Assessment of Your SAM Programme", presentation at Strategic Account Management Association Conference, Paris.

KORNIK, J. (2007). "What's It All Worth?", *Sales & Marketing Management* (May), 27–39.

KROHMER, H., C. HOMBURG, and J. P. WORKMAN (2002). "Should Marketing Be Cross-Functional? Conceptual Development and International Empirical Evidence," *Journal of Business Research* 35, 451–65.

LAFORGE, R. W., T. N. INGRAM, and D. W. CRAVENS (2009). "Strategic Alignment for Sales Organization Transformation," *Journal of Strategic Marketing* 17.3–4, 199–219.

LAMBERT, D. M., H. MARMORSTEIN, and A. SHARMA (1990). "Industrial Salespeople as a Source of Market Information," *Industrial Marketing Management* (17 May), 111–18.

LE MEUNIER-FITZHUGH, K., and N. F. PIERCY (2006). "Integrating Marketing Intelligence Sources: Reconsidering the Role of the Salesforce," *International Journal of Market Research* 48, 38–60.

LONDON, S. (2005). "Xerox Runs Off a New Blueprint," *Financial Times* (September 23), 13.

LUSCH, R. F., and S. L. VARGO (eds.) (2006). *The Service Dominant Logic for Marketing Dialog, Debate, and Directions*, Armonk, NY: Sharpe.

MAIER, J., and J. SAUNDERS (1990). "The Implementation Process of Segmentation in Sales Management," *Journal of Personal Selling & Sales Management* 10 (February), 39–48.

MALTZ, E., W. E. SOUDER, and A. KUMAR (2001). "Influencing R&D/Marketing Integration and the Use of Market Information By R&D Managers," *Journal of Business Research* 52.1, 69–82.

Marketing Week (2003). "Survey Reveals 'Inadequate' State of Internal Marketing," *Marketing Week*, July 3, 8.

MARSH, PETER (2007). "Back on a Roll in the Business of Bearings," *Financial Times* (February 7), 10.

MILLMAN, T. F. (1996). "Global Key Account Management and Systems Selling," *International Business Review* 5.6, 631–45.

MOL, M. J., and J. BIRKENSHAW (2007). *Giant Steps in Management: Innovations That Change the Way We Work*, Harlow: FT–Prentice Hall.

OGBUCHI, A. O., and V. M. SHARMA (1999). "Redefining Industrial Salesforce Roles in a Changing Environment," *Journal of Marketing Theory & Practice* 7.1, 64–71.

OLSON, E. M., D. W. CRAVENS, and S. F. SLATER (2001). "Competitiveness and Sales Management: A Marriage of Strategies," *Business Horizons* (March–April), 25–30.

PFEFFER, J., and R. I. SUTTON (2006). *Hard Facts: Dangerous Half-Truths and Total Answers*, Boston, MA: Harvard Business School Press.

PIERCY, N. F. (2009). *Market-Led Strategic Change: Transforming the Process of Going to Market*, 4th edn, Oxford: Butterworth-Heinemann.

——and N. LANE (2009a). "Corporate Social Responsibility: Impacts on Strategic Marketing and Customer Value," *Marketing Review* 9.4, 335–60.

————(2009b). *Strategic Customer Management: Strategizing the Sales Organization*, Oxford: Oxford University Press.

——G. S. Low, and D. W. CRAVENS (2004). "Examining the Effectiveness of Sales Management Control Practices in Developing Countries," *Journal of World Business* 39, 255–67.

RACKHAM, N., and J. DEVINCENTIS (1999). *Rethinking the Sales Force: Redefining Selling to Create and Capture Customer Value*, New York: McGraw-Hill, 3.

RIGBY, E. (2007). "Shopping Gets Tougher for Online Supermarkets," *Financial Times* (April 9), 19.

ROYAL, W. (1999). "Death of Salesmen," www.industryweek.com, May 17, 59–60.

SEIDENSCHWARTZ, W. (2005). "A Model for Customer Enthusiasm: Connecting the Customer With Internal Processes", presentation at Strategic Account Management Association Conference, February, Paris.

SHAPIRO, B. P. (2002). "Creating the Customer-Centric Team: Coordinating Sales and Marketing," Harvard Business School Note 9-999-006, Boston, MA: Harvard Business School.

——A. J. SLYWOTSKY, and S. X. DOYLE (1998). "Strategic Sales Management: A Boardroom Issue," Harvard Business School Note 9-595-018, Boston, MA: Harvard Business School.

SHETH, J. N., and A. SHARMA (2008). "The Impact of Product to Service Shift in Industrial Markets and the Evolution of the Sales Organization," *Industrial Marketing Management* 37, 260–69.

SHI, L. H., S. ZOU, J. C. WHITE, R. C. MCNALLY, and S. T. CAVUSGIL (2005). "Global Account Management Capability: Insights from Leading Suppliers," *Journal of International Marketing* 13.2, 93–113.

SLYWOTSKY, A., with K. WEBER (2007). *The Upside: From Risk Taking to Risk Shaping: How to Turn Your Greatest Threat Into Your Biggest Opportunity*, New York: Crown Business.

STEPHENS, H., CEO, The H. R. Chally Group (2003). Presentation at the American Marketing Association Educators' Conference, August.

STERN, S. (2008). "The Lofty View from Davos Could Just Be a Mirage," *Financial Times* (January 29), 14.

STEWART, T. A. (2006). "The Top Line," *Harvard Business Review* (July–August), 10.

TALLURI, S., and R. NARASIMHAN (2004). "A Methodology for Strategic Sourcing," *European Journal of Operational Research* 154.1, 236–50.

THE SALES EDUCATORS (2006). *Strategic Sales Leadership: Breakthrough Thinking for Breakthrough Results*, Mason, OH: Thomson.

VARGO, S. L., and R. F. LUSCH (2004). "Evolving to a New Dominant Logic for Marketing," *Journal of Marketing* 68.1, 1–23.

YIP, G. S., and A. J. M. BANK (2007). *Managing Global Customers: An Integrated Approach*, Oxford: Oxford University Press.

——and MADSEN, T. L. (1996). "Global Account Management: The New Frontier in Relationship Marketing," *International Marketing Review* 13.3, 24–42.

ZOLTNERS, A. A., P. SINHA, and S. E. LORIMER (2004). *Sales Force Design for Strategic Advantage*, New York: Palgrave Macmillan.

CHAPTER 3

STRATEGIC LEADERSHIP IN SALES

UNDERSTANDING THE RELATIONSHIP BETWEEN THE ROLE OF THE SALESPERSON AND THE ROLE OF THE SALES MANAGER

KAREN FLAHERTY

3.1 INTRODUCTION

An increasing pace of competition coupled with added resource constraints and shortened product lifecycles have heightened the pressure to internalize new information quickly. Management researchers and practitioners widely recognize the need for organizations to continuously modify their strategies, structures, processes, and programs (Fiol and Lyles 1985). Likewise, sales management scholars have emphasized the importance of implementing new approaches and then learning from their successes and failures in the field (Chonko, Dubinsky, Jones, and Roberts 2003). Handling rapid change has become an essential ingredient of successful sales organizations. To accomplish this task, top management must be open to new initiatives that diverge from its view of strategy, and must use these to shape new competencies (Burgelman 1991). Because of their exposure to external constituents, including customers, frontline salespeople often provide a vital source of divergent thought and creativity (Weitz, Castleberry, and Tanner 2001). As a result, in some organizations the role of the salesperson has moved beyond traditional selling activities to include involvement in shaping strategy.

In many respects the job of the salesperson has changed in an effort to better meet these new role expectations. In fact, today's salespeople often engage in three distinct roles: *competence deployment, competence modification,* and *competence definition* (Floyd and Lane 2000). *Competence deployment* is activity designed to support the existing strategic plan. Salespeople must conform to the formal strategic plan and implement established strategies and processes. However, in today's business atmosphere some salespeople may also engage in *competence modification.* The salesperson is encouraged to engage in adaptive behavior or emergent strategy (Hart 1992). For instance, salespeople may be expected to question the organization's existing strategy and to respond to environmental challenges on the fly. Finally, salespeople may engage in *competence definition* to the extent that they learn and improve (Argyris and Schon 1978), initiate autonomous initiatives (Burgelman 1991), and experiment and take risks (Hart 1992).

Given the changes that are occurring in many sales organizations, it is safe to assume that the tempo of work activity is becoming faster, more dynamic, and less predictable for some salespeople but maybe not for all. The relative importance of the three roles depends on the environmental conditions that the sales organization faces (Floyd and Lane 2000). The roles expected of salespeople are not consistent across all sales organizations, nor should they be. For instance, when organizations face stable competition, then the strategic focus of the organization is directed to the deployment of existing competencies according to the predetermined strategy. The goal is to find optimal solutions to existing problems. There is a good deal of certainty regarding the direction the organization should follow (Floyd and Lane 2000). Thus, the role of the salesperson is competence deployment. In other situations, organizations face changes in product markets and factor markets, and greater flexibility is needed. The existing routines and the established strategy are no longer working. As a result, managers become less certain about the strategic direction of the organization. Under such conditions, salespeople are empowered to respond to changes or to engage in competence modification. Finally, when environmental dynamism is very high across both factor and product markets (i.e. a firm faces a hypercompetitive environment), companies are unable to obtain a sustainable competitive advantage (D'Aveni 1994). These organizations must constantly renew their strategies in order to temporarily differentiate from competitors (Floyd and Lane 2000). In order to achieve this state of constant renewal, salespeople will participate in competence definition.

Despite these differences, sales research often assumes parity in job roles across salespeople and organizations. Furthermore, little consideration has been given to the role the sales manager must play in order to accommodate the various role expectations of the salesperson. The purpose of this chapter is to provide a consideration of the effects that the three strategic roles of the salesperson (competence deployment, competence modification, and competence definition) have for the leadership of the sales force. The chapter reviews the existing leadership literature and then extends this review to consider the relevance of existing leadership theory for future strategic leadership in sales. Based on past research, the chapter proposes that a configuration theory perspective or a 'systems' perspective rather than a 'best practice' approach to leadership is necessary. It is suggested that it is vital to jointly consider the unique role expectations of the salesperson, the subsequent exchange relationship necessary between the salesperson and the sales manager, and various sales management practices including control when determining the best approach to sales leadership. Successful strategic sales leadership will depend on the utilization of leadership techniques that *fit* best with the current environment, salesperson roles, and strategic direction of the organization. On the basis of these considerations, an integrative framework for sales leadership is suggested.

The remainder of this chapter is structured as follows. First, a brief review of the literature on employee roles and job demands is provided. The three roles that salespeople play in the strategy process and the influence of these additional job demands are discussed in detail. Second, the nature of the exchange relationship that exists between the salesperson and the sales manager is considered. The nature of the exchange that is required to accommodate each role complicates matters. For instance, assuming a competence definition role, the salesperson must play a part in initiating information exchange. The salesperson learns from experimentation and then communicates new knowledge to the sales manager. However, to accomplish competency deployment the salesperson must receive information from the manager and implement accordingly. Depending upon the direction and nature of the exchange, certain leadership approaches may be more beneficial than others. Third, the chapter provides a review of the leadership literature. Fourth, the chapter proposes a framework for strategic sales leadership processes and offers propositions for future study.

3.2 OVERVIEW OF SALESPERSON ROLES AND JOB DEMANDS

Every organizational position is associated with a primary role set that reflects expectations regarding the operational tasks and objectives of that position (Merton 1957). Past research suggests that a role is the set of behaviors that others expect of an individual in a certain situation (Floyd and Lane 2000). The primary role expectations or the operational roles (Merton 1957) tend to be explicitly stated or written, and are formally assessed and evaluated (Graen 1976). Based on extant sales practice and research, one might assume that the typical primary role set for the salesperson involves general sales activity including customer retention, database management, building and maintaining customer relationships, problem solving, and satisfying customer needs (Moncrief and Marshall 2005). The primary roles of the salesperson focus on the salesperson's interactions with the customer.

While these primary role expectations are likely to be common to all salespeople, organizational positions also have a secondary set of role expectations (Floyd and Lane 2000) that often brings more variability to the sales position. Secondary roles are not clearly defined, explicitly stated, or written. Sales scholars generally accept the idea that salespeople participate in secondary or extra-role behaviors including various organizational citizenship behaviors (Piercy, Cravens, Lane, and Vorhies 2006; MacKenzie, Podsakoff, and Ahearne 1998) as well as certain elements of strategic decision-making (Ingram, LaForge, and Leigh 2002) that go beyond the operational duties of the salesperson. Likewise, this chapter suggests that some salespeople will participate in competence definition and competence modification rather than solely competence deployment. The extent to which the salesperson participates in these forms of extra-role behavior is likely to vary depending upon the organization as well as the individual. While in some organizations the role of the salesperson may remain consistent with a traditional perspective (i.e. the salesperson's activity is largely limited to competence deployment or the primary role set), in many contemporary sales organizations the role expectations of the salesperson have been expanded to include additional competencies, making the sales job more difficult.

In brief, some salespeople operate in munificent environments, sell for companies that have well-fortified positions, are supported by highly capable co-workers, and have fewer job responsibilities, while others work in more challenging environments and may be asked to take on more challenging roles. The degree of challenge a salesperson faces in his or her job is likely to affect task conduct, performance, satisfaction, and turnover intentions, among other important outcomes, and thus warrants additional attention. Lack of attention to salesperson job roles may partly account for inconsistent or incomplete explanations of effective leadership in sales. In this chapter, it is anticipated that salesperson job roles constitute a crucial omitted variable in previous sales management/leadership research. In particular, the effectiveness of leadership approaches may vary depending upon salesperson role expectations.

In general, role expectations are likely to influence the job demands, or difficulty of the sales job, as perceived by the salesperson. Various definitions and conceptualizations of job demands have been proposed. Most of these definitions suggest that job demands involve the extent to which the employee is required to work hard, work fast, has many activities to perform, has too little time to complete the activities, etc. (Dwyer and Ganster 1991). Given their position as boundary spanners, salespeople are privy to a distinct set of demands that others within the organization do not experience. Salespeople interact both internally (with management and peers) and externally (with customers). Furthermore, as described earlier, some salespeople are now being called upon to fill more challenging strategic roles for the organization.

Job demands is a relatively broad construct that incorporates two dimensions—quantitative demands and qualitative demands (Hambrick, Finkelstein, and Mooney 2005). Quantitative demands include elements of the salesperson's workload (e.g. how many activities does the salesperson have to complete? how large is the salesperson's territory? how much time does the salesperson have to complete activities?). This dimension captures the degree of overall difficulty the salesperson experiences. Within the sales literature, researchers have argued that salesperson work overload is an acute stressor that contributes to a salesperson's overall job stress (Mulki, Lassk, and Jaramillo 2008). Qualitative demands include the salesperson's perceptions of role ambiguity and role conflict. The qualitative dimension captures the extent to which the salesperson is conflicted about which of these activities is most important, or which of his or her constituents needs should be met first. Role conflict and role ambiguity are both widely recognized sources of salesperson job stress (Avlonitis and Panagopoulos 2006).

Prior literature on salesperson job demands may help us better understand the impact of salesperson role expectations. It will provide a guide for how to best manage or lead salespeople under these expanded role demands. When a salesperson is encouraged to participate in competence definition activity, does his or her performance of traditional competence deployment activities decrease or increase? We can also better explain how the deterioration in performance occurs. Does the salesperson become paralyzed by an extended workload? Does the salesperson simply make more mistakes when facing the additional roles and increased complexity? Does the salesperson's expanded role help or hurt customer service behaviors?

It is particularly important to study job demands in a sales context because the salesperson has to deal with pressures that other organizational members are protected from. For instance, the salesperson has to cope with customer demands and the external environment. How can the sales manager lead the salesperson who faces additional challenges? The existing job demands literature largely ignores consideration of these additional demands (Hambrick et al. 2005). For the purposes of this chapter, it is suggested that the extent to which the salesperson operates in an organization wherein competence definition or competence modification is called for is likely to condition that salesperson's experience of the job as more demanding. While the reaction to the demands is often negative, this is not inevitable (Karasek 1979). Exposure to a stressor in and of itself is not a guarantee that felt stress will be incurred. Certain factors may serve as a buffer to the stress. This chapter considers how the sales manager can adjust leadership approaches to best buffer the potential negative effects of the added salesperson demands.

3.3 THE SYSTEM OF RELATIONAL EXCHANGES BETWEEN THE MANAGER AND THE SALESPERSON

Prior research has utilized various exchange models to better understand why some salespeople experience greater success than others. Blau (1964) suggests that when one employee performs a task that is beneficial to another, there is an expectation of reciprocation. The obligation to reciprocate provides balance in the exchange relationship between organizational members. Vertical exchange theory suggests that dyadic relationships (i.e. the relationship between manager and salespeople) are likely to vary on a continuum ranging from high-quality relationships ("cadres") characterized by reciprocal trust to low-quality relationships ("hired hands") characterized by a reliance on formal job contracts and descriptions (Castleberry and Tanner 1986). "Cadres" have strong skill sets, can be trusted without monitoring, and are motivated and able to assume greater responsibilities beyond the formal job description (Liden and Graen 1980). It is likely that these salespeople are given increased job latitude and support from their manager (Castleberry and Tanner 1986). "Hired hands," in contrast, receive little support or latitude. They perform routine tasks and have a more formal exchange with their manager (Liden and Graen 1980).

Facilitating different role expectations affects the nature and direction of the exchange. For our purposes it is particularly important to consider the nature and direction of the exchange of strategic information. In the following discussion the direction and flow of strategic information, content, and ideas between the sales manager and the salesperson is considered. For instance, competence definition requires both exploration and experimentation. Many strategic ideas and initiatives may be explored concurrently within the organization, only some of which will stick and evolve into formal proposals. Given the sheer number as well as the creativity of ideas necessary to this phase, salespeople must all be encouraged to initiate the process. The salespeople must explore new possibilities and experiment with new ideas, before the manager can determine which ideas to champion and pursue. Importantly, the direction of the *strategic* exchange between the sales manager and the salesperson originates with the salesperson (i.e. the salesperson offers an idea/initiative) and flows to the manager.

Conversely, when engaging in competence deployment, the salesperson receives his or her marching orders from the manager, and is then expected to implement or carry out the order. The objective of competence deployment is to effectively and efficiently implement existing procedures, programs, and strategy. Information flows from the sales manager to the salesperson. The exchange of strategic information may be unidirectional. There is less need for the salesperson to initiate strategic communication to the manager.

Finally, during competence modification the sales manager provides direction to the salesperson. These directives are typically based on an existing set of beliefs or assumptions regarding current environmental conditions and customer demands. Given changes to these conditions, the salesperson adjusts the initial direction to respond to the new information. Therefore, the exchange begins with information flow from the manager to the salesperson. The salesperson receives the information

Table 3.1. Information Exchange in Contemporary Sales Organizations

Salesperson Role Expectations	Sales Manager Information Requirements	Salesperson Information Requirements	Focal Direction of Exchange
Competence Definition			
Experiment and Explore Learn and Improve	Identify and Select Proposals; Champion New Ideas	Communicate What Works and What does not	Salesperson ⇨ Manager
Competence Modification			
Adjust to New Information Respond to Challenges	Provide General Vision; Provide Information on Change	Question the Status Quo; Communicate Customer and Technological Developments	Manager ⇨ Salesperson
Competence Deployment			
Conform to the System Follow Directions	Provide Goals and Strategies	Communicate Action Plans	Manager ⇨ Salesperson

and then balances this with an assessment of new environmental and customer information. The salesperson is capable of and expected to adjust and respond to this information.

In summary, this chapter argues that strategic leadership of the sales force can best be studied taking an exchange perspective. Explaining how strategic information moves throughout the sales force is critical to the contemporary sales organization. The social interactions between the manager and the salesperson will be important to the knowledge development and organizational learning required in the new role of the salesperson. Table 3.1 summarizes the relational exchanges proposed under each role expectation.

3.4 Defining the Strategic Role of the Sales Manager

Given a more complex role for the salesperson, it is becoming increasingly important to consider the changing nature of and requirements for effective sales leadership. As the role of the salesperson changes, the role of the sales manager must change as well. The shifting roles also have consequences for the system of exchanges that is necessary between the manager and the salesperson. This section examines several key themes surrounding what is argued to be the changing role of the sales manager. These include a reconsideration of the form of leadership required to be effective when leading today's sales force, and a discussion of how best to manage new salesperson roles via effective management control systems. Against this backdrop, an integrative framework of sales strategic leadership is proposed. Guided by configuration theory, it is suggested that no single best practice for sales leadership exists. Instead, different styles of leadership will outperform others when implemented under the right conditions.

3.4.1 Defining Leadership

Leadership has been an important area of research among social scientists for decades. Not surprisingly, we have witnessed a wide variety of definitions and approaches develop from this area of research. The earliest view of leadership (pre-1980s) involves three key ideas: leadership as an influence process, leadership within a group context, and leadership as direction toward a goal or goals. In this fashion, leadership has been most commonly defined as "the process (act) of influencing the activities of an organized group in its efforts toward goal setting and goal achievement" (Stogdill 1950: 3). Effective leadership is the achievement of the goal. However, after 1980 a shift in the conceptualization of leadership occurred. Researchers began to focus on the leader as the one who defines organizational reality for others. In other words, leadership involves setting the organizational agenda and determining what is important for others in the organization. In this vein, Smirchich and Morgan (1983) viewed leadership, and more specifically a leader, as a "manager of meaning." Similarly, Pfeffer (1981) described leadership as "symbolic action," wherein, a leader plays a vital role in sense-making for the organization, bringing the group to consensus regarding what is important.

A key contention in leadership research has involved distinguishing the leadership construct from the more general management construct. How do leadership behaviors differ from managerial behaviors? For example, some have argued that many of the questions explored in leadership research are simply questions regarding effective management. To distinguish between the two constructs, early leadership scholars suggest that management behaviors are limited to present conceptualizations of strategy or implementation, while leadership behaviors focus on changes. Leaders "change the way people think about what is desirable and necessary" (Bryman 1996), while managers are concerned with the day-to-day tasks and routines. The "manager of meaning" definition of leadership takes this into consideration, suggesting that the purpose of the leader is to engage in more of a visionary role than the three-part definition of leadership focusing on the influence, group, and goal.

3.4.2 A Review of Leadership Approaches

A review of prior research on leadership suggests several theoretical approaches that may prove beneficial to the study of sales leadership in contemporary sales organizations. This research may be categorized as follows: trait approaches, style approaches, contingency leadership, functional team leadership, shared team or dispersed leadership, and flexible leadership. In the following section, each perspective is considered, and its relevance to studying strategic sales leadership is briefly reviewed.

Initially, leadership scholars adopted a trait approach to the study of leaders, whereby the focus of the research was primarily on the personality traits and characteristics of existing leaders. This stream of research is most concerned with determining the set of characteristics that distinguish a leader from followers. A general belief that leaders are born not made is implied in this research. Trait researchers suggest that traits are particularly important to the study of leaders because these traits influence how people perceive the leader (Lord and Maher 1991). It is likely that leaders who depict certain traits (e.g. extroversion, competitiveness, self-confidence) may be perceived to be leaders by others. One goal of the trait approach is to differentiate between effective leaders and less effective leaders on the basis of their personality traits. For instance, past research considers the influence on leadership of physical traits such as height and attractiveness. Abilities such as intelligence have also been considered, and perhaps the most attention has been given to personality traits. For instance, in a review of trait-based research, Bass (1990) found self-confidence, originality, and cooperativeness to be predictors of effective leadership. Others suggest that extraversion (Costa and McCrae 1988, Hogan, Curphy, and Hogan 1994), self-esteem (Hill and Ritchie 1977), and creativity (Yukl 1998) are associated with leadership. In a more recent meta-analysis, Judge, Bono, Ilies, and Gerhardt (2002) found that extraversion, conscientiousness, and openness to experience are strong correlates of both leader effectiveness (i.e. the leader's performance in guiding the unit in the appropriate direction) and leader emergence (i.e. the extent to which an individual is viewed as a leader by others).

On the other hand, the style approach to leadership emphasizes the behaviors of leaders. While trait research calls attention to the specific characteristics of those who are effective leaders, the subsequent style approach provides some practical guidelines regarding the behaviors that are likely to result in effective leadership. In essence, the focus of trait research had been to identify characteristics that may aid in the selection of strong leaders. However, the style approach emphasizes the trainability dimension of leadership. Leaders are capable of studying various techniques and applying these in ways that will enhance the outcome. For example, the "consideration" style of leadership encompasses a style wherein the leader is concerned about the employee as a person. Trust and camaraderie are important aspects of this particular style. Initiating structure is a style wherein the leader clearly defines and schedules employee tasks and requirements. Research has suggested that consideration leads to enhanced employee morale and satisfaction but decreased performance, while initiating structure was associated with poor morale but better group performance.

Contingent theories of leadership argue that situational characteristics moderate the relationship between leader behaviors and outcomes. For example, contingent theories of leadership emphasize the importance of matching the leader's style to characteristics of the situation including the nature of the task at hand, the complexity of the environment, and characteristics of the individual employee. For example, path goal theory proposed that leaders should provide directive leadership when the employee is inexperienced and tasks are more complex (House 1971). Others conclude that leaders should allow employees more latitude in decision-making when the employee buys into the goals of the organization (Vroom and Yetton 1973). Results of leadership studies taking a contingency theory perspective have been somewhat mixed; however, in general this work has provided some important insights into how to lead the sales force. I would also argue that contingency studies continue to offer some insight into leadership within the contemporary sales organization. Understanding the influence of increased job demands on the effect of leadership styles is important.

In the 1980s several new styles of leadership were proposed. For instance, Bass (1985) proposes the idea of transformational leadership. Conger and Kanungo (1988) write about charismatic leadership, and Westley and Mintzberg (1989) add visionary leadership to the list. These new styles all suggest an element of Smircich and Morgan's (1983) definition of leadership as a 'manager of meaning'. Again, the focus of the leader turns toward defining the vision, mission, and goals of the organization for subordinates. Bass proposed that the manager's leadership style is categorized as either transactional or transformational. Transactional leadership involves an exchange between the leader and follower that is focused on the leader providing direction and subsequent rewards for compliance to the follower. A management by exception approach is taken whereby managers take punitive action predominantly when task-related activity is not performed adequately. It emphasizes a contract between the leader and the follower. However, there is no other mutual purpose or goal that binds the two parties together (Bryman 1996).

In contrast, transformational leaders inspire followers to adhere to a common goal or purpose. The aspirations of the followers are raised so that the common purpose is felt. Bass (1985) suggests that the following elements are vital components of a transformational leader. First, leaders must possess charisma and engender trust and respect. They inspire others by setting high goals and expectations for followers (Martin and Bush 2006; MacKenzie, Podsakoff, and Rich 2001). Bass (1985) equates transformational leadership with visionary leadership. The importance of articulating a vision in such a way that other organizational members are compelled to adopt the vision was found to be a central element of this form of leadership.

While these modern approaches have provided substantial insight into the leadership of the sales force, more recent developments in sales organizations calls for additional work. As sales organizations deal with changing structures and changing roles, it is important to consider theoretical perspectives that account for these changes. For instance, one recent theoretical approach to the study of leadership has developed as research attention has turned toward the study of teams. Functional team leadership approaches suggest that the leader should serve his or her team. Key leadership functions include monitoring team performance, monitoring the environment, structuring and directing team activities, actively coaching and training team members, motivating and inspiring team members, and intervening accordingly (Morgeson 2005). This perspective offers some benefits to the study of leadership in a sales context. For one, it points to a distinct set of activities that a sales manager (who must manage the challenging tasks and demands faced by a sales team) should perform to achieve success. In essence, this line of research provides some reasonable guidelines for managers to follow.

Other leadership research suggests that in times of change it is most important for leaders to be flexible, responsive, and adaptive (Yukl and Lepsinger 2004). For example, Zaccaro, Foti, and Kenny (1991) propose that leaders who are socially perceptive and flexible are better able to respond to changes. These leaders interpret the demands and requirements specific to a given organizational problem, and tailor responses quickly. Yukl and Lepsinger (2004) argue that effective leaders are able to balance competing demands. This leadership perspective is useful to the study of sales organizations that are facing increasing demands and rapid change.

Additional leadership scholarship argues that all members of the work unit can enact leadership informally (Avolio 1999, Conger and Pearce 2003). Taking this perspective, leadership has been defined as "a dynamic, interactive, influence process among individuals in work groups in which the objective is to lead one another to the achievement of group goals" (Conger and Pearce 2003: 286). Leading others to lead themselves (Sims and Lorenzi 1992, Bryman 1996) is the common thread across the following set of approaches. Klein, Ziegert, and Knight (2006) propose that leadership requires dynamic delegation, wherein the leader provides quick and repeated delegation of the active leadership role to junior leaders of the team. Here the job of the leader is to provide strategic direction, monitor the team, engage in hands-on activity when necessary, and teach other team members. While a leadership hierarchy exists (i.e. the salesperson reports to the manager, etc.), you will commonly see the active leadership role move up and down the hierarchy. There are moments when the sales manager will lead the group and other times when the salesperson will engage in leadership behaviors. While sales research taking this perspective remains limited, empirical studies in a management context provide some evidence that such a shared team leadership approach results in enhanced team morale and performance (Avolio 1999).

Similarly, dispersed leadership (Bryman 1996, Sims and Lorenzi 1992, Manz and Sims 1991) suggests that a successful leader is one who can develop leadership capacity in others. Nurturing team members so that they are not dependent on formal leaders in the hierarchy is a critical component of leadership. Dispersed leadership suggests that leadership potential is developed in others when the formal leader is able to build followers' confidence and commitment to the organizational goals. The formal leader becomes more of a facilitator within the group as leadership activity is dispersed across committed team members. Thus, the focus of leadership is moving from a focus on the individual who occupies formal authority within the hierarchy of the organization to a focus on the team (Reich 1987). Along these lines, others have also suggested that leadership encompasses something other than a title or formal position given to an individual. Hosking's (1988, 1991) conceptualization of leadership indicates that leadership is in essence "organizing" activity rather than a formal position. For instance, networking may be considered an "organizing" activity that emphasizes social influence within a group, and is in effect leadership. Again, the defining characteristic is the series of activities that the individual engages in that may or may not indicate leadership. In a sales context, Flaherty, Mowen, Brown, and Marshall (2009) suggest that leadership not only exists within sales representatives but also leads to a host of positive outcomes including increased performance of certain sales tasks.

In summary, the leadership perspectives presented above provide insights into strategic sales leadership. These approaches were developed in response to several limitations of previous perspectives. For one, the earlier approaches seem to be focused too much on the upper echelons of the organization, on heroic leaders, and on individuals rather than teams. It is likely that the sales organizations that are evolving towards cross-functional team structures, as well as organizations that seek strategic renewal, will alter their leadership styles to accommodate the new objectives. Dispersed leadership offers a better way to nurture the exchange relationship between the manager and the salesperson so that the salesperson can achieve success in the team structure, and also to effectively balance the multiple roles suggested earlier. In order to facilitate a dispersed leadership approach, the sales manager's key tasks must move beyond those suggested in prior leadership theory. Leaders must do more than just teach, monitor, inspire, and motivate. Perhaps most importantly, contemporary sales managers must build commitment and confidence, remove obstacles, create opportunities, and be part of the team. To accomplish these new objectives, a different skill set is required of the sales manager.

In the following section, a configuration approach to the future study of strategic sales leadership is proposed. This chapter does not advocate one leadership perspective or definition over another. Instead, it is proposed that each perspective has its place.

3.5 Setting the Research Agenda: A Configuration Approach

As the literature review suggests, there has been extensive development in the areas of strategic roles and sales leadership. These streams point to several important and overlapping themes. However, much of our knowledge of the joint influence of salesperson strategic roles and effective sales leadership remains fragmented. An integrative framework that builds on existing strategy and leadership literature to provide a summary of the roles that salespeople and sales managers play in the strategy-making process is proposed. It is argued that a solid consideration of the emerging roles played by sales managers and salespeople in the larger strategy process have been largely omitted in the sales literature. In particular, the sales literature lacks an understanding of how the manager's roles converge or interrelate with those of the salesperson under different job expectations or roles.

From the previous discussion, it is noted that the roles played by salespeople can range from competence definition, where the salesperson is asked to offer strategic ideas and initiatives, to competence deployment, where the salesperson is asked to implement existing strategies and initiatives. Based on a review of current leadership theory, it is proposed that sales managers may engage in a variety of forms of leadership ranging from transactional styles of leadership to heroic styles of leadership to dispersed leadership. The remainder of this chapter jointly considers the unique job expectations of the salesperson and the subsequent exchange relationship necessary between the salesperson and the sales manager. On the basis of these considerations, a framework for sales leadership is suggested. In part, the framework proposed considers the rich literature in strategic management that considers the varying strategic objectives of the organization. A number of typologies have been proposed to classify strategic approaches ranging from organic organizations to mechanistic (cf. Hart 1992). The present framework seeks to expand some of these initial ideas to the sales force level, particularly in regard to strategic sales leadership.

Before we can proceed in our study of sales management practices including control and leadership, we need a general understanding of the leadership process existing within the sales organization. Leadership is not an activity and does not occur in a vacuum. It is a process that involves not just a manager but salespeople as well. The literature suggests that managers can assume a variety of postures to lead the work unit. Specifying who is involved and in what capacity will be useful to future research.

Configuration theory suggests that for each set of strategic characteristics there exists an ideal set of organizational characteristics that yields the best outcomes (Drazin and Van de Ven 1985). The ideal configurations represent complex "gestalts" of multiple, interconnected, and mutually reinforcing characteristics that enable the firm to achieve its strategic goals (Vorhies and Morgan 2003: 201). Consistent with this, this chapter takes a holistic approach via the identification of ideal configurations of sales strategic leadership. Such an approach will enable the evaluation of fit between many variables simultaneously, rather than just the few feasible with typical moderation and interaction approaches.

Taking a configuration approach requires the considerate selection of the characteristics used to calibrate the ideal profile. According to the literature, the ideal profile may be identified either theoretically or empirically (Venkatraman 1990). Based on the earlier literature review, it is proposed that to truly understand sales strategic leadership, the role expectations of the salesperson should be taken into consideration. Therefore, at a minimum the typology must include a consideration of salesperson roles, sales manager roles, and the corresponding leadership approach. It is also important to acknowledge that sales managers focus on different priorities for each of the strategic leadership processes, and must pull different managerial "levers" for each. Therefore, sales management control mechanisms are also included because it is a construct that is critical to the salesperson—sales manager leadership exchange relationship. I selected control because its relevance has been widely established in the literature. Plus, the effects of control systems are especially germane given the added role expectations that salespeople face in contemporary sales organizations.

3.5.1 Strategic Sales Force Control

Previous research on the coordination of the sales force points to the use of various forms of control systems as a mechanism for guiding the behaviors of salespeople. Earlier work debates the effects of various behavior-based controls, output-based controls, and socialization controls. The influence of control on employee job tension and job satisfaction (e.g. Agarwal 1999), teamwork and adaptive selling (e.g. Oliver and Anderson 1994, Baldauf, Cravens, and Piercy 2001), expertise and competence (e.g. Oliver and Anderson 1994, Cravens, Ingram, LaForge, and Young 1993), motivation and performance (e.g. Oliver and Anderson 1994, Cravens et al. 1993) have been studied extensively. Undeniably, control is one of the most important determinants of effective management of salespeople. Many forms of control have been proposed and tested in this research. In this chapter, three forms of control—process controls, output controls, and clan controls—are considered. Process controls involve the use of formal rules, written policies, and hierarchical authority to monitor and evaluate behavior. Using process controls decreases the likelihood of salesperson opportunistic behavior, but it is also dependent upon the ability to monitor salesperson behaviors. Output control provides an objective environment that helps reduce salesperson uncertainty. Salespeople are evaluated and rewarded for the achievement of objective performance goals. Finally, clan control conveys information via organizational traditions. Salesperson commitment is driven by identification with the organization and the leader. The commonality reduces opportunism (Ouchi 1980). Clan controls allow for an increased tolerance for ambiguity (Floyd and Lane 2000).

In the following discussion, the integrative framework is presented. The framework attempts to identify distinct modes of sales leadership. Identifying different leadership modes will hopefully clarify the interactions existing between leadership, salesperson roles, sales manager roles, and management practice. To this end, Table 3.2 details three strategic leadership modes: command, coach, and sponsor. The proposed modes are described below. Also, propositions regarding relationships between the leadership configurations and important salesperson outcomes are offered.

Table 3.2. An Integrative Framework for Strategic Leadership Processes in Sales

	Leadership Modes		
	Command	Coach	Sponsor
Defining Leadership:	Influence group to work toward the goal; Transactional leadership	Heroic or visionary leadership; Transformational leadership	Dispersed leadership; Lead others to lead themselves
Strategic Focus:	Strategy driven by top management	Strategy driven by mission/vision	Strategy driven by initiatives from the bottom-up
Sales Manager Focal Activities:	Provide clear direction; Evaluate and control	Motivate, empower and inspire	Endorse and support; Remove obstacles and create opportunities for salesperson
Sales Control System:	Process control	Combination of output control and clan control	Clan control
Salesperson Focal Activities:	Competence Deployment	Competence Modification	Competence Definition

3.5.2 Command Mode

In this mode, a powerful leader maintains tight control over the sales force. The objective of the sales force is to effectively implement strategies that are delivered from the upper echelons of the sales organization. In the command mode, organizations take a deliberate approach to strategy, where alternatives are weighed carefully and decisions are made based on all available information (Mintzberg 1973). Given this objective, it is important for the salesperson to execute the strategy that is handed down from management as efficiently and effectively as possible. The command mode specifies a leadership process wherein the salesperson's role expectations are limited to competence deployment. Thus, the role of the salesperson is to follow orders coming from the manager. The corresponding role of the sales manager is to give orders and provide direction in how to best carry out the orders. The leadership process may best be described as one where the leader must direct, monitor, evaluate, teach, and engage in other transactional elements of leadership. Here, leadership is best defined as an influence process, directed toward a group, in order to meet the goal at hand. The manager–salesperson information exchange is straightforward: the sales manager supplies information and the salesperson implements.

Here, it is argued that under these conditions increased process controls will enhance the achievement of both individual and sales force short-term performance goals. When the goal is to deploy existing competencies according to a predetermined strategy, process controls offer an effective way to direct the functions of the sales force. Given the focus on a well-defined strategic plan, sales manager and salespeople alike will have adequate information regarding activities and goals. As a result, it is easy to translate these into clear procedures and rules to follow.

3.5.3 Coach Mode

In the coach mode, strategy is more interactive. Learning is emphasized, so the exchange between the manager and the salesperson becomes more interactive. We know that in certain organizations top management's ability to separate the formulation of strategy from its implementation may be limited as a result of environmental uncertainty (March and Simon 1958, Hart 1992). In such contexts, strategy results from an interactive process between employees, suppliers, customers, and other important stakeholders (Hart 1992). Because of the need for consistent feedback in this mode, cross-functional communication becomes critical. While the sales manager provides a general direction or vision for the sales force to follow, it is critical that the salesperson, armed with this vision, continually assesses customer, technological and other environmental changes. The role of the salesperson is to engage in competence modification. That is, the salesperson is required to respond to challenges and modify tactics accordingly. The salesperson will adjust the strategy and/or process according to his or her assessment. The emphasis here is on learning rather than strict implementation of the predetermined plan (Fiol and Lyles 1985).

The coach mode specifies a leadership process that may best be described as heroic or transformational leadership. The role of the sales manager is to motivate and inspire, and to facilitate a process wherein the salespeople are best able to participate and provide feedback in a meaningful and timely fashion. According to this mode, it is also important for the sales manager to provide a clear vision to the sales force, so that the salespeople will be motivated and inspired to take the general direction provided by management and then adjust and adapt to challenges in a way that is consistent with this general direction. The leadership process is driven by an underlying focus on the mission of the organization and common vision for the future. As a result, the extent to which the salespeople identify with the organization will be important. The company's vision gives meaning to the salesperson's activities and provides a sense of identity for them (Dutton and Dukerich 1991). When competence modification is stressed, management recognizes that it is no longer feasible to clearly state rules and processes (i.e. process control is impossible). Sales managers are uncertain about the direction to take and salespeople can no longer conform to expectations. As a result, managers must rely on alternative forms of control. Output controls may best serve to align the interests of the salesperson and the organization in the absence of formal rules and procedures. Also, clan control will promote the shared values necessary to increase the likelihood that the salesperson makes choices that will benefit the organization. Thus, a combination of output control and clan control may be utilized within the coach mode.

3.5.4 Sponsor Mode

Finally, the sponsor mode reflects a leadership process that supports a dispersed leadership perspective. Strategy is influenced by autonomous strategic behavior across all organizational members and not just formal leaders. Strategy takes the form of intrapreneurship (Hart 1992) in that the salespeople are able to provide ideas and initiatives that shape the organization's strategic agenda. In order to accomplish this objective, it is necessary to liberate the salespeople so that they may contribute at this level. The role of the sales manager is to endorse and support the salesperson, while the job of the salesperson is to experiment, take risks, and explore possibilities (i.e. competence definition). Salespeople who are willing and able to participate in the strategic conversation of the firm, to the extent that they match resources with external information from customers, suppliers, etc. to develop new ideas, will be identified and rewarded. Competition among ideas and working for the common good are important elements in the sponsor mode. Thus, clan controls that align the salesperson and the organization's goals will be well suited to dispersed leadership and competence definition.

3.6 THE EFFECT OF LEADERSHIP "FIT" ON SALESPERSON PERFORMANCE

The proposed framework suggests several avenues for future research. For one, it will be essential to empirically verify the existence of the three modes. On the basis of past literature we can propose the command, coach, and support modes; however, empirical testing would reveal the set of characteristics and levels of these characteristics that will result in the ideal configuration. After this, attention should be given to establishing the effect of leadership fit on important salesperson outcomes.

Configuration theory suggests that an organization that resembles its ideal type will be most effective. Increased effectiveness will result from internal consistency (i.e. fit) among the patterns of relevant factors including leadership style, sales-person roles, sales manager roles, control, and identification (Doty, Glick, and Huber 1993). Embedded within this theory is the assumption of equifinality, or the belief that multiple organizations can achieve the same level of effectiveness via a variety of paths. Thus, a given leadership approach is not superior to another in and of itself. Instead, it is the holistic fit between leadership and the other relevant characteristics (i.e. the gestalt) that drives superior performance. In this case, we expect that salesperson performance of both quantity and quality objectives will be greater when the control profile for a particular sales manager–salesperson relationship is closer to that of the ideal type. Various propositions are discussed below.

P1: Deviation from the ideal strategic leadership configuration will have a negative influence on individual sales performance.

With the changing role of the salesperson come new challenges. For one, shifting from competence deployment to competence definition and modification results in increased quantitative job demands as well as potential new sources of qualitative job demands. For instance, the salesperson becomes more susceptible to role conflict. Earlier research on role conflict acknowledges that, due to their position between customers and the organization, salespeople are prone to quantitative and qualitative job demands that may result in felt stress. Also, competence modification and definition require the salespeople to be flexible and to deal with additional role ambiguity.

Exposure to job demands/stressors does not automatically necessitate stress. Cognitive appraisal theory (Lazarus and Folkman 1984) contends instead that cognitive appraisals, representing the ongoing mental processing of a situation with respect to an individual's wellbeing, explain an individual's response to role stressors. Two individuals may be exposed to the same stressor; both will not necessarily react in the same manner. Thus, stress stems from a relationship between the person and the environment that is appraised as taxing resources and endangering wellbeing (Lazarus and Folkman 1984).

For cognitive appraisal theorists, stress is viewed as an outcome of two apprai-sals—primary and secondary. The primary appraisal is a specific evaluation of the impact that an environmental stimulus will have on the individual. Research in cognitive appraisal theory supports the proposition that salespeople make evaluations of potential harm or loss associated with situations of role stress (cf. Lazarus and Folkman 1984: 34). When the individual's evaluation of the environmental stimulus is either positive or irrelevant to the individual's wellbeing, no further appraisal is necessary. However, when the stimulus is evaluated as stressful to the individual's wellbeing, then the primary evaluation of situational stressors leads to the secondary appraisal, which is an individual's assessment of his/her ability (means available) to avoid or minimize harm or loss.

While role stressors activate primary appraisal, it is the secondary appraisal, and the associated environment in which this appraisal is made, that influences the ultimate effect of the stressor variable (Sikora et al. 2004). Thus, the sales manager's approach to leadership and control can influence the extent to which felt stress will result. It is argued that deviation from the ideal configuration of strategic sales leadership will lead to felt stress.

P2: *Deviation from the ideal strategic leadership configuration will have a positive influence on salesperson felt stress.*

While it is proposed that deviation from the ideal leadership configuration will have a negative effect on performance and a positive effect on felt stress, it is also acknowledged that the relationship between these constructs is more complex. The remaining propositions explore these relationships in greater depth. In particular, important intervening constructs that add to the explanation of why deviation from the ideal leadership profile results in detrimental effects for the performance and stress of the salesperson are uncovered.

Again, it is argued that the exchange relationship between the sales manager and the salesperson is of utmost importance in explaining the relationship between the ideal configuration and the outcomes. Trust, information exchange, and the transfer of ideas from the salesperson to the manager is important. To better understand the influence of the ideal configuration on performance and stress, this chapter considers the mediating effect of the salesperson's trust in the manager.

3.6.1 Trust as a Mediator

Trust is defined as the perceived credibility and benevolence of a target of trust (Doney and Cannon 1997). Research findings have generally indicated that trust is a key component in maintaining individual and organizational effectiveness (McAllister 1995, Rich 1997). Creating trust is an important aspect of social exchange (Lambe, Wittmann, and Spekman 2001). Social exchange theorists (Blau 1964) describe trust as one of the key variables in external and internal relationships.

In past research, the social exchange structure of an organization has been found to play an important role in the development of employee trust in a supervisor (Ambrose and Schminke 2003). Building on previous work regarding the effect of social structure on employee attitudes toward an employer, Ambrose and Schminke (2003) demonstrate that organizational norms and policies that are consistent with apparent strategic system goals are the fundamental building blocks of employee trust in a supervisor. Therefore, when an organization structures a leadership approach in a manner that reinforces what employees view to be logical steps toward achieving organizational effectiveness (e.g. a clear linkage between leadership style and the associated environment), employees develop trust through an increase in managerial credibility, as well as a perception of enhanced benevolence, where managers are doing what is "right" for them. Conversely, if the salesperson perceives the leadership approach to be inconsistent with corresponding practices, then the salesperson's perceptions of the manager will suffer. Thus, deviation from the ideal configuration will have a negative effect on trust.

P3: *Deviation from the ideal leadership configuration will have a negative influence on trust.*

A decrease in trust should result in a decrease in performance. Salespeople and their managers will enter into an exchange and actively participate only when both parties trust that the other will reciprocate (Blau 1964). If the salesperson trusts the manager, then he or she will act in the best interest of the employee. The extent to which the salesperson perceives that the manager has his or her best interest in mind is likely to reduce the degree of felt stress experienced by the salesperson. Further, the employee will reciprocate by acting in ways that benefit the manager. Therefore, the employee who trusts the manager will be most likely to perform at a higher level.

P4: *Trust will have a negative influence on felt stress.*
P5: *Trust will have a positive influence on individual performance.*

Integrating the prior hypotheses, it is suggested that lack of leadership fit influences salesperson performance via its effect on trust. To the extent that lack of leadership fit decreases the level of trust in the manager–salesperson relationship, it will hinder salesperson performance.

P6: *Trust mediates the effect of deviation from the ideal leadership configuration on (a) performance and (b) stress.*

3.7 SUMMARY AND CONCLUSION

Existing sales research often assumes uniform role expectations across all salespeople. However, increased competition and environmental dynamism in certain industries has led to a change in the requirements for some salespeople. Given a more complex role for the salesperson, it is becoming increasingly important to consider the changing nature and requirements for effective sales leadership. As the role of the salesperson changes, the role of the sales manager must change as well.

For one thing, a reconsideration of the form of leadership required to be effective when leading today's sales force is essential.

This chapter addresses the impact of the co-alignment of salespersons' roles and the sales manager's leadership and control tactics. Many sales scholars have considered control and leadership individually; however, few have sought to explain the combined influence of the strategic direction of the firm, the corresponding salesperson's role, and the corresponding sales manager's leadership and control as part of a larger system. This chapter provides a framework for strategic sales leadership processes that integrates the strategic process, leadership, and control literatures. Rather than seek to identify one superior strategic leadership approach, it is suggested that leadership must in fact be viewed as a configuration or system. To be effective, leadership tactics must fit the surrounding situation. To the extent that the strategic leadership configuration is internally consistent, improved salesperson outcomes will result.

The three strategic roles of the salesperson (i.e. competence deployment, competence modification, and competence definition) provided the foundation for the organization of the framework. A consideration of the three roles along with prior leadership and control theory led to the identification of three generic modes of strategic leadership (i.e. command, coach, and sponsor). Prior literature acknowledges the importance of the salesperson–sales manager exchange relationship to leadership. All three strategic salesperson roles require certain interactions between the salesperson and the manager. The nature and direction of these exchanges ought to play a critical role in determining effective leadership practice. Adopting this perspective, the required exchange between the salesperson and the manager served as a guiding principle in determining the three strategic leadership modes. Finally, research propositions pointing to the importance of internal consistency, or fit, between leadership, control, and strategy were offered. While in an exploratory fashion a few strategic leadership configurations have been proposed, it should be noted that a more detailed exploration of potential strategic leadership configurations is warranted. Furthermore, an empirical investigation of the existence and prevalence of each configuration, as well as the influence of deviation from the proposed ideal configurations on important salesperson outcomes, should be conducted.

REFERENCES

AMBROSE, M. L., and M. SCHMINKE (2003). "Organization Structure as a Moderator of the Relationship between Procedural Justice, Interactional Justice, Perceived Organizational Support, and Supervisory Trust," *Journal of Applied Psychology* 88.2, 295–322.

AGARWAL, S. (1999). "Impact of Job Formalization and Administrative Controls on Attitudes of Industrial Salespersons," *Industrial Marketing Management* 28.4, 359–68.

ARGYRIS, C., and D. A. SCHON (1978). *Organizational Learning: A Theory of Action Perspective*, Reading, MA: Addison-Wesley.

AVLONITIS, G. J., and N. G. PANAGOPOULOS (2006). "Role Stress, Attitudes, and Job Outcomes in Business-to-Business Selling: Does the Type of Selling Situation Matter?", *Journal of Personal Selling & Sales Management* 26.1, 67–77.

AVOLIO, B. J. (1999). *Full Leadership Development: Building the Vital Forces in Organizations*. Thousand Oaks, CA: Sage.

BALDAUF, A., D. W. CRAVENS, and N. F. PIERCY (2001). "Examining Business Strategy, Sales Management, and Salesperson Antecedents of Sales Organization Effectiveness," *Journal of Personal Selling & Sales Management* 21.2, 109–23.

BASS, B. M. (1985). *Leadership and Beyond Expectations*. New York: Free Press.

——(1990). *Bass and Stogdill's Handbook of Leadership*. New York: Free Press.

BLAU, P. L. (1964). *Exchange and Power in Social Life*. New York: Wiley.

BRYMAN, A. (1996). "Leadership in Organizations," in S. R. Clegg, C. Hardy, and W. R. Nord (eds.), *Handbook of Organization Studies*, London: Sage.

BURGELMAN, R. A. (1991). "Interorganizational Ecology of Strategy Making and Organizational Adaptation: Theory and Field Research," *Organization Science* 2, 239–62.

CASTLEBERRY, S. B., and J. F. TANNER, Jr. (1986). "The Manager–Salesperson Relationship: An Exploratory Examination of the Vertical-Dyad Linkage Model," *Journal of Personal Selling & Sales Management* 6.3, 29–38.

CHONKO, L. B., A. J. DUBINSKY, E. JONES, and J. A. ROBERTS (2003). "Organizational and Individual Learning in the Sales Force: An Agenda for Sales Research", *Journal of Business Research* 56.1, 935–46.

CONGER, J. A., and R. N. KANUNGO (1988). "The Empowerment Process: Integrating Theory and Practice," *Academy of Management Review* 13, 471–82.

——and C. L. PEARCE (2003). "A Landscape of Opportunities: Future Research on Shared Leadership," in C.L. Pearce and J. Conger (eds.), *Shared Leadership: Reframing the Hows and Whys of Leadership*. Thousand Oaks, CA: Sage, 285–303.

COSTA, P. T., and R. R. McCRAE (1988). "Personality in Adulthood: A Six-Year Longitudinal Study of Self-Reports and Spouse Ratings on the NEO Personality Inventory," *Journal of Personality & Social Psychology* 54, 853–63.

CRAVENS, D. W., T. N. INGRAM, R. W. LaFORGE, and C. E. YOUNG (1993). "Behavior-Based and Outcome-Based Salesforce Control Systems," *Journal of Marketing* 57, 47–59.

D'AVENI, R. A. (1994). *Hypercompetition*. New York: Free Press.

DONEY, P. M., and J. P. CANNON (1997). "An Examination of the Nature of Trust in Buyer–Seller Relationships," *Journal of Marketing* 61, 35–51.

DOTY, D. H., W. H. GLICK, and G. P. HUBER (1993). "Fit, Equifinality, and Organizational Effectiveness: A Test," *Academy of Management Journal* 36, 1196–1251.

DRAZIN, R., and A. H. VAN DE VEN (1985), "Alternative Forms of Fit in Contingency Theory," *Administrative Science Quarterly* 30.4: 514–30.

DUTTON, J. E., and J. M. DUKERICH (1991). "Keeping an Eye on the Mirror: Image and Identity in Organizational Adaptation," *Academy of Management Journal* 34.3, 517–39.

DWYER, D. J., and D. C. GANSTER (1991). "The Effects of Job Demands and Control on Employee Attendance and Satisfaction," *Journal of Organization Behavior* 12.7, 595–608.

FIOL, C. M., and M. A. LYLES (1985). "Organizational Learning," *Academy of Management Review* 10.4, 803–13.

FLAHERTY, K. E., J. C. MOWEN, T. J. BROWN, and G. W. MARSHALL (2009). "Investigating the Antecedents and Marketing Consequences of an Enduring Desire to Lead Among Customer Contact Professionals," *Journal of Personal Selling & Sales Management* 29 (Winter), 43–59.

FLOYD, S. W., and P. J. LANE (2000). "Strategizing Throughout the Organization: Managing Role Conflict in Strategic Renewal," *Academy of Management Review* 25.1, 154–77.

GRAEN, G. (1976). "Role-Making Processes Within Complex Organizations", in M. D. Dunnette (ed.), *Handbook of Industrial and Organizational Psychology*. Chicago: Rand McNally, 1201–45.

HAMBRICK, D. C., S. FINKELSTEIN, and A. C. MOONEY (2005). "Executive Job Demands: New Insights for Explaining Strategic Behavior Decisions and Leader Behaviors," *Academy of Management Review* 30.3, 472–91.

HART, S. (1992). "An Integrative Framework for Strategy-Making Processes," *Academy of Management Review* 17, 327–51.

HILL, N. C., and J. B. RITCHIE (1977). "The Effect of Self-Esteem on Leadership and Achievement: A Paradigm and a Review," *Group and Organization Studies* 2, 491–503.

HOGAN, R., G. J. CURPHY, and J. HOGAN (1994). "What We Know about Leadership: Effectiveness and Personality," *American Psychologist* 49, 493–504.

HOSKING, D. M. (1988). "Organising, Leadership and Skilful Process," *Journal of Management Studies* 25.2, 47–66.

——(1991). "Chief Executives, Organising Processes, and Skill," *European Review of Applied Psychology* 41.2, 95–105.

HOUSE, R. J. (1971). "A Path Goal Theory of Leader Effectiveness," *Administrative Science Quarterly* 16.3, 321–39.

INGRAM, T. N., R. W. LaFORGE, and T. W. LEIGH (2002). "Selling in the New Millennium: A Joint Agenda," *Industrial Marketing Management* 31.7, 559–68.

JUDGE, T. A., J. E. BONO, R. ILIES, and M. W. GERHARDT (2002). "Personality and Leadership: A Qualitative and Quantitative Review," *Journal of Applied Psychology* 87.4, 765–80.

KARASEK, R. A., Jr. (1979). "Job Demands, Job Decision Latitude, and Mental Strain: Implications for Job Redesign," *Administrative Science Quarterly* 24.2, 285–308.

KLEIN, K. J., J. C. ZIEGERT, and A. P. KNIGHT (2006). "Dynamic Delegation: Shared Hierarchical, and Deindividualized Leadership in Extreme Action Teams," *Administrative Science Quarterly* 51, 590–621.

LAMBE, C. J., C. M. WITTMANN, and R. E. SPEKMAN (2001). "Social Exchange Theory and Research on Business-to-Business Relational Exchange," *Journal of Business-to-Business Marketing* 8, 1–36.

LAZARUS, R. S., and S. FOLKMAN (1984). *Stress, Appraisal, and Coping*, New York: Springer.

LIDEN, R. C., and G. B. GRAEN (1980). "Generalizability of the Vertical Dyad Linkage Model of Leadership," *Academy of Management Journal* 23, 451–65.

LORD, R. G., C. L. DeVADER, and G. M. ALLIGER (1986). "A Meta-Analysis of the Relation between Personality Traits and Leadership Perceptions: An Application of Validity Generalization Procedures," *Journal of Applied Psychology* 71, 402–10.

——and K. J. MAHER (1991). *Leadership and Information Processing: Linking Perceptions and Performance*. New York: Routledge.

McALLISTER, D. J. (1995). "Affect and Cognition-Based Trust as Foundations for Interpretation," *Academy of Management Journal* 38, 24–60.

MacKENZIE, S. B., P. M. PODSAKOFF, and M. AHEARNE (1998). "Some Possible Antecedents and Consequences of In-Role and Extra-Role Salesperson Performance," *Journal of Marketing* 62.3, 87–99.

—— ——and G. A. RICH (2001). "Transformational and Transactional Leadership and Salesperson Performance," *Journal of the Academy of Marketing Science* 29.2, 115–35.

MANZ, C. C., and H. P. SIMS, Jr. (1991). "SuperLeadership: Beyond the Myth of Heroic Leadership," *Organizational Dynamics* 19, 18–35.

MARCH, J. G., and H. A. SIMON (1958). *Organizations*. New York: Wiley.

MARTIN, C. A., and A. J. BUSH (2006). "Psychological Climate, Empowerment, Leadership Style, and Customer-Oriented Selling: An Analysis of the Sales Manager–Salesperson Dyad," *Journal of the Academy of Marketing Science* 34.3, 419–39.

MERTON, R. K. (1957). *Social Theory and Social Structure*. Glencoe, IL: Free Press.

MINTZBERG, H. (1973). "Strategy Making in Three Modes," *California Management Review* 16.2, 44–53.

MONCRIEF, W. C., and G. W. MARSHALL (2005). "The Evolution of the Seven Steps of Selling," *Industrial Marketing Management* 34.1, 13–24.

MORGESON, F. P. (2005). "The External Leadership of Self-Managing Teams: Intervening in the Context of Novel and Disruptive Events," *Journal of Applied Psychology* 90.3, 497–508.

MULKI, J., F. LASSK, and F. JARAMILLO (2008). "The Effect of Self-Efficacy on Salesperson Work Overload and Pay Satisfaction," *Journal of Personal Selling & Sales Management* 28.3, 285–97.

OLIVER, R. L., and E. ANDERSON (1994). "An Empirical Test of the Consequences of Behavior- and Outcome-Based Sales Control Systems," *Journal of Marketing* 58.4, 53–67.

OUCHI, W. G. (1980). "Markets, Bureaucracies, and Clans," *Administrative Science Quarterly* 25, 120–42.

PFEFFER, J. (1981). "Management as Symbolic Action: The Creation and Maintenance of Organizational Paradigms," *Research in Organizational Behavior* 3: 1–52.

PIERCY, N. F., D. W. CRAVENS, N. LANE, and D. W. VORHIES (2006). "Driving Organizational Citizenship Behaviors and Salesperson In-Role Behavior Performance: The Role of Management Control and Perceived Organizational Support," *Journal of the Academy of Marketing Science* 34.2, 244–62.

REICH, R. B. (1987). "Entrepreneurship Reconsidered: The Team as Hero," *Harvard Business Review* 65.3, 77–83.

RICH, G. A. (1997). "The Sales Manager as a Role Model: Effects on Trust, Job Satisfaction, and Performance of Sales People," *Journal of the Academy of Marketing Science* 25, 319–29.

SIKORA, P. B., E. D. BEATY, and J. FORWARD (2004). "Updating Theory on Organizational Stress: The Asychronous Multiple Overlapping Change (AMOC) Model of Workplace Stress," *Human Resource Development Review* 3.1, 3–36.

SIMS, H. P., and P. LORENZI (1992). *The New Leadership Paradigm: Social Learning and Cognition in Organizations*. Thousand Oaks, CA: Sage.

SMIRCICH, L., and G. MORGAN (1983). "Leadership: The Management of Meaning," *Journal of Applied Behavioral Science* 18, 257–73.

STOGDILL, R. M (1950). "Leadership, Membership, and Organization," *Psychological Bulletin* 90, 307–21.

VENKATRAMAN, N. (1990). "Performance Implications of Strategic Coalignment: A Methodological Perspective," *Journal of Management Studies* 27, 19–42.

VORHIES, D. W., and N. A. MORGAN (2003). "A Configuration Theory Assessment of Marketing Organization Fit with Business Strategy and Its Relationship with Marketing Performance," *Journal of Marketing* 67, 100–115.

VROOM, V. H., and P. W. YETTON (1973). *Leadership and Decision Making*. Pittsburgh, PA: University of Pittsburgh Press.

WEITZ, B. A., S. CASTLEBERRY, and J. TANNER (2001). *Selling: Building Partnerships*. New York: McGraw-Hill.

WESTLEY, F., and H. MINTZBERG (1989). "Visionary Leadership and Strategic Management," *Strategic Management Journal* 10.1, 17–32.

YUKL, G. (1998). *Leadership in Organizations*. Upper Saddle River, NJ: Prentice Hall.

——and R. LEPSINGER (2004). *Flexible Leadership: Creating Value by Balancing Multiple Challenges and Choices*. San Francisco, CA: Jossey-Bass.

ZACCARO, S. J., R. J. FOTI, and D. A. KENNY (1991). "Self-Monitoring and Trait-Based Variance in Leadership: An Investigation of Leader Flexibility Across Multiple Group Situations," *Journal of Applied Pyschology* 76.2, 308–15.

CHAPTER 4

ACHIEVING SALES ORGANIZATION EFFECTIVENESS

DAVID W. CRAVENS

4.1 INTRODUCTION

The sales organization plays a vital role in achieving marketing and business strategy objectives in many companies. The organization's effectiveness contributes to business performance in terms of sales, market position, customer satisfaction, and profits in reference to competition and internal objectives. The traditional role of the sales force is undergoing a transformation in many companies, calling for major new initiatives concerning sales management and salespeople in order to achieve the sales organization's effectiveness requirements.

Effectiveness consists of a summary evaluation of overall organizational outcomes (Churchill, Ford, Hartley, and Walker 1985), and may be assessed for the entire sales organization or for smaller units, such as regions and districts. Sales unit effectiveness provides a composite assessment of the unit's performance, and differs from salesperson performance, which only considers the factors under control of the salesperson. While each salesperson contributes to the unit's effectiveness, it is influenced by other variables including the manager, the business's competencies (e.g. brand strength), and the market and competitive environment (Walker, Churchill, and Ford 1979).

The array of changes impacting sales organizations include greater emphasis on customer relationship management, alterations in sales organization structures, corporate reorganizations and acquisitions/mergers, expense reduction, and expanded use of market segmentation strategies. These important trends create the need to consider uncontrollable influences in developing sales organization strategy, assessing salesperson performance, evaluating alternative methods of organizing the sales force, and understanding the relative importance of sales managers' monitoring, directing, evaluating, and rewarding of salespeople.

Several controllable and uncontrollable factors influence sales organization effectiveness, including sales management, the sales force, company/business competencies, and the business environment. These factors require attention by sales management and, where necessary, proactive initiatives to improve the effectiveness of the sales organization.

The level of analysis of sales organization effectiveness in this chapter considers the sales unit which typically consists of a manager and the assigned salespeople (normally 10 or less). The total effectiveness of all units indicates the overall effectiveness of the sales organization. Each salesperson contributes to unit effectiveness, whereas each unit contributes to the effectiveness of the sales organization. It is assumed that salespeople are involved in business-to-business sales and are deployed in the field.

The sales organization is competing in one or more developed economies. There has been a reasonable degree of consistency in research findings and management practices for sales organization effectiveness across developed economics (Baldauf, Cravens, and Piercy 2001; Babakus, Cravens, Grant, Ingram, and LaForge 1996). However, differences have been reported for studies in developing countries based on analysis of variables concerning political stability, gross national income, and culture (Piercy, Low, and Cravens 2008).

The objective of this chapter is to develop a framework for analysis and decision-making regarding sales organization effectiveness. The intention is to consider existing knowledge and the extent of understanding regarding relevant decision analysis and action guidelines. Important knowledge gaps and the implications are also examined.

4.2 Sales Organization Effectiveness

In this section we define effectiveness, examine the changing role of the sales force, consider the emerging view of service as the dominant form, and discuss the escalating importance of metrics.

4.2.1 Sales Organization Effectiveness

As defined earlier, sales organization effectiveness is a summary evaluation of the performance of the sales organization. There is substantial research support indicating that variations in effectiveness are determined by environmental (markets and competition), organizational, sales management, and salesperson factors (Babakus et al. 1996). Thus, effectiveness indicates overall results of the sales organization, whereas salesperson performance should be assessed using only variables under the control of salespeople.

Sales organization effectiveness is important because it indicates the contribution of the sales organization to the performance of the firm. Assessments of effectiveness may be based on sales, market share, customer satisfaction, profit contribution, and other metrics relative to competition and internal objectives. Importantly, "the overall result on which attention should focus is the effectiveness of the sales organization in implementing business strategy and meeting organizational goals" (Piercy and Lane, 2005, 259). Sales organization effectiveness can be examined at different levels (e.g. the entire sales organization or smaller units).

4.2.2 Changing Role of the Sales Force

Sales organizations around the world are experiencing major transformations in the twenty-first century, influenced by customers demands for superior value from their suppliers:

Personal selling and consequently, sales management are undergoing dramatic changes. These changes are being driven by several behavioral, technological, and managerial forces that are dramatically and irrevocably altering the way salespeople understand, prepare for, and accomplish their jobs. Among the behavioral forces are rising customer expectations, globalization of markets, and demassification of domestic markets; technological forces include sales force automation, virtual sales offices, and electronic sales channels; and managerial forces consist of a shift to direct marketing alternatives, outsourcing of sales functions, and a blending of sales and marketing functions. (Johnston and Marshall 2009: 3–4)

The changing role of the sales force is having a major impact on the determinants of sales organization effectiveness. Perhaps most important, achieving effectiveness has become a much more complex and demanding process compared to the traditional sales organization.

Strategic transformation of the sales force requires directing management attention to several critical issues (Cravens 1995):

- focusing on long-term customer relations, but also assessing customer value and prioritizing the most attractive prospects;

- creating sales organization structures that are nimble and adaptable to the needs of different customer groups;
- gaining greater ownership and commitment from salespeople by removing functional barriers within the organization and leveraging team-based working relationships;
- shifting sales management from "command and control" to coaching and facilitation;
- applying new technologies appropriately;
- designing salesperson evaluation processes to incorporate the full range of activities and outcomes relevant to new types of sales and account management jobs.

Importantly, new business strategies and strategic alignment of the sales force will require both salespeople and sales managers who can proactively respond to the emerging challenges and opportunities.

At the center of the challenges confronting the sales force is a customer who increasingly displays demanding expectations in buyer–seller relationships. Building strong relationships with customers is recognized as a high management priority by academics and executives (Payne and Frow 2005). A Mercer Consultants study of business firms reports that developing and building customer relationships is the most important source of competitive advantage in the twenty-first century (Kale 2004). In another study, some 1000 executives rated customer relationship management and strategic planning highest of ten priority strategic actions for improving business performance (*Economist* 2005). Moreover, customer expectations of salespeople are escalating much faster than salespeople are able to respond to their customers' requirements (Jones, Brown, Zoltners, and Weitz 2005). Increasingly, customers' expectations exceed salesperson knowledge, speed of response, breadth and depth of communication, and customization of information and product/service offerings. This gap presents a serious threat to achieving sales organization effectiveness.

4.2.3 Service-Centered View of Exchange

Instead of the traditional view of tangible goods versus intangible services, a conceptualization has been proposed that this view should be replaced by a service-centered logic, consisting of both goods and services that provide value to customers (Vargo and Lusch 2004) The central issue is determining the composition of the value offering being made to customers. The implication is that the organization must adopt a service-centered perspective. This change in focus from goods to service is obtaining significant support from academics and executives. "A service-centered view of exchange implies customized offerings to better fit customers' needs and identifying firm resources—both internal and external—to better satisfy the needs of customers" (Sheth and Sharma 2008: 262). Related developments include the shift toward the exchange of intangibles, specialized skills, knowledge, and processes, as well as the co-creation of value between buyers and sellers.

The roles of the salesperson and the sales organization will need to change as we move toward a service-dominant logic of marketing. Important implications underlying the service logic include:

- The application of specialized skills and knowledge is the fundamental unit of exchange.
- Goods are distribution mechanisms for service provision.
- Knowledge is the fundamental source of competitive advantage.
- The customer is always a co-creator of value.
- A service-centered view is customer oriented and relational. (Sheth and Sharma 2008: 262)

4.2.4 Metrics

Marketing metrics are receiving significant attention from academics and executives, driven by mounting pressures to develop measures of marketing performance that are related to business performance (O'Sullivan and Abela 2007). Metrics have been designated a top-priority research objective by the Marketing Science Institute's corporate sponsors. Measures may be needed to indicate business position relative to competition, effectiveness in delivering customer value, marketing program effectiveness, and financial performance (Ferris, Bendle, Pfeifer, and Reibstein 2006). Authorities on marketing metrics advise against the use of only one measure (Ambler and Roberts 2006, Lehmann 2004). Eight to ten metrics may be needed by a large firm.

A major challenge is selecting appropriate metrics for use. These guidelines for choosing metrics are recommended: (1) track performance relative to strategy, (2) monitor performance relative to both competitors and customers, (3) measure performance over time, and (4) analyze performance to assess the impact of changes in different strategy components (Clark 2001). A major metrics issue is designing a marketing dashboard which will inform top management with a summary of key measures to report and evaluate the marketing performance of the business (Ferris et al. 2006: 331).

4.3 DETERMINANTS OF SALES ORGANIZATION EFFECTIVENESS

Sales organization effectiveness is determined by several controllable and uncontrollable variables. Each of the types of influences is shown in Figure 4.1, and a discussion of the influences follows.

4.3.1 Sales Management

Sales management is a core determinant of the effectiveness of the sales organization. The relevant aspects of sales management include the *management processes* used by sales managers, the *structure* of the sales organization, and the *performance* of each sales manager.

The management processes used by sales managers range from primary emphasis on salesperson outcomes to emphasis on the work behavior of each salesperson. In using outcome management control, the sales manager is primarily concerned with tracking salespeople's results (sales, market share, new customers, etc.), and motivating salespeople toward results achievement. In contrast, behavior control involves the manager with the salesperson's selling and support processes. The management processes in a sales organization are positioned at a particular point on the behavior/outcome continuum. Importantly, managers' capabilities should correspond to the management process required by the organization.

Determining the structure of the sales organization involves the number of management levels and the design of each salesperson's sales territory. The number of salespeople in each manager's sales unit and deployment of salespeople's efforts (geography, customers, etc.) are major factors in sales unit effectiveness.

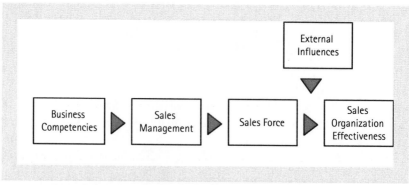

Fig. 4.1. Determinants of Sales Organization Effectiveness

4.3.2 Sales Force

The sales force is the remaining core determinant of the effectiveness of the sales organization. This factor includes *salesperson skills, salesperson structure,* and *salesperson performance.*

The type of selling situation determines the required skills of the sales force. Sales situations may range from a transactional to a collaborative focus. Salesperson structure refers to the role of the salesperson in the buyer-seller relationship. The possibilities include the salesperson working alone with the buyer and the use of sales teams comprising people with different capabilities (product specialist, service expert, salesperson).

Ultimately, the salesperson's impact on sales organization effectiveness is through her/his performance. The salesperson may be evaluated in terms of selling behavior (activities related to generating sales) and/or sales outcomes (sales, new customers, customer retention). Importantly, the sales outcomes should be adjusted to account for results which can be attributable to the salesperson and not other uncontrollable factors (Cravens, Ingram, LaForge, and Young 1993).

4.3.3 Business Competencies and External Influences

The unique competencies of the organization include the products offered and the firm's position in the markets in which it competes, brand position (strength), innovation strengths, financial position, and other competencies. As shown in Figure 4.1, business competencies are likely to influence sales management. Competencies such as brand strength may also impact sales organization effectiveness by making customers and prospects more willing to buy the brand. These influences on sales management and effectiveness tend to be long-term.

External factors such as market potential for the firm's products and the intensity of competition have a moderating long-term influence on sales organization effectiveness. These factors may account for a portion of effectiveness. They are uncontrollable by the business. Markets which are dynamic may introduce substantial uncertainty concerning effectiveness outcomes.

4.4 SALES MANAGEMENT CONTROL

Building on the above examination of various determinants of sales organization effectiveness, the discussion now shifts to a conceptualization of several specific antecedents of effectiveness shown in Figure 4.2. This section considers sales

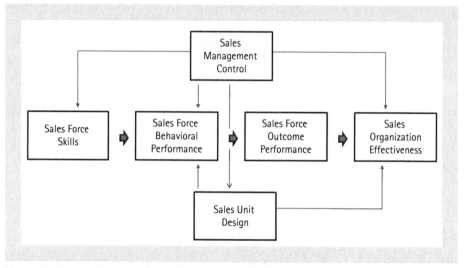

Fig. 4.2. Antecedents of Sales Organization Effectiveness

management control; sales force skills and performance and sales unit design are examined in subsequent sections.

The conceptual framework integrates several research streams which are summarized by Babakus et al. (1996). The conceptualization is based on the basic relationships proposed by Walker, Churchill, and Ford (1979), which provides the foundation for various salesperson and sales manager research studies conducted during the last three decades.

The framework in Figure 4.2 makes explicit the logic of salesperson performance as a separate yet interrelated construct relative to sales organization effectiveness (Walker, Churchill, and Ford 1979). Moreover, sales force performance is conceptualized in terms of behavior and outcome dimensions of performance (Anderson and Oliver 1987). Outcome performance continues to be the focus in some salesperson studies (Jaworski, Stathakopoulos, and Krishnan 1993).

The Figure 4.2 conceptualization includes the sales management control construct proposed by Anderson and Oliver (1987). The researchers indicate that management control may range from behavior control to outcome control. A sales manager may focus on one or the other control form or at some intermediate stage between the two control forms.

The sales unit design construct is an aspect of sales organization research. There have been several studies conducted in this area including organization structure, sales force size, and allocation of selling effort. However, the Babakus et al. (1996) study is the first known research to examine unit design, management control, and effectiveness in the same conceptualization. The design construct considers how well the sales unit has been designed. Design is closely related to the size of the sales force and the allocation of selling effort.

The issue of the sales management level of the organization is also relevant to the Figure 4.2 conceptualization. Levels may range from the chief sales executive to the field sales manager, with one or more intermediate levels. Managers' analysis and decision making activities and issues vary to some extent at the different levels. At the top level, the chief sales executive is interested in the size of the sales force, how the sales organization is structured, and the number of sales units. The first-line field sales manager is concerned with how the sales territories for the assigned salespeople are designed. The conceptualization in Figure 4.2 is relevant to any of the levels, recognizing that measures will need to be modified for certain constructs (Babakus et al. 1996). Moreover, obtaining sensitive measures of some of the constructs may be difficult at the higher levels in the sales organization.

4.4.1 Sales Management Control

Anderson and Oliver (1987) first proposed the use of management control systems for viewing management processes in sales organizations. Their theoretical formulation of sales force control is an important research contribution, with potential impact on sales management practice.

Behavior-based sales force control involves field sales managers in active monitoring of salespeople's activities and results, close management direction of and involvement in the activities of salespeople, and use of subjective and complex methods for evaluating and compensating the sales force (Anderson and Oliver 1987). Compensation of salespeople tends to be fixed under behavior control (rather than incentive-based), with the primary managerial focus on direction and control of salesperson behavior rather than sales outcomes.

Outcome control is exercised by the use of incentive compensation to manage salesperson outcomes. Sales managers are involved in very limited monitoring and direction of salespeople, and they use objective metrics to track salesperson results, rather than the selling and support (behavior) processes of salespeople.

The constructs and relationships shown in Figure 4.2 (except sales unit design) were first examined empirically by Cravens et al. (1993). Behavior control was measured by the extent of activities monitoring and the amount of direction by sales managers. Outcome control was measured by the fixed salary percentage of salespeople. More recent studies have assessed behavior control in terms of the extent of manager monitoring, directing, evaluating, and rewarding salespeople (Babakus et al. 1996).

An alternative conceptualization of management control has been used on a very limited basis in sales force research. The control construct consists of four dimensions: output, process, professional, and cultural control (Jaworski, Stathakopoulos, and Krishnan 1993). Output and process controls are defined as management-focused initiatives and are considered to be formal control. Professional and cultural control are informal and driven by the business environment rather than management. Interestingly, output control is a form of behavior control, rather than outcome-oriented. Control is classified into four categories (high, bureaucratic, clan, and low) based on the extent of the control combinations. A sales force research study involving a large and diverse sample of business-to-business salespeople found that more extensive control had the most favorable impact on salespersons' attitudes and behavior including performance (Cravens, Marshall, Lassk, and Low 2004). This concept of control has not been used to examine the relationships in Figure 4.2. An extensive comparative analysis of the two forms of sales management control can be found in Baldauf, Cravens, and Piercy (2005).

4.4.2 Manager Performance

Surprisingly, the various research studies which examine antecedents of sales organization effectiveness have not included sales manager performance. Logic would argue that manager performance should be related to effectiveness in the Figure 4.2 conceptualization. A poorly performing sales manager may have a negative influence on any of the antecedents in the conceptual framework.

One recent study has partially addressed the sales manager performance issue by proposing a sales manager behavior control competencies construct (Piercy, Cravens, and Lane 2008). The intent of the competencies construct is to consider not only the extent of manager control but also how well control is performed. There is related conceptual support for the competencies construct, since sales management texts discuss the relevance of the leadership role of sales managers. Moreover, a business survey proposes that manager effectiveness will be determined by emerging sales manager competencies (e.g. diagnosing performance) (Rosenbaum 2000).

The control competencies construct is intended to assess managers' performance of behavior control processes. Competencies are expected to be positively related to the extent of behavior control, yet they are proposed to be different variables. In a study involving 301 field sales managers, Piercy, Cravens, and Lane (2008) reported significant positive direct relationships between control competencies, control level, salesperson behavior performance, and critical sales skills. The model also included market orientation, salesperson outcome performance, and sales unit effectiveness. All relationships were positive and significant.

4.5 SALES FORCE SKILLS AND PERFORMANCE

Salespeople play an important role in the Figure 4.2 conceptualization. In this section we examine the sales force skills and performance constructs.

4.5.1 Sales Force Skills

The primary drivers of required skills of the sales force are the selling situations confronting salespeople, and sales executives' decisions on the type of salespeople desired by the sales organization (Anderson and Oliver 1987, Cravens et al. 1993). For example, because of different selling situations sales managers will vary in their preferences concerning salespeople's professional competence, sales support, and customer orientation skills:

Importantly, obtaining favorable levels of sales organization effectiveness requires managers to (1) understand the selling environment of the business and (2) pursue initiatives that are appropriate for the selling situations that their salespeople encounter. The extent of management control implemented and managers' control competencies should correspond with salespeople's required selling skills. (Piercy, Cravens, and Lane 2007: 20)

Anderson and Oliver (1987) identify several categories of salesperson characteristics which are expected to be related to the management control system, including salesperson cognition and capabilities, affects and attitudes, motivation, and behavior. On the basis of these characteristics, Cravens et al. (1993) hypothesized that under behavior control salespeople will be professionally competent, team-oriented, risk-averse, intrinsically and recognition-motivated, planning-oriented, sales support-oriented, and customer-oriented.

Empirical tests by Cravens et al. (1993) and Oliver and Anderson (1994) provide substantial support for a positive relationship between behavior control and the various characteristics. Cravens et al. (1993), using a multi-company sample of sales executives, report a positive relationship between managers' behavior control and team-oriented, risk-averse, recognition-motivated salespeople displaying orientations toward planning, sales support, and customers. This research provides support for a positive relationship between behavior control and sales force skills in the Figure 4.2 conceptualization.

4.5.2 Sales Force Performance

Research studies conceptualize salesperson performance as consisting of *behavior* and *outcome* dimensions (Babakus et al. 1996). Importantly, performance analysis should consider only those aspects of performance which are under the control of the salesperson.

4.5.2.1 *Outcome Performance*

Salesperson performance was often considered in terms of outcomes (e.g. sales) until Anderson and Oliver (1987) conceptualized management control as behavior- or outcome-oriented. A subsequent empirical study by Cravens et al. (1993) conceptualized salesperson performance as consisting of behavior and outcome dimensions. The two views of performance have been shown to be separate constructs but positively related (Babakus et al. 1996, Cravens et al. 1993, Piercy, Cravens, and Morgan 1999). Outcome performance is the consequence of sales-peoples' efforts and capabilities to produce outcomes (results) which are assigned to them and not attributable to other factors (e.g. brand image). Examples of outcome performance include sales, market share, and new customers.

4.5.2.2 *Behavior Performance*

This performance dimension considers the behaviors utilized by salespeople in meeting their job responsibilities (Behrman and Perreault 1984). The relevance of the behavior performance construct is based on the logic that salespeople have more control over their activities and strategies than over the outcomes. Activities included in behavior performance consist of developing and conducting sales presentations, sales support, and planning.

Empirical evidence provides substantial support for a positive relationship between manager behavior control and salesperson behavior performance. For example, Babakus et al. (1996) analyzed the behavior control relationship with the behavior performance components of technical knowledge, adaptive selling, teamwork, sales presentations, sales planning, and sales support. Multiple-item scales were used for each of the performance measures. Significant positive rela-tionships were reported. A strong positive relationship was also found between behavior and outcome performance.

Limited research attention has been given to a possible relationship between behavior control and outcome performance. Cravens et al. (1993) found a signifi-cant positive relationship between manager behavior control and compensation control which was opposite to their hypothesis. The relationship consisted of a direct effect of compensation control and the indirect effects of behavior control and compensation control on achieving sales objectives performance. The researchers commented as follows:

The AO conceptualization and propositions seem to suggest an either/or situation: Either sales organizations emphasize behavioral performance with loss in outcome performance through a BBSCS, or emphasize outcome performance with a loss in behavioral perfor-mance though an OBSCS. (Cravens et al. 1993: 55)

The reality is that, as shown in Figure 4.2, the two dimensions of performance are positively related and are driven by manager behavior control. Behavior performance contributes to outcome performance which displays a positive relationship with sales unit effectiveness.

4.6 Sales Unit Design

The sales unit design construct indicates how well salesperson territories are designed. The field sales manager is responsible for the territories assigned to her/his sales unit. The design of the sales unit considers decisions by sales management about the sales coverage of customers in each territory, products, and geographical area assigned to each salesperson. Territories may be determined based on geography and/or the assigned customers. In this section we examine the design construct and discuss the relationships shown in Figure 4.2.

4.6.1 Design Construct

Sales territory design establishes the work responsibilities for each salesperson assigned to the manager's sales unit:

Sales management must decide the number of accounts to be assigned to the salesperson, product responsibilities, and the geographical area to include (or other basis for identifying accounts such as type of industry). Several considerations may be important in deciding the territory design, including the buying power of the accounts, geographical dispersion of accounts, time required to service each account, and competitive intensity. (Grant, Cravens, Low, and Moncrief 2001: 166)

Territory design should create approximately equal opportunities for salespeople in the sales unit to perform well. Inadequate opportunity in a territory will waste selling effort and limit salesperson productivity. Too much opportunity will prevent advantage being taken of the customer potential available in the territory. Importantly, if the salesperson perceives the territory design to be unsatisfactory, this may have a negative impact on her/his attitude and behavior and eventually performance (plus possible turnover). A poor territory design will limit the salesperson's opportunity to perform well. Too much opportunity may unfairly reward the salesperson and lead to customer dissatisfaction due to lack of coverage.

The number of salespeople assigned to the sales unit will influence the design of individual territories. The decision regarding sales force size needs to be considered by higher-level management. The unit manager will normally obtain approval for increasing or decreasing the number of salespeople assigned to the unit. This requires close coordination between management levels.

The territory/sales unit design construct shown in Figure 4.2 has received limited research attention (Babakus et al. 1996). The construct has also been studied as an antecedent to salesperson attitudes, behavior, and performance (Grant et al. 2001). The design construct has displayed significant positive relationships in the empirical studies. A discussion of the findings follows.

4.6.2 Design Relationships

Relationships concerning sales territory design which have been investigated empirically include sales management control, salesperson performance, and sales organization effectiveness. The design construct has been found to play an important role in the relationships, although design has been included in only a few studies.

When using behavior control, managers are more alert to territory design characteristics and adequacy compared to those using outcome control. The basis of the interest is because managers recognize the potential impact of faulty territory design on salesperson attitudes, behavior, and performance, and sales unit effectiveness. Moreover, the unit manager has the authority to make territory design changes. Surprisingly, given the relevance of the design construct, the topic has received limited research attention.

The design construct is defined as satisfaction with territory design, and can be considered from either a manager or salesperson perspective. The underlying conceptual logic is that a unit design which displays a sound structure, an optimal number of salespeople, good territory designs, and proper allocation of sales effort is expected to have a positive relationship with performance and effectiveness (Babakus et al. 1996). Moreover, higher levels of behavior control should be associated with more favorable sales unit designs.

Research findings concerning sales unit design indicate positive relationships with other constructs (Figure 4.2). A study involving salespeople from a broad cross-section of Australian firms using samples of 146 sales managers and 58 chief sales executives reported several statistically significant relationships involving sales territory design (Babakus et al. 1996). In the sales manager sample, behavior control was positively related to territory design, supporting the conceptual logic that a greater extent of behavior control leads to greater satisfaction with sales territory designs. The manager assessments represented an aggregate measure of design satisfaction for the territories in the sales unit.

In the Australian study, territory design displayed positive antecedent relationships with salesperson behavior and outcome performance and sales unit effectiveness based on the sales manager sample. In the chief sales executive sample, the findings were considerably weaker than the manager sample results. The only significant positive relationships were between management control and design and between design and salesperson behavior performance. The very aggregate assessments of the construct measures made by the chief sales executives may have substantially reduced the sensitivity of the measures.

A study involving 148 salespeople from 27 Australian companies found significant positive relationships of salesperson satisfaction with territory design with intrinsic motivation, performance, and job satisfaction, and was negatively correlated with role ambiguity (Grant et al. 2001). These findings further support the relevance of the territory design construct with some different consequences from those included in Figure 4.2. The performance measure is a multiple-item scale including items for behavior and outcome performance. The study provides strong support on the relevance of territory design to salespeople. Proactive attention to design satisfaction of salespeople by managers is clearly indicated. The largest path coefficient was between design and salesperson performance.

4.6.3 Research Limitations

The research support for the Figure 4.2 antecedents of sales unit effectiveness, while not extensive, is encouraging. However, one issue that should be recognized is that the measure which has been used for territory design is "satisfaction" with territory design. Measuring satisfaction with design may be a possible concern.

The design measure does not address aspects of design including product and/or market specialization, major account and team selling, and vertical design structure (Babakus et al. 1996). However, the scale used to measure the satisfaction with design construct includes several relevant aspects of territory design such as the number and size of accounts, sales productivity, geographical scope, required calls, travel, and workload equivalence. The measurement issue is that these items are addressed in terms of satisfaction rather than magnitude. However, assessing magnitude would create a very complex measure. Moreover, salespeople would find it difficult to make several of the magnitude evaluations.

Another research issue is examining effectiveness antecedents at different levels. Research has typically been conducted at the field sales manager level. Higher-level assessments are challenging, as indicated by the lack of significant findings for the chief sales executive sample discussed earlier (Babakus et al. 1996). The organizational-level issue is further addressed later in the chapter.

4.7 IMPLICATIONS

There are several relevant implications concerning the Figure 4.2 constructs and relationships. Managerial issues are discussed first, followed by consideration of future research directions.

4.7.1 Managerial Issues

There is substantial research support for most of the Figure 4.2 relationships based on several studies conducted in Europe, the US, and Australia. The territory design construct has received less attention. Several antecedents of sales unit effectiveness have been identified and are relevant to sales management.

Perhaps most important is the clearly established role of manager behavior control in the conceptualization. Anderson and Oliver (1987) first proposed the relevance and importance of behavior control. Extensive empirical support for behavior control is available, indicating the construct's pivotal antecedent role in the effectiveness framework. Moreover, territory design has emerged as a promising antecedent.

Research has established a strong link between salesperson behavior and outcome performance. Both constructs are important in the relationships shown in Figure 4.2. They map the path to sales unit effectiveness. Salespeople who perform well in behavior sales/support activities display favorable outcome performance.

The territory design construct points to the importance of directing management attention to organizational design. While research support is less extensive than for the other Figure 4.2 antecedents, the managerial logic in support of territory design is compelling. On the basis of the author's experience with a wide range of firms, there are clear indications that faulty territory design is not an exception in sales management practice. Salesperson motivation initiatives are likely to prove ineffective when there are design imbalances in the sales organization.

Our understanding of management control is limited where higher levels of the sales organization are concerned. The research focus has been at the salesperson and field sales manager level. A few studies have examined the Figure 4.2 relationships at the chief sales executive level. However, the relationships appear most relevant at the salesperson and field manager levels.

The relevance of the behavior control dimensions of monitoring, directing, evaluating, and rewarding salespeople is clearly established. Interestingly, in the Babakus et al. (1996) study the mean values for the four dimensions indicated that the field managers were not heavily involved in the management control activities.

Since the extent of manager involvement was moderate (6–7), based on a 1–10 scale, close day-to-day supervision was not involved or necessary.

4.7.2 Future Research Directions

As discussed earlier, manager performance is a relevant construct that should be incorporated into Figure 4.2. Manager control competencies have been used in one study (Piercy, Cravens, and Lane 2008). However, a construct which considers a more extensive assessment of manager performance should be developed. Performance could be conceptualized as a moderator of the salesperson outcome performance and sales organization relationship in Figure 4.2.

The relative importance of the manager behavior control activities of monitoring, directing, evaluating, and rewarding has not been examined in prior behavior control studies (Babakus et al. 1996). A relevant issue is whether varying the level(s) of the four control dimensions will affect the Figure 4.2 relationships and the effectiveness outcome. The focus of previous studies has been on the overall level of behavior control.

4.8 Global Variations

The discussion up to this point has considered sales organization effectiveness in several developed countries. We now examine the extent of knowledge about the antecedent and effectiveness relationships in developing countries.

4.8.1 Conceptual Foundations

Sales unit effectiveness has received research attention on an international basis. Studies examining the consequences of sales management control have been conducted in Austria, Australia, UK, and the US (Baldauf et al. 2001, Grant and Cravens 1999). Management control consequences have also been investigated in Greece, India, and Malaysia (Piercy, Low, and Cravens 2004). The impact of national culture on sales management control systems has been studied within companies in different European countries (Rouziès and Macquin 2003). Although these findings are relevant, a more extensive international assessment of important antecedents of sales unit effectiveness is needed, particularly in developing countries.

Research findings concerning sales organization effectiveness in developed countries have generally been consistent. The constructs and relationships examined have yielded similar results. Whether these findings are applicable to developing countries is uncertain. In the absence of prior research, developing country investigators assumed that the developed country results would apply for developing countries. If this did not occur, then explanations of the differences would be pursued.

Variations in the levels of income and political stability, together with country culture conditions, may help explain possible differences in the antecedent and sales unit effectiveness relationships in developing countries. For example, uncertainty avoidance and power distance may be relevant (Hofstede 1983). Globalization of sales organizations requires an improved understanding of inter-country variations for antecedent relationships with effectiveness. Global business executives face challenges and uncertainties in recruiting and managing salespeople, and account management calls for complex implementation decisions. For example, should one sales force be employed, or should account responsibilities be assigned to individual country sales forces instead? What antecedents are important in sales unit effectiveness relationships? If the developed country findings do not apply, then the extent of country variations needs to be investigated. It is important to include the above-noted country variation variables in developing country studies.

4.8.2 Research Findings

The most extensive research concerning sales unit effectiveness in developing countries included Bahrain, Greece, India, Malaysia, Nigeria, Saudi Arabia, and the UK (Piercy, Low, and Cravens 2008). The study examined relationships between sales unit design, salesperson turnover, organizational commitment, and outcome performance and effectiveness. The sample consisted of 822 managers of sales units involved in business-to-business sales. The country samples ranged from 80 to 142 respondents, representing multiple companies. The UK was included in the study to provide a developed-country basis of comparison.

The individual country sales unit effectiveness regression findings ranged from one significant relationship (sales unit design) in Bahrain and Greece (salesperson performance); two in India, Malaysia, and Saudi Arabia; and all four relationships were significant in Nigeria and UK. However, turnover satisfaction was negative in Nigeria; all other relationships were positive (Piercy, Low, and Cravens 2008).

In order to determine the impact of possible country differences, the seven countries were divided into three groups based on country political stability and economic wealth using data from the World Bank (Piercy, Low, and Cravens 2008). Bahrain, Greece, Malaysia, and Saudi Arabia were in one group, India and Nigeria were in the second group, and the UK was in the third group. The results for groups

I and III were significant and positive for all four antecedents. Only turnover satisfaction was not significant for India and Nigeria.

4.8.3 Research Implications

The multi-country study findings are very encouraging from a global perspective. While there are some developing-country differences in the antecedent and sales unit effectiveness relationships, there are several similarities in the research findings. Moreover, essentially all the inter-country differences were due to lack of significance rather than to contradictions. The country differences may in part be explained by political instability, gross national income, and culture dimensions in each country.

Importantly, when using country groupings based on political stability and income, essentially all the country differences are eliminated. This finding is very relevant from an international business perspective. The relationships examined are relatively stable across country groups. It is also possible that the individual country differences would be eliminated (or reduced) using larger sample sizes for individual countries.

Accordingly, there do not appear to be large differences between developing and developed countries regarding antecedent and effectiveness relationships in business-to-business sales organizations. Of course, additional studies in other countries are needed to provide support for this position.

4.9 GENDER DIFFERENCES

Variations in research findings concerning sales personnel gender have been investigated in several studies. Since the late 1980s differences have declined somewhat, particularly across female and male salespeople. We briefly examine the extent of differences concerning sales unit effectiveness and related variables for salespeople and field sales managers.

4.9.1 Salesperson Gender

Several studies since 1990 have been conducted to investigate salesperson gender differences regarding attitudes, behavior, and outcomes. Some of the earlier studies found gender differences. However, in the twenty-first century there is no apparent research support for differences between female and male salespeople on several relevant characteristics. A review of sales force gender studies is provided in Moncrief, Babakus, Cravens, and Johnston (2000).

4.9.2 Sales Manager Gender

There is substantial support for gender differences relative to sales managers. A study was conducted in the UK using responses from 267 field sales managers (Piercy, Cravens, and Lane 2003). The study was based on responses from managers representing a broad cross-section of companies. The researchers comment as follows:

The primary differences between the male and female sales managers in our multi-company study are that the females allocate more effort and higher levels of activity to all aspects of behavior-based control. (Piercy, Cravens, and Lane 2003: 229)

One apparent implication of the study findings is that due to greater involvement with salespeople via behavior control, female managers obtain a better understanding of salespeople's weaknesses and are able to identify where improvement is needed. It is also apparent that manager gender is a relevant issue for sales management in the planning and development of effective sales organizations.

4.10 KNOWLEDGE GAPS

As indicated by the discussion so far, there is an extensive base of knowledge concerning sales organization effectiveness and its antecedents. However, the impact of vertical organizational differences on effectiveness relationships is limited. There are also substantial knowledge gaps as to possible effects of longitudinal changes on effectiveness. Moreover, the effects of sales teams on antecedent and effectiveness relationships have received little or no attention from managers and researchers. Finally, there may be additional antecedents of effectiveness that should be examined. Each of these knowledge gaps is examined.

4.10.1 Vertical Relationships

Sales organization effectiveness is the result of the skills and efforts of the entire sales organization. Much of the existing knowledge about effectiveness results is based on findings at the individual salesperson and sales unit manager levels. The effects on effectiveness of different vertical levels have not been examined. While effectiveness is not restricted to the sales unit level, the effects due to management at higher levels have received very limited attention.

One study examined effectiveness relationships from the chief sales executive perspective as previously discussed (Babakus et al. 1996). The findings were not nearly as strong as the sample results obtained from field sales managers in the same companies. However, the chief sales executive results were not in conflict with the manager findings. The differences may be due in part to the sample sizes (146 versus 58).

A key issue is whether vertical organizational levels are relevant to effectiveness relationships. It may be that the salesperson/field manager levels are where effectiveness is determined. Higher levels may aggregate the lower-level findings rather than create new influences concerning effectiveness relationships. Another possibility is that different measures are needed at higher organizational levels. It is apparent that this knowledge gap requires further assessment by managers and researchers.

4.10.2 Longitudinal Effects

There have been no known attempts to examine longitudinal effects on the effectiveness relationships. The research studies have only examined the relationships at one point in time. These relationships are likely to change over time. For example, if one or more of the antecedents improves (e.g. higher salesperson outcome performance), it will have a positive impact on effectiveness. Alternatively, an antecedent may become less effective (e.g. territory design).

The longitudinal issue clearly requires research attention. The antecedents which have the greatest longitudinal impact need to be identified. The rate of change (time span) should be examined. Complicating the process are the sales force transformations occurring in many companies. However, there should be sufficient stability in more than a few companies to provide research locations for study.

4.10.3 Sales Teams

There have apparently been no attempts to examine the antecedent effects of sales teams on the sales unit effectiveness relationships. The expanded use of sales teams highlights the importance of this knowledge gap. All of the prior attention given to effectiveness relationships has examined sales organizations made up of sales territories assigned to individual salespeople.

It may be necessary to assess the adequacy of the Figure 4.2 conceptualization in order to consider the sales team effects. The adoption of customer relationship management in an increasing number of companies is likely to expand the use of sales teams. Variables including management control, sales territory design, and salesperson skills and performance may result in major changes on the antecedent and effectiveness relationships.

4.10.4 Other Antecedents

Finally, consideration needs to be given to other relevant antecedents in the Figure 4.2 conceptualization. While there is a limit to the number of variables to be included in the framework, one or more additional variables could be considered. The key issue is whether other antecedents will enhance the explanation of variations in sales organization effectiveness.

A variable which has received considerable attention in sales force research is organizational citizenship behavior (OCB). It consists of "individual behavior that is discretionary, not directly or explicitly recognized by the formal reward system, and that in aggregate promotes the effective functioning of the organization" (Organ 1988: 4). Relationships with sales management control, salesperson performance, and other variables and OCB have been examined (Piercy, Cravens, Lane, and Vorhies 2006). OCB is a possible antecedent of effectiveness.

4.11 CONCLUSION

This chapter develops a framework for analysis and decision-making in relation to sales organization effectiveness, which is determined by sales management, salesperson, organizational, and environmental (markets and competition) factors. Sales organization effectiveness is distinct from salesperson performance. Importantly, effectiveness indicates the contribution of the sales organization to the performance of the firm. Metrics which track sales organization effectiveness include sales, market share, customer satisfaction, profit contribution, and other relevant measures relative to competition and internal objectives.

The conceptual framework shown in Figure 4.2 draws from several research streams which are relevant to sales organization effectiveness. These include sales management control, sales force skills and performance, and sales unit design. Salesperson performance is considered a separate yet interrelated variable relative to sales organization effectiveness. Sales unit design assesses how well salesperson territories are configured. Management control considers managers' behavior and/ or outcome processes which are relevant in achieving sales organization effectiveness. There is substantial support for most of the Figure 4.2 relationships based on several studies conducted in Europe, the US, and Australia. Territory design has received less research attention. The pivotal role of manager behavior control in the conceptualization is clearly indicated. The evidence suggests that the extent of manager involvement in behavior control is moderate rather than close day-to-day supervision.

The relevance of the sales organization effectiveness framework in developing countries is an important issue. Most of the research has been conducted in developed countries, and the findings have generally been consistent. Global variations concerning sales organization effectiveness and its antecedents for developing countries have not received extensive research attention. However, the findings are very encouraging, and there are several similarities to developed countries. The developing country differences may be explained by political instability, gross national income, and culture dimensions in each country. Moreover, when using country groupings based on political stability and income, essentially all of the country differences are eliminated.

REFERENCES

AMBLER, T., and J. ROBERTS (2006). "Beware the Silver Metric: Marketing Performance Measurement Has to Be Multidimensional," Marketing Science Institute Report 06-003, Cambridge, MA: Marketing Science Institute.

ANDERSON, E., and R. L. OLIVER (1987). "Perspectives on Behavior-Based Versus Outcome-Based Salesforce Control Systems," *Journal of Marketing* 51 (October), 76–88.

BABAKUS, E., D. W. CRAVENS, K. GRANT, T. N. INGRAM, and R. W. LAFORGE (1996). "Investigating the Relationships Among Sales Management Control, Sales Territory Design, Salesperson Performance, and Sales Organization Effectiveness," *International Journal of Research in Marketing* 13.4, 345–63.

BALDAUF, A., D. W. CRAVENS, and N. F. PIERCY (2001). "Examining Business Strategy, Sales Management, and Salesperson Antecedents of Sales Organization Effectiveness," *Journal of Personal Selling & Sales Management* 21.2, 109–22.

————————(2005). "Sales Management Control Research: Synthesis and an Agenda for Future Research," *Journal of Personal Selling & Sales Management* 25.1, 7–26.

BEHRMAN, D. N., and W. D. PERREAULT, Jr. (1984). "A Role Stress Model of the Performance and Satisfaction of Industrial Salespeople," *Journal of Marketing* 48 (Fall), 9–21.

CHURCHILL, G. A., N. M. FORD, S. W. HARTLEY, and O. C. WALKER (1985). "The Determinants of Salesperson Performance: A Meta-Analysis," *Journal of Marketing Research* 22, 103–18.

CLARK, B. H. (2001). "A Summary of Thinking on Measuring the Value of Marketing," *Journal of Targeting, Measurement & Analysis for Marketing* 9.4, 357–69.

CRAVENS, D. W. (1995). "The Changing Role of the Sales Force," *Marketing Management* (Fall), 49–57.

——T. N. INGRAM, R. W. LAFORGE, and C. E. YOUNG (1993). "Behavior-Based and Outcome-Based Salesforce Control Systems," *Journal of Marketing* 57 (October), 47–59.

——G. W. MARSHALL, F. G. LASSK, and G. S. LOW (2004). "The Control Factor," *Marketing Management* (January–February), 39–44.

Economist, The (2005). "The Cart Pulling the Horse," April 9, 5.

FERRIS, P. W., N. T. BENDLE, P. E. PFEIFER, and D. REIBSTEIN (2006). *Marketing Metrics: 50+ Metrics Every Executive Should Master.* Upper Saddle River, NJ: Wharton School/ Pearson Education.

GRANT, K., and D. W. CRAVENS (1999). "Examining the Antecedents of Sales Organization Effectiveness: An Australian Study," *European Journal of Marketing* 33.9–10, 945–57.

———G. S. LOW, and W. C. MONCRIEF (2001). "The Role of Satisfaction with Territory Design on the Motivation, Attitudes, and Work Outcomes of Salespeople," *Journal of the Academy of Marketing Science* 29.2, 165–78.

HOFSTEDE, G. (1983). "The Cultural Relativity of Organizational Practices and Theories," *Journal of International Business Studies* 14 (Fall), 75–89.

JAWORSKI, B. J., V. STATHAKOPOULOS, and H. S. KRISHNAN (1993). "Control Combinations in Marketing: Conceptual Framework and Empirical Evidence," *Journal of Marketing* 57 (January), 57-69.

JOHNSTON, M. W., and G. W. MARSHALL (2006). *Sales Force Management*, 8th edn, Burr Ridge, IL: McGraw-Hill/Irwin.

——(2009). *Sales Force Management*, 9th edn, Burr Ridge, IL: McGraw-Hill/Irwin.

JONES, E., S. P. BROWN, A. A. ZOLTNERS, and B. A. WEITZ (2005). "The Changing Environment of Selling and Sales Management," *Journal of Personal Selling & Sales Management* 25.2, 105–11.

KALE, S. (2004). "CRM Failure and the Seven Deadly Sins," *Marketing Management* 13 (April), 42–6.

LEHMANN, D. R. (2004). "Metrics for Making Marketing Matter," *Journal of Marketing* 68.4, 73–5.

MONCRIEF, W. C., E. BABAKUS, D. W. CRAVENS, and M. JOHNSTON (2000). "Examining Gender Differences in Field Sales Organizations," *Journal of Business Research* 49.3, 245–57.

OLIVER, R. L., and E. ANDERSON (1994). "An Empirical Test of the Consequences of Behavior-Based and Outcome-Based Sales Control Systems," *Journal of Marketing* 58 (October), 53–67.

ORGAN, D. W. (1988). *Organizational Citizenship Behavior: The Good Soldier Syndrome.* Lexington, MA: Lexington Books.

O'SULLIVAN, D., and A. V. ABELA (2007). "Marketing Performance Measurement Ability and Firm Performance," *Journal of Marketing* 72.2, 79–93.

PAYNE, A., and P. FROW (2005). "A Strategic Framework for Customer Relationship Management," *Journal of Marketing* 69 (October), 167–76.

PIERCY, N. F., D. W. CRAVENS, and N. LANE (2003). "Sales Manager Behavior Control Strategy and Its Consequences: The Impact of Manager Gender Differences," *Journal of Personal Selling & Sales Management* 23.3, 221–37.

———(2007). "Enhancing Salesperson's Effectiveness," *Marketing Management* 16.5 (September/October), 18–25.

——————(2008). "Sales Management Control Level and Competencies: Antecedents and Consequences," *Industrial Marketing Management* 37 (June), 459–467.

——————and D. W. VORHIES (2006). "Driving Organizational Citizenships Behavior and Salesperson In-Role Behavior Performance: The Role of Management Control and Perceived Organizational Support," *Journal of the Academy of Marketing Science* 34.2, 244–62.

——————and N. A. MORGAN (1999). "Relationships Between Sales Management Control, Territory Design, Salesforce Performance, and Sales Organization Effectiveness," *British Journal of Management* 10.2, 95–111.

——and N. LANE (2005). "Strategic Imperatives for Transformation of the Sales Organization," *Journal of Change Management* 5 (September), 249–66.

——G. S. Low, and D. W. CRAVENS (2004). "Consequences of Sales Management's Behavior- and Compensation-Based Control Strategies in Developing Countries," *Journal of International Marketing* 12.3, 30–57.

——————(2008). "Country Differences Concerning Sales Organization and Salesperson Antecedents of Sales Unit Effectiveness," working paper.

ROSENBAUM, B. L. (2000). "Identifying Sales Management Competencies for 21st Century Success," *Velocity* Q1, 37–42.

ROUZIÈS, D., and A. MACQUIN (2003). "An Exploratory Investigation of the Impact of Culture on Sales Force Management Control Systems in Europe," *Journal of Personal Selling & Sales Management* 23.1, 61–72.

SHETH, J. N., and A. SHARMA (2008). "The Impact of the Product to Service Shift in Industrial Markets and the Evolution of the Sales Organization," *Industrial Marketing Management* 37.3, 260–62.

VARGO, S. L., and R. F. LUSCH (2004). "Evolving to a New Dominant Logic for Marketing," *Journal of Marketing* 68.1, 1–23.

WALKER, O. C., G. A. CHURCHILL, and N. M. FORD (1979). "Where Do We Go From Here? Selected Conceptual and Empirical Issues Concerning the Motivation and Performance of the Industrial Salesforce," in G. Albaum and G. A. Churchill (eds.), *Critical Issues in Sales Management: State-of-the-Art and Future Research Needs*, Eugene: University of Oregon, 10–75.

....

CHAPTER 5

THE CHANGING SALES ENVIRONMENT

IMPLICATIONS FOR SALES AND SALES MANAGEMENT RESEARCH AND PRACTICE

....

NICK LEE

5.1 INTRODUCTION

....

In 2001, Leigh and Marshall (p. 83) stated that "the sales function is undergoing an unparalleled metamorphosis," driven by changing conditions in the environment, or as Shapiro, Slywotsky, and Doyle (1994: 1) put it, "a dramatically changed world of buying." Leigh and Marshall's paper was published at the dawn of this present century, yet as we move forward, the pace of change does not appear to have slowed, but if anything to have increased. Even so, it is interesting to note the observation by Jones, Brown, Zoltners, and Weitz (2005: 106) that "the more things change, the more they stay the same," insofar that even in the 1960s authors were noting that the sales environment was rapidly changing (e.g. Kahn and Schuchman 1961). Jones et al. (2005) argued that change was a constant, and that while it presents challenges to the sales practitioner and researcher, these challenges tend to occur along similar dimensions—those of changes in the internal organizational environment, the global business environment, and technological advancement. However, within these basic parameters, the specific challenges facing sales vary significantly over time.

Even so, while the picture of the changing sales environment is usually painted in similar broad strokes, there is often some contradiction amongst the detail of the many different agendas for future sales research which have appeared since Leigh and Marshall's (2001) call. For example, Jones et al. (2005) discuss how the changing expectations of customers in terms of communication, product knowledge, and customization have led to increased cognitive demands on salespeople. Leigh and Marshall (2001) would agree with this, yet they focus more strongly on the strategic concept of customer orientation within the firm, which in turn should feed through to enhanced practices of the sales force. However, the findings of Tanner, Fournier, Wise, Hollet, and Poujol (2008) suggest that sales executives themselves have a greater interest in micro-level issues such as what makes a good salesperson – an issue that has somewhat fallen out of favour for researchers – than more strategic issues.

The aim of this chapter of the Handbook is to provide a perspective on the changes which are evident in the contemporary selling environment. However, more than this, the present chapter also looks to discuss critical changes in the sales *research* environment. Taken together, these parallel changes have the potential to usher in a new age of sales and sales management research—one which is both more able to inform sales practice, but also to advance critical sales and sales management theory.

The chapter will begin with a discussion of the changing business environment facing salespeople and their managers. These changes are not limited to the actual business environment the salesperson operates in, although such changes (technology, globalization, and the like) are important. Rather, societal changes also have a significant impact on sales and sales management practices, in particular the increased attention paid to business ethics and the wellbeing of individuals within and outside the workplace. Subsequently, implications are drawn for sales practice and future research. This leads in to a detailed discussion of recent developments across key areas of research on which sales scholars generally draw, and of how these can impact on the research practices of sales academics. Drawing from recent work on social psychology, human interaction, media technology, and organizational cognitive neuroscience, a model is developed both to classify existing sales research topics and to help develop areas which look to be of key importance in the future. This model illuminates what appear to be highly interesting research fields incorporating recent insights from a more biological perspective of human behavior, as well as an enhanced understanding of the individual's relationships with wider social networks.

5.2 The Changing Sales Environment

Figure 5.1 presents a diagram of the various forces which act together to influence the sales environment. The model presents the forces as concentric circles, moving from the individual salesperson at the centre, through the forces that they interact with within their sales role (business and technological forces), to the more abstract forces which operate on the sales and many other environments (culture and society). However, the key to understanding these forces is to recognize that each specific force interacts with the others, as represented by the double-headed arrows. For example, societal changes may change how the individual perceives certain technological advances, or how business is done. Thus, separating out specific forces and describing their effects is a somewhat artificial distinction. Nevertheless, for the sake of clarity it is necessary to provide some form of structure and demarcation between the various forces acting on the sales environment, which will be done below.

Many of the forces represented in Figure 5.1 have received prior attention from sales scholars in agenda-setting articles throughout the previous decade (Tanner et al. 2008). In particular, technological change has proven to be an extremely

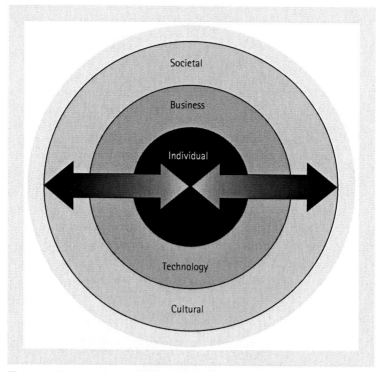

Fig. 5.1. Interactions within the Sales Environment

common theme of the discourse on the changing sales environment (e.g. Leigh and Marshall 2001; Jones et al. 2005). Furthermore, a number of articles pick up on this theme in relation to specific aspects of the individual salesperson's role (e.g. Ingram 2004), or more general business activities (e.g. Robertson, Dixon, and Curry 2006). Yet despite this common interest, Leigh and Marshall's (2001) concerns that not enough is known about effective implementation and use of technology in the sales force appear to hold true even almost a decade later (e.g. Tanner et al. 2008).

5.2.1 Complexity

Perhaps the most prevalent theme running through the various articles which have discussed the changing sales environment since 2001 is that of complexity, and Jones et al. (2005) show that this has in fact been of concern to sales scholars for almost half a century (Kahn and Schuchman 1961). On the one hand, as technology allows product life cycles to shorten, and the customer to come ever closer to the producer, gaining more and more information prior to the sales encounter, the individual salesperson must cope with the significantly more complex demands of their job. Yet changes in society's expectations of working life, and increased integration across cultures—even while cultures become more and more distinct—create even more demands on the salesperson as a member of society. For example, a contemporary salesperson may have to deal with customers who have pre-researched their product and competitors on the internet, including customer weblogs and discussion forums. These customers may reside in far-distant cultures, and require service outside of normal working hours, and also at very short notice. At the same time a typical salesperson may be more aware than in the past of conflicting work–family demands and the impact of such demands on their stress levels. This tension may considerably increase the demands on salespeople in today's environment.

Cutting across these issues is a concern with the role of the salesperson within the firm which is common to prior work (e.g. Ingram, LaForge, and Leigh 2002; Leigh and Marshall 2001; Rackham and DeVincentis 1999; Robertson, Dixon, and Curry 2006). Most common is the question of where the sales function fits in to a market-driven organization (e.g. Leigh and Marshall 2001), which takes in critical issues such as the conflict between sales and marketing (e.g. Jones et al. 2005; Kotler, Rackham, and Krishnaswamy 2006), as well as the need to redefine the role of selling in an environment where customers may do much of the traditional sales-person's role themselves. Drawing from the model presented in Figure 5.1, the following sections present the specific environmental forces influencing the sales environment in more detail, and place each into context with the others.

5.2.2 Globalization

Perhaps the most easily observable of all the forces shaping the sales environment is increasing globalization. Much of this globalization is driven by technological advancement in communication and transport technologies. For example, virtually all companies are now able to operate in the global business environment, thanks to the Internet and other technologies (Lituchy and Barra 2008). Demand can now build for a product across the world, whether or not the manufacturer intended to sell that product outside the home country. This can place a firm in an awkward position at times, requiring decisions to be made regarding the delivery and support of products and solutions far outside their intended markets. In turn, the salesperson may be called upon to interact and work with customers far outside their comfort zone. Companies and salespeople who are unprepared for this risk costly mistakes.

Yet the value chain for many firms is also now a global concern. In many instances, design, manufacture, and marketing of products all take place in different countries, using materials and outsourced functions from countries which are different again. The challenge in this instance is one of diversity for the sales force. Sales representatives may need to link together business functions located across the globe, with customers in another country. In doing so, they become subject to legal and cultural constraints which differ significantly in each environment. All the while, a salesperson may be working within a highly diverse team which presents its own specific challenges (e.g. Richard, Murthi, and Ismail 2007). In turn, the sales manager must develop skills and competencies which differ significantly from those which s/he may have used in the past to manage a domestic sales force in a defined geographic area. For example, skills such as cultural knowledge and sensitivity, highly developed communication skills, ability to work with technology to coordinate and communicate, and many others are now necessary for such a salesperson.

5.2.3 Changes in Channel Delivery and Information Provision

Modern technology has also revolutionized the role of salespeople in a number of more specific senses. First and perhaps foremost is the exponential increase in product-related information which customers now have access to via the Internet. In many instances, rather than relying on a salesperson to provide information regarding the benefits of a product or service, buyers are now able to find this out for themselves. Information is provided both by the company itself and also on the vast number of independent review and interest group sites, which many customers trust more than "official" sources (Brown, Broderick, and Lee 2007).

This leaves a salesperson in a situation where they may face a customer who is pre-armed with a large amount of information—some of which may be inaccurate or opinionated—meaning that they must spend a large proportion of their time repairing perceptions of their offerings, and clarifying misunderstandings. Sales-people in this case may be starting on the back foot.

The increase in information provision can therefore be seen to potentially increase the challenges to the salesperson who is involved in selling value-added solutions to buyers, in that buyers may require significant "re-education" to remove preconceptions they may have developed through their own independent research. However, the most serious implications are likely to arise for sales organizations who are focused on lower-value-added purchasing, and in particular those which primarily work within a reordering context. For example, the tradi-tional role of the retail salesperson has all but disappeared in the contemporary environment, as consumers research product-related information on the Internet, and primarily visit retail stores if they want to try something prior to buying it. In this case, the retail salesperson is reduced to the role of order-taker at best, rather than a component in the consumer decision process. At the same time, electronic delivery methods threaten the role of the more traditional field salesperson, who is mainly focused on repurchasers. In such instances, integrated channel delivery mechanisms can do such tasks automatically, obviating the need for a sales visit (Tanner et al. 2008).

Such a situation could be seen as an opportunity to more clearly define exactly what a salesperson's role is within the firm. More specifically, is it efficient to have an individual representative visit companies merely to take reorders? Skilled salespeople may be better employed working with customers on value-added solutions, or gaining new business, or even educating customers. Self-service technology now enables customers to perform many of the more routine tasks themselves, leaving salespeople free to focus their efforts elsewhere, in areas of more long-term value to the firm.

5.2.4 Customer Co-production and the Demassification of the Marketplace

A critical issue faced by contemporary sales forces is the increased need for the customization of solutions for customers, rather than offering the same product or service to all customers (Jones et al. 2005). Such an approach is attractive to many organizations, since they are able to move away from commodity-based pricing and towards a more defensible competitive position. This can be considered in terms of a significant demassification of the marketplace. In such a case, the existence of defined and substantive market segments is questionable, which makes the use of segmentation strategies even more problematic for firms than Leigh and Marshall reported in 2001. That said, technology can help significantly in the segmentation process, particularly with the growth of demographic classification and segmentation firms and the availability of such data online.

Even so, the further evolution of the demassification process, and the need for customization, brings us ever-closer to the idea of the "co-production" of a solution between sellers and buyers. While advocates of "postmodern marketing" theories have discussed the co-production process for many years (e.g. Firat and Venkatesh 1995), it is only more recently that sales scholars have considered this issue (Jones et al. 2005). "Co-production" refers to the idea that customers are intimately involved in specifying and producing the product or service that they purchase, and it could be considered to be the essence of the value-added solution selling role. However, it is important to note that this process is not just at a business-to-business level, but extends even down to the level of consumer products (Etgar 2008).

While this offers considerable opportunities for salespeople to add value to a sale, Jones et al. (2005) argue that—even though consumers are intimately involved in the production process—any dissatisfaction remains attributed to the selling organization. Furthermore, this is the case even if the source of the dissatisfaction is the customer's own error. This places significant extra demand on the salesperson, who must now manage the customer's role in the co-production process. In this sense, the skills required appear similar to those referred to above in managing a diverse selling team and global value chain. However, the need for these abstract skills has moved further down the chain, to the individual sales operative, who now may find themselves held responsible for many more things which may go wrong in the process. For example, managing the customer expectation and co-production process for a consumer product such as individualized clothing is fraught with potential difficulties—similar to the issues services marketing research has explored.

5.2.5 The Competitive Environment: Hypercompetition and Buyer Concentration

It is in part a combination of the issues covered above which has resulted in a situation Jones et al. (2005) term "hypercompetition." In other words, the increase in competitors has led to a great increase in the intensity of competition within almost all markets (Bogner and Barr 2000). This has also been driven in many markets (particularly FMCGs) by a massive increase in the concentration of buyers—leaving many competitors to complete for fewer but larger accounts (Sudhir and Rao 2006).

On the one hand, product lifecycles are shortening to a great extent, and competition for market leadership has increased, "with firms leapfrogging one another in attempts to gain product advantage" (Jones et al. 2005: 108). In such a situation, salespeople are constantly in need of market-sensing mechanisms and capabilities, as well being used by their organizations as "eyes and ears" in the field (Chen 2005). This adds yet more aspects to the salesperson's role in the firm. Simultaneously, the time available to salespeople to spend with prospects appears to have decreased significantly (Jones et al. 2007), leaving them far less opportunity to perform this role.

The concentration of buying power has been explored by a number of researchers, particularly within the retail and food marketing areas (Gwynne 2008). In many markets the consolidation of a number of smaller buyers, either by buyouts or by joint ventures, has led to a situation where the buyer has unprecedented levels of power in the channel. The large discount retailers such as Wal-Mart are but one example of this phenomenon. Selling organizations are thus forced to act according to the wishes of the buyer, which places additional pressure on the salesperson to deliver in a way tailored to the advantage of the buyer rather than themselves or their firm. In some cases, a single buyer may be responsible for purchasing the entire output of a firm (as is sometimes the case for firms operating in industries such as automotive components), leaving the role of the traditional value-added salesperson at best unclear, and more often completely redundant.

5.2.6 Sales Force Automation and Customer Relationship Management

As well as the aforementioned changes in the business and cultural environment, salespeople must also cope with a revolution in the use of technology to control and automate their field selling tasks. Leigh and Marshall (2001) stressed that the role of information technology was increasing exponentially in terms of enabling a customer-centric sales force culture, focusing on the ability of customer relationship management (CRM) systems to enable a "one-to-one, or enterprise-to-enterprise, marketing vision" (p. 88). This vision has considerable overlaps with some of the issues covered above, including the customization, electronic channel, and order-taking aspects of the changing role of the salesperson. Jones et al. (2005) echo Leigh and Marshall's (2001) focus on CRM technologies, yet they also state that the adoption of such technologies by sales forces has been slow, and research has found that the adoption of CRM and other automation technologies by the sales force can have negative consequences (Speier and Venkatesh 2002).

This is of course unsurprising, since it is often the case that field salespeople see the introduction of CRM and other similar systems into their routines as entailing extra effort which may take them away from what they see as their primary role (Jones, Sundaram, and Chin 2002). Furthermore, salespeople may see the adoption of a CRM system as a method for the company to take power from the sales force, for example by creating a central database of contacts and prospects, or by imposing scripts on salespeople for calls.

Yet technological advances have impacted on other aspects of the salesperson's role in different, perhaps more pervasive, ways. For example, the rise of the "always-on" communication system (such as the almost ubiquitous Blackberry, and other mobile email devices) has blurred the boundaries between work and free time. Expectations of instant response to communications are increasing, from both customers and management, and this is also ratcheting up the demands on the salesperson. The increase in take-up of global positioning devices (which are now inherent to many mobile phones) also has the potential to change how salespeople are managed, with the organization able to keep accurate records of salespeople's movements during their working time, and such concepts will be alluded to in the later discussion.

Taken together, these and similar technological advances may remove some of the perceived flexibility of the field sales role, in terms both of movement and of conduct. While from an organizational perspective, this would appear superficially at least to be desirable, it remains to be seen whether it has more negative implications for salespeople themselves. For example, the selling role is usually an independent one (Anderson and Oliver 1987), which may attract many to the position. If the perception of this is reduced, it may be the case that top-quality candidates target different professions.

5.2.7 Customer Expectations

Drawing the above changes together, it can be seen that they are all likely to raise the expectations of the customer towards the sales force. Indeed, this is exactly the case, with Jones et al. (2005) reporting that customer satisfaction ratings are showing a deflationary trend. This is unsurprising, given the increasing turbulence and competition in the marketplace, which in turn leads to changing customer expectations. Furthermore, with the increase in globalization referred to above, sales forces are likely to be serving an increasingly diverse customer base. In such situations, expectations are likely to differ widely across customers, and each customer will naturally expect that their own needs are catered to effectively.

Yet the increase in technology already discussed also means that customers expect their salespeople to be far better informed than in the past. For example, much basic company information, which salespeople may have expected to gather on their first call, is now able to be gathered from the Internet and public information sources (Jones et al. 2005), meaning that salespeople may be expected to spend time gathering it themselves prior to, rather than during, a sales call. Customers may now demand solutions much earlier in the sales cycle, which provides both a challenge but also an opportunity to the salesperson. For example, rather than the first call being understood by both parties as a process of understanding the buyer's characteristics and needs, customers may expect that the salesperson has already done this via online information, and will be able to offer a customized solution almost immediately. Conversely, customers are also now able to gather far more information about competitors' offerings through the Internet, rather than waiting for sales calls from competitors. In this case, the salesperson must also be expected to have a greater depth of knowledge about how their own products are superior. Instead of presenting this information to the prospect for the first time, they may now be involved in countering pre-formed opinions, often a rather more difficult job.

5.2.8 Ethics

The sales environment has also evolved significantly in terms of societal expectations of appropriate behavior both within and outside the workplace. Perhaps the most prevalent of these changes has concerned the ethics of business itself. While a concern for the ethics of the sales function has been evident for some time (Cadogan, Lee, Tarkiainen, and Sundqvist 2009), in recent years the publicity associated with repeated high-profile cases of unethical business practices has raised public consciousness of business ethics in general. In turn, within the firm, awareness may now be raised of potential unethical practices, possibly leading to a far less flexible environment for salespeople to operate within, and perhaps more pressure to be put on salespeople to act as exemplars of the firm, given their boundary-spanning role.

Whether or (hopefully) not a salesperson considers themselves likely to conduct themselves unethically, such an environment is again likely to lead to greater pressure on the salesperson. Salespeople must now make sure not only that are their practices ethical (which one trusts would be the case anyway) but that they are *perceived* by all as ethical. Salespeople may thus observe a far wider set of stakeholders in their behavior than they may have in the past. Such perceptions may also have an impact on the type of individuals who wish to become salespeople in the future, as well as on stereotypes of salespeople amongst society, which again may influence salespeople's behavior and the pressure they feel. For example, Lee, Sandfield, and Dhaliwal (2007) show that stereotypes of salespeople tend to be rather negative, and this may influence who decides that sales is the appropriate career for them, as well as their expectations of how to behave on the job, potentially creating a vicious cycle.

The global business environment is an additional complication to ethical practices. In particular, it has been noted that businesspeople may have problems in adapting their practices to different cultures with different ethical standards (Rashid and Ho 2003). Furthermore, in such situations, apart from having to deal with different practices across the globe, international salespeople may also have to consider the interaction with the practices of their own country, and which of these practices should take precedence in any given decision situation.

5.2.9 Wellbeing in the Workplace

While the business environment within which the salesperson must operate has evolved considerably over the last two decades, as discussed above, the wider workplace and social environment has also changed significantly. This is particularly the case in terms of prevailing opinions regarding what individuals can expect of their jobs, and the interaction between personal and professional life. These changes are evidenced by the considerable increase in scholarly sales research regarding issues such as job stresses and strains (Bhuian, Menguc, and Borsboom 2005), burnout and emotional exhaustion (Lewin and Sager 2008), and work/family conflict (Netemeyer, Brashear-Alejandro, and Boles 2004). Even so, sales-specific research on these issues appears less prevalent than more general research.

Regarding job stress and strain, it would seem to be the case that contemporary times have seen a recognition that—while stress may be endemic to professional life—it is no longer acceptable to merely tolerate it and consider it as unavoidable. Certainly, the factors already discussed seem likely to have increased demands on sales professionals, which in turn increases stress (Morrison, Payne, and Wall 2003). However, stress has always been a factor in the salesperson's role (Sager and Wilson 1995), and recent concern about stress appears to emerge from new attitudes towards stress as much as from any increase in stress itself.

Related to stress and strain is the concept of burnout. Burnout is defined as a psychological response consisting of the three dimensions of emotional exhaustion, depersonalization, and reduced feelings of personal accomplishment, and is generally considered to be prevalent primarily in the "helping professions," and professions which involve significant human contact and emotional work (Lee and Ashforth 1996, Maslach 1982). While research on burnout began in the social services such as nursing and teaching, more recent work has widened its scope to consider the sales profession as one very likely to suffer from high levels of burnout due to the boundary-spanning, high-contact nature of the job (Singh, Goolsby, and Rhoads 1994).

Finally, a change is also evident in attitudes and expectation regarding the place of work in the wider life of the individual. In more recent times it seems that it is no longer acceptable for one's profession to dominate one's life in the same way as perhaps common stereotypes of the salesperson may describe (as evidenced in dramas such as *Glengarry Glen Ross* or *Death of a Salesman*). Instead, the concept of "work–life balance" is growing in importance to society (Roberts 2007). Also, as already mentioned, recent work has extended the classical notion of "role conflict" to include "work/family conflict", where the employee must reconcile the conflicting demands of the job and the family unit (e.g. Netemeyer, Maxham, and Pullig 2005), showing that such issues can cause considerable harm to the employee.

The increased concern for salesperson wellbeing is also evidenced by the interest in career development of sales people. Rather than seeing salespeople as an expense, it seems that there is an increased recognition of the salesperson as an investment which needs a long-term perspective. This is particularly important given the increased demands on salespeople as shown above, which lead to increased investments in them by the firm. Salespeople therefore need to be managed throughout their career as assets to the firm, rather than as interchangeable "bodies." Interest in salesperson career development is increasingly evident in the literature (Cron, Marshall, Singh, Spiro, and Sujan 2005), and it can be seen that many of the most successful firms treat good salespeople as long-term investments, not short-term expenses (Johnston and Marshall 2008), utilizing ongoing training and development processes and actively managing their career progression.

5.3 IMPLICATIONS OF THE CHANGING ENVIRONMENT

The environmental changes discussed above together have substantial implications for the sales force and its role within the firm. Perhaps most obvious to many is a move towards a more relationship-oriented focus for the sales force. In particular, with the increasing demands on the sales force it is almost certainly no longer the case that "any customer is a good customer." Instead, salespeople and their managers need to select the most appropriate and profitable customers. Especially, it is unlikely to be appropriate to offer all customers the same level of service or support. To enable salespeople to meet the rising expectations of customers, and cope with the demands of globalization, increased technology, and the changing social environment, salespeople must focus their primary energies on the most profitable customers. Lower-potential customers will necessarily therefore receive less specialized and personal services, while high-profit customers will receive higher levels (cf. Johnston and Marshall 2008). For example, a high-profit customer may receive dedicated account executives, perhaps even extending to on-site representatives, while a low-value routinized rebuyer may receive mainly online ordering and support.

Commensurate with this, the role of the sales force must change. However, it is too simplistic to characterize this change as one where the salesperson must become primarily relationship-oriented. In fact, it is likely to be more effective for the sales force to *specialize* across various specific roles, rather than each salesperson trying to play each role simultaneously. In fact, for some time it has been evident that specialization will be likely to accrue some benefits to the selling firm, with for example specialized cold-calling and account maintenance representatives in use at many firms. However, if companies wish to reap the maximum benefits from the changing environment, they must go further than this to more fully develop the specific roles of field salespeople themselves.

In particular, some salespeople will be better suited to the relationship-building and sustaining role, and will therefore be most effective if they focus on these accounts. This role is often characterized as *consultative* selling, involving the salesperson working with the customer in developing a customized solution. Conversely, other salespeople are more likely to suit a role which concentrates on creating and servicing (to a lesser extent) many more accounts, each with simpler needs. Such a role is more *transactional*, and clearly still has a major part to play if utilized effectively. Yet a single salesperson is unsuited to pursuing both these types of opportunities, since each requires distinct competencies, and also varying management structures and reward systems.

Such an approach therefore demands change from the sales managers as well as the salesperson. First of all, the manager must play a key strategic role in determining which accounts require which approach. Importantly, it is not enough to use the account size alone as a determinant of the approach needed. Instead, the distinct characteristics and needs of the account must be taken into account. From there, the manager must decide whether or not their sales force can service both types of account, and if so, who is suited to each account. Most importantly, the manager must then develop motivational tools and reward structures which can motivate high performance in each role, while maintaining equity and fairness perceptions amongst the sales force as a whole. However, on the upside, a structure which incorporates such divergent approaches may have the advantage of providing a ready-made career development structure for salespeople, long considered a problem by scholars (Cron et al. 2005).

However, it is not just sales practice which is experiencing significant change in recent times. Sales research is also undergoing significant changes, which are only likely to increase in future. Certainly, it is clear that sales research has become significantly more interested in research questions related to the above environmental changes. As shown above, such topics include technology adoption and use, global sales issues, sales ethics, job stress, and the like. Yet in future the very nature of sales research may be revolutionized by advances in other fields of research, such as psychology and organizational science. The balance of this chapter will develop a sales research model based on these advances, and use it both to structure recent advances in sales research and to define areas which are likely to prove fruitful in the future.

5.4 THE CHANGING SALES RESEARCH ENVIRONMENT

As already noted, societal conditions have changed in a fundamental way over the last two decades, leading to major changes in the research topics which sales scholars have either pursued or have argued are in need of investigation in the future. These topics can be usefully categorized by the scope of their interest, as can be seen in the horizontal axis of Figure 5.2, which presents a selection of major sales research topics which have been explored over the last two decades. Additionally, recently emerging topics in the sales literature, or topics in other fields which look likely to be of great interest in the sales research context, are shown in bold. These topics include some in this Handbook, as well as very recent articles in the marketing and general psychology and scientific literature. The list of previously explored and potential topics is in no way intended to be exhaustive, since this would clearly be impossible, given the diversity of research in the last 20 years. Instead the selection is meant to be indicative of key issues, and representative of overall trends. Emerging topics have been selected to illustrate important directions of future work, given emerging trends across other disciplines and existing directions in sales research.

At one end of a continuum are placed research topics which are concerned with the salesperson as an individual. Much early academic research covered issues such as salesperson characteristics (e.g. Bagozzi 1978), and this interest continues today. Moving to the right along the axis, we find topics that deal with the dyadic relationship between members of the sales force, such as the sales manager–salesperson relationship, or the salesperson–customer relationship (e.g. Lagace 1990). Such work has proved popular since the 1980s, and has made significant contributions to our understanding of the sales force. However, in more recent times the need to understand the sales force in the context of a team or wider organizational situation has been a significant driver of research activity in the sales

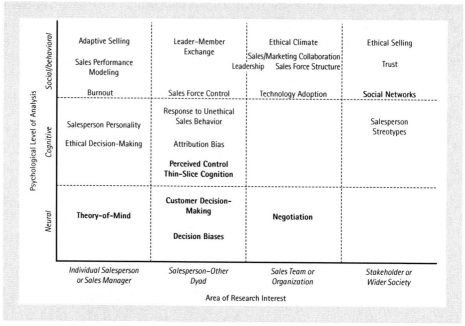

Fig. 5.2. Levels of Analysis and Sales Research

force (e.g. Brown, Evans, Mantrala, and Challagalla 2005). Finally, to the extreme right we have research themes and topics which concern the sales force in relation to wider stakeholders, society, and social trends. Such work has been the most recent development in sales research, and has been clearly influenced both by environmental changes and by recent calls for research (e.g. Jones et al. 2005). It can be seen that as the topics move along the horizontal axis of Figure 5.2, the scope of the research widens, from the individual to the dyadic relationship, to the work team or organization, through to those external to the firm. As already mentioned, it is interesting to note how this widening of scope has also partly at least corresponded to an evolution over time, from the emergence of academic sales research to more contemporary times.

However, while the scope of sales research has varied significantly in the last three to four decades, the underlying theoretical basis of sales research has also been fragmented, drawing from fields as diverse as strategy, ethics, organization studies, economics, sociology, and gender studies. Nevertheless, a convincing argument could be made for psychology as a fundamental theoretical foundation for the major part of sales research. That said, a large proportion of this founda-tion has been drawn secondhand from other business-related disciplines which themselves have a psychological basis. The disadvantage of this is that sales research has tended to rely on advances to be made in other disciplines before it moves forwards itself. This is important because massive theoretical and methodological advances in human psychology have been made since 1990, and have only very recently have begun to filter into business research in general. Sales research, as an application of more general research areas, has seen very little progress in this regard, and the need is clear for a reconceptualization of the psychological basis of sales research.

The vertical axis of Figure 5.2 provides a first step towards such a reconsideration, providing a classification of sales research topics by their psychological *level of analysis*. More specifically, one can theoretically understand and explain any human behavior at various levels. At the social level, we are particularly concerned with how humans behave in socially relevant contexts, and within this are organizational contexts such as the sales force. Yet theories of social behavior are not independent of our understanding of cognitive psychology (which refers to processes associated with thought, such as information processing). Even more fundamentally, theories of cognitive psychology are dependent ultimately on an understanding of base-level brain systems and physiology—which is termed in Figure 5.2 the neural level of analysis. Recent research on *organizational cognitive neuroscience* (e.g. Lee and Chamberlain 2007) has drawn from social neuroscience (e.g. Cacioppo, Berntson, and Crites 1996) to more fully explore this concept.

The essence of such a model is that it is impossible to fully understand or explain any sales force-relevant concept purely in a top-down manner, by focusing purely on behavioral approaches or high-level sales or organizational theories. Yet focusing only on basic-level neuroscientific research is likely to lack relevance, and runs the risk of theoretical sterility. Instead, by taking an integrative or multidisciplinary approach we can develop research themes, programmes, and topics which either (a) use an understanding of more fundamental levels of theory to untangle key research questions at a higher level or (b) are completely original, contributing to both higher- and lower-level theories. Figure 5.2 thus classifies existing key sales research topics in various cells of a two-dimensional matrix, and suggests fruitful avenues for new research that are relevant to the key environmental changes already discussed. These emerging directions are presented in **bold**. In the final major section of this chapter, these topics will be briefly discussed and key directions for future research suggested. In the process, the utility of integrating an enhanced understanding of cognitive and/or neuropsychological theories and methods will be explicitly discussed and pointed out using key examples of cross-disciplinary work. At the same time, key directions at the other end of the spectrum—that of the sales force's relationship to wider society—will also be discussed. As a result, what is presented below is a wide (though by no means comprehensive) agenda for key future work that taps into both the changing environment of sales practice and the correspondingly changing environment of sales research.

5.5 The Potential for Biological and Neuroscientific Insights into Sales Force Performance and Behavior

From Figure 5.2, it can be seen that theories based on a cognitive psychology foundation have had some influence in sales research, particularly when exploring individual or dyadic-level theories. Cognitive psychology refers to the study of the mental processes associated with thought, and in this sense it is a field rich in theory. In general cognitive psychology, basic topics of interest include; perception, memory, representation, and categorization, knowledge, language, problem solving, reasoning, and decision-making. In more recent times emotion has also entered the cognitive framework, particularly with regard to recent work on emotions in decision-making (e.g. Bechara, Tranel, and Damasio 2000, Damasio 1994).

5.5.1 Managerial Decision-Making and Control

Topics which have used (whether knowingly or not) cognitive foundations within sales research are not especially rare, although it is clear that they are less prevalent than the higher-level topics that take a behavioral or social approach. Probably the most common topic of interest within this area is that of decision-making—which is a rather high-level cognitive topic (in that it depends on a number of more basic theories). For example, sales researchers have long been interested in how managers make decisions regarding how to attribute responsibility for performance, or conversely blame for an undesirable sales behavior, and various biases have been explored (e.g. Gentry, Mowen, and Tasaki 1991, DeConinck 1992). A particularly relevant thread of this work within the current environment is that of making decisions on how to punish unethical behavior. Although some of this has looked at the situation through a cultural lens (e.g. Lee, Beatson, Garrett, Lings, and Zhang 2009), which is clearly at the social level, much of the seminal work has explored the influences of key perceptual factors on the decision process of the sales manager (e.g. Bellizzi and Hite 1989, Hunt and Vasquez-Parraga 1993).

A good example of how an increased incorporation of cognitive-level concepts can help unpack our understanding of key sales research topics is provided by the area of sales management control systems. At present, control systems research can be understood as based on theory that is broadly located within a social or behavioral framework. Such work has often considered a sales management control system to be defined by the actions taken or intended by the sales manager—the controller (e.g. Jaworski 1988). However, a significant proportion of research in the area has operationalized these theories by measuring salespeople's perceptions of managerial activities (Oliver and Anderson 1994). Thus, it is not entirely surprising that there is no uniform agreement on the consequences of different sales management control systems, in terms either of objective salesperson behavior or of salesperson psychological states (Baldauf, Cravens, and Piercy 2005). Incorporating a cognitive model into sales management control theory would involve a recognition of the role of attention, perception, learning, knowledge, and the like. In practical terms, the upshot would be an explicit recognition that control systems may work across different levels, with different consequences on salespeople. For example, how are managers' intended control actions perceived and acted upon by salespeople? Cognitive theories would suggest that salespeople's perceptions and evaluations of sales managerial control would have the most significant influence, but in a context where managers can control behavior directly (i.e. by manipulating pay), is this still feasible? In other words, does it matter what the salesperson perceives as the intention when a manager removes a performance bonus, or will they change their behavior anyway? Will this situation lead to some kind of negative psychological outcome, such as a lack of motivation? These questions are difficult to theorize about without a base in cognitive psychology, and work in this area will undoubtedly advance our understanding of how control systems may work in practice. For example, such work may help practicing managers understand the correct manner in which to implement their intended controls, and in which situations salespeople's perceptions do or do not override the manager's intention.

5.5.2 Salesperson–Customer Interactions

Cognitive theories can also be of significant impact on our understanding of the salesperson–customer interaction, and in fact any dyadic interaction involving a salesperson. For example, Sujan (this volume) presents a review of psychological theories which show the influence of salespeople on customers. One of the most promising psychological theories in this area involves what are known as "thin slices" of an interaction (cf. Ambady and Rosenthal 1993). In essence, a thin slice is a very short "slice" of time (ranging from around 5 to 300 seconds) within an interaction. Psychological researchers have studied thin slices in the context of how accurately humans can evaluate the characteristics of others using a thin slice of an interaction rather than by participating in or observing a longer interaction. It has been found that when judging negative characteristics, or the intelligence and competence of a dyadic partner, individuals can do this accurately from a slice of only 5 seconds. However, when it comes to positive characteristics such as agreeableness, longer slices yielded significantly higher accuracy (Carney, Colvin, and Hall 2007). Interestingly, Carney, Colvin, and Hall (2007) also found that slices extracted from the 3rd and 5th minute of a 5-minute interaction are generally the most accurately judged by subjects. Further, recent work has found that "ultrathin" slices of as little as 50 milliseconds are enough for humans to judge certain characteristics (Rule and Ambady 2008). In a sales context, the relevance of such work is clear, and both Ambady, Krabbenhoft, and Hogan (2006) and Hari, Stros, and Marriott (2008) have explored such situations. Ambady et al. (2006) found that thin slices (20 seconds) of audio (both solely tone, and also tone and actual semantic content) could predict judgements of personality, which in turn differentiated between high- and low-rated sales managers. Hari et al. (2008) used videoed interactions to include behavioral material rather than audio, and found that slices of 30 seconds were enough for potential customers to clearly differentiate their likelihood of purchasing from a given salesperson. Taken together, such results show the relevance of such theories for exploring sales interaction, although considerably more research is needed here.

Further work on human interaction, drawing from neuroscientific and psychophysiological theory, may help to extend this understanding. More specifically, Pentland (2004) developed a theory explaining exactly which specific voice tone and conversational interaction features were likely to serve as accurate predictors of future behavior from thin slice judgements. In a later research thesis by one of Pentland's students, these features were shown to accurately predict interest and attraction in 3-minute and 5-minute dyadic interactions, as well as to predict decision-making in group situations (Madan 2005). In fact, Madan (2005) showed how to build a real-time monitor of such key features into a PDA device, which could indicate how well an individual was doing in the interaction. It is not hard to see how sales interaction research (and practice) could be influenced by such work. Curhan and Pentland (2007) extended this work to a business negotiation context, showing that a computer could be programmed to accurately judge these interaction features, and that they could thus predict individual success in negotiation. The variety of possible applications of this in a sales context is vast. For example, mobile computing devices such as PDAs or mobile phones could be used to provide real-time advice on the likely success of sales interactions—even allowing remote monitoring of key features by a trainer or manager.

5.5.3 Sales Research and Cognitive Neuroscience

Pentland and colleagues' research shows how an understanding of human biology and psychophysiology, as well as cutting-edge technology, can enhance our ability as sales researchers to explore and explain the situations and research questions of interest to us. In turn this will allow us to be more confident and creative in drawing implications for sales practice in the contemporary selling environment.

However, this is not unique to sales research as a subfield of marketing, organizational, social, or human science research in general. As Gazzaniga (2000: p. xiii) puts it, "understanding each nucleus or program in the brain can only be helped by examining the pieces with which it interlocks in this scrupulously well-turned machine." In other words, only by understanding the fundamental components can one understand fully our ultimate behavior.

Perhaps the clearest recent example of this within a sales context is the study by Dietvorst, Verbeke, Bagozzi, Yoon, Smits, and van der Lugt (2008). The authors show how a cognitive neuroscientific approach can enhance our understanding of key sales force research topics in two key ways, which map almost exactly onto the multi-level approach introduced above. First, they use an understanding of existing psychological theory drawn from recent neuroscientific findings to develop a theory of brain functioning as applied to the research question of whether or not salespeople can recognize customer intentions and cues—or, in common phraseology, to "read their minds." Second, they build up an incremental research strategy, which incorporates best practice social and behavioural research tools (e.g. confirmatory factor analysis and structural equation modelling) and also a functional magnetic resonance imaging approach drawn from cognitive neuroscience research. In this way, the middle ground between top-down and bottom-up theorizing is reached, allowing each to illuminate the other, and providing a significant contribution to our understanding or a critical sales question.

5.6 AN ENHANCED UNDERSTANDING OF THE SALES FORCE'S RELATIONSHIP TO WIDER SOCIETY

While much of the previous discussion has focused on how a more biological view incorporating a cognitive neuropsychological or psychophysiological understanding can help us to explore sales theories which deal with individual or dyadic-type theories, sales researchers are also becoming interested in the wider social aspects of the sales force. In particular, the *social network* approach has received significant interest (e.g. Seevers, Skinner, and Kelley 2007). Social network approaches go beyond traditional dyadic relationship research (e.g. Leader–Member Exchange) to explore aspects of the position of individuals (such as sales managers) in a wider network of formal and sometimes informal relationships. While the approach is popular in many fields, it is only recently that is has begun to filter into sales contexts (e.g. Mehra, Dixon, Brass, and Robertson 2006), and even more recently into the specific sales literature.

Biological and technological views can also provide significant insight here. For example, Pentland and colleagues' work has already been mentioned here, and it also contains some interesting implications for a network-based approach (e.g. Olguin, Waber, Kim, Mohan, Ara, and Pentland 2009, Waber, Olguin, Kim, and Pentland 2008). Pentland calls his approach "reality mining," and it involves the use of technological tools to track social interaction for later analysis. The use of what are called "sociometers" has received significant attention in the practition-er-based press (e.g. Buchanan 2008), and in fact Pentland's work was awarded the 2009 Breakthrough Idea of the Year from the *Harvard Business Review*. Socio-meters are small electronic devices that can track the physical location of subjects, as well as their body language and voice cues (such as the key conversational and voice tone features discussed earlier). Such devices can track social networks accurately, as well as potentially indicating how "well" that interaction is going. Choudhury, Philipose, Wyatt, and Lester (2006) on the other hand have used RFID (radio frequency ID) tags to explore social networks in communities. Such tools could have major utility for sales managers in understanding the pattern of relationships and networks of their most versus least successful salespeople—although there are significant practical hurdles to be negotiated before this is realistic.

Similarly, Madan (2005) develops the principles behind a cellular phone-based network which would use the capabilities of smartphones to detect and evaluate the key conversational features, detect where it is to within a communications cell or WiFi access point, and then be able to transmit this information to a central server. Such information could be used for social networking purposes (e.g. a text message to your phone saying "Your best friend Mike is having a great time at Bar X"). Of course, it could also be used for real-time monitoring of salesperson location and more importantly of interaction success. While this has—for most—uncomfortable connotations of "Big Brother," it also has the potential to be one of the most effective training tools ever created, allowing trainers to pinpoint what goes wrong in sales calls, and when, potentially in real time—allowing instant feedback.

5.7 CONCLUSIONS

The primary objective of this chapter was to present a number of key changes in the contemporary business and social environment, and to draw out the implications of these changes for sales practice and for sales research. A complimentary goal was to present directions for future research that can be perceived from recent advances in the psychological sciences, tied to the environmental changes previously discussed. In doing so, what has been presented can be taken to be (at least from some viewpoints) a call for a more biological approach to sales research. What is meant by this is not necessarily the blanket employment of research tools such as brain scanners and psychophysiological measurements, but instead an incorporation into sales research theories of human behavior which are based on an appreciation of the biological and evolutionary basis of the human species.

Many of the theories discussed in the present work concern cognitive and neuroscientific approaches to sales and sales management. However, in recent times researchers have also explored the link between evolutionary theory and these approaches. Such theories have revolutionized the human sciences in the last two decades, and have the potential to do the same to the organizational sciences, with sales and sales management no exception. Garcia and Saad (2008) argue that a complete understanding of the human mind (and thus of our behavior) cannot occur without understanding the evolutionary adaptations that have shaped it. In essence, such an approach aims to understand the reasons *why* certain physical behaviors and physiological activities may have evolved, which allows an understanding of why certain behaviors manifest in similar ways across different individuals and situations. Such an approach has major potential benefits for the understanding of behavior in the workplace, including the sales force, and the design of effective workplaces and jobs. It is also evident in much of the work mentioned herein (e.g. Pentland 2004). For example, how should a manager design the most effective motivational plans, in sympathy with our evolved nature?

Thus, we take the position here that greater understanding of sales and sales management behaviors is dependent on the incorporation into sales research of the theoretical advances discussed in the present chapter. Of course, as already mentioned, this does not depend on the use of sophisticated equipment such as that used in Dietvorst et al. (2008), but instead on an appreciation of the biological and evolutionary underpinnings of human behavior, and their incorporation into the theoretical explanations used in the sales context. In doing so, sales researchers are thus able to make a significantly greater impact on the theoretical understanding, and also on the practice, of sales and sales management in today's environment. It is hoped that this chapter both provides an integrative function and also inspires more consideration of how sales and sales management research can benefit from a greater assimilation of methods and theories from recent advances in the human sciences.

REFERENCES

AMBADY, N., M. A. KRABBENHOFT, and D. HOGAN (2006). "The 30-Sec Sale: Using Thin-Slice Judgements to Evaluate Sales Effectiveness," *Journal of Consumer Psychology* 16.1, 4–13.

——and R. ROSENTHAL (1993). "Half a Minute: Predicting Teacher Evaluations from Thin Slices of Nonverbal Behavior and Physical Attractiveness," *Journal of Personality & Social Psychology* 64.3, 431–41.

ANDERSON, E., and R. L. OLIVER (1987). "Perspectives on Behavior-Based Versus Outcome-Based Salesforce Control Systems," *Journal of Marketing* 51.4, 76–88.

BAGOZZI, R. P. (1978). "Salesforce Performance and Satisfaction as a Function of Individual Difference, Interpersonal, and Situational Factors," *Journal of Marketing Research* 15, 517–31.

BALDAUF, A., D. W. CRAVENS, and N. F. PIERCY (2005). "Sales Management Control Research: Synthesis and an Agenda For Future Research," *Journal of Personal Selling & Sales Management* 25.1, 7–26.

BECHARA, A., D. TRANEL, and H. DAMASIO (2000). "Characterization of the Decision-Making Deficit of Patients with Ventromedial Prefrontal Cortex Lesions," *Brain* 123, 2189–202.

BELLIZZI, J. A., and R. E. HITE (1989). "Supervising Unethical Salesforce Behaviour," *Journal of Marketing* 53, 36–47.

BHUIAN, S. N., B. MENGUC, and R. BORSBOOM (2005). "Stressors and Job Outcomes in Sales: A Triphasic Model Versus a Linear-Quadratic-Interactive Model," *Journal of Business Research* 58, 141–50.

BOGNER, W. C., and P. S. BARR (2000). "Making Sense in Hypercompetitive Environments: A Cognitive Explanation for the Persistence of High Velocity Competition," *Organization Science* 11.2, 212–26.

BROWN, J., BRODERICK, A. J., and N. LEE (2007). "Word of Mouth Communication within Online Communities: Conceptualizing the Online Social Network," *Journal of Interactive Marketing* 21.3, 2–20.

BROWN, S. P., K. R. EVANS, M. K. MANTRALA, and G. CHALLAGALLA (2005). "Adapting Motivation, Control, and Compensation Research to a New Environment," *Journal of Personal Selling & Sales Management* 25.2, 155–67.

BUCHANAN, M. (2008). "The Science of Subtle Signals," *Strategy + Business* 48 (Autumn), 1–10.

CACIOPPO, J. T., G. G. BERNTSON, and S. L. CRITES, Jr. (1996). "Social Neuroscience, Principles of Psychophysiological Arousal and Response," in T. E. Higgins and A. W. Kruglanski (eds.), *Social Psychology: Handbook of Basic Principles*. New York: Guilford Press, 72–101.

CADOGAN, J. W., N. LEE, A. TARKIAINEN, and S. SUNDQVIST (2009). "Sales Manager and Sales Team Determinants of Salesperson Ethical Behavior," *European Journal of Marketing* 43.2–3, 907–37.

CARNEY, D. R., R. C. COLVIN, and J. A. HALL (2007). "A Thin Slice Perspective on the Accuracy of First Impressions," *Journal of Research in Personality* 41, 1054–72.

CHEN, F. (2005). "Salesforce Incentives, Market Information, and Production/Inventory Planning," *Management Science* 51.1, 60–75.

CHOUDHURY, T., M. PHILIPOSE, D. WYATT, and J. LESTER (2006). "Towards Activity Databases: Using Sensors and Statistical Models to Summarize People's Lives," *IEEE Data Engineering Bulletin* 29, 1–8.

CRON, W. L., G. W. MARSHALL, J. SINGH, R. L. SPIRO, and H. SUJAN (2005). "Salesperson Selection, Training, and Development: Trends, Implications, and Research Opportunities," *Journal of Personal Selling & Sales Management* 25.2, 123–36.

CURHAN, J. R., and A. PENTLAND (2007). "Thin Slices of Negotiation: Predicting Outcomes from Conversational Dynamics within the First 5 Minutes," *Journal of Applied Psychology* 92.3, 802–11.

DAMASIO, A. R. (1994). *Descartes' Error: Emotion, Reason, and the Human Brain.* London: Macmillan.

DeCONINCK, J. B. (1992). "How Sales Managers Control Unethical Sales Force Behavior," *Journal of Business Ethics* 11, 789–98.

DIETVORST, R. C., W. J. M. I. VERBEKE, R. P. BAGOZZI, C. YOON, M. SMITS, and A. VAN DER LUGT (2008). "A Salesforce-Specific Theory of Mind Scale Tests: Of Its Validity by Multitrait-Multimethod Matrix, Confirmatory Factor Analysis, Structural Equation Models, and Functional Magnetic Resonance Imaging," *Journal of Marketing Research* 45, 1–68.

ETGAR, M. (2008). "A Descriptive Model of the Consumer Co-production Process," *Journal of the Academy of Marketing Science* 36, 97–108.

FIRAT, A. F., and A. VENKATESH (1995). "Postmodernism and the Reenchantment of Consumption," *Journal of Consumer Research* 22.3, 239–67.

GARCIA, J. R., and G. SAAD (2008). "Evolutionary Neuromarketing: Darwinizing the Neuroimaging Paradigm for Consumer Behavior," *Journal of Consumer Behaviour* 7.4–5, 397–414.

GAZZANIGA, M. S. (2000). *The New Cognitive Neurosciences.* Boston, MA: MIT Press.

GENTRY, J. W., J. C. MOWEN, and L. TASAKI (1991). "Salesperson Evaluation: A Systematic Structure for Reducing Judgmental Biases," *Journal of Personal Selling & Sales Management* 11.2, 27–38.

GWYNNE, R. (2008). "UK Retail Concentration, Chilean Wine Producers and Value Chains," *Geographical Journal* 174.2, 97–108.

HARI, J., M. STROS, and J. MARRIOTT (2008). "The 30-Second-Sale: Snap Impressions of a Retail Sales Person Influence Consumers' Decision Making," in F. U. Sims, M. Brandstatter, and H. Golzner (eds.), *Anspruchsgruppenorientierte Kommunikation*, Berlin: Springer, 53–66.

HUNT, S. D., and A. Z. VASQUEZ-PARRAGA (1993). "Organizational Consequences, Marketing Ethics, and Salesforce Supervision," *Journal of Marketing Research* 30, 78–90.

INGRAM, T. N. (2004). "Future Themes in Sales and Sales Management: Complexity, Collaboration, and Accountability," *Journal of Marketing Theory & Practice* 12.4, 18–28.

——R. W. LaFORGE, and T. W. LEIGH (2002). "Selling in the New Millennium: A Joint Agenda," *Industrial Marketing Management* 31.7, 559–67.

JAWORSKI, B. J. (1988). "Toward a Theory of Marketing Control: Environmental Context, Control Types, and Consequences," *Journal of Marketing* 52, 23–39.

JOHNSTON, M. W., and G. W. MARSHALL (2008). *Churchill/Ford/Walker's Sales Management*, 9th edn, Irwin, IL: McGraw-Hill.

JONES, E., S. P. BROWN, A. A. ZOLTNERS, and B. A. WEITZ (2005). "The Changing Environment of Selling and Sales Management," *Journal of Personal Selling & Sales Management* 25.2, 105–11.

Jones, E., L. Chonko, D. Rangarajan, and J. Roberts (2007). "The Role of Overload on Job Attitudes, Turnover Intentions, and Salesperson Performance," *Journal of Business Research* 60, 663–71.

——Sundaram, S., and W. Chin (2002). "Factors Leading To Sales Force Automation Use: A Longitudinal Analysis," *Journal of Personal Selling & Sales Management* 22.3, 145–56.

Kahn, G. N., and A. Schuchman (1961). "Specialize Your Salesmen!", *Harvard Business Review* 39.1, 90–98.

Kotler, P., N. Rackham, and S. Krishnaswamy (2006). "Ending the War between Sales and Marketing," *Harvard Business Review* 84.7–8, 68–78.

Lagace, R. R. (1990). "Leader–Member Exchange: Antecedents and Consequences of the Cadre and Hired Hand," *Journal of Personal Selling & Sales Management* 10, 11–19.

Lee, N., A. Beatson, T. C. Garrett, I. Lings, and X. Zhang (2009). "A Study of the Attitudes Toward Unethical Selling Amongst Chinese Salespeople," *Journal of Business Ethics*, 497–515.

——and L. Chamberlain (2007). "Neuroimaging and Psychophysiological Measurement in Organizational Research: An Agenda for Research in Organizational Cognitive Neuroscience," *Annals of the New York Academy of Sciences* 1118, 18–42.

——A. Sandfield, and B. Dhaliwal (2007). "An Empirical Study of Salesperson Stereotypes Amongst UK Students and Their Implications for Recruitment," *Journal of Marketing Management* 23, 723–44.

Lee, R. T., and B. E. Ashforth (1996). "A Meta-Analytic Examination of the Correlates of the Three Dimensions of Job Burnout," *Journal of Applied Psychology* 81.2, 123–33.

Leigh, T. W., and G. W. Marshall (2001). "Research Priorities in Sales Strategy and Performance," *Journal of Personal Selling & Sales Management* 21.2, 83–93.

Lewin, J. E., and J. K. Sager (2008). "Salesperson Burnout: A Test of the Coping-Mediational Model of Social Support," *Journal of Personal Selling & Sales Management* 28.3, 233–46.

Lituchy, T. R., and R. A. Barra (2008). "International Issues of the Design and Usage of Websites for E-commerce: Hotel and Airline Examples," *Journal of Engineering & Technology Management* 25, 93–111.

Madan, A. P. (2005). "Thin Slices of Interest" master's thesis, Massachusetts Institute of Technology.

Maslach, C. (1982). *Burnout: The Cost of Caring*. Englewood Cliffs, NJ: Prentice Hall.

Mehra, A., A. L. Dixon, D. J. Brass, and B. Robertson (2006). "The Social Network Ties of Group Leaders: Implications for Group Performance and Leader Reputation," *Organization Science* 17.1, 64–79.

Morrison, D., R. L. Payne, and T. D. Wall (2003). "Is a Job a Viable Unit of Analysis? A Multi-Level Analysis of Demand-Control-Support Models," *Journal of Occupational Health Psychology* 8.3, 209–19.

Netemeyer, R. G., T. Brashear-Alejandro, and J. S. Boles (2004). "A Cross-National Model of Job-Related Outcomes of Work Role and Family Role Variables: A Retail Sales Context," *Journal of the Academy of Marketing Science* 32.1, 49–60.

——J. G. Maxham III, and C. Pullig (2005). "Conflicts in the Work–Family Interface: Links to Job Stress, Customer Service Employee Performance, and Customer Purchase Intent," *Journal of Marketing* 69, 130–43.

Olguin, D., B. N. Waber, T. Kim, A. Mohan, K. Ara, and A. Pentland (2009). "Sensible Organizations: Technology and Methodology for Automatically Measuring

Organizational Behavior," *IEEE Transactions on Systems, Man, & Cybernetics: Part B, Cybernetics* 39.1, 43–55.

OLIVER, R. L., and E. ANDERSON (1994). "An Empirical Test of the Consequences of Behavior- and Outcome-Based Sales Control Systems," *Journal of Marketing* 58 (October), 53–67.

PENTLAND, A. (2004). "Social Dynamics: Signals and Behavior," paper presented at the International Conference on Developmental Learning, Salk Institute, San Diego, CA.

RACKHAM, N., and J. R. DeVINCENTIS (1999). *Rethinking the Sales Force*, New York: McGraw-Hill.

RASHID, A. Z. M., and A. J. Ho (2003). "Perceptions of Business Ethics in a Multicultural Community: The Case of Malaysia," *Journal of Business Ethics* 43, 75–87.

RICHARD, O. C., B. P. S. MURTHI, and K. ISMAIL (2007). "The Impact of Racial Diversity on Intermediate and Long-Term Performance: The Moderating Role of Environmental Context," *Strategic Management Journal* 28, 1213–33.

ROBERTS, K. (2007). "Work–Life Balance: The Sources of the Contemporary Problem and the Probable Outcomes," *Employee Relations* 29.4, 334–51.

ROBERTSON, B., A. L. DIXON, and D. CURRY (2006). "An Agenda for Selling and Sales Management Research: Using the Financial Industry's Forward Thinkers for Insight," *Journal of Personal Selling & Sales Management* 26.3, 293–303.

RULE, N. O., and N. AMBADY (2008). "Brief Exposures: Male Sexual Orientation is Accurately Perceived at 50ms," *Journal of Experimental Social Psychology* 44, 1100–1105.

SAGER, J. K., and P. H. WILSON (1995). "Clarification of the Meaning of Job Stress in the Context of Sales Force Research," *Journal of Personal Selling & Sales Management* 15.3, 51–63.

SEEVERS, M. T., S. J. SKINNER, and S. W. KELLEY (2007). "A Social Network Perspective on Sales Force Ethics," *Journal of Personal Selling & Sales Management* 27.4, 341–53.

SHAPIRO, B. P., A. J. SLYWOTZKY, and S. X. DOYLE (1994). "Strategic Sales Management: A Boardroom Issue," Boston, MA: Harvard Business School.

SINGH, J., J. R. GOOLSBY, and G. K. RHOADS (1994). "Behavioral and Psychological Consequences of Boundary-Spanning Burnout for Customer Service Representatives," *Journal of Marketing Research* 31.4, 558–69.

SPEIER, C., and V. VENKATESH (2002). "The Hidden Minefields in the Adoption of Sales Force Automation Technologies," *Journal of Marketing* 66, 98–111.

SUDHIR, K., and V. R. RAO (2006). "Do Slotting Allowances Enhance Efficiency or Hinder Competition?" *Journal of Marketing Research* 42, 137–55.

TANNER, J. F., Jr., C. FOURNIER, F. A. WISE, S. HOLLET, and J. POUJOL (2008). "Executives' Perspectives of the Changing Role of the Sales Profession: Views from France, the United States, and Mexico," *Journal of Business & Industrial Marketing* 23.3, 193–202.

WABER, B. N., D. OLGUIN, T. KIM, and A. PENTLAND (2008). "Understanding Organizational Behavior with Wearable Sensing Technology," (August 12, 2008), available at http://ssrn.com/abstract=1263992

PART II

SALES MANAGEMENT

CHAPTER 6

STRUCTURING THE SALES FORCE FOR CUSTOMER AND COMPANY SUCCESS

ANDRIS A. ZOLTNERS

PRABHAKANT SINHA

SALLY E. LORIMER

6.1 INTRODUCTION

The structure of a sales force defines roles and reporting relationships for salespeople and their managers. A sales force structure is defined by two main decisions.

1. The *specialization* decision defines the mix of generalist and specialist sales roles. Sales roles specify product, customer, and selling activity responsibilities for various members of the sales force.
2. The *reporting relationship* decision defines how sales activity will be coordinated and controlled. Reporting relationships are specified by sales force organization charts that represent the relationships and the hierarchy of different sales positions.

6.1.1 The Specialization Decision

In some sales force structures, salespeople are generalists who perform all selling activities and sell the company's full product and service line to all types of customers in a territory. In other structures, salespeople specialize in specific selling activities, products, or markets. Many structures include a mix of generalists and specialists. Consider the following examples:

- A company that sells bottled water to residential and commercial accounts uses *generalist* salespeople to sell water coolers and bottled water delivery contracts. The salespeople are also responsible for installing the coolers and making bottled water deliveries on a regular basis. Each salesperson covers both the residential and commercial accounts that fall within a compact geographic territory. Since just one salesperson is responsible for each account, there is clear accountability for meeting customer needs, and travel time and costs are kept to a minimum.

- At a medical diagnostics company, salespeople specialize by *product*. The company has a broad, complex portfolio of medical diagnostic products, including research equipment and its reagents, analyzers and their reagents, glucose meters and strips, and diagnostic tests. The sales force is organized as four separate product-specialty teams that share hospitals as major customers. Having product specialists allows the sales force to be very knowledgeable and effective at selling the company's large and technical product line.

- A division of a computer company organizes its sales force by *sales activity* into a "hunter"/"farmer" structure. "Hunters" specialize in finding business at new accounts. Once a sale is made, a "farmer" takes over the account to cultivate the relationship and generate repeat business. These two sales roles allow the company to better match salespeople's personalities and skills to the tasks at hand and thus provide more customer value while increasing overall effectiveness.

- A networking equipment manufacturer specializes its sales force by *market*. Three main sales groups are organized around customers of different sizes: the enterprise account group covers the company's largest accounts, a mid-market account group covers moderately large accounts, and a geographic account team calls on the smallest accounts. To enhance effectiveness with enterprise accounts, salespeople in that group are assigned to different industry teams. One team focuses on carriers and service providers (such as AT&T and Sprint); another calls on government, education, and utility accounts; a third calls on finance and retail accounts; and a fourth calls on healthcare and hi-tech accounts.

- A company that develops microprocessors that are embedded in electronic products uses a *hybrid* sales force structure that includes a mix of market and activity specialists. The company sells to manufacturers of electronic products, such as computers and telecommunications equipment. Acquiring new business requires many months of collaboration between a prospective customer and one of the company's sales teams. Some teams are dedicated to serving the needs of a single major customer, while others have responsibility for mid-market accounts in a geographic territory. Teams include both application engineers and account representatives. Application engineers assess a prospective customer's technological needs and work with the company's design engineers to develop a competitively superior functional prototype. Account representatives are responsible for the commercial details of the relationship with the customer, including supply chain logistics, legal contracts, volume requirements, and price. Account representatives also work with customers on an ongoing basis to support their needs and to look for new opportunities.

Each of the companies in these examples has decided to specialize its salespeople in a way that it feels best enables the sales force to meet customer needs and achieve company objectives.

6.1.2 The Reporting Relationship Decision

Reporting relationships define how sales activity will be coordinated and controlled. When salespeople are generalists, reporting structures are typically defined geographically. At the bottled water company, for example, salespeople report to branch managers who report to market managers who report to regional sales directors, each of whom is accountable for the total business in a geographic area.

When sales roles are specialized around products, markets, or selling activities, the reporting structure decision becomes more complex. Figure 6.1 shows two

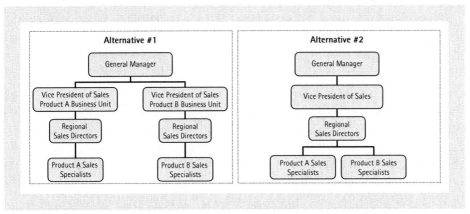

Fig. 6.1. Two Alternative Reporting Structures for a Sales Force of Product Specialists

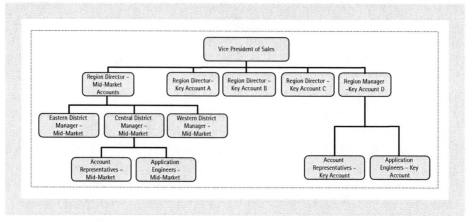

Fig. 6.2. Reporting Structure for a Microprocessor Manufacturer with Multiple Sales Specialist Roles

alternatives for structuring reporting relationships in a sales force that sells two product lines using product specialists. Alternative #1 reinforces the product expertise and focus of the sales force, while alternative #2 encourages customer focus because regional sales directors can coordinate the sales effort for customers who have need for both product lines.

When there are multiple types of sales specialists or a combination of generalists and specialists, reporting structure decisions become even more complex. Figure 6.2 shows how the microprocessor manufacturer designed its reporting structure to achieve a high level of customer focus, particularly for its largest customers.

Each of the companies in these examples has structured sales force reporting relationships to achieve what it feels is the best possible coordination and control of sales activity for meeting customer needs and achieving company objectives.

Sales management textbooks (such as Johnston and Marshall 2009) discuss the major issues involved in determining the best sales force specialization and reporting structures. This chapter summarizes these issues and extends the literature by providing:

- new frameworks showing how sales force structure decisions affect company results within the context of the broader sales system, and showing how salesperson bandwidth and company strategy influence the specialization decision;
- specific ways to deal with the tensions that different types of sales force specialization and reporting structures can create;
- strategies for successfully implementing sales force structure changes.

6.2 THE IMPACT OF SALES FORCE STRUCTURE DECISIONS

Before we discuss the various sales force structure options in more detail, it is useful to step back and view the context of sales force structure decisions and how they affect company results. Figure 6.3 provides a framework for understanding sales force structure and its impact. This framework is extracted from a comprehensive sales system framework showing the impact of a broader set of decisions that sales leaders are responsible for (Zoltners, Sinha, and Lorimer 2009).

Sales force structure decisions ultimately affect company results by directly influencing salespeople and their activities. Structure affects salespeople by defining the skills and capabilities that they need to be successful in their jobs, by determining who each salesperson's manager is, and by influencing how salespeople and managers interact with one another. Sales force structure decisions also directly affect sales force activities. They affect what salespeople do everyday and how much effort gets directed towards different customers, products, and selling tasks. Sales force activity affects customer results. Sales force structure affects which salespeople customers will interact with and how responsive the sales force can be to customer needs. Customer results are a key influencer of company results. The sales force structure helps determine how effectively the sales force generates revenues, how efficiently it manages costs, and how likely it is to achieve company objectives.

As Figure 6.4 suggests, sales force structure decisions should align with and reinforce a company's business strategy. This strategy is driven by customer needs, and is influenced by competitors' strategies and the business environment (e.g. the economic or regulatory climate). The right sales force structure enables the sales

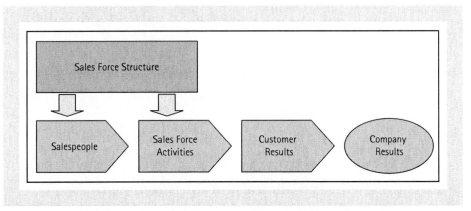

Fig. 6.3. A Framework for Understanding the Impact of Sales Force Structure Decisions

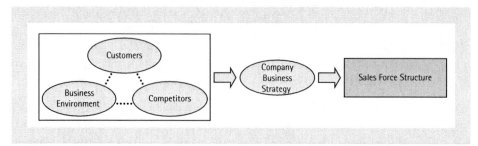

Fig. 6.4. A Framework for Understanding the Influences on Sales Force Structure Decisions

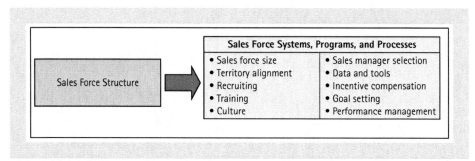

Fig. 6.5. The Influence of Sales Force Structure on Sales Force Systems, Programs, and Processes

force to carry out the company's business strategy by executing a sales process that delivers an effective value proposition to every targeted market segment. A business strategy that calls for selling many diverse and complex products, for example, will require a different sales force structure to meet the needs of customers than a strategy that requires salespeople to sell a more limited product line.

As Figure 6.5 shows, sales force structure affects many sales force systems, programs, and processes. Consequently, sales leaders should consider how these downstream sales force needs will be affected when they make sales force structure decisions.

6.3 THE SPECIALIZATION DECISION

6.3.1 How Specialized Should the Sales Force Be?

Should salespeople be *generalists*, selling all products and performing all selling tasks for all types of customers (as salespeople do at the bottled water company)?

Or should they be *specialists*, focusing on a particular product (as at the medical diagnostics company), market (the networking equipment company), and/or selling activity (the computer company)? Or are multiple types of specialists needed to serve customers effectively (as they are at the microprocessor company)? The framework in Figure 6.6 shows the two primary influences for the specialization decision. The first influence is the sales process that needs to be executed in order to deliver value to customers. A sales process that is complex and diverse and exceeds a single salesperson's skill and capability bandwidth requires specialization, while a sales process that is straightforward can be accomplished more efficiently with generalists. The second influence on the specialization decision is company objectives and strategy. Some typical examples of company objectives and strategies are listed in the right-hand column of Figure 6.6 and are organized into logical categories. Goals and strategies like these affect what type of sales force structure is best.

6.3.2 Sales Processes That Require Complex and Diverse Skills Lead to Sales Force Specialization

Members of a single generalist sales force are *efficient*—they will have smaller sales territories, less travel time, and usually will have more face-to-face time with customers. Figure 6.7 compares the efficiency of a generalist sales force with that of a specialized sales force.

However, while a generalist sales force is efficient, it may not be very *effective*—in other words, the impact that sales calls have with customers may be low. If meeting customer needs requires diverse skills, necessitates knowledge of a broad and complex product line, and/or entails employing a wide range of activities for different types of customers, then one salesperson may not be able to acquire the skills and knowledge needed to do everything that is required.

6.3.3 What is the Bandwidth of the Sales Force?

In the world of telecommunications, "bandwidth" refers to the amount of information that can be carried through a communication channel such as a phone line or satellite connection. The bandwidth concept can also be applied to salespeople. There is a limit to how many products, sales activities, and types of customers an individual salesperson can understand and be effective with. A salesperson who in order to meet customer needs has to understand a large, complex, or diverse product and service portfolio, or who has to perform many selling tasks for several customer segments with complex and diverse needs, at some point will not be able

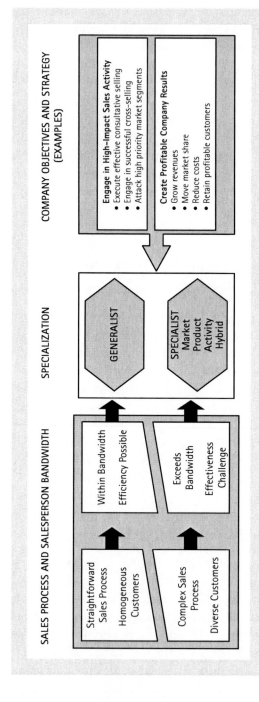

Fig. 6.6. A Framework that Guides the Specialization Decision

	Scenario I	Scenario II
Sales Force Organization	A single geographic team	Two speciality teams by product or market
Number of Salespeople	100	70 and 30
Sales Territory Description	Each sales territory has roughly 1% of the country	Overlapping territories: The 70-person team has territories that are on average 43% larger in size than the geographic team. The 30-person team has territories that are on average 3.3 times as large as those in the geographic team.

Fig. 6.7. A Comparison of Efficiency for a Generalist versus a Specialized Sales Organization

to perform the job effectively. The job will exceed the salesperson's bandwidth. When this happens, salespeople are likely to ignore the customers, products, or selling activities that are most difficult or unpleasant for them. Unfortunately, these customers, products, and activities may have strategic importance or represent a large profit opportunity. As a result, a salesperson trying to do a job that exceeds his bandwidth may not be able to produce the results the company wants.

Companies that sell many complex products to multiple diverse markets require a sales bandwidth that is much greater than the capacity of a single salesperson. For example, IBM has customers all over the world who need technology solutions for a wide array of business challenges. To meet the diverse needs of these customers, IBM offers hundreds of different hardware and software products, as well as professional services. It sells to numerous industries in over 200 countries and to customers ranging from huge multinational corporations to small businesses. Figure 6.8 lists the major categories of products, services, and markets sold by IBM in 2009, according to the company's website. The bandwidth required for a salesperson to understand all of these in order to add value to customers is enormous. A single salesperson, no matter how intelligent or hardworking, could never be successful working alone as a generalist at IBM. In order to bring the needed expertise to its customers, IBM has created a highly specialized sales force structure. More than 40,000 people are organized into many sales divisions with dozens of types of sales specialists, structured around markets, products, and activities. The company also relies on thousands of business partners—distributors, value-added resellers, software vendors—to sell many of its products in many markets.

Services Sold	Products Sold	Markets Sold To
Business Consulting •Business analytics and optimization •Customer relationship management •Financial management •Human capital management •Strategy and change •Supply chain management **IT Services** •Business continuity and resiliency •End user services •Integrated communications •Internet security systems •IT strategy and architecture services •Maintenance and technical support •Middleware services •Outsourcing services •Server services •Site and facilities services •Storage and data services **ServicePacs** **Training** **Note:** This list includes just the major service categories. The alphabetical list of services on the company website lists more than 500 different IBM service offerings.	**Software** •Application servers •Applications–desktop and enterprise •Business integration •Business intelligence and financial performance management •Commerce •Data management •Data warehouse and industry data models •Enterprise content management •Host transaction processing •Information integration and master data management •Messaging applications •Mobile, speech, and enterprise access •Networking •Operating systems •Organizational productivity, portals, and collaboration •Product lifecycle management •Security •Software development •Storage management •Systems and asset management **Storage** •Disk storage •Storage area network (SAN) •Storage media •Storage software •Tape storage •Network attached storage (NAS) **Systems and Servers** •Blades (BladeCenter) •Mainframe (System z) •Powersystems •System i •System p •Clusters •x86 (System x) **Small Business Products** **Medium Business Products** **Workstations** **Certified Used PCs and Systems** **Upgrades and Accessories**	**By Size** •Multi-national corporations •Large business •Medium-sized business •Small business •Home and home office **By Industry** •Aerospace and defense •Automotive •Banking •Chemicals and petroleum •Consumer products •Education •Electronics •Energy and utilities •Financial markets •Government •Healthcare •Insurance •Life sciences •Media and entertainment •Retail •Telecommunications •Travel and transportation **By Geography** •Africa •The Americas •Asia Pacific •Europe •Middle East •200+ countries •30+ languages

Fig. 6.8. Sales Bandwidth Required for IBM in 2009

If products are simple, target markets are homogeneous, and the sales processes across products and markets are similar or require similar skills, salespeople can handle a larger number of products, markets, and selling activities while adding value to customers.

6.3.4 Specializing for Strategy

Sales force specialization can reinforce company strategies and make it easier to accomplish important objectives. Following are several examples that show how sales force structure solutions have helped companies achieve specific objectives for revenue growth, profitability, customer focus, company culture, and market penetration.

6.3.4.1 *Microsoft's Strategy: Grow Revenues Through Increased Emphasis on Solution Selling*

In 2002, Microsoft's customers were looking for more than software—they wanted integrated solutions to business problems. Microsoft developed a sales strategy aimed at growing revenues and income through increased emphasis on selling customers not just software but business solutions (Sliwa 2001). This required developing greater industry expertise within the sales force. Microsoft expanded its sales force by 20 percent and established seven new vertical selling teams to serve the needs of large customers in the retail, healthcare, automotive manufacturing, high-tech manufacturing, oil and gas, media and entertainment, and professional service industries (Rooney 2002). These industry-specific vertical teams were added to five vertical teams established two years earlier for the financial services, telecommunications, state and local government, federal government, and education sectors. According to the Microsoft website, the new sales teams included industry specialists in sales, service and support, partnering, and marketing. The vertical teams allowed Microsoft to get closer to the business challenges faced by its customers, enabling the sales force to sell more complete solutions that addressed specific industry needs.

6.3.4.2 *SAP's Strategy: Improve Profitability Through Cost Reductions*

In contrast to Microsoft's strategy of becoming more specialized to increase sales force effectiveness and drive revenue growth, SAP, another large provider of business software, had a different approach to dealing with its market challenges in 2002 (Cowley 2003). Bleak economic conditions had led to sharp declines in SAP's revenues. To improve profitability, the company's strategies focused on cost reduction. In addition to eliminating 132 sales positions in the US (a 3 percent reduction in its sales force), SAP restructured its sales force. Instead of each salesperson specializing in one industry, sales territories were reorganized geographically so that each salesperson sold a wider array of products to a local group of customers. The new geographic territories allowed salespeople to be more efficient in covering their customers and helped the company reduce costs.

6.3.4.3 *Black & Decker's Strategy: Grow Sales and Profits by Focusing on Key Customers*

As retailers consolidated and gained power in the early 1990s, power tool manufacturer Black & Decker wanted to strengthen its relationships with its largest national chain retail customers in the US (Sellers 1992). The company established vertical selling teams dedicated to serving the needs of two important and fast-growing customers—Wal-Mart and Home Depot. Each vertical team had a vice-president who led a group composed of salespeople, a marketer, an information systems expert, a sales forecaster, and a financial analyst. Team members partnered with the appropriate people at these two retailers to help them increase profitablity by selling more Black & Decker products. A year after the vertical teams were established, Black & Decker sales to Wal-Mart were up over 10 percent and those to Home Depot had increased almost 40 percent.

6.3.4.4 *W. L. Gore's Strategy: Create Success Through a Culture of Innovation and Teamwork*

At W. L. Gore, the maker of Gore-Tex lining for weatherproof jackets and other innovative products, a unique culture is built around innovation, empowerment, and teamwork (Weinreb 2003). The company's sales force structure is designed to encourage that culture. The sales force is organized into what Gore calls a lattice structure—there are no titles and no official lines of reporting. Every salesperson has a sponsor who functions as a mentor, not a boss, and sales leaders function like coaches and help salespeople set their own sales goals. Salespeople work together in teams to meet the needs of their customers. This structure helps perpetuate the team-oriented and entrepreneurial culture of the company. Salespeople stay focused on long-term customer success and are willing to help each other out as needed to respond to customer needs.

6.3.4.5 *ADP's Strategy: Increase Market Penetration While Managing the Cost of Sales*

For many years, Automatic Data Processing (ADP) focused on payroll processing for companies of all sizes around the world. In the mid-1990s, the company recognized a need among its customers for a broader range of employer-related business process outsourcing solutions, and made a strategic decision to offer an array of new services to customers, such as administration of worker's compensation insurance, taxes and compliance, and human resources and benefits (McCue 2008). With 585,000 clients around the world (including more than 400,000 small-to-medium sized businesses), ADP's field sales force did not have the capacity to achieve the depth of penetration into customers' businesses that the company desired. Yet adding headcount to the already 5,000 salespeople that the company employed in the US alone would increase the cost of sales beyond desired levels. In 2005, ADP created a telesales organization to supplement the efforts of the field sales organization, creating a cost-effective way to provide coverage to customers with needs that could be met with traditional products. This freed up field sales-people's time for complex solution sales. Telesales also provided quality leads to field salespeople. The addition of the telesales group enabled ADP to increase market penetration while keeping the cost of sales at a manageable level.

6.4 DETERMINING THE BEST WAY TO SPECIALIZE

Sales force specialization along the three main dimensions—market, product, and activity—can take many forms. Markets can be divided up among specialists using criteria such as account size, industry, purchasing status (new versus existing account), and needs (such as product and price or solution and value-added services). Products too can be partitioned in different ways across specialists based on product-selling process similarities and differences. Selling activities can also be assigned to specialists in different ways. When the sales process is long and complex, critical steps can be assigned to different specialists who can perform those steps more effectively. Alternatively, if there are activities that can be performed by less expensive resources, such as telesales, efficiency gains are possible through activity specialization. Determining what type of sales force specialization is best starts with answering several questions about sales force bandwidth, effectiveness, attention, and efficiency with respect to products, markets, and selling activities (see Figure 6.9). The answers to these questions provide insight about the dimensions on which the greatest opportunity exists to create value through specialization.

Coverage cubes, like the ones shown in Figure 6.10, are useful tools for viewing specialization possibilities. The cubes in the example show four sales force speciali-zation alternatives for a sales force that sells wine and spirits to liquor stores and restaurants/bars. This company selected two market attributes (liquor store or

---

Bandwidth:
Which of the following tasks requires skills and knowledge that are too broad for one salesperson to master?
1. Selling all the products
2. Selling to all market segments
3. Performing all the selling activities

Effectiveness:
Which type of specialization of job responsibilities could lead to significantly enhanced impact with customers?
1. Selling a subset of products
2. Selling to a subset of marketing
3. Performing a subset of selling activities
(Note that specialization resolves bandwidth concerns but can also increase effectiveness even when bandwidth is not exceeded.)

Attention:
Which of the following would likely get ignored if a generalist was expected to do everything?
1. Some important products
2. Some important markets
3. Some important selling activities

Efficiency:
Which of the following job responsibilities could be performed by lower cost resources such as telesales?
1. Selling some products
2. Selling to some customers
3. Performing some selling activities

Fig. 6.9. Questions for Assessing the Need for Product, Market, or Activity Specialization

restaurant/bar; small or large account) and products (wine or spirits) as the most important dimensions for possible sales force specialization. Each cell in the cubes requires sales force coverage. Groupings or clusters of cells represent the responsibilities of different types of specialists. The company considered alternative specialization plans that included generalists, product specialists, market specialists, and a hybrid combination of these roles.

The best alternative for partitioning the coverage cube requires assessing salesperson bandwidth, effectiveness, attention, and efficiency for each alternative. The questions in Figure 6.9 guide this assessment. For example, selecting choice "1" for the questions in Figure 6.9 suggests that a structure with product specialists like alternative B should be considered. Similarly, selecting choice "2" suggests that a structure with market specialists like alternative C may be best. Selecting both

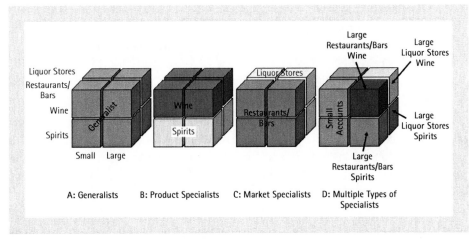

Fig. 6.10. Alternative Sales Force Specialization Plans for a Wine and Spirits Distributor

choices "1" and "2" suggests that a structure with multiple types of specialists like alternative D should be considered.

In addition, the following tests can help determine the appropriateness of a particular partitioning of a coverage cube.

1. *Within-cluster homogeneity.* Are cells that have similar selling process requirements clustered together in the same partition? For example, if selling spirits is very similar to selling wine, then these two products should be clustered together, as in alternatives A and C. If selling to restaurants is very similar to selling to liquor stores, then these two markets should be clustered together, as in alternatives A and B.

2. *Between-cluster heterogeneity.* Are selling requirements different across the various partitions or clusters? For example, if selling spirits is very different from selling wine, then the two products should be clustered into different partitions, as in alternative B. If selling to liquor stores is very different than selling to restaurants, then the two markets should be clustered into different partitions, as in alternative C.

3. *Communication and coordination needs.* Are cell combinations that require communication and coordination clustered together in the same partition? For example, if it is important for the salesperson who sells spirits to an account to know about the wine purchase needs of that account, then the company should consider clustering spirit sales and wine sales to accounts together, as in alternatives A and C.

4. *Cluster potential.* Clusters need to be large enough in sales potential to support a team of specialists. For example, alternative D recognizes that the individual

cells for small accounts may not have enough sales potential to economically justify dedicated specialists. Thus, all small account cells are clustered together and are covered by salespeople who sell both products to both markets in a geographic territory.

Sales force specialization has helped many companies achieve their objectives by enabling the sales force to be more effective at delivering value to customers. Yet it is possible for a sales force to become overspecialized. Sales specialization is likely to increase a company's revenues, but it also increases costs. Overspecialization can create confusion for customers and for salespeople about who is responsible for what selling tasks. Specialization also adds complexity to sales systems, processes, and programs. Further, more sales managers are usually required to manage a more complex organization. Specialization can also reduce the flexibility of the sales force to adapt to changing conditions. A decision to specialize the sales force must consider both the incremental sales that increased effectiveness delivers and the incremental cost of managing a more complex organization. A general rule of thumb for sales force specialization: use the smallest number of specialists required to create the effectiveness and focus needed to drive customer and company results.

6.5 RESOLVING STRUCTURE TENSIONS WHEN EMPLOYING DIFFERENT TYPES OF SALES FORCE SPECIALIZATION

Different types of specialization facilitate the accomplishment of certain business objectives, but may also create tensions that require mechanisms such as training, incentives, coaching, performance management, and information support for maximal effectiveness. For example, a generalist structure facilitates travel efficiency within the sales force, while relying on programs such as training and coaching to provide salespeople with the knowledge and skills they need to effectively sell many products and perform many selling activities for a diverse set of customers. A product specialist structure encourages product expertise, while relying on mechanisms such as incentives and customer information sharing to ensure that different product specialists who share common customers are attuned to the customer's overall needs. In this section we describe strategies for meeting customer needs and achieving business objectives with different types of sales force specialization.

6.5.1 Achieving Success with Generalists

The bottled water company described earlier in this chapter uses generalists to sell water coolers and bottled water delivery contracts to residential and commercial accounts. Each salesperson is responsible for selling, installing coolers, and making bottled water deliveries to all customers in his geographic sales territory.

A sales force of generalists helps a company accomplish several business objectives:

- *Efficiency.* There is no duplication of effort, since just one salesperson calls on each customer. Salespeople can live close to their accounts, minimizing travel time and costs and maximizing the time devoted to face-to-face selling. At the bottled water company, some territories in downtown Manhattan consisted of a single building.
- *Customer focus and accountability.* There is no confusion regarding who is responsible and accountable for each customer; customers always know who to talk to.
- *Attractive jobs for salespeople.* The generalist approach encourages entrepreneurship among salespeople who "own" their customers and have freedom to make decisions about how to spend their time.
- *Flexibility.* It is possible to reallocate sales effort to different customers or product lines fairly easily as company priorities change. It is also relatively easy to change sales force size or to evolve to become more specialized, if needed.

Sales forces made up of generalists who sell many products to many diverse customers typically need systems, processes, and programs to help them achieve two additional business objectives:

- *Effectiveness.* Generalists with diverse job responsibilities need help to be effective at everything: they may need to master multiple products and markets and a wide array of selling tasks, ranging from complex selling activities to administrative tasks that take time away from selling.
- *The right allocation of sales effort.* Generalists with many choices of how to spend their time often chose to work within their comfort zone, and need support and direction to ensure that all important products, customers, and selling activities get the attention they deserve.

Figure 6.11 presents some solutions that companies have used to help generalists who have many diverse responsibilities be more effective and allocate their time appropriately.

Examples of companies that have employed some of the solutions described in Figure 6.11 include:

- *Improving effort allocation using training, goals, and performance management.* An executive search firm encouraged *new* salespeople to spend their time

Solutions	Enhancing effectiveness	Ensuring the right allocation of sales effort
Information Support and Targeting	Provide detailed product information, "how to" guidance for critical selling activities, good target lists, and processes for sharing market and customer knowledge.	Provide information that helps salespeople make good decisions about how to spend their time across products, selling activities, and customers.
Training and Development	Provide training that develops knowledge and skills needed for success with important products, markets, or selling activities.	------
Incentives	------	Pay salespeople varied commission rates or bonus amounts for different products or customers to influence effort allocation.
Goal Setting	------	Give salespeople specific product, activity, or market/customer goals.
Performance Management and Coaching	------	Track metrics for product, market, or selling activity success and manage and evaluate salespeople on these metrics. Have sales managers coach salespeople on how to best spend their time.

Fig. 6.11. Solutions for Enhancing Effectiveness and Ensuring the Right Allocation of Sales Effort with Generalists

effectively by teaching and directing them to engage in activities that the firm knew would drive success—like calls to potential job candidates and company visits. Training for new salespeople focused on developing skills to help them excel in these activities. In addition, salespeople received daily and weekly goals for these activities and were evaluated based on achievement of these goals.

- *Improving effort allocation with targeting information.* One company educated its generalist salespeople about how they could use their time more effectively to earn more incentive pay. The company analyzed data from the previous year to formulate a plan that reflected the best allocation of sales effort across customers and products for each salesperson. Management tracked salespeople's activities for a year to see how closely they followed the recommended plan, and also tracked their performance. The evidence was clear: salespeople who followed the plan (i.e. they allocated their time as the company recommended across customers and products) had greater success in attaining their goals and therefore earned higher incentive pay than those who did not adhere to the plan. The company shared this information with every salesperson, and empowered the sales force to make the right decisions about how to allocate its time.

Some companies have had success in helping generalists be more effective and improve time utilization by adding a few specialists, while preserving their basic generalist structure. A small number of product, market, or activity specialists—say one per sales region—can act as a resource for generalists. In addition, some companies will add less expensive resources—such as sales assistants or a telesales group—to take on some of the tasks that the generalists perform. For example, a number of generalist salespeople in the xpedx office products distribution division of International Paper hire their own sales assistants to help with routine tasks, freeing time for selling. The commissions the salespeople receive from their incremental sales more than cover the cost of paying a sales assistant's salary.

6.5.2 Achieving Success with Market Specialists

The networking equipment manufacturer described earlier in this chapter has a sales force of market specialists. Salespeople at this company specialize according to both account size and industry.

Market specialization helps a company accomplish several business objectives:

- *Customer expertise and focus.* Market specialization increases salespeople's knowledge of customers and enhances their ability to meet the complex needs of a specific set of customers within a diverse customer base. Salespeople become highly adaptable to changes in customer needs and buying processes.
- *Control of effort allocation across customers.* Sales leaders can more easily control sales effort toward any group of customers.
- *Customer accountability.* There is clear accountability for sales that meet the customer's overall needs.

Companies that structure the sales force to specialize by market typically need systems, processes, and programs to help them achieve two additional business objectives:

- *Product and selling activity effectiveness.* With sales force attention centered on markets and customers, salespeople may not have complete knowledge of a large portfolio of products and brands or may not be effective at performing a broad and diverse set of selling activities.
- *Control of effort allocation to products and activities.* A market-focused sales structure can make it hard for sales leaders to properly allocate effort across

products or selling activities. Special challenges can arise at companies with product-based business units, where unit leaders want control of their own sales force resource.

Market specialists are product and activity generalists for their customers. Consequently, the solutions that companies have used to help market specialists achieve product and activity effectiveness and effort allocation objectives are similar to the solutions described for helping generalists achieve these objectives (see Figure 6.11). A company can encourage the effectiveness of market specialists by providing information support and training to develop critical product and selling activity skills and knowledge. For example, Microsoft helps its channel partners (such as value-added resellers) who sell to small and mid-market accounts to be more effective selling Microsoft products by providing a Partner Learning Center website with training programs to help partners understand the complexity and diverse nature of Microsoft's business software solutions (Doyle and DeMarzo 2004). A company can also leverage information support, as well as incentives, goal setting, performance management, and sales manager coaching, to encourage appropriate time allocation across products and selling activities

Because market specialists are responsible for focused market segments, they have larger geographic territories than generalists do. Companies have been successful at reducing travel for market specialists by segmenting their accounts according to size and location, and assigning smaller, geographically remote customers to a telesales organization.

6.5.3 Achieving Success with Product or Activity Specialists

The medical diagnostics company described earlier in this chapter uses product specialists to sell its portfolio of medical diagnostic products. Four separate product-specialty teams share hospitals as customers.

A sales force of product specialists helps a company accomplish several business objectives:

- *Product expertise and focus.* When a product line is broad or complex, a specialized sales force that divides up the responsibility for the product portfolio has better product knowledge and thus is more effective.
- *Control of effort allocation across products.* Sales leaders can more easily intensify and control sales effort toward strategically important products.
- *Product accountability.* The sales force becomes more accountable to product-based business units.

The division of a computer company described earlier in this chapter uses selling activity specialists to "hunt" for new accounts. Once an account is sold, responsibility for the customer is transferred to a specialist who "farms" and sustains the relationship.

A sales force of activity specialists helps a company accomplish several business objectives:

- *Selling activity expertise and focus.* When activities require diverse skills and knowledge, dividing them among different types of salespeople increases effectiveness. The company can match salespeople's personalities and skills to the tasks at hand.
- *Control of effort allocation across selling activities.* Sales leaders can more easily control sales effort toward defined sets of activities, such as hunting for new customers.
- *Efficiency of performing routine selling activities.* If some tasks can be assigned to cheaper selling resources, such as sales assistants or telesales, the company may be able to improve efficiency as well as effectiveness.

Companies that structure the sales force to specialize by product or selling activity typically need systems, processes, and programs to help them achieve two additional business objectives:

- *Customer focus.* Customers may dislike dealing with multiple salespeople from the same company, preferring the convenience of working with a single salesperson that is accountable for all products and activities. In addition, product specialists may miss opportunities to cross-sell other company products that can meet customer needs. These issues can be especially important at major accounts, and many companies designate account managers as a single point of contact for important customers (see section 6.5.4).
- *Synchronization of sales effort and efficient coordination.* In order to be effective with customers, salespeople may need to spend time documenting customer information or communicating internally with sales colleagues who call on shared customers—activities that are necessary for delivering customer value yet reduce the amount of time with the customer.

Figure 6.12 illustrates some solutions that companies have used to help product and activity specialists achieve customer focus and facilitate coordination.

Many companies employ information systems to help product and activity specialists achieve customer focus and enhance efficiency. For example, by the mid-1990s, the sales force at airplane parts supplier Allied Signal (which merged with Honeywell in 1999) had become very large and specialized (Levinson 2002). The company had a broad and technical product line, and major customers had as many as 50 different contact points with product and activity specialists within Honeywell's sales force. Lack of coordination among salespeople who called on the same accounts frustrated customers, who often had to spend their time getting the appropriate people from Allied Signal to talk to one another so that a workable solution could be developed. To improve the coordination of sales efforts, Allied

Solutions	Achieving customer focus	Facilitating coordination
Sales Process and Information Support	Clarify responsibilities and specify the communication flows that need to occur to execute each stage of the sales process effectively. Provide CRM systems that are a centralized source of customer information and allow sales specialists to easily obtain information about company-wide contacts with their customers. Provide other forums for information exchange, such as email, voice mail, or meetings.	Provide sales processes that define the steps where different salespeople may need to collaborate, and CRM or other systems that improve the efficiency of information exchange between specialists who are responsible for common customers.
Incentives	Offer team-based incentives to encourage specialists who work with common customers to share leads and coordinate their efforts in the customer's best interest.	------
Goal Setting and Performance Management	Give salespeople customer-centric goals that are shared by the specialists who work with common customers. Manage and evaluate the entire team based on team goal attainment.	------
Hiring and Culture	Hire cooperative and team-oriented people who can work together to meet customer needs. Strive to build a culture of trust, respect, and teamwork.	------

Fig. 6.12. Solutions for Achieving Customer Focus and Enhancing Efficiency with Product and Activity Specialists

Signal developed a company-wide CRM system. By 2002, this system provided a single source of customer information for sales reps, field service engineers, product-line personnel, and response center agents across three business units. Quick access to customer information allowed sales efforts to be easily coordinated at the customer level.

With a product or activity specialist structure, multiple salespeople may travel to the same customers, thereby increasing sales force costs and reducing selling time. Some companies have successfully offset a portion of these increased travel costs by using telesales to perform some selling and servicing activities. An interesting model-based approach for designing a product-based sales force structure is provided in Rangaswamy, Sinha, and Zoltners (1990).

6.5.4 Achieving Success with Multiple Types of Specialists

Very many companies have "hybrid" sales force structures that include a mix of generalists and market, product, and activity specialists. With hybrid structures, teams of salespeople with different expertise work together to serve the needs of customers. The microprocessor company described earlier in this chapter had sales teams made up of both market and activity specialists.

Hybrid structures often evolve over time as the bandwidth of a sales force gets challenged by product line growth or market expansion. As the sales process becomes more complex and diverse, companies find it necessary to add more types of specialists to maintain sales force effectiveness. Hybrid structures can also evolve as companies find it necessary to amend their sales force structures to encourage the accomplishment of multiple business objectives simultaneously. For example, in the early 1990s, customers of 3M's medical products group complained that too many 3M people were calling on them (Borzo 1991). As part of a corporate quality improvement effort, 3M restructured the sales force for all medical products divisions, establishing corporate account managers. With the new structure, account managers visited major customers regularly and brought in product specialists as needed to clarify details or provide technical expertise. Small customers were still visited by product specialists or served over the telephone. Microsoft also uses account managers to coordinate sales efforts at major accounts. According to the company's web site, the job description for these account manager positions includes responsibilities such as "lead a virtual team of sales specialists at assigned accounts," "act as the point person for customer questions and concerns," "be the predictable and consistent interface from Microsoft to the customer," and "be a thought leader at accounts for 'One Microsoft' positioning"—a philosophy that emphasizes one account team and one opportunity pipeline per account.

Hybrid sales force structures sometimes evolve in response to a regional diversity of customer needs. A "one size fits all" national structure does not always work well, and many sales forces find that they can achieve more sales with a reduced headcount by varying their structure and resource allocation to match local conditions. A common example of this is to deploy specialists in urban areas where customers are geographically concentrated, and generalists in rural areas where travel demands are greater.

Figure 6.13 shows how a pharmaceutical company varied the design of its sales structure and resource deployment to match local conditions in one sales district in Texas. Depending on the needs and density of customers in different markets, the company varied the number and types of sales specialists, the products that the specialists sold, the emphasis placed on different products and customer types, and the sales incentive plan. Local managers had authority to modify their sales structure and resource allocation as needed to best serve the needs of customers in their local market.

The customer intimacy and effectiveness that hybrid specialization can create for a company can be a significant source of competitive advantage. Yet companies will

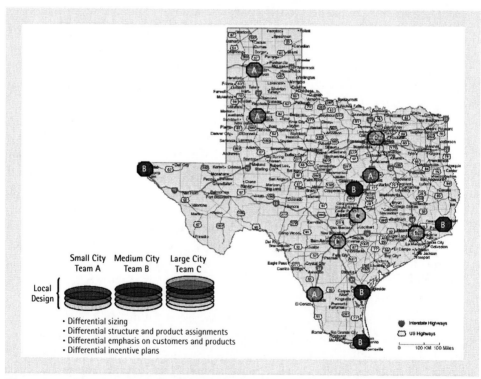

Fig. 6.13. Matching the Sales Force Structure to Local Needs at a Pharmaceutical Company – Example of One Sales District in Texas

need programs, processes, and systems to manage the complexity of a hybrid structure. Companies have used many of the methods suggested earlier in this chapter (see Figures 6.11 and 6.12) to maintain effectiveness, efficiency, customer focus, and appropriate effort allocation with a hybrid structure. Some additional issues that often need to be addressed with hybrid structures are:

- *Internal coordination.* Hybrid structures require much internal coordination, which means more sales managers or salespeople spending more time synchronizing their activities and less time selling. Salespeople not only need to learn their customers' organizations and buying processes; they must also learn the complexities of their own sales organization in order to assemble the right resources to address customer needs. CRM and other information-based support tools can facilitate information exchange between members of the sales force in hybrid structures.

- *Accountability.* Since several people work together to meet the needs of each customer, individual accountability is diminished in a hybrid structure, making it important to encourage a team-oriented sales culture. This culture is reinforced by hiring team players, providing them with the tools they need to work together effectively, and challenging them with team goals while reducing the role of individual incentives.

- *Flexibility.* When salespeople are highly specialized and when a sales organization has many interdependent parts, it can take a lot of effort to overcome organizational inertia and retrain salespeople or redesign the sales organization as the customer or company needs change. A sales culture that encourages a flexible, change-friendly sales force is important for allowing a hybrid structure to evolve as the business needs change.

Hybrid sales force structures add complexity to sales force support and administration. In order to meet the needs of different types of sales specialists, companies with hybrid structures must anticipate investing more to develop and manage a diverse set of hiring profiles, training programs, sales systems, incentive plans, and other sales support needs.

6.6 THE REPORTING RELATIONSHIP DECISION

The sales force structure specifies the hierarchy of sales force reporting relationships which affects how sales activity is coordinated and controlled. With the simplest type of reporting structure, salespeople with similar responsibilities report to a first-level sales manager, groups of first-level managers report to a second-level manager, and so on. Reporting structures can get complex when multiple product or activity specialists have responsibility for the same customers. Geographic reporting, separate reporting, integrated reporting, matrix reporting, and mirrored sales organizations are discussed here.

6.6.1 Geographic Reporting with Generalists

The bottled water company described earlier in this chapter has a sales force of generalists organized into a geographic reporting structure (see Figure 6.14).

A geographic reporting structure with generalists provides clear accountability for customers and the sales process. The lines of communication are unambiguous and the career path is straightforward. When a geographic reporting structure is used for a generalist sales force that sells several products, the company may have to implement mechanisms for managing the alignment between sales and marketing. If the marketing organization has multiple product managers, those product managers may compete for sales force time. Sales force attention can become focused on products that have aggressive product managers, and not necessarily on products that have the highest strategic importance. Centralized marketing or sales force control is needed to ensure that all products get appropriate levels of sales force support. At a financial services company that sold investment products to individuals, dozens of product managers competed for the sales force's time by running sales campaigns on specific investment products. Salespeople received so many demands from product managers that they became overwhelmed with information. To help the sales force sift through the information and decide which products to offer customers, the company created several market segment manager positions to complement the efforts of product managers. Market segment managers recommended the best product offering for specific market segments, such as families with young children or people nearing retirement. Segment managers helped salespeople find the best offerings for their customers and also freed up more of their time for selling.

6.6.2 Separate Geographic Reporting with Specialists

Geographic reporting structures are not only for generalist salespeople—they can be used for product, market, or activity specialists, too. With separate geographic reporting, a company structures its sales organization into several separate specialty sales forces, each with its own geographic reporting structure. The separate sales forces report to a common manager at a high level within the organization. Figure 6.15 gives an example of such a structure for a company organized around two separate product-based business units. Each business unit has its own dedicated sales force, thereby encouraging excellent sales force product knowledge and

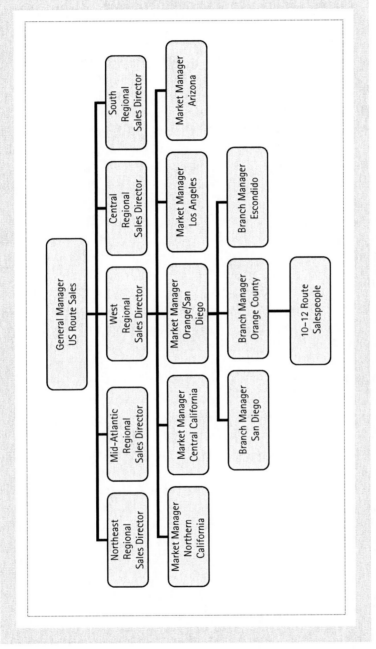

Fig. 6.14. Geographic Reporting Structure for a Bottled Water Company

focus, accountability to product-based business units, and control of product effort up and down the organization. The structure also enables a strong alignment between the sales force and product managers in marketing.

Figure 6.16 provides an example of separate reporting with activity specialists in a medical device sales organization. The activities of the sales process are divided among three different types of salespeople—sales, clinical support, and service—and each type of specialist reports up through its own management structure. The number of people in each position is also indicated on the chart.

The company in this example kept the sales, support, and service reporting relationships separate for two reasons. First, the skills required for the three roles are very different, and it was felt that a single manager could not manage and coach all three types of people. Second, if the company had to choose a manager for all three types, they would likely select someone with a sales background, and as a result, the clinical coordinators and service people would feel that their career path was limited.

Structures with separate reporting of multiple specialists who share the same customers require systems, processes, and programs to ensure customer focus and synchronization of sales effort. This is important in product-based sales structures if customers value a unified or bundled offering from the company. It is also important when customer success requires coordination among specialists who perform different steps of the sales process, as is the case at the medical device company. The separate reporting structure at this company provides little incentive, for example, for a salesperson to coordinate his efforts with clinical coordinators or field service technicians. Doing so would require reaching out to several coordinators, technicians, and managers in two different business units—a process that is time-consuming and may be perceived to be of little value by the salesperson's immediate manager who is responsible for delivering results on a single activity: sales. One must go up four levels in the sales hierarchy before finding someone who is directly accountable for the entire sales process and could therefore resolve conflicts.

Since a separate reporting structure may not encourage strong coordination across multiple specialists who share customers, mechanisms such as sales process and information support, incentives, goal setting and performance management, and hiring and culture (see Figure 6.12) are very important for achieving customer focus and coordination efficiency in sales organizations with separate reporting. Companies have also had success using mirrored territory alignments to encourage teams of different types of specialists to work together to provide coordinated customer effort when there is a separate reporting structure (see section 6.6.5).

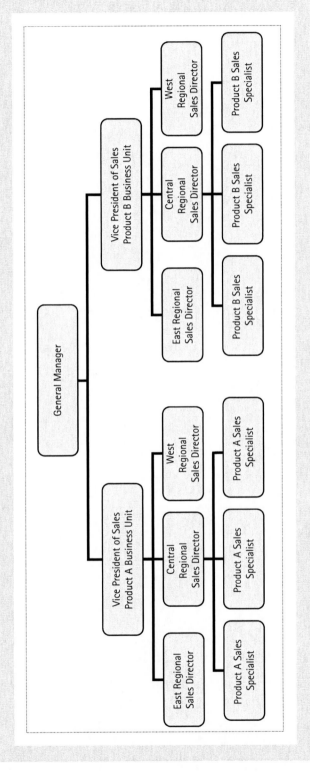

Fig. 6.15. Example of Product Specialists in a Product–based Reporting Structure

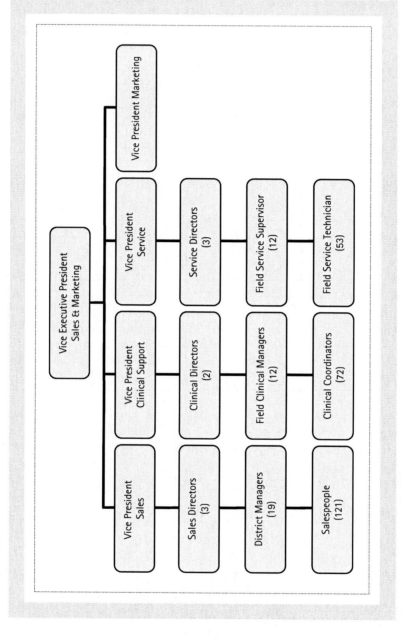

Fig. 6.16. Organization Chart for a Medical Device Sales Force of Activity Specialists

6.6.3 Integrated Reporting with Specialists

Integrated reporting is another possibility for sales forces that have multiple types of sales specialists. With integrated reporting, the different types of specialists report into a common manager at a low level in the sales organization.

The sales force in Figure 6.17 has two types of product specialists (Product A and Product B). These specialists report to common regional sales directors who have responsibility for both products. The structure makes regional sales directors accountable for all sales in their geography, and encourages them to facilitate coordination between Product A and Product B specialists for customers who value an integrated offering. It also enhances flexibility at a regional level: regional directors can shift resources as needed across the two specialty groups without requiring approval from a vice-president or general manager. Companies with large sales organizations may have more management levels—for example, sales-people may report to district managers who report to regional directors. In such cases, Product A and Product B specialists can report to common district managers, or may have their own dedicated district managers who report to a common regional sales director.

Integrated structures do require sales managers at a low level in the organization to manage a more diverse group of people. First-level managers may need to understand a broader product line, more types of customers, or many dissimilar selling tasks. Managers of integrated structures may need to be creative in running regional or district sales meetings, because of the diverse needs and perspectives of the different salespeople who report to them.

6.6.4 Matrix Reporting with Specialists

Matrix reporting superimposes a horizontal structure on top of a traditional hierarchical reporting structure in order to encourage multiple lines of communication and control across the organization. Matrix reporting is needed when a simple hierarchy cannot capture the necessary channels of collaboration needed to meet customer and company needs. For example, if a company is organized in product business units but the sales force is organized by market, a "dotted-line" or secondary reporting relationship may be needed between the salespeople and the product organization. Geographic scope of a customer can also lead to the need for matrix reporting. For example, a salesperson handling the German division of a large global account such as IBM may report to the German sales director, but he may also need to collaborate with a sales director who is responsible for IBM worldwide who is based near IBM's headquarters in New York.

Figure 6.18 shows an organization chart with matrix reporting for one region of a maintenance, repair, and operational supply (MRO) sales force that sells three

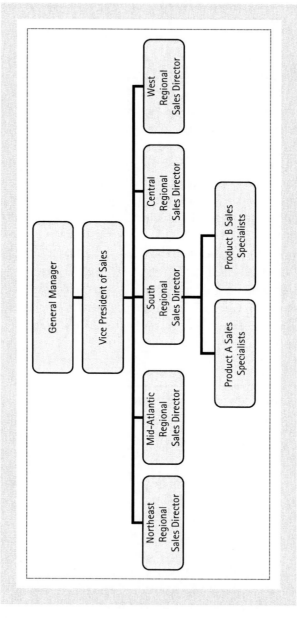

Fig. 6.17. **Example of Product Specialists in a Geographically-based Reporting Structure**

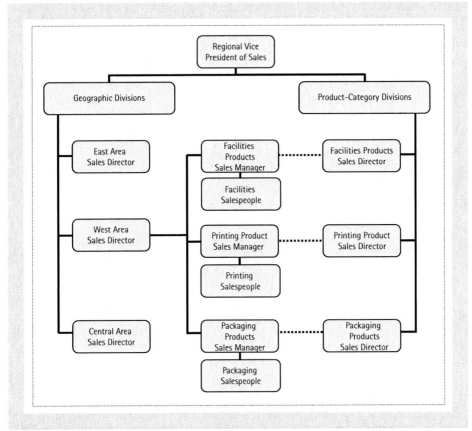

Fig. 6.18. Organization Chart for a Maintenance, Repair, and Operational Supply (MRO) Company

product categories. A regional vice-president has overall responsibility for sales of all products in the region. Three sales directors have geographic responsibility: each of them oversees sales of all product categories in approximately one-third of the geography in the region. Another three sales directors have product-category responsibility: each of them oversees sales of one product category across the entire region. Sales managers and the salespeople who report to them specialize by product category but are allocated geographically. Every sales manager is accountable to two different sales directors; directly to the geographic director and indirectly to the product-category director.

Matrix reporting structures for sales forces with multiple types of specialists—market, product, and activity—can be even more complex. Primary and secondary reporting relationships need to be clearly defined if a matrix reporting structure is to work well. A good rule is that the primary reporting structure (whether it is geography, product, activity, or customer) should be determined by the dimension that requires the most control, collaboration, and communication. Other dimensions can form the "dotted-line" reporting relationships.

The market (customer) dimension has emerged as an important way to specialize in many recent sales force reorganizations. For example, beginning in 1990, Xerox had a major account management program for the largest revenue accounts in the United States (Canaday 2008). Accounts in other countries were served by the Xerox headquarters in the region in which they were based, making geography the dominant dimension in the company's sales reporting structure. As many large customers expanded their operations around the world, they increasingly wanted to buy globally. In 2006, Xerox responded to this need by centralizing global account management at its corporate headquarters, making the customer dimension dominant to geography for managing global accounts. Xerox upgraded the global account management job to the vice-president level, raising the bar for talent, pay, requirements, and skills. A typical global account team at Xerox includes 5–15 dedicated people, and the structure and roles of team members are tailored around how each customer likes to buy and where they are located. The new global account management structure helped Xerox better meet the needs of its most important customers while increasing global reach and penetration.

Whatever the dominant reporting dimension is, the other dimensions still have to be managed to ensure a smooth working system.

6.6.5 Mirrored Alignment of Specialists

In a mirrored alignment, sales territories for two or more types of sales specialists are geographically identical or in synch with one another. This enables sales specialists who are responsible for the same set of customers to work as a team, regardless of whether or not they report to the same manager. Mirrored territories create efficiencies in coordination required between specialists who share customers. For example, if the sales and service organizations share a mirrored alignment, one salesperson coordinates with one service person for all customers in the territory. Without a mirrored alignment, a single salesperson may have to interact with dozens of different service people, depending on which customers need service.

If a mirrored alignment is successful at promoting teamwork among specialists who share customers, customers get a more integrated and coordinated effort, co-promotion and cross-selling of products and services can occur, a culture of internal cooperation is encouraged, and salespeople who call on the same customers can share insights and positively affect results through peer influence. Mirrored alignments can also help to minimize the impact of salesperson turnover. When one salesperson leaves the company, a mirrored partner that already has a relationship with that salesperson's customers can cover the required responsibilities until a replacement is hired. All of these benefits are especially evident in integrated reporting structures where mirrored partners report to a common manager who can facilitate and encourage teamwork within each mirrored group; however, mirrored alignments have been used to successfully encourage teamwork among specialists in separate reporting structures as well.

A mirrored alignment can define a one-to-one relationship or a many-to-one relationship between sales territories for different specialists. For example, one company's sales force and telephone service organization have territories that overlay one another in a four-to-one ratio. Each telephone customer service rep provides support for all the customers covered by exactly four salespeople, allowing each salesperson to coordinate with just one service rep and each service rep to coordinate with just four salespeople. The mirrored territories encourage teamwork between the sales and service organizations, providing salespeople with a greater awareness of customer support issues. This enhances the credibility of the sales force with customers, and enables them to better manage customer expectations so that there are fewer demands on customer service. At software maker Oracle, inside (telesales) and outside (field) salespeople are organized into mirrored sales teams. One outside salesperson located in the US is matched with two inside salespeople—one in the US and one in India. Inside sales team members handle telephone prospecting, online product demonstrations, and selling tasks that can be done remotely. Team members work together to meet the needs their assigned US customers and achieve territory sales goals.

Mirrored alignments are also common in the pharmaceutical industry. Companies will have multiple product-based sales teams that co-promote or cross-sell important products. This allows increased access and higher frequency of calls to key customers, and strengthens the company's relationship with its most important customers.

With a mirrored alignment, there is less flexibility to realign sales territories easily. A change proposed by a single salesperson or manager affects all layers of the overlay. Thus, many people need to be involved in evaluating and approving a change, slowing down the process. Mirrored arrangements work best when there is substantial overlap in the customer base that each specialist on the team works with. This helps to ensure that each common territory has the right workload and potential for each of the individual salespeople in the different specialist roles. Another issue that sales organizations with mirrored alignments need to address is that free-riders can emerge. One or more salespeople in a mirrored team can coast, relying on other team members to drive results. Good management and peer pressure can be leveraged to eliminate free-riders.

6.7 Implementing Sales Force Structure Change Successfully

6.7.1 Sales Force Structures Must Adapt as Business Needs Evolve

Almost all companies will face the challenge of restructuring their sales organization as forces for change emerge. Some forces come from outside the company. Changing customer needs, the actions of competitors, and changes in the economic, regulatory, or technological environment can drive a need to change selling processes. Other forces from within the company—product portfolio evolution, entry and exit from markets, new channel strategies, and company performance challenges—can compel companies to adapt sales force structures to better serve customers and achieve company objectives.

A 2005 restructuring of the Hewlett Packard (HP) sales organization illustrates the need to evolve sales force structure as business needs change. HP restructured its corporate sales organization of some 17,000 employees in an effort to address many challenges, including flat sales, unhappy customers, and a demoralized sales force (Tam 2006, Hosford 2006). Prior to the restructure, the sales force was a company-wide function, reporting to a group that operated independently from the company's product-based business units. Many HP salespeople sold the entire portfolio of HP products, a task which had become increasingly difficult as HP's product line had grown organically and through acquisition. Product line breadth and complexity challenged the bandwidth of individual salespeople. Further, the business units had little or no control over the sales process and sales budget. To deal with these challenges, HP decentralized the sales force and dispersed it among three business divisions: the IT needs of large enterprises, printers and printing, and personal computers. Salespeople were given responsibility for a smaller set of products, allowing them to develop stronger product expertise. The new structure also sought to improve the product divisions' ability to control the sales process. Several administrative layers within the sales organization were eliminated in order to cut costs and improve responsiveness to customer needs. These sales force changes at HP are credited with boosting income, driving revenues, and improving the company's reputation with customers and on Wall Street.

As a business evolves and responds to ongoing challenges and opportunities, sales force structure change is inevitable. Opportunities to change sales force structure often evolve with the business lifecycle (Zoltners, Sinha, and Lorimer 2006). As a company's product line expands and the sales job becomes more complex, sales force bandwidth and effectiveness get challenged, creating a need for specialists to better serve customer needs. Then, as customers have to interact with an increasing number of specialists over time, they may benefit from a more coordinated sales effort, prompting the company to change its sales force structure again by using account managers to coordinate sales activity for increased effectiveness with important customers.

Other sales force structure changes are driven by a desire to be more efficient as the business lifecycle evolves. Often customers become more knowledgeable and savvy as a market matures, and may no longer require the specialized sales force support that was needed when the market was new. In addition, as market growth slows, a specialized sales force structure can become too expensive to maintain. Less expensive structures may be implemented to keep the company profitable— for example, some specialists can be replaced with generalists. In addition, effective use of lower-cost sales resources like telesales becomes even more important as market growth slows.

6.7.2 Encourage Successful Structure Change by Focusing on Customer Value

Sales force restructures can fail if customers see too little value to the change. Consider an example of a very common structure change that companies make to encourage coordination across multiple sales specialists who have responsibility for the same customers—adding an account manager at major accounts to coordinate sales activity to satisfy customer needs (see the 3M and Microsoft examples earlier in this chapter). This type of structure is more likely to be successful when customers derive value from the coordinated sales effort. At Microsoft, for example, customers perceive high value to coordination since the different software products that sales specialists sell may have to work together for the solution to succeed. At a medical products company, as with 3M, account managers are likely to be successful because even if the products that specialists sell are used independently (say in different hospital departments), a hospital's purchasing department may value having a single account manager with whom it can negotiate the best price and logistics across multiple purchases.

An account management structure like this is likely to fail, however, if it is put in place primarily to benefit the company rather than the customer. One large financial institution had several separate product groups, each with its own sales force, selling a variety of investment and financial products to corporate customers. The financial institution wanted to leverage the relationships that salespeople in the various product groups had with customers in order to cross-sell each customer a broader range of products. The financial institution invested heavily in restructuring its sales effort by adding corporate account coordinators to facilitate cross-selling at major accounts. While the goal of the initiative was to increase the financial institution's revenues, customers perceived little or no value to having a coordinator for the sales effort. Salespeople from the product groups were reluctant to include the coordinators in their interactions with customers, since the coordinators added little customer value and in fact were sometimes a distraction. The corporate account coordinators failed to produce any significant results and eventually were eliminated.

6.7.3 Why Sales Force Structure Change Can Be Difficult

Changing the structure of a sales force is rarely easy. Xerox discovered this in 1999 when it restructured its 4,300-member sales organization to shift more selling effort toward large, global customers while enhancing sales force expertise by creating industry-specific selling teams (Zoltners, Sinha, and Lorimer 2004). The changes were very disruptive: almost two-thirds of Xerox customers were reassigned to a different salesperson. Performance fell well short of company goals, as many Xerox salespeople left the company and customers complained of neglect. One commercial printing customer, whose long-time Xerox service rep was reassigned in the restructuring, reported seeing eleven different service reps over a five-month period, none of whom knew how to service his machines. As a result, the customer replaced his Xerox machines with those of a competitor. The disruption caused by the sales force restructure contributed to serious financial troubles for Xerox, and it took until 2002 for the company to return to a full year of profitability.

As the Xerox experience illustrates, sometimes a sales force structure change creates so much chaos and disruption for customers and salespeople that the benefits of a theoretically better sales force structure are never realized. Though the intent of the structure change may be good, excessive disruption of long-standing customer relationships can lead to reduced customer service levels, creating customer frustration and uncertainty, and providing an opportunity for competitors. Significant change also makes it difficult for the sales force to adapt. Uncertainty creates stress for salespeople who may need to acquire new skills and knowledge, give up familiar relationships with customers, report to a new boss, or relocate to fill new positions. If salespeople earn a portion of their pay through incentives, restructuring can redistribute earnings opportunities among salespeople. If top performers feel uncertain about the changes or fear that their earnings opportunity is threatened, they may leave the company.

Many companies experience a long, painful transition of their support systems and processes—such as information support, communication flows, and incentive administration—as they change to a new sales structure. For example, shifting the sales force from product-based specialization to market-based specialization can be especially difficult. If the sales force is restructured around markets while the rest of the company remains organized in product-based business units, it can be hard to match sales force requirements with the needs of other departments. If the accounting department measures profit and loss by product and not by market, it is difficult to hold a market-based sales force accountable for results. If the marketing department is organized around products, alignment between product managers and a market-oriented sales force may be strained. A significant sales force structure change like this can also necessitate considerable change to sales support systems.

6.7.4 Encourage Successful Structure Change by Focusing on Implementation

Success in changing a sales force structure requires attention to effective implementation. The following guidelines can help companies implement sales force structure change successfully.

6.7.4.1 *The Devil is in the Details of a Restructure Proposal*

Evaluating whether or not a sales force restructure can be implemented successfully requires looking at proposed changes at a very detailed level. A true sense of the cost and feasibility of making a structure work becomes clear only when the impact of the new structure on specific customers, salespeople, and sales support systems is examined. The questions in Figure 6.19 provide a starting point for understanding this impact.

The analysis required goes well beyond a top-down strategic look by a task force at headquarters that produces a "macro" list of goals, advantages, challenges, and a new organization chart. We have seen many companies head down the path of restructuring based on macro-level analysis, only to discover late in the process that the amount of change required for salespeople and customers makes implementing the restructure infeasible. For example, Xerox underestimated the disruption that would be required to reorganize its sales force into industry-specific teams.

6.7.4.2 *Protect the Best Customers*

Before implementing a sales force structure change, it is important to develop a plan for taking care of customers during the transition, particularly those who contribute most to company sales and profits. Customers may be concerned about the changes taking place, and a well-thought-out relationship transition plan can reassure them and help them establish a trusted relationship with a new salesperson or sales team. The experience of an industrial distribution company shows that a formal relationship transition plan can reinforce customer connections and help a company maintain sales after a restructure. The company implemented a major sales force reorganization that resulted in many accounts being assigned to a

A customer perspective	• What salesperson or team will serve each important customer after the restructure? • How will the change affect how the customer engages with the company? (For example, will the customer need to purchase through telesales rather than through a field salesperson?) • Will the customer need to establish a relationship with a different salesperson or team? • If the salesperson or team changes, how will knowledge be transferred?
A salesperson perspective	• How will the job responsibilities of each salesperson change? • Who will be asked to relocate? • Who will be reassigned to a different manager? • How will the company prepare salespeople for their new responsibilities?
A systems perspective	• How will sales reporting need to change? • How will the sales incentive plan be affected? • How will planning and communication processes be impacted? • What is required to make these and other sales systems, processes, and programs compatible with the new structure?

Fig. 6.19. Questions for Understanding the Detailed Impact of Sales Force Structure Change

different salesperson. Sales performance at reassigned accounts declined only when relationship transition was not taken seriously. If the former salesperson introduced the reassigned customer to the new salesperson and worked together with the new salesperson to serve the customer's needs for a brief period, then sales to that customer were unaffected. However, at reassigned accounts where relationship transition was neglected, a sales decline of up to 20 percent was observed. For this company, a relatively small investment in careful customer relationship transition had a high impact on sales performance.

6.7.4.3 *Protect the Top Salespeople*

Before implementing a sales force structure change, it is important to understand how the change affects the responsibilities and earnings opportunities of the top producers, and to ensure that they are on board with the change so they do not leave the company. This is particularly important in situations where salespeople control customer relationships, have customer knowledge that is a significant source of competitive advantage, and/or are viewed by customers as the primary face of the company. A plan for protecting top salespeople includes two main elements. First, top performers should keep job responsibilities that they enjoy and excel at, and/or they should gain new responsibilities that are well suited to their skills and interests. Second, their earnings opportunity should be protected. If a top performer gives up an established account that has been a steady source of commission income, and replaces it with a new but largely undeveloped account, a transition compensation plan may be needed to keep the salesperson's earnings "whole" for a period until the new account can be penetrated.

6.7.4.4 Begin Implementation Planning at Design

A plan for transitioning to a new structure should be developed almost as soon as the process of designing the structure begins. Information needs to be gathered about key stakeholders, including customers, salespeople, sales managers, and other company departments, both to ensure the best possible structure and to identify implementation challenges early while there is time to develop approaches for dealing with them. Appropriate involvement of key stakeholders also helps to build consensus around the new structure and makes implementation easier. The scope and timing of stakeholder involvement depends upon the extent of the changes and the amount of organizational anxiety that they are likely to create. One of the key reasons that the 1999 Xerox restructure was initially unsuccessful is that the changes were pushed down from the highest management levels, the sales force was not sufficiently involved in the structure design process, and the sales management team did not endorse the new structure.

6.7.4.5 Reinforce Sales Force Structure Change by Adapting Sales Systems, Processes, and Programs

While the decision of how to structure the sales force has a powerful influence on sales results, it is just one component of good decision-making by sales leaders. The downstream decisions that sales leaders make regarding issues such as sales force hiring and training, performance management, compensation, and culture need to be compatible with and reinforce the structure decision. Implementation of a sales force restructure will not be successful unless there are consistent, high-quality sales force programs, systems, and processes to support it.

The 2005 restructuring of the HP sales organization illustrates this need for consistency. To help the new decentralized and specialized structure succeed, HP implemented several sales force changes. More than 30 different sales force automation systems were combined into a single, company-wide system, giving HP better analytic control of its sales pipeline and making it easier to manage the sales compensation system. New performance metrics tracking customer follow-up and support were put in place to emphasize the need to become more customer-centric. HP also made significant investments to improve sales force performance management, training, hiring, and compensation. The alignment of all of these programs, systems, and processes with the new sales structure helped to successfully transform the HP sales culture and drive company results.

6.8 Conclusion

Sales force structure decisions affect customer and company results by directly influencing salespeople and their activities. Creating an effective sales force structure involves:

- finding the mix of generalists and product, market, or activity specialists that achieves the right balance of sales force effectiveness and efficiency;
- designing reporting relationships for salespeople and managers that facilitate coordination and control of sales activity;
- implementing mechanisms such as training, incentives, coaching, performance management, and information support to manage tensions and encourage the accomplishment of business objectives.

As companies need to change their sales force structures as business needs evolve, careful attention to implementation helps ensure that sales force structure changes are well received by customers and salespeople.

References

Anon. (2002). "Microsoft Expands US Sales Force to Deliver Greater Value to Customers" and "Q and A: Microsoft Continues to Invest in Next Evolution of Customer and Partner Focus," *PressPass Information for Journalists*, available at www.microsoft.com/presspass/, June 24.

Anon. (2008). *Microsoft Careers*, available at www.microsoft.com/careers, October.

Anon. (2008). *Jobs at IBM*, available at www.ibm.com, October.

Borzo, G. (1991). "3M promotes quality inside, outside company Minnesota Mining and Manufacturing's Medical Products Group," *Health Industry Today*, March.

Canaday, H. (2008). "A Global Sales Approach," *Selling Power*, October, 19.

Cowley, S. (2003). "SAP Reorganizes US Sales Force," *InfoWorld Daily News*, January 8.

Doyle, T. C., and R. C. DeMarzo (2004). "Cutting to the Chase: Vendors' Channel Executives Get Right to the Issues That Matter Most Today to Solution Providers," *VARbusiness*, October 25, 35.

Hosford, C. (2006). "Rebooting Hewlett Packard," *Sales & Marketing Management*, July/August, 32.

Johnston, M. W., and G. W. Marshall (2009). *Churchill/Ford/Walker's Sales Force Management*, 9th edn, Burr Ridge, IL: McGraw-Hill Irwin.

LEVINSON, M. (2002). "Honeywell Retools Business Processes for CRM," *CIO*, April, available at: http://www.cio.com/article/30972/Honeywell_Retools_Business_Processes_ for_CRM

McCUE, M. (2008). "The Low Cost Sales Leader: ADP's John Gleason Champions Diversity and Flexibility," salesandmarketingmanagement.com, September/October.

RANGASWAMY, A., P. SINHA, and A. ZOLTNERS (1990). "An Integrated Model-Based Approach for Sales Force Structuring," *Marketing Science* 9.4, 279.

ROONEY, P. (2002). "Microsoft to Expand its US Sales Force," *CRN—The Newsweekly for Builders of Technology Solutions*, July 1–8.

SELLERS, P. (1992). "How to Remake Your Sales Force," *Fortune*, May, 98.

SLIWA, CAROL (2001). "Microsoft Changes Sales Strategy," *Computerworld*, July 23, 1.

TAM, PUI-WING (2006). "System Reboot: Hurd's Big Challenge at H-P: Overhauling Corporate Sales; Years of Acquisitions Led to a Bloated Bureaucracy; Improving Client Relations; Mr. Ditucci Gets the Contract," *Wall Street Journal* (Eastern Edition), April 3, A.1.

WEINREB, MICHAEL (2003). "Power to the People: W. L. Gore Succeeds by Eliminating the Rules and Boundaries," *Sales & Marketing Management*, April, 30.

ZOLTNERS, A. A., P. SINHA, and S. E. LORIMER (2004). *Sales Force Design for Strategic Advantage*, Basingstoke: Palgrave Macmillan.

————————(2006). "Match Your Sales Force Structure to Your Business Lifecycle," *Harvard Business Review* (July–August), 80.

——————(2009). *Building a Winning Sales Force*, New York: AMACOM.

————and G. A. ZOLTNERS (2001). *The Complete Guide to Accelerating Sales Force Performance*, New York: AMACOM.

CHAPTER 7

.....

SALES FORCE-GENERATED MARKETING INTELLIGENCE

.....

KENNETH R. EVANS

C. FRED MIAO

7.1 INTRODUCTION

.....

In the formulation of business strategy, management has long recognized the need for effective and efficient market information systems. The strategic management and marketing literatures have addressed both conceptually and empirically the role superior marketing intelligence plays in effective strategy formulation. As noted by Makadok and Barnet (2001: 1623), achieving competitive advantage may well be based on the asymmetry among firms in their "skill in collecting, filtering and interpreting information about the future value of resources." Regarding the acquisition of superior market information, Maltz and Kohli (1996) discovered that managers' perceptions of market information quality was a function of intentional communication efforts by firms that sought to make the information acquisition process formal and sufficiently frequent, thereby instilling perceived value. This notion is further reinforced by the characterization of a firm's market orientation, which is depicted as relying extensively on how firms access and integrate market information (Kohli, Jaworski, and Kumar 1993). Therefore, a firm's performance is highly dependent on its ability to effectively build and integrate marketing intelligence systems into its strategic formulation process.

The concept of Marketing Information System (MIS) was first defined by Cox and Good (1967) as a set of procedures and methods for planning and presenting information required in making marketing-related decisions, which involves "an organized system of direction, collection, analysis, and dissemination of intelligence to operating units of a business enterprise" (Pinkerton 1969: 51). Because of their "boundary-spanner" role in the organization, the sales force can gather such important market information as customers' product preferences, competitors' new product and promotional strategies, current and potential distributor information, and point-of-purchase promotional effectiveness (Thietart and Vivas 1981). The sales force is in an excellent position to "observe, filter, and transmit information about the sales environment to aid managerial decisions" (Grove, LaForge, Knowles, and Stone 1992: 65), especially when such information is not readily available via other means. The rapidly changing business environment not only elevates the role of the sales force as an important source of market information but also places greater challenges on salespeople to assist the organization in adapting to ever-rising standards of performance. Three dimensions of change are particularly relevant to the salespeople's role in the MIS—Customers, Competitors, and Technology (Jones, Brown, Zoltners, and Weitz 2005).

Customer satisfaction and loyalty are at the core of modern marketing thought, and are probably the best measures of long-term marketing effectiveness as opposed to short-term sales or profits. With ever increasing customer expectations of salespeople and their firms in delivering superior products and services, salespeople must be more informed, increase their responsiveness to customers' concerns, enhance communication efficiency, and provide customized solutions to these changing customer expectations. Given that the sales force is on the frontline in dealing with customers, they are especially positioned to help inform customer prioritization based on customer lifetime value (Homburg, Droll, and Totzek 2008). In key account management systems, salespeople play the role of "internal orchestrator" (Jones et al. 2005), where they have to coordinate efforts within cross functional teams such that market information can be tapped to its full potential. External to the selling organization, the salesperson must deal with a greater number and variety of individuals within client organizations. Contact density, or number of relational ties, has been found to have a direct impact on customer value (Palmatier 2008); therefore, the extent to which a salesperson can extract valuable information from each contact point within the customer organization becomes an important antecedent to the selling organization's performance. However, it should be noted that there may be trade-offs between the depth and breadth of communication where more contact ties may reduce the ability of sales representatives to secure the depth of information from each contact point. Therefore, there is an increased need for salespeople to differentiate the potential quality of information from each source and allocate their time accordingly.

Parallel to customer information analysis and communication across the selling organization's functional units is the need for an MIS that recognizes current and potential competitors in terms of their capabilities and strategies (Narver and Slater 1990). In today's hypercompetitive markets, as product lifecycles decline in duration, salespeople must update their knowledge of competitors' products and technologies on a continuous basis. Timely and accurate competitor information enables the selling organization to shift its course of action in the marketplace. In order for the sales force to better handle rapidly changing customer expectations, many sales organizations have adopted sales-based technology such as those used in customer relationship management (CRM) and sales force automation (SFA). While these technologies can assist the sales force in collecting, analyzing, and transmitting customer and market information within the selling organization, salespeople's resistance to sales force automation has been a subject of considerable interest to practitioners and academics alike. Reporting on the use and role of SFA among various industries, Cotteleer, Inderrieden, and Lee (2006) noted that it is estimated that companies expended about $3 billion on global SFA in 2004 with no guarantee of a payoff. Common sales force reaction has been a sense of loss of autonomy (a sales manager closely scrutinizing their every move) and loss of power by having the customer relationship wrested from their oversight and placed in the company's control. Of course the common complaint is the time invested in SFA data input, which detracts from time invested in sales activities (Cotteleer, Inderrieden, and Lee 2006). How to help salespeople manage this trade-off and motivate them to actively participate in market information generation and dissemination have thus become a crucial questions with the advent of sales-based technology. A more behavior-based compensation system (Anderson and Oliver 1987) and/or an easy-to-use reporting and feedback system of MIS (Evans and Schlacter 1985) might be especially relevant in addressing these issues.

In today's service-centered economy, recently denoted the "new dominant logic" (Vargo and Lusch 2004), knowledge of the customers, competitors, technical know-how, and the market environment as a whole has become the fundamental source of competitive advantage. With the customer becoming more like a co-producer, a company's ability to continuously acquire "real-time" customer and market information through the field sales force becomes a vital part in its value propositions. How to integrate the sales force into a well-designed MIS is thus elevated in its strategic importance.

The remainder of this chapter seeks to provide an in-depth examination of the role of the sales force in the MIS (see Figure 7.1). We first define the domain of the sales force-generated marketing intelligence, including product planning, sales forecasting, setting competitive strategy, pricing strategy, sales territory knowledge,

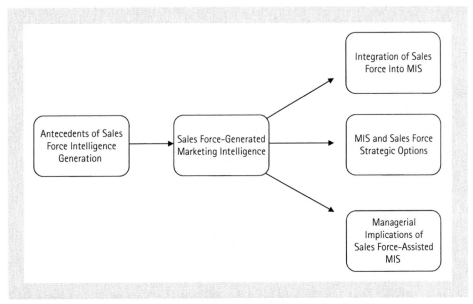

Fig. 7.1. An Overview of Sales Force–Generated Marketing Intelligence

and international marketing intelligence. Next, we discuss important antecedents to sales force intelligence generation at both the organizational and personal level, after which we take a look at the implementation of marketing intelligence generation and dissemination—integrating the sales force into MIS. We then discuss the relationship between integrated marketing intelligence and sales force strategic options, focusing on how a well-implemented MIS can influence sales strategies. To help readers better grasp applications of the concepts discussed in this chapter, we have included examples and case materials throughout. Lastly, we provide managerial implications and conclusions regarding the role of the sales force in the design and implementation of an effective MIS.

7.2 Domain of Sales Force-Generated Marketing Intelligence

This section examines the scope of sales force-generated marketing intelligence depicted in the middle of Figure 7.1. Specifically, we examine the key dimensions of sales force intelligence and their pivotal roles in aiding effective managerial decisions.

7.2.1 New Product Planning and Development

New product development lies at the heart of a company's survival and growth if the traditional management directive "Successfully innovate or perish" holds any merit. Successful new product introductions provide increased sales, profits, and competitive advantage (Sivades and Dwyer 2000); however, the failure rate of new products and services for US companies is in the range of 40–90 per cent (Judson, Schoenbachler, Gordon, Ridnour, and Weilbaker 2006). One of the main reasons for this unfortunate statistic, according to a survey of corporate respondents conducted by *Industry Week*, is poorly defined customer needs (Osborne 2002). As Chandy and Tellis (1998) note, the success of product innovation relies not only on the newness of technology but also on how it fulfills customer needs better than existing offerings.

One functional area that is particularly positioned to collect customer needs-related intelligence for new product development is the sales force. An example from the pharmaceutical industry reveals that field salespeople working with a major hospital were unable to get doctors to buy a standard drug administration kit because of demands by these physicians for major kit modifications. While the salesperson's company generally discourages taking "special orders" like this due to possible strains on profitability, the sales manager approved the exception because he believed it would be a great new product development opportunity. A year later, one of the doctors published a paper on a new technique he developed utilizing the specially modified drug administration kit, which boosted demand and eventually generated millions of dollars in sales and profits. The competition was caught completely off guard by the advantage the supplier created in the marketplace (Falvey, 1992).

Judson et al. (2006) note that in early stages of new product development sales force involvement is particularly critical because (1) close ties between boundary-spanners (i.e. salespeople) and customers can facilitate exchange of information necessary to guide the product development process, (2) new information technology (e.g. CRM, SFA) facilitates the incorporation of key customers as co-producers for new products, and (3) cross-functional new product teams involving salespeople will benefit from the availability of timely market information from the customer's perspective.

7.2.2 Sales Forecasting

Sales forecasting seeks to estimate customer demand of a company's goods and/or services during a given time period (Moon and Mentzer 1999). Outstanding performance in sales forecasting is a very desirable yet difficult task for companies to achieve, especially those operating in volatile environments that render predictions based on historical data unreliable and risky (Wotruba and Thurlow 1976). In a case study conducted by Palmatier, Miao, and Fang (2007), it was found that sales forecasting based on historical data was very susceptible to unique economic conditions. A more effective approach would be to integrate historical data with sales force input. According to a longitudinal study of sales forecasting performance at 33 companies including such well-known firms as Coca Cola, Exxon, and Hershey Foods, researchers at the University of Tennessee (Moon and Mentzer 1999) found that the judgement of a company's sales force was a valuable input in estimating future sales.

When should companies actively solicit forecasting information from their sales force? The study conducted by Moon and Mentzer (1999) identified two primary conditions. In one condition, salespeople may have unique insights into potential significant demand changes by customers away from their historical patterns due to close relationships with accounts. In another context, if a company has a small number of large customers making up the majority of its sales, substantial forecasting errors could result if one of these customers were to unexpectedly place a large order, or if one customer that had previously been a major purchaser suddenly had a need to significantly reduce its order. Under such circumstances, the valuable insights from salespeople who work closely with these key accounts would be critical in improving forecasting accuracy.

Companies should also try to lessen the burden placed on their sales force in performing the forecasting-related responsibilities. For example, a European pick-and-mix confectionery company employed a new forecasting approach—assortment forecasting—to significantly reduce time spent on the forecasting process. This new technique allowed salespeople to work on an entire assortment at a time instead of producing a forecast for individual products. By using a less time-consuming approach, the company was better able to involve its sales force in forecasting (Smaros and Hellstrom 2004).

7.2.3 Setting Competitive Strategy

In addition to securing important customer information, market-oriented companies also need to actively collect, analyze, and respond to competitive information (Narver and Slater 1990). Sales executives have noted: "Keeping an eye on the competition is tantamount to surveying the periphery to protect yourself in battle" (Rottenberger 1991: 24), but they often complain about the inadequacy of the competitive intelligence they receive (Ligos 1997).

Two questions are particularly germane to competitive intelligence: (1) What is the scope of competitive intelligence? and (2) How may such information be obtained? Competitive intelligence includes all information about a competitor that typically involves such information as pricing, quality, service, emerging technologies, sales volume, and market share change. Although the sales force is by no means the sole source of competitive intelligence, most experts in the field agree that it is by far the most useful, because information from other sources such as trade publications tend to be historical and are less valuable (Mellow 1989). Salespeople often interact with their clients, distribution partners, and vendors, from whom they can garner important competitor information. A case in point is Rockwell Collins—an aviation electronics supplier that bids on government contracts to produce certain types of information technology. Rockwell Collins solicited feedback from its sales force regarding what they were hearing about their main competitor's intention to bid on a project. After an extensive investigation by a cross-functional team including engineers and salespeople, Rockwell Collins concluded that its main competitor's strategy was to focus its bid on price. Armed with this information, Rockwell Collins prepared its bid with an emphasis on its experience, quality, and superior customer service in return for a higher price. It was this understanding of the competitor's bidding strategy that ultimately helped Rockwell Collins win the contract (Mellow 1989). Therefore, managers need to recognize the value of information generated by their salespeople when compiling competitor intelligence.

7.2.4 Pricing Strategy

Most companies face pricing decisions that entail internal financial requirements—cost-driven pricing—and external market considerations—customer-driven pricing (Peter and Donnelly 2007). While finance and accounting departments provide relevant cost information for breakeven analysis, salespeople are often called upon to provide market information such as prices of competitive products, prices customers indicate they are willing to pay, and segment-specific price elasticity. Smith and Nagle (1994) identified two scenarios when salespeople's input can be particularly germane—*proactive price change* and *reactive price change*. In the scenario of *proactive price change*, if the breakeven analysis determines that a 10 percent price cut would require a 25 percent sales increase to break even; similarly, a 10 percent price increase would require that sales volume fall by no more than 17 percent in order to break even. The likelihood of meeting those sales quotas can best be judged by the sales manager through feedback from the field sales force. In the *reactive price change* scenario, the general manager needs to make a decision whether the company should match a major competitor's 10 percent price cut. Supposing that no price cut is made, the general manager figures out the company can still break even at a 20 percent decrease in sales volume (especially if the company is sensitive to its price–quality image). Then it would be the sales manager's job to determine how likely it is that the company will lose more than 20 percent in sales if the company does not match the price cut. Field sales forces are particularly well positioned to collect information on competitors' and customers' reactions to different pricing strategies; therefore a sales force-integrated MIS should be designed to capture information on customers' willingness to pay, competitors' responses, and the subsequent demand elasticity.

7.2.5 Sales Force and Territorial Customer Knowledge

When a company serves different customer groups across a vast geographic area beyond the reach of the company headquarters, regional or territorial differences in economic conditions, customer demographics, and buying preferences can vary quite significantly. Since the field sales force or sales channel operates in local territories, salespeople should have the best insight and knowledge of distinct customer preferences because of their closeness to the target market. A case in point is General Electric (GE). GE has incorporated its sales force into its Quick Marketing intelligence (QMI) system (Keenan 1994) that allows the field sales force to quickly communicate customers' new product/service requirements back to the company. Once a week field salespeople have a conference call with the headquarters to review activity in the field and what needs to be done to accommodate customers' requirements. In one instance an appliance salesperson came across a contractor who needed clothes dryers for an apartment complex but needed the dryer doors to open right to left (GE's dryer doors open left to right). After a phone call to the corporate office, a decision was made to redesign the product for the contractor and an order was subsequently secured. In another example, McDonald's franchisee sales channel is known for its innovative ideas and solutions because of its territory-focused customer knowledge (Falvey 1992). Many years ago a franchisee in a devout Catholic area discovered a need for a non-meat item for Fridays, resulting in the introduction of "Filet-O-Fish." Still another McDonald's innovation came from a franchisee located near an air force base. Because all base personnel were required to be in uniform when entering local stores, the franchisee developed the "drive-thru" service. Unless a company has a system to collect and act on territory-specific information from the field sales force, such valuable information will not be used for strategic opportunities.

7.2.6 Sales Forces in Foreign Countries

Selling in domestic markets is often significantly different from selling in a foreign country (1) because of added social, political and economic risks involved in the firm's operations and (2) because international market research is difficult to perform, costly, and unreliable (Cavusgil 1985). For these reasons, salespeople operating in foreign countries may be the company's only link to customers and, as a result, may be the most reliable source of market data. In an in-depth study of US companies that operate sales forces in international markets, Chonko, Tanner, and Smith (1991) grouped sales force-generated marketing intelligence into three distinct stages: market entry phase, growth phase, and maturity phase.

In the market entry phase, sales forces operating in a foreign country are valuable assets to the company due to the high costs of sending research teams or hiring consultants to evaluate the new market. In the entry stage, the sales force can assume the responsibility of marketing research by collecting information regarding market potential (e.g. size) and entry logistics such as packaging, distribution channels, and local regulations. In the case of market entry with a new product, salespeople operating in international markets can be asked to conduct new product trial research, investigate customer expectations, and provide sales volume predictions. To summarize, at the market entry stage international salespeople can provide a variety of essential marketing intelligence such as competitor information, government regulations, entry logistics, customers' needs and expectations, customers' willingness to try products, product trial implementation and results, customers' awareness of the company and its products, natural resource availability for production, socioeconomic climate and political stability, data from local trade and industry publications, data from government published statistics, and market volatility.

During the growth phase, companies can use international salespeople to gather information on the competition and new market requirements. Specifically, salespeople can collect information on the service needs and overall customer satisfaction once the product has secured a foothold in the international market. Alternatively, the sales force can focus on customers' likes or dislikes of the product compared to that of the competition such that customers' intention to switch can be detected early. In the growth stage, it is also very important to monitor competitors' moves. The sales force can, for instance, gather information about competitor pricing, competitor sales force structure and allocation, advertising intensity, distribution strategy, and production capacity, etc. that may inform market share and growth potential. To summarize, important data that international salespeople can collect in the growth phase include: competitor information, new market requirements, customer surveys, product quality and features, customer relationships, profitability, market expansion, sales growth potential, and distributor information.

During the maturity phase, many companies want to hold on to their established market position for as long as possible due to the significant amount of capital investment in the previous stages. Salespeople can provide early warning information regarding competitor trends that may undermine the company's competitive pricing and market share, which can guide the planned phase-out decision for a particular product. Essential marketing data that an international sales force can collect during the maturity phase include: competitor information, government data on product usage, type of businesses using the product, potential improvement in distribution, customers' desire for change to current product, and emerging new customer needs.

Due to the remote locations and socioeconomic differences between the US domestic and international markets, multinational companies frequently rely on international salespeople as sources of marketing intelligence for product, price, promotion, and distribution decisions in those markets. In order to encourage international salespeople to actively participate in marketing intelligence collection, companies must ensure that marketing information systems are easy to use, and that salespeople are made aware that market information collection is a job expectation. (Evans and Schlacter 1985, Grove et al. 1992).

7.3 ANTECEDENTS OF SALES FORCE INTELLIGENCE GENERATION

There are primarily two levels of variables that can influence marketing intelligence generation by the sales force in the field (see Figure 7.1). They can be grouped at the firm and personal level, respectively. At the firm level, relevant variables include organizational culture, sales force control philosophy, training, job description, compensation and rewards; at the personal level, role conflict and role ambiguity are particularly relevant.

7.3.1 Organizational Culture

As Narver and Slater (1998) note, organizational activities cannot be successfully ingrained without an underlying belief system reflected in the firm's organizational culture/climate. Organizational culture is defined as "The pattern of shared values and beliefs that help individuals understand organizational functioning and thus provide them norms for behavior in the organization" (Deshpandé and Webster 1989: 4). As such, organizational culture can encourage salespeople's market-oriented behaviors in generating and disseminating marketing intelligence (Homburg and Pflesser 2000). Cultivation of a market-oriented culture committed to marketing intelligence generation within the sales organization requires top management support. Management must also encourage an environment where new product ideas are fostered within the sales organization by placing a unique emphasis on the role of intelligence generation and dissemination (Jaworski and Kohli 1993). When top management gives clear signals to its sales staff of the importance and role of marketing intelligence generation, a market-oriented culture will likely emerge and persist.

7.3.2 Sales Force Control Philosophy

Anderson and Oliver (1987) conceptualized two types of sales control systems—outcome control and behavior control. Outcome control uses incentives to reward salespeople in direct proportion to their sales outcomes (e.g. sales volume), whereas behavior control often entails extensive management involvement in guiding, monitoring, and evaluating salespeople according to their selling behaviors rather than focusing on immediate sales outcomes. More recently, Challagalla and Shervani (1996) disaggregated behavior control into activity control and capability control. Activity control refers to the specification of the activities a salesperson is expected to perform (e.g. activity reports), whereas capability control emphasizes the mastery of skills in the selling process. In practice most sales organizations employ both behavior and outcome control with varying degrees (Oliver and Anderson 1994). Therefore, we consider sales control systems as a combination of activity, capability, and outcome control.

Theory and empirical evidence in the sales control literature suggest that behavior and outcome control philosophies will have differential impacts on salespeople's behavior in the selling process. Under the outcome control philosophy, a salesperson is rewarded by incentives such as commission or bonus with little managerial intervention during the selling process. Outcome control approximates a market contracting arrangement that transfers most of the risk associated with selling to the salesperson in the event sales quotas cannot be met. This type of control system would be more likely to focus salespersons' attention on activities that lead to immediate payoffs (Anderson and Oliver 1987). Due to salespeople's tendency to minimize non-selling activities under the outcome-based control, it would be harder to get the sales force to actively engage in marketing intelligence collection and dissemination because time spent on those activities will be viewed as a distraction from the primary objective of selling.

Behavior control, on the other hand, can either specify what activities salespeople must perform or emphasize what types of skills salespeople must develop and master (Challagalla and Shervani 1996). If behavior control is employed, salespeople will be evaluated by how they perform not only selling activities but also required non-selling activities. Since salespeople are not evaluated by their immediate sales outcome, they are more likely to comply with company procedures and to perform non-selling activities such as market information collection (Cravens, Ingram, LaForge, and Young 1993; Oliver and Anderson 1994).

In order to engage the sales force in market information collection and dissemination, the sales organization should incorporate some use of behavior control. That is, managers should monitor, evaluate, and reward salespeople's marketing intelligence generation. This can be achieved by specifying such intelligence collection as a required activity (i.e. activity control) and/or by monitoring and improving salespeople's ability to detect and report high quality market information (i.e. capability control). While behavior control does increase supervisory time, it can prove rewarding by quality and timely marketing intelligence.

7.3.3 Training, Job Description, Compensation, and Reward

Traditional sales force training focuses on such aspects as knowledge about products/services, the company's strengths and weaknesses, consumer profiles, competitors, and market and industry characteristics (Cron, Marshall, Singh, Spiro, and Sujan 2005). However, most companies' training programs failed to identify and reinforce intelligence gathering activities (Festervand, Grove, and Reidenbach 1988). Training should be provided to help salespeople identify desired types of marketing intelligence such as pricing policy changes by competitors, promotional activities, new product development processes, and customer feedback on product features. In addition, sales training should focus on various sources of marketing intelligence, emphasizing that valuable market information can be retrieved from interactions with customers and channel members such as distributors and retailers. In short, the sales force's role in securing market information will be severely compromised if individuals are not clear on what information they should acquire and how to secure it (Ligos 1997). This also entails consideration of what constitutes the proper boundaries of ethical gathering of marketing intelligence (Ligos 1997, Neuborne 2003). Finally, salespeople need to be trained on (1) what reporting systems are available and (2) how to use these reporting systems for intelligence gathering and dissemination. As Thietart and Vivas note (1981: 21), "relying upon salesmen as a strategic information source also implies training them as environmental scanners and informers."

It has been well documented that many companies do not include market information generation as part of their salespeople's job description (Rottenberger 1991). The importance of explicitly including marketing intelligence generation in the job descriptions of the sales force has been identified in previous sales management research as a vital means of clearly stipulating management's expectation of the sales organization (Evans and Schlacter 1985). By clearly communicating the responsibility of the sales organization in securing market information, this becomes an expected part of performance evaluations and is integrated into sales controls. Salespeople will thus anticipate their performance in this area to be an integral part of regularly scheduled review processes (Webster 1965). Therefore, marketing intelligence must be formalized, explicitly identified as the salespersons' responsibility, and clearly articulated in their job description. Failure to clarify the sales role in MIS results in sales managers receiving sporadic and non-systematic reports from the sales force.

Reinforcement of salespeople's effort in market information generation requires the sales organizations to design compensation structures that link financial rewards to the frequency and quality of market information provided by the salesperson (Vroom 1964). Such a behavior-based compensation scheme was demonstrated to be effective in reinforcing salespeople's performance in providing required information and reports (Cravens et al. 1993). Other reinforcement tools include formal recognition and managerial feedback. Specifically, when salespeople excel in providing timely and high quality market information, management should formally recognize this outstanding performance (e.g. salesperson of the year). This in turn serves as an important motivational factor to encourage future market information generation activity. Moreover, to enhance the salesperson's intrinsic motivation to engage in market information-related tasks, managers need to provide timely feedback (especially positive feedback) to the salesperson regarding the results. Such positive feedback can improve the salesperson's sense of accomplishment, which can further reinforce the desirability of participating in market information generation (Vroom 1964).

7.3.4 Role Conflict and Role Ambiguity

As boundary spanners, salespeople often operate in environments that give rise to high levels of uncertainty, conflict, and ambiguity. The importance of salesperson role perception was highlighted in the analysis of sales performance by Churchill, Ford, Hartley, and Walker (1985), who found role perception to be the strongest antecedent of overall sales performance. Two important aspects of role perception are of primary interest in sales management research, namely role conflict and role ambiguity. Role conflict is "the degree of incongruity or incompatibility of expectations associated with the role" (Behrman and Perreault 1984: 2), whereas role ambiguity refers to "the perceived lack of information a salesperson needs to perform his or her role adequately and his or her uncertainty about the expectations of different role set members" (Singh 1998: 70). In the MIS context, when salespeople face ambiguous and/or conflicting information requests from multiple organizational units, motivation and effectiveness in collecting relevant market information can be significantly compromised. To the extent that role conflict and role ambiguity may negatively affect the salesperson's wellbeing and job performance, sales managers have been advised to use managerial tools such as empowerment (Hartline and Ferrell 1996), salesperson participation (Teas 1983), and behavior-based sales control (Challagalla and Shervani 1996) to enhance the salesperson's role clarity and performance.

While it is important for management to mitigate the negative impact of role stressors on the salesperson's marketing intelligence performance, a recent study of salesperson role perception suggests that salesperson selection also plays an important role in how salespeople cope with role stressors. Miao and Evans (2007) reveals that sales managers should seek to recruit salespeople who exhibit certain motivational characteristics. Salespeople's motivation has been shown to have distinct cognitive and affective dimensions (Miao, Evans, and Zou 2007). Specifically, intrinsic motivation has been found to include challenge orientation (cognitive) and task enjoyment (affective), whereas extrinsic motivation has been found to include compensation orientation (cognitive) and recognition orientation (affective). According to Miao and Evans' (2007) findings, salespeople with higher levels of task enjoyment or compensation seeking are better able to handle role ambiguity, whereas those who exhibit higher levels of challenge seeking can better cope with role conflict. Therefore, sales managers might seek to recruit salespeople with motivational traits that mitigate the negative impact of role ambiguity and role conflict on the performance of market information generation.

7.4 Integrating the Sales Force into the Marketing Information System

In order for the marketing intelligence generated by the sales force to be captured and disseminated across functional boundaries in a timely fashion, the sales force must be fully integrated into the MIS system (see Figure 7.1). This section describes how the sales force can become an integral part of the MIS.

7.4.1 Evaluation of Sales Intelligence and Formal Feedback Process

The inclusion of the sales force in marketing intelligence generation and dissemination is becoming more strategic in nature due to the rapidly changing environment (Le Meunier-FitzHugh and Piercy 2006). Since salespeople frequently interact with customers and distribution channel members, collection of salesperson-generated market information should incur little additional cost to the

marketing budget; however, proper intelligence evaluation and processing mechanisms need to be in place to maximize the full potential of sales force-provided
MIS (Festervand, Grove, and Reidenbach 1988). Initial information needs must be
articulated to establish early MIS design parameters; however, it is also important
that the MIS be sensitive to emerging needs and new types of information to
prevent valuable information loss. In other words, the MIS must be flexible in its
scope and format. Sales managers play an important role in the market information generation process, as they are the "central processing unit" that receives and
analyzes market information and aids in the formulation of strategic decisions (Le
Meunier-FitzHugh and Piercy 2006). However, relying on the sales manager as a
lone "central processing unit" is far from adequate or effective because of the sales
manager's knowledge constraints and possible information overload. Therefore,
market information collected through the sales force will be much more effective,
especially in sales organizations that have well-designed information evaluation
and feedback systems.

A good example of integrating the sales force into the MIS by using a formal
feedback instrument was illustrated by Grove et al. (1992). Using a well-known
consumer food manufacturer as the background, these researchers demonstrated a
seven-step feedback instrument that helped the sales force identify, filter, and
condense relevant marketing intelligence data. These steps are as follows:

Step 1. Assemble call reports that have occurred over a period of time such that
they provide an accurate representation of the sales representatives' initial
MIS effort.

Step 2. Select a panel of independent judges to examine the content of the reports
in order to (a) identify general foci of concerns and (b) specify topics with
respect to each focus.

Step 3. Create a matrix for tallying the number of times each topic appears in call
reports for each representative and for the sales force overall.

Step 4. Evaluate the call reports to identify (a) patterns of "under-reporting" and
"over-reporting" by the sales force at large and (b) areas requiring more
attention or improvement by the individual sales representative.

Step 5. Use 4(a) to develop and adapt call report forms that are more conducive to
broader or more relevant observations.

Step 6. Share results of the analysis with each of the sales representatives to provide
constructive direction and motivation for their continued participation.

Step 7. Monitor the flow of information to adapt the instrument to changes in the
firm's internal and external environment.

Grove et al. reported that, in the quarter following the implementation of this
feedback instrument, the number of call reports remained approximately the same
but useful information generated by each sales report increased tenfold. Apparently, the availability of a well-designed and easy-to-use market information analysis

and feedback mechanism is crucial in the successful integration of the sales force into the MIS.

7.4.2 Sales Intelligence Dissemination and MIS Use

High-quality market information generated by the sales force will be of little value if it stays localized and is not disseminated across functional units to aid managerial decisions. Evidence shows that many companies fail to use market knowledge readily available to them. Nothing discourages the sales force from intelligence gathering more than the perception that management is not intentional in its use of the data acquired. Similarly, management can demotivate sales force participation in intelligence gathering if negative information is met with displeasure and denial (Falvey 1992). Therefore, it is important to understand (1) what constitutes the sales/marketing intelligence dissemination process and (2) what may facilitate or inhibit sales intelligence dissemination and market information use.

The marketing intelligence dissemination process is composed of two elements, namely dissemination frequency and dissemination formality. "Dissemination frequency" refers to the number of dissemination events between a sender and a receiver during a given period of time, whereas "dissemination formality" can be assessed by verifiability and spontaneity (Maltz and Kohli 1996). "Verifiability" refers to the documented or witnessed evidence that certain intelligence was transmitted by a sender to a receiver during a dissemination event (meetings with three or more participants; memos, etc.), and spontaneity is the extent to which the intelligence dissemination is pre-planned as opposed to informal. Therefore, dissemination formality can be measured with the ratio of formal dissemination events to the combined total of both formal and informal dissemination events in a given time period.

Two issues are of primary interest regarding the intelligence dissemination and usage: (1) what the optimal levels are of dissemination frequency and formality such that marketing intelligence usage can be maximized, and (2) what can organizations do to influence dissemination frequency and formality. Maltz and Kohli (1996) reported interesting non-linear effects of dissemination frequency and formality on marketing intelligence usage mediated through perceived intelligence quality by the receiver. Specifically, a threshold of dissemination frequency has to be reached before perceived intelligence quality starts to increase, which will then dip after reaching the peak. This S-shaped relationship suggests that too frequent intelligence dissemination will decrease a receiver's perceived intelligence quality just as much as too infrequent dissemination. The possible explanation is potential information overload by the intelligence receiver. When perceived intelligence quality is lower, the likelihood of the information receiver making use of such intelligence is significantly reduced. On the other hand, dissemination formality was found to have an inverted U-shaped relationship with perceived intelligence quality. That is, when the information dissemination is too informal or too formal, the perceived intelligence quality will be compromised. The optimal level of formality will call for a combination of formal dissemination complemented by informal dissemination such that maximum marketing intelligence usage can be encouraged (Maltz and Kohli 1996).

Given the propensity for the non-linear relationships between dissemination frequency/formality and perceived intelligence quality and usage, what factors influence the dissemination process? Maltz and Kohli's (1996) empirical evidence suggests that dissemination frequency can be increased through more joint customer visits, shorter inter-functional distances between the receiver and the sender, and relatively lower organizational standing of the sender. The implications for the sales organization are:

(1) Intelligence receivers and the salespeople should form cross-functional teams and jointly visit customers resulting in increased interactions and mutual understanding.

(2) Cross-functional teams composed of the salesperson and potential intelligence receivers and users need to be physically proximate.

(3) Salespeople (as opposed to managers), due to their lower ranking in the organizational hierarchy, are in better positions to disseminate intelligence frequently.

Moreover, structural changes in an organization (e.g. frequent modifications of company rules, personnel, and procedures) can increase dissemination formality beyond the optimal point (recall the inverted U shape). Increased information reporting formality in sales organizations often results in excessive formal documentation used to track internal and external changes. Last but not least, developing a trusting relationship between the salespeople and other participants in the intelligence dissemination process will motivate a higher degree of informal intelligence dissemination, thereby improving perceived intelligence quality, spontaneity in information acquisition, and intelligence usage.

To summarize, effectively integrating the sales force into the MIS hinges on the shaping of dissemination frequency and formality to optimal levels. Sales organizations should cultivate an internal environment that will not only encourage their sales force to generate high-quality marketing intelligence but also, perhaps more importantly, make good use of the marketing intelligence in formulating effective business strategies.

7.5 Integrated Marketing Intelligence and Sales Force Strategic Options

The power of an effective MIS lies in its ability to guide tactics and strategy formulation in response to opportunities and threats in the market. This section, therefore, zooms in on the link between sales force-generated marketing intelligence and sales force strategic options depicted in Figure 7.1.

7.5.1 Customer Relationship Strategy

As more and more sales organizations move toward building closer relationships with customers, the concept of relational exchange or relationship marketing has gained a solid footing in both practice and academia (e.g. Morgan and Hunt 1994). However, relationship marketing in which the sales force plays a critical role in seller–buyer interactions may not always be the most effective exchange approach because (1) some customers may prefer short-term/less complex transactions and (2) the resources required of the sales organization to accommodate a relational exchange may exceed the potential profit derived from the customer's lifetime value (CLV). A well-maintained MIS will make the sales force both a contributor to and a beneficiary of a system that helps allocate relational investments across individual customers. The marketing intelligence system can and, in many cases does, maintain separate profiles for each customer and inform the salespeople how to best allocate their time, develop customer-specific knowledge, and apply their selling expertise.

For instance, when a customer is identified with whom a long-term relationship is merited, salespeople with more suitable experience and sales expertise may be assigned/matched with this customer. Often similarity between salesperson and the customer is an important antecedent of relationship quality (Crosby, Evans, and Cowles 1990); hence, the matching of customer and salesperson culture, values, and beliefs can enhance the likelihood of successful buyer–seller relationship outcomes. Ongoing training becomes especially important to these relational salespeople as "skills and knowledge are the fundamental unit of exchange" in these relational contexts (Vargo and Lusch 2004: 3). More frequent communication and high-quality information exchange should be encouraged between the sales force and the relational customer because it helps deepen mutual understanding and trust in the long run. It is due to the idiosyncrasies of these buyer–seller relationships that continuous reporting of vital client data by the sales staff becomes particularly critical.

A high-quality MIS is useful in helping sales organizations identify customer groups according to their lifetime value/contribution to the company (CLV). Classifying customers into top-tier and bottom-tier groups based on their respective CLVs can inform strategic options with regard to the deployment of marketing resources inclusive of its sales force. CLV-based customer prioritization has proven to increase financial returns through operational efficiencies and revenue enhancements by increasing the likelihood of top-tier customer satisfaction (Homburg, Droll, and Totzek 2008). It was found that preferential treatment directed toward top-tier customers does not jeopardize the satisfaction level of bottom-tier customers, further reinforcing the value of focusing resources on top-tier clients. The successful implementation of such a customer prioritization strategy is dependent on the quality of customer information provided by the sales force (Homburg et al. 2008), suggesting that superior sales force performance is dependent on a highly effective MIS. To make the MIS a true strategic tool, the sales force must commit itself to intelligence gathering and reporting, especially customer-related information, to achieve superior return on their sales efforts.

An effective MIS will not only direct salespeople's effort toward more profitable relational customers, but it can also help the sales force build a much stronger relational tie with those customers through (1) sharing market knowledge and (2) proposing integrative solutions (Hunter and Perreault 2007). Sharing market knowledge refers to the extent to which salespeople impart their market-based expertise and knowledge (e.g. customer or competitor knowledge) with customers during their interactions. Proposing integrative solutions is how salespeople use market information and knowledge to construct a mutually beneficial solution to the selling and buying firms. For instance, a salesperson with little knowledge of a customer's cost structure may promise a higher-quality component to help reduce the customer's repair/maintenance rate. However, this more costly solution on the part of the seller's firm may not meet the customer's cost control objectives. With the customer cost structure information derived from the seller's MIS, the salesperson could propose a much more effective, less costly solution such as shorter order-cycle time. A salesperson who has superior customer knowledge and strategically deploys it in the provision of integrative solutions serves the best interests both of the customer and of the selling firm.

Personal selling is the only form of market communication that allows messages to be adapted to unique customer needs and preferences. Adaptive selling refers to "the altering of sales behaviors during a customer interaction or across customer interactions based on perceived information about the nature of the selling situation" (Spiro and Weitz 1990: 62). Adaptive selling is more likely practiced under the following situations: (1) salespeople encounter a wide variety of customers with different needs, (2) the typical sales situation involves large orders, and (3) the salespeople have the capability to adapt effectively. These situational characteristics require salespeople to have a well-developed knowledge structure of customer categories/types and appropriate selling strategies. While a salesperson's experience can guide his or her adaptive behavior, a well-maintained MIS can further enhance a salesperson's ability in identifying customers' distinct needs, and inform the salesperson of the customer's industry and other relevant information, as well as key differentiating features between the seller's company and its competitors' offerings, thereby helping to better articulate the seller's unique value proposition. While an experienced salesperson may engage in successful adaptive selling due to a highly developed knowledge structure, an advanced MIS can enhance the capability of less experienced salespeople to achieve selling success in settings that demand adaptations to customers' specific needs.

7.5.2 Key Account Management and Team Selling

Key account management and team selling are beginning to draw more attention from sales researchers. As the supply chain experiences consolidation among suppliers and customers, larger customers are gaining influence such that developing customer relationship strategies to serve and retain key accounts is of paramount importance to the selling organization. Companies are increasingly deploying cross-functional selling teams to serve these key accounts. The complexity of information flow and coordination between the selling team and the key account buying center gives rise to a pressing need for better knowledge management (Tanner, Ahearne, Leigh, Mason, and Moncrief 2005).

Key account management strategies that use teams usually operate with performance outcomes that have two levels of focus—interorganizational and intraorganizational. At the interorganizational level, sales teams are positioned to detect changes in the business environment. Teams gain knowledge about the customer and improve customer alignment strategy through continuous market-based learning (Jones et al. 2005). From a knowledge management perspective, these teams improve their understanding of key accounts through continuous interactions, recording these interactions and relying on this archival data for future client services improvement. Marketing intelligence in these team selling contexts must be stored in an MIS that will build firm-level memory and allow for easy retrieval. At the intraorganizational level, the cross-functional nature of the selling team requires the sales force to develop skills in the collection, analysis, and dissemination of information which can help direct the overall team as it adapts to changes and develops customer-focused strategies. The sales force in the cross-functional team environment must communicate valuable information in a timely fashion to team members while guarding against the risk of information loss or inaccuracies due to hasty actions. A well-functioning MIS can facilitate this process by regulating the appropriate levels of information dissemination frequency and formality (Maltz and Kohli 1996). Team-based selling outcomes depend heavily on relational learning. MIS can benefit the entire selling team in monitoring changing environments, setting feasible goals, and determining appropriate strategies in serving customers that have been identified as key accounts.

7.6 Managerial Implications and Conclusions

This section concludes by reflecting on the managerial implications associated with the sales force generated MIS, which corresponds to the last link depicted in Figure 7.1. Achieving sustainable differential advantages in today's business environment calls for unique capabilities that distinguish firms from one another. Among these asymmetric strategic advantages, the effective acquisition and dissemination of market information has been often noted as a particularly valuable means of achieving competitive superiority. Among firms that strive to distinguish themselves in the quality of their customer relationships, the sales force is particularly valuable as a source of information on customer needs and market responses to the selling firm's offerings.

Customer information content primarily focuses on the buyer's needs and wants with an eye toward customer lifetime value. In addition, the sales force is uniquely positioned to secure competitor data, as customers who often interact with competitors' representatives can provide first-hand information on pricing, promotion, distribution, and overall offering characteristics which otherwise may not be accessible. While there has been considerable argument for the need and value of incorporating the sales force into the marketing information system of the firm, the key to successfully engaging the sales force in MIS lies in securing timely market information, minimizing the cost of these non-selling distractions, capturing these data in an ethical fashion, and assuring high levels of information quality. The advantage of effective integration of the sales force in intelligence gathering has been documented to include: product development/modification, enhanced customer services, improved pricing, efficiencies in distribution, improvements in the content and allocation of promotional efforts, and more accurate sales forecasts to name but a few. These advantages are further highlighted when the firm is relying on the sales force for representation in international markets where the disadvantages of their remoteness can be partially addressed by improved market/field communication.

Challenges abound for management to achieve the desired type, frequency, and quality of market information from the field sales force. Of primary concern to both management and the field sales force is producing sales outcomes (e.g. sales volume—dollars/units, margin, new customer acquisition) that meet the firm's annual projections. Any distraction from sales-generating activity may be seen as non-productive and outside the salesperson's job description. How to build an effective motivational tool to obtain market information from the sales force in light of these perceived contradictions is no easy challenge. In addressing this issue management has used such tools as:

- instilling organizational cultures that commit to intelligence gathering and promote its value to the enterprise;
- using a sales control approach that measures and rewards/recognizes MIS engagement by the sales force; and
- integrating the role of securing marketing intelligence into the sales training and salesperson job description coupled with a suitable recognition and reward system—thereby resulting in market information acquisition that is less likely to be subject to salesperson role conflict and ambiguity. (These role stressors have often plagued individual perceptions of the value of salesperson–MIS behaviors.)

Another important issue regarding sales force participation in MIS is less focused on what it takes to secure valuable market information from the field sales force, but rather on how it is used. Unless marketing intelligence from the sales force is effectively incorporated into strategic (or for that matter tactical) decision-making, the firm receives little ROI on the marketing intelligence investment and the field sales force will perceive participation in information collection to be a senseless act. What then needs to take place to achieve more effective field market information integration? Information retrieval and formatting which has been, in part, the domain of the customer relationship management system (CRM) must provide management with effective ways to access information provided by the field sales force. These formal mechanisms, however, are only part of the answer. Occasional meetings, one-on-one or collectively among two or more salespeople and management, can serve to elicit observations, stimulate previously unarticulated impressions, and in general offer often richer data than more automated/structured systems. These informal means of acquiring data have been demonstrated to be a valuable way of securing quality market information (Maltz and Kohli 1996); however, assuring that this information is acquired, reported, and acted upon is the key.

The increased use of sales teams offers a valuable context for market data acquisition, interpretation, and integration. Data secured by team members may be subjected to periodic discussion, vetting and queries by team members. Spurious or otherwise inconsequential information can be quickly screened out, leaving more substantive market information to surface and encouraging constructive debate from multiple perspectives that leads to possible alternative courses of action. Management, in turn, receives information that is more than raw observations and disjointed data but rather robust interpretations of competitive strategies, customer reactions to the firm's offerings, and/or other key elements of valuable marketing intelligence. In the absence of cross-functional sales teams, periodic sales meetings where marketing intelligence is a regular part of the agenda may fall short of this multi-perspective scrutiny. The information that is ultimately passed along from this process is less likely to be encumbered by self-interest-seeking biases (often a criticism of field sales-provided market data) that diminish the perceived usefulness of these potentially valuable sources of marketing intelligence.

Tracking of marketing intelligence data also serves as a valuable tool for elevating quality and ultimately perceived usefulness. The impact of intelligence can and should play a role in how it is recognized in the MIS. Thoughtful attention to information that has a meaningful impact on firm performance is best achieved by finding mechanisms to record and credit valuable input into strategic management/marketing. One of the authors recalls sitting in on a Saturday morning meeting in Bentonville, Arkansas, where one of the assistant store managers at store X was recognized for having discovered that the same item (glassware) was being inventoried under two different stock-keeping unit IDs in the Wal-Mart store system. That single correction represented multiple thousands of dollars of savings. The tracking of the impact and related recognition (he was awarded employee of the week for the Wal-Mart system) is part of the Wal-Mart information acquisition culture.

No information system would be complete without recognition of the effort extended by the management team to cultivate and acquire timely and useful data. Promotion within the management hierarchy must capture sales manager performance in MIS design and supervision. As noted earlier, the balance between sales performance and information acquisition (among other selling tasks) is challenging. Often the bias is toward objective performance criteria which diminish the MIS and other qualitative metrics/roles. If a culture of market information acquisition is to be fostered and maintained, care must be taken when seeking objective performance that other biases are not introduced.

An area that has received modest attention in the practitioner literature but scant attention in the academic area is the notion of using the customer as a market information acquisition partner. Often the speed and salience of market information (whether customer- or competitor-specific) is more effectively obtained from the customer not by direct solicitation but by voluntarily offered information when it is pertinent to strategic planning. Cultivating relationships with customers (often salesperson-specific) can provide access to these unique information channels. Customer rewards come from perks provided by the salesperson, often in the form of market information salient to the customer's industry, that would otherwise be delayed or unobtainable, among other benefits. These partnerships are valuable parts of the information conduit between the firm and its marketplace made possible by a well-trained and market information-acculturated sales force. No single individual in the firm has his/her hand on the pulse of the customer and competitor marketplace quite like that of the sales staff. The role of salespeople as a data acquisition resource is further evident given the unique position they occupy in often long-term/complex relationships with their customers. MIS is dramatically enhanced by a fully engaged sales force that clearly sees the strategic value and rewards of their role in marketing information acquisition and dissemination. One might go so far as to suggest that sustainable differential advantage can be leveraged from a commitment to building and sustaining an effective sales force supported MIS.

REFERENCES

ANDERSON, E., and R. L. OLIVER (1987). "Perspectives on Behavior-Based Versus Outcome-Based Salesforce Control Systems," *Journal of Marketing* 51 (October), 76–88.

BEHRMAN, D. N., and W. D. PERREAULT, Jr. (1984). "A Role Stress Model of the Performance and Satisfaction of Industrial Salespersons," *Journal of Marketing* 48 (Fall), 9–21.

CAVUSGIL, S. T. (1985). "Guidelines for Export Market Research," *Business Horizons* 28.5, 27–33.

CHALLAGALLA, G. N., and T. A. SHERVANI (1996). "Dimensions and Types of Supervisory Control: Effects on Salesperson Performance and Satisfaction," *Journal of Marketing* 60 (January), 89–105.

CHANDY, R. K., and G. J. TELLIS (1998). "Organizing for Radical Product Innovation: The Overlooked Role of Willingness to Cannibalize," *Journal of Marketing Research* 35.4, 474–87.

CHONKO, L. B., J. F. TANNER, and E. R. SMITH (1991). "Selling and Sales Management in Action: The Sales Force's Role in International Marketing Research and Marketing Information Systems," *Journal of Personal Selling & Sales Management* 11.1, 69–79.

CHURCHILL, G. A., Jr., N. M. FORD, S. W. HARTLEY, and O. C. WALKER, Jr. (1985). "The Determinants of Salesperson Performance: A Meta-Analysis," *Journal of Marketing Research* 22 (May), 103–18.

COTTELEER, M., E. INDERRIEDEN, and F. LEE (2006). "Selling the Sales Force on Automation," *Harvard Business Review* (July/August), 18–22.

COX, D. F., and R. E. GOOD (1967). "How to Build a Marketing Information System," *Harvard Business Review* 45.3, 145–54.

CRAVENS, D. W., T. N. INGRAM, R. W. LaFORGE, and C. E. YOUNG (1993). "Behavior-Based and Outcome-Based Salesforce Control Systems," *Journal of Marketing* 57 (October), 47–59.

CRON, W. L., G. W. MARSHALL, J. SINGH, R. L. SPIRO, and H. SUJAN (2005). "Salesperson Selection, Training, and Development: Trends, Implications, and Research Opportunities," *Journal of Personal Selling & Sales Management* 25.2, 123–36.

CROSBY, L. A., K. R. EVANS, and D. COWLES (1990). "Relationship Quality in Services Selling: An Interpersonal Influence Perspective," *Journal of Marketing* 54 (July), 68–81.

DESHPANDÉ, R., and F. E. WEBSTER (1989). "Organizational Culture and Marketing: A Research Agenda," *Journal of Marketing* 53.1, 3–15.

EVANS, K. R., and J. L. SCHLACTER (1985). "The Role of Sales Managers and Salespeople in a Marketing Information System," *Journal of Personal Selling & Sales Management*, November, 49–58.

FALVEY, J. (1992). "Salesforce Management," *Sales & Marketing Management* 144.14, 10–12.

FESTERVAND, T. A., S. J. GROVE, and E. R. REIDENBACH (1988). "The Sales Force as a Marketing Intelligence System," *Journal of Business & Industrial Marketing* 3.1, 53–9.

GROVE, S. J., M. C. LaFORGE, P. A. KNOWLES, and L. H. STONE (1992). "Improving Sales Call Reporting for Better Management Decisions," *Journal of Consumer Marketing* 9.4, 65–72.

HARTLINE, M. D., and O. C. FERRELL (1996). "The Management of Customer-Contact Service Employees: An Empirical Investigation," *Journal of Marketing* 60 (October), 52–70.

HOMBURG, C., and C. PFLESSER (2000). "A Multiple-Layer Model of Market-Oriented Organizational Culture: Measurement Issues and Performance Outcomes," *Journal of Marketing Research* 37.4, 449–62.

——M. DROLL, and D. TOTZEK (2008). "Customer Prioritization: Does It Pay Off, and How Should It Be Implemented?" *Journal of Marketing* 72 (September), 110–30.

HUNTER, G. K., and W. D. PERREAULT, Jr. (2007). "Making Sales Technology Effective," *Journal of Marketing* 71 (January), 16–34.

JAWORSKI, B. J., and A. K. KOHLI (1993). "Market Orientation: Antecedents and Consequences," *Journal of Marketing* 57 (July), 53–70.

JONES, E., S. P. BROWN, A. A. ZOLTNERS, and B. A. WEITZ (2005). "The Changing Environment of Selling and Sales Management," *Journal of Personal Selling & Sales Management* 25.2, 105–11.

JUDSON, K., D. D. SCHOENBACHLER, G. L. GORDON, R. E. RIDNOUR, and D. C. WEILBAKER (2006). "The New Product Development Process: Let the Voice of the Salesperson be Heard," *Journal of Product & Brand Management* 15.3, 194–202.

KEENAN, W. (1994). "How GE Stays on Top of Its Markets," *Sales & Marketing Management* 146.8, 61.

KOHLI, A. K., B. J. JAWORSKI, and A. KUMAR (1993). "MARKOR: A Measure of Market Orientation," *Journal of Marketing Research* 30 (November), 467–77.

LE MEUNIER-FitzHUGH, K., and N. F. PIERCY (2006). "Integrating Marketing Intelligence Sources: Reconsidering the Role of the Salesforce," *International Journal of Market Research* 48.6, 699–716.

LIGOS, M. J. (1997). "Leading Edge: The News Digest for Sales and Marketing Executives," *Sales & Marketing Management* (June), 13.

MAKADOK, R., and J. B. BARNEY (2001). "Strategic Factor Market Intelligence: An Application of Information Economics to Strategy Formulation and Competitor Intelligence," *Management Science* 47.12, 1638.

MALTZ, E., and A. K. KOHLI (1996). "Market Intelligence Dissemination Across Functional Boundaries," *Journal of Marketing Research* 33 (February), 47–61.

MELLOW, C. (1989). "The Best Source of Competitive Intelligence," *Sales & Marketing Management* 141.15, 24–8.

Miao, C. F., and K. R. Evans (2007). "The Impact of Salesperson Motivation on Role Perceptions and Job Performance: A Cognitive and Affective Perspective," *Journal of Personal Selling & Sales Management* 27 (Winter), 89–101.

——and S. Zou (2007). "The Role of Salesperson Motivation in Sales Control Systems: Intrinsic and Extrinsic Motivation Revisited," *Journal of Business Research* 60, 417–25.

Moon, M. A., and J. T. Mentzer (1999). "Improving Salesforce Forecasting," *Journal of Business Forecasting Methods & Systems* 18.2, 7–12.

Morgan, R. M., and S. D. Hunt (1994). "The Commitment-Trust Theory of Relationship Marketing," *Journal of Marketing* 58 (July), 20–38.

Narver, J. C., and S. F. Slater (1990). "The Effect of a Market Orientation on Business Profitability," *Journal of Marketing* 54 (October), 20–35.

——(1998). "Additional Thoughts on the Measurement of Market Orientation: A Comment on Deshpande and Farley," *Journal of Market-Focused Management* 2.3, 233–6.

Neuborne, E. (2003). "Know Thy Enemy," *Sales & Marketing Management* (January), 29–33.

Oliver, R. L., and E. Anderson (1994). "An Empirical Test of the Consequences of Behavior- and Outcome-Based Sales Control Systems," *Journal of Marketing* 58 (October), 53–67.

Osborne, R. (2002). "New Product Development: Lesser Royals," *Industry Week* (April): http://www.industryweek.com/articles/new_product_development_–_lesser_royals_1049.aspx

Palmatier, R. W. (2008). "Interfirm Relational Drivers of Customer Value," *Journal of Marketing* 72.4, 76–89.

——C. F. Miao, and E. Fang (2007). "Sales Channel Integration after Mergers and Acquisitions: A Methodological Approach for Avoiding Common Pitfalls," *Industrial Marketing Management* 36.5, 589–603.

Peter, J. P., and J. H. Donnelly (2007). *Marketing Management: Knowledge and Skills*, 8th edn., New York: McGraw-Hill.

Pinkerton, R. L. (1969). "How to Develop a Marketing Intelligence System," *Industrial Marketing*, April, 41–4.

Rottenberger, K. (1991). "Is Competitor Intelligence Important to Your Sales and Marketing Efforts?" *Sales & Marketing Management*, September, 24–5.

Singh, J. (1998). "Striking a Balance in Boundary-Spanning Positions: An Investigation of Some Unconventional Influences of Role Stressors and Job Characteristics on Job Outcomes of Salespeople," *Journal of Marketing* 62 (July), 69–86.

Sivades, E., and F. R. Dwyer (2000). "An Examination of Organizational Factors Influencing New Product Success in Internal and Alliance-Based Processes," *Journal of Marketing* 64.1, 31–49.

Smaros, J., and M. Hellstrom (2004). "Using the Assortment Forecasting Method to Enable Sales Force Involvement in Forecasting: A Case Study," *International Journal of Physical Distribution & Logistics Management* 34.1–2, 140–57.

Smith, G. E., and T. T. Nagle (1994). "Financial Analysis for Profit-Driven Pricing," *Sloan Management Review* 35.3, 71–84.

Spiro, R. L., and B. A. Weitz (1990). "Adaptive Selling: Conceptualization, Measurement, and Nomological Validity," *Journal of Marketing Research* 27 (February), 61–9.

TANNER, J. F., M. AHEARNE, T. W. LEIGH, C. H. MASON, and W. C. MONCRIEF (2005). "CRM in Sales-Intensive Organizations: A Review and Future Directions," *Journal of Personal Selling & Sales Management* 25.2, 169–80.

TEAS, R. K. (1983). "Supervisory Behavior, Role Stress, and the Job Satisfaction of Industrial Salespeople," *Journal of Marketing Research* 20.1, 84–91.

THIETART, R. A., and R. VIVAS (1981). "Strategic Intelligence Activity: The Management of the Sales Force as a Source of Strategic Information," *Strategic Management Journal* 2, 15–25.

VARGO, S. L., and R. F. LUSCH (2004). "Evolving to a New Dominant Logic for Marketing," *Journal of Marketing* 68 (January), 1–17.

VROOM, V. H. (1964). *Work and Motivation*, New York: Wiley.

WEBSTER, F. E. (1965). "The Industrial Salesman as a Source of Market Information," *Business Horizons* (Spring), 77–82.

WOTRUBA, THOMAS R., and MICHAEL L. THURLOW (1976). "Sales-Force Participation in Quota Setting and Sales Forecasting," *Journal of Marketing*, 40.2, 11–16.

CHAPTER 8

MANAGEMENT OF A CONTRACTED SALES FORCE (MANUFACTURER REPRESENTATIVES)

THOMAS E. DECARLO

8.1 INTRODUCTION

A critical issue facing companies today is how to effectively and efficiently distribute and sell products in the marketplace. The tough competitive landscape is forcing managers to dissect every aspect of their operations in an attempt to improve productivity, reduce costs, and, at the same time, meet customer demand. Increasingly, many organizations are realizing that the distribution channel not only represents an untapped opportunity for major efficiency gains (Narus and Anderson 1996) but, if properly configured, can enhance a company's ability to respond to customer needs in a cost-effective manner. The same is true with respect to decisions about outsourcing a company's field sales force. For many business-to-business firms, the field sales force is the primary window to the market and the disseminator of market information. As a result, strategic decisions about whether the selling function should be performed using a direct company sales force, an outsourced partner, or some combination will likely have a direct impact on a firm's competitive advantage.

This chapter deals with the "rent" option of sales force management (i.e. manufacturer reps as opposed to an in-house sales force). Gaining an understanding of the important decision criteria as to when to outsource the sales force and how to manage the outsourced sales organization relationship is an important prerequisite for devising marketing strategies aimed at enhancing a firm's sales performance. To that end, this chapter will begin with a review of the factors affecting the decision to outsource the sales force, in an attempt to answer questions such as: Is it possible to build committed relationships between a manufacturer (principal) and independent rep agents (reps)? If so, how is such commitment built? What, if any, benefits are realized in such relationships? In doing so, I will evaluate the trade off between using a "market-" based governance typically associated with using reps as compared with the "hierarchical" governance structure of an in-house sales force (Williamson 1985). In addition to the governance issues associated with interfirm relationships (e.g. Wathne and Heide 2000), the chapter will consider how reps contribute to market coverage efficiencies and selling effectiveness (Ross, Dalsace, and Anderson 2005).

The chapter will also identify some unique challenges in maintaining the principal–rep relationship. In particular, managing independent reps requires a different set of management competencies from those used in leading a conventional in-house sales force. For example, principal managers are exhorted to develop firm-level economic incentives and relationship ties to motivate reps to increase sales volume, profits, and market share. In developing these different perspectives, the chapter will review existing literature regarding such decisions and offer practical tools for maximizing the return on the rep relationship. Before we address these differences, however, I begin our discussion with a definition of a manufacturer rep and briefly illustrate how reps differ from an in-house sales force.

8.1.1 What Is a Manufacturer Representative?

A manufacturer representative provides selling services for its principals' goods and services on a contractual basis. While the typical principal–rep contract is relatively short-term (two years or less) and cancellable by either party, reps typically represent their principals for extended periods. Unlike a distributor, the business model for reps is unique in that they do not take title of the product, do not set their own prices, and typically do not handle merchandise. They are paid by commission on realized sales, and market a portfolio of complementary products with each brand representing a non-competing category from a variety of suppliers. An important aspect of reps' marketplace value to manufacturers is their deep contextual knowledge of a particular regional market and customer base. That is, they know the buyers and distributors in their regional markets, call on them regularly, and have developed a high level of trust and credibility with them over time.

Med Tech, Inc., for example, is a manufacturer's rep for medical products. The primary advantage of Med Tech is its ability to leverage its multiple product lines to completely outfit a doctor's office. As pointed out by Mark Hughes, sales director of Med Tech, "we have a greater opportunity to influence a variety of buying decisions because of our broad product line and our (in-supplier) status with the physician." For example, a typical sales call might require the salesperson to lead with a GE scanner, but because of Med Tech's multiple product lines, the salesperson can ask questions about other needs. The value to the customer is the time efficiencies gained by one-stop shopping which, in turn, promotes a more consultative relationship. According to Mark Hughes, "a rep may be able to sell two or three different products in a new account because the physicians and office staff understand the time efficiencies associated with working with one rep instead of multiple salespeople." The medical product distributors also recognize and support these efficiencies. As a result, Med Tech reps are able to quickly develop trust and credibility as a *solutions* provider.

Despite recognizing the benefits of outsourcing the sales force over 30 years ago (Shapiro 1977), firms have generally overlooked this channel when compared to the number of businesses that have outsourced functions such as payroll, human resources, or transportation services. In fact, rep firms have historically constituted a relatively small percentage (approximately 10 percent) of business-to-business sales volume. However, there has been a recent growth trend (of approximately 20 percent per year) of companies who have started using rep firms (Gschwandtner 2008). One reason for the recent surge can be attributed to the fact that many firms have seen the costs associated with developing and managing a direct sales force continue to increase over the recent years, to as much as 40 percent of revenue (Ross et al. 2005). While costs are certainly an important input into the "make or buy" sales force decision, there are a number of other unique advantages to the manufacturer rep model. These will be discussed next.

8.1.2 Principal Benefits of the Manufacturer Rep Model

As shown in Table 8.1, outsourcing the sales function provides a number of advantages to a manufacturer (see Anderson and Trinkle 2005 for more on the benefits of the rep selling model). Perhaps the most overlooked advantage is the staying power of rep firms. Such firms are designed for one function—selling. Top-performing reps are driven to develop long-term relationships at all organizational levels in a given geography in order to maintain their strategic advantage (Anderson and Trinkle 2005). Failure to leverage these relationships into sales will result in a bankrupt rep firm, since there is no other way to generate resources. Thus, rep firms place a premium on hiring and developing their top salespeople for the long term. Direct salespeople, on the other hand, have a tendency to perceive sales as the first stop in their career. A mindset of being promoted to better territories, better accounts, or out

Table 8.1 Benefits of Manufacturer Reps

Reps are Stable	Reps are small business enterprises entrenched in a local or regional market through their strong relationships developed over time.
Reps are Market Focused	Reps typically work on 100% commissions and only succeed when they convert customer problems into sales. As a result, they are specialists in closing sales and running an efficient and effective sales infrastructure.
Reps are Agile	Top performing reps have adapted to changing marketplace shifts in order to survive. Manufacturers reap the benefits of such marketplace knowledge.
Reps Use Portfolio Selling	Relative to selling one product line, a rep's portfolio-selling capabilities provide greater economies of scope by leveraging product synergies with a variety of customers.
Reps Provide Greater Scale	Because reps market a full line of noncompeting products and are able to aggregate demand, they can increase the size of their sales force beyond that of a single line manufacturer; hence providing greater market coverage.
Reps Reduce Risk	Reps finance the sales effort by getting paid only after a sale is completed; thus they provide a float of cash between when the sale is made and thirty days after shipment. Reps also reduce a principal's opportunity cost of the time spent on a lost sale.

of sales altogether is more typical of the direct sales career track. As a result, the relationship between the direct salesperson and customer becomes disconnected when a new salesperson enters a territory and needs to be "retrained" by the customer.

Because rep firms are so well entrenched in a particular geographic region, the use of this channel has also been used by smaller firms as a cost-effective way to reach international markets. Although the ongoing reduction of trade barriers, innovations in logistics and transportation, and advances in communication technologies (e.g. Internet) continue to erode the barrier between suppliers and prospective customers in foreign markets, significant cultural barriers remain. Local rep firms provide a channel for immediate growth because of the ability to leverage existing relationships that they have developed in their home country markets. SiliconSystems, Inc., for example, attributes its recent ascent as a world leader in advanced storage technology to its use of internationally based manufacturer's reps. Headquartered in California, SiliconSystems selected the rep model for its foreign market entry strategy "based on their [the reps'] superior knowledge and long-standing relationships in the enterprise system OEM and embedded systems market" ("Silicon Systems . . ." 2009). Since signing a number of Europe's leading rep firms, SiliconSystems has experienced tremendous sales growth in the region and has quickly become the preferred solid-state storage system by European enterprise system OEMs.

Another key advantage of reps is their strategic focus on the sales process and an ability to align customer needs and principal capabilities. Strategic marketing theory suggests that market-oriented firms operationalize business strategies by providing guidelines that influence customers in a manner that corresponds with organizational goals (Moorman and Rust 1999, Noble, Sinha, and Kumar 2002, Walker and Ruekert 1987). When a firm's strategy is successfully aligned with customer needs and how it treats those customers, significant performance results will likely accrue (e.g. Day and Wensley 1988, Moorman and Rust 1999, Noble, Sinha, and Kumar 2002, White, Varadarajan, and Dacin 2003). Indeed, Porter (1991: 108) underscores this by noting: "Resources are only meaningful in the context of performing certain activities to achieve certain competitive advantages." Given that a rep firm's sole focus is on leveraging established relationships to satisfy customer needs, principals have the opportunity to reap the benefits of such marketplace knowledge with a relatively low cost/sales ratio (Anderson and Trinkle 2005). According to Dan Maloy of the Maloy Group, "Because reps constantly work on gaining a deep understanding of their customer needs, they are uniquely capable in aligning those needs with manufacturer capabilities. For manufacturers, having such a fanatical focus on the customer, through the rep, is invaluable in today's competitive marketplace."

The factors affecting a rep's market focus (e.g. commission-based, stability) also create an agile organization capable of adapting to market swings. Direct sales forces, on the other hand, are typically less agile due to their fixed cost structures. Thus, reps are able to create relatively quicker returns under a variety of market conditions. As discussed earlier, reps are also uniquely qualified to propose an assortment of complementary, non-competing products to solve customer problems. Such portfolio-selling capabilities provide greater economies of scope than a typical direct sales force that may be constrained by the manufacturer's product line. Similarly, portfolio selling provides reps with greater selling opportunities to reach more types of customers, which leads to increases in the scale of its selling operations.

Finally, reps can reduce the risk associated with a direct sales force. Because the reps get paid a commission only after the sales has been completed and the product shipped, the risk of financing a nonproductive sales force is removed. According to Bob Jones, former manufacturer rep for Intel products, "The ability to consistently maintain the cost of sales at a known percentage of your revenue is one of the greatest strengths, along with the ability to share a line card to leveraging products/ services and business contacts that are synergistic with your product or service. It also increases your strength in the distribution channel" (Jones 2005). In addition to the value reps offer to manufacturers, there are similar benefits accrued to customers. These will be discussed next.

8.1.3 Customer Benefits of a Manufacturer Rep

Manufacturer reps provide a number of customer advantages. From a solutions-selling perspective, customers look to salespeople for insights and suggestions to solve their problems (e.g. Weitz and Bradford 1999). They expect sales personnel to be able to diagnose and discern implicit needs and offer wise counsel. In this process, a salesperson learns about, and reacts to, the goals, needs, preferences, and sales potential of the prospect. Thus, the added customer value of a rep, relative to a direct salesperson, is the ability to provide customers economies of scope by exploiting the bundle of benefits of all the products in its line card. Multi-line or portfolio selling affords the rep more time per call by allowing him or her to ask additional questions without being perceived as wasting the customers' time. As a result, reps can learn more about a customer's current and future needs, which in turn may reduce a customer's transaction costs by increasing efficiencies in purchasing. In the same way, such interactions provide an opportunity to enhance the salesperson's problem-solving and persuasiveness by aggregating demand for a variety of principals. This, in turn, affords rep firms the opportunity to reach operating efficiencies with a larger sales force, i.e. economies of scope leading to economies of scale (Anderson and Trinkle 2005). Interestingly, transaction cost analysis scholars have recognized that pooling of demand is an important reason why outsourcing is more efficient than vertical integration (Williamson 1996).

It is important to note, however, that reps are limited in their ability to develop economies of scope. Recall that reps carry one brand in each product category. While this provides an assortment of products, a rep's depth of assortment is limited. On the one hand, the lack of depth means that the rep is likely to become more interdependent with the principal in regard to product knowledge and recent product updates. On the other hand, the rep will have no contingency offering if the customer has specific needs that are better served by a competitor's product.

Thus far, the arguments presented in favor of the manufacturer rep have not considered the contingencies that might affect the decision to use a rep model of selling. Research studies that have investigated the question of how and under what conditions the rep model can enhance the sales function have been explored through the lens of transaction cost analysis. The next section will begin with a brief review of transaction cost analysis and then discuss relevant findings associated with the outsourced sales function.

8.2 FACTORS AFFECTING THE DECISION TO OUTSOURCE THE SALES FORCE

8.2.1 Transaction Cost Analysis

As noted above, the decision to outsource some or all of a principal's sales function remains a critical strategic decision. Inherent in this decision is the trade off between using a "market-" based governance typically associated with using reps as compared with the "hierarchical" governance structure of an in-house sales force (Williamson 1985). One commonly used theory to frame such decisions is transaction cost analysis (TCA).[1] Transaction cost analysis (Williamson 1975, 1985) provides an appealing framework for examining the "make or buy" sales force decision because it identifies a set of theoretical constructs for determining the appropriate governance mechanism for economic activities. Indeed, much of the empirical research dealing with the manufacturer–rep relationship has been conducted using the TCA framework. Prior to reviewing these studies, however, I will provide a brief discussion of the TCA framework.

The fundamental underpinnings of TCA deal with transaction costs (actual and opportunity costs under different governance structures) rather than production costs. It posits that markets and firms are alternative governance structures that differ in their transaction costs. In the manufacturer rep context, for example, the "costs of running the system" include ex ante costs such as drafting and negotiating rep contracts and ex post costs such as monitoring rep performance and enforcing contracts, whereas a direct sales force includes costs such as hiring costs, salary, incentives, selling expenses, and management oversight. According to the basic tenets of TCA, if the costs for initiating and managing a rep channel are low (e.g. interviewing process, consulting fees, legal costs, marketing and training support), then firms will favor the market governance approach (i.e. use manufacturer reps). If these costs are higher than those associated with the in-house sales force, then firms will favor a direct sales force.

Extending the basic TCA framework, Williamson (1975, 1985, 1996), suggests that transaction costs include not only the direct costs of managing relationships but also the possible opportunity costs of making inferior governance decisions. TCA assumes that decision-makers intend to act rationally, but are naturally constrained in their capabilities (i.e. bounded rationality) to make such decisions. Moreover, these behavioral constraints will be affected by the uncertainty of the environment in which the circumstances cannot be specified ex ante (i.e. environmental uncertainty and asset specificity) and/or when performance is not easily verified ex post (i.e. behavioral uncertainty). The behavioral assumptions and environmental uncertainty characteristics can independently and/or in combination affect managerial decision-making. For example, a manufacturer may respond to a new competitive product by developing its own version (i.e. environmental uncertainty). In doing so, the manufacturer would need to modify the contract with its reps to include the new product. It is quite possible that the manufacturer may also need to assume considerable transaction costs associated with preparing for the contract renegotiation process. Alternatively, the manufacturer may have difficulty determining whether its reps are providing customers with the necessary services (i.e. behavioral uncertainty) as reorders from current customers have been dropping. As a result, adequately monitoring rep behaviors may require incurring substantial information-gathering and processing costs.

In addition to these key assumptions, Williamson (1985) argues that some decision-makers tend to act in their own self-interest whenever this is profitable. Opportunistic behavior, according to Williamson (1985: 47), is "self-interest seeking with guile," and includes a wide-ranging variety of behaviors from outright lying and cheating to more subtle forms of deceit such as violating agreements. While there has been some attempt to develop a framework of opportunistic behaviors along with a corresponding governance strategy (see Wathne and Heide 2000), much work is needed because of the considerable resources needed to control and monitor such behaviors (Heide, Wathne, and Rokkan 2007). Opportunistic behaviors are particularly damaging in situations where the specific assets invested in a particular relationship are unique and have limited value outside the confines of the two companies. Referring to the previous example, assume that the executives of a manufacturer's rep organization know that it would be difficult for the manufacturer to replace the rep firm. The incumbent rep can exploit the situation opportunistically by demanding additional support (e.g. increased marketing and advertising dollars) and other concessions from the manufacturer. In this case, the effect of the market competition no longer serves as a restraint against opportunism (i.e. specific asset).[2]

Against this background, relevant research findings dealing with the decision for implementing a rep sales strategy will be presented next.

8.2.2 When to Use Manufacturer's Reps: The Make vs. Buy Decision

The applicability of TCA in the decision to outsource the sales function decision is well established. In a series of studies, Anderson and colleagues (e.g. Anderson 1985, Anderson and Schmittlein 1984, Weiss and Anderson 1992) use TCA to identify factors that influence the "make or buy" decision. Indeed, there are a number of arguments that justify forgoing a rep strategy for a direct sales force. Anderson (1985), for example, found that the decision to use direct sales was positively associated with complex, hard-to-learn products (e.g. requiring idiosyncratic salesperson skills). Idiosyncratic products or sales processes typically require firms to invest significant resources in training and educating a field sales force. Under these conditions, the costs associated with training and developing the sales force were economically justifiable under the direct sales model. It is interesting to note, however, that idiosyncratic products and processes are not as common as one might think. Anderson and Trinkle (2005) argue that for a firm to truly have an idiosyncratic product, the knowledge needed to sell one brand cannot be redeployed to sell a competitive brand. CT scanners, for example, are highly technical products, but since most CT scanners use similar basic technology, the product knowledge needed to sell such equipment would not be considered idiosyncratic. Thus, product knowledge that is relatively easy to redeploy to a competitive brand is not considered idiosyncratic.

A vertically integrated sales force is also recommended when sales performance is ambiguous (i.e. difficult to evaluate). The TCA model would suggest that the decision to use a direct sales force (and avoid the rep model) is an attempt to reduce "internal uncertainty" (Williamson 1985) by gathering information about the activities of their salespeople. An ambiguous performance condition is one in which the manufacturer cannot specify with confidence how well a salesperson is performing. Examples include long, complex sales cycles with many people involved in the selling and buying process; team selling, where it is difficult to assign specific roles; missionary selling, where salespeople are not responsible for order taking (e.g. pharmaceutical and textbook reps); and sales positions with a high demand for non-selling activities by the salesperson. Firms with idiosyncratic internal processes such as unwritten, nonstandard rules or proprietary "language" may also realize a lower cost/sales ratio by vertically integrating the sales force (Anderson and Trinkle 2005).

Despite the apparent advantages to reducing internal uncertainty with a direct sales force, there are a number of factors that justify consideration for the rep sales model. In addition to the benefits of the rep model discussed in the previous section, a rep's value proposition can be summarized in terms of the knowledge advantages gained between customer needs and manufacturer capabilities. In other words, recognizing situations where customer needs and manufacturer capabilities match up is an important part of the rep's marketplace value. Leveraging this type of expertise often requires pledges from both the rep and principal (Anderson and Weitz 1992, Ross, Anderson, and Weitz 1997), which in turn creates idiosyncratic marketplace knowledge between the firms. As illustrated in Figure 8.1, a rep's idiosyncratic knowledge investments in the principal's customers, products, and company are important drivers of a principal's trust and commitment of the rep–principal relationship. For example, when a rep learns about a customer's unique application of a particular product, the customer intelligence, understanding, and insights gleaned from the interactions are not readily transferable and thus become an idiosyncratic investment. Investments of this nature help solidify the relationship between the principal and rep.

Similarly, a rep's investment of time and energy to learn about the principal's factory personnel, management, and even supplier base is another illustration of the non-transferable knowledge base that is often used to create strong principal–rep relationships. Consistent with this rationale, Weiss and Anderson (1992) found that principal dissatisfaction with reps is significantly reduced when reps make the effort to learn the manufacturer's idiosyncrasies. In addition, the more the reps cultivate loyalty among customers for the principal's products, the greater the principal's satisfaction with the relationship. The study also found that principals

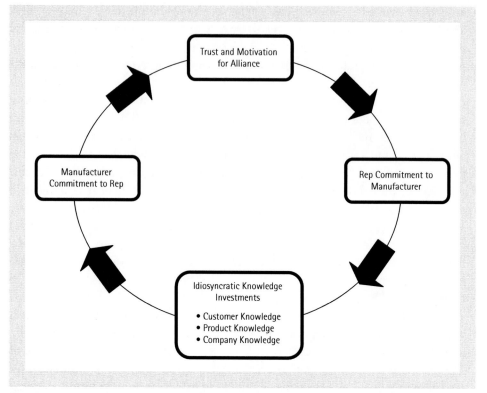

Fig. 8.1. Idiosyncratic Investment Model of the Manufacturer–Rep Relationship

will avoid converting from reps to a direct sales force when there are perceptions of high switching costs. Thus, reps who invest in transaction-specific factors, such as knowledge of the principal and its customers, not only increase principal satisfaction with the rep but also reduce the risk of being replaced by a direct sales force.

In a similar study, Anderson and Weitz (1992) investigated whether such idiosyncratic investments create and sustain commitment in a channel relationship. Their findings indicate that manufacturers and distributors signal their commitment toward each other, most notably in the form of additional idiosyncratic investments and grants of exclusivity. When distributors recognize that a manufacturer has made non-redeployable investments in the relationship, they perceive the manufacturer to be more committed to the relationship. From a transaction cost perspective, signaling pledges between two channel partners appears to reduce the chance of either party abandoning the relationship due to the increased exit barriers in the form of idiosyncratic investments.

A common theme across both studies is the importance of pledges in creating durable relationships. However, these unique investments also tie each partner to the other, and increase the pledger's exposure to opportunistic behaviors by the other party. While this seems to be a rather precarious position for a firm to be in, there is evidence suggesting that, under certain conditions, such an investment increases the motivation to maintain the relationship. Indeed, Jap (1999) argues that idiosyncratic investments are enablers of strategic outcomes instead of a transaction cost to be minimized. Among the findings reported, Jap (1999) notes that dynamic business environments appear to motivate both parties to make idiosyncratic investments in an effort to create a closer relationship to more effectively deal with environmental change. Termination of the relationship would result in significant losses for both parties, and the threat of losing the pledge appears to motivate commitment to the relationship and reduce opportunistic behaviors. Moreover, Jap (1999) reports that interpersonal trust between the two parties facilitates coordination efforts and idiosyncratic investments, but only if the investments are considered balanced by each party. Perceived asymmetry in the commitment to the relationship can lead to an increase in conflict and a decrease in profits (Ross et al. 1997). In total, these findings underscore the reciprocal nature the rep–principal relationship.

A rep's motivation to commit to a manufacturer, however, can be tenuous, particularly when the rep perceives greater power in the relationship (e.g. Anderson and Narus 1984, Dutta, Bergen, Heide, and John 1995, Frazier 1983). In particular, Dutta et al. (1995) posit that a rep-only channel is best governed using the standard market safeguard of competition (i.e. termination), but that this safeguard is undermined when the firm is locked in with an incumbent rep. They argue that one way to mitigate the potential power struggle is to introduce house accounts (i.e. specific accounts where a direct sales force manages the customer instead of the rep). Introducing house accounts in the rep's territory restores the credibility of the termination safeguard. In addition, house accounts provide performance benchmarks that permit a better assessment of the rep's performance. Essentially, house accounts re-establish termination as a credible sanction by making it clear to the rep that the manufacturer is in a better position to replace the rep if necessary. It is not suggested that the manufacturer actually intends to terminate the rep. Rather, house accounts are a safeguard that allows the firm to continue enjoying the cost and motivational benefits of the rep channel. In essence, Dutta et al. (1995) conclude that one go-to-market channel (i.e. house accounts) is needed to effectively use the other (desired) rep go-to-market channel.

8.2.3 Market Considerations Affecting the Use of Manufacturer Reps

In addition to the control issue, manufacturers tend to use the direct sales force–rep model hybrid channel strategy more frequently under specific market conditions. For example, in a study of large multinational firms, Sa Vinhas and Anderson (2005) report that firms use the hybrid strategy more frequently under higher market growth conditions. They argue that the two sales channels will be more likely to find new customers and/or better satisfy current customers when the market is growing as compared to stagnating or declining markets. Their findings also indicate that hybrid sales forces are used less when buyers band together to buy as a group. It appears that under these conditions, the balance of power tips toward buyers and they use their power to pit one sales channel against another. Finally, hybrid sales strategies were used more often in markets comprising heterogeneous customer segments that exhibit variability in purchase behaviors.

To successfully execute such a hybrid sales strategy, the rep firm should perceive the dual channel as non-threatening to the long-term viability of the relationship. While there are a number of ways to achieve a collaborative relationship, evidence suggests that the two sales channels should be developed around specific, non-competing sales roles and for reasons other than safeguarding power. Sa Vinhas and Anderson (2005) also provided evidence that the rep and principal will engage in less destructive behaviors the more the two channels have differentiated offers and the more the manufacturer adopts a system that clarifies order (i.e. sales) ownership. Otherwise, if one channel is perceived as a threat, destructive behaviors between the two channel forms may occur which can lead to serious channel conflict and ultimately to decreased performance in the entire channel system (Moriarty and Moran 1990).

Even if the two channels do not perceive each other as a threat, it is difficult, if not impossible, for manufacturers to prevent the channels from competing with each other. This is due to the fact that both channel types will likely contact the same customer or, more importantly, because the customer will contact both channels because of a perception that they are in competition against each other. When the rep and the direct salesperson interact with the same customer for a given order, it is frequently difficult to clearly establish which channel member generated the sale. In such cases, the issue of which channel member to reward becomes a relevant question. Indeed, the perceived fairness of the reward system plays a critical role in motivating the two channels to put forth selling effort of the manufacturer's product line. Under such conditions, many firms use a double compensation program where both the direct sales force and rep receive a commission regardless of which channel made the sale. However, recent research suggests that double compensation occurs more frequently when customers are larger, when there are fewer customers, when behavioral uncertainty is higher, and when there are more integrated supply contracts with distribution channels (Sa Vinhas and Anderson 2008). Prior to adopting a double compensation program, however, a cost–benefit analysis is recommended that considers factors such as the costs of gathering information and monitoring both sales channels, the potential for free riding between the two channel types, and the strategic need to maintain a high selling effort in both channels.

Sa Vinhas and Anderson's (2005, 2008) research is notable, given that it represents an initial investigation into the influence that market characteristics and compensation exert on managing an effective hybrid sales strategy. However, the importance of the general topic of hybrid personal selling channels suggests that further work exploring questions such as to why some firms double compensate their channel members is needed. Gaining a richer understanding of potential moderating factors (e.g. relative power of the manufacturer vs. the rep) underlying such decisions would be a logical next step for future theory development.

8.2.4 Considerations in Motivating and Compensating Reps

Principals are faced with a number of unique management challenges as compared to those faced with captive or in-house salespeople. Unlike managing and leading an in-house sales force, a principal is charged with developing and maintaining enterprise-to-enterprise management systems with their rep firms. Thus, an important aspect of managing the rep channel is to continuously develop firm-level economic incentives and emotional ties designed to improve the principal–rep relationship that should, in turn, improve the manufacturer's sales volume, profits, and market share for its particular product line (e.g. Vazquez, Iglesias, and Alvarez-Gonzalez 2005). Unfortunately, this task remains a challenge for many firms (e.g. Jap 1999, Jap and Anderson 2003, Wathne and Heide 2004).

Recent work dealing with how conflict arises between manufacturers and re-sellers can offer insight into the potential factors affecting the principal–rep relationship. Although conflict can arise from many sources, research has identified fundamental differences in the basic operating models between a supplier and a reseller firm which may contribute to the difficulties in these relationships (Marks, Horan, and Emerson 2006). Based on a content analysis of their interviews of 154 channel managers, Marks and his colleagues (2006) conclude that the lack of alignment between a supplier and reseller can be attributed to two consistent themes of miscommunication. The authors dub these two themes *the law of legitimate cross-purposes* and *the law of perpetual change*.

The law of legitimate cross-purposes refers to the notion that supplier firms and reseller firms rely upon different profit models that are sometimes at odds with one another. Specifically, supplier firms tend to operate using the economies of scale model where profits are generated from producing and shipping large quantities of a limited number of products. Ideally, manufacturers would like their reseller partners to direct their undivided attention to selling large quantities of the suppliers' products to all prospective customer firms. Rep firms, on the other hand, profit through economies of scope from selling unique bundles or solutions comprising small quantities of a wide variety of products and services to their customers. Reps sell a portfolio of products from numerous supplier firms that are often perceived by their customers as high-value, customized bundles or solutions, and because of their regular customer interaction, they perceive themselves as truly understanding customer needs. Thus, pressure to sell larger quantities from a manufacturer is likely to be met with resistance.

The law of perpetual change operates on the principle of environmental dynamism (Jap 1999) where changes in the market may dramatically and unexpectedly alter the goals and resources of channel partners. As complementary resources and mutual self-interest start to diverge, the research findings of Marks et al. (2006) suggest there will inevitably be counterproductive claims and actions that threaten the continued prosperity of a principal-reseller relationship. For example, if a manufacturer develops a new product that directly competes with a product its rep firm currently markets from one of its other alliances, the rep firm will likely experience higher transaction costs in formulating a decision as to which product to endorse. Such changes in the relationship may lead to lower idiosyncratic investments and coordination problems between the supplier and reseller (e.g. Jap 1999). Alternatively, a manufacturer may see its sales volume growing to a point where it begins to consider replacing the rep firm with its own in-house sales force. If so, such intentions would be difficult to hide from the reps and would likely be perceived as a signal to begin disengaging from the relationship.

Scholars have long pointed to a third and more malicious (though less common) threat to channel alignment, opportunism. As mentioned earlier, opportunism refers to self-interest seeking with guile. In contrast to the legitimate pursuit of individual firm goals, a destructive reseller partnership characterized by opportunistic behaviors is one where a firm may resort to calculated efforts to mislead, disguise, obfuscate, or otherwise confuse in order to claim a greater share of relational benefits than warranted under existing contracts. Even the mere suspicion of opportunism will weaken an alliance. Indeed, related research suggests that the fact that a decision-maker becomes suspicious of an influence agent's ulterior motives will significantly alter the decision-maker's attitudes and opinions concerning the agent (e.g. DeCarlo 2005, Campbell and Kirmani 2000). It is reasonable to assume, therefore, that one channel partner's suspicion of opportunism by the other will erode trust and invite reciprocity with real opportunism. However, additional research is needed to investigate this possibility.

8.2.4.1 *Recommendations for Effective Rep Management*

Given these potential sources of conflict, what recommendations can be made for effective management of manufacturer–rep alliances? Extensive research has identified four principal mechanisms through which managers can enhance channel alignment: (1) careful selection of partner firms, (2) the provision of incentives designed to thwart counterproductive behaviors, (3) diligent monitoring of partner firm activities, and (4) socialization of partner firm managers to the norms and values associated with the pursuit of shared goals (e.g. Wathne and Heide 2000, Heide, Wathne, and Rokkan 2007).

First, it is essential that management develop a deep understanding of their channel partners' business models and the valid, though possibly counterproductive, tendencies they spawn (i.e. law of cross purposes). As noted earlier, supplier firms tend to focus their resources to maximize return on fixed assets. They are inclined to be product-oriented and are driven to achieve growth in sales and market share for each of their offerings. As a result, they implicitly (or explicitly) expect their resellers to focus almost exclusively on their lines and aggressively market them to all their customers. All too often, supplier managers interpret reseller efforts of any other suppliers' products that they carry to be a sign of disloyalty (Marks, Horan, and Emerson 2006). Reseller firms, on the other hand, tend to focus on net quick assets (e.g. accounts receivable, cash flow). At the same time, successful rep firms are motivated to increase the share of customer business and profitability of each customer account they serve. Thus, it is not surprising that some scholars attribute the underlying causes of channel conflict to differences in goals, misunderstandings of the allocation of partnership responsibilities, and divergent perceptions of the marketplace (Anderson, Narus, and Narayandas 2008).

Similarly, it is critical that channel managers identify and pay particular attention to changes in the marketplace that stand to misalign the partners' mutual self-interests (i.e. law of perpetual change). Although disruptive market forces may take many forms, as demonstrated by the recent global financial crisis, the market forces posited to have the greatest impact on business-to-business marketing channels are cost-to-serve customers, customer demand requirements, channel member capabilities, the distribution of power among channel members, and competitive actions (Rangan 2006). Changes in these forces often arise subtly and unexpectedly, and hence managers are exhorted to monitor them and to forecast their consequences.

In addition to environmental monitoring activities, interfirm monitoring programs can be an effective control mechanism for reducing partner opportunism (e.g. Ghosh and John 1999). Indeed, the recent availability of performance data from advances in information technology is expected to increase the level of monitoring between exchange partners (e.g. Jacobides and Croson 2001). The rationale used to support the monitoring of partner firms is to suppress opportunism and enhance the norms and values associated with the pursuit of shared goals.

Along these lines, a recent study of how channel partners react to output monitoring (e.g. delivery time, order accuracy, product quality) and behavior monitoring provides some unique insights into the two forms of monitoring (Heide, Wathne, and Rokkan 2007). Heide and his colleagues found that firms who used output monitoring reduced partner opportunism, similar to the predictions of transaction cost theory. However, the study also reports that behavior monitoring will enhance partner opportunism. The authors argue that since behavior monitoring focuses on evaluating the processes that are expected to produce the desired outcomes, it is a more intrusive form of monitoring. Interestingly, the relationship between a manufacturer and reseller has an important effect on behavior monitoring and opportunism. Heide, Wathne, and Rokkan (2007) report that micro-level social contracts (i.e. informal relationship elements such as a mutual agreement on production schedules and product quality) serve as a buffer that both enhances the effects of output monitoring and permits behavior monitoring to suppress opportunism. This result not only highlights interaction between formal agreements and social contracts on supplier–reseller relationships, but also illustrates the importance of trust when managing such relationships. According to Joe Rini of Joseph Rini Consulting, "the manufacturer must make sure there is a high degree of trust that the reps are the type of people they will want not only representing the company in its greatest light, but also the type of people who they will be working with everyday for years to come."

Although it has been argued that close, collaborative relationships are important for effective rep performance, it is also important to remember that a rep's motivation to perform is calculated and based on the perceived return on effort. To this end, an important consideration in motivating reps is the growth potential of the principal's product category. Anderson and Trinkle (2005) argue that declining or flat growth potential will eventually reduce the rep's time invested in a product, since experienced reps understand the tradeoffs between effort and sales commissions. The forward-looking nature of the rep firm suggests that it will invest resources in products that have momentum in the marketplace. If a category has growth potential, the rep will anticipate future returns and will allocate more time than its current economics are worth. Indeed, a study by Anderson, Lodish, and Weitz (1987) suggests that reps allocate their selling effort according to potential commissions. The study indicated that reps will perceive an optimal level of selling effort given a finite amount of selling time, and will maximize their selling time with products that have greater potential. However, reps will reduce their effort level as they reach a saturation level of sales for a particular product line. A question remains, however, as to what factors affect reps' decisions in their time allocation among different product lines.

Evidence from a series of studies by Barone and DeCarlo (2009) offer some insights into how perceived product momentum may affect a rep's future sales effort. In these studies, the authors had the participants gauge the relative attractiveness of two segments for market entry (segments A and B depicted in Table 8.2) based on category sales over the preceding twelve-month period. While monthly sales in segment A are initially high and remain at that level, sales in segment B begin at a relatively low level but continuously increase to reach the final sales volume achieved in segment A.

The primary questions investigated in this study are: How would a reseller rate the attractiveness between these two segments? And what factors might influence a rep's preferences? Within the context of the information presented in Table 8.2, a preference for the trending option (segment B) is somewhat counter-intuitive, given that multiple performance metrics highlight its inferiority (an average

Table 8.2. Market Segment Sales Profiles

Month	Market Segment A Sales Volume	Market Segment B Sales Volume
1	$92,000	$44,500
2	$91,020	$49,250
3	$92,750	$53,950
4	$92,000	$58,700
5	$92,800	$63,450
6	$91,500	$68,250
7	$92,000	$73,000
8	$90,800	$77,750
9	$91,500	$82,450
10	$91,005	$86,950
11	$92,025	$90,050
12	$92,000	$92,000
Total*	$1,101,400	$840,300
Monthly* Average	$91,783	$70,025

*Column totals and monthly averages were added for illustration purposes and were not included in the data the respondents evaluated in the study.

monthly sales volume of $70,025 and a cumulative sales volume for all twelve periods of $840,300) relative to the steady option, segment A (average monthly sales = $91,783; total sales = $1,101,400). Viewed in this manner, a preference for the trending segment is compatible with the "hot hand" preferences for stocks that display improving prior earnings (e.g. Johnson, Tellis, and MacInnis 2005, Morrin, Jacoby, Johar, He, Kuss, and Mazursky 2002).

Analogously, relying on the trend of improving sales in segment B over a finite past evaluation period may also result in biased prospective decisions. Though providing a salient frame of reference to decision-makers, this positive trend may constitute a non-representative sample of the entire distribution of past sales volume in this market (Roggeveen and Johar 2004) and may simply signal that the upcoming evaluation period is likely to be marked by a downturn towards an average level of sales that might better typify segment volume (i.e. regression to the mean will occur: Tversky and Kahneman 1974). As a consequence, this historical trend in market B's sales volumes may not be objectively diagnostic in predicting future segment sales. In light of these competing theories, the authors report that the percentage of participants selecting the trending option was significantly greater than choosing the steady option. Evidence on multiple indicators of information diagnosticity showed that this performance trend was consistently viewed as more diagnostic (i.e. an important input into the decision) with regard to prospective effort decisions.

A number of factors moderated these results. In particular, the authors argue that the effect of trend information on decision-making will be contingent upon the level of experience possessed by the decision-maker. Specifically, the preferences of less experienced managers should exhibit greater sensitivity to trend information than should those of more experienced managers. The results support these predictions, as less experienced managers exhibited a greater tendency to select the trending performer as compared to more experienced managers.

In addition to experience effects, the study also found that sales executives' level of risk tolerated during decision-making altered category preferences. The authors argue that future growth projections involve speculative extrapolations from historical information and, as such, represent a relatively risky input to rely on during decision making. In supporting this hypothesis, risk-taking managers exhibited stronger preferences for the trending option than risk-averse managers. Finally, the authors report that a firm's strategic orientation will influence choice of product category. Respondents working for firms with a low-cost defender culture (i.e. firms that compete by achieving operational efficiencies) appeared to make their decision using a risk-avoidance mindset, resulting in a preference for the steady choice option. Conversely, respondents from prospector firms (i.e. organizational cultures that tolerate risk-taking) opted for the trending prospect. This study provides support for the notion that business strategy will dictate how firms compete by "trickling down" to shape employee behaviors and actions in a manner that corresponds with organizational goals (Moorman and Rust 1999, Noble et al. 2002, Walker and Ruekert 1987, White, Varadarajan, and Dacin 2003).

As this research suggests, the management of reps' time can be influenced by a number of factors. In line with Anderson, Lodish, and Weitz (1987), reps will likely reallocate selling time from product lines with relatively flat elasticities to product lines with more elastic returns. However, the findings of Barone and DeCarlo (2009) also suggest that a person's level of experience and risk tolerance may affect a rep's decision-making. Moreover, the research supports other claims that business strategy will likely affect manager interpretation of a market situation, which in turn will affect the solutions and changes in resource commitment (White, Varadarajan, and Dacin 2003). There is much work to be done, however, to better understand rep decision-making regarding such choices.

8.3 SUMMARY AND OPPORTUNITIES FOR FUTURE RESEARCH

Today's sales and marketing executives are under more pressure than ever and are being held accountable to additional enterprise-level scorecard metrics beyond sales volume dollars. This is not to say that the traditional revenue-generation targets will no longer drive managerial decision-making; they will. However, executives and managers can also be expected to face a scorecard that broadens responsibility to the costs associated with generation of these revenues. As we have witnessed in the recent global recession, the nature and quality of the revenue and profitability is coming under closer scrutiny. To that end, a wider variety of customer-related activities are becoming part and parcel of the new scorecards (similar to those discussed by Srivastiva, Shervani, and Fahey 1999 and Leigh and Jones 2005). For example, today's assessments are emphasizing such outcomes as sales/service costs, gross margin percentages, perceived product and/or service quality, speed to market acceptance, share of customer category expenditures (or share of wallet), product availability in key channels, and customer satisfaction (Leigh and Jones 2005). In such cases, the outsourced sales rep can provide a competitive advantage for many firms. In particular, reps can fulfill the tasks that once belonged exclusively to the direct field sales force, usually at a lower cost. As discussed above, reps are nimble, are extremely focused on matching principal capabilities with customer needs in a defined geography, provide synergies with multiple product lines, and are highly specialized to get results quickly.

Despite these advantages, many manufacturers have generally overlooked reps as a viable channel. One might attribute the general disregard of reps to the notion that businesspeople are conservative and outsourcing the sales function may be perceived as a risky endeavor (i.e. perceived loss of direct control over the revenue-generating function). Does this suggest that the rep model is destined to be relegated to smaller manufacturers who cannot afford the start-up costs of a direct sales force? Perhaps not. The objective of the present inquiry was to review extant research to provide a better understanding of the viability of the rep model and management considerations of an outsourced sales organization. To that end, this chapter focused on three distinct areas of inquiry, each of which presents a unique perspective in understanding the rep model. The first highlighted the benefits of the rep model; the second offered insights as to the appropriate conditions for using manufacturer reps; the third examined motivational and reward drivers of successful principal–rep relationships.

Within each of these perspectives there are a number of unanswered questions and opportunities for additional research. In terms of the benefits reps provide to the marketplace, researchers should do more to understand the antecedents of the sales force structures that predict superior rep performance. For example, one of the benefits discussed in this chapter is a rep's lower cost/sales ratio than the direct sales model. Additional research is needed to quantify the hypothesized efficiency gaps between the rep and direct sales models. Investigations of this nature would not only provide useful guidance to managers and executives, but the results of such studies would also offer insights into theories such as TCA, which holds that firms are highly concerned about efficiencies.

Future research should also investigate managers' "mental models" of outsourcing the sales function. Sales and marketing managers typically play an important strategic decision-making role in responding to threats and opportunities posed by a changing environment, and how managers interpret a market situation directly affects the solutions they consider (White, Varadarajan, and Dacin 2003). Thus, a fruitful area for further research is to gain an understanding of the mediating and moderating variables that affect such strategic go-to-market decisions. The results of such studies will offer important insights into the critical contingencies that affect such decisions.

In terms of the motivational and reward attributes of successful principal–rep relationships, previous research suggests that idiosyncratic investments and coordination will enhance profits and create a competitive advantage (Jap 1999). Clearly, such outcomes would be important motivational drivers for forming the interdependencies of close collaboration. However, we cannot state for certain which actions a principal should take to prevent a relationship from going awry. Studies that identify how coordination is achieved and how conflict is resolved between groups is central to understanding this, and, surprisingly, inter-organizational coordination has received scant attention in strategy implementation research.

NOTES

1. Agency theory has also been used to investigate various sales force outsourcing issues. Although agency theory and TCA appear to be complementary, this chapter focuses on TCA as it was originally advanced to understand and study issues related to the boundaries of the firm (e.g. make-or-buy decisions of a firm), while agency theory has been proposed to understand the contractual arrangements between a firm and its employees (i.e. salary vs commission).
2. The complete TCA framework also includes risk neutrality and transaction frequency as a third behavioral assumption and transactional dimension, respectively. Because of the lack of research investigating these two factors, they will not be discussed further in this chapter.

REFERENCES

ANDERSON, E. (1985). "The Salesperson as Outside Agent or Employee: A Transaction Cost Analysis," *Marketing Science* 4 (Summer), 234–54.
——L. M. LODISH, and B. WEITZ (1987). "Resource Allocation Behavior in Conventional Channels," *Journal of Marketing Research* 24 (February), 85–97.
——and D. SCHMITTLEIN (1984). "Integration of the Sales Force: An Empirical Investigation," 15 *RAND Journal of Economics*, 385–95.

——and B. Trinkle (2005). *Outsourcing the Sales Function*, Mason, OH: Thomson.

——and B. Weitz (1992). "The Use of Pledges to Build and Sustain Commitment in Distribution Channels," *Journal of Marketing Research* 29 (February), 18–34.

Anderson, J. C., and J. A. Narus (1984). "A Model of the Distributor's Perspective of Distributor–Manufacturer Relationships," *Journal of Marketing* 48 (Fall), 62–74.

————and D. Narayandas (2008). *Business Market Management: Understanding, Creating, and Delivering Value*, 3rd edn, Upper Saddle River, NJ: Prentice Hall.

Barone, M. J., and T. E. DeCarlo (2009). "Performance Trend Effects on Managers' Evaluations of Employees: The Influence of Evaluation Task and Strategic Orientation," working paper.

Bergen, M., S. Dutta, and O. C. Walker, Jr. (1992). "Agency Relationships in Marketing: A Review of the Implications and Applications of Agency and Related Theories," *Journal of Marketing* 56 (July), 1–24.

Bukszar, E., and T. Connolly (1988). "Hindsight Bias and Strategic Choice: Some Problems in Learning from Experience," *Academy of Management Journal* 31.3, 628–41.

Campbell, M. C., and A. Kirmani (2000). "Consumers' Use of Persuasion Knowledge: The Effects of Accessibility and Cognitive Capacity on Perceptions of an Influence Agent," *Journal of Consumer Research* 27 (June), 69–83.

Day, G. S., and R. Wensley (1988). "Assessing Advantage: A Framework for Diagnosing Competitive Superiority," *Journal of Marketing* 52 (April), 1–20.

DeCarlo, T. E. (2005). "The Effects of Suspicion of Ulterior Motives and Sales Message on Salesperson Evaluation," *Journal of Consumer Psychology* 15.3, 238–49.

Dutta, S., M. Bergen, J. B. Heide, and G. John (1995). "Understanding Dual Distribution: The Case of Reps and House Accounts," *Journal of Law, Economics, & Organization* 11 (April), 189–204.

Frazier, G. L. (1983). "On the Measurement of Interfirm Power in Channels of Distribution," *Journal of Marketing* 20 (May), 158–66.

Ghosh, M., and G. John (1999). "Governance Value Analysis and Marketing Strategy," *Journal of Marketing* 63 (Special Issue), 131–45.

Gschwandtner, G., "Should You Outsource Your Sales Force?", accessed October 5, 2008, http://www.sellingpower.com/magazine/editorial/v26n7_editorial.asp

Heide, J. B., and G. John (1990). "Alliances in Industrial Purchasing: The Determinants of Joint Action in Buyer–Supplier Relationships," *Journal of Marketing Research* 27.1, 24–36.

——K. H. Wathne, and A. I. Rokkan (2007). "Interfirm Monitoring, Social Contracts, and Relationship Outcomes," *Journal of Marketing Research* 44 (August), 425–33.

Jacobides, M. G., and D. C. Croson (2001). "Information Policy: Shaping the Value of Agency Relationships," *Academy of Management Review* 26.2, 202–23.

Jap, S. D. (1999). "Pie-Expansion Efforts: Collaboration Processes in Buyer–Supplier Relationships," *Journal of Marketing Research* 36 (November), 461–75.

——and E. Anderson (2003). "Safeguarding Interorganizational Performance and Continuity Under Ex Post Opportunism," *Management Science* 49 (December), 1684–1701.

Johnson, J., G. J. Tellis, and D. J. MacInnis (2005). "Losers, Winners, and Biased Trades," *Journal of Consumer Research* 32 (September), 324–9.

Jones, B. (2005). "A New Wrinkle on Outsourcing," *Business Week*, September 15 (accessed January 19, 2009: http://www.businessweek.com/the_thread/techbeat/archives/2005/09/a_new_wrinkle_o_1.html)

LEIGH, T. W., and E. P. JONES (2005). "Creating Customer Relationship Strategies", in R. L. LaForge, T. N. Ingram, J. Bauer, T. W. Leigh, E. P. Jones, A. Dixon, M. H. Morris, and G. Marshall, *Strategic Sales Leadership: Breakthrough Thinking for Improving Results*, Chicago: American Marketing Association, 90–125.

MARKS, M., T. HORAN, and M. EMERSON (2006). *Working at Cross-Purposes: How Distributors and Manufacturers Can Manage Conflict Successfully*, Washington, DC: Distribution Research and Education Foundation.

MOORMAN, C., and R. T. RUST (1999). "The Role of Marketing," *Journal of Marketing* 63 (Special Issue), 180–97.

MORIARTY, R. T., and U. MORAN (1990). "Managing Hybrid Marketing Systems," *Harvard Business Review* 68.6, 146–55.

MORRIN, M., J. JACOBY, G. V. JOHAR, X. HE, A. KUSS, and D. MAZURSKY (2002). "Taking Stock of Stockbrokers: Trend versus Contrarian Investor Strategies and Profiles," *Journal of Consumer Research* 29 (September), 188–98.

NARUS, J. A., and J. C. ANDERSON (1996). "Rethinking Distribution: Adaptive Channels," *Harvard Business Review* (July–August), 112–20.

NOBLE, C. H., R. K. SINHA, and A. KUMAR (2002). "Market Orientation and Alternative Strategic Orientations: A Longitudinal Assessment of Performance Implications," *Journal of Marketing* 66 (October), 25–39.

PORTER, M. E. (1991). "Toward a Dynamic Theory of Strategy," *Strategic Management Journal* 12 (Winter), 95–117.

RANGAN, V. K. (2006). "The Promise and Rewards of Channel Stewardship," *Supply Chain Management Review* 10 (July/August), 42–9.

ROGGEVEEN, A. L., and G. V. JOHAR (2004). "Integration of Discrepant Sales Forecasts: The Influence of Plausibility Inferences Based on an Evoked Range," *Journal of Marketing Research* 41 (February), 19–30.

ROSS, W. T., Jr., E. ANDERSON, and B. A. WEITZ (1997). "Consequences of Perceived Asymmetry of Commitment to the Relationship," *Management Science* 43.5: 680–704.

——F. DALSACE, and E. ANDERSON (2005). "Should You Set Up Your Own Sales Force or Should You Outsource It? Pitfalls in the Standard Analysis," *Business Horizons* 48, 23–36.

SA VINHAS, A., and E. ANDERSON (2005). "How Potential Channel Conflict Drives Channel Structure: Concurrent (Direct and Indirect) Channels," *Journal of Marketing Research* 42 (November), 507–15.

————(2008). "The Antecedents of Double Compensation Systems in Concurrent Channel Systems in Business-to-Business Markets," *Journal of Personal Selling & Sales Management* 28 (Spring), 133–44.

SHAPIRO, B. (1977). *Sales Program Management: Formulation and Implementation*, New York: McGraw-Hill.

"Silicon Systems Strengthens European Sales Channel; Signs Five of Europe's Leading Manufacturers Representatives" (February 22, 2007); accessed January 8, 2009 at: http://www.mechdir.com/press/catalog/785/index.html

SRIVASTAVA, R. K., T. A. SHERVANI, and L. FAHEY (1999). "Marketing, Business Processes, and Shareholder Value: An Organizationally Embedded View of Marketing Activities and the Discipline of Marketing," *Journal of Marketing* 63 (October), 168–79.

STERN, L. W., A. I. EL-ANSARY, and A. T. COUGHLAN (1998). *Marketing Channels*, Englewood Cliffs, NJ: Prentice Hall.

TVERSKY, A., and D. KAHNEMAN (1974). "Judgment Under Uncertainty: Heuristics and Biases," *Science* 185, 1124–31.

VAZQUEZ, R., V. IGLESIAS, and L. I. ALVAREZ-GONZALEZ (2005). "Distribution Channel Relationships: The Conditions and Strategic Outcomes of Cooperation between Manufacturer and Distributor," *International Review of Retail, Distribution & Consumer Research* 15 (April), 125–50.

WALKER, O. C., Jr., and R. W. RUEKERT (1987). "Marketing's Role in the Implementation of Business Strategies: A Critical Review and Conceptual Framework," *Journal of Marketing* 51 (July), 15–33.

WATHNE, K. H., and J. B. HEIDE (2000). "Opportunism in Interfirm Relationships: Forms, Outcomes, and Solutions," *Journal of Marketing* 64 (October), 36–51.

——————(2004). "Relationship Governance in a Supply Chain Network," *Journal of Marketing* 68 (January), 73–89.

WEISS, A. M., and E. ANDERSON (1992). "Converting From Independent to Employee Salesforces: The Role of Perceived Switching Costs," *Journal of Marketing Research* 29 (February), 101–15.

——————and D. J. MacINNIS (1999). "Reputation Management as a Motivation for Sales Structure Decisions," *Journal of Marketing* 63 (October), 73-89.

WEITZ, B. A., and K. BRADFORD (1999). "Personal Selling and Sales Management: A Relationship Marketing Perspective," *Journal of the Academy of Marketing Science* 27.2, 241–54.

WHITE, J. C., VARADARAJAN, P. R., and P. A. DACIN (2003). "Market Situation and Interpretation: The Role of Cognitive Style, Organizational Culture, and Information Use," *Journal of Marketing* 67 (July), 63–79.

WILLIAMSON, O. E. (1975). *Markets and Hierarchies: Analysis and Antitrust Implications*, New York: Free Press.

——(1985). *The Economic Institutions of Capitalism*, New York: Free Press.

——(1996). *The Mechanisms of Governance*, New York: Oxford University Press.

CHAPTER 9

TRAINING AND REWARDS

MARK W. JOHNSTON[*]

9.1 INTRODUCTION

Two of the most important elements in sales management are providing the tools for salespeople to improve critical skills and creating a reward platform that motivates salespeople and encourages success, while offering financial security. At the same time, creating effective training programs and reward systems are two of the hardest challenges facing any sales manager. Every sales manager has a story, often many, of the training seminar that didn't work, cost too much, or both. Companies spend billions of dollars on training every year, yet sales managers and HR professionals are often hard pressed to identify the long-term benefits of the training. The challenge of reward systems is balancing individual circumstances, limited budgets, competitive pressure, and customer concerns.

Fortunately, the challenges are not insurmountable; in this chapter we present a plan for developing and assessing successful training programs. We will talk about the important of setting objectives, developing programs that actually add value to the sales force, and creating useful success metrics. In addition, we define a winning reward strategy and create an action plan for implementing it. Sales managers balance the effectiveness of individual reward systems with the efficiency of

* The foundation for this chapter is based on material from *Sales Force Management*, 9th edn (McGraw-Hill) by Mark W. Johnston and Greg W. Marshall (2009).

"one size fits all." We will examine the process of aligning company objectives with individual goals.

9.2 ISSUES IN SALES TRAINING

Given the importance of sales training, it is not surprising that the subject produces considerable interest and concern throughout the company (Johnston and Marshall 2009). Managers at all levels have a variety of concerns and objectives for training. National account managers, for example, want sales training to provide specific details about certain industries and teach the sales reps to develop close relationships with customers—a critical issue, especially with large national accounts. Marketing managers are interested in how much training sales representatives receive in dealing with the complex customer problems. Product managers, of course, hope the salespeople have been well schooled in product knowledge, specifications, and applications. Even departments external to marketing, such as Human Resources, have a stake in the sales training process, and everyone is concerned about balancing training needs with cost.

When determining sales training needs, three issues must be considered:

- *Who should be trained?* In most organizations new sales recruits receive a combination of training and orientation to company policies and procedures. But this raises the issues of training for different types of salespeople and, depending upon how market or competitive changes may have altered the nature of sales tasks, training for different stages of the same salesperson's career.
- *What should be the primary emphasis in the training program?* Sales training can encompass the following: product knowledge, company knowledge, customer knowledge, or selling skills (e.g. time management or presentation skills). All of these may be important, but the relative importance of each type of training differs depending upon the selling situation, the feasible scope and costs of sales training, and the nature of the company's marketing strategy.
- *How should the training process be structured?* The following methods are options: on-the-job training and experience versus a formal and more consistent centralized program; Web-based or instructor-based; and in-house training versus outside expertise.

These issues suggest that sales training is vitally important to the organization; at the same time, they also reinforce the challenge of delivering the right training to the right people in the right format (Attia, Honeycutt, and Leach 2005). Figure 9.1 summarizes the training topics discussed in the chapter.

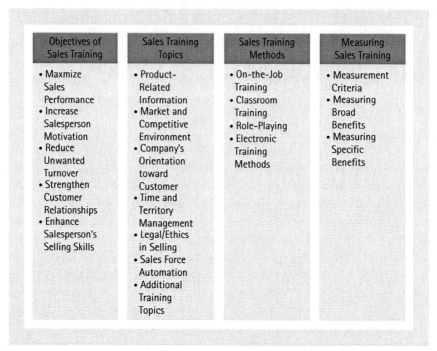

Fig. 9.1. Sales Training Objectives, Topics, Methods, and Measurement

9.3 OBJECTIVES IN SALES TRAINING

Although the specific objectives of sales training may vary from firm to firm, there is some agreement on the broad objectives. Sales training is undertaken to increase productivity, improve morale, lower turnover, improve customer relations, and produce better management of time and territory.

9.3.1 Maximize Sales Performance

With limited budgets and time, sales managers face the constant challenge of improving sales performance (Skiera and Albers 2008). A critical tool for improving sales productivity is sales training which, when properly conceived and implemented, should provide valuable skills to improve selling performance. Sales training attempts to teach and enhance critical selling skills. The time it takes for a new member of the sales force to achieve satisfactory levels of productivity is thus shortened considerably (Artis and Harris 2007, Leach, Liu, and Johnston 2005).

9.3.2 Increase Salesperson Motivation

As noted previously, one sales training objective is to improve a salesperson's productivity. Appropriate training enables salespeople to function more efficiently and effectively. Evidence indicates that salespeople who are uncertain about their job requirements tend to be less satisfied with their jobs. Conversely, this same evidence shows that salespeople who are well aware of the job requirements are also more satisfied with their company's sales training activities. Creating the right format for sales training is a challenging task. Competent sales training is not a function of motivational hype but consists rather of delivering specific skills and techniques designed to enhance the salesperson's ability to be successful in the field. Research suggests that effective training does affect motivation which indirectly affects performance (Wilson, Strutton, and Farris 2002)

9.3.3 Reduce Unwanted Turnover

If sales training can lead to increased productivity and improved morale, then the result should be lower turnover in the sales force; however, as noted previously, training is not "one size fits all" and training designed to lower turnover should be focused on that issue (Barksdale, Bellenger, Boles, and Brashear 2003). The pharmaceutical industry has focused a great deal of effort on improving its sales training programs. The industry estimates that turnover can cost as much as 200 per cent of a salesperson's total compensation package, and cites training as the most significant factor in improving the retention rate of high-performing salespeople (O'Grady 2003).

9.3.4 Strengthen Customer Relationships

One benefit of sales training that accompanies lower turnover is continuity in customer relationships. Having the same sales representative call on customers on a regular basis promotes customer loyalty, especially when the salesperson can handle customer questions, objections, and complaints. In addition, salespeople represent one of the best sources of information about customers and the competitive environment which is critical to creating effective customer relationship management (CRM) systems. Training on how to collect this type of information is really important to improving CRM systems throughout the company (Liu and Comer 2007). Finally, training can provide tools to identify areas of similarity between the salesperson and buyer that can serve to strengthen the customer relationship (Lichtenthal and Tellefsen 2001)

9.3.5 Enhance Salesperson Selling Skills

Research suggests that improving basic selling skills is essential in improving a wide range of performance metrics including customer orientation (Wachner, Plouffe, and Grégoire 2009). For example, time and territory management is a frequent sales training topic. How much time should be devoted to existing accounts versus calling on potential new accounts? Sales training programs provide answers to these and other questions. In addition, over time research on the relationship between salesperson and customer can lead to new approaches in sales training. Recent research suggests that it can be beneficial for salespeople to provide more structure to the sales presentation in dealing with inexperienced customers. A focused selling strategy designed to create an "agenda" for the customer as they move through the decision-making process can be helpful for new customers who are unaware of the product/services performance characteristics or benefits. This kind of information can be conveyed to salespeople very effectively in a sales training program (Wagner, Klein, and Keith 2001).

9.4 The Development of Sales Training Programs

Sales training is an important sales management function; unfortunately, all too often developing and implementing an effective sales program presents a number of challenges. Senior training managers were asked to identify their most important training issues and priorities (Hall and Boehle 2004). They reported that linking training programs with business strategy was the top priority. This means training salespeople to be customer-focused and consulting-oriented, and providing them with tools necessary to build strong customer relationships by adding value to the customer's business (Pelham 2002). What factors adversely influence the effectiveness of training programs? Research suggests the following (Ricks, Williams, and Weeks 2008):

- limited assessment of training needs;
- lack of training objectives;
- no alignment between training objectives and corporate goals;
- poor or inadequate sales training content;
- ineffective sales trainer.

These issues raise an important question. What is management doing that allows some of these problems to occur? These issues have created a growing awareness among training professionals and sales managers that sales training needs to be re-evaluated and new programs developed (Cron, Marshall, Singh, Spiro, and Sujan 2005).

Many sales trainers believe their programs lack credibility. Budget-cutting efforts are too often directed at existing sales training programs (Hahne 1981). This may reflect management's feelings that these programs are accomplishing little, and are expendable. Sales training programs have to fit the long-term goals and objectives of the organization, and just like the company's own products and services, they must deliver value to the organization (Kumar, Venkatesan, and Reinartz 2008). The process of developing sales training programs consists of the following steps:

- *Analyze needs.* The starting point in creating credibility is to conduct a sales training analysis that analyzes the training needs of the sales force. This analysis should answer three basic questions: Where in the organization is training needed? What should be the content of the training program? Who needs the training?
- *Determine objectives.* Setting specific, realistic, and measurable objectives for the sales training program is critical. The objectives may include learning about new products, sales techniques, or company procedures. Keep the objectives simple and measurable.
- *Develop and implement program.* At this point, a decision has to be made as to whether to develop the training program or to hire an outside organization to conduct it. Many companies, both large and small, outsource at least a part of their sales training. Small companies often outsource most of their training. Large companies usually develop most of their own programs and use outside agencies to handle specific or special training needs. When considering an outside training supplier, it is critical to conduct a careful investigation.
- *Evaluate and review program.* A critical step that must address several questions: What do we want to measure? When do we want to measure? How do we do it? What measuring tools are available? Using tests to measure learning is not difficult; however, measuring the application of training in the field is very difficult. Whether a salesperson can demonstrate a product can be evaluated during a training session. But whether that same individual demonstrates the product effectively in front of a customer is harder to assess. This is why field sales managers are an important link: They can provide follow-up and feedback information on the salesperson's ability to retain and use sales training take-aways in the field. The field sales managers can also coach the salesperson if there is a need for follow up.

Finally, evaluations of sales performance provide additional evidence on the value of training, although such information must be used carefully. Changes in perfor-mance, i.e. sales increases, may be due to factors not related to sales training; and when training managers claim they are it casts doubts on the sales training efforts. Most of the time some groups are targeted for training before others, and it is also important to remember that not every salesperson needs the same training. Certainly, newly hired recruits need training, whether on the job, more centralized, or some other arrangement. When procedures or products change, everyone needs training. If certain salespeople are having specific problems related to performance or attitude, the training needs to be directed at them individually. To include the entire force wastes resources and creates problems, especially among those not experiencing the same issues. When a new training method is being tested, it is wise to use a group that will be receptive. This increases credibility, creating a favorable climate for continuation. Since measurement is crucial, the sales trainer needs to collect data before training starts. The needs analysis discussed earlier provides relevant information pertaining to program content. For example, if management knows some salespeople had difficulty managing their sales calls, observation by the trainer or the field sales manager after the program should provide data indicating the value of the training. Call reports would be another source of information. Follow-up must continue beyond the initial check, because the use of new skills may drop off over time and reinforcement is necessary

9.5 SALES TRAINING TOPICS

For new salespeople, the content of sales training tends to remain relatively constant over time. Product or service knowledge appears in the majority of programs as well as an orientation on the market/industry, company, and basic selling skills. Beyond these standard topics, there exists a vast array of different subjects.

9.5.1 Product-Related Information

Although product knowledge is one of the most important topics, knowing when and how to discuss the subject in a sales call is probably even more important. More time is typically spent on product knowledge than any other subject, although the time spent varies with the product sold (Pelham 2006).

Product knowledge involves knowing not only product specifications but also how the product is used and, in some cases, how it should not be used. Product knowledge is not limited to the company's products. Customers often want to know how competitive products compare on price, construction, performance, and compatibility with each other. As a result, the importance of product knowledge training is linked to training on other critical sales skills (Pettijohn, Pettijohn, and Taylor 2007).

9.5.2 Market and Competitive Environment

Sales training in the market/industry orientation covers both broad and specific factors (Pelham 2002). From a broad viewpoint, economic fluctuations affect buying behavior, which affects selling techniques. Information about inflationary pressure, for example, may be used to persuade prospective buyers to move their decision dates ahead. If the sales force is involved in forecasting sales and setting quotas, knowledge of the industry and the economy is essential.

More specifically, salespeople must have detailed knowledge about present customers. They need to know their customers' buying policies, patterns, and preferences and the products or services these companies produce. In some cases, sales reps need to be knowledgeable about their customers' customers. This is especially true when sales representatives sell through wholesalers or distributors that often want salespeople to assist them with their customers' problems. These salespeople are expected to know the needs of both wholesalers and retailers, even though the retailers buy from the wholesalers.

9.5.3 Company's Orientation toward the Customer

Salespeople expect customers to request price adjustments, product modifications, faster delivery, and different credit terms. Most companies have policies on such matters arising from customer orientation, legal requirements, or industry practices. Too often, however, avoidable problems result when salespeople do not understand important company policies (Pelham and Kravitz 2008).

9.5.4 Time and Territory Management

New salespeople frequently need assistance in managing their time and territories. More experienced salespeople often need to learn about more efficient and effective time management technologies as well as to sharpen existing skills. It is not surprising that management also considers time management a critical issue. Research suggests that good time management, goal setting, and prioritization techniques reduce role ambiguity and improve performance (Leach, Liu, and Johnston 2005).

9.5.5 Legal/Ethical Concerns in Selling

The statements—or, rather, misstatements—and behaviors of salespeople have legal and ethical implications. Increasingly, sales management puts ethical and legal aspects high on the list of sale training topics (Schwepker and Good 2007).

Research suggests that ethical behavior and decision-making is positively associated with job satisfaction and performance (Amyx, Bhuian, Sharma, and Loveland 2008).

9.5.6 Sales Force Automation

Despite the documented potential benefits of sales force automation (SFA), successful implementation of SFA strategies has met with mixed success (Bush, Moore, and Rocco 2005). Sufficient IT training and support has been shown to be a critical factor in increasing salesperson efficiency and effectiveness. Too little training can reduce salesperson performance (Ahearne, Jelinek, and Rapp 2005; Buehrer, Senecal, and Pullins 2005).

9.5.7 Additional Training Topics

Companies understand that training is most effective when it is specialized and tailored to individual job functions. One issue of significant concern that is not limited to sales is building diversity in the workplace. Selling presents some unique challenges because salespeople must build diversity in their own workplace but work successfully in the customer's environment. As a result, cultural diversity is a major training topic for many organizations (Bush and Ingram 2001).

Sales training is also effective in helping salespeople work through problems or issues that may limit their performance. Research reports that sales call anxiety (SCA) can lead to real problems in both a salesperson's effectiveness and efficiency. One of the results of the research is a focus on better training methods to reduce SCA before it becomes a problem for salespeople (Verbeke and Bagozzi 2000).

9.6 SALES TRAINING METHODS

There are a variety of methods used in sales training. Companies use many techniques, recognizing that different subjects require different methods (Jantan, Honeycutt, Thelen, and Attia 2004). Overlap exists within a given method. On-the-job training includes individual instruction (coaching and/or on-line) as well as in-house classes held at various locations. Let's examine some of the more widely used training methodology.

9.6.1 On-the-Job Training

The thought of "learning by doing" is psychologically discomforting for many people, particularly new sales recruits. When done properly, however, OJT is a carefully planned process in which trainees learn by doing while being productively employed. Furthermore, a good OJT program contains established procedures for evaluating and reviewing a salesperson's progress (Lupton, Weiss, and Peterson 1999).

Research has been mixed on the effectiveness of formal on-the-job training (Van der Klink and Streumer 2002). A key aspect of OJT is the coaching salespeople receive from trainers, who may be experienced sales personnel, sales managers, or personnel specifically assigned to do sales training (Deeter-Schmelz, Kennedy, and Goebel 2002). Managers are aware that helping a salesperson reach his or her full potential means spending time with the person one on one. OJT often involves job rotation—assigning trainees to different departments where they learn about such things as manufacturing, marketing, shipping, credits and collections, and servicing procedures. After OJT, many sales trainees proceed to formal classroom training.

9.6.2 Classroom Training

For most companies, formal classroom training is an indispensable part of sales training, although very few of them rely on it solely (Roman, Ruiz, and Munuera 2002). Classroom training has several advantages. First, formal training sessions often save substantial amounts of executive time because executives can meet an entire group of salespeople at once. Second, there is a much more opportunity for interaction between salespeople.

Classroom training also has its disadvantages. It is expensive and time-consuming. It requires recruits to be brought together and facilities, meals, transportation, recreation, and lodging to be provided for them. Sales managers, who are cognizant of these costs and time demands, sometimes attempt to cover too much material in too short a time. This results in less retention of information. Sales managers must avoid the natural tendency to add more and more material, because the additional exposure is often gained at the expense of retention and opportunity for interaction.

9.6.3 Role-Playing

A popular technique used in many companies has an individual act out a part (role) in a simulated work environment; this is known as role-playing, and is widely regarded as a valuable training methodology (Sogunro 2004). In sales role-playing, the simulated environment is most often the meeting between the customer and sales person. Role-playing is widely used to develop selling skills, but it can also be used to determine whether the trainee can apply knowledge taught via other methods of instruction. The salesperson, trainer, and other salespeople critique the trainee's performance immediately following the role-playing session.

9.6.4 Electronic Training Methods

Electronic training methods and, more specifically, the Internet have revolutionized the delivery of training, not just in sales but across the entire organization (Lim, Lee, and Nam 2007). In addition to sales training, companies increasingly are also delivering product and service training to their customers online. Companies find the Internet effective and efficient in delivering just-in-time information. Internet-based training involves a wide range of tools, from distributing product information and service updates to on-line chat groups with customers and other salespeople that enable salespeople to share information or provide feedback on current activities.

Do these programs work? Can they train salespeople to effectively interact with customers? Answers to these questions have not been well documented. Online training can be very effective in delivering certain kinds of information, but are unlikely to eliminate the need for one-on-one training for salespeople (Abbott, Klein, Hamilton, and Rosenthal 2009, Erffmeyer, Russ, and Hair 1991).

9.7 MEASURING THE COST AND BENEFITS OF SALES TRAINING

Sales training is a time-consuming and very costly activity. If done properly, it can be one of the most helpful tools to increase the satisfaction and performance of salespeople; but there are many obstacles in the way of a successful training strategy (Attia, Honeycutt, and Jantan 2008).

Sales training and increased profits have an obscure relationship at best. At the beginning of this chapter, we identified some broad objectives of sales training: improved selling skills, increased productivity, improved morale, lower sales force turnover, better customer relations, and better time and territory management. Unfortunately, pinning down the relationship between sales training and these broad objectives is not easy (Honeycutt, Karande, Attia, and Maurer 2001). Very little research has been done to determine what effect, if any, sales training has on the sales force. Most sales organizations simply assume on blind faith that their sales training programs are successful. After all, if a company has high sales and high profits, why should a sales manager assume sales training is anything but effective?

9.7.1 Measurement Criteria

Even though intervening variables such as changes in competitive activities make evaluation of sales training programs difficult, it is still important to measure training effectiveness (Leach and Liu 2003, Pelham and Kravitz 2008). This raises the question: What characteristics of sales training should be assessed? A strong argument can be made that several criteria should be used in assessing the results of any sales training program. Measuring what was learned, for example, does not mean much if the company does not also measure changes in behavior. However, it is important to assess sales training programs, because the program should deliver value to the salesperson and organization (Wilson, Strutton, and Farris 2002). The solution rests in properly specifying the objectives and content of the sales training program, the criteria used to evaluate the program, and the proper design of the research so that benefits can be unambiguously determined.

9.7.2 Measuring Broad Benefits

Measuring reactions and learning is important in sales training for both new and experienced personnel. Most companies measure reactions by asking those attending the training to complete an evaluation form either immediately after the session or several weeks later. Emotions and enthusiasm may be high right after a session, but sales training effectiveness is much more than a "warm feeling." Measuring what was learned requires tests. To what extent did salespeople learn the facts, concepts, and techniques included in the training session? Objective examinations are appropriate.

9.7.3 Measuring Specific Benefits

Liking the program and learning something are not enough. Specific measures to examine behavior changes and results are needed to assess effectiveness. For example, the effectiveness of a mentoring program linking experienced with inexperienced sales people should measure how well the relationship is improving specific behaviors (Pullins and Fine 2002) such as customer satisfaction. The measurement of specific and broad benefits is predicated on the assumption that the sales training program is designed to achieve certain goals. The goals should be established before sales training begins. When specific objectives have been determined, the best training program is developed to achieve these objectives. Most training programs have several objectives. Multiple measurements of the effectiveness of the training program are then a necessary part of evaluating the benefits.

Most sales training evaluation measures are simple, consisting primarily of reactions to the program. Meaningful evaluation measures, such as learning, behavior, and results, are used much less frequently. Often, the easiest-to-collect measures—staff comments and feedback from supervisors and trainees—are used the most. Bottom-line evaluation (e.g. changes in sales volume) is used less frequently or not at all. The most frequently used measure is course evaluation, but course evaluation is a reaction measure that fails to reveal learning, behavioral, and results changes associated with the sales training. Evaluating the benefits of sales training is difficult. One study asked sales managers to identify the most important restrictions on sales training evaluation. The most common restrictions were time and money and difficulty in gathering the data or gaining access to data (Honeycutt and Stevenson 1989, Jaramillo, Carrillat, and Locander 2005).

9.8 REWARDS

Salespeople perform to receive rewards and increase job satisfaction. It sounds simple; however, the relationship of performance to rewards and rewards to other salesperson attitudes and behaviors is complex and changes over time (Johnston and Marshall 2009). Indeed, reward systems bring together many areas of management expertise. For example, research suggests that effective rewards systems incorporate clear goals (motivation theory) and performance metrics (management control)—skills that go beyond simply creating a compensation program (Brown, Evans, Mantrala, and Challagalla 2005).

The way the reward system is implemented in a sales organization is primarily through the compensation plan. Three basic questions drive successful compensation programs:

1. Which compensation method is most appropriate for motivating specific kinds of selling activities in specific selling situations?
2. How much of a salesperson's total compensation should be earned through incentive programs?
3. What is the appropriate mix of financial and non-financial compensation and incentives for motivating the sales force?

Today, sales managers seek the proper balance between individual salesperson reward preferences and the needs of the firm. In most firms, the total financial compensation paid to salespeople comprises several components, each component designed to achieve different objectives. The core of sales compensation plans consists of a salary and incentive payments. The amount of salary is usually a

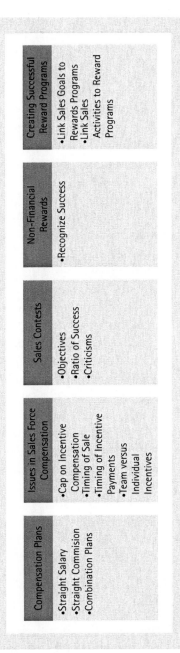

Fig. 9.2. Rewards

function of that person's experience, competence, and time on the job, as well as the sales manager's judgements about the quality of the individual's performance.

Many firms that pay a salary also offer incentives to encourage good performance. These incentives take several forms but most often are commissions tied to a particular sales metric (e.g. unit sales), or bonuses for meeting or exceeding specific performance targets. Such incentives direct salespeople's efforts toward specific strategic objectives, as well as providing additional rewards for the top performers within the sales force. Since a direct link exists between sales volume and the amount of commission received, commission payments are particularly useful for motivating a high level of selling effort (Chonko, Tanner, and Weeks 1992, Lopez, Hopkins, and Raymond 2006).

A bonus is a payment made at the discretion of management for achieving or surpassing some set level of performance. Whereas commissions are typically paid for each sale, a bonus is typically not paid until the salesperson surpasses some level of total sales or other performance criteria. Bonuses are usually additional incentives designed to motivate salespeople rather than part of the basic compensation plan, and are almost never used alone; rather, they are combined with one or more other compensation elements. Attaining a quota is often the minimum requirement for a salesperson to earn a bonus. Quotas can be based on goals for sales volume, profitability of sales, or various account-servicing activities. To be effective, quotas (like goals) should be specific, measurable, and realistically attainable. Therefore, bonuses can be offered as a reward for attaining or surpassing a predetermined level of performance on any dimensions for which quotas are set.

In addition to the above incentives, a foundation of most compensation plans is a package of benefits. These are designed to satisfy the salesperson's basic need for security. They typically include such things as medical and disability insurance, life insurance, and a retirement plan. The types and amount of benefits included in a compensation plan are usually a matter of company policy, and apply to all employees. Figure 9.2 summarizes the topics discussed on reward systems.

9.9 STRAIGHT SALARY, STRAIGHT COMMISSION, AND COMBINATION PLANS

The three primary methods of compensating salespeople are (1) straight salary, (2) straight commission, and (3) a combination of base salary plus incentive pay in the form of commissions, bonuses, or both. Combination plans are the most common form of compensation. In essence, managers seek to create a "pay for performance" plan that rewards people using salary and incentive programs to maximize the salesperson's performance. These programs are complex, however, and usually require additional time and resources to create (Talgan 2001, Liang, Wu, and Jung 2009). The following sections highlight the three principal compensation approaches.

9.9.1 Straight Salary

Two sets of conditions favor the use of a straight salary compensation plan: (1) salespeople need to achieve objectives beyond short-run sales volume; and (2) the salesperson's impact on sales volume is difficult to measure in a reasonable time. Because consultative, relationship selling may involve both of these conditions, it is not uncommon for sales jobs with heavy customer care to be compensated by straight salary.

9.9.1.1 *Advantages*

The primary advantage of straight salary is that management can require salespeople to spend their time on activities that may not result in immediate sales. Therefore, a salary plan or a plan offering a large proportion of fixed salary is appropriate when the salesperson is expected to perform a great deal of customer service or other non-selling activities (e.g. market research, customer problem analysis, customer education).

Straight salary compensation plans are also desirable when it is difficult for management to measure the individual salesperson's actual impact on sales volume or other aspects of performance. Thus, firms tend to pay salaries to their sales force when (1) their salespeople are engaged in missionary selling, as in the pharmaceutical industry; (2) other parts of the marketing program, such as advertising or dealer promotions, are the primary determinants of sales success, as in some consumer packaged goods businesses; or (3) the selling process is complex and involves a team or multilevel selling effort. Research suggests that buyers consider the salesperson's compensation scheme in evaluating product claims, and expect the true value of the feature to be less than the claimed value when the salesperson has a high percentage of incentive compensation involved with the sale (Kalra, Shi, and Srinivasan 2003).

Finally, salary plans are easy for management to compute and administer. They also give management more flexibility. It is easy to reassign salespeople to new territories or product lines, because managers do not have to worry about how such changes will affect their sales volumes. Also, since salaries are fixed costs, the compensation cost per unit sold is lower at relatively high levels of sales volume.

9.9.1.2 *Disadvantages*

The major limitation of straight salary compensation is that financial rewards are not tied directly to any specific aspect of job performance. In addition, salaries do not provide any direct financial incentive for improving sales-related aspects of performance. Consequently, over the long run salary plans appeal more to security-oriented than to achievement-oriented salespeople.

9.9.2 Straight Commission

A commission is payment for achieving a given level of performance (Johnston and Marshall 2009). Salespeople are paid for results. Usually, commission payments are based on the salesperson's dollar or unit sales volume; however, additional criteria are also incorporated in base commissions such as profitability of sales. The most common method is called variable commissions, where relatively high commissions are paid for sales of the most profitable products or sales to the most profitable accounts. Such a variable commission rate can also be used to direct efforts toward a variety of sales objectives, such as paying a higher commission on a new product line being introduced.

9.9.2.1 *Advantages*

Direct motivation is the key advantage of a commission compensation plan, since a clear and direct link exists between sales performance and financial compensation earned by the salesperson. Consequently, salespeople are strongly motivated to improve their sales productivity to increase their compensation, at least until they reach such high pay that further incremental increases become less attractive.

Commission plans also have advantages from a sales management viewpoint. Commissions are usually easy to compute and administer. Also, compensation costs vary directly with sales volume. This is an advantage for firms that are short of working capital, because they do not need to worry about paying high wages to the sales force unless it generates high sales revenues.

9.9.2.2 *Disadvantages*

Straight commission compensation plans do have limitations that cause many firms—especially those engaged in more consultative, relationship selling—to limit their use. Perhaps the most critical weakness is that management has less control over the sales force than other compensation plans. When all their financial rewards are tied directly to sales volume, it can be difficult to motivate salespeople to engage in relationship-building activities that do not lead directly to short term sales. Consequently, salespeople on commission are likely to sell to existing customers rather than working to develop new accounts and sustain long-term relationships.

From the salesperson's perspective, straight commission plans can make earnings unstable and hard to predict. To combat the inherent instability of commission plans, some firms provide their salespeople with a draw, or drawing account. In a draw, money is advanced to a salesperson in months when commissions are low to ensure that he or she will always take home a specified minimum amount of pay. The amount of the salesperson's draw in poor months is deducted from earned commissions when sales improve. This gives salespeople some secure salary, and it allows management more control over their activities. A problem arises, however, when a salesperson fails to earn enough commissions to repay the draw. Then the person may quit or be fired, and the company must absorb the loss (Fine and Franke 1995).

9.9.3 Combination Plans

Compensation plans that offer a base salary plus some proportion of incentive pay are popular because they have many of the advantages but avoid most of the limitations of both straight salary and straight commission plans. The base salary provides the salesperson with a stable income, and gives management some ability to reward salespeople for performing customer service and administrative tasks that are not directly related to short-term sales. At the same time, the incentive portion of such compensation plans provides direct rewards to motivate the salesperson to expend effort to improve sales volume and profitability.

9.10 PROPORTION OF INCENTIVE PAY TO TOTAL COMPENSATION

What proportion of total compensation should be incentive pay? The decision on the proportion of incentivized pay in an overall compensation package is based on several factors, including the degree of consultative selling involved in the job. When the firm's business model is focused on short-term sales (such as increasing sales volume, profitability, or new customers), a large incentive component works effectively. Alternatively, when customer service and other non-sales objectives are deemed more important, the major emphasis is more appropriately on the base salary component of the plan. This gives management more control over rewarding the sales force's relationship selling activities.

If a particular combination plan is not very effective at motivating salespeople, one of the most common reasons is that the incentive portion is not large enough to motivate the salesperson. One approach is to open up the incentive component to negotiation on a salesperson-by-salesperson basis, thus creating a very individualized combination plan. In this way, salespeople who seek greater compensation security can focus on more fixed compensation (salary), while others can opt for the potential to earn even higher total compensation by taking greater risks through gaining more of their compensation from incentive-based rewards (Ho, Lee, and Wu 2009). Such individualized approaches must allow a salesperson to change his or her compensation allocation periodically, perhaps annually.

9.11 ISSUES IN SALES FORCE COMPENSATION

Beyond the basic compensation package, there are a number of other issues in creating the most effective, efficient compensation plan.

9.11.1 Cap on Incentive Compensation

Should there be a ceiling or cap on incentive earnings to ensure top salespeople do not earn substantially more money than other employees? This issue is dealt with in very different ways across companies and industries, and strong arguments can be made on both sides. Part of the variation in how different firms handle this issue seems to reflect variation in average compensation levels, with firms in relatively low-paying industries being more likely to impose caps than those in higher-paying lines of trade.

One argument in favor of ceilings is that they ensure top salespeople do not accrue such high earnings that other employees in the firm, sometimes even managers, suffer resentment and low morale. Ceilings also protect against wind-falls, such as increased sales due to the introduction of successful new products, where a salesperson's earnings might grow substantially without corresponding effort. Finally, ceilings make a firm's maximum potential sales compensation expense more predictable and controllable. A strong counterargument can be made, however, that such ceilings ultimately have a bad effect on motivation and dampen the sales force's enthusiasm. Also, when ceilings are in place, some salespeople may reach the earnings maximum early in the year and be inclined to put in less effort.

The issue of incentive ceilings has become a growing problem in relationship selling, particularly when compensating a salesperson in a team-selling environ-ment. As team selling brings together individuals from around the company, the question becomes: What is the appropriate compensation for the salesperson, given that the sale is the result of the many people's efforts throughout the firm? This problem is made worse as the size of each sale grows, and is especially relevant when dealing with key accounts. Another problem with incentive ceilings occurs as customers move around the world. How much should the sales representative be compensated for a sale in another part of the world even though that person is servicing the customer's headquarters in his or her territory? The solution to these problems that many companies have chosen is limiting or capping a salesperson's incentive compensation (Sharma 1997).

9.11.2 Timing of a Sale

When incentives are based on sales volume or other sales-related aspects of performance, the precise meaning of a sale should be defined to avoid confusion and irritation. Most incentive plans credit a salesperson with a sale when the order is accepted by the company, less any returns and allowances. Occasionally, though, it makes good sense to credit the salesperson with a sale only after the goods have been shipped or payment has been received from the customer. This is particularly true when the time between receipt of an order and shipment of the goods is long and the company wants its salespeople to maintain close contact with the customer to prevent cancellations and other problems. As a compromise, some plans credit salespeople with half a sale when the order is received and the other half when payment is made.

9.11.3 Timing of Incentive Payments

In general, plans offering salary plus commission are more likely to involve monthly incentive payments, whereas salary plus bonus plans more often make incentive payments on a quarterly or annual schedule.

Shorter intervals between performance and the receipt of rewards increase the motivating power of the plan. However, short intervals add to the computation required, increase administrative expenses, and may make the absolute amount of money received by salespeople appear so small they may not be very impressed with their rewards.

9.11.4 Team versus Individual Incentives

The increasing use of sales or cross-functional teams to win new customers and service major accounts raises some important questions about the kinds of incentives to include in a combination compensation plan. Should incentives be tied to the overall performance of the entire team, should separate incentives be keyed to the individual performance of each team member, or both? If both group and individual incentives are used, which should be given the greatest weight? These questions have yet to be addressed in sales research, and represent a growing issue for sales managers designing team-based incentives.

9.12 SALES CONTESTS

Sales contests are short-term incentive programs designed to motivate sales personnel to accomplish specific sales objectives. Although contests should not be considered part of a firm's ongoing compensation plan, they offer salespeople the opportunity to gain financial as well as non-financial rewards (Murphy, Dacin, and Ford 2004). Contest winners often receive prizes in cash, merchandise, or travel. Winners also receive non-financial rewards in the form of recognition and a sense of accomplishment.

9.12.1 Contest Objectives

Because contests supplement the firm's compensation program and are designed to motivate extra effort toward some short-term goals, their objectives are very specific and clearly defined. Equally important, incentive compensation needs to be consistent with stated corporate objectives (Murphy and Dacin 2009). Unfortunately, although companies may believe an objective is important, they do not always create incentives for salespeople that reflect those objectives.

Sales contest time frames are, most often, relatively short. This ensures that salespeople maintain their enthusiasm and effort throughout the contest. But the contest should be long enough to allow all members of the sales force a reasonable chance of winning. As a result, the average duration of sales contests is about three months.

9.12.2 The Ratio of Success

While there are a number of different formats, three contest formats are popular. In the first, salespeople compete with themselves by trying to attain individual quotas so that everyone who reaches or exceeds quotas during the contest period wins. A second form requires that all members of the sales force compete with each other. The people who achieve the highest overall performance on some dimension are the winners. A third format organizes the sales force into teams, which compete for group and individual prizes.

Historically, individual sales quotas have been the most popular of the three formats. This reliance on individual quotas allows firms to design contests that focus salespeople's effort on specific objectives, do not put salespeople in low-potential territories at a disadvantage, and do not undermine cooperation in the sales force by forcing salespeople to compete against each other.

Whichever format is used, it is essential that every member of the sales force has a reasonable chance of winning an award. If there are to be only one or a few winners, salespeople may think their chances of winning are remote, and give up on the contest.

In addition, average or below-average performers may automatically assume the top performers will win the award and not try as hard to hit sales goals. In this respect, contests that provide rewards to everyone who meets quotas during the contest period are desirable. Increasingly, companies are focusing on incentive programs, including contests that seek to reward more rather than fewer salespeople.

9.12.3 Criticism of Sales Contests

Although many sales managers believe contests are effective for motivating special efforts from salespeople, contests can potentially cause a few problems, particularly if they are poorly designed or implemented.

Some critics argue that contests designed to stimulate sales volume may produce results that are largely fleeting, with no lasting improvement in market share. Salespeople may "borrow" sales from before or after the contest to increase their volume during the contest. As a result, customers may be overstocked—causing sales volume to fall off for some time after the contest is over. Contests may also hurt the cohesiveness and morale of the company's salespeople. This is particularly true when contests force individual salespeople to compete with one another for rewards and the number of rewards is limited.

Finally, some firms tend to use sales contests to cover up faulty compensation plans. That is, salespeople are compensated a second time for what they are already being paid to do. Contests should be used on a short-term basis to motivate special efforts beyond the normal performance expected of the sales force. If a firm finds itself conducting frequent contests to maintain an acceptable level of sales performance, it should re-examine its compensation and incentive program.

9.13 NON-FINANCIAL REWARDS

Most sales managers consider opportunities for promotion and advancement second only to financial incentives as an effective sales force motivator. This is particularly true for young salespeople who view their sales positions as stepping-stones to top management. One common career path is from salesperson to district sales manager to top sales management. Thus, if a person has been with a firm for several years without making it into sales management, the individual may start to believe such a promotion will never happen. Consequently, veteran salespeople may begin to concentrate solely on financial rewards, or they may lose motivation and not work as hard (Miao, Lund, and Evans 2009).

To overcome this problem, some firms have instituted two different career paths for salespeople. One leads to management, while the other leads to more advanced sales positions. The latter usually involves responsibility for dealing with key accounts or leading sales teams. To make advanced sales positions more attractive as promotions, many firms provide people in those positions with additional benefits such as higher compensation.

9.13.1 Recognize Success

Contest awards and promotions to positions with more responsibility provide recognition for good performance, but many firms also have separate recognition programs to provide non-monetary rewards. As with contests, effective recognition programs should offer a reasonable chance of winning for everyone in the sales force. But if a very large proportion of the sales force achieves recognition, the program is likely to lose some of its appeal because the winners feel no special sense of accomplishment. Consequently, effective recognition programs often recognize the best performers across several different performance dimensions (e.g. the highest sales volume for the year, the biggest percentage increase in sales, or the best customer retention record). Recognition is an attractive reward because it makes a salesperson's peers and superiors aware of outstanding performance. Communicating the winner's achievements, through recognition at a sales meeting, publicity in the local press, announcements in the company's internal newsletter, or other ways is an essential part of a good recognition program. Also, firms typically give special awards as part of their recognition program, and these are often awards with low monetary but high symbolic value, such as trophies, plaques, or rings.

9.14 CREATING SUCCESSFUL REWARD PROGRAMS

The complexity of these issues makes designing and implementing an effective compensation and incentive program difficult. Many managers wonder whether their company's program is as effective as possible in motivating the kinds and amounts of effort they desire from salespeople (Ramaswami and Singh 2003). And sometimes compensation plans just get so complicated that they have to be retooled to make them understandable to the sales force. To make matters worse, even well-designed motivational programs can lose their effectiveness over time.

Recognizing such problems, an increasing number of firms frequently review their compensation and incentive policies. Many firms adjust their total compensation levels at least annually, and they are increasingly willing to make more substantial adjustments in their programs when circumstances demand. Some firms have established compensation and incentive committees to regularly monitor sales motivation programs for fairness and effectiveness. Two major issues involve (1) linking sales goals to reward programs and (2) linking sales activities to reward programs.

9.14.1 Linking Sales Goals to Rewards Programs

A major purpose of any sales compensation program is to stimulate and influence the sales force to work toward accomplishing the objectives of securing, building, and maintaining long-term relationships with profitable customers. As a first step in deciding what job activities and performance dimensions a new or improved motivation program should stimulate, a manager should evaluate how salespeople are allocating their time. On what job activities do they focus, and how much time do they devote to each? How good are their current outcomes on various dimensions of performance, such as total sales volume, sales to new customers, or retention of existing customers? Much of this information can be obtained from job analyses conducted by the firm as part of its recruitment and selection procedures, as well as from performance evaluations and company records.

This assessment of the sales force's current allocation of effort and levels of performance can then be compared to the firm's specific selling objectives. Such comparisons often reveal that some selling activities and dimensions of performance are receiving too much emphasis from the sales force, while others are not receiving enough. This situation necessitates an adjustment in the incentive plan; in particular, it requires an immediate look at the quotas salespeople are working against. An important sales management function is monitoring whether the compensation and incentive plan, as well as associated quotas, continue to be effective over time in motivating the sales force. Remember, to be effective, quotas (which are goals for attaining some aspect of the sales job) must be specific, measurable, and realistically attainable.

9.14.2 Linking Sales Activities to Reward Programs

When the firm's relationship selling objectives are misaligned with its sales force's allocation of time, the compensation and incentive program can be redesigned to more strongly reward desired activities or performance outcomes, thus motivating the sales reps to redirect their efforts.

It is a mistake to try to motivate salespeople to do too many things at once. When rewards are tied to numerous different aspects of performance, (1) it becomes difficult for a salesperson to focus on improving performance dramatically in any one area, and (2) the salesperson is more likely to be uncertain about how total performance will be evaluated. In short, complex compensation and incentive programs may lead to great confusion among salespeople. Thus, it is better for compensation and incentive plans to link rewards to only the key aspects of job performance (Widmier 2002). They should be linked to those aspects consistent with the firm's highest priority and relationship selling objectives.

The complex relationship between today's customers and their suppliers has created the need for salespeople to cooperate and work with many individuals within their own firm as well as within the customer's business. Many performance outcomes will not be achieved unless salespeople cooperate with others. Linking financial compensation programs with the need for cooperation is critical in building long-term relationships with customers (Yilmaz and Hunt 2001).

Some companies choose to link compensation with customer-oriented metrics such as customer satisfaction. One reason for the reluctance of many firms to base rewards on customer satisfaction is the difficulty of measuring changes in satisfaction over time. Also, while there is some evidence that strong satisfaction-based incentives improve customer service by salespeople, some managers worry that such incentives may distract sales reps from the tasks necessary to capture additional sales volume in the short term. To offset this problem, some firms combine customer satisfaction-based incentives with bonus or commission payments tied to sales quotas or revenue. Unfortunately, such mixed incentive plans can sometimes add confusion for the sales force and even lead to reductions in customer service levels (Sharma and Sarel 1995). The bottom line, then, is that although rewarding customer service is an attractive goal, it can present some thorny measurement and design issues for the sales manager.

9.15 Conclusion

This chapter has focused on two critically important aspects of sales management: training and rewards. Improving the performance of the sales force means improving the performance of each salesperson and training is essential in making salespeople better. As discussed, training is critical for the entire sales force, not just for the new, inexperienced salespeople. The benefits of training extend through the sales organization; few management activities can have a greater impact on sales performance than training. At the same time, many aspects of sales training are not well understood. For example, practitioners and academics struggle with linking training with specific sales objectives, and long-term benefits are, more often than not, assumed rather than verified.

One of the most significant challenges facing sales managers today is to create an effective reward system that balances the needs of the individual salesperson while achieving corporate goals of effectiveness and efficiency. Coupled with that are increasing customer expectations of better service, more responsive suppliers, and, of course, lower costs. Few management responsibilities require more time to create and manage than the sales reward system. However, as we discussed here, sophisticated reward systems incorporating the latest technologies are being created and implemented with success.

REFERENCES

ABBOTT, J., B. KLEIN, C. HAMILTON, and A. J. ROSENTHAL (2009). "The Impact of Online Resilience Training for Sales Managers on Wellbeing and Performance," *E-Journal of Applied Psychology* 5.1, 89–95.

AHEARNE, M., R. JELINEK, and A. RAPP (2005). "Moving Beyond the Direct Effect of SFA Adoption on Salesperson Performance: Training and Support as Key Moderating Factors," *Industrial Marketing Management* 34.4, 379–88.

AMYX, D., S. BHUIAN, D. SHARMA, and K. LOVELAND (2008). "Salesperson Corporate Ethical Values (SCEV) Scale Development and Assessment Among Salespeople," *Journal of Personal Selling & Sales Management* 28.4, 387.

ARTIS, A. B., and E. G. HARRIS (2007). "Self-Directed Learning and Sales Force Performance: An Integrated Framework," *Journal of Personal Selling & Sales Management* 27.1, 9.

ATTIA, A., E. HONEYCUTT, and M. JANTAN (2008). "Global Sales Training: In Search of Antecedent, Mediating, and Consequence Variables," *Industrial Marketing Management* 37.2, 181.

————and M. P. LEACH (2005). "A Three-Stage Model for Assessing and Improving Sales Force Training and Development," *Journal of Personal Selling & Sales Management* 25.3, 253–68.

BARKSDALE, H. C., Jr., D. N. BELLENGER, J. S. BOLES, and T. G. BRASHEAR (2003). "The Impact of Realistic Job Previews and Perceptions of Training on Sales Force Performance and Continuance Commitment: A Longitudinal Test," *Journal of Personal Selling & Sales Management* 23.2, 125–38.

BROWN, S. P., K. R. EVANS, M. K. MANTRALA, and G. CHALLAGALLA (2005). "Adapting Motivation, Control, and Compensation Research to a New Environment," *Journal of Personal Selling & Sales Management* 25.2, 155–67.

BUEHRER, R. E., S. SENECAL, and E. B. PULLINS (2005). "Sales Force Technology Usage— Reasons, Barriers, and Support: An Exploratory Investigation," *Industrial Marketing Management* 34.4, 389.

BURNTHORNE LOPEZ, T., C. D. HOPKINS, and M. A. RAYMOND (2006). "Reward Preferences of Salespeople: How Do Commissions Rate?" *Journal of Personal Selling & Sales Management* 26.4, 381–90.

BUSH, A. J., J. B. MOORE, and R. ROCCO (2005). "Antecedents and Consequences of CRM Technology Acceptance in the Sales Force," *Industrial Marketing Management* 34.4, 355–68.

BUSH, V. D., and T. N. INGRAM (2001). "Building and Assessing Cultural Diversity Skills: Implications for Sales Training," *Industrial Marketing Management* 30.1 (January), 65–76.

CHONKO, L. B., J. F. TANNER, Jr., and W. A. WEEKS (1992). "Reward Preferences for Salespeople," *Journal of Personal Selling & Sales Management* 12.3, 67–75.

CRON, W. L., G. W. MARSHALL, J. SINGH, R. L. SPIRO, and H. SUJAN (2005). "Salesperson Selection, Training, and Development: Trends, Implications, and Research Opportunities," *Journal of Personal Selling & Sales Management* 25.2, 123–36.

DEETER-SCHMELZ, D. R., K. N. KENNEDY, and D. J. GOEBEL (2002). "Understanding Sales Manager Effectiveness: Linking Attributes to Sales Force Values," *Industrial Marketing Management* 31.7, 617–26.

ERFFMEYER, R. C., R. K. RUSS, and J. F. HAIR, Jr. (1991). "Needs Assessment and Evaluation in Sales-Training Programs," *Journal of Personal Selling & Sales Management* 11.1, 17.

FINE, L. M., and J. R. FRANKE (1995). "Legal Aspects of Salesperson Commission Payments: Implications for the Implementation of Commission Sales Programs," *Journal of Personal Selling & Sales Management* 15.1, 53–68.

HAHNE, G. (1981). "Creating Credibility for Your Sales Training," *Training & Development Journal* (November), 34.

HALL, B., and S. BOEHLE (2004). "Top Training Priorities for 2004: The Second Annual Leaders of Learning Survey," *Training* (February), 26–33.

HO, J., L. LEE, and A. WU (2009). "How Changes in Compensation Plans Affect Employee Performance, Recruitment, and Retention: An Empirical Study of a Car Dealership," *Contemporary Accounting Research* 26.1, 4.

HONEYCUTT, E. D., Jr., K. KARANDE, A. ATTIA, and S. D. MAURER (2001). "An Utility Based Framework for Evaluating the Financial Impact of Sales Force Training Programs," *Journal of Personal Selling & Sales Management* 21.3, 229–38.

——and T. H. STEVENSON (1989). "Evaluating Sales Training Programs," *Industrial Marketing Management* 18.3, 215.

JANTAN, M. A., E. D. HONEYCUTT, Jr., S. T. THELEN, and A. M. ATTIA (2004). "Managerial Perceptions of Sales Training and Performance," *Industrial Marketing Management* 33.7, 667–73.

JARAMILLO, F., F. A. CARRILLAT, and W. B. LOCANDER (2005). "A Meta-Analytic Comparison of Managerial Ratings and Self-Evaluations," *Journal of Personal Selling & Sales Management* 25.4, 315–28.

JOHNSTON, M. W., and G. W. MARSHALL (2009). *Sales Force Management*, 9th edn, Burr Ridge, IL: McGraw-Hill/Irwin.

KALRA, A., M. SHI, and K. SRINIVASAN (2003). "Sales Force Compensation Scheme and Consumer Inferences," *Management Science* 49.5, 655–72.

KUMAR, V., R. VENKATESAN, and W. REINARTZ (2008). "Performance Implications of Adopting a Customer-Focused Sales Campaign," *Journal of Marketing* 72.5, 50.

LEACH, M. P., and A. H. LIU (2003). "Investigating Interrelationships Among Sales Training Evaluation Methods," *Journal of Personal Selling & Sales Management* 23.4, 327–39.

——and W. J. JOHNSTON (2005). "The Role of Self-Regulation Training in Developing the Motivation Management Capabilities of Salespeople," *Journal of Personal Selling & Sales Management* 25.3, 269–81.

LIANG, X., S. WU, and J. Y. JUNG (2009). "Re-coupling Compensation-Performance Relationship: A Mediating Role of Performance," *International Journal of Human Resource Development & Management* 9.4: 317–33.

Lichtenthal, J. D., and T. Tellefsen (2001). "Toward a Theory of Business Buyer–Seller Similarity," *Journal of Personal Selling & Sales Management* 21.1, 1–14.

Lim, H., S. Lee, and K. Nam (2007). "Validating E-learning Factors Affecting Training Effectiveness," *International Journal of Information Management* 27.1, 22.

Liu, S. S., and L. B. Comer (2007). "Salespeople as Information Gatherers: Associated Success Factors," *Industrial Marketing Management* 36.5, 565.

Lopez, T. B., C. D. Hopkins, and M. A. Raymond (2006). "Reward Preferences of Salespeople: How Do Commissions Rate?" *Journal of Personal Selling & Sales Management* 26.4: 381.

Lupton, R. A., J. E. Weiss, and R. T. Peterson (1999). "Sales Training Evaluation Model (STEM): A Conceptual Framework," *Industrial Marketing Management* 28.1, 73–86.

Miao, C.F., D. J. Lund, and K. R. Evans (2009). "Re-Examining the Influence of Career Stages on the Salesperson: A Cognitive and Affective Perspective," *Journal of Personal Selling & Sales Management* 29.3, 243–56.

Murphy, W., and P. Dacin (2009). "Sales Contest Research: Business and Individual Difference Factors Affecting Intentions to Pursue Contest Goals," *Industrial Marketing Management* 38.1, 109.

————and N. M. Ford (2004). "Sales Contest Effectiveness: An Examination of Sales Contest Design Preferences of Field Sales Forces," *Academy of Marketing Science Journal* 32.2, 127–43.

O'Grady, G. (2003). "Every Rep a Star," *Pharmaceutical Executive: Successful Sales Management* (May), 76–80.

Pelham, A. M. (2002). "An Exploratory Model and Initial Test of the Influence of Firm Level Consulting-Oriented Sales Force Programs on Sales Force Performance," *Journal of Personal Selling & Sales Management* 22.2, 97–109.

————(2006). "Sales Force Involvement in Product Design: The Influence on the Relationships between Consulting-Oriented Sales Management Programs and Performance," *Journal of Marketing Theory & Practice* 14.1, 37–55.

————and P. Kravitz (2008). "An Exploratory Study of the Influence of Sales Training Content and Salesperson Evaluation on Salesperson Adaptive Selling, Customer Orientation, Listening, and Consulting Behaviors," *Journal of Strategic Marketing* 16.5, 413–35.

Pettijohn, C. E., L. S. Pettijohn, and A. J. Taylor (2007). "Does Salesperson Perception of the Importance of Sales Skills Improve Sales Performance, Customer Orientation, Job Satisfaction, and Organizational Commitment, and Reduce Turnover?" *Journal of Personal Selling & Sales Management* 27.1, 75.

Pullins, E. B., and L. M. Fine (2002). "How the Performance of Mentoring Activities Affects the Mentor's Job Outcomes," *Journal of Personal Selling & Sales Management* 22.4, 259–71.

Ramaswami, S. N., and J. Singh (2003). "Antecedents and Consequences of Merit Pay Fairness for Industrial Salespeople," *Journal of Marketing* 67.4, 46–66.

Ricks, J., J. Williams, and W. Weeks (2008). "Sales Trainer Roles, Competencies, Skills, and Behaviors: A Case Study," *Industrial Marketing Management* 37.5, 593.

Roman, S., S. Ruiz, and J. L. Munuera (2002). "The Effects of Sales Training on Sales Force Activity," *European Journal of Marketing* 36.11–12, 1344–66.

Schwepker, C. H., Jr., and D. J. Good (2007). "Sales Management's Influence on Employment and Training in Developing an Ethical Sales Force," *Journal of Personal Selling & Sales Management* 27.4, 325–39.

SHARMA, A. (1997). "Customer Satisfaction-Based Incentive Systems: Some Managerial and Salesperson Considerations," *Journal of Personal Selling & Sales Management* 17.2, 61–70.

——and D. SAREL (1995). "The Impact of Customer Satisfaction-Based Incentive Systems on Salespeople's Customer Service Response: An Empirical Study," *Journal of Personal Selling & Sales Management* 15.3, 17.

SKIERA, B., and S. ALBERS (2008). "Prioritizing Sales Force Decision Areas for Productivity Improvements Using a Core Sales Response Function," *Journal of Personal Selling & Sales Management* 28.2, 145.

SOGUNRO, O. A. (2004). "Efficacy of Role-Playing Pedagogy in Training Leaders: Some Reflections," *Journal of Management Development* 23.3–4, 355–71.

TALGAN, BRUCE (2001). "Real Pay for Performance," *Journal of Business Strategy* (May–June), 19–22.

VAN DER KLINK, M. R., and J. N. STREUMER (2002). "Effectiveness of On-the-Job Training," *Journal of European Industrial Training* 26.2–4, 196–9.

VERBEKE, W., and R. P. BAGOZZI (2000). "Sales Call Anxiety: Exploring What It Means When Fear Rules a Sales Encounter," *Journal of Marketing* 64.3, 88–101.

WACHNER, T., C. PLOUFFE, and Y. GRÉGOIRE (2009). "SOCO's Impact on Individual Sales Performance: The Integration of Selling Skills as a Missing Link," *Industrial Marketing Management* 38.1, 32.

WAGNER, J. A., N. M. KLEIN, and J. E. KEITH (2001). "Selling Strategies: The Effects of Suggesting a Decision Structure to Novice and Expert Buyers," *Academy of Marketing Science Journal* 29.3, 289–306.

WIDMIER, S, (2002). "The Effects of Incentives and Personality on the Salesperson's Customer Orientation," *Industrial Marketing Management* 31.7, 609–15.

WILSON, P. H., D. STRUTTON, and M. T. FARRIS II (2002). "Investigating the Perceptual Aspect of Sales Training," *Journal of Personal Selling & Sales Management* 22.2, 77–86.

YILMAZ, C., and S. D. HUNT (2001). "Salesperson Cooperation: The Influence of Relational, Task, Organizational, and Personal Factors," *Academy of Marketing Science Journal* 29.4, 335.

CHAPTER 10

....

ADDRESSING JOB STRESS IN THE SALES FORCE

....

THOMAS N. INGRAM
RAYMOND W. LAFORGE
CHARLES H.
SCHWEPKER, JR.

10.1 INTRODUCTION

....

Within the sales context, job stress has been defined as "a psychological process wherein a salesperson perceives personal resources as taxed, resulting in an unknown potential for negative outcomes" (Sager and Wilson 1995: 59). Well before the worldwide economic downturn of 2008/2009, there were clear indications that job stress was a widespread problem in sales and other "high-pressure" occupations. Researchers in the mid-1990s predicted that job stress would increase, noting that the dynamics of change, lack of employee control, and higher workload were fueling an epidemic in job stress (Cartwright and Cooper 1997). Almost a decade later, Jones, Brown, Zoltners, and Weitz (2005) noted that an increasingly complex business environment, intensifying competition, and pace of change were imposing escalating demands and expectations on salespeople in virtually all industries. For example, new communications technology allows instant contact with customers around the clock. This can be positive, but it also contributes to a stressful environment in which the salesperson is rarely separated from the job. Today's salespeople are working smarter and harder than their predecessors, yet feel the stress of not knowing if their efforts will be sufficient.

Several factors contribute to job stress in sales occupations, including the undeniable pressure to perform at an acceptable level. Salespeople's performance is critical not only to their own success but also to the success of their employers and customers. The inability of salespeople to minimize their responsibilities to significant others contributes to their job stress. Key performance metrics such as sales versus quota are easily observed, while the sometimes excruciating efforts that lead to results are not so easily observed. Stress is further increased as salespeople regularly face non-routine situations, and often work without the support that comes with supervision on a daily basis. This can create a lack of clarity about how to proceed, thus adding to job stress. Because salespeople occupy boundary-role positions, additional stress is generated when the demands of customers, employers, and other parties conflict.

Salespeople in many organizations also experience stress due to various forms of work overload. Of particular interest in sales organizations is role overload, which is the perception that role demands are overwhelming relative to available resources (Brown, Jones, and Leigh 2005). Another contributor to salesperson job stress is ethical conflict, which occurs when salespeople face ethical dilemmas on the job (Dubinsky and Ingram 1984, Schwepker, Ferrell, and Ingram 1997). Unfortunately, ethical conflict is a fairly common occurrence in the sales field.

Eliminating job stress in most sales organizations is not feasible, and may not be desirable. Some stress can be positive, as it can improve employee motivation and lead to higher performance levels. Nonetheless, the significant negative effects of excess work-related stress call for management efforts to achieve a reasonable level of control over salespeople's job stress. Unreasonable levels of job stress can negatively impact individual salesperson performance and lead to excessive employee turnover. Negative customer perceptions and actions can result when salespeople are stressed and exhibit behaviors that are deleterious to the establishment and enhancement of customer relationships. Excess stress can also reduce overall sales force effectiveness and sales manager performance, as dealing with stressed employees can take an inordinate amount of time away from dealing with other crucial matters.

Our objective in this chapter is to summarize three decades of research on job stress in the sales field and offer managerial suggestions for reducing job stress among salespeople. Existing research is used to generate suggested organizational and managerial actions to reduce salespeople's job stress and ultimately improve their job satisfaction and other important job outcomes. Important directions for future research are also identified.

At the outset, it is important to note that this chapter will not consider the medical and healthcare ramifications of job stress among salespeople. Serious physiological problems such as increased blood pressure and heart rate have been associated with occupational stress, as have mental health concerns, including depression and anxiety. Further, some coping behaviors such as excessive drug or alcohol usage have been linked with job stress. We regard these as medical issues that should be addressed with the guidance of medical professionals. Our focus in this chapter will be on the managerial actions, organizational factors, and individual salesperson characteristics that impact job stress in sales organizations, and on how sales managers and sales organizations can reduce excess levels of job stress.

10.2 RESEARCH INSIGHTS: A MODEL OF SALESPERSON JOB STRESS

The model of salesperson job stress shown in Figure 10.1 will guide our summary of existing research. As depicted in the model, salesperson job stress is impacted both directly and indirectly by sales manager leadership behaviors (training, empowerment, control system, etc.), organizational characteristics (culture, climate, span of control, etc.) and salesperson characteristics (e.g. experience, locus of control, self-efficacy). These antecedents affect two key role stressors, role conflict and role ambiguity, which significantly impact salesperson job stress. Both role stressors and job stress ultimately affect several job consequences (e.g. job satisfaction, performance, motivation). Furthermore, as seen in Figure 10.1 and discussed here, several factors (e.g. upward influence tactics, gender, education) have been found to moderate the relationship between role stressors and job consequences.

10.2.1 Key Stressors: Role Conflict and Role Ambiguity

Research in the sales literature has focused on two primary stressors: role conflict and role ambiguity. An employee sees his or her role as a pattern of expected behaviors. Roles, however, differ from job tasks in that roles are the set of expected behaviors while performing job tasks (cf. Tubre and Collins 2000).

Role conflict develops when two or more role expectations occur simultaneously in which compliance with one would make compliance with the other difficult or impossible (Kahn, Wolfe, Quinn, Snoek, and Rosenthal 1964). This construct has been conceptualized in terms of the following five conflict types (cf. Michaels, Day, and Joachimsthaler 1987: 31):

1. Intrasender: the extent to which two or more role expectations from a single role sender are mutually incompatible.

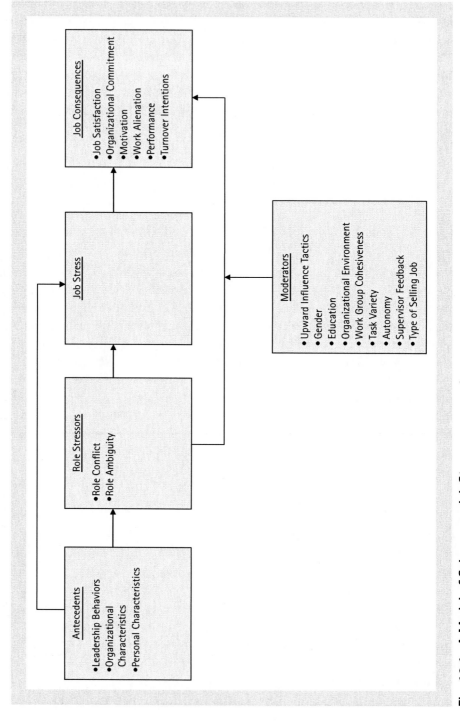

Fig. 10.1. A Model of Salesperson Job Stress

2. Intersender: the extent to which role expectations from one role sender oppose those from one or more other role senders.
3. Person–role: the extent to which expectations are incongruent with the orientation of values of the role incumbent.
4. Interrole: the extent to which expectations for performance of one role are incompatible with the expectations for performance of a different role.
5. Role overload: the extent to which the various role expectations communicated to a role incumbent exceed the amount of time and resources available for their accomplishment.

In an attempt to measure aspects of person–role conflict commonly found in the sales environment, Chonko, Howell, and Bellenger (1986) developed a measure that assesses the compatibility of the salesperson's expectations with those of his or her supervisor, customers, family, personal principles, and the job itself. They found these to be important dimensions of salesperson role conflict.

Role ambiguity stems from intra-role stress caused by the lack of information concerning role expectations (Kahn et al. 1964). It is the extent to which one is uncertain regarding expectations about a role, the most appropriate ways to fulfill these expectations, and the consequences of role performance (Behrman and Perreault 1984). Kahn et al. (1964) believe that boundary spanners, who produce innovative solutions to non-routine problems and face a variety of role expectations from those both inside and outside the organization, are more likely to experience role ambiguity. Salespeople certainly qualify as such individuals.

Like role conflict, ambiguity is believed to have several dimensions. Chonko et al. (1986) developed a scale that measures role ambiguity stemming from five sources: the job, the salesperson's family, supervisor, customers, and the sales organization. Studying boundary spanners, Singh and Rhoads (1991) developed a scale that measures seven distinct facets of boundary role ambiguity. This measure is similar to the Chonko et al. (1986) measure, but does not include the job dimension and adds ethical, co-worker, and other manager ambiguity dimensions. Salesperson role ambiguity was further partitioned into internal (boss, other managers, co-workers, company, ethical involving internal role members) and external (family, customer, ethical involving external role members) dimensions (Rhoads, Singh, and Goodell 1994). It appears that salespeople experience more internal than external ambiguity (Rhoads, Singh, and Goodwell 1994).

The relationship between the two role stressors is not clear, as role ambiguity has been found to both positively (Sager 1994, Babakus, Cravens, Johnston, and Moncrief 1999) and negatively (Jaramillo, Mulki, and Solomon 2006) impact role conflict, while role conflict has been found to positively impact role ambiguity (Behrman and Perreault 1984, Johnston, Parasuraman, Futrell, and Black 1990) as well as be positively associated with it (Brown and Peterson 1993, Jones et al. 1996).

10.2.2 Leadership Behaviors and Role Stressors

The most consistently found antecedent to both role conflict and ambiguity is leadership consideration (Teas 1983, Hampton, Dubinsky, and Skinner 1986, Fry, Futrell, Parasuraman, and Chmielewski 1986, Johnston et al. 1990, Hafer 1986, Agarwal and Ramaswami 1993, Sager 1994, Jones et al. 1996, Sager, Yi, and Futrell 1998). Leadership consideration involves leader behaviors that create a climate of psychological support, mutual trust, helpfulness, and friendliness (House 1971). Salespeople who perceive that such a climate is created by their sales leader will experience less role conflict and ambiguity. One common form of support is sales training (Russ, McNeilly, Comer, and Light 1998). Through training, sales managers have the opportunity to delineate sales roles and clarify desired actions, thus reducing conflict and ambiguity. Researchers (e.g. Russ et al. 1998) who have conceptualized consideration as leader–member exchange quality, in which a superior fosters a relationship with a subordinate that involves mutual trust, respect, and goals, have found similar results.

Leadership role clarity involves the extent to which a sales manager is perceived by salespeople as having clearly established role tasks and performance expectations (Fry et al. 1986). As might be expected, there is an inverse relationship between leadership role clarity and role ambiguity (Fry et al. 1986, Johnston et al. 1990, Tanner, Dunn, and Chonko 1993, Jones et al. 1996), as clearly outlined duties and expectations should result in less ambiguity, at least in terms of these job aspects. Leadership clarity has likewise been found to lead to less role conflict (Fry et al. 1986, Tanner, Dunn, and Chonko 1993).

In addition, when salespeople are allowed to influence decisions about their job (i.e. participation), they are likely to experience less conflict (Teas 1983) and role ambiguity (Teas 1983, 1980, Agarwal and Ramaswami 1993). Specifically, this would include the ability to provide input in formulating standards (Walker, Churchill, and Ford 1975). Perhaps this in part explains why salespeople who feel empowered in the job will experience less conflict and ambiguity (Ruyter, Wetzels, and Feinberg 2001). Moreover, salespeople who are given more autonomy experience less role ambiguity (Hafer 1986, Agarwal and Ramaswami 1993).

Participation involves communication, which has been found to impact role stress. When sales managers use indirect communication to influence salespeople's actions by sharing information and decision-making responsibility with them, rather than specifically telling them what to do, they can reduce salesperson role ambiguity (Johlke, Duhan, Howell, and Wilkes 2000). Moreover, bidirectional communication between sales manager and salesperson, in which the manager solicits salesperson input and provides task-related instructions and feedback to salespeople, who in turn respond with their reactions and market feedback, reduces salesperson role ambiguity (Johlke et al. 2000). Communication in terms of feedback regarding job duties is particularly important, as it has been found to reduce salesperson ambiguity (Teas 1983, Agarwal and Ramaswami 1993).

Finally, the sales management control system, level of supervision, and style of leadership also have been examined in relationship to role stress. Management control involves the activities used by sales managers to influence salesperson behavior to achieve organizational objectives (Cravens, Lassk, Low, Marshall, and Moncrief 2004). Research shows that high control systems, those using output (e.g. setting performance standards that are monitored and evaluated), process (e.g. managers influence important sales activities), professional (e.g. encouraging information sharing and cooperation among salespeople), and cultural (e.g. driving behavior through strong shared values and beliefs) controls are more effective at reducing role conflict and role ambiguity than other combinations of control systems (Cravens et al. 2004).

With higher control comes closer supervision. The more closely salespeople are supervised, the lower their role ambiguity (Walker, Churchill, and Ford 1975, Teas 1980, Behrman and Perreault 1984). Conversely it appears that a laissez-faire style of leadership will result in greater salesperson role conflict (Dubinsky et al. 1995).

Some research has found that salespeople who are supervised by high-performing sales managers (those classified by the researchers as exhibiting more transactional and transformational leadership behaviors) exhibit less role conflict and less role ambiguity (Russ, McNeilly, and Comer 1996, Dubinsky, Yammarino, Jolson, and Spangler 1995, MacKenzie, Podsakoff, and Rich 2001). While transactional leaders understand what followers want and get it for them in exchange for support, transformational leaders raise the consciousness of followers about the importance of outcomes and how to attain them by going beyond their own self-interests (Burns 1978). Transactional leadership leans heavily on contingent reward and punishment behaviors (Bryman 1992). The transformational leader, however, motivates one to do more than one would originally expect to do by articulating a vision, fostering the acceptance of group goals, providing an appropriate role model, providing individualized support and intellectual stimulation, and expressing high performance expectations (Podsakoff, MacKenzie, Moorman, and Fetter 1990).

It should be noted, however, that one aspect of transformational leadership, intellectual stimulation, tends to increase role ambiguity (MacKenzie, Podsakoff, and Ahearne 2001). This is not surprising, given that intellectual stimulation involves sales manager behaviors that challenge salespeople to question common work assumptions and to search for creative ways to improve their performance (MacKenzie, Podsakoff, and Ahearne 2001). Such tasks, by nature, are likely to create ambiguity.

10.2.3 Organizational Characteristics and Role Stressors

The firm's organizational structure plays an important role in impacting job stressors. When salespeople have clearly defined roles, tasks, administrative rules, policies, and procedures they tend to experience less role ambiguity (Hampton,

Dubinsky, and Skinner 1986, Michaels et al. 1988, Sager, Yi, and Futrell 1998) as they become clear on expectations. However, it is not entirely clear what effect this formalization has on role conflict, as it has been found to both increase (Teas 1983) and decrease it (Michaels et al. 1988, Sager, Yi, and Futrell 1998). While greater formalization may increase role clarity, having to abide by rules that salespeople may believe need to be "bent" to achieve customer satisfaction may result in increased role conflict (Agarwal and Ramaswami 1993). This may be particularly true when the sales position calls for developing and executing innovative solutions to customer problems. In such cases, salespeople may require a great need for flexibility. However, this need for flexibility may conflict with the firm's established rules and procedures. In this case, role conflict is likely to be higher (Behrman and Perreault 1984).

By providing salespeople with autonomy to deal with the unique demands of their role, the organization may be able to diminish role ambiguity (Hafer 1986, Singh 1993). Further, allowing such autonomy may be useful the more salespeople are required to negotiate compromises between the selling company and the customer (i.e. the greater the salesperson integration). This is because there is a positive relationship between salesperson integration and role conflict (Behrman and Perreault 1984). Perhaps additional autonomy is achieved through a greater span of control, which has been found to reduce both role conflict and ambiguity (Avolonitis and Panagopoulos 2007). When designing the structure, keep in mind that outside salespeople tend to experience more role ambiguity than inside salespeople (Tanner, Dunn and Chonko 1993).

Not only must policies and procedures be in place, but it is important for them to be enforced (Agarwal and Ramaswami 1993). Formalization with regard to ethical behavior appears to be particularly important, as it is likely to influence the firm's ethical climate. An ethical climate is believed to exist when the firm has ethical practices and procedures in place, such as ethical codes and ethical policies, which are practiced and enforced (Schwepker, Ferrell, and Ingram 1997). Ethical climate has been found to influence role conflict both directly (Jaramillo et al. 2006) and indirectly, through ethical conflict (differences in shared ethical values between salesperson and sales manager) (Schwepker, Ferrell, and Ingram 1997). An ethical climate should result in less ethical conflict concerning shared ethical values between salespeople and their sales manager. This in turn should result in lower role conflict. Likewise, ethical climate has been found to be inversely related to role ambiguity (Jaramillo et al. 2006). Having guidelines for handling ethical situations provides salespeople with a sense of clarity in a typically "grey" area.

Another critical organizational factor impacting salesperson role stress is the firm's organizational culture. Organizational culture can be defined as "the pattern of shared values and beliefs that help individuals understand organizational functioning and thus provide them norms for behavior in the organization" (Deshpande and Webster 1989: 4). When an organization has a strong culture in which its beliefs and values are widely shared by its members, those members are likely to experience less role conflict and role ambiguity (Barnes, Jackson, Hutt, and Kumar 2006). More specifically, Singh, Verbeke, and Rhoads (1996) found that organizations characterized by high levels of open communication, professional attitude, employee focus, and customer orientation (i.e. an affective archetype) result in boundary spanners who experience less role stress.

10.2.4 Individual Characteristics and Role Stressors

A limited number of individual characteristics have been associated with both role conflict and role ambiguity. Despite one recent study to the contrary (Alvolonitis and Panagopoulos 2007), experience on the job is generally thought to reduce salesperson role conflict (Onyemah 2008, Teas 1983, Walker, Churchill, and Ford 1975) and role ambiguity (Behrman and Perreault 1984, Singh and Rhoads 1991) as salespeople apparently become more familiar with role expectations and how to deal with conflicting demands. Additionally, salespeople who have an internal locus of control are likely to experience less role conflict (Behrman and Perreault 1984) and less ambiguity (Singh and Rhoads 1991) than those with an external locus of control. Individuals with an internal locus of control believe they have the power to influence events in their environment. As such, they tend to be more informed about their role and task environment than do those with an external locus of control (Singh and Rhoads 1991). Finally, salespeople high in self-efficacy tend to experience less role stress (Mulki, Lassk, and Jaramillo 2008). "Self-efficacy" relates to an individual's belief in their ability to perform a certain task. Salespeople's confidence in the ability to perform their job is likely to extend to their confidence in understanding role expectations and in effectively dealing with different role demands. Such findings support research showing that salespeople who tend to confront situations head-on and who tend to transform situations into opportunities are less vulnerable to the effects of role stressors (Onyemah 2008).

Salespeople's level of job involvement also impacts their job stress. Individuals who are involved with their job identify psychologically with it, consider work to be very important, and are impacted personally by it (Dubinsky and Hartley 1986). This involvement leads salespeople to have a clearer grasp of role expectations. As such, highly involved salespeople tend to experience less ambiguity (Dubinsky and Hartley 1986). Furthermore, male salespeople tend to experience less ambiguity than female salespeople (Singh and Rhoads 1991).

10.2.5 Consequences of Role Conflict and Role Ambiguity

Three decades of research indicate that higher levels of role conflict and role ambiguity are generally detrimental to the salesperson and the organization. In our review of sixteen studies over this period, a consistent finding is that salesperson job satisfaction can be increased by diminishing salesperson role conflict (e.g. Bagozzi 1978, Behrman and Perreault 1984, Johnston et al. 1990, Brown and Peterson 1993, Sager 1994, Singh 1998, Jaramillo et al. 2006, Jones, Chonko, Rangarajan, and Roberts 2007). There is also an inverse relationship between role ambiguity and job satisfaction, as indicated in twenty studies over the past three decades (e.g. Busch and Bush 1978, Teas 1980, Hafer and McCuen 1985, Rhoads, Singh, and Goodell 1994, MacKenzie et al. 1998, Johlke et al. 2000, Jaramillo et al. 2006, Singh 1993).

Likewise, both role conflict (Brown and Peterson 1993, Jones et al. 2007, Michaels et al. 1988, MacKenzie, Podsakoff, and Ahearne 1998, Singh 1998) and role ambiguity (Michaels et al. 1988, Johnston et al. 1990, Rhoads, Singh, and Goodell 1994, Agarwal and Ramaswami 1993, MacKenzie, Podsakoff, and Ahearne 1998, Singh 1998, Johlke et al. 2000) are inversely related to organizational commitment. Further, role ambiguity can lead to increased work alienation in which salespeople psychologically detach from their work, give little effort, and focus on extrinsic rewards (Michaels et al. 1988). Although there is little evidence linking role conflict directly to turnover intention (Jones et al. 2007, Nonis, Sager, and Kumar 1996), there is strong support for a positive relationship between role ambiguity and turnover intention (Busch and Bush 1978, Singh and Rhoads 1991, Brown and Peterson 1993, Rhoads et al. 1994, Singh et al. 1996, Jaramillo et al. 2006). Apparently the tension created by the lack of clarity in the salesperson's position makes salespeople lean toward leaving the organization.

Role stressors also impact salesperson motivation and job performance. Although the findings are limited in sales research, it appears that both role conflict (Tyagi 1985) and role ambiguity (Hampton, Dubinsky, and Skinner 1986) can have detrimental effects on salesperson work motivation. While two meta-analyses examining a variety of occupations find that role stress is negatively related to job performance (Gilboa, Shirom, and Fried 2005, Tubre and Collins 2000), the findings in the sales literature are less clear. Though some recent research suggests that moderate levels of ambiguity and role conflict may be beneficial to performance (Onyemah 2008), overall the results are mixed. In a meta-analysis of salesperson performance, Churchill et al. (1985) found that role perceptions have the largest average size association with performance. With regards to observed variation in correlations across studies in the meta-analysis that is real variation (i.e. not attributable to sampling effort), role perceptions rank third in their relationship to performance amongst the variables studied. It is fairly evident that role ambiguity negatively affects performance (Busch and Bush 1978, Behrman and Perreault 1984, Churchill, Ford, Hartley, and Walker 1985, Dubinsky and Hartley 1986, Singh and Rhoads 1991, Hafer 1986, Brown and Peterson 1993, Rhoads, Singh, and Goodell 1994, Singh 1993, Singh, Verbeke, and Rhoads 1996, MacKenzie, Podsakoff, and Ahearne 1998, Singh 1998, Babakus et al. 1999, MacKenzie, Podsakoff, and Rich 2001).

The effect of role conflict is less clear, as it has been found to be both positively (Behrman and Perreault 1984, Dubinsky and Hartley 1986, Singh et al. 1996, Babakus et al. 1999) and negatively (Bagozzi 1978, MacKenzie et al. 1998, Singh 1998) related to performance. Thus, some role conflict may actually be beneficial to salesperson performance. However, if the organization wants its salespeople to practice customer-oriented selling, in which salespeople focus on satisfying customer needs while attaining firm objectives, it should take steps to reduce role conflict and role ambiguity, as both tend to diminish its application (Flaherty, Dahlstron, and Skinner 1999).

Besides the potentially negative consequences to the organization resulting from role stressors, there are several detrimental individual consequences. Increases in both role conflict (Boles, Johnston and Hair 1997, Babakus et al. 1999) and role ambiguity (Babakus et al. 1999) can result in increases in salesperson emotional exhaustion. Emotional exhaustion, considered a key to job burnout, is characterized by a shortness of energy and the feeling that the individual's emotional "tank" is empty (Babakus et al. 1999). Furthermore, salespeople's conflicting demands tend to bring on greater job anxiety (Fry et al. 1986, Jones et al. 1996), while a lack of role clarity induces greater job tension (Singh and Rhoads 1991, Rhoads, Singh, and Goodell 1994). Role ambiguity likewise negatively impacts specific self-esteem (Bagozzi 1978), or how well an individual believes that he or she performs required duties of the sales job relative to other salespeople in the company, and positively influences salespeople's perceptions of diminished personal accomplishments (Lewin and Sager 2007).

Role stressors have also been found to affect the use of upward influence tactics by salespeople on their sales managers in an attempt to lessen role stress. Upward influence tactics are means by which salespeople influence their superiors to win their approval. Salespeople who perceive high role conflict use exchange (i.e. remind superior of a prior favor), ingratiation (i.e. act humble, praise superior), coalition-building (i.e. seek the aid of others to persuade superior), upward appeal (i.e. bypass immediate superior to appeal to higher authority), and assertiveness (i.e. demand or threaten superior) influence tactics more than those who perceive low role conflict (Nonis, Sager, and Kumar 1996). Similarly, salespeople high in role ambiguity are more likely to use exchange, ingratiation, coalition-building, and assertiveness influence tactics to influence their superior than those with low role ambiguity. Those with low role ambiguity are more likely to use the rationality upward influence tactic (i.e. logical arguments, facts) than those with high role ambiguity (Nonis, Sager, and Kumar 1996).

An important type of role conflict, role overload, has received limited attention in the sales area. Role overload, a form of person–role conflict, amounts to perceptions that role demands are overpowering relative to available capabilities and resources, which results in distraction and stress (Jones et al. 2007). Both role conflict and role ambiguity have been found to positively impact role overload (Mulki et al. 2008). Also, salespeople high in self-efficacy tend to experience less role overload (Mulki et al. 2008). In turn, role overload has been found to be both positively (Singh 1998) and negatively (Jones et al. 2007) related to organizational commitment, positively related to turnover intentions (Jones et al. 2007) and emotional exhaustion (Lewin and Sager 2007), and negatively related to job motivation (Tyagi 1985), job satisfaction (Jones et al. 2007), pay satisfaction (Mulki et al. 2008), and capability rewards (i.e. rewards based on selling skills) (Mulki et al. 2008).

10.2.6 Additional Antecedents of Job Stress

Although salesperson job stress can be defined in a number of ways, Sager and Wilson (1995: 59) synthesize the varied conceptualizations of job stress and define it as "a psychological process wherein a salesperson perceives personal resources as taxed, resulting in an unknown potential for negative outcomes." Role conflict and role ambiguity are believed to positively affect job stress (Sager 1994). Research has examined additional antecedents of role stress, several of which are similar to those for role conflict and role ambiguity. In terms of leadership behaviors, sales leaders need to make sure not to overload the salesperson with too many tasks and responsibilities, as this tends to result in greater job stress (Roberts, Lapidus. and Chonko 1997). Moreover, job stress can be reduced when sales leaders make job expectations clear (Tanner, Dunn, and Chonko 1993) and provide appropriate support to salespeople to help them succeed (Roberts, Lapidus, and Chonko 1997).

Several individual characteristics, attitudes, and behaviors have likewise been found to affect salesperson job stress. While several studies have found role stress to negatively impact salesperson job satisfaction, Sager (1994) found job satisfaction to negatively impact job stress. Apparently, more satisfied salespeople will feel less stressed out. Additionally, salespeople who feel more attached to the selling environment and subsequently have greater organizational commitment, job involvement, and growth-need strength tend to experience less job stress (Sager, Yi, and Futrell 1998). Salespeople high in growth-need strength want their sales environment to provide them with an opportunity to use and develop personal capabilities (Sager, Yi, and Futrell 1998). As was true with role stressors, salespeople with an internal locus of control likewise experience less job stress than those with an external locus of control. Salespeople's influence strategies also impact their job stress. Salespeople's use of threats and promises leads to greater physical and mental stress, resulting in less influence over the sale. However, the level of felt stress caused by using threats is moderated by a learning orientation (i.e. a strong desire to continuously improve and master selling skills) (McFarland 2003). Finally, the longer salespeople have been on the job with their firm and the greater their income, the less their job stress (Roberts, Lapidus, and Chonko 1997).

10.2.7 Consequences of Job Stress

Although much of the sales research has focused on role stressors, ambiguity and conflict, some research has found several negative consequences of salesperson job stress. Salespeople who experience job stress tend to be less involved in their jobs, less committed to the organization, and to experience lower levels of work and life satisfaction (Sager 1991a). Moreover, these salespeople do not perform as well (Roberts, Lapidus, and Chonko 1997) and are more likely to leave the organization (Sager 1991b).

While the findings in the sales literature show the negative consequences of job stress, as alluded to in the introduction, some stress can be beneficial. A meta-analysis of 82 articles comprising 101 samples found that hindrance stressors negatively affect performance both directly and indirectly through negative effects on strains and motivation. Challenge stressors, however, positively affect performance directly and indirectly through their positive impact on motivation, yet they negatively affect performance via their negative impact on strains (i.e. anxiety, exhaustion, depression, and burnout). Hindrance stressors comprise constraints, resource inadequacy, hassles, role conflict, role ambiguity, role dissensus, role interference, role strain, lack of role clarity, role overload, supervisor-related stress, and organizational politics. Job/role demands, pressure, time urgency, and workload constitute challenge stressors (LePine, Podsakoff, and LePine 2005).

10.2.8 Moderators

A variety of moderators have been found to influence the relationship between role stressors and job-related outcomes. Several individual factors, including upward influence tactics, gender, and education, are among these moderators. As mentioned earlier, upward influence tactics are means by which salespeople influence their superiors to win their approval. Upward influence tactics ingratiation, assertiveness, and upward appeal moderate the relationship between role ambiguity and satisfaction with a supervisor such that the use of these tactics increases the negative impact of role ambiguity on job satisfaction. In addition, as role ambiguity increases, greater use of ingratiation increases the likelihood that the salesperson intends to quit. When role conflict exists, the more a salesperson uses coalition-building as an upward influence tactic, the more likely it is he or she will quit (Nonis et al. 1996). When it comes to gender, role ambiguity and role conflict are negatively related to males' satisfaction with work, co-workers, supervisors, promotion, and policy, but are only negatively related to females' satisfaction with supervisors, co-workers, promotion, and policy. For females, there is a positive relationship between role ambiguity and supervisor satisfaction. Work/family conflict is negatively related to satisfaction with work, co-workers, and policy for women, and to increased satisfaction with pay, supervisor, promotion, and policy for men (Boles, Wood, and Johnson 2003). In terms of education, when role ambiguity exists, more educated salespeople are less likely to be committed to the organization than less educated salespeople. Moreover, role conflict is likely to have a greater impact on organizational commitment the higher the level of education of the salesperson (Michaels and Dixon 1994).

A variety of organizational characteristics have been found to act as moderators between role stressors and job-related outcomes. Role ambiguity's effect on job satisfaction is significantly more dysfunctional for a procedural organizational environment (i.e. one highly focused on processes relative to outcomes and least customer-oriented) than an affective environment that is characterized by high levels of open communication, professional attitude, employee focus, and customer orientation. However, role ambiguity's effect on performance is more dysfunctional for the affective environment (Singh et al. 1996). The more cohesive the work group, the smaller the negative impact of both role conflict and ambiguity on organizational commitment (Michaels and Dixon 1994).

With regard to structuring the sales position, task variety buffers the negative effects of role conflict on performance, but autonomy enhances the dysfunctional effects of role ambiguity on performance (Singh 1998). Thus, greater task variety may help improve performance, while greater autonomy increases it due to lower role stress. Caution must be given to improving task variety, however, as it enhances the dysfunctional effect of role ambiguity on turnover intentions (Singh 1998).

The research on leadership behaviors as moderators has been limited. It appears that supervisor feedback buffers the negative effects of role conflict on job performance but enhances the dysfunctional effects of role ambiguity on organizational commitment (Singh 1998).

The type of selling job impacts the interrelationships among role stress, affective attitude, and job outcomes of B-to-B salespeople such that role stressors have different impacts depending upon whether the selling job is missionary, trade, or technical (Avolonitis and Panagopoulos 2006). While role conflict had no impact on the missionary salesperson's intention to leave the job, its intention on trade salespeople's intention to leave is negative and it is positively related to technical salespeople's turnover intentions. Furthermore, role ambiguity is the only predictor of job performance in the missionary sample, while role conflict significantly affects the performance of technical salespeople (Avolonitis and Panagopoulos 2006). In a related study, it was determined that missionary salespeople experience less job stress than other B-to-B salespeople (Avolonitis and Panagopoulos 2007).

Studies examining role overload have found it to be both a moderator and a moderated variable. Role overload refers to the perception of overwhelming role demands relative to available resources (Brown, Jones, and Leigh 2005). When role overload is high, salespeople's perceptions of organizational resources provided by the firm are not related to self-efficacy, but when role overload is low, organizational resource perceptions are positively related to self-efficacy. Further, both self-efficacy and goal level are positively related to performance when role overload is low, but neither is related to performance when role overload is high (Brown et al. 2005). The positive effects achieved on salesperson performance through self-efficacy and goal setting may be negated by burdening salespeople with too much work and providing them with inadequate resources (Brown, Jones, and Leigh 2005).

In terms of moderators impacting the effect of role overload, experience seems to play a role. Although increased role overload tends to lead to increased turnover intentions, these may be mitigated by sales experience (Jones et al. 2007) and increasing the task variety of the salesperson's job (Singh 1998). In addition, role overload tends to have a more negative impact on the job satisfaction of experienced salespeople (Jones et al. 2007).

10.3 Managerial Implications

The results from our review of previous research provide general directions for actions that sales organizations and sales managers can take to reduce the negative consequences of job stress in the sales force. Research findings are reasonably consistent concerning the linkages between role stressors, job stress, and job consequences (see Figure 10.1). However, the antecedent factors and relationships are less clear due to the large number of potential antecedents, complex antecedent relationships, and limited research attention to some important areas. Although there are no simple actions sales organizations can take to reduce job stress in the sales force, the research literature suggests a number of approaches likely to create an environment that limits salesperson job stress to an acceptable level.

A broad interpretation of these research results indicates that sales organization and management efforts to achieve an effective balance between providing salespeople with direction as to role expectations, but also allowing salespeople reasonable discretion in responding to specific situations, are likely to produce the best results. Although the appropriate balance depends on the unique situation of each sales organization, the research does provide several general guidelines in the leadership, organizational, and individual areas that are potentially applicable to all sales organizations. The critical task is to determine the proper blending of decisions and activities within and across these areas.

It is clear that leadership has a significant impact on salesperson job stress. Sales force control systems and leadership style are particularly important. Low levels of role ambiguity and role conflict are most likely when sales force control systems achieve the appropriate balance between behavioral-based and outcome-based orientations. The basic objective is to ensure that salespeople understand the specific behavioral and outcome expectations for performing their job. An effective blend of transactional and transformational leadership styles can also have a significant impact. The use of rewards and punishments (transactional leadership) to clarify job expectations and direct salesperson behavior in conjunction with creating a supportive and trusting climate (transformational leadership) helps salespeople address ambiguity and conflict in their job situations.

Sales organizations also need to determine the proper balance between formalization and flexibility in their structure and policies. One key decision trade-off is the span of control and level of supervision. The objective is to determine the span of control that will provide the desired level of both sales manager supervision and salesperson empowerment. Sales organization policies need to be scrutinized and revised to ensure the right balance between direction and discretion. Different areas are likely to require different types of policies. For example, ethical policies might be more formalized with specific expectations and little salesperson discretion, as this should result in a more ethical climate and less role stress. Account management policies, in contrast, might provide a basic process framework, but allow salespeople considerable flexibility in the activities used at each stage of this process to develop and maintain account relationships.

Another key organizational aspect driving role stress is the organization's culture. Fostering a strong culture in which the organization's beliefs and values are widely shared by its members should lead to less role stress. In particular, an organization that promotes open communication, a professional attitude, an employee focus, and a customer orientation will find that its salespeople will experience less role stress. Thus the organization must develop and encourage two-way communication in the organization, so that salespeople are informed but also are given ample opportunity to voice their concerns. Furthermore, training should focus on professionalism in the sales force, as well as actions salespeople should be taking to put the customer first. Finally, the organization needs to engage in activities (e.g. financial and non-financial rewards) that communicate to its employees that they are valued. Together, these initiatives should help develop a culture that is conducive to less role stress.

The individual factors have somewhat more direct implications. Sales organizations can focus on hiring salespeople less likely to suffer from job stress. One approach is to use psychological tests to identify and then hire applicants who score high in locus of control and self-efficacy. Another possibility is to hire only experienced salespeople. If this is not desired or possible and inexperienced salespeople are hired, mentor programs might be used. The experienced salespeople can mentor new hires and transfer their insights about how to handle ambiguous and conflicting situations most effectively.

The management implications discussed to this point represent an attempt to create an environment intended to limit or reduce role stress for the entire sales force. Sales managers must also be attuned to specific salespeople experiencing high levels of job stress that are having especially negative consequences. Closer supervision with continuous communication and frequent feedback can help identify salespeople suffering from job stress. Although the appropriate sales management actions depend on each salesperson's situation, coaching and sales training programs can be tailored to the specific needs of individual salespeople and are effective approaches to reducing job stress to a manageable level.

10.4 DIRECTIONS FOR FUTURE RESEARCH

Over the past three decades, we have learned a great deal about job stress in the sales force. Nevertheless, much remains to be learned. Faced with ever-increasing demands in a progressively more complex sales environment, salespeople are turning to new technologies to cope. Research is needed to understand the effect of these technologies on salespeople's job stress. For instance, are advanced communication technologies making life less stressful for salespeople or are they actually generating more stress? Such technologies enable salespeople to more easily keep in contact with customers, but consequently they can make it difficult for salespeople to separate work from personal life. Is the relationship between stress and technology impacted by the salesperson's age or even generational group? Perhaps younger salespeople, familiar with the latest technology, are more adept at using technology and thus it creates less stress for them as opposed to those who are not accustomed to using the latest technology. How do we manage the stress associated with this technology?

The impact creating an entrepreneurial sales force may have on salesperson job stress is an area in need of investigation. As organizations create structural changes to compete in today's turbulent competitive environment, there has been a call for a more entrepreneurial organization, and in particular a more entrepreneurial sales force (The Sales Educators 2006). To cope with today's ever-changing environment, leading-edge firms are becoming more flexible and adaptable, which creates greater uncertainty. Entrepreneurship by its nature is about creating change—it is disruptive (The Sales Educators 2006). With the fluid roles and uncertainty created by fostering an entrepreneurial sales force, there is ample opportunity for increased role stress. We could benefit from more clearly understanding the dynamics between salesperson entrepreneurial behavior and job stress.

As teamwork continues to play an increasingly vital role in sales organizations, its effects on job stress are little known. Salespeople work as members of teams both formally and informally and within and outside the organization. Teamwork enhances the opportunity for uncertainty and conflicting roles as salespeople try to understand and meet the expectations of different role partners. What type of effect does teamwork have on job stress? How can any negative effects of teamwork on job stress be minimized?

There has been limited research investigating environmental influences on salesperson role stress. Russ et al. (1998) found that positive critical sales events lowered role ambiguity, but had no effect on role conflict. However, negative critical sales events increased both role ambiguity and role conflict. The authors defined a critical sales event as one that is out of the ordinary, and gave facing a significant new competitor as an example of a negative critical sales event. Given this lack of research on the environment, it may be a fruitful area for further research. In their book *Achieve Sales Excellence*, Stevens and Kinni (2007) point out that salespeople must be easily accessible. Do the demands of the market for greater accessibility generate greater salesperson stress? Does being easily accessible to one customer diminish the salesperson's ability to be easily accessible to another? If so, what impact does this have on role conflict for salespeople trying to effectively meet the needs of multiple demanding customers? How does any resulting stress impact customer relationships? Could these demands, along with the competitive environment, result in greater ethical conflict?

Today's sales force often includes multiple generations (e.g. boomers, generation X, generation Y) who bring differing values, attitudes, and interpersonal styles to the workplace. What are the effects of generational differences on role stress across organizational members as salespeople work with others within the organization? While generational differences may cause stress in teamwork, the relationship between salesperson job stress and teamwork dynamics in general needs further investigation. Moreover, does role stress result from salespeople working with customers across different generations? Given that different generations tend to operate under different value sets, could conflict between salespeople and customers of different generations result, ultimately impacting job stress?

There is an increasing need for sales specialists, and salespeople are being required to possess in-depth specialized knowledge. Undoubtedly such knowledge can assist the salesperson in creating customer value. Little is known regarding how the demands to provide additional value beyond the basic product or service affect salesperson job stress. Salespeople add value in many ways, including serving as advocates for customers to ensure their desired results. In doing so, conflicts may arise. As much as 50–60 percent of a salesperson's time is spent resolving customer problems caused or left unresolved by the salesperson's company (Stevens and Kinni 2007). Are these conflicts between the salesperson's desire to satisfy the customer and the problems caused by the salesperson's company creating undue stress? Which types of conflict are likely to result in the greatest stress?

There are several different approaches (e.g. stimulus response, mental states, need satisfaction, problem solving, consultative) to personal selling. Furthermore, some salespeople practice adaptive selling in which they alter their sales messages and behaviors during a sales presentation or as they encounter unique sales situations and customers. We do not know, however, how these approaches and behaviors affect salesperson job stress. Does the use of certain approaches result in greater job stress? What factors would affect the stress level associated with the use of each approach (e.g. is proper training simply the key to stress reduction with any approach?)? Furthermore, do salespeople who practice adaptive selling experience lower levels of stress?

Most of the sales research focuses on the negative consequences associated with salesperson job stress. Hence, there is a need to more closely examine stressors that may contribute to positive job outcomes. Challenge stressors (i.e. job/role demands, pressure, time urgency, and workload) have been found to positively impact performance and motivation (LePine, Podsakoff, and LePine 2005) in a variety of occupational settings. Yet the sales literature is remiss in examining their impact in a sales setting. We could greatly benefit by learning the effects of such factors on role stress so that positive stress (i.e. eustress) can be promoted to maximize salesperson effectiveness.

Job stress in the sales force is an increasingly important issue for sales organizations around the world. The global economic downturn, the complex and rapidly changing business environment, increased intensity of competition worldwide, and continuous introduction of new technologies will expand the job stress associated with sales jobs. Salesperson job stress research has increased our understanding of this important area and provided sales organizations with general guidelines to address this critical challenge. However, more research is needed to build on the current knowledge base, and to begin to address the impact of new trends on salesperson job stress relationships.

10.5 SUMMARY AND CONCLUSIONS

Job stress is a widespread and increasing problem in sales occupations. Excessive job stress has a negative relationship with a number of important salesperson job consequences. Fortunately, this area has received considerable attention from sales researchers. Our Model of Salesperson Job Stress (see Figure 10.1) provides a framework for organizing important job stress relationships. Based on this framework, we reviewed previous research results, discussed key findings, suggested important managerial implications, and suggested future research directions.

Considerable research has found that role conflict and role ambiguity are major determinants of salesperson job stress. Research also indicates that various leadership behaviors, organizational characteristics, and personal characteristics are antecedents to salesperson role conflict and role ambiguity, but also have a direct effect on job stress. In addition to a direct effect on job stress, role conflict and role ambiguity are related to various job consequences, with these relationships moderated by a number of personal and organizational factors.

These research results provide several management guidelines for sales organizations trying to limit salesperson job stress to acceptable levels. Among the most important management implications are the need for sales organizations to find an effective balance between providing salespeople with direction as to role expectations and discretion in responding to specific situations, between behavioral-based and outcome-based sales force control systems, between transformational and transactional leadership approaches, and between formalization and flexibility in sales organization structure and policies. Recruiting efforts to hire salespeople high in locus of control and self-efficacy, and coaching efforts to deal effectively with salespeople experiencing high job stress, are also important management actions suggested by research results.

Although previous research has improved our understanding of salesperson job stress relationships, there are many opportunities for future research efforts. Especially important issues needing attention are the effect of new and emerging technologies, environmental influences such as critical sales events, generational differences within sales organizations, developing an entrepreneurial sales organization, increasing teamwork within sales organizations, and the impact of different sales approaches on salesperson job stress. Sales researchers need to build on the strong foundation of past research and expand salesperson job stress research to address critical issues facing contemporary sales organizations. This research would expand the knowledge base on salesperson job stress, and provide important implications for managing salesperson job stress in the future.

References

AGARWAL, S., and S. N. RAMASWAMI (1993). "Affective Organizational Commitment of Salespeople: An Expanded Model," *Journal of Personal Selling & Sales Management* 13.2, 49–70.

AVOLONITIS, G. J., and N. G. PANAGOPOULOS (2006). "Role Stress, Attitudes and Job Outcomes in Business-to-Business Selling: Does the Type of Selling Situation Matter?" *Journal of Personal Selling & Sales Management* 24.1, 67–77.

—— —— (2007). "Exploring the Influence of Sales Management Practices on the Industrial Salesperson," *Journal of Business Research* 60.7, 765–75.

BABAKUS, E., D. W. CRAVENS, M. JOHNSTON, and W. C. MONCRIEF (1999). "The Role of Emotional Exhaustion in Sales Force Attitude and Behavior Relationships," *Journal of the Academy of Marketing Science* 27.1, 58–70.

BAGOZZI, R. (1978). "Salesforce Performance and Satisfaction as a Function of Individual Difference, Interpersonal and Situational Factors," *Journal of Marketing Research* 15.4, 517–31.

BARNES, J. W., D. W. JACKSON, M. D. HUTT, and A. KUMAR (2006). "The Role of Culture Strength in Shaping Sales Force Outcomes," *Journal of Personal Selling & Sales Management* 26.3, 255–70.

BEHRMAN, D. N., and W. D. PERREAULT, Jr. (1984). "A Role Stress Model of the Performance and Satisfaction of Industrial Salespersons," *Journal of Marketing* 48.4, 9–21.

BOLES, J. S., M. W. JOHNSTON, and J. F. HAIR, Jr. (1997). "Role Stress, Work–Family Conflict and Emotional Exhaustion: Inter-Relationships and Effects on Some Work-Related Consequences," *Journal of Personal Selling & Sales Management* 17.1, 17–28.

—— J. A. WOOD, and J. JOHNSON (2003). "Interrelationships of Role Conflict, Role Ambiguity, and Work–Family Conflict with Different Facets of Job Satisfaction and the Moderating Effects of Gender," *Journal of Personal Selling & Sales Management* 23.2, 99–113.

BROWN, S. P., E. JONES, and T. W. LEIGH (2005). "The Attenuating Effect of Role Overload on Relationships Linking Self-Efficacy and Goal Level to Work Performance," *Journal of Applied Psychology* 90.5, 972–9.

—— and R. A. PETERSON (1993). "Antecedents and Consequences of Salesperson Job Satisfaction: Meta-Analysis and Assessment of Causal Effects," *Journal of Marketing Research* 30.1, 63–77.

BRYMAN, A. (1992). *Charisma and Leadership in Organizations.* London: Sage.

BURNS, J. M. (1978). *Leadership.* New York: Harper & Row.

BUSCH, P., and R. F. BUSH (1978). "Women Contrasted to Men in the Industrial Salesforce: Job Satisfaction, Values, Role Clarity, Performance, and Propensity to Leave," *Journal of Marketing Research* 15.3, 438–48.

CARTWRIGHT, S., and C. L. COOPER (1997). *Managing Workplace Stress.* Thousand Oaks, CA: Sage.

CHONKO, L. B., R. D. HOWELL, and D. N. BELLENGER (1986). "Congruence in Sales Force Evaluations: Relations to Sales Force Perceptions of Conflict and Ambiguity," *Journal of Personal Selling & Sales Management* 6.1, 35–48.

CHURCHILL, G. A., Jr., N. M. FORD, S. W. HARTLEY, and O. C. WALKER, Jr. (1985). "The Determinants of Salesperson Performance: A Meta-Analysis," *Journal of Marketing Research* 22.2, 103–18.

—— —— and O. C. WALKER, Jr. (1976). "Organizational Climate and Job Satisfaction in the Salesforce," *Journal of Marketing Research* 13.4, 103–18.

CRAVENS, D. W., F. G. LASSK, G. S. LOW, G. W. MARSHALL, and W. C. MONCRIEF (2004). "Formal and Informal Management Control Combinations in Sales Organizations: The Impact on Salesperson Consequences," *Journal of Business Research* 57.3, 241–8.

DESHPANDE, R., and F. E. WEBSTER, Jr. (1989). "Organizational Culture: Defining the Research Agenda," *Journal of Marketing* 53.1, 25–49.

DUBINSKY, A. J., and S. W. HARTLEY (1986). "A Path-Analytic Study of a Model of Salesperson Performance," *Journal of the Academy of Marketing Science* 14.1, 36–46.

—— and T. N. INGRAM (1984). "Correlates of Salespeople's Ethical Conflict: An Exploratory Investigation," *Journal of Business Ethics* 3, 343–53.

—— F. J. YAMMARINO, M. A. JOLSON, and W. D. SPANGLER (1995). "Transformational Leadership: An Initial Investigation in Sales Management," *Journal of Personal Selling & Sales Management* 15.2, 17–31.

FLAHERTY, T. B., R. DAHLSTROM, and S. J. SKINNER (1999). "Organizational Values and Role Stress as Determinants of Customer-Oriented Selling Performance," *Journal of Personal Selling & Sales Management* 19.2, 1–18.

FRY, L. W., C. M. FUTRELL, A. PARASURAMAN, and M. A. CHMIELEWSKI (1986). "An Analysis of Alternative Causal Models of Salesperson Role Perceptions and Work-Related Attitudes," *Journal of Marketing Research* 23.2, 153–63.

GILBOA, S., A. SHIROM, and Y. FRIED (2005). "A Meta-Analysis of Stress and Performance at Work: Moderating Effects of Gender, Age and Tenure," *Academy of Management Proceedings*, A1–A6.

HAFER, J. C. (1986). "An Empirical Investigation of the Salesperson's Career Stage Perspective," *Journal of Personal Selling & Sales Management* 6.3, 1–7.

—— and B. A. McCUEN (1985). "Antecedents of Performance and Satisfaction in a Service Sales Force as Compared to an Industrial Sales Force," *Journal of Personal Selling & Sales Management* 5.2, 7–17.

HAMPTON, R., A. J. DUBINSKY, and S. J. SKINNER (1986). "A Model of Sales Supervisor Leadership Behavior and Retail Salespeople's Job-Related Outcomes," *Journal of the Academy of Marketing Science* 14.3, 33–43.

HOUSE, R. (1971). "A Path–Goal Theory of Leadership Effectiveness," *Administrative Science Quarterly*, 321–39.

JARAMILLO, F., J. P. MULKI, and P. SOLOMON (2006). "The Role of Ethical Climate on Salesperson's Role Stress, Job Attitudes, Turnover Intention and Job Performance," *Journal of Personal Selling & Sales Management* 26.3, 271–82.

JOHLKE, M. C., D. F. DUHAN, R. D. HOWELL, and R. W. WILKES (2000). "An Integrated Model of Sales Managers' Communication Practices," *Journal of the Academy of Marketing Science* 28.2, 263–77.

JOHNSTON, M. W., A. PARASURAMAN, C. M. FUTRELL, and W. C. BLACK (1990). "A Longitudinal Assessment of the Impact of Selected Organizational Influences on Salespeople's Organizational Commitment During Early Employment," *Journal of Marketing Research* 27.3, 333–44.

JONES, E., S. P. BROWN, A. A. ZOLTNERS, and B. W. WEITZ (2005). "The Changing Environment of Selling and Sales Management," *Journal of Personal Selling & Sales Management* 25.2, 105–11.

—— L. CHONKO, D. RANGARAJAN, and J. ROBERTS (2007). "The Role of Overload on Job Attitudes, Turnover Intentions and Salesperson Performance," *Journal of Business Research* 60.7, 663–71.

—— D. M. KANTAK, C. M. FUTRELL, and M. W. JOHNSTON (1996). "Leader Behavior, Work Attitudes, and Turnover of Salespeople: An Integrative Study," *Journal of Personal Selling & Sales Management* 16.2, 13–23.

KAHN, R. L., D. M. WOLFE, R. P. QUINN, J. D. SNOEK, and R. A. ROSENTHAL (1964). *Organizational Stress: Studies in Role Conflict and Ambiguity.* New York: Wiley.

LePINE, J. A., N. P. PODSAKOFF, and M. A. LePINE (2005). "A Meta-Analytic Test of the Challenge Stressor–Hindrance Stressor Framework: An Explanation for Inconsistent Relationships Among Stressors and Performance," *Academy of Management Journal* 48.5, 764–75.

LEWIN, J. E., and J. K. SAGER (2007). "A Process Model of Burnout Among Salespeople: Some New Thoughts," *Journal of Business Research* 60.12, 1216–24.

MCFARLAND, R. G. (2003). "Crisis of Conscience: The Use of Coercive Sales Tactics and Resultant Felt Stress in the Salesperson," *Journal of Personal Selling & Sales Management* 23.4, 311–25.

MACKENZIE, S. B., P. M. PODSAKOFF, and M. AHEARNE (1998). "Some Possible Antecedents and Consequences of In-Role and Extra-Role Salesperson Performance," *Journal of Marketing* 62.3, 87–98.

—— —— and G. A. RICH (2001). "Transformational and Transactional Leadership and Salesperson Performance," *Journal of the Academy of Marketing Science* 29.1, 115–34.

MICHAELS, R. E., W. L. CRON, A. J. DUBINSKY, and E. A. JOACHIMSTHALER (1988). "Influence of Formalization on the Organizational Commitment and Work Alienation of Salespeople and Industrial Buyers," *Journal of Marketing Research* 25.4, 376–83.

—— R. L. DAY, and E. A. JOACHIMSTHALER (1987). "Role Stress Among Industrial Buyers: An Integrative Model," *Journal of Marketing* 51.2, 28–45.

—— and DIXON, A. L. (1994). "Sellers and Buyers on the Boundary: Potential Moderators of Role Stress–Job Outcome Relationships," *Journal of the Academy of Marketing Science* 22.4, 62–73.

MULKI, J. P., F. G. LASSK, and F. JARAMILLO (2008). "The Effect of Self-Efficacy on Salesperson Work Overload and Pay Satisfaction," *Journal of Personal Selling & Sales Management* 28.3, 285–97.

NONIS, S. A., J. K. SAGER, and K. KUMAR (1996). "Salespeople's Use of Upward Influence Tactics (UITs) in Coping with Role Stress," *Journal of the Academy of Marketing Science* 24.1, 44–56.

ONYEMAH, V. (2008). "Role Ambiguity, Role Conflict, and Performance: Empirical Evidence of an Inverted-U Relationship," *Journal of Personal Selling & Sales Management* 28.3, 299–313.

PODSAKOFF, P., S. B. MACKENZIE, R. H. MOORMAN, and R. FETTER (1990). "Transformational Leader Behaviors and Their Effects on Followers' Trust in Leader Satisfaction and Organizational Citizenship Behaviors," *Leadership Quarterly* 1.2, 107–42.

RHOADS, G. K., J. SINGH, and P. W. GOODELL (1994). "The Multiple Dimensions of Role Ambiguity and their Impact upon Psychological and Behavioral Outcomes of Industrial Salespeople," *Journal of Personal Selling & Sales Management* 14.3, 1–24.

ROBERTS, J. A., R. S. LAPIDUS, and L. B. CHONKO (1997). "Salespeople and Stress: The Moderating Role of Locus of Control on Work Stressors and Felt Stress," *Journal of Marketing Theory & Practice* 5.3, 93–108.

RUSS, F. A., K. M. MCNEILLY, J. M. COMER, and T. B. LIGHT (1998). "Exploring the Impact of Critical Sales Events," *Journal of Personal Selling & Sales Management* 18.2, 19–34.

—— —— —— (1996). "Leadership, Decision Making and Performance of Sales Managers: A Multi-Level Approach," *Journal of Personal Selling & Sales Management* 16.3, 1–15.

RUYTER, K. D., M. WETZELS, and R. FEINBERG (2001). "Role Stress in Call Centers: Its Effects on Employee Performance and Satisfaction," *Journal of Interactive Marketing* 15.2, 23–35.

SAGER, J. K. (1991a). "Type A Behavior Pattern (TABP) Among Salespeople and Its Relationship to Job Stress," *Journal of Personal Selling & Sales Management* 11.2, 1–14.

—— (1991b). "A Longitudinal Assessment of Change in Sales Force Turnover," *Journal of the Academy of Marketing Science* 19.4, 25–36.

—— (1994). "A Structural Model Depicting Salespeople's Job Stress," *Journal of the Academy of Marketing Science* 22.4, 74–84.

SAGER, J. K. and P. H. WILSON (1995). "Clarification of the Meaning of Job Stress in the Context of Sales Force Research," *Journal of Personal Selling & Sales Management* 15.3, 51–64.

——J. YI, and C. M. FUTRELL (1998). "A Model Depicting Salespeople's Perceptions," *Journal of Personal Selling & Sales Management* 18.3, 1–22.

SCHWEPKER, C. H., Jr., O. C. FERRELL, and T. N. INGRAM (1997). "The Influence of Ethical Climate and Ethical Conflict on Role Stress in the Sales Force," *Journal of the Academy of Marketing Science* 25.1, 99–108.

SINGH, J. (1993). "Boundary Role Ambiguity: Facets, Determinants, and Impacts," *Journal of Marketing* 57.2, 11–31.

—— (1998). "Striking a Balance in Boundary-Spanning Positions: An Investigation of Some Unconventional Influences of Role Stressors and Job Characteristics on Job Outcomes of Salespeople," *Journal of Marketing* 62.3, 69–86.

—— and G. K. RHOADS (1991). "Boundary Role Ambiguity in Marketing-Oriented Positions: A Multidimensional, Multifaceted Operationalization," *Journal of Marketing Research* 28.3, 328–38.

—— W. VERBEKE, and G. K. RHOADS (1996). "Do Organizational Practices Matter in Role Stress Processes? A Study of Direct and Moderating Effects for Marketing Oriented Boundary Spanners," *Journal of Marketing* 60.3, 69–86.

STEVENS, H., and T. KINNI (2007). *Achieve Sales Excellence*. Avon, MA: Platinum Press.

TANNER, J. F., M. G. DUNN, and L. B. CHONKO (1993). "Vertical Exchange and Salesperson Stress," *Journal of Personal Selling & Sales Management* 13.2, 27–36.

TEAS, R. K. (1980). "An Empirical Test of Linkages Proposed in the Walker, Churchill, and Ford Model of Salesforce Motivation and Performance," *Journal of the Academy of Marketing Science* 8.4, 58–72.

—— (1983). "Supervisory Behavior, Role Stress, and the Job Satisfaction of Industrial Salespeople," *Journal of Marketing Research* 20.1, 84–91.

THE SALES EDUCATORS (2006). *Strategic Sales Leadership: Breakthrough Thinking for Breakthrough Results*. Mason, OH: Thomson.

TUBRE, T. C., and J. M. COLLINS (2000). "Jackson and Schuler (1985) Revisited: A Meta-Analysis of the Relationships Between Role Ambiguity, Role Conflict, and Job Performance," *Journal of Management* 26.1, 155–69.

TYAGI, P. K. (1985). "The Effects on Stressful Organizational Conditions on Salesperson Work Motivation," *Journal of the Academy of Marketing Science* 13.1, 290–309.

WALKER, O. C., Jr., G. A. CHURCHILL, Jr., and N. M. FORD (1975). "Organizational Determinants of the Industrial Salesman's Role Conflict and Ambiguity," *Journal of Marketing* 39.1, 32–9.

CHAPTER 11

SIZING THE SALES FORCE AND DESIGNING SALES TERRITORIES FOR RESULTS

ANDRIS A. ZOLTNERS

PRABHAKANT SINHA

SALLY E. LORIMER

11.1 INTRODUCTION

The size of the sales force and the design of sales territories affect customers, salespeople, and company results. If the sales force is too small, it will be unable to serve the needs of customers effectively, salespeople are likely to be overworked, and the company will miss key sales opportunities. If the sales force is too large, salespeople can inconvenience customers by being around too much. In addition, salespeople probably are not challenged, the costs of maintaining the force will be too high, and productivity will be low. These same productivity challenges can exist in sales forces that are the right size but have poorly designed sales territories. If the workload and opportunity in every territory is not well matched to the capacity of the salesperson or team assigned to cover it, some customers will get too little attention while others get more than what is justified by their potential, some salespeople will be overworked while others are underutilized, and sales and profits will fall short of what the company could achieve.

11.2 Sizing the Sales Force for Long-Term Success

11.2.1 Common Decision Rules that Lead to Sales Force Sizing Errors

Determining the right size for a sales force is not easy. Sales force size affects both revenues and costs. While it is fairly easy to predict the cost side of sizing decisions (variable expenses for items such as compensation, benefits, field support, and travel are straightforward to estimate using historical data), it is much more difficult to predict the revenue impact. The relationship between sales force size and revenues depends on various factors, many of which are difficult to control and predict. Some of these factors are external to the sales force. Customer needs, competitive intensity, and the economic outlook, for example, are all hard to forecast yet can impact the ability of a sales force to create sales. Other factors originate within the sales force. The skills, knowledge, and capabilities of salespeople, for example, and the effectiveness of the sales force systems, programs, and processes that the company provides all affect sales. Because it is impossible to foresee the precise effect of these complexities on a sales force's ability to generate revenues, sales leaders often use decision rules that rely on common sense rather than precise analytics to determine how large their sales forces should be. Unfortunately, these heuristic approaches often do not lead to the best sales force-sizing decisions (Zoltners, Sinha, and Lorimer 2004). Four commonly used decision rules are described here.

11.2.1.1 *Add Salespeople when the Current Sales Force Generates Enough Sales to Afford an Increased Investment*

When expanding a sales force, many companies take a conservative "wait and see" approach to adding salespeople. As sales increase, they grow the sales force slowly, viewing the sales force as a cost item that needs to be justified by sales, rather than an investment that drives sales. This "earn-your-way," risk-averse strategy is sometimes necessary in markets with high uncertainty or when a company is cash-strapped. However, many companies take this conservative growth approach even when there is reasonable certainty of success and available financing. As a result, they undersize their sales forces and miss out on considerable opportunity. One company estimated that an overly cautious sales force expansion strategy to support an important new product launch cost the company 17 percent of profits—over $50 million over a three-year period (Zoltners, Sinha, and Lorimer 2006a).

11.2.1.2 *Split a Territory as Soon as Its Sales Hit a Certain Threshold Level*

At one company, as soon as a territory hits $3 million in sales, sales leaders split the territory and give a portion of it to a new salesperson. The current salesperson's "reward" for working hard to build business is to have his territory reduced. As a result, over time too many salespeople are placed in geographies where salespeople were successful initially and too few salespeople are placed in other geographies. The company does not consider how much sales potential exists in a given territory or how much of that potential remains untapped. Another downside to this decision rule: It gives salespeople who have a territory with sales approaching the threshold level an incentive to stop selling in order to maintain their customer base and keep their territory intact.

11.2.1.3 *Maintain a Sales Force Size That Keeps Sales Force Costs at a Constant Percentage of Sales*

Many companies determine sales force size by looking at the industry or company historical average sales force cost as a percentage of sales. They determine how many salespeople they can "afford" while keeping their costs in line with this average. Maintaining the sales force cost to sales ratio is not the same as maximizing profits. While it may seem counterintuitive, when the sales force is undersized, adding salespeople increases the sales force cost to sales ratio and at the same time increases profitability. It is always possible to reduce the sales force cost to sales ratio by cutting headcount, yet the impact on profitability will be positive only if the sales force is already too large. The practice of maintaining an industry average cost to sales ratio can especially hurt small-share companies who, in order to get adequate share of voice with customers, may need to maintain a higher sales force cost to sales ratio than that of their larger-share competitors. Maintaining a historical cost to sales ratio is also dangerous during a business downturn, as it may suggest significant sales force downsizing that could amplify the impact of the downturn and leave the company poorly positioned for a turnaround.

11.2.1.4 *If the Current Sales Force Size Worked Last Year, Avoid Disruption and Keep the Same Size this Year*

While it's tempting to avoid "rocking the boat" when things are working, most markets are fairly dynamic, and sales force size needs to be re-evaluated annually. External market forces can create a need to change the size of the sales force: for example, customers may change their buying processes, competitors may increase or decrease the size of their sales forces, or economic swings may affect market opportunity. Internal company forces also prompt a need to change sales force size: for example, the company may launch a new product, exit from a key market, or seek to improve its financial performance. External and internal forces create constant new challenges and opportunities for companies, and a non-decision to keep sales force size the same is in fact a decision that may not be the best option.

11.2.2 Sales Force Sizing Dynamics

The decision rules that sales leaders commonly rely on when considering whether to resize a sales force can lead to non-productive conclusions because they ignore several dynamics about sales force size and its impact on performance. First and foremost, all of the rules overlook the relationship between sales force size and customer and product coverage. The size of the sales force influences how many customers the company can cover, how much time is spent with those customers, and how much sales effort products receive. Larger sales forces can reach more customers and prospects, can visit important customers more frequently, and can sell more products and/or spend more time on important products. Therefore, a larger sales force will create more sales and gross contribution margin (sales less variable product costs) than a smaller sales force. At the same time, most companies define a target income level for their salespeople and also provide salespeople with benefits such as automobiles, travel expense reimbursement, computers, and administrative support. These sales force costs increase roughly linearly with the number of salespeople. Figure 11.1 shows the relationship between sales force size and some commonly used performance metrics. Several observations from these graphs that have implications for sales force sizing are described below.

11.2.2.1 *There Are Diminishing Returns to Sales Force Effort*

The relationship between sales force size and sales or gross contribution margin yields diminishing returns (Graph A). This happens for two reasons. First, new salespeople need time to learn the company's products, markets, and selling process, and to establish effective customer relationships; their effectiveness in the first year may only be 50 to 60 percent of that of an experienced salesperson.

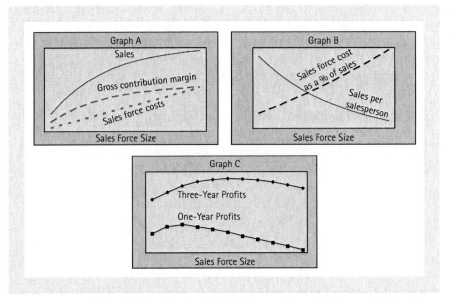

Fig. 11.1. The Relationship between Sales Force Size and Several Sales Force Performance metrics

Second, even after they have become fully effective, additional salespeople bring down the average sales per salesperson. The existing sales force has gathered the low-hanging fruit, and, when the sales force expands, all the salespeople will have to dig deeper into the universe of customers and work harder to earn their sales. Only in very rapidly growing markets or in sales forces that are significantly undersized is it reasonable to expect additional salespeople to incrementally match the average sales of current salespeople.

11.2.2.2 *Sales Force Size Affects Financial Ratios*

The relationships between sales force size, sales, and sales force costs have implications for the financial ratios that many companies use to manage their sales force investment. The relationship between sales force size and two commonly used financial ratios—sales per salesperson and sales force costs as a percent of sales—is not intuitive (Graph B). Many sales leaders feel that high sales per salesperson and low sales force cost as a percentage of sales imply high sales force effectiveness and productivity. Yet high sales per salesperson or low sales force cost as a percentage of sales can also be signs that the sales force is undersized. When the sales force is too small, adding salespeople increases profits even though it decreases sales per salesperson and increases sales force costs as a percentage of sales. The dynamics are more intuitive when the sales force is too large—cutting headcount increases profits, increases sales per salesperson, and decreases sales force cost as a percentage of sales. Cutting sales force size always increases sales per salesperson and decreases sales force cost as a percentage of sales, but the impact on profitability can be either positive or negative. In fact, a company maximizes sales per salesperson and minimizes sales force cost as a percentage of sales by firing all but one salesperson!

11.2.2.3 *There is a Sales Force Size that Maximizes Profits*

The relationship between sales force size and profits (gross contribution margin less sales force costs) can be measured across different timeframes—for example, one year, and three years as shown in Graph C. Profits are highest when the size of the sales force is such that the incremental contribution of the last-added salesperson is equal to the incremental cost. Compare Graphs B and C, and note that if the sales force is smaller than the profit-maximizing size, adding salespeople to increase profitability reduces sales per salesperson and increases sales force costs as a percentage of sales. These relationships tend to be a little counterintuitive, since many sales leaders view high sales per salesperson and low sales force cost ratios as surrogates for profitability.

11.2.2.4 *The Sales Force Size that Maximizes One-Year Profits is Smaller than the Size that Maximizes Three-Year Profits*

Changes in the size of a sales force have both short-term and long-term impacts on costs and sales. As salespeople are added, incremental sales increase slowly at first and accelerate over time as new salespeople become acclimatized to their jobs and the new customers they acquire make repeat purchases. Alternatively, when sales force size decreases, a decline in sales may not be immediate, as repeat purchases by loyal customers continue to contribute to sales for a period of time despite reduced sales force coverage. Only over time does the impact of the size reduction become apparent as repeat business gradually dwindles.

The long-term impact of sales force sizing changes is better understood when sales leaders take into account *carryover sales*—sales that will occur in future years even without future sales force effort because they result from this year's effort. Carryover sales occur when a product meets the needs of a customer who continues to buy it even if a salesperson is no longer promoting it. Carryover is especially likely when switching products is costly. The impact of carryover increases as products mature. In some markets, carryover sales represent a large portion of total sales.

Because of carryover, the multi-year sales impact of adding or reducing salespeople is much larger than the one-year impact. Upsizing a sales force can result in an incremental profit reduction in the first year because sales force costs increase immediately while sales increase slowly, but a significant profit improvement can be attained as the impact of carryover sales is fully realized over three, four, and five years. Similarly, reducing sales force size can have an immediate and positive profit impact because costs are reduced right away, but the positive profit impact will dwindle over time as carryover sales are lost.

Across 50 sales force sizing studies conducted by our consulting company ZS Associates, the sales force size that maximized one-year profits was 18 percent smaller on average than the size that maximized three-year profits (Zoltners and Sinha 2001). Maximizing profitability across a time horizon longer than three years requires an even larger sales force size. The considerable difference between the one-year and longer-term profit-maximizing sizes creates a dilemma for sales leaders who recognize that multi-year revenue streams are less predictable than one-year streams, and who at the same time are under pressure to deliver short-term results.

11.3 Assessing the Current Size of a Sales Force

Five quick tests can provide insights to different company stakeholders about the current size of the sales force. Sales management is likely to care most about the results of the customer, sales force morale, and selling activity tests. Marketing leaders will be most interested in the competitive position test results, while finance leaders are likely to focus on the findings of the financial test. A synthesis across of all of the tests is required in order to make a final sales force sizing assessment.

11.3.1 Customer Test

Listening to what customers say about your salespeople can provide important insights about the size of the sales force. Figure 11.2 depicts typical customer reactions to a sales force that is either too large or too small.

While customer input could be collected through a formal survey, most companies gather input by simply asking customers for feedback or by conducting informal customer interviews.

11.3.2 Sales Force Morale Test

One company had 28 salespeople covering the United States. Some territories encompassed several large states; the salespeople in these territories were almost never home and consequently suffered a great deal of stress. The sales force had a high turnover rate (40 percent per year) that the company attributed to the heavy travel requirements. Because the company's products were very complex and specialized, the cost to hire and train new salespeople was significant. The company increased the

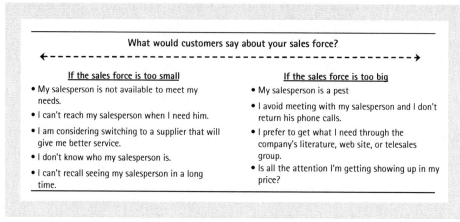

Fig. 11.2. The Customer Test of Sales Force Size

number of salespeople and thus reduced each individual's need to travel. The additional salespeople not only generated incremental sales, but also had positive impact on sales force retention because morale improved when salespeople no longer had to spend so many nights away from home. Improved sales force retention led to lower hiring and training costs and greater customer loyalty.

The morale of the sales force can be linked to its size. When there are either too many or too few salespeople, morale suffers. While many salespeople have complaints whenever they speak to their managers, the frequency and strength of complaints intensifies when a sales force is not the right size. Figure 11.3 lays out some typical comments from salespeople that may be important indicators about the size of a sales force. High sales force turnover can be a signal that a sales force is not sized correctly.

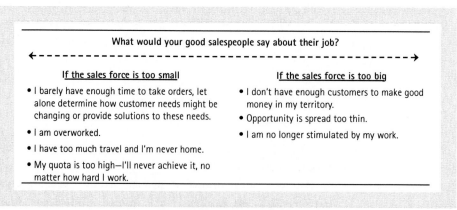

Fig. 11.3. The Sales Force Morak Test of Sales Force Size

11.3.3 Selling Activities Test

Information about how salespeople spend their time provides insight about sales force size. Some sales forces track sales force activity data—for example, how much time is spent by customer or how much time is devoted to non-selling activities such as meetings or administration—through a CRM (customer relationship management) or other sales reporting system. Other sales forces do not routinely track these data, but will ask salespeople to complete surveys of how they spend their time in a given period, or will ask sales managers or other observers to monitor and report back on how salespeople spend their time. Figure 11.4 provides some signs that the sales force is either too large or too small.

11.3.4 Competitive Position Test

Another way to judge the size of a sales force is to compare the company's sales force investment with that of competitors. Market share often depends more upon "effective share of voice" with customers than on the absolute amount of time the sales force spends with them. Companies can increase their effective share of voice in two ways. First, they can increase the number of salespeople they employ relative to competitors. Second, they can invest in systems, programs, and processes that make their salespeople more effective than competitors' salespeople. If competitors are increasing their sales staff, a company's sales force also needs to expand and/or to get more effective in order to maintain effective share of voice and thus preserve market share. Similarly, if major competitors are reducing their sales staffs, a company may be able to downsize its sales force and/or give up some effectiveness without losing market share. Sales may

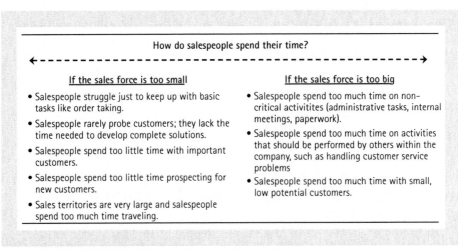

Fig. 11.4. The Selling Activities Test of Sales Force Size

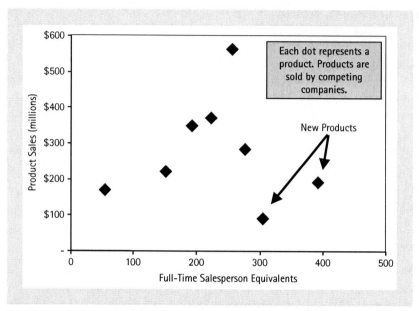

Fig. 11.5. A Competetive Benchmarking Analysis for One Market

decline if the entire market is declining, but a company often maintains or strengthens its competitive position by maintaining or increasing its effective share of voice. A competitive benchmarking analysis, like the example shown in Figure 11.5, can help a company determine a sales force size that ensures that its sales force is not out-shouted by competitors. The analysis shows the annual sales and the level of sales force support for the major products sold by competing companies in one market. In general, products with higher sales have higher levels of sales force support. New products require even higher levels of support at first in order to build their brand. If a company plans to launch a new product in this market, it can use the analysis to determine what sales force investment it needs to become a major player—300 or more full time salesperson equivalents to launch and 200 or more equivalents on an ongoing basis in order to be competitive.

11.3.5 Financial Test

A break-even analysis can help determine whether a sales force is too large, too small, or about the right size (Zoltners, Sinha, and Lorimer 2006a). Follow seven steps to conduct the analysis.

1. *Estimate the annual cost of a salesperson.* Include all costs that vary with the number of salespeople, including salary, benefits, taxes, bonuses, automobiles, travel expenses, computers, and administrative support.

2. *Estimate the gross contribution margin rate.* This is the percentage of sales that the business keeps, after taking out variable product costs. Variable product costs include raw materials, manufacturing, royalties, freight to factory, and shipping to customers. Variable costs do not include allocations of fixed costs, such as factory overheads and R&D.

3. *Calculate breakeven sales.* This is the amount a salesperson must sell in a year to cover his or her cost. Divide the annual cost of a salesperson by the gross contribution margin rate.

4. *Estimate the incremental sales that an additional salesperson could generate in a year.* The current average annual sales per salesperson provides a reference point for what this level of sales might be. Incremental annual sales per additional salesperson will be less than the average annual sales per current salesperson because of the diminishing return on additional sales force effort and because of the lower effectiveness of new salespeople.

5. *Divide incremental annual sales per additional salesperson by breakeven sales to get the breakeven ratio.* The ratio reflects the extent to which an additional salesperson will generate sales to cover his or her costs. For example, a ratio of 2.00 implies that, on average, a new salesperson will generate gross margin equal to twice his or her cost within a year.

6. *Estimate the percentage of this year's sales that will be maintained next year without any sales force effort next year.* This is the carryover rate.

7. *Use the table in Figure 11.6 to find out what the breakeven ratio and the carryover rate imply about sales force size.* The numbers in each cell of the table represent a three-year ROI on incremental sales force investment. The sizing recommendations are based on the following ROI targets:

   • ROI of less than 50 percent: The sales force is too large.
   • ROI of 50–150 percent: The sales force is the right size.
   • ROI of more than 150 percent: The sales force is too small.

These ROI targets are consistent with those commonly used by sales organizations we have worked with; however, an ROI target can be adjusted to a specific situation and the sizing recommendation adjusted accordingly.

For a given breakeven ratio, the ROI (and therefore the sales force sizing recommendation) varies depending upon the carryover rate. For example, a ratio of 1.00 implies that in a low carryover environment (i.e. less than 40 percent of sales would be maintained next year without effort) the sales force may be too large. In a moderate carryover environment (more than 40 percent but less than 90 percent of sales maintained next year without effort) the sales force is about the right size. In a high carryover environment (90 percent or more of sales would be retained next year without effort) the sales force may be too small.

Figure 11.7 shows an example of the financial test calculations for one sales organization.

New Salesperson Sales / BE Sales	Carryover									
	0%	10.0%	20.0%	30.0%	40.0%	50.0%	60.0%	70.0%	80.0%	90.0%
0.25	-75%	-72%	-69%	-65%	-61%	-56%	-51%	-45%	-39%	-32%
0.50	-50%	-45%	-38%	-31%	-22%	-13%	-2%	10%	22%	36%
0.75	-25%	-17%	-7%	4%	17%	31%	47%	64%	83%	103%
1.00	0%	11%	24%	39%	56%	75%	96%	119%	144%	171%
1.25	25%	39%	55%	74%	95%	119%	145%	174%	205%	239%
1.50	50%	67%	86%	109%	134%	163%	194%	229%	266%	307%
1.75	75%	94%	117%	143%	173%	206%	243%	283%	327%	374%
2.00	100%	122%	148%	178%	212%	250%	292%	338%	388%	442%
2.25	125%	150%	179%	213%	251%	294%	341%	393%	449%	510%
2.50	150%	178%	210%	248%	290%	338%	390%	448%	510%	578%
2.75	175%	205%	241%	282%	329%	381%	439%	502%	571%	645%
3.00	200%	233%	272%	317%	368%	425%	488%	557%	632%	713%
3.25	225%	261%	303%	352%	407%	469%	537%	612%	693%	781%
3.50	250%	289%	334%	387%	446%	513%	586%	667%	754%	849%
3.75	275%	316%	365%	421%	485%	556%	635%	721%	815%	916%
4.00	300%	344%	396%	456%	524%	600%	684%	776%	876%	984%
4.25	325%	372%	427%	491%	563%	644%	733%	831%	937%	1052%
4.50	350%	400%	458%	526%	602%	688%	782%	886%	998%	1120%

Matrix contains the 3-year sales force ROI

☐ = Oversized   ■ = Right-sized   ▨ = Undersized

Fig. 11.6. Implications of the Incremental Sales per Additional Salesperson/Breakeven Sales Ratio and carryover for Sales Force Size

Test Step	Example Calculation
1. Estimate the annual cost of a salesperson.	$75,000 salary and bonus (total compensation) + 22,500 benefits (30% of total compensation) + 11,250 field support (15% of total compensation) + 9,250 T&E, automobile, computer, phone, etc. $118,000 total annual cost of a salesperson
2. Estimate gross contribution margin rate.	($900 MM sales - $300 MM variable product costs)/ ($900 MM annual sales) = 66.7% gross contribution margin rate.
3. Calculate breakeven sales.	$118,000 cost of a salesperson /.667 gross contribution margin rate = $176,912 breakeven sales.
4. Estimate annual incremental sales revenue that an additional salesperson could generate.	$525,000 incremental sales revenue per year per salesperson, according to management estimate.
5. Calculate the breakeven ratio.	$525,000 incremental sales/$176, 912 breakeven sales = 2.97 breakeven ratio.
6. Estimate the carryover rate.	60% carryover according to management estimate.
7 Use the table in Figure 11.6 to find out what the estimates imply about sales force size.	The three-year ROI on incremental sales force investment is about 488%. According to the criteria used in most sales organizations, the sales force is undersized.

Fig. 11.7. Finacial Test Calculation Example

The financial test is useful for most sales forces selling either products or services, but it should be used cautiously in some environments. The approach typically does not work well for key account sales forces that have responsibility for a small number of very large accounts. In such environments, sales leaders can usually specify what work an additional salesperson could do, but they often find it difficult to estimate the incremental sales that the additional salesperson will generate by doing this work. Also, the approach does not work well for companies that pay salespeople all of their pay in the form of commissions. In these cases, costs vary directly with sales so every additional salesperson exceeds breakeven. Other analyses, described later in the chapter, are more useful for sizing commission-only sales forces.

11.4 Determining the Right Size for the Sales Force

Sales leaders should use a market-focused approach to determine the best sales force size. Market-focused approaches involve understanding and segmenting customers according to their needs, and then determining what sales process and how much sales force time is required to meet those needs. By aggregating the time required across all customer segments, sales leaders can estimate the necessary sales force size. Greater coverage of customers creates more incremental sales, but since more salespeople are needed, it also increases costs. Similarly, reducing customer coverage results in lower incremental sales, but costs are also lower since fewer salespeople are needed. Determining the right sales force size and level of coverage is critical to maximizing profits.

The best approaches for measuring the link between sales force size, segment coverage, and segment financial value (such as sales or profits) combine analysis with management input to create good, data-driven recommendations for sizing the sales force. Some companies rely heavily on management input to develop segment coverage needs; others have data and analytical capabilities that allow them to measure the link between coverage, sales, and profits directly using historical data. Market-based sales force sizing models have been developed by several researchers, including Lodish (1980), Zoltners and Sinha (1980), LaForge and Cravens (1985), Horsky and Nelson (1996), and Darmon (2005). Four market-based approaches that companies have used to size their sales forces, listed in increasing order of sophistication, are described here. An additional approach is also described for a special situation: when the company does not set a target level of pay but rather pays salespeople entirely through a commission on sales or margin. More detail on how to implement these and other market-based sales force sizing methods is provided in Zoltners, Sinha, and Lorimer (2004).

11.4.1 Approach 1: Activity-Based Analysis

Activity-based analysis links sales force size to the time it takes salespeople to complete all the activities required to serve the needs of different types of customers. Figure 11.8 provides a simplified example of an activity-based sizing analysis for a consumer products sales force that performed merchandising activities in retail stores.

Activity-based sizing requires the following steps:

1. Segment accounts according to their sales force coverage needs. The company in the example segmented stores according to sales volume, but other segmentation criteria can also be used, such as industry, account potential, or customer buying process.
2. Develop a list of the sales activities to be performed at accounts in each segment in a year.
3. Estimate the time it takes to complete these activities. Companies can obtain data for developing these estimates by examining historical call data, by observing successful salespeople, or by asking salespeople, sales managers, and customers for input.
4. Calculate the total hours per year required for the sales force to cover each account segment. It is useful to compare the total time required to the sales volume in each segment as a check that the time estimates are reasonable and justified.

Segment: Direct Retail Stores	# of Accounts	Calls/ Year	Hours/ Call	Total Hours	Sales- people Needed
Over $25 K	112	12	2.0	2,688	2.0
$12 –25 K	784	6	2.0	9,408	7.1
$5 –12 K	2,543	4	2.0	20,344	15.4
Under $5 K	6,559	3	1.0	19,677	14.9
Total Direct Retail	9,998	--	--	52,117	39.4

Hours per salesperson per year = 1,325

Fig. 11.8. Example of Activity-based Analysis for Sizing a Consumer Products Merchandising Sales Force

5. Estimate the call capacity of a salesperson, calculate the number of salespeople required to cover each segment, and sum across segments to determine a desired sales force size.

Activity-based analysis is a relatively quick and easy method of sizing a sales force. It works well for sales forces that perform well-defined selling activities, that have limited resources for performing sales force sizing analysis, and that have difficulty estimating the relationship between sales force effort and sales. Often companies will conduct an activity-based sizing analysis in addition to using one of the more sophisticated sizing approaches, as it provides a good baseline recommendation and check for reasonableness.

11.4.2 Approach 2: Pipeline Analysis

Pipeline analysis enriches activity-based analysis for sales forces that utilize multi-step sales processes consisting of a series of milestones that advance the probability of a sale. Figure 11.9 provides a simplified example of a pipeline sizing analysis used by a medical device sales force to determine how many salespeople it needed to cover one of its market segments.

Pipeline sizing requires the following steps:

1. Segment accounts according to their sales force coverage needs.
2. Map out the sales process stages or steps for each segment.

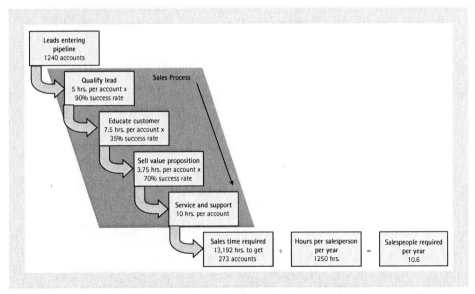

Fig. 11.9. Example of Pipeline Analysis for sizing a Medical Device Sales Force

3. Estimate the number of prospects in each segment entering the sales pipeline in a year.
4. Estimate the average sales time required to complete each stage and the success rate resulting from that effort. Historical company data as well as the input of salespeople, sales managers, and customers is useful for developing these estimates.
5. Calculate the total sales time required and the number of accounts successfully sold.
6. Estimate the call capacity of a salesperson, calculate the number of salespeople required to cover each segment, and sum across segments to determine a desired sales force size.

Like activity-based analysis, pipeline analysis is relatively easy to do. In addition to helping with sales force sizing decisions, it provides insights about sales process effectiveness, customer response, and sales force effort allocation. Pipeline analysis can also link sales force sizing to the achievement of a desired sales goal; the success rate at each sales process stage helps the company determine how many leads must enter the pipeline in order to achieve the goal, and the sales time estimates help it determine how many salespeople are needed to create those leads and move them successfully through the pipeline. The pipeline analysis shown in the example provides a steady state size assuming that leads enter and move through the pipeline in a stable flow over time. Companies facing dynamic situations where there is instability in lead flows, sales time requirements, and success rates can enhance the analysis by using Monte Carlo simulation techniques to model the pipeline flow. Companies can also enhance pipeline analysis by modeling across multiple years or by using sales response analysis (see Section 11.4.4) to estimate the link between effort and the success rate at each stage of the sales process.

11.4.3 Approach 3: Target-Return-per-Call Analysis

Target-return-per-call analysis enhances activity and pipeline analysis by allowing companies to use a targeted rate of return on investment as a guideline for determining which customer segments the sales force should cover. Figure 11.10 provides a simplified example of a target-return-per-call analysis used by a not-for-profit sales force to determine whether or not its salespeople should contact four different segments of corporate accounts to solicit sponsorship revenues.

Target-return-per-call sizing requires the following steps:

1. Use activity or pipeline analysis to estimate the number of salespeople needed to meet the needs of customers in different market segments.
2. Estimate the cost of coverage for each segment by multiplying the number of salespeople by the annual cost of a salesperson (include all variable costs such as

	Segment 1	Segment 2	Segment 3	Segment 4
Salespeople needed to cover accounts in market segment (determined by activity-based analysis)	4.2	2.9	1.5	0.8
Cost to cover @ $250,000 per salesperson per year (000)	$1, 050	$725	$375	$200
Expected value of sales force coverage (000)	$8,423	$2,441	$832	$141
Segment ROI – (Value – Cost) ÷ Cost	702%	237%	122%	–30%
Target ROI	200%	200%	200%	200%
Cover segment?	Yes	Yes	No	No

Fig. 11.10. Example of Target-Return-per-Call Analysis for Sizing a Not-for-Profit Sales Force

   salary and incentives, benefits, taxes, automobiles, travel expenses, computers, and administrative support).

3. Estimate the value of sales force coverage—the incremental contribution generated by deploying the suggested number of salespeople against the segment. At a minimum, this involves developing a sales forecast for each market segment and subtracting variable product costs. The analysis can be enriched by accounting for carryover sales from prior years and into future years. Companies can use analysis of historical data as well as input from customers, the sales force, and company leaders to develop these estimates.
4. Calculate a segment return on investment (ROI).
5. Compare to a company target ROI to determine if each segment should be covered.
6. Sum the estimated number of salespeople across all segments to be covered to determine a desired sales force size.

Target-return-per-call analysis provides a fairly easy way for companies to link sales force activity to financial projections so they can assess the reasonableness of a sales force sizing recommendation. The analysis is especially useful for companies wanting to determine what depth of coverage of a large universe of prospective customers is affordable and represents a good investment for the company.

11.4.4 Approach 4: Sales Response Analysis

Sales response analysis directly measures the relationship between sales force investment and sales, allowing companies to assess the profit consequences of alternative sales force sizing decisions. Figure 11.11 provides a simplified example of a sales response analysis conducted by a pharmaceutical company to determine what sales force size would maximize one-year and three-year profitability.

   Sales response analysis requires the following steps:

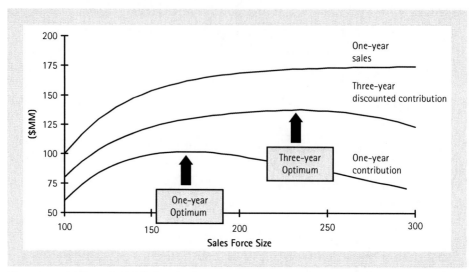

Fig. 11.11. Example of Sales Response Analysis for Sizing a Pharmaceutical Sales Force

1. Segment accounts according to their sales force coverage needs.
2. For each segment, measure the relationship between sales force effort and sales for each product. Companies with rich historical data on account potential, sales, and sales force effort have had success deriving sales response curves using statistical analysis of cross-sectional and time-series data. These forecasts tend to be quite accurate in stable markets. In dynamic markets, companies often augment historical data analysis with judgmental data obtained from salespeople and managers, company leaders, and customers when developing sales response curves.
3. Develop a contribution curve by subtracting two types of costs from the sales forecasts: (1) variable product costs and (2) variable sales force costs (such as salary and incentives, benefits, taxes, automobiles, travel expenses, computers, and administrative support). The peak of the contribution curve suggests a profit maximizing sales force size.
4. Enrich the analysis by developing sales and contribution curves that acknowledge carryover sales. Looking at longer time horizons (e.g. three years) suggests a larger sales force size because current sales effort becomes more profitable when the carryover sales that it creates in future years are accounted for.
5. Use the models to evaluate the short- and long-term sales and profit consequences of alternative sales force sizes, and select a size that maximizes profits while achieving other important company objectives.

Sales response modeling is theoretically the best way to determine sales force size, as it is the only approach that directly links sales effort to results, allowing companies to predict the sales and profit consequences of their sales force sizing decisions. However, not all companies can develop reliable sales response models. The models require detailed, accurate data; in many industries, these data are not available. Even when data are available, the analysis requires complex statistical modeling. Developing the data and modeling capabilities can be expensive for many companies. Sales response models also do not work well in situations where marketing instruments other than the sales force, such as advertising or alternative selling channels, have large impact on sales, as it can be difficult to isolate the impact of each instrument. Like target-return-per-call analysis, sales response analysis is appropriate for companies that set a target level of pay for salespeople, rather than those that pay salespeople only through commissions.

11.4.5 Approach for a Special Case: When the Sales Force is Paid Exclusively by Commission

When a company pays its salespeople all of their pay in the form of commissions, it incurs sales force costs only when salespeople bring in sales that cover those costs. Since the company makes gross margin on every sale, its first inclination might be to continue adding salespeople indefinitely to maximize profits. However as Figure 11.12 suggests, several dynamics occur in commission-only sales forces that prevent sales and contribution from rising indefinitely as the company adds salespeople. Understanding these dynamics helps companies with commission-only sales forces determine the best sales force size.

In a commission-only sales force, as the size of the sales force increases, the opportunity to generate sales and earn money gets divided among more and more salespeople, and income per salesperson decreases (Graph A). At some point, the sales force becomes so large that some salespeople are unable to earn a lifestyle-sustaining income and they leave the company. As earnings opportunity declines, the quality of the people that the company attracts to the job goes down. Thus, as the sales force grows, salesperson turnover increases (Graph A) and sales force effectiveness goes down. We know of many insurance companies and distributor businesses that have commission-only sales forces with turnover rates in excess of 50 percent per year. Excessive sales force turnover and reduced effectiveness have a negative impact on company sales and contribution (Graph B), as turnover puts customer relationships in jeopardy, and at the same time, experienced salespeople are replaced with newer, less effective salespeople. Commission-only sales forces can be oversized if they overlook these dynamics.

As Graph B shows, the best size for a commission-only sales force is the size that produces maximal company sales and profits by providing enough income opportunity per salesperson to keep sales force turnover at a manageable level while keeping sales force effectiveness high.

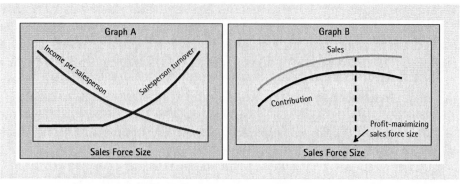

Fig. 11.12. Sales Force Size and Income per Salesperson, Salesperson Turnover, Sales, and Contribution in a Commission-only Sales Force

The commission rate that salespeople earn affects the shape of the Figure 11.12 curves. Companies can model the impact of commission rate changes on the optimal sales force size and company profitability to derive the best commission rate and sales force size combination.

Companies that pay their sales forces exclusively through commissions can also gain insights through non-financial analyses when sizing their sales forces. Several of the non-financial tests for assessing sales force size described earlier in the chapter are quite useful, as they evaluate sales force size from the perspective of customers, sales force morale, selling activities, and competitive position.

11.5 Designing Sales Territories that Match Sales Effort with Market Opportunity

11.5.1 Sales Leaders Often Overlook Sales Territory Design

A sales force that is the right size needs to be deployed effectively across customers and prospects in order to achieve maximal productivity. Sales leaders encourage the right deployment by designing sales territories that have workload and market opportunity that are well matched to the capacity of the salespeople or teams assigned to cover them.

Sales leaders often overlook the power of sales territory design as a sales effectiveness tool, and they often misdiagnose symptoms of poor territory design as they focus on other sales effectiveness concerns (Zoltners, Sinha, and Lorimer 2004). Here are six examples:

1. *Targeting problem?* "Why can't our sales force target more effectively?" wonders a marketing manager. "The salespeople in Dallas have visited only 10 percent of the good leads that we passed on. No wonder our market share is so low in Dallas! And in Atlanta, salespeople are spending too much time with low-potential prospects that aren't even on the target list."

2. *Hiring and retention problem?* "The Detroit territory is vacant again," says a frustrated Midwest regional director. "This is the fifth vacancy in just two years. In their exit interviews, the people who left implied that they were not given enough opportunity to succeed."

3. *Compensation problem?* "I can't make any money with this incentive compensation program," complains an office products salesperson who has just completed his first year on the job. "I'm working twice as hard as veteran salespeople who are milking their well-established books-of-business, yet I earned just a small fraction of what they made this year."

4. *Award trip criteria problem?* "This is the same group of salespeople who went on the award trip last year," observes a vice president of sales. "I wonder why several of the salespeople who I thought worked really hard this year didn't make the cut."

5. *Rank ordering problem?* "Why do they insist on publishing these district market share rankings?" complains a pharmaceutical district sales manager in Denver. "My district has so much potential spread out across a huge geography and I don't have enough salespeople to possibly cover it all. The rankings are unfair."

6. *Quota setting problem?* "I had a good year, and now I'm rewarded with a huge quota for next year," complains a medical supply sales rep. "I'll never achieve that quota. Why can't my manager understand that the potential in my territory has been maxed out?"

Sales leaders can at least partially remedy all of these situations through better territory design. In example 1, targeting may improve if salespeople are redeployed from Atlanta (where low-potential prospects are over-covered) to Dallas (where good leads are neglected because salespeople are too busy to follow up). In example 2, the Detroit salesperson may stay on the job if the territory is enlarged so that he or she has more opportunity to generate sales. In the other examples, better territory design can lead to fairer recognition and rewards for the salespeople.

If sales leaders have not evaluated and adapted territory design to current business needs within the last year or two, it is likely that sales territory misalignments are keeping the sales force from achieving maximum effectiveness. Poor territory design makes it impossible for the sales force to give all valuable customers the attention they deserve and, at the same time, underutilizes many talented salespeople. Poor territory design also makes it extremely difficult to identify and reward the true top performers, and thus affects sales force morale and motivation. Poor territory design can also result in high travel costs.

11.5.2 Good Sales Territory Design Encourages Sales Success

11.5.2.1 *Well-Designed Sales Territories Enhance Customer Coverage*

Well-designed territories allow salespeople to improve customer and prospect coverage, leading to higher sales. A salesperson in a territory with too much work or travel cannot cover all assigned customers and prospects. He probably spends his time traveling to and calling on accounts he's comfortable with, ignoring other more challenging but potentially more profitable accounts. As a result, the company misses out on important sales opportunities. Likewise, a salesperson in a territory with too little work will spend a disproportionate amount of time on non-productive activities, such as calls on low-potential customers, despite the fact that the sales generated from those customers are likely to be lower than potential sales from the accounts not covered in high-workload territories. When sales leaders redesign territories, they can assign under-covered profitable accounts from high-workload territories to salespeople who have time to call on them, increasing sales force effectiveness. This leads directly to higher sales and profits—without increasing sales force headcount.

A cosmetics company's sales force provides a good example of the how poor sales territory design often leads to a mismatch between customer coverage needs and sales force capacity. This sales force performed merchandising duties at retail stores—stocking shelves, setting up displays, taking inventory. The company's intention was to match each territory's store workload to the capacity of a full-time salesperson. However, when the company conducted an assessment of how long merchandising tasks should take at the different types and sizes of stores in each territory, it discovered that the majority of territories had workloads that deviated by more than 15 percent from a full-time salesperson's capacity. Approximately 33 percent of territories had too much work for a salesperson to complete effectively, and some important customers in these territories were being neglected. At the same time, approximately 27 percent of the territories had too little work to keep the salesperson fully busy, and some customers in these territories were getting too much attention for the sales volume they could generate. This type of misalignment is quite typical. Data for a convenience sample of over 4,800 territories from 18 sales territory redesigns that ZS Associates conducted in four industries in the US and Canada showed that the majority of sales territories either had too much work for a salesperson to handle effectively (25 percent of territories) or had too little work to keep a salesperson fully busy (31 percent). Because of these mismatches, those businesses missed opportunities to add 2–7 percent to their revenues every year (Zoltners and Lorimer 2000).

11.5.2.2 *Well-Designed Sales Territories Improve Morale and Enhance the Power of Reward Systems*

There is high correlation between territory potential and territory sales. Across companies and industries, territory potential is often a better predictor of territory sales than any other characteristics, including the salesperson's experience, ability, or effort (Lucas, Weinberg, and Clowes 1975, Ryans and Weinberg 1979; 1987). Territories with high market potential often have high sales regardless of sales force effort. In fact, in environments with significant carryover, it is not uncommon for a vacant sales territory with high sales potential to have higher sales than a fully staffed territory with low sales potential. Similarly, territories with low potential tend to have low sales, but high market share.

Frequently, sales leaders do not place enough emphasis on differences in territory potential when they evaluate, compensate, reward, and acknowledge salespeople. When leaders underestimate the importance of these differences and treat salespeople as if their territories were identical, sales force morale suffers. Few salespeople will be content with what they feel are inferior account assignments while their colleagues make more money and get more recognition with less effort because they have superior territories. Territories with low potential, intense competition, or too many small accounts, but a high quota, lead to low job satisfaction and low motivation for salespeople. For this reason, unfair sales territories often lead to salesperson turnover.

The link between territory design and sales force morale is especially strong when a large proportion of the pay and rewards for salespeople is tied to their level of sales. For example, most of salespeople's earnings at a one company came from incentives paid as a commission on sales. Morale was quite low because the sales force did not feel that the wide range of incentive pay across salespeople accurately reflected true performance differences. The skills, capabilities, and motivation of the bottom 20 percent of salespeople did not appear to be substantially different from those of the top 20 percent, yet the top people earned more than four times as much incentive pay as the bottom people. Sales leaders assumed that something was wrong with the incentive plan. However, analysis revealed that poor territory design was the major cause of the variation in payout, and that the incentive plan could work quite well if territories were redesigned so that potential was distributed more equitably across the sales force (Zoltners, Sinha, and Lorimer 2006b).

The link between territory design and sales force morale is also strong when non-monetary recognitions—plaques, award trips, invitations to join select groups such as the President's Club—are tied to territory sales. And territory balance is a *must* for those companies that publicly publish a forced ranking of all salespeople on any sales metric.

11.5.2.3 *Well-Designed Sales Territories Keep Travel Time and Costs Under Control*

Sales territories that minimize sales force travel allow more face time with customers and have a positive impact on sales force morale, especially when sales leaders distribute travel requirements fairly. The high cost of gasoline and other travel expenses make travel-efficient territories critical for managing sales force costs. Companies often discover that the time and cost required for a salesperson to travel a great distance to reach one potentially large customer cannot be justified; they find that they get a greater return from calls on several mid-size customers closer to home. Differences in travel requirements sometimes create a need for different territory structures in remote and urban areas.

11.5.3 How to Redesign Territories

When companies take an "update as needed" and decentralized approach to territory design, the inevitable consequence is territories that do not effectively match sales force effort to customer needs, that compromise methods for evaluating and rewarding sales force performance, and that require excessive travel. Companies can create and maintain well-designed territories by developing accurate measures of account workload and potential, auditing sales territory design at least every one or two years, and using well-thought-out, structured processes and efficient tools to change territories as necessary to support business needs.

11.5.3.1 *Evaluate Territory Design Decisions Using Defined Business Objectives*

A structured territory design process begins with stated objectives that reinforce sales force strategy. Sales leaders can then evaluate proposed territory changes according to these unbiased business objectives.

Maximize profits. This is an important objective for most companies; due to modeling complexity, however, it is often impractical to measure the profit impact of territory design directly. While profit-maximizing territory alignment models have been developed to solve moderate-sized problems (Skiera and Albers 1998), most companies rely on territory design objectives such as those listed below that are easier to model and measure and that correlate with profit maximization.

Match territory workload to salesperson capacity. Having the right workload distribution across the sales force improves responsiveness to customers, ensures that salespeople are challenged but not overworked, and improves sales force morale. Territory workload measures vary in sophistication. Simple measures can include counts of accounts and prospects, perhaps weighted according to account size or potential. The most complex measures rely on sales response models that predict a profit-maximizing level of sales force effort for every account and prospect (see the Pharmacia example in section 11.7.2).

Distribute sales potential fairly to salespeople. Equitable distribution of potential to salespeople improves sales results and morale. Depending upon the compensation plan, the right distribution of sales potential can be critical to providing all salespeople with a fair opportunity to earn money. Some industries have direct measures of territory potential—for example, when competitive sales data can be obtained at the account level. In many industries, it is necessary to use creative approaches to develop surrogate measures of territory potential based on available data from sources such as government agencies, industry trade associations, and other data and research companies. More information about methods used by companies to develop measures of territory potential is provided in Zoltners, Sinha, and Lorimer (2009).

Develop compact, travel-efficient territories. Territories that are geographically compact and efficient to reach make it easier for salespeople to be responsive to customer needs. Compact territories also reduce the need for overnight trips and keep travel costs down.

Unfortunately, these business objectives cannot always be achieved simultaneously. For example, it may be necessary to build territories with lighter workload or potential in sparsely populated areas in order to make them geographically compact or to compensate for a large travel requirement. Often it is not even possible to achieve equitable workload and equitable sales potential distribution simultaneously. While workload and potential are closely correlated, territories with a greater proportion of large accounts will have a higher potential to workload ratio, while those with a greater proportion of small accounts will have a lower potential to workload ratio. The importance of each objective depends upon the mission of the sales force, the compensation plan, and the nature of the sales force's relationship with customers.

Companies frequently make the mistake of designing sales territories around the needs and desires of individual salespeople. While this strategy may keep a few salespeople happy in the short term, it can result in gerrymandered sales territories that do not make good business sense yet are likely to outlast the tenure of the people they were designed for. Sales territories are best designed from a customer and company perspective first; then the salespeople can be wisely matched with jobs that are consistent with long-term business needs.

11.5.3.2 *Use Structured Processes and Efficient Tools*

A successful sales territory redesign needs to be handled carefully and intentionally using a well-thought-out process. The best processes start with a centrally developed territory design proposal, based on objective business criteria and consistent logic for determining staffing needs. The proposal acts as a benchmark providing quantifiable criteria (such as profitability, territory workload and potential balance, and travel time) against which all territory design alterations can be judged. By allowing field sales managers to make local adjustments to the centrally developed proposal, sales leaders ensure that the redesign takes local conditions into account. Incorporating local input also makes it easier for the entire sales organization to accept territory changes.

Computer-assisted analysis, when coupled with structured processes, makes it possible for sales managers to create good territories quickly without frustration and without losing significant time in the field. Optimization software is available that uses mathematical algorithms to evaluate millions of potential territory designs to find one that best meets a company's objectives for profitability, equitable workload and sales potential, reasonable territory size and manageable travel requirements, as well as involving minimal disruption. These optimization models are based on the work of several researchers, including Hess and Samuels (1971), Easingwood (1973), Lodish (1975), Heschel (1977), Segal and Weinberger (1977), Richardson (1979), Zoltners (1979), Zoltners and Sinha (1983), and Skiera and Albers (1998). Practical implementation of these models within companies did not take off until two developments occurred, beginning in the early 1980s. First, software became available for use on personal computers (and later, on the Internet), allowing sales managers to create their own "what if" territory design scenarios using computerized maps and worksheets. Second, structured processes were invented that encouraged sales managers to use these tools within their companies to make appropriate local adjustments to a centrally developed (sometimes mathematically developed) initial territory design. More information about how companies have used structured processes and tools to successfully implement sales territory design changes is provided in the Pharmacia example in section 11.7.2, as well as in Zoltners, Sinha, and Lorimer (2004) and Zoltners and Sinha (2005).

11.6 Implementing Changes in Sales Force Size and Territory Design

Success in changing the size and territory design of a sales force requires attention to effective implementation. Here are some insights for successful implementation for sales force growth, downsizing, and realignment.

11.6.1 Growing the Sales Force

Companies may face several challenges when increasing the size of the sales force. Two of the most significant include addressing the resistance of the sales force to expansion and establishing effective processes for assimilating new salespeople.

Salespeople, particularly those paid largely on commission, often fight sales force expansion. For example, at a medical device company, when sales leaders set out to implement an expansion plan of 25 additional sales territories, salespeople and sales managers strongly resisted. Salespeople feared that the change would have an adverse impact on their commission earnings. They had worked hard to develop their "book of business," and felt they deserved to reap the benefits of their past efforts by earning commissions on easy repeat sales to current customers. They argued that the new territories were not justified, and they did whatever they could to make sure that their will prevailed, including threatening to resign and go to work for competitors (and take accounts with them) if their account base was reduced. Salespeople put so much pressure on management that only 12 of the 25 proposed new territories were ultimately implemented.

For sales forces that receive a significant portion of their earnings through commissions, several incentive compensation plan strategies can reduce the resistance to expansion. These strategies include designing a goal-based plan that does not penalize salespeople who give up accounts to expansion territories, establishing temporary transition compensation plans that keep salespeople's compensation "whole" for a period following expansion, and phasing in compensation changes over time. Sales leadership can reduce the resistance of the sales force to expansion by carefully managing the expansion—for example, establishing objective and quantifiable business criteria for territory size, such as an ideal level of untapped market potential or a maximum number of key accounts per territory. Expansion decisions based on consistent criteria are more likely to be perceived as uniformly fair. If expansion decisions are based primarily on executive opinions rather than on data, salespeople will come up with countless reasons why new territories are not needed.

When the size of a sales force increases, recruiting and training new salespeople adds significantly to the workload of sales managers. Managers in rapidly growing businesses often struggle to keep up with their day-to-day coaching and selling responsibilities, and they may lack sufficient time for hiring and training large numbers of new salespeople. One way to ease this stress is to keep the sales force span of control (the average number of people that report to each sales manager) at a reasonable level while the sales force is growing. This will ensure that managers have enough time to manage their people well and, at the same time, recruit and train effectively. Another way to help managers in rapidly growing sales forces is to leverage external resources and build strong support programs to assist sales managers with their hiring and training responsibilities. One company hired a recruiting/training manager and paid him incentives based on the second-year performance of all new hires.

11.7 Downsizing the Sales Force

During downsizing—a painful process that can be devastating for sales force morale—sales leaders are challenged to reduce the sales force headcount strategically while minimizing the pain to the organization and keeping a core group of salespeople who will retain key customers. Protecting the company's top customers and best salespeople should be highest priorities when a sales force must be downsized.

Sometimes it is possible to avoid massive layoffs by anticipating a need for future downsizing and using attrition to slowly reduce the sales force to a desirable size. To be successful, attrition management programs need to be systematic. Too often, companies implement across-the-board hiring freezes which result in insufficient coverage of important customers when top salespeople in high-potential territories leave the company. Intelligent attrition management programs consider "territory opportunity," closing down vacant territories in low-potential areas but retaining those in high-opportunity areas, and transferring current salespeople into them or selectively hiring to fill important vacancies.

When a significant decline in sales opportunities is not anticipated sufficiently in advance, the only viable strategy is to rapidly reduce the sales force. Survivors will know quickly that they have a job and some reasonable level of job security, customers will have greater confidence about what the future holds, and sales leaders can begin to rebuild a new, smaller, and more focused sales organization.

11.7.1 Realigning the Sales Force

At most companies, a need to make minor sales territory design adjustments occurs frequently. Changes in the customer base, new promotional cycles, and turnover of sales force personnel are just some of the situations that can require the fine-tuning of sales territories on a regular basis. Major changes to territory design occur every few years at many companies. Typically, these major realignments are in response to an important sales force design change, such as a major sales force restructuring or a significant sales force expansion or contraction. Major realignments can also be prompted by significant changes in market conditions, new product launches, or significant shifts in company strategy. Because sales territory design issues arise on a regular basis, companies need processes for evaluating and developing territory design quickly while ensuring acceptance of territory changes by the sales force.

Sometimes companies are reluctant to redesign sales territories because they do not want to disrupt the continuity of sales force relationships with customers. Particularly in industries where salespeople's customer knowledge is a source of competitive advantage, an ineffective transition from one salesperson to another could result in inadequate servicing of the customer and ultimately loss of business.

A well-thought-out, comprehensive account transition plan for important customers makes it less likely that the company will lose sales during a transition.

Companies in which sales territory design has not been evaluated for long periods of time are usually seriously out of alignment with current market needs. Many valuable customers are not getting the attention they deserve, and many talented salespeople are not being fully utilized. Sales leaders should assess territory design on a regular basis to ensure that it keeps pace with ongoing market and product-line change, and that territory workload and opportunity is well matched to the talents and capacity of salespeople.

11.7.2 An Example: Resizing the Sales Force and Redesigning Sales Territories at Pharmacia

In June 2001, pharmaceutical company Pharmacia (acquired by Pfizer the following year) employed several of the approaches described in this chapter to implement sales force sizing and territory design changes (Zoltners and Sinha 2005). At that time, Pharmacia had 3,080 salespeople calling on primary care physicians. These salespeople were organized into seven sales teams that came from what had previously been three separate companies (see Figure 11.13)—Pharmacia, Upjohn (from a 1995 merger), and Searle (from a 2000 merger). Following the mergers, the company had retained the name Pharmacia. Pharmacia had never fully integrated the sales teams from these three companies. This created inefficiencies, particularly when the company asked multiple sales teams to co-promote key products. Effective co-promotion required several salespeople to coordinate their activities at the physician level, and the territory misalignment across the different sales teams made this difficult. Salespeople had to interact with an average of 8.2 other company salespeople in order to coordinate their co-promotion activity.

With a goal of integrating the sales organization into a more cohesive structure that would position the company more effectively for the future, the company launched "Project Genesis" to resize and realign the sales organization. Specific project objectives included:

- enhancing copromotion coordination by reducing the number of required inter-salesperson interactions and streamlining managmeent coordination across sales teams;
- increasing sales force capacity slightly to support planned new product launches;
- balancing the workload across sales territories, as sales territory design for most teams had not changed in years even as the product line had evolved.

The project included three major steps:

- *Step 1: Physician Segmentation and Sales Response Estimation.* Pharmacia started by focusing on customer needs. It developed critiera for segmenting physicians according to their likely responsiveness to sales force effort. Segmentation criteria included a physician's speciality, product category usage, and market share of Pharmacia and key competitive products. The company analyzed physician-level call and prescription data to develop sales response estimates that reflected the historical sales impact of sales force effort for each physician segment for each product. Input from company sales and marketing team members helped to shape future sales response estimates, particularly for new products, using a decision calculus methodology (Little 1970).

• *Step 2: Sales Force Sizing and Workload Allocation.* Pharmacia used the sales response functions from step 1 in an optimization model that determined a profit-maximizing sales force effort allocation across the company's products and physician segments (Zoltners and Sinha 2005). The company used the model to evaluate several alternative sales force sizes and team structures. As shown in Figure 11.13, it selected a new structure with six teams of 550 salespeople, each team with an identical sales territory and sales management configuration. This structure had several advantages. It enhanced efficiency of co-promotion coordination by drastically reducing the number of salesperson interactions and by making cross-team management coordination easier. The total number of salespeople increased by 7 percent, providing additional sales force capacity to support new products. Since the team size of 550 matched the size of the former Upjohn sales teams, the new structure minimized disruption of these two teams and helped keep the overall disruption of customer–salesperson relationships to a manageable 28 percent.

• *Step 3: Design and Rollout New Territories.* Pharmacia applied the segment call effort allocations or "workloads" from Step 2 to over 100,000 US physicians and summed the physician workload estimates to the zip code level. The company then used a territory optimization model to develop an effective and efficient design for 550

Before		After	
Sales Team	Size	Sales Team	Size
Searle 1	482	Pharmacia 1	550
Searle 2	482	Pharmacia 2	550
Searle 3	466	Pharmacia 3	550
Upjohn 1	550	Pharmacia 4	550
Upjohn 2	550	Pharmacia 5	550
Pharmacia 1	275	Pharmacia 6	550
Pharmacia 2	275		

Fig. 11.13. Sales Force Team Sizes Before and After "Project Genesis" at Pharmacia

territories with profit-maximizing workloads across all six sales teams. Pharmacia rolled out these optimized territory designs to 500 managers in five cities over a two-week period. Alignment consultants assisted sales managers using software to match salespeople to territories and to assess and fine-tune sales territory design. Web-based tools assisted with fine-tuning of territory alignments after the face-to-face meetings. Every salesperson and manager received maps and reports to help them understand and visulize their new responsibilities.

Pharmacia's Vice President of Sales, Rick Keefer, described two important benefits of using structured processes and efficient tools to complete this challenging project.

- "The project took just four months from start to finish. Without the models and structured processes, the project would have taken six months or more."
- "The process produced significant results for the organization while creating sales force buy-in."

11.8 DIRECTIONS FOR FUTURE RESEARCH

Some important knowledge gaps in sales force sizing and territory design can benefit from additional research.

11.8.1 Sales Force Sizing Research Directions

The best sales force sizing approaches described in this chapter have been used most successfully by many companies that execute relatively simple, defined sales processes and that can measure the link between sales activity and performance metrics, such as sales and profits. Yet at the majority of companies, sales processes are complex, requiring salespeople to use creative problem-solving and consultative selling approaches to meet a wide array of customer needs. For these companies, the best sales process for all targeted market segments is often challenging to determine, and the link between sales activity and company performance metrics may be difficult to quantify. Companies that face these complexities tend to quickly abandon attempts to use analytical sales force sizing methods in favor of "gut feel" appoaches. Research focused around two issues can help these companies size their sales forces more effectively.

1. When the sales process is complex and results measurement is difficult, what performance metrics are best for evaluating and comparing the effectiveness of alternative sales processes? Many companies prefer results metrics such as

company sales and profits, but measurability challenges can create a need to
consider alternative metrics such as customer satisfaction and account coverage.
2. How can companies in complex selling situations search through the vast array
   of possible selling activities to craft the best sales process for driving performance for the chosen metrics?

11.8.2 Sales Territory Design Research Directions

Many companies have used the territory design approaches described in this
chapter to make significant territory design improvements. Their biggest challenges frequently lie in the implementation of change. Three implementation-
focused issues that companies often find challenging are:

1. There are many thousands of good territory designs for any sales force, but there
   are also billions of bad ones. Companies need good metrics for evaluating and
   comparing alternative sales territory designs. For example, what is the best way
   to measure profitability, utilization of salesperson capacity, customer coverage,
   travel costs, and disruption costs?
2. Ongoing market and company product-line changes continuously impact the
   workload and potential of sales territories. At the same time, salesperson
   turnover creates opportunities to redeploy sales effort without relocating salespeople. Companies need processes for proactively managing territory vacancies
   so that they can take advantage of sales force attrition to continually keep sales
   territory design aligned with market and company needs.
3. Some of the most stressful territory redesign situations occur when companies
   downsize, perhaps following a merger or acquisition or in response to a missed
   financial goal. Companies need structured processes for personnel placement
   following sales force downsizing—processes that are objective and legally defensible while ensuring that the company keeps its best people.

ZS Associates has devised situation-specific processes for addressing these issues,
but the development of theoretical constructs for approaching these challenges
could further enhance the process of successfully implementing sales territory
design changes.

11.9 CONCLUSION

Sales force size and territory design decisions have considerable impact on salespeople, customers, and company results. Good management decisions regarding

these important sales effectiveness drivers help to ensure that salespeople are appropriately challenged but not overworked, customer needs are well served, and company financial goals are achieved.

Because sales force size directly affects both revenues and costs, many company stakeholders, including leaders in sales, marketing, and finance, take a keen interest in the sales force sizing decision. Companies often use cost-control-based decision rules for determining how many salespeople they need, but unfortunately these rules often lead to critical sales force sizing errors. The best approaches for determining how large a company's sales force should be require assessing customer needs, determining how much sales force time is required to execute a sales process that meets those needs, and understanding the link between sales force size, customer coverage, and financial value (such as sales or profits). The right sales force size results in high sales, reasonable costs, and strong long-term profitability for a company.

In addition to determining the right size for the sales force, companies that seek to maximize effectiveness need to deploy salespeople effectively across customers and prospects by designing sales territories that match account workload and market opportunity to the capacity of each salesperson or sales team. By improving sales territory design, most companies can add 2–7 percent to their revenues every year without adding salespeople.

Companies need to change their sales force size and territory design as business needs evolve, and careful attention to implementation helps ensure that changes are well received by customers and salespeople. Researchers can continue to make progress by developing processes and models that enhance sales force sizing decision-making while making it possible to implement those decisions successfully.

References

Darmon, R. Y. (2005). "Joint Assessment of Optimal Sales Force Sizes and Sales Call Guidelines: A Management-Oriented Tool," *Canadian Journal of Administrative Sciences* 22.3, 206–19.

Easingwood, C. (1973). "Heuristic Approach to Selecting Sales Regions and Territories," *Operations Research Quarterly* 24.4, 527–34.

Heschel, M. S. (1977). "Effective Sales Territory Development," *Journal of Marketing* 41.2, 39–43.

Hess, S. W., and S. A. Samuels (1971). "Experiences with a Sales Districting Model: Criteria and Implementation," *Management Science* 18.4(2), 41–54.

Horsky, D., and P. Nelson (1996). "Evaluation of Salesforce Size and Productivity Through Efficient Frontier Benchmarking," *Management Science* 15.4, 301–20.

LaForge, R. W., and D. W. Cravens (1985). "Empirical and Judgment-Based Sales Force Decision Models: Comparative Analysis," *Decision Sciences* 16, 177–96.

LITTLE, J. D. C. (1970). "Models and Managers: The Concept of a Decision Calculus," *Management Science* 16, 466–85.

LODISH, L. M. (1975). "Sales Territory Alignment to Maximize Profit," *Journal of Marketing Research* 12, 30–36.

——(1980). "A User-Oriented Model for Sales Force Size, Product, and Market Allocation Decisions," *Journal of Marketing* 44.3, 70.

LUCAS, H. C., C. B. WEINBERG, and K. W. CLOWES (1975). "Sales Response as a Function of Territorial Potential and Sales Representative Workload," *Journal of Marketing Research* 12.3, 298.

RICHARDSON, R. J. (1979). "A Territory Realignment Model: MAPS," presented at the New Orleans ORSA/TIMS meeting, May 1.

RYANS, A. B., and C. B. WEINBERG (1979). "Territory Sales Response," *Journal of Marketing Research* 16.4, 453.

————(1987). "Territory Sales Response Models: Stability over Time," *Journal of Marketing Research* 24.2, 229.

SEGAL, M., and D. B. WEINBERGER (1977). "Turfing," *Operations Research* 25.3, 367–86.

SKIERA, B., and S. ALBERS (1998). "COSTA: Contribution Optimizing Sales Territory Alignment," *Marketing Science* 17, 196–213.

ZOLTNERS, A. A. (1979). "A Unified Approach to Sales Territory Alignment," in R. Bagozzi (ed.), *Sales Management: New Development from Behavioral and Decision Model Research*, Cambridge, MA: Marketing Science Institute, 360–76.

——and S. E. LORIMER (2000). "Sales Territory Alignment: An Overlooked Productivity Tool," *Journal of Personal Selling & Sales Management* 20.3, 139–50.

——and P. SINHA (1980). "Integer Programming Models For Sales Resource Allocation," *Management Science* 26.3, 242.

————(1983). "Sales Territory Alignment: A Review and Model," *Management Science* (November), 1237–56.

————(2001). "Sales-Force Decision Models: Insights from 25 Years of Implementation," *Interfaces* 31.3 (part 2 of 2), S8–S44.

————(2005). "Sales Territory Design: Thirty Years of Modeling and Implementation," *Marketing Science* 24.3, 313–31.

————and S. E. LORIMER (2004). *Sales Force Design for Strategic Advantage*, New York: Palgrave Macmillan.

——————(2006a). "Match Your Sales Force Structure to Your Business Lifecycle," *Harvard Business Review* (July–August).

——————(2006b). *The Complete Guide to Sales Force Incentive Compensation: How to Design Plans That Work*, New York: Amacom.

——————(2009). *Building a Winning Sales Force: Powerful Strategies for Driving High Performance*, New York: Amacom.

PART III

THE SALES FORCE AND THE CUSTOMER

CHAPTER 12

CUSTOMER SELECTION TO ACQUIRE, RETAIN, AND GROW

ANDREA L. DIXON

12.1 INTRODUCTION

Ask a senior sales and marketing executive what causes sleep loss, and "creating satisfied customers" is frequently close to the top of the list (Yoon 2002). According to the Insurance Advisory Board Agenda Poll conducted by the Corporate Executive Board, the top priority for 2009 among financial services and insurance executives was customer retention and service management. Yet, having 99 percent, or even 90 percent, satisfaction levels reported by the organization's customers while failing to return the profit level desired by the organization's stakeholders will not ensure the long-term viability of the organization (Keiningham, Cooil, Aksoy, Andreassen, and Weiner 2007). Nor will such an approach guarantee career advancement opportunities for the sales and marketing executive.

In "Managing Through Rose-Colored Glasses," Keiningham, Vavra, and Aksoy (2006) share the results of a study which examines the beliefs and misconceptions of executives on a similarly important topic, customer loyalty. They found that many of the popularly held beliefs about customer loyalty were patently untrue, when current research results are taken into account. Consequently, sales and marketing executives may be seeking the holy grail of customer loyalty because they have embraced one of these myths:

- *Existing customers spend more money on an organization's products/services than do new customers.* While this statement sounds as though it could be true, research shows that this may or may not be the case (Burritt 2009).
- *Current customers are more lucrative to serve because they purchase at full margin and are less likely to demand deep discounts.* The picture evoked by this statement is the demanding new customer saying, "If you want my business, sharpen your pencil." In fairness, research runs counter to this statement as well, suggesting that the existing customer is the more demanding one, requiring concessions of the organization in order to keep the customer's business (Reinartz and Kumar 2002).
- *Existing customers are easier to serve since they understand the organization's business operations and will align their business to the supplier organization.* This thinking leads to the assumption that current customers are essentially cheaper to serve. In fairness, current customers may demand more or more expensive contact approaches (e.g. personalized web access, dedicated sales teams) that make them more costly to serve.
- *Current customers who are loyal to the organization are more profitable.* "Documented studies across many industries show that all companies serve three types of customers. Generally, less than 20 percent of customers generate the lion's share of the profits; another 60–70 percent of customers are break-even to marginal in their contribution to profit; and the remaining 20 percent or so eat up profits based on the high costs of serving them. However, there are loyal customers in each category" (Keiningham, Vavra, and Aksoy 2006: 15).

Sales and marketing executives' sleep loss is aided and abetted by the increased complexity of recommendations emanating from consulting circles and academic scholars. Research studies and textbooks listed at the close of this chapter urge sales and marketing professionals to attend to a variety of measures and data in order to ensure a healthy customer base:

- Satisfaction
- Loyalty: behavioral and attitudinal
- Net promoter scores
- Word of mouth
- Repurchase rates
- Historical purchases
- Share of wallet/share of spending
- Customer lifetime analysis
- Upgrading and cross-buying
- Returns and defections
- Referrals and word of mouth
- Frequency of contact
- Voice of the customer

The focus of this chapter is to synthesize the current knowledge in the area of customer management and to encourage the organization to fully engage in this essential activity for business success. Keeping some existing customers may be more profitable and less costly than finding and developing new customers, but new customers might be necessary in the organization's portfolio to maintain long-term financial health.

The first section of this chapter includes a discussion of who is the right customer—which prompts the question of how should the organization identify the right customers from among its existing customers. The second section of the chapter examines the common metrics or dimensions used for customer analysis and insights. Next, the chapter provides a discussion of the measurement issues associated with the composite profitability measure, CLV. To select the right customers to add to the firm's portfolio, we discuss how lifetime valuation analysis can yield important insights. Since not all customers are necessarily good for the firm, we devote a section of this chapter to the process of identifying and firing the right customers. Lifetime valuation analysis provides the foundation for a pro-posed model for identifying the right "lost" customers (or defectors) to prioritize for winning-back strategies. Then, a composite model of lifetime valuation, current profitability, and loyal advocacy is introduced as a tool for identifying the custo-mers to prioritize for retention efforts. Following a discussion of retention, the last section of this chapter focuses on customer portfolio management. The closing perspective focuses on the value of systematic customer assessment for acquiring, growing, and retaining the right mix of customers to generate the strongest return in investment.

To begin, the right customers have to be identified to truly engage in profitable customer management. These right customers need to be given the right attention in order to properly grow their business with the supplier organization. These concepts will be explored next.

12.2 THE RIGHT CUSTOMER

To select the right customers to acquire, retain, and grow requires that sales and marketing professionals first identify who are the "right customers." Defining the right customer has escalated in complexity, moving beyond simply customers who are satisfied, or customers who are loyal, or those who recommend the supplier organization, and so forth. These various indicators of a customer's relationship with the supplier organization do not guarantee that the organization is focused on the most profitable customers (Reinartz and Kumar 2003). Today, as organizations seek to define the right customers, they place increased emphasis on measuring the value of individual customers and viewing customers as assets. Sales and marketing professionals recognize today that all customers are not alike. In addition, such professionals are charged with understanding the impact of marketing expenditures on immediate sales (marketing ROI) and on long-term customer value (customer lifetime value, or CLV). All marketing and sales strategies are not equally appropriate in various contexts. The goal today is to actively use marketing channels (such as web and salespersons) and marketing activities (such as email campaigns and special promotions) to maximize customer and firm value (Venkatesan, Kumar, and Bohling 2007).

As sales and marketing professionals develop a stronger understanding of various customer segments, they can focus their efforts on one or more of several general strategies:

1. identify the segment(s) most likely to respond to anticipated marketing actions and stimulate their consumption rates in the next planning period;
2. focus on retaining key customer segment(s) in an effort to extend their patronage and improve the overall contribution margin to the organization;
3. streamline the costs associated with acquiring new customers and/or improve the efficiency by which new customers are acquired;
4. focus on finding new customer segment(s) which might be profitable for the organization (Jones, Stevens, and Chonko 2005).

The first two activities call for sales and marketing professionals to focus on existing customers. But the question remains: How should the organization identify the right customers, among its existing customers, upon which to focus its marketing efforts?

12.2.1 Identifying the Right Customers Among Existing Customers

There is not a single or simple metric, scale, or data set that allows organizations to easily identify the right customers for their marketing efforts. This section explores the most common and potentially useful metrics to consider when identifying the right customers. Opportunities, concerns, and challenges associated with such metrics are also offered (see Figure 12.1).

12.2.1.1 *Identify the Right Customers Based on Customer Satisfaction*

Having satisfied customers is important: satisfaction is a key driver of customer loyalty and retention (Gupta and Zeithaml 2006, Rust and Zahorik 1993). In addition to its widespread use among practitioners, customer satisfaction measures are the most widely studied in academic circles (Gupta and Zeithaml 2006). Typically defined as a customer's judgement that a product/service meets or exceeds expectations (this is a disconfirmation of expectations model), customer satisfaction can be operationalized as transaction-specific (based on a given

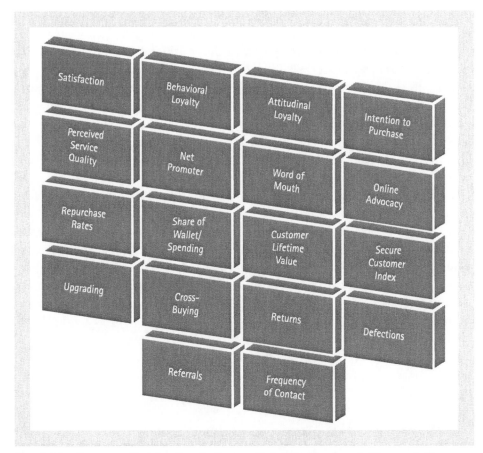

Fig. 12.1. Common Metrics for Customer Relationship Acquisition and Management

customer–organization encounter) or at an overall level. While an improvement in customer satisfaction is shown to have significant and positive impact on organizational financial performance, the strength of the satisfaction–profitability linkage shows substantial variance across industries and companies, with the largest variances evident when comparing organizations within a given industry (Gupta and Zeithaml 2006). Consequently, satisfaction in the aggregate is a helpful but not complete measure, suggesting that satisfied customers cannot be the sole criterion used when identifying the right customers.

12.2.1.2 *Identify the Right Customers Based on Customer Loyalty*

Customer loyalty is also an important metric as keeping the right customers is likely through either contracts (contractual loyalty) or non-contractual means (behavioral or attitudinal loyalty). Behavioral loyalty can be defined simply as purchasing the same product (product loyalty) or other additional products (company or supplier loyalty) from the same organization over time (Weitz,

Castleberry, and Tanner 2007). Or, Oliver (1997) offers a comprehensive definition where loyalty is viewed as a deeply held commitment to rebuy a product/service consistently in the future, despite the efforts of other marketers to prompt switching behavior or other situational influences that can impede or reshape consumption habits. Some researchers and practitioners operationalize customer loyalty as a higher-order construct comprising repurchase intentions, share of wallet, positive advocacy/word-of-mouth referrals, emotional attachment to the brand, and so forth. The issue of composite measures will be examined shortly. Meanwhile, typical behavioral measures used to capture customer loyalty include repeat purchase frequency or relative volume of purchase, while attitudinal loyalty is often captured as repurchase intent, word of behavior activity, and propensity to refer (Gupta and Zeithaml 2006).

In "The Mismanagement of Customer Loyalty," Reinartz and Kumar (2002) report that customer loyalty measures not accounting for profitability are not appropriate measures for identifying the right customers. These researchers reported correlational coefficients between loyalty and profitability as low as 0.20 for a mail order company to 0.45 for a grocery retailer, "hardly a ringing endorsement of the loyalty mantra" (p. 88). Their work challenges several long-standing myths about customer loyalty, noting that long-time customers are (1) not less costly to serve, (2) not paying higher prices than newer customers for the same bundle of products/services, (3) not necessarily the strongest market mavens (creating active or passive positive word of mouth about the organization). In fact, in the case of word-of-mouth advocacy, behavioral loyalty alone was not a strong predictor of positive word-of-mouth behavior. Inertia, convenience, contracts, and other forces can be driving what appears to be behavioral loyalty. Reinartz and Kumar (2002) recommend that attention be paid to the use of attitudinal indicators of loyalty (i.e. *Are you loyal to xyz organization? Are you interested in switching to another organization?*) to examine true customer commitment or loyalty. They believe that "the reason the link between loyalty and profits is weak has a lot to do with the crudeness of the methods most companies currently use to decide whether or not to maintain their customer relationships" (p. 90).

Bolton, Lemon, and Verhoef (2004) note: "the marketing discipline is in the midst of a shift from a managerial focus on allocating resources to customers who are currently loyal (i.e. a reactive strategy) to a focus on allocating resources to customers to create, maintain, and enhance loyal behaviors (i.e. a proactive strategy)" (p. 286).

12.2.1.3 *Identify the Right Customers Based on Purchase History*

Traditional customer analysis examines fine-grained data such as the customer purchases, including recently purchased upgrades (Bolton, Lemon, and Verhoef 2008), repurchase rates (Boulding, Kalra, Staelin, and Zeithaml 1993), cross-purchasing situations (purchasing other products from the same organization but perhaps a different division) (Li, Sun, and Wilcox 2005), as well as returns and purchase disruptions. Historical customer purchase behavior is a very common approach used to segment an organization's customer database to identify the right customers. The typical assumption is that a specific element of a customer's purchase history—for example, whether the customer purchases from more than one part of an organization—serves as a driver (or antecedent) to important organizational outcomes. Yet, as Reinartz, Thomas, and Bascoul (2008) demonstrate, the nature of such relationships may be quite the opposite. In their study, these researchers examined whether or not cross-buying (or purchasing products from multiple product categories offered by the organization) drives customer retention, revenues, and loyalty. They found that "cross-buying is a consequence and not an antecedent of behavioral loyalty" in industry contexts where there is no natural sequencing of purchases (general merchandise catalog, direct mail book retailer) (Reinartz, Thomas, and Bascoul 2008: 5).

A common approach in a method using historical purchase data is to score customers on the basis of how recently they made a purchase (recency), how often they purchase (frequency), and how much the customer typically spends (monetary). While this Reach Frequency Monetary (RFM) model promises to help an organization identify whether a particular customer is worthy of investment, RFM evaluations cannot distinguish the buying pattern differences that customers exhibit. Typical RFM scoring approaches often result in an overinvestment of lapsed customers (Reinartz and Kumar 2002).

While individual-level behaviors can play an important role in defining the right customer, marketing models have moved beyond individual-level transactional analysis to predictive modeling of customer purchase patterns. Firms typically employ individual-level purchase data to determine promotion strategy targets and possible marketing campaigns. An alternative modeling approach using historical customer purchase data, event history analysis, determines the probability of future purchases based on statistical patterns of past purchases, which will be discussed more fully in a later section.

12.2.1.4 *Identify the Right Customers Based on Share of Wallet*

Prediction of the right customers can rely on survey data to determine the customer's share of wallet, which is the percentage of a customer's purchases (wallet) for a product category that the customer purchases from the supplier organization. Share of wallet (or, share of spending as it is sometimes called) provides an indication of various customer groups' potential value, important input for directing marketing and sales strategies, and guiding promotional programs. Share of wallet is a behavioral indicator of loyalty; however, although organizations may have large groups of customers for whom their share of wallet is very high, when the cost of marketing and serving those customers is subtracted from the customers' gross margins, profitability may be actually negative.

Consequently, share of wallet measures provide more insight and value when used in combination with other measures for selecting the right customers.

12.2.1.5 *Identify the Right Customers Based on Net Promoter Scores*

Some researchers and practitioners suggest that the right customers must be advocates for the brand, product, and/or organization. Customer advocacy as determined through customer surveys is one type of word-of-mouth (WOM) measure. The Net Promoter® Score, introduced by Reichheld and commercialized by Bain & Company, represents a loyalty and advocacy metric calculated via a single question (Reichheld 2006; www.netpromoter.com). The single question: *How likely is it that you would recommend [organization x] to a friend or colleague?* is posed to current customers in order to classify them into three groups: promoters, passives, and detractors. Reichheld (2006) recommends classifying customers into these groups according to their responses on a 0–10 point rating scale as follows:

Promoters (score 9–10): these are loyal enthusiasts, who continue buying and referring other customers, thereby fueling an organization's organic growth.

Passives (score 7–8): these are satisfied, but not particularly enthusiastic customers. Given their lack of attitudinal loyalty, they are particularly vulnerable to competitors' marketing activities.

Detractors (score 0–6): these are truly dissatisfied customers, who may damage the organization's brand image and reputation, thereby hampering new customer acquisition, hastening existing customer defections, and impeding an organization's growth through negative word-of-mouth. (www.netpromoter.com)

While Reichheld (2006) recommends how survey results be used to classify individual customers (above), the loyalty movement and Net Promoter Community (www.netpromoter.com/netpromoter_community) provide industry-level benchmarking data for comparing an organization's overall Net Promoter Score (NPS).

To calculate the overall NPS for an organization, the firm subtracts the percentage of Detractors from the total percentage of customers classified as Promoters (the overall NPS calculations ignore the percentage of Passives in an organization's portfolio). A partner organization in the Net Promoter space, Satmetrix, has released their 2009 benchmark data on Net Promoter Scores for close to 100 companies in the United States. NPS company scores vary widely from a high of 45 percent for Vonage in the telecommunications sector to almost double that score in the financial services sector (USAA having an 89 percent NPS). Apple carries a leading NPS score of 77 percent in the computer hardware segment of the technology sector (www.netpromoter.com).

While the Net Promoter Score concept has made inroads and gained fairly broad organizational adoption, other research suggests that reliance upon a single question/single dimension approach for identifying the right customers is not without caution. According to Keiningham, Cooil, Andreassen, and Aksoy (2007), who analyzed over 15,000 interviews from two country-level satisfaction studies (the Norwegian Customer Satisfaction Barometer and the American Customer Satisfaction Index) and attempted to replicate the original Net Promoter analysis, no single measure from either country-level database "did an adequate job of predicting firm growth. For example, Net Promoter was only best two out of 19 times." Through a second study comprising longitudinal data from 8,000+ interviews among US customers, these same researchers examined the impact of commonly used measures of satisfaction and loyalty on future purchase behaviors. Their results suggest that future customer loyalty behaviors, such as retention, share of wallet, and word of mouth, are distinct. Consequently, no single measure appears to adequately predict future loyalty behaviors among customers (Keiningham and Aksoy 2008).

Focusing specifically on the Net Promoter Scores, Keiningham and Aksoy (2008) explain that the correlations between NPS and various measures of financial performance across a spectrum of industry settings are wide-ranging. Sample correlations between Net Promoter Score and Sales at the district level results in three industries range from a correlation of r=.36 for a specialty retailer, to a correlation of r=.17 for a grocery retailer, to r=−.65 for a home improvement retailer. Standard satisfaction and brand preference measures also exhibit inconsistency in tracking with financial performance across grocery, home improvement, and specialty retailer sectors (Keiningham and Aksoy 2008). Consequently, the value of a single-measure Net Promoter Score appears to be less than originally proposed.

12.2.1.6 *Identify the Right Customers Based on Customer Advocacy*

Most research on customer selection focuses on individual behavior, individual attitudes, and/or organizational results. However, recent research in the online area shows that internet shoppers choosing an online retailer as a result of WOM referrals yield stronger organizational benefits (more sales) in response to local market conditions than do internet shoppers who "search" the Internet to find a product (Choi, Bell, and Lodish 2008). Thus, the impact of a customer on other customers through social networks and word of mouth needs to be an important part of the "right customer" discussion (Blackshaw 2008).

In today's business environment, WOM or customer advocacy measures no longer need to be self-reported via a survey methodology. In fact, organizations are beginning to identify, track, and measure the impact that individual customers may have on their organization through the customer's online activities, such as blogging, conducting product reviews, posting to message boards, participating in product and brand communities, answering questions for other customers in online forums, etc. Researchers are just beginning to understand and incorporate these measures into analysis for defining the right customer (Blackshaw 2008). Sales and marketing professionals will likely experiment with a variety of

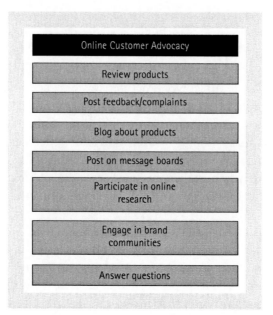

Fig. 12.2. Measures for Online Customer Advocacy

Adapted from Blackshaw (2008)

measurement approaches while scholars and consultants create a foundation of current research (see Figure 12.2).

12.2.1.7 *Identify the Right Customers Based on Customer Security*

Managing a customer base to optimize customer relationships, ensure that the organization's products and services match (or exceed) customer needs, and provide for the growth targets set by shareholders has yielded several composite measures used for determining the right customers. One such tool, introduced by Burke, Inc., a leading US-based marketing research organization, is the Secure Customer Index® (SCI®). The SCI® involves measures of satisfaction, repurchase likelihood, recommendation likelihood, the degree to which customers prefer the brand or organization to all others, and whether customers believe the organization has earned the customer's loyalty (see Figure 12.3).

According to Burke, customer loyalty at the individual level or for a customer segment is determined by the percentage of points attained for these five dimensions: satisfaction, repurchase, recommendation, brand preference, and loyalty owed. Customers are classified as "secure" if their scores are notably high in each category.

To validate their SCI® measure, Burke used a longitudinal research methodology spanning five industries (including business to business and business to consumer). Evaluating two supplier organizations with which they do business, research participants provided SCI® measures at two points in time as well as share of wallet information for validation purposes. Burke's SCI® represents a composite measure

Fig. 12.3 Burke, Inc's Secure Customer Index®

Source: http://www.Burke.com

of key customer attitudinal and behavioral dimensions linked to retaining customers who purchase from the organization. If the goal of sales and marketing executives is to secure, build, and maintain long-term relationships with *profitable* customers (Johnston and Marshall 2007), organizations need to consider more than a composite measure that has been validated against a revenue (share of wallet) measure.

12.2.1.8 *Identify the Right Customers Based on Profitable Loyalty*

Clearly, it should be evident by now that defining the right customers requires attending to multiple dimensions of customer behavior, customer attitudes, and customer profitability—both historical and future profitability.

Customer profitability analysis refers to the practice of estimating the profitability of individual customers and identifying both customers that create value for the company and, just as importantly, those customers that destroy value. Effective customer profitability analysis provides the company with a strong competitive advantage by improving key strategic and operating decisions involving customer selection and retention. (Heitger and Heitger 2008: 261)

A proprietary composite measure is Profitable Loyalty, offered by IPSOS, an international marketing research firm with 9000+ employees and offices in 64 countries (http://www.ipsos.com/who/fastfacts). Using this Profitable Loyalty measure to help its customers create stronger financial performance, IPSOS directs its clients to focus on the customer segments showing greatest Profitable Loyalty across three dimensions: attitude (affective commitment, brand preference), behavior (share of wallet, momentum, which is recent change in behavior), and value (profitability) (Keiningham and Aksoy 2008). This Profitable Loyalty measure appears to comprise a good balance of dimensions to drive customer selection toward a profitable end. However, since this is a proprietary measure, few independent assessments of the measure are published in the literature.

12.2.1.9 *Identify the Right Customers Based on Customer Lifetime Value (CLV)*

While IPSOS' Profitable Loyalty measure presumably captures behavior, attitudes, and profits, the information published about this composite measure suggests that this approach might be considered a backward-looking modeling approach. Profitable loyalty composite measures, as described above, assume that the past patterns of behaviors, attitudes, and profits remain unchanged for the future. Consequently, organizations also need customer profitability assessments that are forward-looking, not just historical (Joelson 2009). This is an important activity: "many companies spend millions of dollars conducting profitability analysis of their customers. For instance, the banking industry alone spends an estimated $400 million per year on customer profitability analyses" (Heitger and Heitger 2008: 261).

When attempting to prioritize which customers to retain, an organization must look at both present profitability and future profit potential (Niraj, Gupta, and Narasimhan 2001). One such measure, the lifetime value of a customer (CLV), is defined as the present value of all future profits achieved from a specific customer during the length of the customer's relationship with the organization. If a firm calculates the CLV for each individual customer and then aggregates those values into an overall organizational level measure, this disaggregated (bottom-up) approach yields an overall customer equity valuation for the firm as well as customer-specific data useful for segmenting the customer base and targeting marketing activities (Kumar and George 2006). Aggregate level (or top-down) approaches, of which there are several advanced by scholars, yields only an average CLV for the organization's customers and is a less useful measure for identifying the right customers for future marketing efforts (Rust, Lemon, and Zeithaml 2004).

A measure that focuses on long-term profit not short-term profit or market share, customer lifetime value has a strong positive impact on the organization's financial performance—almost by definition. "Therefore, maximizing CLV is effectively maximizing the long-run profitability and financial health of a company" (Gupta and Zeithaml 2006: 730). Rationale for using CLV to guide an organization's approach to customer relationship management lies in CLV's role in guiding customer selection decisions as well as strategic direction provided by CLV for allocating marketing dollars or resources.

In the area of customer selection, Gupta and Zeithaml (2006) summarize eighteen separate research studies confirming the value of CLV-based models for guiding the organization's selection of the right customers. Venkatesan, Kumar, and Bohling's (2007) research suggests that in a typical organizational environ-ment, where marketing funds are not unlimited, using a Bayesian decision theory-based framework for selecting customers to target provides the highest profits for the organization. The Bayesian framework leverages the maximized expected CLV of a customer (Venkatesan, Kumar, and Bohling 2007).

CLV results appear to have industry boundary conditions, whereby some industries experience a higher service context (face-to-face contact is required or demanded by customers) which requires a higher level of investment on the part of the organization. Yet service demands for all industries and customer perceptions of required levels of service quality increase over time. For example, single-channel contact with custo-mers is no longer "accepted" as adequate in most industries. As social networking platforms become standard, having an information-based web portal will no longer be the "minimum required." Interactivity and 24/7 access and support via handheld devices will be the baseline of acceptable service. All of these marketing changes, demanded by customer expectations, have financial implications for the companies' go-to-market strategies. In many companies, data warehouse systems serve as the central repository of customer data, and analyzing that data to create consumer profiles or target segments is an important part of the "right customer" process.

12.3 MEASURING CUSTOMER LIFETIME VALUE

Calculating the lifetime value of a single customer or prospect can be quite challenging. While there are an array of CLV formulas, the basic components of most formulas include current revenues and expenditures for a customer, pro-jected duration of the customer relationship, projected revenues and expenses for the customer for each year of the projected duration of the customer relationship, and projected interest rates for each year of the projected duration of the customer relationship (see Figure 12.4 for two CLV approaches).

One of the key challenges with measuring (or forecasting) a customer's lifetime value lies in predicting the expected duration of a customer relationship. Will the customer relationship span five months, five years, or fifty years? Consequently, a common approach used to address this challenge is to limit the calculation to a three-to five-year range. Even within this shorter time horizon, calculating a single custo-mer's lifetime value (or, importantly, a firm's entire portfolio of current or prospective customers) is challenging, considering the probabilistic nature of the equation inputs.

If the firm (or its accountants) is already calculating the current profitability of each customer, an important question arises: What additional value does the CLV calculation bring to the table? And, importantly, does the added value of this

$$CLV_i = \sum_{t=0}^{T^*} \frac{(p_t - c_t)}{(1+i)^t} - AC$$

Where

p_t = price paid by a consumer at time t
c_t = direct cost of servicing the customer at time t
i = discount rate or cost of capital for the firm
T^* = expected lifetime of a customer
AC = acquisition cost

Source: Gupta and Zeithaml (2006)

$$CLV_i = \sum_{j=T^*+1}^{T^*+T} \frac{\hat{Q}_{i,j} * M}{(1+r)^{\hat{t}_{i,j}}} - \sum_{t=1}^{n} \frac{\sum c_{i,q,t} * x_{i,q,t}}{(1+r)^{t-1}}$$

CLV_i = lifetime value of customer i
$\hat{Q}_{i,j}$ = predicted purchase quantity for customer i in purchase occasion j
M = contribution margin or gross profits for a single item
r = discount rate for money
$c_{i,q,t}$ = unit marketing cost for customer i in channel q in year t
$x_{i,q,t}$ = the number of contacts to customer i in channel q in year t
$\hat{t}_{i,j}$ = predicted period of purchase for customer i for the jth purchase occasion
n = number of years to forecast
T^* = current time period
T = predicted number of purchases made by customer i over n after T^*

Source: Venkatesan, Kumar, and Bohling (2007)

Fig. 12.4. Two CLV Formulations

lifetime value information exceed the administrative costs associated with calculating a CLV for each customer and prospect?

An important aspect of the nature of lifetime valuation analysis must be mentioned here. In fairness, like marketing, CLV is less of a specific formula or calculation and more of an orientation or mindset embraced by the firm. The calculations can be quite onerous (see the second calculation in Figure 12.4). So, the firm embracing the lifetime valuation process must begin with small assessments of customer lifetime valuations, calibrate their results against their predictions, learn, and then adjust. Consequently, the conceptual equation shown at the top of Figure 12.4 will be a useful starting point for most organizations.

However, lifetime valuation may not be as useful for all industry settings. Industry contexts where the CLV orientation works better include those industries marked by high transaction volumes with relatively low per-transaction costs to serve their customers, and those industries having a high cost of acquiring, retaining, and growing customers (SAS 2005). Using a lifetime valuation orientation is less likely in those industries capturing limited data about their customers or having indirect channels wherein other channel members capture and mine the customer data. Since business-to-business relationships tend to be more stable and more enduring than business-to-consumer relationships, CLV tends to add less value on top of the historical customer profitability analysis. However, projecting the CLV of a prospective business-to-business customer is an important part of determining which prospective customers to target.

Johnson and Selnes' (2004) recent modeling efforts show . . . that a key to increasing CLV, aggregated across the firm's customers, lies in acquiring new customers (who initially have weaker relationships to the firm) to build the long-term value of the customer portfolio. (Bolton et al. 2004: 286)

12.3.1 Leveraging Customer Lifetime Value Estimates for Selecting New Customers

Though many firms and industries are focused on retaining existing customers, all organizations must have strategies and processes in place to acquire new customers. Even firms with high retention rates will lose customers, and will need to actively engage in replacing them (Blattberg, Getz, and Thomas 2001).

While some firms, consultants, and scholars define the customer acquisition process as ending with the customer's first purchase, Blattberg, Getz, and Thomas (2001) recommend taking a *process* perspective wherein the acquisition process includes all non-purchase encounters (web, call center, sales representative, etc.) that *precede* and *follow* the initial purchase. The acquisition process phase ends with the execution of a repeat purchase. However customer acquisition is defined within a company, all costs (hard and soft) associated with customer acquisition need to be taken into account when estimating the lifetime value of a prospective customer.

Generally speaking, when prospecting for new customers, sales and marketing personnel can be asked to estimate the expected lifetime value of their prospect pool (or target market segments) to identify those prospects worthy of pursuit as potential customers (Niraj, Gupta, and Narasimhan 2001). The process involves two key steps: gathering information, and determining the basis for segmenting and targeting the right prospective customers.

Gathering information to assess prospective customers involves information from within and outside the firm and its existing customers. The relevant information for estimating prospective customers' lifetime value includes, but is not limited to:

- the firm's estimated cost to acquire a customer (for that region, if regional differences are relevant, and many times they are);
- average revenues generated by existing customers operating in that industry and of similar size and/or market position (to be used as a proxy for the prospective customers);

- projected products to be purchased based on the prospect's industry, size and/or market position, etc.;
- estimated cost of goods sold for the estimated purchases; and
- estimated costs to service and maintain similar customers (Jones et al. 2005).

Once the appropriate data are at hand, the organization must engage in a process of determining the appropriate basis for segmenting prospective customers in order to prioritize the most attractive prospects for marketing efforts. Segmentation of prospects can be guided by strategic priorities such as desired industries and/or geographies for increased market share or strategic presence. The prospective customers with the highest estimated lifetime value would be the top priority for action in these industries or geographies.

Another approach to prioritizing targets is to identify those prospective customers with a high estimated lifetime value who are likely to yield the highest volume of purchases (highest revenue) in the short term. An approach such as this allows a firm to maximize both short-term results and longer-term profitability. Similarly, prospects with strong estimated lifetime values who are also likely to be highly responsive to marketing programs can yield long-term profits and the often much-needed short-term sales gains (Jones et al. 2005).

Now, the preceding discussion implies that this process of leveraging CLV for the acquisition of the right customers is quite easy. In reality, part of the challenge of understanding which customers a firm should focus upon for acquisition efforts is that lifetime value and customer retention data used to profile customer segments are based on incomplete or limited data. Company databases typically comprise data from existing customers, and have little (if any) data on prospective customers. According to Thomas (2001), the models and their coefficients resulting from such data limitations yields biased estimates of model coefficients. To ensure that the firm addresses this bias, Thomas (2001) recommends using a particular model, the Tobit model with selection, to simultaneously address the data limitations known as censoring and truncation. For more information on this modeling approach, see Thomas (2001).

12.3.2 Leveraging Customer Lifetime Valuation for "Firing" the Right Customers

An important idea in the landscape of customer selection is knowing which current customers ought to be "de-selected" or, as Donald Trump says on *The Apprentice*, be "fired." Intuitively, firing customers appears to be *not* in the company's best interest. All customers are providing sales to the organization, so, no matter what, all customers should be considered valuable. However, the thinking that all customers are valued emanates from the perspective that a firm ought to pursue increasing sales volume at any cost.

Yet, in fairness, the company may have some customers in its portfolio purchasing low-margin products and services which yield absolutely no profits at all when the cost to serve such customers is considered. Similarly, even among customers purchasing high-margin products and services, these customers may require such a high level of service (personal and e-mediated) that they too fail to yield a profitable bottom line. Either type of customer really detracts value from the firm. In these cases, "sending an unprofitable customer to your competitor isn't a bad thing" (SAS 2005: 5).

The real key to identify which customer ought to be fired is to consider both the current profit contribution and the future long-term potential (or CLV). Considering the interplay of current profitability and long-term profitability, we can clearly see where the customers are who ought to be let go (see Figure 12.5). Those customers with a low current profit contribution and also having a limited long-term profit potential are the ready target for customer portfolio trimming. Again, if such customers are not yielding profitability (now or the promise of such in the future), we should want our competitors to be serving these customers and experiencing the resource drain these customers represent.

Once the right customers are identified who detract from the firm's value-creation efforts, sales leaders focused on building a strong customer portfolio will strategically work to disengage from such customers. While the disengagement or firing tactics may vary from company to company, strategies for firing customers range from *immediate* to *calculated migration,* where the migration occurs along the continuum from the customer's "current degree of access" to "no access" over time.

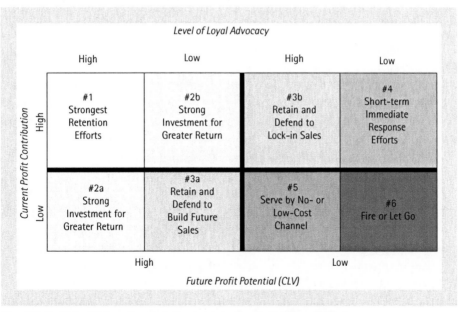

Fig. 12.5. Prioritizing Current Customers for Retention Efforts

Adapted from SAS 2005

A business-to-consumer example of an *immediate* firing strategy can be seen in the property and casualty (P&C) insurance industry. Offering automotive insurance at a very slim margin, some P&C companies leverage the automotive insurance sale to gain access to the consumer's home insurance coverage needs, products often offering a stronger margin than automotive insurance products. A consumer who purchased the firm's home insurance and then chose to purchase that product from another firm may receive a cancellation letter (regarding the household's automobile insurance) instead of a renewal form or invoice upon the anniversary of their coverage. *Calculated migration* strategies for firing a customer, common in many business-to-business settings, involve moving a customer from having a dedicated customer sales/service representative to having access to call center personnel, to having only web-based access to purchases. Moving a customer through reduced levels of access requires a communication strategy with clear messages delivered to key customer contacts explaining how business contacts and processes will occur in the future. At the final migration to "no access," the firm must clearly explain that they are no longer able to service this customer, given the current business context. Such communications are frequently brief and unapologetic.

12.3.3 Leveraging Customer Lifetime Valuation to Recapture the Right Lost Customers

Another important part of the customer relationship management strategy includes the process of winning back customers lost by or defecting from the organization. "Customer winback focuses on the re-initiation and management of relationships with customers who have lapsed or defected from a firm" (Thomas, Blattberg, and Fox 2004: 31). However, organizations cannot focus on winning back all customers, since all customers may not have been profitable assets for the organization before they were lost. The first strategic issue that organizations must address is developing the ability to know when customers have defected or been lost.

Once the organization has the ability to identify and classify lost customers, Griffin and Lowenstein (2001) provide a four-step process for winning back lost customers. Part of their four-step model includes two steps for segmenting lost customers provided by Strauss and Friege (1999): (1) segment lost customers on the basis of second lifetime value, and then (2) segment those segmented customers on their basis of their reason(s) for defecting from the organization.

Customers leave a firm for a variety of reasons, many of which have very industry-specific contexts. Strauss and Friege (1999) have developed a defector typology that transcends industry-specific drivers; they propose five unique defector categories:

- those customers who were intentionally pushed away (indicating that they were difficult or unprofitable to serve);
- those customers who were unintentionally pushed away, where the firm failed to meet expectations, fumbled the handling of a complaint, made a change (product, price, policy, etc.) that offended the customer, or failed to fully appreciate the customer during customer encounters;
- those customers who were pulled away by the competition (attracted by the competitor's product, new innovation, etc.);
- those customers who were lured away by a low-ball pricing offer;
- those customers who moved out of the target market (either via a geographical move or due to a change in needs).

Griffin and Lowenstein (2001) recommend that a firm take several specific steps to understand the real reasons for customer defections. These researchers suggest there is a need to understand both the firm's view and the customer's view. The firm's view can be examined by reviewing the customer's history with the account team, reading through customer files, reviewing orders and call reports, etc. By conducting an exit interview with defecting customers, a lost customer can share his/her view of the activities which led to the decision to leave the supplier/firm. Two critical watch-outs recommended for these exit interviews are (1) to focus on gaining real understanding of the situation, not on trying to resell the customer, and (2) to allow some time to elapse (i.e. not call too soon) after the termination, as the customer likely needs time and distance before being able to speak freely (Griffin and Lowenstein 2001).

Once a customer leaves the organization, the relationship must be reassessed relative to a new lifetime value. The second lifetime value (SLTV) recognizes that a customer's second lifecycle can be quite different from that customer's first lifetime value (prior to defection) (Strauss and Friege 1999). Griffin and Lowenstein (2001) suggest that there are four reasons prompting a customer's second lifetime value to vary from the first lifetime value:

- The defected customer is already familiar with the organization's products/services.
- The organization has more information concerning this customer's preferences than it does for a first-time customer.
- Successful win-back strategies could lead to higher sales results than the results had for a first-time customer.
- Second life cycles may offer shorter prospecting and new customer phases.

Once the SLTV has been estimated for the defecting customers, Griffin and Lowenstein (2001) recommend that a firm:

1. categorize "defected" customers into four groups based on their SLTV score:
   A (top 10 percent);
   B (next 20 percent);

C (next best 30 percent); and

D (last 40 percent).

2. within each of these four groups, further segment the defectors according to whether they were unintentionally pushed away, pulled away, or left for some other reason. The unintentionally pushed away customers and the pulled away customers in each of the four groups are the best win-back candidates, since the other defectors (bought away, moved away, and intentionally pushed away) defected from the firm for reasons that make them less attractive for the future.

3. research the present needs and purchases of lost customers;

4. create a communication and action plan focused on rebuilding trust;

5. measure the results of the plan so the firm understands how the communications/ actions have impacted lost customers;

6. evaluate the results against goals;

7. refine the plan going forward (Griffin and Lowenstein 2001).

Winning back lost customers entails segment- or customer-specific strategies that require listening and responding based on customer feedback. In some instances, bringing the customer or customer segment back into the firm's portfolio will be a longer-term process. In such cases, the appropriate strategy will involve acknowledging and accepting the customer's decision (not making the customer feel guilty) and repositioning the firm for future business. In a business-to-business context, ask for the opportunity to keep in touch and to be reconsidered in the future should the account be opened to review (Griffin and Lowenstein 2001).

Some firms choose to use a pricing strategy (i.e. offering lower prices for the same product) in order to win a customer back. According to Thomas, Blattberg, and Fox (2004), who studied the customer win-back process in the context of newspaper subscriptions, reacquisition of a customer is more likely if a reacquisition price is lower; however, customers who restart a relationship based on a lower price offering are likely to lapse or defect even more rapidly than the length of the first relationship. Based on their research context of newspaper subscriptions, we learn that "customers who are acquired at higher prices have longer second tenures" (Thomas, Blattberg, and Fox 2004: 44). Obviously, more research is needed in this area to determine the generalizability of their findings. In the meanwhile, firms should test any win-back efforts among lost customers that involve offering a lower price to returning customers.

12.3.4 Leveraging Customer Lifetime Valuation for Identifying Priority Customers to Retain

Clearly, the most crucial customers to retain are those providing the highest level of current profit margin and promising the highest levels of future profit potential (largest lifetime valuation). Such customers are likely designated (or perhaps should be designated) as key accounts in the firm's existing customer portfolio. In addition to these current and future profitability dimensions, we propose that firms also consider using a third dimension for segmenting and targeting current customers. We believe it is also important to assess each customer's propensity to be loyal advocates, and that the firm place priority on those demonstrating loyal advocacy (see cell 1 in Figure 12.5).

While the CLV measure captures *loyalty* in expected length of relationship for future financial calculations, loyal advocacy represents the domains of several measures discussed previously: net promoter (intention to recommend the firm to others), word-of-mouth customer advocacy (report of the extent to which the customer reports that s/he advocates about the firm to others), and online customer advocacy. The last dimension, online customer advocacy, represents a newly emerging area of customer behavior requiring attention and measurement for guiding a firm's strategy and operations.

Many firms are already using customer relationship management data, profitability analysis, and lifetime valuation analysis to guide their investments in customer selection, targeting, and strategies.

Using technology from business analytics provided by SAS Institute, Cary, N.C., and consulting services from Daemon Quest to carry out its customer segmentation and client orientation strategy, Genesis the Spanish subsidiary for Liberty Mutual Group, has been 'outperforming the market in terms of retention rate and growing significantly in terms of cross-selling,' according to Enrique Huertas, Genesis' GM. The firm, which chiefly focuses on auto insurance, is segmenting clients by their value, total volume of premium, social demographics, age, and loyalty. (Joelson 2009: 2)

Other key customer segments to focus upon, which may or may not represent current key accounts, are found in cells 2, 3, and 4 in Figure 12.5. Customers exhibiting a high future lifetime value coupled with a high current profit contribution but lacking loyal advocacy behaviors (2a) need to be retained. For this segment, the firm's strategy may focus on engaging such customers in referral or advocacy behaviors. Customers exhibiting a high future lifetime value and a high level of loyal advocacy need to be nurtured, even if their current profit contribution is low (2b). Additional data/analysis that might prove fruitful among these customers is a share-of-wallet analysis to determine whether their current profit contribution is low due to business captured by a competitor. It is possible that the firm is capturing a large share of the customer's spending, and that their current need for the firm's products/services is hampered by some other business condition.

Similarly, customers representing high future profit potential but low loyal advocacy and low current profit contribution (3a) typically represent a part of the customer portfolio worthy of additional analysis and attention. Customers providing high current profit contributions but lower future profit potential are worthy of investment and retention efforts when they also serve as loyal advocates for the firm (3b). Firms must ensure that they serve these customers well enough to retain and satisfy them without overspending the margin they provide. These five segments (cells 1, 2a, 2b, 3a, and 3b) in the customer portfolio represent the most important areas for customer retention and marketing investment (see Figure 12.5).

Three final segments revealed by this 2×2×2 matrix all represent low future profit potential (low lifetime customer values). Customers representing low future profit potential but high current profit potential may or may not yield requisite payback from a firm's marketing efforts (cell 4). Lacking loyal advocacy behaviors, such customers are less likely to fuel the firm's revenue growth or bring new customers to the organization. Consequently, marketing investment and activities should be carefully targeted toward this customer segment (4) to yield short-time, immediate profitable results.

Customer segment 5, yielding low current and low future profitability but engaging in high loyal advocacy behaviors, needs to be served by no- or low-cost channels while being targeted by occasional marketing strategies to reinforce their advocacy behavior. The cost of such strategies must be carefully considered to ensure that the firm retains a profitable position for this customer. If serving this customer segment (5) via a no- or low-cost channel is not possible, then this customer segment is a likely candidate for firing. Clearly, the firm needs to disengage customers in segment 6 offering low current profitability, low future profit potential, and low loyal advocacy. While moving this customer segment to a no- or low-cost channel would seem to be an option, most firms operate with limited resources, and the firms are better served to identify new customers having high current or future profit potential for the firm.

12.3.5 Making Customer Retention Happen

Getting the right customers is critical. Keeping the right customers is equally important. According to Jeremy Bowler, senior director of the insurance practice at J.D. Power and Associates,

For any of the 50 largest U.S. personal auto insurers, improving retention by one percent for the next five years can equate to tens of millions of dollars over that time period, so even seemingly small differences in retention rates can have a substantial impact on an insurance company's bottom line...Making strides to improve satisfaction and retain customers clearly has a significant financial incentive for carriers. (J.D. Power and Associates 2009)

In the midst of defining who are the right customers, organizations also must consider how they measure this issue of customer retention. A market research firm specializing in the financial services and insurance areas, LIMRA International asked the companies in its industry how they measure customer retention (Moss 2008). Methods reported by companies include using client satisfaction surveys, measuring lapse rates (in which a product payment schedule is not met), reporting the number of contract cancellations and reasons why customers have cancelled, measuring cross-sell and up-sell rates, and measuring the percentage of maturing policies reinvested in the company (which is like an upgrade situation; for example, Microsoft's parallel measure is the percentage of customers purchasing a new Windows operating system to replace their old Windows operating system) (Moss 2008).

A common approach to measuring retention among scholars focuses on modeling the duration of a customer relationship. According to Gupta and Zeithaml (2006: 722), "customer retention is the probability of a customer being 'alive,' or repeat buying from a firm." While the probabilistic focus of the definition dictates use of a predictive model, scholars have proposed two classes of retention models: permanent and transient. The permanent retention model predicts the probability of customer defection using either an accelerated failure time (AFT) or proportional (PH) hazard model. The transient retention model generally relies on migration or Markov models to estimate the probability that various customer groups will migrate into a different customer "state." (See Gupta and Zeithaml 2006 for a complete discussion of the mathematical equations and distributional assumptions associated with these different approaches.) Suffice to say, industry practitioners and academic researchers provide a very broad spectrum of possible measures of customer retention.

Once the operationalization of a retained customer is determined, firms must identify the right activities for keeping these valued customers. Some firms have mistakenly assumed that retaining customers results in cross-selling the customer on other offerings from the firm. Booz Allen Hamilton (2003) suggest that the cross-selling strategy to drive retention is actually a transactional approach, operating at odds with customer desires. To retain the customer requires aligning the firm's product and service offerings to the customer's cycle of changing needs. Such alignment is only possible when the firm maintains an ongoing and transparent dialogue with customers. A customer-centric approach leads to higher retention if a firm takes the following strategic steps:

1. Align the business model with customer life cycle.
2. Create life-cycle-based advice/product modules.
3. Devise innovative ways to further "open the window" with customers [wherein both the customer and the firm have access to the same information and understanding].
4. Earn and retain the right to deeper relationship through superior service (Booz Allen Hamilton 2003: 2).

Retention strategies include a vast array of organizational activities, including customer complaint response/recovery, contractual review (where penalties can be instituted to discourage early termination), customer retention teams, staff retention initiatives, and adjusting culture and climate work to ensure a positive work environment. Several of the retention strategies mentioned above require the organization to understand the buying and engagement experience from the customer's point of view. One approach to understanding the customer's perspective is to use a customer experience storyboard technique which identifies all customer contact points across various channels. The storyboards depict the entire customer experience via a visually compelling presentation. The actual development of the storyboards provokes internal engagement and alignment work that shapes a more holistic understanding of the customer's experience. By involving key stakeholders (marketing planning, marketing research, brand/product managers, interactive, field sales, operations, external agencies) in the developments of the board, key personnel participate at a very engaged level in the development of the storyboards, which serve as a physical cue during a facilitated discussion to identify priorities for action. Like the dot exercise used for prioritizing action, teams of marketing personnel can use color codes to identify where and what deserves greater organizational focus and resources. By visually grounding the decision-making team in the customer experience, decisions are more likely to focus on the actual customer issues rather than on internal turf wars. The result should be faster and better customer-focused decisions which should allow for more consistent internal alignment. The real key to successfully using this technique, as with any customer research tool, appears to be in creating a shared understanding of how the customer experiences a relationship with the organization. (One example of this tool can be seen at: clarity-international.com/customer_experience.html.)

Retaining customers also involves eliminating the annoyance factors that push customers away: over-communicating (snail or email sent too frequently or at inappropriate times from the customer's perspective) or disruptive changes of control (e.g. when a pop-up avatar keeps a customer from controlling his/her own navigation on the firm's website). Over-communicating and disruptive changes of control can create distance between the firm and its customers. Kumar, Venkatesan, and Reinartz (2006: 136) report on a series of experiments that show:

purchase acceleration was linked to marketing communication in a highly nonlinear fashion. Below a certain threshold frequency of marketing contact, customers were held back from purchasing; but above a certain threshold, customers were put off. In other words, communicating too much can harm you as much as communicating too little.

Based on research in the financial services sector, conducted in the United States and the United Kingdom, "creating personal, relevant and timely communications for each individual customer, via a number of different channels, has now become critical to building and maintaining strong relationships and retaining valuable customers" (Moss 2008: 7).

Kumar, Venkatesan, and Reinartz (2008) advocate the adoption of a customer-focused approach to the sales campaign process as a key to increasing firm profits and return on investment for marketing dollars. In their field experiments, these researchers also found that those exposed to a customer-focused sales campaign demonstrated a higher likelihood of repurchasing from the firm than those exposed to a product-focused sales campaign. So, stronger retention is achieved by communicating at the right frequency (not too little and not too much) and communicating with the right message (customer-relevant message focused on identified customer needs). Using customer data, sales and marketing leaders need to identify when such customers are likely to make their next purchase and what product(s) are most likely to be purchased—then they need to communicate with customers on the customers' cycle and interests. Purchase sequence analysis can help organizations determine which products to target to which customers at what time (Kumar, Venkatesan, and Reinartz 2008). Knowing who, what, and when equips the organization to determine just how much it ought to spend on various segments of customers over the next planning period. Results to expect from a customer-focused sales campaign include: higher revenues, lower marketing costs, improved customer relationships, improved efficiency and effectiveness of sales calls, improved sales campaign results (Kumar, Venkatesan, and Reinartz 2008), and probably increased positive social media because the customer is more likely to recommend the organization and to repurchase from the same.

12.4 MANAGING THE CUSTOMER PORTFOLIO

Scholars and industry practitioners find that success in the customer realm does not lie in identifying and keeping only the "best customers." In fact, current thinking suggests that a firm should actively engage in the management of a portfolio of customers, representing the full range of relationships from transactional to strategic partnerships.

Johnson and Selnes (2004) developed a model of customer portfolio lifetime value (CPLV) which differentiates between acquaintances (weak relationships), friends (intermediate relationships), and partners (close relationships). Based on their analysis, they propose that firms having a large leaky bucket (meaning a base

of weaker customer relationships) will experience long-term growth and profitability, since the weaker relationships serve as the base from which stronger, more
profitable relationships are sourced. Having a large base of weaker relationships
plays an important role in providing scale economies for amortizing the firm's
organizational capacity (Johnson and Selnes 2004).

Firms adopting a customer portfolio management orientation look to integrate
the analysis, strategy, and implementation activities associated with customer
acquisition, customer retention, and profitability rather than have these activities
handled by different sales and marketing teams (Thomas, Reinartz, and Kumar
2004). As seen in Figure 12.6, customer portfolio analysis begins with the assessment of the key metrics that have been discussed in this chapter. Considering
measures of current profitability, future profitability (lifetime value), loyal advocacy, and others, the firm needs to identify the customer segments (or, in some
business-to-business contexts, the individual customers) that create different types
of value for the firm. Some customer segments are important to the firm for the
cash they generate today. Simply put, their current cash flow is far more important
to the firm's overall objectives and health than might be any lifetime valuation
analysis. However, the customer portfolio cannot only contain those providing
short-term cash to the firm. The portfolio needs to contain a healthy mix of
customers (customer segments) that also serve the firm's future needs. The premise
of the portfolio approach to customer lifetime value (CPLV) is the need to focus
more on "accumulated value creation of a customer portfolio, not on the value
created in single relationships" (Johnson and Selnes 2004: 15).

Once the customer segments are understood, marketers need to develop a more
comprehensive view of the various marketing strategies (offensive and defensive)
that are represented in Figure 12.5. Testing of strategies against various customer
segments should involve alternative marketing approaches as well as levels of
marketing investment. Research in the area of customer return on investment
suggests that "underspending is more detrimental and results in smaller ROIs
than does overspending . . . a suboptimal allocation of retention expenditures will
have a greater impact on long-term customer profitability than will suboptimal
acquisition expenditures" (Reinartz, Thomas, and Kumar 2005: 77). Consequently,
the testing phase shown in Figure 12.6 is crucial for determining the range of
returns possible from each level of marketing investment targeted against each
customer segment.

By identifying the right strategies for the right customer segments and taking
those strategies to full implementation (last stage in Figure 12.6), the firm is actively
engaged in increasing the value of the firm's customer base and the overall value of
the firm. Growing current customers means more future lifetime valuation (CLV)
from such customers. Actively focusing on creating stronger loyal advocacy can

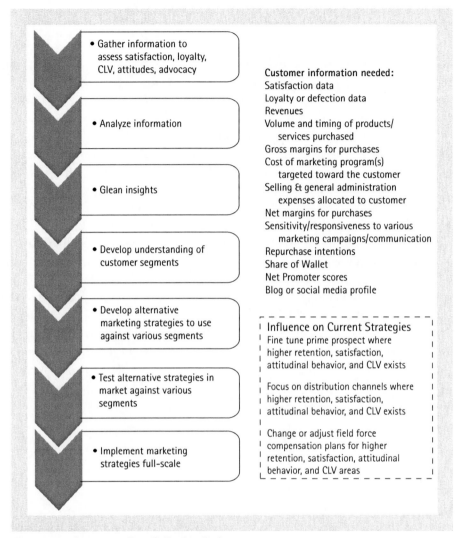

Fig. 12.6. Customer Portfolio Analysis

result in driving the equity yields of customer retention as well as resulting in increased brand equity. Systematic assessment of current and prospective customers allows a firm to take the right actions to acquire, grow, and retain the right mix of customers. In the end, this process of managing the customer portfolio enables the firm to focus the right efforts on those marketing strategies that will generate the strongest return in investment.

12.5 CLOSING OUT CUSTOMER SELECTION

After introducing the idea of building a firm's customer portfolio on the right customers, we initially focused on how to identify the right customers. Finding the right metrics to assess the firm's customer base can be confusing: myriad different metrics are promoted in the academic literature and popular press. To clarify the choices, we delineated the pros and cons associated with the most common customer analysis metrics: customer satisfaction, behavioral and attitudinal loyalty, customer purchase history, share of wallet, net promoter, word-of-mouth advocacy, online advocacy, secure customer index, profitable loyalty, and customer lifetime value. While conceptually logical, the most promising metric—customer lifetime valuation—is challenging to operationalize. Therefore, we provide several alternative formulas for measuring Customer Lifetime Value. Building on our discussion of customer lifetime valuation, we discuss how this CLV measure can be used to identify the right customers to add, to "fire," and to retain in the firm's customer portfolio. Lifetime valuation analysis can also serve as a foundation for identifying the right defectors to prioritize for win-back strategies. We recommend using lifetime valuation, current profitability, and loyal advocacy measures to guide the firm's efforts for retaining the right customers. In the chapter's closing discussion of customer portfolio management, we discuss the value of systematic customer assessment for acquiring, growing, and retaining the right mix of customers to generate the strongest return in investment.

REFERENCES

ANON. (1988). "Why Customers Leave," *Sales & Marketing Management* (May).

BAKER-PREWITT, J. (2009). *Advances in Customer Loyalty Management*, White Paper from www.burke.com/library, accessed March 10, 2009.

BLACKSHAW, P. (2008). *Satisfied Customers Tell Three Friends, Angry Customers Tell 3,000: Running a Business in Today's Consumer-Driven World*, New York: Doubleday Publishing.

——(2009). *Satisfied Customers Tell Three Friends, Angry Customers Tell 3,000: Running a Business in Today's Consumer-Driven World*, presentation to University of Cincinnati's MS-Marketing program, May 8.

BLATTBERG, R. C., G. GETZ, and J. S. THOMAS (2001). *Customer Equity: Building and Managing Relationships as Valuable Assets*, Boston, MA: Harvard Business School Press.

BOLTON, R. N., K. N. LEMON, and P. C. VERHOEF (2004). "The Theoretical Underpinnings of Customer Asset Management: A Framework and Propositions for Future Research," *Journal of the Academy of Marketing Science* 32.3, 271–92.

——————(2008). "Expending Business-to-Business Customer Relationships: Modeling the Customer's Upgrade Decision," *Journal of Marketing* 72 (January), 46–64.

Booz Allen Hamilton (2003). "The Customer-Centric Bank: Debunking the Myth that Cross-Sell = Customer Centric," from www.boozallen.com.

Boulding, W., A. Kalra, R. Staelin, and V. Zeithaml (1993). "A Dynamic Process Model of Service Quality: From Expectations to Behavioral Intentions," *Journal of Marketing Research* 30 (February), 7–27.

Burritt, C. (2009). "Wal-Mart U.C. Chief Says New Customers Spending More," www.bloomberg.com, April 29.

Choi, J., D. R. Bell, and L. M. Lodish (2008). "The Role of Local Environments in Customer Acquisition Online," MSI Reports Working Paper Series, 4.

Corporate Executive Board (2008). *2009 Insurance Advisory Board Agenda Poll for 2009,* Washington, DC: Corporate Executive Board, October.

Griffin, J., and M. W. Lowenstein (2001). *Customer Winback: How to Recapture Lost Customers—and Keep Them Loyal,* San Francisco, CA: Jossey-Bass.

Gupta, S., and V. Zeithaml (2006). "Customer Metrics and Their Impact on Financial Performance," *Marketing Science* 25.6, 718–39.

Heitger, L. E., and D. L. Heitger (2008). "Jamestown Electric Supply Company: Assessing Customer Profitability," *Issues in Accounting Education* 23.2, 261–80.

J.D. Power and Associates (2009). *Personal Insurance Retention Special Report,* released April 22.

Joelson, D. (2009). "Know Your Customer and Segment Accordingly," accessed at: www.insurancenetworking.com/issues, February 1.

Johnson, M., and F. Selnes (2004). "Customer Portfolio Management: Toward a Dynamic Theory of Exchange Relationships," *Journal of Marketing* 68.2, 1–17.

Johnston, M. W., and G. W. Marshall (2007). *Relationship Selling,* New York: McGraw-Hill Irwin.

Jones, E., C. Stevens, and L. Chonko (2005). *Selling ASAP: Art, Science, Agility, Performance,* Mason, OH: Thomson.

Keiningham, T., and L. Aksoy (2008). "The Quest for Profitable Loyalty," presentation to Marketing Science Institute Conference "Marketing Metrics for the Connected Organization", September 10–12, Dallas, TX.

——B. Cooil, T. W. Andreassen, and L. Aksoy (2007). "A Longitudinal Examination of Net Promoter and Firm Revenue Growth," *Journal of Marketing* 71.3, 39–51.

————L. Aksoy, T. W. Andreassen, and J. Weiner (2007). "The Value of Different Customer Satisfaction and Loyalty Metrics in Predicting Customer Retention, Recommendation and Share-of-Wallet," *Managing Service Quality* 17.4, 361–84.

——T. Vavra, and L. Aksoy (2006). "Managing Through Rose-Colored Glasses," *Sloan Management Review* 48.1, 15–18.

Kumar, V. (2008). *Marketing Metrics for the Connected Organization,* presented at Marketing Science Institute Conference "Marketing Metrics for the Connected Organization," September 10–12, Dallas, TX.

——and M. George (2006). "A Comparison of Aggregate and Disaggregate Level Approaches for Measuring and Maximizing Customer Equity," *American Marketing Association 2006 Winter Educator Conference Proceedings,* 142–3.

KUMAR, V., R. VENKATESAN, and W. REINARTZ (2006). "Knowing What to Sell, When and to Whom," *Harvard Business Review* (March), 131–7.

————(2008). "Performance Implications of Adopting a Customer-Focused Sales Campaign," *Journal of Marketing* 72 (September), 50–68.

LI, S., B. SUN, and R. T. WILCOX (2005). "Cross-Selling Sequentially Ordered Products: An Application to Consumer Banking Services," *Journal of Marketing Research* 42 (May), 233–9.

MOSS, N. (2008). "Strategies for Customer Retention," *LIMRA's Marketfacts Quarterly* (Fall), 5–7.

NIRAJ, R., M. GUPTA, and C. NARASIMHAN (2001). "Customer Profitability in a Supply Chain," *Journal of Marketing* 65 (July), 1–16.

OLIVER, R. (1997). *Satisfaction: A Behavioral Perspective on the Consumer,* New York: McGraw-Hill.

REICHHELD, F. (2006). *The Ultimate Question: Driving Good Profits and True Growth,* Boston, MA: Harvard Business School Press.

REINARTZ, W., and V. KUMAR (2000). "On the Profitability of Long-Life Customers in a Noncontractual Setting: An Empirical Investigation and Implications for Marketing," *Journal of Marketing* 64 (October), 17–35.

————(2002). "The Mismanagement of Customer Loyalty," *Harvard Business Review* (July), 86–94.

————(2003). "The Impact of Customer Relationship Characteristics on Profitable Lifetime Duration," *Journal of Marketing* 67 (January), 77–99.

——J. S. THOMAS, and G. BASCOUL (2008). "Investigating Cross-Buying and Customer Loyalty," *Journal of Interactive Marketing* 22.1, 5–20.

————and V. KUMAR (2005). "Balancing Acquisition and Retention Resources to Maximize Customer Profitability," *Journal of Marketing* 69 (January), 63–79.

RUST, R. T., K. N. LEMON, and V. A. ZEITHAML (2004). "Return on Marketing: Using Customer Equity to Focus Marketing Strategy," *Journal of Marketing* 68.1, 109–27.

——and A. J. ZAHORIK (1993). "Customer Satisfaction, Customer Retention and Market Share," *Journal of Retailing* 69.2, 193–215.

SAS (2005). "How to Measure and Manage Customer Value and Customer Profitability," White Paper.

STRAUSS, B., and C. FRIEGE (1999). "Regaining Service Customers," *Journal of Service Research* 1.4, 347–61.

THOMAS, J. S. (2001). "A Methodology for Linking Customer Acquisition to Customer Retention," *Journal of Marketing Research* 38 (May), 262–9.

——R. C. BLATTBERG, and E. J. FOX (2004). "Recapturing Lost Customers," *Journal of Marketing Research* 41 (February), 31–45.

——W. REINARTZ, and V. KUMAR (2004). "Getting the Most out of All Your Customers," *Harvard Business Review* (July–August), 117–23.

VENKATESAN, R., and V. KUMAR (2004). "A Customer Lifetime Value Framework for Customer Selection and Resource Allocation Strategy," *Journal of Marketing Research* 68 (October), 106–25.

————and T. BOHLING (2007). "Optimal Customer Relationship Management Using Bayesian Decision Theory: An Application for Customer Selection," *Journal of Marketing Research* 44 (November), 579–94.

WEBSTER, F. E., Jr. (1992). "The Changing Role of Marketing in the Corporation," *Journal of Marketing* 56 (October), 1–17.

WEITZ, B. A., S. B. CASTLEBERRY, and J. F. TANNER, Jr. (2007). *Selling Building Partnerships*, New York: McGraw-Hill Irwin.

WINER, R. S. (2001). "A Framework for Customer Relationship Management," *California Management Review* 43.4, 89–105.

www.netpromoter.com

www.netpromoter.com/netpromoter_community

YOON, L. (2002). "What Executives Worry About," *CFO.com*, November 13.

....

CHAPTER 13

CUSTOMER RELATIONSHIP MANAGEMENT AND THE SALES FORCE

....

THOMAS W. LEIGH

13.1 INTRODUCTION

....

As firms seek to become more market-driven, systematically defining the nature of their relationships with their core customers promises to enhance firm performance (Day, 1994). Market-driven firms segment their customers in terms of how these customers *prefer to buy and relate to their suppliers,* typically arraying customers from the purely transactional to highly collaborative (Dwyer, Schurr, and Oh 1987; Anderson and Narus 1991). They then selectively target customer segments in which they have the capabilities to compete. Market-driven firms have "superior market sensing, customer linking and channel-bonding capabilities" that are aligned toward "measurable improvements in customer satisfaction and retention" (Day 1994, p. 41). However, despite the recognized strategic importance of customer relationships, the role of the direct sales force as a resource and capability has received only limited attention. As Day (1994) has noted, "despite the recent emphasis on . . . collaborative relationships, few firms have mastered this capability" (p. 45), or for that matter, the possibilities of customer "linking" capabilities for even purely transactional customers. The role of the sales force in CRM and strategy is rigorously debated today as firms press to cut costs (Anderson and Trinkle 2005).

The purpose of this chapter is to conceptually specify the role of the direct sales force as a core enterprise strategy and capability in the context of the firm's CRM system. To ground the role of the sales force in corporate strategy and CRM, the CRM models implied by the product leadership, cost leadership, and customer intimacy enterprise strategies are first introduced (Treacy and Wiersma 1993). This is important because each of these three corporate strategies involves a realized, if not formally intended and defined, firm-level CRM model. In turn, these CRM models provide a context for defining the role of the sales force versus alternative go-to-market channels in accessing and relating to customers.

Next, a customer relationship framework for positioning the sales force in the context of CRM strategy and practices is articulated. In specifying this framework, *customer relationship strategy* is defined as the customer segments targeted by the firm and the attendant strategic selling models required to effectively and efficiently build competitive advantage in these segments. The role of the sales force is explicated in terms of four customer archetypes: transactional, solution-selling, relationship selling, and strategic partnerships (Wotruba 1991). An important aspect of this framework is the notion that the sales may perform either *agentic* or *learning* functions for the firm. The relative emphasis on each of these roles will depend on the nature of the dialogue that the firm needs to have with its customers and how this dialogue is best managed. In fact, a direct sales force may be a wasteful use of corporate resources.

Third, since market-driven firms are supposedly better at organizational learning about markets and customers than their more internally-oriented competitors, the role of the direct sales force is explicated in terms of four specific CRM processes: market sensing, customer sensing, customer linking, and cross functional spanning. Nonaka's (1994) model of organizational learning is employed to provide conceptual basis for conceptually examining the learning role of the sales force, the nature of the information or learning required, and the learning process for each of the four customer archetypes. For example, at the *individual salesperson* level, the learning and knowledge factors driving sales effectiveness and efficiency will be elaborated and differentiated according to customer relationship type. At the *organizational* level, the role of the sales force as a core CRM capability, a source of sustainable competitive advantage, and a strategic asset will be explored.

Finally, consistent with the RBV perspective (Srivastava, Shervani, and Fahey 1999), a core set of CRM capabilities and processes is identified. These include customer acquisition, customer retention, customer revenue expansion, customer relationship expansion, market sensing, customer segmentation and selection, customer linking, strategic customer management, and cross-functional spanning. Each of these is illustrated by a practical example.

From a practical perspective, this chapter may provide a basis for improving sales force decisions. The practical problems in "rethinking" sales force decisions are not inconsequential (Donath 1995). In the first place, the shift from transactional to relational buyer-seller exchanges apparently requires complex changes in salesperson and organizational strategies, capabilities, support systems, and reward programs. Firms that are effective and efficient in employing simpler selling models may find the transition to more complex models to be challenging, especially on cultural and human capital issues (Chzranowski and Leigh 1998).

In the second place, firms that choose to target multiple customer segments must be able to manage the possible conflicts that these "hybrid marketing systems" (Moriarty and Moran 1990) engender as customers pursue their own best interests. Understanding the learning, knowledge, and management implications associated with a broad scope strategy may sharpen these decisions. Ironically, examining CRM from an organizational learning perspective may yield "best practices" for the transactional selling model itself. In transactional sales contexts, sales strategy is still largely set by the day-to-day decisions of field sales personnel. This relatively "casual" selling strategy may not be adequate for market-driven firms. As Day (1994) notes, even in transactional selling, "there are still possibilities for gaining (competitive) advantages by nurturing some elements of a linking capability . . . and seeking ways to maintain continuity" (p. 45). In practice, transactional sellers largely ignore the learning capabilities of the sales force, probably compromising CRM leverage.

13.2 ENTERPRISE CUSTOMER RELATIONSHIP STRATEGY

Every company has a CRM strategy, whether or not it is *explicitly* defined. Hence, it is relevant to identify the CRM models that underlie the product innovation leadership, operational excellence, and customer intimacy enterprise strategies (see Figure 13.1). It is critical to realize that each of these enterprise strategies requires the specification and implementation of a suitable CRM model. For example, operational excellence depends critically on market share and operational scale as critical success factors. Dell's success was lionized for years as it scaled an inimitable model of order-getting, order-taking, and supply chain efficiencies. Consistent with this strategy, it minimized its investment in product innovation, service excellence, and customer relationships. Product innovation was largely left up to judiciously selected suppliers such as Intel, Symantec, or Microsoft. Services were outsourced to UPS and Unisys. Customer relationships were

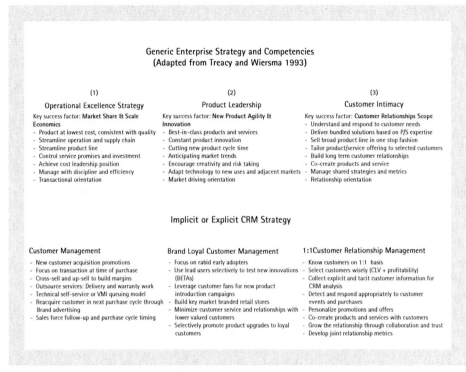

Fig. 13.1. Enterprise Customer Relationship Strategy

largely transactional in nature. Dell's implicit CRM focus was on the "bundle" sold to the customer at a point in time. Customer acquisition using traditional promotions, call center cross-selling and up-selling, and rapid order and credit processing were core business processes. It was also incumbent on Dell to identify low value customers in order to reduce or eliminate unnecessary services and promotions. Relational databases were used primarily to test sales promotion effectiveness and efficiency, rather than customer retention or loyalty. We term this Customer Management.

On the other hand, Apple's resurrection reflects its almost magical capability to identify latent customer needs and creatively position their products at the center of a converging communications ecosystem. Apple is quite willing to cannibalize and make obsolete its own products. Although it occasionally provides its customers a promotional offer as compensation, the quality leap in its new product is expected to generate customer loyalty. Apple's CRM strategy is clearly secondary to its product leadership and appears to be tightly focused on leveraging its core "early adopter" fans. For these fans, Apple manages the nature of the customer experience through its retail stores, sales force and internet releases. However, for the broader customer base, its CRM model is deliberately limited in scope. For example, repair services after the sale, warranty programs, and attention to customer feedback lag competitors.

Concerning customer intimacy, companies such as RBC Bank, Harrah's, Wesco, and IBM have been recognized for stressing customer relationships, share of wallet, and customer lifetime value as core business strategies. They seek to build best-in-class relationships or collaborative partnerships with their customers, sell bundled solutions, co-create business processes and systems, and define shared business metrics to judge relational success. In short, customer intimacy is their primary competitive strategy. However, the strategic requirements undergirding a successful customer intimacy approach in B2B contexts present tough challenges.

In light of the above, it is clear that each firm must recognize its need to define a customer relationship strategy that "fits" its dominant focus on operational excellence, product leadership, or customer intimacy. For example, a cost leader firm intends to use competitive pricing as its core marketing strategy. Hence, it must maximize its customer scale and minimize its investments in unnecessary and underused customer information and knowledge. To do otherwise would compromise its pricing or margins. Similarly, product leaders should limit their consumer relationships to those customers that directly impact its product innovation ambitions. To do otherwise might compromise new idea generation or divert capital from engineering. Finally, customer intimacy requires a selective and clear focus on the customers who are willing to collaborate and invest in mutually advantageous exchanges. So, selecting customers wisely and managing customer loyalty is necessary.

13.3 CRM: Strategic and Organizational Perspectives

CRM definitions vary (Plouffe, Williams, and Leigh 2004) depending on: 1) whether a strategic or tactical perspective on CRM is taken; 2) the organizational role of the individual providing the CRM definition (i.e., marketing, sales, or logistics); and 3), in the case of CRM providers, the nature of the solution that they offer, an enterprise suite or a "best of breed" application. We examine CRM at the strategic and the organizational levels.

13.3.1 CRM: A Strategic Perspective

From a *strategic* perspective, CRM is the process that identifies customers, creates customer knowledge, builds customer relationships, and shapes customers' perceptions of the firm and its products (Srivastava, Shervani, and Fahey 1999). This executive point of view emphasizes that customer value creation, and hence a firm's competitive position in its desired market spaces, depends critically on its ability to 1) define a distinctive customer-centric perspective on what drives demand in its markets; and 2) translate this customer knowledge into customer-valued solutions that can be profitably produced and sold. It is important to note that an organizational role for a direct sales force is not a necessary aspect of the CRM definition. The firm's decision to employ a sales force depends on its customer's buying preferences and how it prefers to generate and manage its customer relationships.

This strategic CRM perspective is important to senior sales executives because their role in the firm is likely to be affected when CRM strategies, processes, and metrics become aspects of corporate decision making. In the first place, strategic accounts may require that top management play a direct, proactive role in account development and management. Cisco's CEO John Chambers, by his own accounts, is in regular contact with the firm's strategic customers. Also, Procter & Gamble signaled the strategic importance of its Wal-Mart partnership by appointing Tom Muccio to be President for P&G/Wal-Mart business unit (Sebenius and Knegel 2007). Hence, one implication is that customer acquisition, customer retention and loyalty, and revenue and margin expansion become core enterprise strategies and capabilities, rather than mere sales force tactics. To the extent that the CRM strategy is a firm-level strategy, then customer value creation, sales force models, and channel partner relationships would be part and parcel of the corporate strategic planning process itself. If this is true, then sales executives will need to be well-versed in the corporate strategic planning process, in particular their role in articulating "local" market and customer information to shape firm-level customer and sales channel strategic choices.

In the second place, CRM investments will be valued as market-based assets (see Figure 13.2). Brand equity has long been considered to be a market-based asset by senior marketing and finance executives because it provides future strategic options. For example, brand extensions are presumed to require less marketing effort due to image transfer from parent brands. In contrast, sales channel expenditures have historically been evaluated as direct costs of generating transactional sales. However, customer intimacy strategies accord more attention to customer scope (share of wallet) and customer lifetime value. Hence, the size and quality of an established customer base become assets of the firm as well. Sales channel expenditures may thus be evaluated according to the future strategic options and value they offer.

In the third place, given this new strategic emphasis on the customer and sales force, sales executives can expect to be held accountable to a more diverse and firm-level scorecard (See Figure 13.2, Column 2). In addition to revenue generation, sales executives and managers can be expected to be held accountable for the nature and quality of the revenue stream and its profitability in specific customer-related terms. For example, assessments may examine such traditional intermediary market/customer outcomes as speed to market acceptance, share of customer category spend, perceived product or service quality, product availability in key channels, in-store

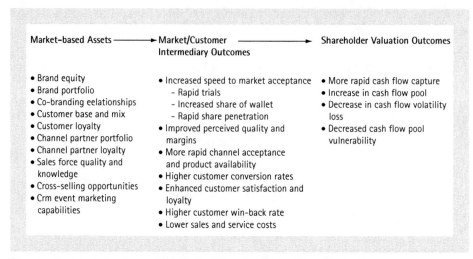

Fig. 13.2. Assessing Financial Payback on CRM in Sales Force Terms

(Adapted from Srivastiva, Shervani, and Fahey 1998)

merchandising acceptance and positioning, customer satisfaction and retention rates, customer win-back rates, and sales/service costs. However, they may also involve additional intermediary metrics such as customer learning and knowledge, cross-functional relationships, and new product success and profitability.

Finally, an enterprise view of CRM strategy brings into play the CFO's financial valuation methods for assessing the return on CRM investments (Srivastava et al. 1998). Hence, sales executives will need to be able to translate customer-level, intermediate outcomes such as increasing customer acquisition, enhancing customer loyalty, or revenue expansion into firm-level financial metrics such as free cash flow, ROI, economic value-added, and net present value (see Figure 13.2, column 3). For example, investments in building closer relationships with core customers may enable more rapid adoption of new products and solutions among highly visible and loyal customers who can in turn provide prestige, referrals, and proof of purchase evidence to support new product rollouts. In turn, given that time is money, quicker speed to market enhances the NPV of these cash flow streams.

Similarly, CRM investments in collaborative relationships may affect cash flow from existing customers due to: 1) higher margins; 2) increased cross-selling; 3) reduced service, inventory, or receivables costs; and 4) reduced direct selling costs. For example, a national accounts program at Wesco, a leading electronics distributor, was credited with enhancing customer value through supply chain efficiencies (reduced search and inventory costs), improved procurement demand forecasting, and a new product alert system, while enhancing Wesco's cash flow as its own SCM (electronic catalogs, wireless ordering) costs decreased.

Finally, since NPV analysis is risk-adjusted, CRM initiatives that reduce cash flow volatility, customer churn, or enhance loyalty should increase shareholder value. For example, investments in strategic accounts may increase customer loyalty and thereby reduce purchase volatility, customer quality, or credit risk. They might also reduce the need for customer "win-back" or new customer acquisition campaigns to replace lost demand.

13.3.2 CRM: An Organizational Perspective

From an organizational perspective, the goal of CRM is to systematically select the right target customers that fit the firm's generic competitive strategy (be it product leadership, cost leadership, or customer intimacy). Then, the firm can go about designing a selling and channel model, organizational structure, customer interaction strategy, human resource policies, business systems, and technology to serve these customers profitably. If the firm's generic strategy is customer intimacy, then Day's (2001) CRM definition is a good fit: CRM is "a cross-functional process for achieving a continuing dialogue with customers, across all of their contact and access points, with personalized treatment of the most valuable customers, to increase customer retention and the effectiveness of marketing initiatives" (p. 4). However, when the firm has adopted a product or cost leader strategy, the definition of CRM is less clear, in particular on the nature of the dialogue with its customers and the degree of personalization. Nevertheless, it appears reasonable that explicitly articulating the firm's CRM strategy and practices might enhance effectiveness or efficiency regardless of the type of generic strategy employed. This is consistent with findings that market-oriented firms find performance advantages regardless of whether they follow a cost leader or differentiation strategy (Narver and Slater, 1990).

Analytical CRM is the analysis of customer-level data and general market intelligence in order to provide strategic and tactical customer and market insights (See Figure 13.3, top half). Analytical CRM processes include the specifics of the analytical methods and tools used to provide strategic insights that drive the firm's choices in four general, interlinked strategy arenas: marketing strategy, customer relationship strategy, services delivery strategy, and go-to-market strategy. Executive-level decisions in each of these strategic domains directly affect customer selection criteria, customer value creation, customer service and experience expectations, the relative price/value tradeoff that customers face, and the relative ease and convenience of the customers' interactions with the selling firm. Critical analytic processes relevant to establishing the role of the selling function and sales force involve: defining a coherent customer relationship typology (or competitive playing field) the firm faces; selecting desirable target market and customer choices;

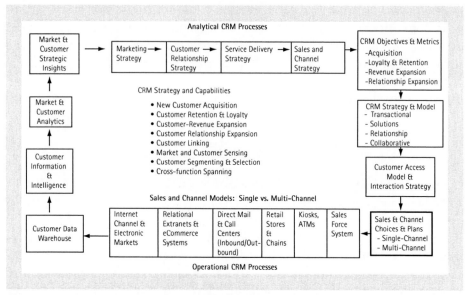

Fig. 13.3. Organization–Level CRM Model and Processes

and specifying the customer relationship strategies and tactics that might best suit each type of customer targeted.

Operational CRM involves translating the core marketing and selling function strategies, developed in the analytical CRM phase, into a coherent and replicable customer access model and interaction strategy (see Figure 13.3 bottom half). The fundamental objective is to generate the customer demand targeted in the analytical CRM phase, among the desired customers, and employing the core marketing-related strategies chosen to drive the customer value versus cost model. This is the implementation phase of the right customer → right strategy → right organization → right processes → right systems → right people → right rewards success cycle that was designed to deliver customer value at a profit to the selling firm.

It is critical at this juncture to note the conceptual distinctions in the roles of the sales function and the sales force, respectively. In essence, the role of the sales function will determine the role of the sales force, if any. Rather, environmental conditions, buyers preferred buying strategies and motivations, and selling firm CRM strategies will interact to define a fundamental role for the selling function and the selling process. Once this role is defined, the firm can then decide whether to employ a direct sales force or other customer access channels. This distinction is similar to that proposed for the role of marketing as a fundamental function of the organization versus the specification of a formal marketing department (McKenna, 1991). It is also consistent with the hybrid marketing systems perspective that there are a variety of channel options available to resolve the firm's revenue-generation function (Moriarty and Moran 1990).

13.3.3 The Role of the Sales Force in a CRM Model

The role of the sales force in a CRM model depends on how the firm decides it can best manage its dialogue with desired customers and channel partners. The days of the territorial sales force, in which a salesperson is implicitly responsible for all customers, products, and services, may no longer be cost-effective for some firms in light of the specialized expertise required for relational customers, and the availability of lower cost channels such as the internet or call centers. Sales force investments may have to be justified on NPV basis, relative to alternate ways to reach, interact with, and relate to the customer.

In thinking about the role of the sales force, demand generation is a fundamental CRM process (revisit Figure 13.3). This is the *agentic role*, or the involvement of the direct sales force in generating and managing customer demand. The key capabilities or processes involved are customer acquisition, customer retention, and revenue expansion. However, adopting a CRM model may also place a premium on customer knowledge in order to enhance customer loyalty and relationship quality. Hence, customer learning may be a fundamental CRM process as well. And, the *learning role* of the sales force (if any) must be clearly delineated and balanced against the requirements of the agentic role.

In establishing the role of the direct sales force, four selling models will be overviewed. In the first place, the agentic role may be implemented using a talent-based model in which the direct sales force, perhaps supported by CRM technology, fully manages customer acquisition, customer retention, revenue expansion, and relationship management. This approach is commonly used when the customer prefers to buy transactionally. The sales territory model may best fit this sales context. Hence, the salesperson selects desirable customers, develops a customer coverage strategy, executes appropriate selling approaches and messages, and manages future transactions. This decentralized, talent-based model stresses sales productivity over customer learning. In fact, a fundamental challenge is the difficulty of engaging the field sales force in the CRM learning loop.

A second alternative is to disintermediate the field sales organization by using an indirect channel, such as a distributor or the internet. The presumption is that the CRM process may be effectively managed by a third-party partner at a lower total cost. Since direct control by the firm is lessened, a common requirement for the selling firm is to work closely with its indirect channel partners to ensure that customer acquisition, retention, and revenue goals are met. This selling model may compromise control, customer learning, and customer loyalty. For rapidly changing markets, sophisticated customers, or commoditized products the notion is that the selling firm can substitute more technology driven and less costly selling models for the services of a talent-based field sales system. However, for B2B customers firms often employ an integrated multi-channel sales model. Customers are provided a set of channel choices, including Internet, call center, retail, direct sales, and account manager. Transactional customers tend to use the Internet and call centers; relational customers often prefer account managers.

A third selling model is account management, usually employed when the CRM strategy targets relational or strategic customers. In either case, the salesperson is assigned a single account, or limited set of customers. The account manager's task is to build a dominant or sole supplier position with the firm. However, an integrated multi-channel model may also be used to supplement the account manager's efforts. Hence, this selling model may be both talent and technology based and is centralized to achieve tighter control over selling efforts.

A final selling model is the customer-focused team (CFT) for a strategic customer. In this selling model, an enterprise-to-enterprise (E2E) relationship is established to build and manage a strategic relationship with a collaborative customer. The strategic account manager often manages the partnership as a distinct business unit with joint goals and metrics. Hence, the selling function and sales force model is both strategic and centralized to ensure the full attention and support of the partnership. CFT managers require business acumen and executive skills and knowledge. These partner relationships may be supported with enterprise-level CRM processes, shared technology, and e-business solutions.

Historically, these operational CRM issues were considered tactical in nature. Sales personnel were not usually privy to the firm's marketing strategies or costs, often in the belief that they might compromise the firm's proprietary position. One consequence of this was a marketing and sales disconnect that often compromised customer value and satisfaction, as promises were not kept (Kotler 1977). Adopting an organizational CRM perspective may provide a better link between marketing and sales. In the first place, marketing and sales force roles may be more clearly integrated at the analytical CRM phase in terms of: 1) target segments and customer priorities; 2) the intended customer value contribution by both marketing and selling; and 3) the customer relationship roles of all "customer-facing" employees.

In the second place, the intended CRM strategy and practices may be more clearly defined in terms of the best approaches for customer access and engagement. In Figure 13.3, the set of alternate customer "touch points" includes the sales force, ATMs and kiosks, retail stores, direct mail, call centers, relational extranets, and e-Commerce platforms. Hence, the firm must carefully consider the appropriate channels to meet the selling firm's demand generation, control, and profitability requirements. Furthermore, customers are increasingly sophisticated in their use of these channels. For example, a distributor or retailer may be highly valued by customers for local availability, expertise, or personal attention. A call center may be valued for its immediacy. An e-Business system may be valued because it simplifies search and comparison effort. Finally, a dedicated account manager may be valued for her business acumen and customer knowledge. Buyers may also prefer a multi-channel approach, perhaps favoring a direct sales force when expertise matters, a distributor for emergency purchases, and a call center for service problems.

A final issue in operational CRM is customer learning. A centerpiece in organizational CRM is a centralized data warehouse that captures, integrates, analyzes, and shares data from all "points of contact" with the customer in a "closed loop" learning system. This involves the acquisition of explicit customer information, such as hits to a web site, call center contacts, requests for quotes (RFQs), transactions completed, or complaints made. However, capturing the implicit (or tacit) knowledge and insights from sales call dialogues, which are personal and context specific, is also critical. Hence, operational CRM systems have the challenge of engaging sales personnel in the customer feedback and learning process.

13.4 CRM in B2B Sales Force Intense Contexts

13.4.1 Customer Relationship Typology and Strategy

Building close customer relationships with *all* customers is neither feasible nor necessary. In my experience, an inspection firm that verified the qualities of oil arriving in large oil tankers found that one customer accounted for over 50% of its revenue, but none of its profits. This large powerful customer was an aggressive transactional buyer who focused strictly on the cost of an inspection. The selling firm instead targeted medium-sized firms that understood the enterprise risks associated with accepting lower grade shipments and, hence, desired a relationship with a best-in-class inspection firm. Similarly, a chemical firm found that its largest customer was a diversified sports product manufacturer. However, its profits were higher with firms that produced leading edge performance boats and, hence, were willing to pay for engineering expertise. Nevertheless, these firms continued to sell to the large transactional accounts in the belief that this covered overhead, built brand equity, or erected entry barriers.

Market-driven firms seek to understand their markets in terms of a customer relationship typology that defines the set of customer segments in the product/ market, the specific customers in each segment, and the attendant marketing, selling, and servicing models that fit each segment. The most common way to specify a customer relationship typology is to analyze customers in terms of their propensity to buy in either transactional or relational terms (Dwyer, Schurr and Oh 1987; Bhote, 1989). These researchers opine that there has been a fundamental paradigm shift from transactional buying, with its emphasis on product-based,

Discrete Transaction	Solution Transaction	Relationship Partner	Collaborative Partner
• Buy product at best price	Bring solution to a business application problem	Build relationship based on value chain synergies	Joint strategic collaboration targeting end-users
• Discrete transaction	Solution life cycle transaction	Open-ended relationship	Partnership presumed (strategic soul mate)
• Always open to buy	Open to switch	Open to suggestions to improve the relationship	Open-ended "Green" agreements and contracts
• Classic adversarial buying process	Reasoned bargaining (Asymmetric)	Open negotiation of relational agreement	Collaborative political exchange model
• Win-Lose on purchase price	Win-Lose on Relative Power	Win-Win through relational qualities	Win-Win through joint problem solving
• Product Quality only	Product and Service Value-in-use	Best-in-class supplier qualities	TQM leadership through collaboration
• Resolute and distant	Respect and satisfaction	Trust and responsiveness	Reciprocity and Trust

Fig. 13.4. Customers Vary in Their Buying Sophistication and Relational Preferences

adversarial negotiation, to the relational buying, with its emphasis on "best-in-class" supplier relationships and strategic partnerships (see Figure 13.4). The strategic choice facing the firm is to define the *breadth* and *depth* in its customer relationship strategy, or the set of targeted customers segments it intends to pursue, realizing that each segment will require a distinct business model. A narrow scope allows specialization in resource capability development and deployment. However, delimiting the scope of an intended customer relationship strategy is a decision that many firms are unwilling to make. For example, the specialty chemical company above identified six customer segments in its boating manufacturer CRT, with the large transaction considered a "segment of one." Only after considerable debate did the selling firm decide to walk away from the major account in order to rationalize its resources to the product leader manufacturers and a set of firms that, while lacking engineering expertise, nevertheless sought to compete on an innovation basis. This relatively selective customer relationship strategy allowed the firm to specialize its engineering, sales, and service capabilities.

On the other hand, a firm may decide to compete in several or all of the customer segments available. For example, a leading healthcare firm decided to compete in all five hospitable segments it identified (Chrzanowski and Leigh 1998). Hence, it found it necessary to develop and execute multiple selling models, including territorial sales, account management, customer-focused teams, local distributors, and a call center. Needless to say, this firm faced many challenges as it sought to simultaneously develop these selling approaches.

13.4.2 CRM: The Sales Force Role in Managing Customer Dialogues and Learning

The goal here is to examine the role of the sales force within each of four customer archetypes. Consistent with RBV (Day 1994), we define the fundamental role of the sales force in terms of the organizational tasks, activities, and processes specifically focused on *establishing and managing an ongoing dialogue with desirable customers*. The focus is on the sales force's role in four CRM learning capabilities: market sensing, customer sensing, customer linking, and cross-functional spanning (Day 1994). Drawing on Nonaka's (1994) organizational learning model the predominant learning role of the sales force, the nature of the dialogue and learning indicated, and the learning processes involved are identified for each buyer archetype. Since the unique aspect of the sales force is interpersonal interaction with the customer, several aspects of the selling process are emphasized, in particular information collection and provision processes, skills and knowledge concerning how to relate to and converse with customers, customer learning and sense-making processes, and cross-functional coordinating activities.

13.4.2.1 *The Discrete Transaction Context*

The *discrete transaction context* is the classic economic model. The product is the focus of exchange and the discrete transaction is the unit of analysis. Essentially, the buyer defines product requirements on the basis of what is available in the market. An adversarial negotiating stance stressing the immediate product transaction is adopted in the belief that supplier competition will yield the best price as the market adjusts to relative supply and demand. Hard bargaining, purposeful distrust, and bluffing are employed to negotiate the best deal. Value chain and SCM costs are not typically considered. Since product quality is presumed to be similar across suppliers and price is the key to choice, the basis for buyer loyalty is to the product. The buying firm is open to buy in the next purchase cycle. Hence, repeat sales are often a function of the seller's attentiveness and likeability. This transactional process is often described as "win-lose" in the sense that the buyer and seller compete for relative advantage. Win-lose may be a misnomer for highly competitive markets; however, when buyers and sellers have asymmetric information or power, hard bargaining may yield a loss for the more dependent party.

In this discrete transactional selling context, the role of the sales force in CRM is aptly characterized as the "salesperson-as-persuader" model (see Figure 13.5). The salesperson's agentic role is stressed; the organizational learning role is relatively limited. The selling firm in essence sets its strategic direction, develops a product mix and marketing programs, builds its business processes, and so forth. The sales force's task is demand generation by actively working the territory for prospects, making sales presentations, and closing sales. Sales presentations may be scripted (Leigh and McGraw 1989) or adaptive (Weitz, Sujan, and Sujan 1986). In each case,

	Discrete Transaction	Solution Transaction	Relationship Partner	Partner Collaborative
CRM Sales Model	Salesperson-as-Persuader	Salesperson-as-Problem Solver	Salesperson-as-Account Manager	Salesperson-as-Executive
CRM Role of Sales Force	Customer Management	Customer Knowledge Management	Account Development and Management	Enterprise-to-Enterprise Linking
Predominant Learning Role	Market Sensing	Market and Customer Sensing	Customer Learning and Linking	Customer Linking and Knowledge Co-creation
Nature & Level of Learning	Sales Transactions and Touchpoints	Product-in-Application Solutions	Relational Qualities and Value-added Solutions	Strategic Directions and Business Processes
Learning Process	Information Acquisition (Explicit)	Knowledge Elicitation (Explicit & Complex)	Adaptive Relational (Explicit & Tacit)	Knowledge Co-Creation (Embodied & Embedded)
Focus of Learning	Individual Salesperson	Individual Salesperson; cross-functional	Account Manager; Account Team	Organization-to-Organization

Fig. 13.5. CRM Customers Learning Typology in Sales-Intense Contexts

the nature of the customer dialogue is focused on standardized probing processes and learning about the customer is limited to the immediate transaction. The buyer is not typically willing to share more general information. Once the buyer's needs have been narrowed down, the process of persuading and closing proceeds iteratively until a sale is made or rejected. Repeat sales are generated by re-calling and re-selling the customer in the next purchase cycle. However, the customer will likely be open to buy from alternate suppliers.

Considering the salesperson's learning role, it is best described as market and customer sensing at the level of the individual transaction. Buyers are usually fairly guarded about sharing information beyond the immediate purchase. And sales personnel, because they are typically paid for their success at the agentic role of closing the sale, are not concerned about future transactions. Furthermore, the information that is collected is typically tactical in a nature, such as who is the current supplier, what are the competitor's pricing and financing options, what are the product benefits and features that seem to be influencing supplier choice, what are the firm's future plans to purchase, and so forth. The learning process stresses information acquisition in which the salesperson asks questions and probes for explicit answers. Hence, any information or knowledge developed is encapsulated in the memories or records of the sales force. Sharing this explicit information to drive market sensing or customer sensing depends critically on the sales force's ability and willingness to share the information. Often the sales force guards this information jealously as it is only rewarded for its agentic sales role, it fears that sales management may increase its sales targets or workload, or the CRM is not intuitive to use.

This sketch of the transactional selling model is very elemental; the purpose here is not to perjure it. Significant business enterprises are built on transactional selling models because they can be cost-effective for their price-oriented target customer base. Progressive firms are linking their transactional sales forces into the CRM system to enhance the selling process and cut costs. For example, several pharmaceutical companies provide sales representatives with hand held devices that automatically score the doctor's responses to detailing initiatives. Firms employ transactional databases to track customer purchase cycles and show exceptions and share this information with the sales force to help enhance their productivity. However, these are the exceptions. In general, little is known academically about how to sharpen the CRM and sales force roles in the context of an enterprise CRM system for transactional customers.

13.4.2.2 *The Solution Transaction Selling Context*

The *solution selling context* is signaled by a more sophisticated perspective concerning the product in the context of a larger business application or market bundle. The buying firm typically adopts a value-in-use, value chain, or total life cycle cost orientation on the exchange. Often the set of qualified sellers is screened to 3–4 highly qualified suppliers based on their solutions expertise and reputation. A solution engagement may extend over a period of years and may involve a bundle of products and services. Nevertheless, the purchase is market-based in that it is bought through a reasoned bargaining process and the buyer is open to new providers on the next purchase cycle. The competitive, arms-length bargaining process is typically socially-defined and ritualistic, with limited information exchange focused on the problem and solution at hand. Sophisticated analyses and/ or projections may guide this evaluation process. The effective purchaser (or seller) is one who can strike the best value/cost bargain in this purchase occasion.

It is important to note that the buyer and seller act unilaterally in defining the existence and nature of the problem and its potential solutions. This is a major contrast to the subsequent relational approaches in that the buyer may be unwilling to share full information. Hence, sales personnel employ sophisticated questioning processes in order to surface customer problems and needs. The buying process may be complicated by the existence of a buying center, or multiple decision-makers. Despite this inherent complexity, the buying firm typically attempts to remain "open to buy" on future purchases. However, the buying process may be somewhat sticky due to insider information, switching costs, and tendencies on the buyer's part to simplify the purchasing process and cut transactions costs (i.e., to treat repurchases as modified or straight rebuys).

In light of this *solution selling context*, the role of the sales force is best described as the "salesperson-as-problem solver" model (see Figure 13.5). Given the types of products and applications the selling firm is competitively able to offer, the agentic role of the sales force is to identify suitable prospects that fit the value chain proposition and application segment profile and then actively engage the buying firm in a dialogue designed to identify and define purchasing needs and require- ments relevant to selling a solution. The presumption is that this consultative selling process will yield a suitable set of customers, profitable engagements, customer satisfaction, and repeat purchases as a consequence of the focused attention of the salesperson on selling the right solutions to the right customers. As a result, the in-supplier may gain buying firm loyalty as the firm streamlines its buying processes (Leigh and Rethans 1984). However, given the buyer's likely openness to buy, the salesperson must maintain dialogue with the customer.

Solution selling elevates the importance of customer knowledge and feedback to the selling firm and, hence, the sales force's customer sensing and market sensing learning roles. On the one hand, the sales force must expertly and efficiently manage the customer dialogue in order to identify quality prospects, collect customer information, diagnose problems and application needs, and develop suitable solutions. In Nonaka's (1994) terms, this represents a knowledge elicita- tion, or externalization, process in which the salesperson surfaces explicit informa- tion concerning the firm's situation, problems, needs and value/cost implications. On the other hand, it involves a *customer knowledge generation function*, as the salesperson goes beyond formal questioning procedures to employ his/her every- day knowledge of how businesses operate to make interpretations and inferences to guide the learning process. This is a sophisticated knowledge capability that is developed by employing and retaining experienced sales personnel.

Market sensing remains the sales force's dominant learning role, but the stakes for transferring knowledge within the firm grow. There is greater emphasis on developing and sharing the contextual knowledge that enables the firm to develop solutions to fit problems that are common across customers and market segments. In some cases, this salesperson knowledge may lead to new product innovations. Hence, the sales force must be able to cross-functionally communicate the nature of the solution context. This *knowledge sharing function* places a premium on the sales force's intra-firm networks, credibility, and internal selling skills.

Given that buyers remain open to buy, the struggle among in-suppliers and out- suppliers is continuous in solution selling contexts. In-suppliers push the buyer toward rebuy decisions; out-suppliers seek to reopen the buying process at the slightest sign of concern or dissatisfaction. Hence, a third sales force learning role is *customer monitoring and feedback*. One aspect is verifying satisfaction; the second is internal prospecting to meet repurchase cycles and find new engagement possibilities.

13.4.2.3 *The Relationship Partner Selling Context*

The *relationship partner selling context* involves a fundamental shift to "adminis- tered" exchange (Arndt 1979), particularly in that any products or solutions are embedded in the context of a presumed longer-term business relationship. The essence of this view is that close relationships with a preferred set of "best-in-class" suppliers will yield mutual competitive advantages through "win-win" actions to resolve key value chain and business process requirements. Joint action on value chain issues requires the parties to share information and trust, to involve each other in core business decisions (i.e., new product development, information management systems), to build joint business initiatives, and to establish multi-level communication linkages to support relational bonds.

These relationships are often "open ended" on the presumption that best-in-class suppliers will, with continued investments in their core capabilities and attention to buyer interests, maintain their preferred supplier status. Hence, "openness to buy" as a risk management strategy is replaced by a problem resolution model intended to maintain relationship integrity while flexibly renegotiating the terms of exchange. A key aspect of the P&G/Wal-Mart relationship is a shared focus on how the relationship helps each party gain share in end user markets. Nevertheless, buyers may prefer to maintain relationships with primary and secondary suppliers in order to avoid over-dependency. Relationships may dissolve as technology and market forces change the relationship calculus (Dwyer, Schurr, and Oh 1987).

Joint actions by buyers and sellers to solve core business problems and drive value chain advantages critically differentiate relationship buying from market-based contexts. However, relationship buyers do not typically share their strategic imperatives. That is, relationship buyers unilaterally defined their generic strategic posture and, hence, their value chain and business capability requirements. Similarly, the selling firm unilaterally develops its strategic plan and capabilities, although it may have done so with an eye toward desirable customer segments. Thus, while joint action is a distinctive characteristic of relationship selling, strategic collaboration is not. Thus, Levitt's (1960) admonition that the salesperson is asymmetrically central in building and maintaining customer relationships is crucial.

In *relationship selling*, the role of the sales force is best described as the "Salesperson-as-Account Manager" model (see Figure 13.5). Since relationship selling involves a fundamental shift to firm-to-firm issues, but without strategic collaboration, the role of the salesperson is to identify a set of customers that are a strategic "fit" with the selling firm's business strategy, establish a trust-based customer dialogue at many organization levels, assess the buying firm's likely strategic business context and value chain implications, build relationship-specific solutions, and manage the relationship (including problem-resolution and re-negotiation).

Relationship selling is implemented through a key or strategic account management program. In this sophisticated agentic role, the salesperson is the selling firm's customer *expert* and *strategic thinker*. She is expected to understand the strategic concerns of the buying firm, how the buying firm adds value and incurs costs, and how its business processes relate to its performance. *Solution-selling* skills are employed to embed transactions and solutions into the fabric of the relationship. The salesperson is also a *service-provider* who identifies customer service expectations and manages the service delivery process. Finally, the account manager adds value through personal rapport and liking, immediacy and consistency, listening and empathy, and advocacy to the supplier organization. Given these demands, it is no wonder that account managers are considered the "*creme de la crème*" of selling (Shapiro, 1992, p. 129).

As with solution selling, the *customer knowledge generation function* is a critical learning role for the salesperson. However, it is now punctuated by a strong emphasis on strategic business assessment, including inferring the buying firm's mission, strategic direction, competitive strategy, value chain and cost structure, key organizational processes, and so forth. Although some of this knowledge is publicly available, some of it has to be externalized by the salesperson through dialogues with key buyer executives, and some of it is tacit and must be internalized by the salesperson through direct experience with the buying firm (Nonaka, 1994). Given the desire for a long term relationship, a significant amount of up-front learning is indicated on both sides to ensure that strategic fit exists. The account manager typically initiates and manages these relationship learning processes.

The *knowledge-sharing* role is also critical in relationship selling. However, this knowledge-sharing role is more complex than in the solution selling model. The account manager must be an astute student of the selling firm itself, its key decision makers, and its capabilities in order to marshal commitment and resources to support the buyer-seller relationship. This may involve internal selling to mobilize top management support, ensure cross-functional investments, and generate relationship specific solutions and systems.

Customer linking is also a core distinction of relationship selling. Account managers are the "face" of the selling firm, operating to link both firms. The account manager is typically expected to quarterback the relationship. The quality of the account manager's personal and professional relationships with key executives, initiative and responsiveness in serving the customer, and commitment to the account provide the glue for the relationship. Customer monitoring and feedback are also embedded in this customer linking role.

From a learning perspective, account management requires a range of complex and higher-order skills, abilities, and processes. Account managers must be strategic thinkers, entrepreneurs, social network managers, problem-solvers, intrapreneurs, and cross-functional negotiators. They require the declarative (know what) and procedural (know how) knowledge that underlie transactional and solution selling. However, they also require wisdom, or business acumen, causal knowledge (know why), and motivation to learn (care why). Such knowledge, skills, and attitudes are complex, tacit, and difficult to imitate. Hence, they meet the conditions of RBV theory and, properly developed and employed, may be a core capability of the firm.

13.4.2.4 *The Strategic Partnership Selling Context*

The core characteristic of the *strategic partnership selling context* is that it involves enterprise-to-enterprise strategic collaboration with a focus on building leadership positions *for the partners jointly* in key end-user markets. Strategic partnerships are single source relationships which take on the "mutuality of a long marriage" (Shapiro 1992, p. 133). These relationships have three characteristics (Shapiro, 1992): (1) mutual importance (strategic, technical, organizational, and financial); (2) intimacy (beyond trust to shared strategic information, bilateral actions, matching structures and teams, and shared outcomes; and (3) longevity (shared commitment over market opportunism). Some recognized characteristics of these partnerships are a total supply chain focus; emphasis on TQM; enhanced cycle times; reduced transactional costs; supplier certification and shared engineering; technology sharing; JIT delivery and inventory systems; and, supplier involvement in NPD processes (Bhote 1989).

With this *strategic partnership selling context*, the role of the sales force can be best described as the "Salesperson-as-Executive" (see Figure 13.5). The core issue for the sales force is that the customer dialogue is mutually and openly strategic. Hence, unlike the prior selling models, strategic partner selling is neither salesperson nor account centered. The role of the sales force is embedded in the strategic business that defines the partner firms' exchange. The boundaries between the firms blur as the firms develop joint business plans, business processes, and performance metrics. We characterize this new role as the salesperson-as-executive role to reflect the fact that the senior account manager is in most senses the leading executive representing the selling firm in a jointly defined business entity. In fact, P&G defined the role of the President of the P&G/ Wal-Mart partnership to reflect this executive role.

The salesperson-as-executive role involves the management of a customer as a domesticated "market of one." Domesticated markets are political alliances, characterized by long-term strategic orientations, mutual stake, reciprocal exchange and influence, strategic negotiation, shared processes and systems, administered solutions and procedures, and the use of political models to negotiate terms and resolve disagreements (Arndt 1979). The essence of the salesperson-as-executive role is "a strong emphasis on strategic marketing thinking and the development of the art and science of the management of coalitions" (Arndt 1979, p. 74).

Customer learning is a central component to the salesperson-as-executive role. However, since the firms are interested in developing mutually advantageous positions in desirable consumer end user markets, the customer learning is embedded in a knowledge co-creation process that is partly explicit (shared marketing research and customer tracking data) and partly tacit, or learning about the partner through socialization and day-to-day interactions (Nonaka, 1994). In fact, after living in a strategic partnership, the senior sales executive will be very likely to become acculturated in the business values, practices, and behaviors of the strategic partnership entity to the extent that these cultural realities are embodied in the executive's mind-set.

Building the partnership coalition requires strategic design and negotiation capabilities; managing it requires sophisticated understanding of inter-organizational systems, administrative procedures, conflict resolution skills, and social influence strategies. Removing the market as a mechanism of exchange places considerable stress on the bilateral communications and bargaining processes. The salesperson-as-executive is the linchpin that is politically astute enough to bring the partners into strategic co-alignment and then is able to negotiate compromises as market conditions and internal exigencies change. These are higher order learning and knowledge skills that involve complex reasoning and conceptual skills, as well as "knowing how to learn" (Nonaka 1994). Hence, the salesperson-as-executive role legitimately reflects dynamic meta-learning capabilities (Teece 2007).

13.5 CRM: Core Strategies and Capabilities

In this section, a representative set of CRM capabilities that involve the sales force in its agentic and learning roles under the generic enterprise CRM strategies and customer learning models are identified and illustrated. There is a general need for academic research concerning the role of the sales force in: 1) the customer management process when operational excellence is at issue; 2) the brand loyal customer management process when product leadership is at issue; and 3) the customer relationship management process when customer intimacy is at issue.

13.5.1 New Customer Acquisition Capability

Customer acquisition through lead generation and management kicks off the customer equity management process and sets the table for future transactions and relationships. For transactional firms, in particular operational excellence firms, lead generation, lead quality assessment, and lead sharing timeliness processes may be key CRM capabilities. In the telecom business, customer acquisition is a continuous process to counter churn among deal-prone customers. The advent of database marketing has been a major enhancer of the effectiveness and efficiency of customer acquisition efforts (Reinartz and Kumar 2002). And, data mining of customer tracking data has allowed firms such as Best Buy to monitor the on-deal purchasing behaviors, returns, and allowances, and service warranty claims of customers and profile their customers (e.g., angels and devils) in order to enhance promotional efficiency. While a major purpose of these predictive models is to enable judicious customer retention investments, they can also be used to predict the likely quality and profitability of a potential new customer and the likely return on a promotional investment.

Generating a prospect list has always been a problem and over-spending on promotions has been common due the relatively low quality of purchased lists. However, the advent of the internet has impacted this lead generation process significantly. John Deere and GM now provide very sophisticated websites that allow prospects to peruse the availability of products, configure a product, check financial package possibilities and availability, search regional dealer inventories, and leave behind contact information. Dealers can then respond in a timely fashion to what should be a quality lead.

Another emerging option is social media. IBM has developed a Marketing 2.0 model that presents what it claims is a new paradigm for marketing (Carter 2009). A key aspect of this model is to energize the peer-to-peer channel, including the possible use of outgoing blog messages; external blog tracking; social media such as Twitter to create "buzz;" online communities such as Facebook and LinkedIn to create social relationships; and YouTube to share information. While little academic research has been done on how these new media relate to sales force issues, IBM's strategy in both B2C and B2B markets is to actively participate in them as a form of viral marketing, lead generation, and customer engagement. If IBM is correct, then the capability to link these social media to the sales force deserves more research attention.

13.5.2 Customer Retention Capability

Managing customer equity involves retaining profitable customers, growing the relationship with loyal and profitable customers, and rewarding customer loyalty. Customer churn is inevitable in transactional contexts. However, managing it is critical to a company's customer lifetime value metrics (Gupta and Lehmann, 2005). Operational excellence firms must be particularly attentive to managing churn. The research of Reinartz and Kumar (2002) stresses the use of transactional data in predicting the customer's likelihood of defecting by employing hazard analysis based on exceptions to the client's normal purchase or touch point data. The firm could signal the sales force of an impending defection, send out a timely promotion offer, or evaluate the net worth of a customer win-back offer.

Relationship oriented firms may require a different perspective on customer defections. In B2C, markets, product leadership firms such as Apple or Harley Davidson often have brand loyal "fans" and communities to reinforce their customers' loyalty and minimize the likelihood of defection. In these cases, event-based customer sensing tools can be employed to monitor their customer's recent purchases, satisfaction, complaints, website contacts, social media use, and participation in community events. These firms may develop the capability to directly share or collect such information with the sales force. They may also selectively involve the sales force in these customer community interactions and events. Customer intimacy firms, of course, seek to immerse themselves in these brand and online communities in a fashion that respects the trust-based learning relationship and allows them to personalize their interactions with these brand loyal enthusiasts.

13.5.3 Customer Revenue Expansion

Customer revenue expansion refers to the capability of a firm to leverage its installed customer base to generate new revenue or cash flows. Typically, firms lever new customer acquisitions through the relatively simple process of cross-selling or up-selling. However, at issue here is the firm's demonstrated capacity to expand revenue or cash flow as a fundamental business strategy, rather than execute a tactical revenue program. One such strategy is to expand the revenue from the installed customer base by constantly upgrading products and services in a generational pattern. In a sense, these firms cannibalize on themselves by adding value and getting their current customers to replace the old with the new. Microsoft has for years leveraged its customer base with new Windows generations. Many customers note feeling a "master and slave" relationship with Microsoft, given the switching costs of moving legacy applications to Apple or Red Hat. Clearly, Microsoft's strategy requires its sales force to maintain strong relationships with key accounts in order to execute this strategic option.

Oracle is applauded for its business acumen in identifying and integrating acquisitions of smaller rivals, such as PeopleSoft in the HRM space, Siebel Systems in the CRM space, and Sun Microsystems with its JAVA software. Oracle has a strong reputation for its capabilities to integrate distinct sales cultures, to maintain solid relationships with its core enterprise customers, and its sales success culture that celebrates sales people who can leverage engagement revenue with established customers.

A final strategy involves enhancing the cash flow or margins on a revenue stream from the installed customer base. Some of the processes involved include: constantly monitoring the quality of the installed customer base to eliminate risky customers, reducing selling and servicing costs as the sales force homes in on key customer expectations, and reducing working capital and inventory costs.

13.5.4 Customer Relationship Expansion Capability

Relationship expansion refers to the continual increase in benefits obtained by exchange partners and to their increasing dependence (Dwyer, Schurr, and Oh 1987). GE Medical Systems is a good B2B example of how a firm may open a customer relationship with one product, an MRI machine, and then subsequently sell other imaging products, such as a CT scanner, imaging rooms design, or imaging training programs. Relationship expansion on the surface appears to be relatively straightforward. However, the challenges to be bridged in realizing it involve complex customer prospecting, relationship building, and credibility selling processes.

The most common example of the difficulty of relationship expansion occurs when a firm employs a foot-in-the-door approach to open an account, perhaps low balling its pricing. The major problem with this foot-in-the door gambit is that the firm's initial position establishes its reputation as a discounting firm. Often the customer is a transactional buyer, at least in the product category sold, and, hence, the selling firm faces the problem of persuading the buyer to adopt a more relational approach, establishing its credibility as a relational supplier with other customer departments, or attempting to sell to the firm's executive suite. Since the customer was not initially selected because of its inclination to buy solutions or relationships, accomplishing the transactional→solution→relationship→strategic partner transition is difficult. The seller faces credibility limitations, the inability or unwillingness of its sales personnel to sell solutions, the selling firm's own inexperience at team selling and cross-functional co-ordination, and the lack of a demonstrable strategic partner capability. Nevertheless, the evolution of the P&G/Wal-Mart exchange from transactional to strategic partnership provides testimony to the fact that, with significant interest on both the buyer and seller's sides, it can be accomplished.

13.5.5 Market Sensing Capability

Market sensing shares conceptual content with market orientation (Kohli and Jaworski 1990; Slater and Narver 1995). However, Day (1994) articulates market sensing as a capability, not a firm's orientation or culture. He notes four market sensing processes: *open-market inquiry,* or active scanning by customer-facing employees who are charged to inform top management; *systematic bench-marking* of key competitor capabilities and activities; *continuous experimentation;* and *informed imitation,* including feedback concerning how customers are responding to competitor offers. Hence, a systematic learning role for the sales force is strongly implied to the degree that these are issues that fit the firm's CRM strategy. Market sensing also requires the breaking down of functional silos and the development of accessible business intelligence systems.

13.5.6 Market Segmentation and Customer
Selection Capability

Market-driven firms select their customers wisely for the longer term strategic opportunities they provide the selling firm. Selecting strategic customers is an investment decision that ranks with new technology and NPD in terms of its strategic impact on the firm. Misadventures in selecting a strategic account can lead to investments in initiating, building, and managing a strategic account management system, high costs in terms of extracting the selling firm from the relationship, and opportunity costs in the sense of forgone investments in better qualified customers. Moreover, the selling firm must also be willing to conduct strategic and financial reviews of strategic customers to determine if they are meeting their side of the strategic agreement (Anderson and Narus 1991).

In general, there are three customer selection criteria for selecting key and strategic accounts. First, these accounts are strategic with respect to their revenue stream, market share, margins, and revenue or relationship expansion opportunities. Second, they represent a good strategic fit with respect to the nature of the selling firm's strategic direction and its desire for long term relationships with its key customers. Third, they are strategic with respect to the development of new products and services, new capabilities and processes, customer references, and entry into new markets. A leading software firm emphasizes corporate prospects that are large in sales force size, have executive sponsorship, compete in multi-national markets, use multiple channels, are industry leaders, and that offer the potential to advance the selling firm's technology roadmap. Similarly, a leading electronics firm stresses customers who advance the seller's technology roadmap by providing channel access to lead-users, a dominant sales position with the customer (share of wallet), absolute sales potential (size of wallet), acceptance of a total cost orientation as its business philosophy, and are willing to put equity at stake (skin in the game). It is clear from these examples that the establishment and use of a business process capability for enabling the sales force to identify and manage relationships with suitable customers is critical for market-driven firms.

Strategic partnerships are organization-to-organization in nature. The overriding criterion for selecting strategic partners is the existence of a compelling reason to partner. In general, a compelling reason to partner would involve an analysis of desired end-markets of mutual interest to both parties, and the recognition that joint strategic efforts might provide a distinct competitive advantage in these markets. For example, Ford finds it tough to compete on a power/gas mileage basis with such competitors as Honda and Toyota. Hence, Ford had a compelling reason to develop a strategic partnership with Eaton, the leading innovator in air flow systems. The Wal-Mart/P&G partnership is another. In this, the relationship evolved from a transactional to a relationship model, as the respective firms built trust and came to a realization that each could benefit from a joint focus on driving share in a mutually desirable end-user market, while at the same time, adopting a TQM focus on increased efficiency. In essence, a compelling reason to partner, and ultimately mutual respect for each other's business process capabilities, fueled the development of a collaborative partnership in terms of joint end-user market strategies, a joint enterprise vision, partnership operating principles, a shared TQM perspective, and ultimately a partnership intelligence model. Thus, candidates for strategic partnership may exist among the selling firm's present customer base, in particular among relationship accounts. Hence, the deep knowledge of the customer possessed by the account manager is an asset that may be creatively and strategically leveraged.

13.5.7 Customer Linking

Customer linking refers to the organization's capacity to create durable relationships with customers (Day, 1994). Day (1994) indicates that the sales force adopts a "different—possibly subordinate—role in a collaborative relationship" (p. 45). The view here is that the salesperson-as-account manager and salesperson-as-executive roles elevate, not depreciate, the strategic role of the sales force. Cardinal Health's relationships with its collaborative partner and potential partner hospitals provide extensive descriptions of the development of customer linking strategies and processes (Chrzanowski and Leigh 1998). Furthermore, the fact that customers must be strategically selected for their collaboration potential and payback, as well as the need to develop complex go-to-market strategies that involve multi-function teams, B2B eCommerce solutions, and multi-channel communication opportunities, suggest that the sales force may be considered a combinative or organizational capability of the firm (Barney, 1991).

Finally, the role of customer-facing processes, such as the order generation→order entry and prioritization→order scheduling→order fulfillment→billing→post-sale servicing cycle (Day 1994), in linking a firm's outside-in and inside-out processes may represent a strategic capability regardless of the firm's generic enterprise strategy. For the firm competing on customer intimacy, these customer-facing capabilities and their cross-process dialogues may be central to the firm's value proposition and customer learning. Hence, the sales force may be critical from an agentic and learning role perspective. For the product leader firm, this customer linking capability may be of only secondary value, except for the truly loyal fan base that fuels its NPD adoption process. For the cost leader firm, the focus may be more on enhancing the efficiency of customer management to minimize its prices and customer churn. In a sense, this is an aspect of the debate concerning operational CRM choices, multi-channel systems, and outsourcing the sales force. Given channel options to reach and serve customers, firms must assess the agentic and learning value of owning a sales force internally or employing distributors, web channels, or eCommerce systems.

Empirical research on customer linking is limited. Hunter and Perreault (2007) examine the role of two *customer relationship forging* constructs that link the effect of sales technology on firm performance. *Sharing market knowledge* is the extent to which sales personnel develop relevant market related expertise and share this knowledge with their customers. *Proposing integrative solutions* is the extent to which sales personnel apply their expertise to propose recommendations that are mutually beneficial to both firms. They propose and find that the impact of sales technology on sales performance is mediated by these customer relating capabilities. They conclude that more research should be directed to how sales IT resources, salesperson relationship building capabilities, and consultative selling drive sales performance.

Tuli, Kohli and Bharadwaj's (2007) grounded theory study of customer solutions as relational processes in B2B markets offers a process-oriented view of a customer solution as a set of "customer-supplier relational processes comprising (1) customer requirements definition, (2) customization and integration of goods and services, (3) their deployment, and (4) post deployment customer support" (p. 5). It is clear from their elaborate explication of each of these relational processes that they meet the conditions of rarity, inimitability, and value that define knowledge-based resources and capabilities (Barney, 1997). It is also apparent that further research concerning the organizational structures, complex informational and cultural processes and routines, and incentive systems that drive these solutions is indicated.

13.6 SUMMARY AND CONCLUSIONS

In this chapter, the role of the sales force in the context of an enterprise, organizational and operational customer relationship management model is examined. A critical contribution to the previous literature is made by explicitly developing CRM strategy perspectives for each of three generic enterprise strategic models: operational excellence, product leadership, and customer intimacy (Treacy and Wiersma, 1993). This is a missing piece of the CRM puzzle at most firms. The customer intimacy model of CRM has to a large degree become the implied prototype for market-driven management and customer relationship management. However, this model best fits the firms that have adopted a matching enterprise strategy that stresses genuine customer relationships and learning. In most cases, the firm's actual CRM strategy is embedded in its culture and practices and customer-facing and sales personnel learn it through experience. It is only in recent years, as firms have struggled with adopting CRM technology, that firms have realized the need to explicate and articulate their CRM strategy. Hence, there have been many misunderstandings and failures in delivering CRM promises (Fournier, Dobscha, and Mick 1998).

In Figure 13.1, a template for each of Treacy and Wiersma's (1993) three enterprise strategies is presented (revisit Figure 13.1.1). Then, a tentative corresponding CRM model is developed for each of these enterprise strategies (revisit Figure 13.1.2): Customer Management for Operational Excellence; Brand Loyal Customer

Management for Product Leadership; and 1:1 Customer Relationship Management for Customer Intimacy. In a sense, the goal was to alert researchers and practitioners to formally examine the nature of the strategic fit between the firm's generic strategy and its CRM and sales force strategy as a predictor of firm-level performance. This is similar to Miles and Snow's (1978) notion of the fit between domain selection and domain navigation strategies (for prospectors, analyzers, and defenders, respectively) as a driver of firm performance. CRM and sales force strategic investments in this view should be evaluated in ROI and NPV terms as core strategic options and assets, rather than period expenses.

The notion that the sales force's role in CRM strategy involves both agentic and learning functions was advocated. The sales force role will vary according to the nature of the customer dialogue the firm needs to have with its core customers because of the enterprise and CRM strategy it has adopted. Hence, two frameworks were developed to more closely examine the nature of these customer dialogues. First, the nature of the customer buying process was explicated in terms of four archetype customer models derived from the purchasing literature: discrete transaction, solutions transaction, relationship partner, and collaborative partner. The nature of the distinctions in the customer dialogue and the customer learning process across these buying models was explored (revisit Figure 13.4). Second, the implications of each of these customer buying types for specifying the nature of the salesperson role in selling, customer learning and knowledge management was articulated in terms of Day's (1994) RBV model of the customer relationship management process and Nonaka's (1994) model of organizational learning (revisit Figure 13.5). This allowed a conceptual exploration of the role of the sales force in the CRM context according to four distinct agentic roles: salesperson-as-persuader, salesperson-as-problem solver; salesperson-as-account manager; and salesperson-as-executive. Finally, the learning role of the salesperson were specified for each of these customer buying types in terms of the predominant learning role (market sensing; customer sensing; customer linking), the nature and learning level indicated for each learning role (transactions; applications; value chain solutions; or strategic learning), the nature of the learning process (information acquisition; knowledge elicitation; relational and tacit; or knowledge co-creation), and the organizational focus of the learning effort (salesperson; account manager and team; or organization-to-organization). This conceptual model should provide the substance for considerable debate and research.

Finally, a representative, but not exhaustive, set of CRM and sales force capabilities that are central to the sales force's customer learning and management roles in the firm, given its generic enterprise and CRM strategy, the nature of the customer segments it chooses to target, and the learning and knowledge management implications for the sales force were presented (see the summary list in Figure 13.3, center). It is clear from the nature of the these CRM and sales force capabilities and resources that RBV (Barney 1997) is the appropriate theoretical lens for formulating conceptual and empirical research on the strategic role of the sales force in the firm. Such research should examine the direct effects of these sales force capabilities as well as their interactions with the firm's generic competitive strategy, the nature of the customer dialogue, and the learning role that the firm intends to employ with its core customers.

REFERENCES

ANDERSON, E., and B. TRINKLE (2005). *Outsourcing the Sales Function: The Real Costs of Field Sales*, Mason, OH: Thomson.

ANDERSON, J. C., and J. A. NARUS (1991). "Partnering as a Focused Market Strategy," *California Management Review* 33, 95–113.

ARNDT, J. (1979). "Toward a Concept of Domesticated Markets," *Journal of Marketing* 43 (Fall), 69–75.

BARNEY, J. B. (1991). "Firm Resources and Sustained Competitive Advantage," *Journal of Management* 17, 99–120.

——(1997). *Gaining and Sustaining Competitive Advantage*, Reading, MA: Addison-Wesley.

BHOTE, K. R (1989). *Strategic Supply Management*, New York: Amacom.

CARTER, S. (2009). *The New Language of Marketing 2.0: How to Use Angels to Energize your Market*, Boston, MA: Pearson.

CHRZANOWSKI, K., and T. W. LEIGH (1998). "Customer Relationship Strategy and Customer-Focused Teams," in R. LaForge and T. Ingram (eds.), *New Horizons in Sales Force Strategy and Management*, Westport, CT: Greenwood.

DAY, G. S. (1994). "The Capabilities of Market-Driven Organizations," *Journal of Marketing* 58, 37–52.

——(2001). "Capabilities for Forging Customer Relationships," MSI Report 00-118, 1-33, 4.

DONATH, B. (1995). *Transfiguring the Sales Force*, State College, PA: Institute for Study of Business Markets.

DWYER, F. R., P. SCHURR, and S. OH (1987). "Developing Buyer–Seller Relationships," *Journal of Marketing* 51, 11–27.

FOURNIER S., S. DOBSCHA, and D. G. MICK (1998). "Preventing the Premature Death of Relationship Marketing," *Harvard Business Review* (January–February), 42–51.

GUPTA, S., and D. LEHMANN (2005). *Managing Customers as Investments*. Upper Saddle River, NJ: Pearson.

HUNTER, G. K., and W. D. PERREAULT, Jr. (2007). "Making Sales Technology Effective," *Journal of Marketing* 71, 16–34.

KOHLI, A., and B. J. JAWORSKI (1990). "Market Orientation: The Construct, Research Propositions and Managerial Implications," *Journal of Marketing* 54, 1–18.

KOTLER, P. (1977). "From Sales Obsession to Marketing Effectiveness," *Harvard Business Review* (November–December), 1–10.

LEIGH, T. W., and P. F. McGRAW (1989). "Mapping the Procedural Knowledge of Industrial Sales Personnel: A Script–Theoretic Investigation," *Journal of Marketing* 53 (January), 16–34.

——and A. J. RETHANS (1984). "A Script-Theoretic Analysis of Industrial Purchasing Behavior," *Journal of Marketing* 48 (Fall), 22–33.

Levitt, T. (1960). "Industrial Sales Personnel: A Script-Theoretic Investigation," *Journal of Marketing* (January), 16–34.

McKenna, R. (1991). "Marketing is Everything," *Harvard Business Review* (January–February), 1–23.

Miles, R. E., and C. C. Snow (1978). *Organizational Strategy, Structure and Process.* New York: McGraw-Hill.

Moriarty, R. T., and U. Moran (1990). "Managing Hybrid Marketing Systems," *Harvard Business Review* (November–December), 146–55.

Narver, J. C., and S. F. Slater (1990). "The Effect of Marketing Orientation on Business Profitability," *Journal of Marketing* 54.4, 20–35.

Nonaka, I. (1994). "A Dynamic Theory of Organizational Knowledge Creation," *Organizational Science* 5.1, 14–37.

Plouffe, C. R., B. C. Williams, and T. W. Leigh (2004). "Who's on First? Stakeholder Differences in Customer Relationship Management and the Elusive Notion of Shared Understanding," *Journal of Personal Selling and Sales Management* 24.4, 323–38.

Reinartz, W., and V. Kumar (2002). "The Mismanagement of Customer Loyalty," *Harvard Business Review* (July), 86–94.

Sebenius, J., and E. Knebel (2007). "Negotiating the P & G Relationship With Walmart (A)," Harvard Business School Cases, available online at: http://harvardbusinessonline. hbsp.harvard.edu/b01/en/common/Fitem_detail.jhtml?id=907011&referral=2342

Shapiro, B. P. (1992). "Close Encounters of the Four Kinds," in R. J. Dolan (ed.), *Strategic Marketing Management*, Boston, MA: Harvard Business School, 127–55.

——A. J. Slywotsky, and S. X. Doyle (1994). "Strategic Sales Management: A Boardroom Issue," Boston, MA: Harvard Business School (Case 9-595-018), 1–23.

Slater, S. F., and J. C. Narver (1995). "Market Orientation and the Learning Organization," *Journal of Marketing* 59, 63–74.

Srivastava, R. K., T. A. Shervani, and L. Fahey (1998). "Market-Based Assets and Shareholder Value: A Framework," *Journal of Marketing* 62.1, 2–18.

————(1999). "Marketing, Business Processes, and Shareholder Value: An Organizationally Embedded View of Marketing Activities and the Discipline of Marketing," *Journal of Marketing* 63, 168–79.

Teece, D. J. (2007). "Explicating Dynamic Capabilities: The Nature and Micro-foundations of (Sustainable) Enterprise Performance," *Strategic Management Journal* 28, 1319–50.

Treacy, M., and F. Wiersma (1993). "Customer Intimacy and Other Value Disciplines," *Harvard Business Review* (January–February), 84–93.

Tuli, K. R., A. K. Kohli, and S. G. Bharadwaj (2007). "Rethinking Customer Solutions: From Product Bundles to Relational Processes," *Journal of Marketing* 71: 1–17.

Weitz, B. A., H. Sujan, and M. Sujan (1986). "Knowledge Motivation, and Adaptive Behavior: A Framework for Improving Selling Effectiveness," *Journal of Marketing* 50 (October), 174–91.

Wotruba, T. R. (1991). "The Evolution of Personal Selling," *Journal of Personal Selling & Sales Management* 11.3, 1–12.

CHAPTER 14

THE USE OF ORGANIZATIONAL CLIMATE IN SALES FORCE RESEARCH

STEVEN P. BROWN

MANOSHI SAMARAWEERA

WILLIAM ZAHN

14.1 INTRODUCTION

Building a sustainable competitive advantage through the sales force involves motivating talented representatives to achieve sales and profit objectives by serving customer needs effectively, within limitations imposed by resource constraints and policy restrictions. This requires attainment of multiple performance goals and reconciliation of disparate and often conflicting requirements of customers and management. Directing the efforts of sales representatives toward the most productive ends, and keeping them on track as they encounter inevitable obstacles, is a formidable challenge, but one that must be overcome to achieve a high level of sales force effectiveness.

Existing research discusses three components of sales force effort: intensity, persistence, and direction (e.g. Brown and Peterson 1994, Naylor, Pritchard, and Ilgen 1980). This chapter focuses on the least investigated of these: how organizations direct sales force effort toward achievement of organizational goals. Our central focus is on: (1) how organizational climate signals the types of activities and accomplishments that are valued by organizations and directs salesperson behavior to these ends and (2) the conceptual and methodological implications of conducting organizational climate research in sales force contexts.

To better understand the role of organizational climate in directing employee efforts toward organizational goals, we also discuss closely related concepts, such as culture, psychological climate, and control systems and their relationships to organizational climate. We use a stream of research we are in the process of developing on a new construct we refer to as sales climate to suggest the utility of the climate concept and the types of questions that can and should be addressed to provide a better understanding of sales force effectiveness.

14.2 ORGANIZATIONAL CLIMATE

Organizational climate refers to employees' shared perceptions of organizational policies and practices and the types of activities that are supported and rewarded by the organization (Ashkanasy, Greenbaum, Wilderom, and Peterson 2004, Reichers and Schneider 1990). As such, according to Schneider (2000), climate represents the way employees experience their work environment and participate in the "psychological life" of the organization.

Although organizational climate has previously been studied as an influence on salesperson behavior (e.g. Churchill, Ford, and Walker 1976), we believe its importance in directing sales force effort toward organizational goals has not been fully appreciated. Schneider (2000) speculates that methodological problems, such as establishing the extent to which employees share perceptions of the organizational environment, have limited the development of climate research. He also notes, however, that these problems have largely been resolved, and climate research has contributed importantly to understanding how organizations can focus employee efforts on collective goals (e.g. de Jong, de Ruyter, and Lemmink 2004, 2005, Zohar and Tenne-Gazit 2008). Multi-level modeling approaches capable of partitioning variance attributable to individual- and group-level sources constitute an important methodological advance for understanding the subtle and complex effects of organizational climate on employee motivation and performance (e.g. Mehta and Neale 2005).

We view organizational climate, and the sales climate construct in particular, as useful ways of describing and explaining variation in organizational orientations toward the sales force. Whereas the preponderance of extant research on sales force motivation and performance has been conducted from a micro-organizational behavior perspective, focusing narrowly on individual-level variables, the climate perspective assesses employees' shared perceptions of the types of activities that are supported and rewarded by the organization and the influence these perceptions have on individual and organizational performance. In essence, it provides a holistic characterization of the sales force with respect to its roles in communicating and enhancing value to customers and in extracting value from customer relationships (Rackham and DeVincentis 1999). We describe the construct in more detail in a subsequent section of the chapter.

The definition of climate as shared perceptions of the types of activities that are supported and rewarded by the organization highlights its function in directing employee efforts toward organizational goals. Recent climate research has emphasized this directive function by focusing on specific aspects of climate that are aligned with important organizational goals. For example, a stream of research has explored the nature and effects of a climate for service (e.g. de Jong, de Ruyter, and Lemmink 2004, 2005, Schneider, Wheeler, and Cox 1992, Schneider, White, and Paul 1998), whereas other research has investigated climate for safety (Zohar 2002, Zohar and Tenne-Gazit 2008), and climate for diversity (McKay, Avery, and Morris 2008). Each of these research streams has successfully related specific climate dimensions to closely matched performance criteria. For example, evidence indicates positive relationships between service climate and customer-perceived service quality (Schneider, White, and Paul 1998), safety climate and safety performance (Zohar 2002), and diversity climate and equality of performance across ethnic groups (McKay, Avery, and Morris 2008).

Motivating the sales force to a superior level of achievement would be relatively easy if it were simply a matter of performing well on a single criterion. However, as previously noted, it typically involves pursuing multiple goals (e.g. sales and service) and satisfying the needs and interests of multiple parties (customers and management). Thus far, climate research has not been extended to studying the effects of multiple dimensions of climate on disparate performance criteria. An important focus of our developing research program is to assess the interrelationships among multiple dimensions of climate and how they influence diverse performance outcomes and trade-offs between them (e.g. how a climate for service influences sales performance and sales climate influences customer satisfaction).

14.3 ORGANIZATIONAL CLIMATE AND RELATED CONSTRUCTS

A research focus on organizational climate requires clarity regarding its similarities and distinctions with respect to related constructs. In particular, organizational climate is conceptually closely related to organizational culture, psychological climate, and organizational control systems. Table 14.1 compares and contrasts organizational climate with these related constructs. The following discussion develops the distinctions among them, and suggests their interrelated roles in directing sales force effort toward organizational goals.

14.3.1 Climate and Culture

Numerous authors have addressed the distinctions between climate and culture (e.g. Ashkanasy et al. 2004). Fundamentally, organizational culture refers to the configuration of stories, legends, artifacts, symbols, and rituals that pervade organizational environments and provide a context that enables employees to make sense of new developments (e.g. Deshpandé and Webster 1989, Homburg and Pflesser 2000, Schein 1999). As such, it refers to features that inhere in and constitute properties of the organization (as opposed to being characteristics of individuals). Homburg and Pflesser (2000) employed constructs rooted in organizational culture (e.g. shared values, norms, artifacts related to market orientation) to explain variation in market and financial performance of SBUs (strategic business units) across five industries.

The most salient distinction between organizational culture and climate is that the former consists of features that inhere in and are properties of the organization, whereas the latter consists of employees' shared perceptions of the kinds of actions that are supported, rewarded, and facilitated in the organization. To the extent that these perceptions are shared, organizational climate, like culture, can be considered to be characteristic of the organization (i.e. rather than exclusively a property of individuals within the organization). A vigorous literature has recently developed around the idea that the extent of perceptual agreement represents climate strength, and that this in itself is a meaningful construct that influences the efficacy of efforts to direct employee behaviors toward achievement of organizational goals (e.g. Lindell and Brandt 2000, Luria 2008, Sanders, Dorenbosch, and de Reuver 2008). We return to the issue of climate strength later in the chapter.

As employee perceptions of the types of behavior that are supported, rewarded, and facilitated by the organization, organizational climate represents a more proximal influence on employee behavior than organizational culture does (Schneider 1990, 2000). That is, perceptions of the environment constitute a more immediate

Table 14.1 A Comparison of Climate, Culture, and Controls

	Psychological Climate	Organizational Climate	Organizational Culture	Organizational Controls
Conceptual definition	Individuals' interpretation of the implications of their work environment for their own status and well-being (Brown and Leigh, 1996, James et al., 2008, James et al., 1990)	The shared perception among organizational employees of the behaviors that are facilitated, supported, and rewarded by the organization. Organizational climate encompasses the shared understanding among employees regarding what they need to focus on and what to direct their effort towards in their day-to-day work.	The pattern of shared values and beliefs among organizational members that helps them understand the way the organization functions (Deshpandé and Webster, 1989). Organizational culture includes values, beliefs, norms and artifacts (stories, rituals, arrangements, language) that guide the way individuals function within the organization (Homburg and Pflesser, 2000).	Mechanisms that are designed to direct employee behavior, organizational controls are of two types: formal controls and informal controls (Jaworski, 1988). Formal controls include procedures adopted by the organization to monitor, evaluate, and reward its employees (Anderson and Oliver, 1987, Babakus et al., 1996, Challagalla and Shervani, 1996, Jaworski, 1988). Informal controls include unwritten worker initiated mechanisms that guide employee behavior (Jaworski, 1988).
Property of the	Individual	Organization	Organization	Organization
Level of analysis	Individual	Organization	Organization	Organization/Individual
Representative studies	Brown and Leigh (1996) Brown et al. (1998) Burke et al. (1992) D'Amato and Zijlstra (2008)	Schneider et al. (1998) de Jong et al. (2005) de Jong et al. (2004) Schneider et al. (2005) Salanova et al. (2005)	Deshpandé and Webster (1989) Homburg and Pflesser (2000) Narver and Slater (1990) Barnes et al. (2006)	Anderson and Oliver (1987) Babakus et al. (1996) Challagalla and Shervani (1996) Cravens et al. (1993) Cravens et al. (2004)

	Psychological climate	Climate	Culture	Management controls
	James et al. (1977) James et al. (1979) Parker et al. (2003) James and James (1989)	Salvaggio et al. (2007) Zohar (2000) Zohar and Luria (2005) McKay et al. (2008)	Lassk and Shepherd Ridnour et al. (2001)	Jaworski(1988) Jaworski and MacInnis (1989) Jaworski et al. (1993) Oliver and Anderson (1994) Piercy et al. (2004) Piercy et al. (2006)
Typical research questions	Does the level of organizational climate impact psychological climate? Does organizational climate moderate the relationship between psychological climate and its various outcomes (e.g., motivation)? How does perceptual disagreement (i.e., lack of climate consensus) regarding the strategic focus of a work unit affect employees' interpretation of their work environments (i.e., psychological climate)?	How do we measure climate? What is climate strength? Does a specific climate relate to a matched performance criteria (e.g. does a service climate result in greater customer satisfaction, does a safety climate result in greater safety performance, etc.)? What are the antecedents of a service climate?	What are the different layers of organizational culture and how do they impact an organization's performance? Does market orientation affect business performance? How does culture strength relate to employee attitudes and role perceptions and performance?	How do different types of controls (output controls vs. behavior controls) relate to individual/organizational performance? How do behaviorally based management control activities (e.g. monitoring, directing, evaluating, and rewarding activities) relate to organizational/individual performance? How do different types of controls relate to employee job attitudes and role perceptions?
Questions for future research	Does the level of organizational climate impact psychological climate?	Do multiple climates exist within an organization? How do they relate to one another?	Does organizational culture influence employee attitudes towards the organization?	How would formal and informal controls interact with one another in predicting

(continued)

Table 14.1. Continued

	Psychological Climate	Organizational Climate	Organizational Culture	Organizational Controls
Questions for future research	Does organizational climate moderate the relationship between psychological climate and its various outcomes (e.g., motivation)? How does perceptual disagreement (i.e., lack of climate consensus) regarding the strategic focus of a work unit affect employees' interpretation of their work environments (i.e., psychological climate)?	What factors contribute to the nature of this relationship? How would a specific climate relate to an unmatched performance criteria (e.g. how would service climate relate to sales performance, how would sales climate relate to customer satisfaction)? How do the different dimensions of sales climate relate to one another in predicting organizational outcomes? What organizational, industrial, and transactional factors affect the different dimensions of a sales climate?	Does a lack of climate consensus influence the development of subcultures in an organization? How can firms successfully resolve disputes between subcultures? How do subcultures impact an individual's feeling of psychological climate within an organization?	organizationally relevant outcomes? Would a climate for sales enhance or impede the effectiveness of the sales force controls adopted by the organization? What factors influence the effectiveness of different types of formal controls adopted by the organization?

driver of behavior than do objective features of the environment. Thus, beyond considerations of culture, climate perceptions need to be considered in efforts to understand how organizations direct employee efforts toward organizational goals.

Also, organizational climate research has focused on its directive function and related climate dimensions specifically to organizational goals, such as delivering customer satisfaction (e.g. de Jong, de Ruyter, and Lemmink 2004, Schneider, White, and Paul 1998). The perspective of this research has been that climate signals valued types of behavior, and these behaviors in turn improve performance against organizational goals.

Although culture research has also investigated linkages between market-oriented culture and organizational outcomes (e.g. SBU market performance, financial performance; Homburg and Pflesser 2000, Jaworski and Kohli 1993, Narver and Slater 1990), its perspective has been different in a subtle but meaningful way. The conceptualization and measurement of market-oriented culture, grounded on a measurement model with formative indicators (Jarvis, MacKenzie, and Podsakoff 2003), implicitly considers such culture to be an outcome, rather than a cause, of employee behavior. The formatively indicated second-order construct, market orientation, is represented as an outcome of first-order dimensions, such as information gathering, information sharing, cross-functional co-ordination, that consist of employee behaviors characteristic of a market-oriented culture. Market-oriented culture, then, is said to exist when these behaviors are regularly practiced in the organization. In this sense, market orientation is conceived of as being a result, rather than a cause, of employee behavior (Jarvis, MacKenzie, and Podsakoff 2003).

In several respects, organizational climate is better aligned with the goal of understanding how organizations direct employee efforts toward organizational goals. First, as shared perceptions of behaviors that are supported, rewarded, and facilitated by the organization, "organizational climate" represents a summary description of the way the environment is experienced by employees. Second, as perceptions of what is valued by the organization, organizational climate represents a proximal influence on employee behavior with resulting substantive effects on performance against organizational goals. Third, the climate perspective, which posits a causal relationship between employee perceptions and goal-directed effort, is consistent with the objective of understanding mechanisms organizations can use to direct employee behavior toward collective goals.

14.3.2 Organizational Versus Psychological Climate

Another important distinction needs to be made to differentiate organizational climate from psychological climate. Whereas organizational climate represents shared perceptions of what really matters in the organization and what types of behavior are supported, rewarded, and facilitated, psychological climate refers to individuals' interpretations of the implications of their work environment for their own status and wellbeing in the organization (Brown and Leigh 1996, James, Choi, Ko, McNeil, Minton, Wright, and Kwang-Il 2008, James, James, and Ashe 1990). An important implication of this distinction is that organizational climate (as shared perceptions) constitutes a property of the organization, whereas psychological climate (as individuals' interpretation of the personal significance of the environment) is a property of the individual.

Because organizational climate refers to employees' *shared* perceptions of the environment, whereas psychological climate refers to an *individual's* interpretation of the personal significance of the environment, conceptual and methodological treatments necessarily differ. Models of psychological climate effects require no indices of perceptual agreement, and are typically operationalized at the individual level of analysis, rather than aggregated to a team or unit level (e.g. Brown, Cron, and Slocum 1998, Brown and Leigh 1996, Chan 1998).

In contrast, models of organizational climate often estimate effects at a team or unit level of analysis. In the typology of compositional models offered by Chan (1998), these models would typically be classified as direct consensus models, in which, given acceptable evidence of perceptual agreement, the group level construct (e.g. climate for service, sales climate) has the same conceptual meaning as it does at the individual level. Our only caveat here is that, as it is made up of shared perceptions of the environment, it is debatable whether organizational climate actually has meaning at the individual level of analysis.

Although Chan (1998) avers that when climate measures do not show acceptable indices of perceptual agreement within units, they can simply be construed as indicators of psychological (as opposed to organizational) climate, we believe that conceptually the two types of climate refer to qualitatively distinct types of perceptions. Organizational climate dimensions, such as climates for service, sales, safety, diversity, etc., are strategically focused, and indicate organizational priorities toward which effort and resources must be allocated. On the other hand, psychological climate dimensions, such as challenge, loyalty, recognition, competition, self-expression, etc., relate to individuals' cognitive interpretations of the implications of features of the workplace for their own status and wellbeing (Brown, Cron, and Slocum 1998, Brown and Leigh 1996, James et al. 2008, James, James, and Ashe 1990). These interpretations represent the translation of the perceived environment into the individual's personal psychological space, filtered through his or her own cognitive schemas and meaning structures.

As cognitive interpretations of the personal significance of the perceived environment, psychological climate gets still closer to the motivational force driving goal-directed behavior than does organizational climate. Individuals carry out work routines valued by the organization because behaving in a manner consistent with organizational mandates enables them to improve their stature and wellbeing and avoid incurring sanctions.

Generally, researchers have chosen to focus on either organizational climate or psychological climate, but not on both. Even so, theoretically it is possible, indeed desirable, to assess their combined effects. For example, in a multi-level modeling context, it would make sense to consider the effects of psychological climate on effort and performance at an individual level, while also assessing how organizational climate at a unit level affects the individual-level constructs and relationships between them. Such studies would be capable of providing a more nuanced understanding of how individuals' perceptions and performance are affected by group membership. For example, research might investigate how individuals' perceptions of challenge (as an element of psychological climate) affect performance and how climate for service (as a unit-level dimension of organizational climate) moderates the relationship.

14.3.3 Summary

In brief, then, the sequence organizational culture $\rightarrow$ organizational climate $\rightarrow$ psychological climate represents a chain that begins with features that inhere in the organizational environment, proceeds into shared perceptions of the strategic directions pursued by management, and culminates in interpretations of these perceptions through the filter of individuals' cognitive structures. The sequence describes a process through which organizations direct employee effort toward collective goals. In the next section, we consider another very important way of directing employee effort, organizational control systems, and how they relate to organizational climate.

14.4 CLIMATE AS INFORMAL CONTROL

Organizational control systems specify the criteria by which employees are evaluated and rewarded and against which progress toward goal attainment is monitored (Jaworski 1988). Jaworski makes a fundamental distinction between *formal* and *informal* control systems. Formal controls consist of the specific metrics and criteria that mark the organization's stated goals for the individual, as well as the interactions with supervisors that provide feedback on progress toward goal attainment. In contrast, informal controls consist of signals rooted in the cultural and social fabric of the organization that indicate the types of activities and behaviors that are expected of employees and rewarded by the organization (Jaworski 1988, Jaworski and MacInnis 1989, Jaworski, Stathakopoulos, and Krishnan 1993). In essence, formal controls focus on manager-initiated mechanisms that indicate and provide feedback on specific performance criteria and standards, whereas informal controls are the means by which employees acquire a functional understanding of how things really work in the organization through everyday experience.

   Although a substantial amount of research has investigated the effects of formal controls on sales performance (e.g. Anderson and Oliver 1987, Challagalla and

Shervani 1996, Cravens et al. 1993), considerably less research has specifically con-sidered the effects of informal controls. Following studies by Jaworksi and MacInnis (1989) and Jaworski, Stathakopoulos, and Krishnan (1993), research has largely neglected the role of informal controls in directing employee effort. These early studies indicated beneficial effects of informal controls (in the form of professional, self, and cultural controls) in reducing role ambiguity and conflict and improving job satisfaction and performance. Since the early 1990s, however, informal controls have been neglected in the literature to the extent that organizational controls often tend to be construed narrowly as formal control systems. It is important for empirical research to reinstantiate the distinction between formal and informal controls, and to assess the individual and conjoint effects of these two aspects of organizational control systems on directing employee effort toward collective goals.

In our view, organizational climate is a pervasive manifestation of informal control that reinforces and interacts with formal controls to direct employee effort toward organizational goals. Whereas formal controls specify targets and mark progress toward their attainment, informal controls, such as organizational cli-mate, inform individuals continuously regarding what really matters in the orga-nization. They speak to any doubts employees may have regarding whether the prevailing formal controls "have teeth" (i.e. does management really mean what it says about the importance of customer satisfaction scores?). They also add the considerable influence of peer opinion to that of management's judgement (e.g. management specifies quota, but co-workers suggest the importance and implica-tions of making it) in signaling how effort should be allocated.

14.4.1 Interactive Effects of Climate and Formal Controls

Alternative ways of conceptualizing organizational climate offer opposing predic-tions regarding its effects on the relationship of formal controls to performance. As implied above, conceptualization of organizational climate as informal control leads to prediction of a positive interaction with formal control systems (Jaworski 1988). In this view, when organizational climate is well aligned with formal controls (e.g. when service performance is a key metric and climate for service is strong), it is likely to have a reinforcing effect that augments the effects of formal controls on perfor-mance (Jaworski 1988). In support of this view, Jaworski and Kohli (1993) found that marketing managers working in organizations that combined high formal with high informal controls experienced less role ambiguity and greater job satisfaction than managers working in organizations that combined formal controls with low infor-mal controls. An alternative viewpoint (i.e. viewing organizational climate as a substitute for leadership), however, suggests just the opposite effect.

Another way of thinking about organizational climate is to construe it as a substitute for leadership. Kerr and Jermier (1978: 395) defined substitutes for leadership as variables (e.g. organizational formalization, cohesive work groups) that "render leadership not only impossible but also unnecessary." From this point of view, to the extent that organizational climate fosters a particular type of behavior (e.g. sales, service), formal organizational controls specifying targets for performance on the same dimension (e.g. sales revenue, service quality) will have less influence on performance. Both perspectives are plausible, and which is correct remains an open question.

14.5 CLIMATE STRENGTH

As previously noted, organizations must perform effectively on diverse goals to be successful. For example, they must sell aggressively to meet short-term financial objectives, while at the same time providing a high level of customer satisfaction. In some cases (e.g. when maximizing performance against one goal detracts from performance on another), performing against these diverse criteria involves trading off between disparate goals to achieve an optimal balance. Thus, an important question for climate research concerns the extent to which organizations can simultaneously foster a climate supportive of *both* performance domains. For example, if aggressive selling and customer service are negatively correlated (as they are in de Jong et al. 2004), can organizations maintain an equally supportive climate for both dimensions of performance, or must support for one be subordinated to support for the other?

The concepts of climate strength and climate level figure importantly in efforts to address these questions. Climate level refers to the aggregated mean level within a managerial unit (e.g. a sales district or region) regarding the extent to which a certain type of performance (e.g. sales or service) is supported, rewarded, and facilitated in that unit. In contrast, climate strength, as it has been used in the literature, refers to the extent to which individuals within the managerial unit agree in their perceptions. In other words, climate level is assessed by within-group means, whereas climate strength is assessed using a measure of within-group dispersion, such as the within units standard deviation of employee perceptions.

The climate strength construct is central to what Chan (1998) refers to as the dispersion composition model. This model is distinct from the direct consensus model of organizational climate (referred to above), in which acceptable indices of perceptual agreement are necessary to justify aggregation to a unit level to establish that an organizational climate in fact exists. In contrast, the dispersion model treats within-group variances as constructs capable of explaining incremental variance in individual and organizational outcomes beyond that explained by climate level (e.g. Chan 1998,

Dickson, Resick, and Hanges 2006, Gonzalez-Roma, Peiro, and Tordera 2002, Lindell and Brandt 2000, Schneider, Salvaggio, and Subirats 2002, Zohar and Luria 2005).

The results of climate strength research have generally been weak and inconclusive in terms of the ability of within-group dispersion to explain incremental variance in individual and organizational outcomes. Lindell and Brandt (2000) found no incremental effects of climate strength over and above those of climate level, whereas Gonzalez-Roma, Peiro, and Tordera (2002) found incremental predictive validity for climate strength for one of three climate dimensions. Similarly, Schneider, Salvaggio, and Subirats (2002) found incremental predictive validity for climate strength for one of four climate dimensions tested.

Beyond its weak empirical track record, important conceptual and methodological caveats about the climate strength construct should be noted. First, as illustrated by Lindell and Brandt (2000), climate level and climate strength have a curvilinear functional relationship. Scores at the polar ends of the climate scale can only be obtained in one way, by consensus, whereas mid-level scores can be obtained by a variety of combinations. Therefore, climate strength, as the inverse of within-group variance, is high when climate level is very high *or* very low, but low for mid-range climate level scores. Lindell and Brandt (2000) specify the functional relationship between climate level and climate consensus (see Figure 14.1).

The non-independence of climate level and climate strength also has a troubling conceptual implication: the meaning of strong consensus for a low climate level is unclear. Does strong agreement for a low climate level truly indicate a strong climate? Conceptually, this is doubtful. Moreover, in conjunction with the functional non-independence of level and strength, the meaning of climate strength effects is also unclear. For example, researchers typically hypothesize linear effects of climate level and strength, but the two constructs are functionally related in a curvilinear manner, where strength is high for both high and low levels of climate level. One would intuitively expect different effects for climate strength depending

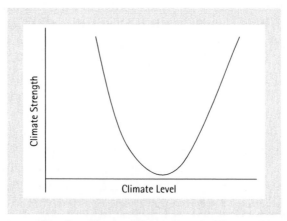

Fig. 14.1. The Curvilinear Climate Level–Climate Strength Relationship

on whether high strength was combined with high or low climate level. Such effects have not generally been predicted or tested in the extant literature. Because of the conceptual fuzziness regarding the meaning of high consensus for low climate level, we prefer the term "climate consensus," as used by Lindell and Brandt (2000), to the more common label "climate strength."

Despite these caveats, we believe that both climate level and climate consensus must play meaningful roles in addressing the question of whether organizations can foster and maintain climates for multiple and disparate strategic imperatives. Both are key metrics in determining whether organizations can maintain climates that simultaneously direct employee efforts toward achieving multiple, disparate goals.

14.6 BUILDING CLIMATE

Rooted in culture, organizational climate is shaped by numerous influences in the social fabric of the organization. Antecedent influences on climate include leader behavior, peer group dynamics, training programs, and attraction, selection, and attrition processes that work toward attracting and retaining individuals who fit well with the culture and strategic direction of the organization (e.g. Dickson, Smith, Grojean, and Ehrhart 2001, Schneider 1987). Although it is not within the scope of this chapter to provide a comprehensive discussion of influences that shape the character of organizational climate, it is important to provide an overview of the dynamics that lead to shared perceptions of behaviors that are supported, facilitated, and rewarded in the organization. Dickson et al. (2001) and Grojean, et al. (2004) provide more comprehensive discussions. Our overview focuses on four types of influences: leader behaviors, control systems, peer group dynamics, and attraction, selection, and attrition processes. Figure 14.2 depicts the antecedents and consequences of an organizational climate for selling.

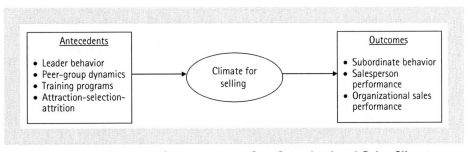

Fig. 14.2. Antecedents and Consequences of an Organizational Sales Climate

14.6.1 Leader Behaviors

Leaders affect climate profoundly through their personalities, values, leadership styles, and the reward structures and value systems they instill in the organization. Leaders who are founders have a particularly profound influence, and often personify the culture and climate of their organizations (Schein 1999). Bill Gates, Sam Walton, and Michael Dell exemplify founder leaders whose personalities, values, styles, and beliefs put an indelible stamp on the cultures and climates of their organizations (Of course, we could also cite more notorious examples of climate-setting, such as the leaders of Enron, financial institutions bent on predatory lending practices, and so forth.) Legions of less prominent leaders also condition their organizations' climates through their personalities, attitudes, and behavior. In so doing, they also help direct employee actions toward the types of actions the organization signals as desirable.

Perhaps the primary means leaders have to influence allocation of employee effort is through decisions regarding the appropriate control and reward system for the organization. Such systems provide employees with explicit direction regarding the types of performance that will be measured and rewarded. This is the essence of formal control, and decisions regarding the types of measures to employ and the levels at which they should be set are leaders' responsibility and prerogative. Much research has been conducted on the effects of formal controls. It is important to note, however, that formal controls and their effects on organizational outcomes are essentially manifestations of leader influence. The types of formal controls managers deploy importantly influence the character of organizational climate.

Despite the existence of a few studies, research regarding leader influence on organizational climate remains underdeveloped. Focusing on personality, Mayer et al. (2007) found that agreeableness, conscientiousness, and neuroticism predicted aspects of the organizational justice climate, whereas extraversion did not. Overall, the effect sizes were quite modest. Zohar and Tenne-Gazit (2008) investigated the effect of transformational leadership on safety climate strength and found a positive relationship, mediated by the density of individuals' social network within the organization. Zohar (2002) found that training and feedback for field supervisors improved safety practices. Generally, these results are supportive of the notion that leader personalities, training, and behavioral styles influence organizational climate. They also support the idea that individuals (i.e. leaders) attempt to influence situations (e.g. organizational climate) to achieve a closer fit with the environment. Much more research is needed to understand how leader behavior affects the direction, level, and strength of organizational climate. Such research would have direct implications for informing leaders regarding how to better establish a climate for directing employee behavior toward organizational goals.

14.6.2 Attraction—Selection—Attrition

Schneider's (1987) attraction—selection—attrition (ASA) model suggests the mechanisms by which organizations attract and retain individuals whose dispositions and goals are aligned with organizational goals and strategies. Organizational controls, including climate, constitute means of inducing compliance with organizational norms and reducing variance outside of a normative range of employee behavior. Through attraction and selection processes, organizations take in those individuals who are perceived as matching the profile desired by the organization. When Type I errors inevitably occur (i.e. the organization selects people who do not match the profile), attrition processes act to rectify mistakes, as employees who do not fit leave, either voluntarily or through forced exit. These processes ideally yield a workforce that shares the core values of the organization and works cohesively in pursuit of organizational goals. One outcome, of course, is a strong climate aligned with organizational goals that clearly signals behavioral expectations to newcomers.

14.6.3 Peer Influence

An effective organizational climate contributes to a strong workforce that is well aligned with strategic imperatives of the organization. Through ASA processes, such climates are self-reinforcing. Its ability to direct employee behavior increases as the climate is internalized and personified by employees. Of course, at the same time, behavior in the organization becomes more state dependent as climate becomes stronger (i.e. it becomes more difficult to change and adapt to new strategic imperatives that require behavioral changes). Peer influence processes lie at the heart of such dynamics.

Individuals are often more responsive to peers than they are to superiors (Pfeffer 1998). This is an important reason why organization of tasks into team structures is an effective way of getting work done and why many organizations assign fundamental tasks to teams (Huselid 1995, Pfeffer 1998). It is simply hard to shirk when one is immediately accountable to one's peers. In line with these observations, Zohar and Tenne-Gazit (2008) found that the density of individuals' social networks in the organization positively influences climate strength and mediates the effect of transformational leadership. In other words, the denser their social networks, the more employees shared perceptions of safety climate.

14.7 SALES CLIMATE AND CLIMATE FOR SERVICE

In developing our framework, we adopt the perspective of Schneider (e.g. 1990, 2000): to be managerially useful, an organizational climate must be strategically focused (i.e. a *climate for something*). The extensive stream of literature on climate for service (de Jong, de Ruyter, and Lemmink 2004, Schneider, White, and Paul 1998) is central to our discussion because cultivating and maintaining customer relationships through excellent service is critical for salespeople, who must balance the roles of relationship manager, service provider, and revenue producer. We also develop a new construct, *sales climate,* that is at least equally important in directing the efforts of sales personnel toward organizational goals (i.e. for revenue production). We discuss the relationship of sales climate to climate for service, and the relationships of both to customer satisfaction and sales force productivity.

Of particular interest is whether sales climate and climate for service are positively or negatively related (if they are related at all), and how sales climate and climate for service influence customer satisfaction and sales productivity. In other words, we consider whether sales climate is compatible with climate for service and the extent to which each contributes to (or detracts from) customer satisfaction and sales productivity. Figure 14.3 provides a representation of the potential interactive effects of having climates for seemingly disparate objectives.

Extant research has demonstrated that climate for service relates positively to customer perceptions of service quality and satisfaction (e.g. Schneider, White, and Paul 1998). Important as these outcomes are, however, they are not the only ones that affect firm performance. For example, short- and long-term revenue production goals obviously must also be considered. Thus, a more holistic appraisal of the strategic effects of organizational climate must involve consideration of how *multiple* dimensions of climate affect diverse performance outcomes. In particular,

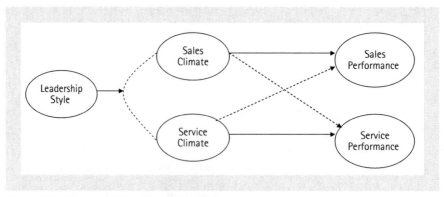

Fig. 14.3. The Ambidextrous Organization

knowledge of how sales climate affects customer satisfaction and how climate for service influences sales performance would be useful in fostering climates that lead to sustained and balanced performance. Existing evidence suggests a negative relationship. For example, de Jong, de Ruyter, and Lemmink (2004) found a negative relationship between service climate in self-managed teams and sales productivity, suggesting the difficulty of balancing aggressive selling and customer service.

It seems likely that, at least in some contexts, high levels of service and aggressive selling may be incompatible, and thus negatively correlated (e.g. when focus on aggressive selling overrides efforts to understand and fulfill customers' unique needs and requirements, or vice versa; Saxe and Weitz 1982). If sales climate and climate for service are negatively correlated, then one must be subordinated to the other, and balanced performance must involve trade-offs between the two. This would not be an appealing scenario for firms with aggressive sales goals and climates that also emphasize excellent service and customer satisfaction.

Our perspective is that trading off one objective for the other (e.g. sub-optimizing service for aggressive revenue production, or vice versa) is not inevitable and that synergies between sales climate and climate for service are possible. That is, sales organizations can be "ambidextrous" (Tushman and O'Reilly 1996) and simultaneously foster climates for both sales and service. The key to doing so lies in the nature of sales leadership. We will return to the issue of leadership as a unifying force in the pursuit of disparate performance goals after describing climate for service and sales climate.

14.7.1 Climate for Service

Schneider, White, and Paul (1998: 151) define climate for service as "employee perceptions of the practices, procedures, and behaviors that get rewarded, supported, and expected with regard to customer service and customer service quality." Empirical research has found climate for service to be positively related to service quality and customer satisfaction (de Jong, de Ruyter, and Lemmink 2004, 2005, Dietz, Pugh, and Wiley 2004, Schneider, White, and Paul 1998). When employees perceive that service-oriented behaviors are supported, rewarded, and facilitated by the organization, they self-regulate their own actions accordingly.

Impressive as these results are, they paise several questions. For example, what is the contribution of climate for service relative to that of formal control systems in driving delivery of service quality and customer satisfaction, and how does a climate for service affect other organizational outcomes (e.g. what is the relationship between climate for service and sales productivity)? Investigation of these questions is integral to a thorough understanding of the effects of climate for service in promoting organizational effectiveness.

When organizations focus on delivering service quality and customer satisfaction, they do so with the goal of creating future revenues and profits (e.g. Reichheld 1996). However, creating *present* revenue streams is also essential. The need to create sufficient present revenue streams (i.e. to close sales *now*) may sometimes motivate salespeople to use tactics that are not service- or customer-oriented (e.g. overselling or using high pressure tactics; Saxe and Weitz 1982). Presumably, this is what led to a negative climate for service–sales productivity relationship in the de Jong, de Ruyter, and Lemmink (2004) study.

14.7.2 Sales Climate

Firms cannot survive without profitable revenue streams, and the primary function of the sales force is to assure a continuous flow of revenue sufficient to achieve financial objectives. However, extracting value from customer relationships follows from a process that includes prospecting for potential customers, communicating the potential value the firm can provide, and customizing offerings to suit the specific needs of individual customers. Investigating the extent to which organizations focus on each of these stages of the value delivery and exchange process can potentially contribute to the development of a useful typology of sales force strategies and assessment of the relative effectiveness and impact of the resulting strategies.

In our conceptualization, the sales climate construct assesses the extent to which organizations support, reward, and facilitate three aspects of the value chain: value communication, value enhancement, and value extraction (Rackham and DeVincentis 1999). As such, it provides a means of classifying sales forces in terms of the strategic importance they attach to each link in the value-delivery chain. This focus on the sales force as a unit of analysis fills a noteworthy gap in a literature (i.e. on sales force effectiveness and performance) that is dominated by studies conducted at the individual level of analysis. Considering organizations' focus on different stages of the value-delivery process is likely to contribute meaningfully toward understanding the performance effects of sales force strategies from a top management perspective (Leigh and Marshall 2001, Shapiro, Slywotzky, and Doyle 1994). We describe the three dimensions of the sales climate construct, illustrated in Figure 14.4, in the following sections.

14.7.2.1 *Value Communication*

The value communication dimension refers to the role of the sales force in functioning as an element of the marketing communications mix to promote customer awareness of product offerings and the benefits they provide. This encompasses sales force activities such as prospecting to identify and qualifying potential customers as a way of allocating selling effort effectively and efficiently (e.g. Gensch

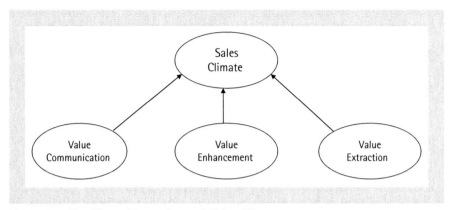

Fig. 14.4. The Three Dimensions of Sales Climate

1984). Organizations that rank highly on value communication are likely to place importance on behavioral inputs to the selling process and closely monitor sales-people's activities to ensure that they are communicating company and product information to numerous customers.

14.7.2.2 *Value Enhancement*

We use the term "value enhancement" to refer to efforts by salespeople to co-produce value with customers and provide custom-tailored solutions for individual customers (Fang, Palmatier, and Evans 2008). In most selling contexts, one size does not fit all, and responsibility for overseeing adaptation of product offerings to serve the idiosyncratic needs of individual customers generally falls to salespeople. In this respect, the value enhancement dimension is inherently customer-oriented, as it involves an understanding of customer needs and efforts to satisfy them as completely as possible with custom-tailored solutions. Organizations that emphasize value enhancement are deeply invested in relationship marketing, and utilize salespeople as primary managers of customer relationships (Palmatier, Gopala-krishna, and Houston 2006). They are responsive to salesperson efforts to marshal the resources needed to provide exactly what individual customers need.

14.7.2.3 *Value Extraction*

The value extraction dimension refers to organizations' focus on current period sales numbers. Just as organizations and units within organizations differ in the extent to which they support, reward, and facilitate customer service (Schneider 2000, Schneider, White, and Paul 1998), they also differ in the degree to which they emphasize aggressive selling to achieve current period sales quotas.

We refer to the degree to which organizations or units within organizations focus on short-term revenue production as "value extraction." It refers to a pervasive concern with "making the numbers." Firms that rank highly on value extraction reward status and material benefits to salespeople who meet or exceed quota and deny them to those who do not. They publicize sales production results and make sure that salespeople know where they stand with respect to quota attainment at all times. They leave little doubt that what really counts in getting ahead in the organization is delivering one's allotted share of sales revenue.

14.7.3 Anticipated Effects of Climate Dimensions

This conceptualization of the sales climate construct considers its three first-order dimensions as formative indicators of the higher-order construct. The three indicators are more properly considered as causes rather than effects of the latent construct, do not constitute interchangeable reflections of it, and are not likely to covary in a systematic manner (Jarvis, MacKenzie, and Podsakoff 2003). That is, an organization that ranks highly on value extraction may or may not also rank highly on the other two dimensions.

  We view the most interesting applications of sales climate as ones in which the individual and interactive effects of the three first-order dimensions are assessed in relation to performance outcomes, such as sales revenue, customer satisfaction, or share of customers. In this regard, our expectation is that the most effective sales forces are likely to be those that combine high levels of value enhancement and value extraction focus. Firms that focus on value extraction but not on value enhancement are likely to have difficulty sustaining balanced performance on financial metrics and customer reactions over time, as their customer satisfaction and retention performance is likely to be lower than that of firms who devote more attention to providing maximum value for individual customers. We are currently collecting data to validate our measures of the three dimensions and test these hypotheses.

14.7.4 Relationship of Sales Climate to Climate for Service

In our view, there is likely to be considerable conceptual and operational overlap between the value enhancement dimension of sales climate and Schneider's climate for service construct. We view the former as being narrower in referring specifically to activities that salespeople engage in jointly with customers to provide custom-tailored solutions for unique problems. Even so, there is likely to be a high correlation between our value enhancement dimension of sales climate and operational measures of climate for service. Thus, in research applications focused on climate for service, it may be worthwhile to adopt a narrower view of the sales climate construct and, for example, compare and contrast the effects of climate for service and sales climate on individual and organizational sales and service performance outcomes. Such research has the potential to advance climate research and understanding of sales force effectiveness by indicating how multiple dimensions of organization influence simultaneous pursuit of disparate performance goals.

14.7.5 Leadership and Organizational Ambidexterity

As suggested previously, we believe that effective leadership is likely to be a key for enabling firms to achieve balanced high performance on disparate criteria (e.g. sales and service). Transformational leaders strive to bring subordinates' intrinsic motivation into play in performing their work, and to inspire them to achieve excellence through the power of positive effect and emotional connection to the leader (Bass 1990). When employees internalize the aspirational values espoused by the leader and the organization, they are likely to exert extraordinary effort on behalf of the organization, not because of extrinsic compulsion but because they see it as the right thing to do. Under such circumstances, employees are likely to be able to perform well simultaneously on disparate criteria, such as sales and service. Transformational leaders are likely to reduce the necessity of making trade-offs between disparate performance criteria by inspiring subordinates to perform well on both. Such dynamics are likely to lead to organizational ambidexterity, or the ability of the organization to do multiple things well.

14.7.6 Managerial Implications

An effective sales force is a key to sustainable competitive advantage, and fostering a healthy organizational climate in the sales force is critical to achieving sales force effectiveness. But sales force effectiveness requires performing well on multiple, disparate criteria. Salesperson effort can be directed toward achievement of organizational goals by informal as well as by formal control mechanisms. It is important for management to think through carefully the most appropriate performance metrics to specify as targets for formal control. It is also important that social influence processes in the organization, realized through employees' experience of organizational climate, work to support the formal control system. That is, employees' experience of the organizational environment must confirm that the organization means what it says when it assigns accountability for organizational goals.

It may be difficult for organizations to foster strong climates supportive of efforts to attain multiple, diverse performance objectives. In this regard, the nature and quality of leadership is critical. Leaders who inspire lofty visions and identification with the high standards of the organization tap into the wellsprings of deeply held employee values and intrinsic motivation. As a result, employees rise to the challenge of performing effectively on the disparate aspects of performance that must be accomplished to achieve a high overall level of sales force effectiveness. Thus, selection, training, and evaluation of sales managers should focus on their capability to communicate visions of what can be accomplished and inspire employee identification with and internalization of organizational objectives. When salespeople see these objectives as their own, superior overall performance is likely to follow.

Such intrinsically motivated efforts contribute toward sustaining performance by creating and reinforcing organizational climates in which peer influence indicates the types and levels of performance that are expected. Peer communication dynamics condition employee attitudes, which in turn strongly influence the effectiveness of managerial communications. This suggests that management should cultivate a cadre of leaders among the ranks of salespeople who personify organizational ideals and help to spread them to others. Giving leading salespeople a voice in recruiting and having them lead training sessions can help build climates that direct employee efforts in support of organizational objectives.

Performing effectively on multiple disparate performance criteria requires a high level of salesperson capability and flexibility. It is likely to be difficult for management to specify clear, predictable paths toward achievement of such sets of goals. This has important implications for recruiting and supervision. First, salespeople must be capable of carrying out courses of action that lead to accomplishment of disparate goals. Second, they must be able to deal with contingencies that arise in a diversity of situations to solve problems for individual customers subject to resource and policy constraints. Organizations can facilitate their efforts to do this by empowering them to do what is necessary to solve customer problems without having to contend with a tangle of policy restrictions and inability to access needed resources. A strong climate involves supporting and facilitating salesperson efforts to advance organizational efforts. Organizations need to recruit highly qualified salespeople and then clear the path for them to be able to do what is necessary to achieve organizational objectives.

Organizations should analyze and understand the process through which the sales force provides value to customers and, in turn, to the organization, and support each stage in the process. The value the sales force provides to the organization depends on, and is enhanced by, the value that it is able to provide to customers. Focusing too narrowly on attainment of current period sales numbers may result in neglect of value communication and value enhancement activities that are integral to this process. The organization should support, facilitate, and reward efforts in all phases of the value chain, as they all ultimately contribute to greater value received from customers in return for value delivered.

14.8 SUMMARY AND CONCLUSIONS

Organizational climate research, and the sales climate construct in particular, have the potential to inform sales management research in several important ways. First, it provides a holistic perspective on organizations' strategic deployment of the sales force that contrasts with the individual-level perspective that has been pervasive in sales force research. That is, the climate perspective captures shared perceptions of the organization's strategic priorities, and the sales climate construct, in particular, describes the organization's strategic focus on three broad aspects of the value chain. At the same time, however, organizational climate research, operationalized using multi-level models, is able to assess the effects of the organization's strategic focus on individual-level motivation, effort, and performance. Although the climate perspective has considerable potential to advance understanding of sales management theory and practice, it has seen relatively little use in this domain to date. We enthusiastically recommend application of climate research in the sales force context to develop broad strategic classifications of sales force climates and assess their effects on an array of relevant performance criteria.

We also believe sales force research applications have considerable potential for advancing knowledge of organizational climates, a long-standing focus of study in organizational psychology. To date, climate research has not addressed the critical issues of the extent to which organizations are capable of sustaining climates supportive of multiple dimensions of the performance and to what extent climates supportive of one dimension of performance affect other, disparate performance indices. In sales force research, performance on both sales and service is important for achieving overall effectiveness, and it is important to understand not only how a strategically focused dimension of climate (e.g. for sales or service) affects a matched performance criterion, but also how it affects a mismatched criterion (e.g. how sales climate affects service and customer satisfaction). Our developing program of research addresses these issues, and we would encourage related research in sales force contexts.

Organizational climate research also has the potential to inform and advance understanding of sales force control systems. At present, control system research has focused predominantly on the nature and effects of formal control systems. Assessing the incremental effects of organizational climate, as informal control, over and above the effects of formal controls has the potential to provide a richer understanding of the mechanisms by which organizations direct employee effort toward collective goals.

Given these opportunities, we hope researchers will increasingly adopt the climate perspective to advance the theory and practice of sales management. We believe it has substantial potential to inform scholars and executives in their efforts to understand and improve the underpinnings of sales force effectiveness.

REFERENCES

ANDERSON, E., and R. L. OLIVER (1987). "Perspectives on Behavior-Based Versus Outcome-Based Salesforce Control Systems," *Journal of Marketing* 51, 76–88.

ASHKANASY, N. M., T. L. GREENBAUM, C. P. M. WILDEROM, and M. F. PETERSON (eds.) (2004). *Handbook of Organizational Culture and Climate*, Thousand Oaks, CA: Sage.

——C. P. M. WILDEROM, AND M. F. PETERSON (EDS.) (2000). *Handbook of Organizational Culture and Climate*, 2nd edn, Thousand Oaks, CA: Sage.

BABAKUS, E., D. W. CRAVENS, K. GRANT, T. N. INGRAM, and R. W. LAFORGE (1996). "Investigating the Relationships among Sales, Management Control, Sales Territory Design, Salesperson Performance, and Sales Organization Effectiveness," *International Journal of Research in Marketing* 13, 345–63.

BARNES, J. W., D. W. JACKSON, M. D. HUTT, and A. KUMAR (2006). "The Role of Culture Strength in Shaping Sales Force Outcomes," *Journal of Personal Selling & Sales Management* 26, 255–70.

BASS, B. M. (1990). "From Transactional to Transformational Leadership: Learning to Share the Vision," *Organizational Dynamics* 18, 19–31.

BROWN, S. P., W. L. CRON, and J. J. W. SLOCUM (1998). "Effects of Trait Competitiveness and Perceived Intraorganizational Competition on Salesperson Goal Setting and Performance," *Journal of Marketing* 62, 88–98.

——and T. W. LEIGH (1996). "A New Look at Psychological Climate and its Relationship to Job Involvement, Effort, and Performance," *Journal of Applied Psychology* 81, 358–68.

——and R. A. PETERSON (1994). "The Effect of Effort on Sales Performance and Job Satisfaction," *Journal of Marketing* 58, 70–80.

BURKE, M. J., C. C. BORUCKI, and A. E. HURLEY (1992). "Reconceptualizing Psychological Climate in a Retail Service Environment: A Multiple-Stakeholder Perspective," *Journal of Applied Psychology* 77, 717–29.

CHALLAGALLA, G. N., and T. A. SHERVANI (1996). "Dimensions and Types of Supervisory Control: Effects on Salesperson Performance and Satisfaction," *Journal of Marketing* 60, 89–105.

CHAN, D. (1998). "Functional Relations among Constructs in the Same Content Domain at Different Levels of Analysis: A Typology of Composition Models," *Journal of Applied Psychology* 83, 234–46.

CHURCHILL, G. A. J., N. M. FORD, and O. C. J. WALKER (1976). "Organizational Climate and Job Satisfaction in the Salesforce," *Journal of Marketing Research* 13, 323–32.

CRAVENS, D. W., T. N. INGRAM, R. W. LaFORGE, and C. E. YOUNG (1993). "Behavior-Based and Outcome-Based Salesforce Control Systems," *Journal of Marketing* 57, 47–59.

——F. G. Lassk, G. S. Low, G. W. Marshall, and W. C. Moncrief (2004). "Formal and Informal Management Control Combinations in Sales Organizations: The Impact on Salesperson Consequences," *Journal of Business Research* 57, 241.

D'Amato, A., and F. R. H. Zijlstra (2008). "Psychological Climate and Individual Factors as Antecedents of Work Outcomes," *European Journal of Work & Organizational Psychology* 17, 33–54.

de Jong, A., de Ruyter K., and Lemmink, J. (2004). "Antecedents and Consequences of the Service Climate in Boundary-Spanning Self-Managing Service Teams," *Journal of Marketing* 68, 18–35.

————(2005). "Service Climate in Self-Managing Teams: Mapping the Linkage of Team Member Perceptions and Service Performance Outcomes in a Business-to-Business Setting," *Journal of Management Studies* 42, 1593–1620.

Deshpandé, R., and F. E. J. Webster (1989). "Organizational Culture and Marketing: Defining the Research Agenda," *Journal of Marketing* 53, 3–15.

Dickson, M. W., C. J. Resick, and P. J. Hanges (2006). "When Organizational Climate Is Unambiguous, It Is Also Strong," *Journal of Applied Psychology* 91, 351–64.

——D. B. Smith, M. W. Grojean, and M. Ehrhart (2001). "An Organizational Climate Regarding Ethics: The Outcome of Leader Values and the Practices that Reflect Them," *Leadership Quarterly* 12, 197.

Dietz, J., S. D. Pugh, and J. W. Wiley (2004). "Service Climate Effects on Customer Attitudes: An Examination of Boundary Conditions," *Academy of Management Journal* 47, 81–92.

Fang, E., R. W. Palmatier, and K. R. Evans (2008). "Influence of Customer Participation on Creating and Sharing of New Product Value," *Journal of the Academy of Marketing Science* 36, 322–36.

Gensch, D. H. (1984). "Targeting the Switchable Industrial Customer," *Marketing Science* 3, 41–54.

Gonzalez-Roma, V., J. M. Peiro, and N. Tordera (2002). "An Examination of the Antecedents and Moderator Influences of Climate Strength," *Journal of Applied Psychology* 87, 465–73.

Grojean, M. W., C. J. Resick, M. W. Dickson, and D. B. Smith (2004). "Leaders, Values, and Organizational Climate: Examining Leadership Strategies for Establishing an Organizational Climate Regarding Ethics," *Journal of Business Ethics* 55, 223–41.

Homburg, C., and C. Pflesser (2000). "A Multiple-Layer Model of Market-Oriented Organizational Culture: Measurement Issues and Performance Outcomes," *Journal of Marketing Research* 37, 449–62.

Huselid, M. A. (1995). "The Impact of Human Resource Management Practices on Turnover, Productivity, and Corporate Financial Performance," *Academy of Management Journal* 38, 635.

James, L. A., and L. R. James (1989). "Integrating Work Environment Perceptions: Explorations into the Measurement of Meaning," *Journal of Applied Psychology* 74, 739–51.

James, L. R., C. C. Choi, C.-H. E. Ko, P. K. McNeil, M. K. Minton, M. A. Wright, and K. Kwang-Il (2008). "Organizational and Psychological Climate: A Review of Theory and Research," *European Journal of Work & Organizational Psychology* 17, 5–32.

——M. J. Gent, J. J. Hater, and K. E. Coray (1979). "Correlates of Psychological Influence: An Illustration of the Psychological Climate Approach to Work Environment Perceptions," *Personnel Psychology* 32, 563–88.

JAMES, L. R., A. HARTMAN, M. W. STEBBINS, and A. P. JONES (1977). "Relationships between Psychological Climate and a VIE Model for Work Motivation," *Personnel Psychology* 30, 229–54.

——L. A. JAMES, and D. K. ASHE (1990). "The Meaning of Organizations: The Role of Cognition and Values," in B. Schneider (ed.), *Organizational Climate and Culture*, San Francisco, CA: Jossey-Bass, 40–84.

JARVIS, C. B., S. B. MacKENZIE, and P. M. PODSAKOFF (2003). "A Critical Review of Construct Indicators and Measurement Model Misspecification in Marketing and Consumer Research," *Journal of Consumer Research* 30, 199–218.

JAWORSKI, B. J. (1988). "Toward a Theory of Marketing Control: Environmental Context, Control Types, and Consequences," *Journal of Marketing* 52, 23–39.

——and A. K. KOHLI (1993). "Market Orientation: Antecedents and Consequences," *Journal of Marketing* 57, 53–70.

——and D. J. MacINNIS (1989). "Marketing Jobs and Management Controls: Toward a Framework," *Journal of Marketing Research* 26, 406–19.

——V. STATHAKOPOULOS, and H. S. KRISHNAN (1993). "Control Combinations in Marketing: Conceptual Framework and Empirical Evidence," *Journal of Marketing* 57, 57–69.

KERR, S., and J. M. JERMIER (1978). "Substitutes for Leadership: Their Meaning and Measurement," *Organizational Behavior & Human Performance* 22, 375–403.

LEIGH, T. W., and G. W. MARSHALL (2001). "Research Priorities in Sales Strategy and Performance," *Journal of Personal Selling & Sales Management* 21, 83–93.

LINDELL, M. K., and C. J. BRANDT (2000). "Climate Quality and Climate Consensus as Mediators of the Relationship Between Organizational Antecedents and Outcomes," *Journal of Applied Psychology* 85, 331–48.

LURIA, G. (2008). "Climate Strength: How Leaders Form Consensus," *Leadership Quarterly* 19, 42–53.

McKAY, P. F., D. R. AVERY, and M. A. MORRIS (2008). "Mean Racial-Ethnic Differences in Employee Sales Performance: The Moderating Role of Diversity Climate," *Personnel Psychology* 61, 349–74.

MAYER, D., L. NISHII, B. SCHNEIDER, and H. GOLDSTEIN (2007). "The Precursors and Products of Justice Climates: Group Leader Antecedents and Employee Attitudinal Consequences," *Personnel Psychology* 60, 929–63.

MEHTA, P. D., and M. C. NEALE (2005). "People Are Variables Too: Multilevel Structural Equations Modeling," *Psychological Methods* 10, 259–84.

NARVER, J. C., and S. F. SLATER (1990). "The Effect of a Market Orientation on Business Profitability," *Journal of Marketing* 54, 20–35.

NAYLOR, J. C., R. D. PRITCHARD, and D. R. ILGEN (1980). *A Theory of Behavior in Organizations*, New York: Academic Press.

OLIVER, R. L., and E. ANDERSON (1994). "An Empirical Test of the Consequences of Behavior- and Outcome-Based Sales Control Systems," *Journal of Marketing* 58, 53.

PALMATIER, R. W., S. GOPALAKRISHNA, and M. B. HOUSTON (2006). "Returns on Business-to-Business Relationship Marketing Investments: Strategies for Leveraging Profits," *Marketing Science* 25, 477–93.

PARKER, C. P., B. B. BALTES, S. A. YOUNG, J. W. HUFF, R. A. ALTMANN, H. LACOST, and J. E. ROBERTS (2003). "Relationships between Psychological Climate Perceptions and Work Outcomes: A Meta-Analytic Review," *Journal of Organizational Behavior* 24, 389–416.

PFEFFER, J. (1998). *Human Equation: Building Profits by Putting People First*, Boston, MA: Harvard Business School Press.

PIERCY, N. F., D. W. CRAVENS, N. LANE, and D. W. VORHIES (2006). "Driving Organizational Citizenship Behaviors and Salesperson In-Role Behavior Performance: The Role of Management Control and Perceived Organizational Support," *Journal of the Academy of Marketing Science* 34, 244–62.

——G. S. LOW, and D. W. CRAVENS (2004). "Consequences of Sales Management's Behavior- and Compensation-Based Control Strategies in Developing Countries," *Journal of International Marketing* 12, 30–57.

RACKHAM, N., and J. R. DEVINCENTIS (1999). *Rethinking the Sales Force*, New York: McGraw-Hill.

REICHERS, A. E., and B. SCHNEIDER (1990). "Climate and Culture: An Evolution of Constructs," in B. Schneider (ed.), *Organizational Climate and Culture*, San Francisco, CA: Jossey-Bass, 5–39.

REICHHELD, F. F. (1996). *The Loyalty Effect: The Hidden Force Behind Growth, Profits, and Lasting Value*, Boston, MA: Harvard Business School Press.

RIDNOUR, R. E., F. G. LASSK, and C. D. SHEPHERD (2001). "An Exploratory Assessment of Sales Culture Variables: Strategic Implications Within the Banking Industry," *Journal of Personal Selling & Sales Management* 21, 247.

SALANOVA, M., S. AGUT, and J. M. A. PEIRÃ, (2005). "Linking Organizational Resources and Work Engagement to Employee Performance and Customer Loyalty: The Mediation of Service Climate," *Journal of Applied Psychology* 90, 1217–27.

SALVAGGIO, A. N., B. SCHNEIDER, L. H. NISHII, D. M. MAYER, A. RAMESH, and J. S. LYON (2007). "Manager Personality, Manager Service Quality Orientation, and Service Climate: Test of a Model," *Journal of Applied Psychology* 92, 7141–50.

SANDERS, K., L. DORENBOSCH, and R. DE REUVER (2008). "The Impact of Individual and Shared Employee Perceptions of HRM on Affective Commitment: Considering Climate Strength," *Personnel Review* 37, 412–25.

SAXE, R., and B. A. WEITZ (1982). "The SOCO Scale: A Measure of the Customer Orientation of Salespeople," *Journal of Marketing Research* 19, 343–51.

SCHEIN, E. H. (1999). *The Corporate Culture Survival Guide: Sense and Nonsense about Culture Change*, San Francisco, CA: Jossey-Bass.

SCHNEIDER, B. (1987). "The People Make the Place," *Personnel Psychology* 40, 437–53.

——(1990). "The Climate for Service: An Application of the Climate Construct," in B. Schneider (ed.), *Organizational Climate and Culture*, San Francisco, CA: Jossey-Bass, 383–412.

——(2000). "The Psychological Life of Organizations," in Ashkanasy et al. (2000: xvii–xxi).

——M. G. EHRHART, D. M. MAYER, J. L. SALTZ, and K. NILES-JOLLY (2005). "Understanding Organization–Customer Links in Service Settings," *Academy of Management Journal* 48, 1017–32.

——A. N. SALVAGGIO, and M. SUBIRATS (2002). "Climate Strength: A New Direction for Climate Research," *Journal of Applied Psychology* 87, 220–29.

——J. K. WHEELER, and J. F. COX (1992). "A Passion for Service: Using Content Analysis to Explicate Service Climate Themes," *Journal of Applied Psychology* 77, 705–16.

SCHNEIDER, B., S. S. WHITE, and M. C. PAUL (1998). "Linking Service Climate and Customer Perceptions of Service Quality: Tests of a Causal Model," *Journal of Applied Psychology* 83, 150–63.

SHAPIRO, B. P., A. J. SLYWOTZKY, and S. X. DOYLE (1994). "Strategic Sales Management: A Boardroom Issue," Boston, MA: Harvard Business School (Case 9-595-018), 1–23.

TUSHMAN, M. L., and C. A. O'REILLY (1996). "Ambidextrous Organizations: Managing Evolutionary and Revolutionary Change," *California Management Review* 38, 8–30.

ZOHAR, D. (2000). "A Group-Level Model of Safety Climate: Testing the Effect of Group Climate on Microaccidents in Manufacturing Jobs," *Journal of Applied Psychology* 85, 587–96.

——(2002). "The Effects of Leadership Dimensions, Safety Climate, and Assigned Priorities on Minor Injuries in Work Groups," *Journal of Organizational Behavior* 23, 75–92.

——and G. LURIA (2005). "A Multilevel Model of Safety Climate: Cross-Level Relationships Between Organization and Group-Level Climates," *Journal of Applied Psychology* 90, 616–28.

——and O. TENNE-GAZIT (2008). "Transformational Leadership and Group Interaction as Climate Antecedents: A Social Network Analysis," *Journal of Applied Psychology* 93, 744–57.

CHAPTER 15

SALESPEOPLE'S INFLUENCE ON CONSUMERS' AND BUSINESS BUYERS' GOALS AND WELLBEING

HARISH SUJAN

15.1 INTRODUCTION

The study of sales management has stayed quite distinct from the study of consumer behavior. Nonetheless, as evidenced in many chapters in this volume, the needs and wants of consumers constitute the springboard to an understanding of the effectiveness of salesperson actions. To illustrate, how much and in what manner to train salespeople, or whether or not a particular offering can be considered a value proposition have as their basis an understanding of consumer behavior. In evaluating the appropriateness of salesperson influence strategies, an understanding of consumer needs and wants is no less—perhaps even more—central. Dale Carnegie, through his book *How to Win Friends and Influence People,* suggested that this understanding needs to be a deep not a superficial one. This suggestion has been echoed in the call to alter the criterion for effective selling to the achievement of customer loyalty (Weitz and Bradford 1999). Customer satisfaction, although an improvement over evaluating effectiveness through sales alone, Weitz and Bradford argue, does not take a long enough view of the achievement of customers' needs and wants. It is only through developing a mutually nourishing relationship, one that keeps the customer as a partner, they suggest, that a salesperson is successful.

The view that salespeople's understanding of customer needs should be deep and fulfilling, and that these needs should nourish the relationship between the customer (the firm the customer represents for the business buyer) and the salesperson (the firm the salesperson represents), raises the question of the difference between needs and wants. The maxim "The customer is king (or queen)", often followed when customer satisfaction is the end goal, pays more attention to stated wants than unstated needs. What if what the customer asks for runs counter to their long-term wellbeing? For example, a student in class (customer to the university her teacher works/sells for) wants tests that do not ask about integration of concepts, just for a memory of main points. Adhering to this request generally raises teacher evaluations—an index of customer satisfaction—but within the bounds of the illustration runs counter to serving the need for an education that imparts wisdom and enlightenment. So, as a starting point for evaluating good salesperson influence, I consider the question of needs versus wants for consumers and business buyers. Much of what has been written about the difference between needs and wants relates to the American consumer. So, rather than evaluate consumers in other parts of the globe, or evaluate business buyers in America, I work through arguments focusing on the American consumer. I do suggest that these arguments globalize, geographically and to other categories of buying populations.

Through this analysis I suggest that the two needs that matter, critically, are learning and social connectedness. Both consumers and business buyers are looking for ways to develop themselves and the entities they represent, and though they say they are unwilling to sacrifice short-term pleasure, or hedonism, for this (illustratively, for the business buyer, ease of task completion), they tend to form deeper, more lasting, stronger relationships with salespeople (and the entities they represent) if their learning needs are achieved. Similarly, both consumer and business buyers are looking for ways to alleviate loneliness and increase meaningful connections with other people, and though they may say that speed and efficiency are their top goals, they tend to form deeper, more lasting, and stronger relationships with salespeople (and the entities they represent) if their social needs are achieved. The consequence that follows from this suggestion is that salespeople, quite often, need to not provide customers with what they ask for but instead influence them to recognize that their more profound needs will be harmed by shallow purchases and consumption. They need to influence them to consume smarter, sometimes leading to greater consumption and often to lesser or more efficient consumption. By evaluating good influence through a contrast between short-term wants and long-term needs, I hope to raise questions spurring research that changes conventional wisdom.

15.2 THE WELLBEING OF THE AMERICAN CONSUMER

Is the American consumer getting a good bang for his or her buck? Ed Diener, a psychologist at the University of Illinois, has made it his business to discover where—in which countries—people have higher levels of personal happiness or subjective wellbeing. He has compared subjective wellbeing with economic wellbeing (Diener 2000). This is so much the focus of what he researches, and so much of this research is attributed to him, that in the popular press he is called Dr Happy (*Wall Street Journal*, October 3, 2008)! Based on his research, he reports that the United States has the highest of all purchasing power parity, 100. The life satisfaction of its residents (judged by asking: "How satisfied are you with life as a whole these days?") is on average 7.73, with 10 being the highest. As a contrast, those who live in the Netherlands have lower purchasing power parity, 76, and a slightly higher satisfaction, 7.77. Switzerland, just behind the United States in purchasing power parity, 96, has a higher life satisfaction at 8.36. The life satisfaction index and purchasing power potential of these three, as well as several other countries, are set out in Table 15.1. Compared to residents of the Netherlands and Switzerland, residents of the US are not getting as much happiness for their buck/Euro/Swiss franc (after adjustment for differences in currency value)!

When purchasing power parity is very low, in less developed countries, a "buck" goes a long way. For example, residents of India have an extremely high ratio of life satisfaction (6.70) to purchasing power parity (5). This ratio represents the extreme importance money has for the wellbeing of the very poor (Myers 2000). Because economic disparity in the United States is higher than many other countries, certainly than that in the Netherlands and Switzerland, this suggests that relatively wealthy American consumers are getting an even lower bang for their buck than is indicated by the aggregate country index. The deal that affluent US consumers get, with happiness as the criterion, is not as good as the deal affluent consumers from several other wealthy countries get. Why? What is wrong in the US?

Evaluating the wellbeing of Americans longitudinally, rather than comparing this cross-nationally, David G. Myers (2000) has reported that the percentage of Americans who described themselves as very happy corresponded with the growth

Table 15.1. Mean Life Satisfaction and Income across Nations . . . from Diener (2000)

Nation	Life Satisfaction	Purchasing Power Parity 1992
Bulgaria	5.03	22
Russia	5.37	27
Belarus	5.52	30
Latvia	5.70	20
Romania	5.88	12
Estonia	6.00	27
Lithuania	6.01	16
Hungary	6.03	25
Turkey	6.41	22
Japan	6.53	87
Nigeria	6.59	6
Korea (South)	6.69	39
India	6.70	5
Portugal	7.07	44
Spain	7.15	57
Germany	7.22	89
Argentina	7.25	25
China (PRC)	7.29	9
Italy	7.30	77
Brazil	7.38	23
Chile	7.55	35
Norway	7.68	78
Finland	7.68	69
United States	7.73	100
Netherlands	7.77	76
Ireland	7.88	52
Canada	7.89	85
Denmark	8.16	81
Switzerland	8.36	96

in per person after tax income from 1930 to 1960. From that point onwards, while income growth continued (into the 1990s) the percentage of the population describing themselves as very happy leveled off at about 30 percent. Money ceased to buy happiness. Myers suggests that saturation or declining rates of happiness spring from the failure of residents to develop a meaningful life philosophy. Economic wellbeing can be antithetical (although not necessarily so) to a meaningful philosophy, he has suggested (see Figure 15.1).

Given that both a cross-sectional and a longitudinal analysis suggest that the American consumer is getting ripped off, it is important to understand who is at fault. Since social psychology teaches us that behavior is a result of not just the individual but also the situation, *caveat emptor* (let the buyer beware) is not sufficient as an explanation. Marketing has an impact. Marketers communicate

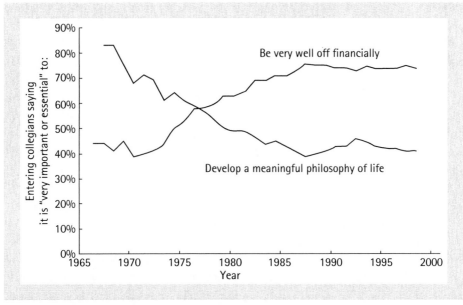

Fig. 15.1. The Contrast between Economic and Psychological Well-Being . . . from Meyer (2000).

with their customers primarily through advertising, sales promotion, and personal selling. Judging by expenditure, contact through personal selling has the highest influence on the goals, decisions, and behavior of buyers in the United States. The influence of sales promotion comes second and the influence of advertising a distant third (Cron and DeCarlo 2006). Using marketing and sales jobs as the yardstick, the influence of personal selling is seen as even larger. According to the US census for the year 2000, from a working population of about 130 million people, about 15 million work in sales and related professions (U.S. Census Bureau 2000). Current estimates, notwithstanding a recession, are as high as 20 million (Zoltners, Sinha, and Lorimer 2008). Even though many salespeople—about half—work only part-time, they far outnumber other marketing personnel, estimated to be less than a million strong. The 10 million full-time salespeople split about evenly into business-to-business (B2B) and retailing salespeople. Since advertising is skewed, decidedly, towards the consumer and away from the industrial buyer, the relative influence of personal selling is not as strong with consumers. Nevertheless, quite inescapably, salespeople have a large influence on consumer buying. Furthermore, judging by the fact that businesses are faltering as a result of poor procurement and B2B buyers becoming jobless in this recession, there is reason to extend the argument to B2B buyers; salespeople can alleviate or worsen the low-bang-for-buck problem among both consumer and industrial buyers.

If salespeople have been instrumental in disabling consumers from pursuing meaningful life goals and business to business buyers from pursuing wellbeing enhancing corporate goals, why is this? Is it because they have too much of a sales orientation? They still have not developed a customer orientation, leave aside a relationship orientation (Weitz and Bradford 1999). Or have they tried, and found that their consumer customers are little interested in meaningful life goals, being far too hedonistic, and that their business customers are far too short-term-oriented to be interested in broader corporate goals? Consistent with this notion of acting without keeping the broader meaning in mind, Vallacher and Wegner (2000) suggest that people can be action-oriented and lose sight of the underlying purpose of their actions. A third, more subtle possibility is that consumers do in fact wish to pursue meaningful life goals, business buyers do want to take a long view, and salespeople do wish to move beyond a sales orientation; but both constituencies have become so lost in the language of hedonism and crisis management, so much the norm, that their better goals have become suppressed. Wilson (2002) argues that in our subconsciousness can lie considerable good intention, unexpressed until we let our subconscious take control. In this chapter I will pursue these questions while developing a frame for good salesperson influence.

15.3 WHY DO PEOPLE BUY?

While developing the idea of mapping human intelligence onto robots, Schank and Abelson (1977) suggested that humans pursue six general goals: (1) owning desirable objects, (2) having servants, (3) vacationing a lot, (4) having rich friends, (5) having lots of money, and (6) having one or more fancy houses. Only "having rich friends" is, albeit questionably, independent of consumption. The human clone will have to be taught why people buy! There have been considerable efforts to give the range of buying goals people pursue more structure. The most notable of these efforts is documented in a book called *The Meaning of Things* (Csikszentmihalyi and Rochberg-Halton 1981). In this treatise on why people buy, the authors document eleven categories of meaning. They include memories such as family heirlooms, the loss of which is particularly painful, utilitarian objects such as vacuum cleaners and toasters, the embodiment of personal ideals represented for example in the books one owns, and things that connect people to their immediate family such as photographs. Seeking a more parsimonious categorization, Csikszentmihalyi and Rochberg-Halton define three levels of meaning:

(1) hedonistic pleasure or buying what makes one feel good with little concern for the effect this may have on the other goals one has or on the goals of other people;

(2) enjoyment or buying what enables learning and the meeting of longer-term valued goals more readily described as challenges; and

(3) kinship or buying to help in linking oneself to other people, family, or friends.

At an even more abstract level, this distinction implies that consumers either pursue shallow goals, which may make them feel good in the short run but will do little for them in the long run, or pursue meaningful goals. The shallow, short-term goals may be even more harmful than just not providing meaning to life: they may be counterproductive, as evidenced by the prevalence of credit card debt—$2,600 billion, with 5.5 per cent written off as losses (Christopher 2008).

It may be argued that, for consumers, hedonistic goals, although shallow, bring happiness. The key issue is matching offerings to goals. As an example, Sndyer and DeBono (1985) separated out the goal of enhancing one's image from the goal of buying for the inherent features of the product or service. They showed that image goals—hedonistic and shallow from some people's standpoint—were preferred by high self-monitors, while inherent product features were sought by low self-monitors. Based on this, they suggest that good advertising targeted at high self-monitors focuses on image offerings, and good advertising targeted at low self-monitors focuses on inherent product attributes. The reason this argument—that matching leads to wellbeing—is questionable is that marketing theory and practice has for a consider-able while focused on personalizing offerings. In retailing this has occurred through both on-line and bricks and mortar selling. If the mismatching of hedonistic offerings to those not hedonistically inclined and higher-level offerings to those hedonistically inclined were the issue, then the plateau in life satisfaction that Myers reported would have lasted only until sophisticated personalization became the personal selling norm; once it did, life satisfaction should have begun spiraling upwards again. This has not happened. Consumption for valued hedonistic goals, whether wanted or not, much like alcohol addiction, appears to hurt human wellbeing.

15.3.1 Research on Materialism

Kasser (2002) suggests that the pursuit of materialistic values degrades human wellbeing. What are these materialistic values? While research on what is material-ism is plentiful, six values dominate the answer. Richins and Dawson (1992) suggest that materialistic things are pursued because (a) they are symbols of success, (b) they are central to what one wants out of life, and (c) they lead to happiness. Belk (1985) suggests that materialistic things are pursued (a) to alleviate envy of people who own more or better, (b) to enable an inherent lack of generosity towards others, and (c) to foster possessiveness. Mapped onto the Csikszentmihalyi and Rochberg-Halton framework, interestingly, success, envy, and non-generosity are the antithesis of kinship: they distance people from other people. Centrality, happiness, and possessiveness appear to be hedonistic and consistent with the Kasser perspective on why materialism works against wellbeing. Because Csikszentmihalyi and Rochberg-Halton suggest that learning and kinship are powerful positive influences on wellbeing while hedonism, although a negative influence, is not as powerful in its effects, research that contrasts the combination of success, envy, and non-generosity with the combination of centrality, happiness, and possessiveness may find the former combination to be more lethal to wellbeing.

Materialism can be pursued for positive kinship. As an illustration, I once found myself in a grocery store following a married couple with a shared cart. The wife carefully selected high-quality items; as she pursued the next item on her list, her husband replaced some of what she had bought with less expensive alternatives. When some rather attractive tomatoes were replaced with cheaper, greener, and more squashed tomatoes, she told him with considerable emotion that if he kept doing this he might have to do all the cooking and, depending on the nature of his substitutions, all the eating too. I remember thinking that this, notwithstanding the difference of opinion and the resulting conflict, was quite a bonding experience for the married couple—that materialism can enable kinship. Materialism can also be pursued for learning. Some video games, like Wii's Grand Slam Tennis, are highly challenging and require considerable effort and concentration to master. The real game of tennis, of course, offers an even higher potential for learning!

If the conceptualization of what constitutes materialism were to include positive and negative learning and kinship, it should lead to an understanding of when consumers gain wellbeing from buying and consuming, when they lose wellbeing, and when it does not matter. In a similar fashion, among B2B buyers, buying that enables organizational growth and social connectedness among members of the buying organization (or across organizations) should enable greater wellbeing, while buying that is in essence a band-aid fix to a crisis should hurt wellbeing.

How can salespeople move away from hedonistic and quick-fix offerings to focus more on learning and social connectedness? If they do, it should help turn the negative correlation between economic and subjective wellbeing into a positive correlation.

15.4 How do Salespeople Sell?

15.4.1 Selling Skills: Reading and Writing

For a long while it has been understood that selling skills require both reading skills (understanding customer needs) and writing skills (developing and implementing good selling strategies); successful selling is the adaptive implementation of writing skills (Weitz, Sujan, and Sujan 1986). A seminal contribution by Mayer and Greenberg (2006, a reprint of a 1964 article) led to the belief that salespeople with highly developed skills balanced their reading and writing skill development: they were not skewed towards either one of the two. More specifically, Mayer and Greenberg answered the question: "What makes a good salesperson?" by suggesting that a balance between ego (writing) and empathy (reading) was the best, and through this argument altered the belief that ego or writing was the more important skill: in terms of the sales process, they suggested that closing was not the most important skill because, given a good balance between empathy (customer needs) and ego (persuasive sales pitches), closing should follow effortlessly.

Has this balance been achieved? I would argue that because sales had always been an action-oriented profession, an emphasis on enacting sales strategies rather than understanding the customer has stayed the vogue. This is in contrast to a profession such as that of a counselor or a therapist, where reading is considered far more important. Other than salespeople's own proclivity to write in preference to read, customers often make reading their needs exceptionally hard (Rackham 1988). Both these considerations suggest that, although the seminal contribution of Mayer and Greenberg did much to alert those interested in practicing and theorizing sales issues to the skew away from ego (writing) towards empathy (reading), it may not have been enough to create a balance. There is a need for a greater emphasis on reading; this increase in emphasis may enhance a positive association between materialism and subjective wellbeing.

15.4.1.1 *Good Writing*

With very little controversy, the most influential perspective on what makes salespeople persuasive is the research on influence by Robert Cialdini (1993). Identified in this research are six highly effective strategies. *Reciprocation* is the idea that if a customer is given a gift, he or she feels obligated to reciprocate. If it is not possible to reciprocate equivalently, he or she is more likely to over-reciprocate rather than under-reciprocate. As an example, a car salesperson who lets you test drive his car overnight is much more likely to make a sale than if he took you on a standard 10-minute test drive. *Commitment and Consistency* is the idea that if we agree to take a tiny first step the rest of us is likely to follow. If we indicate a liking for theatre, then resisting expensive tickets for an amateur production is very hard, even if we know the play will be terrible. A significantly better example of the commitment and consistency principle, taken from Cialdini (1993), is shown in Figure 15.2. *Social Proof* is the idea that if we believe others are buying a particular product we feel compelled to go along too. Teenage consumption of beer—a beverage that tastes like medicine to some—is an example. *Liking* is the idea that if we like someone personally, we will buy almost anything this person sells. The effectiveness of flattery is a validation of this idea. *Authority* is the idea that people

Dear Mother and Dad,

Since I left for college I have been remiss in writing and I am sorry for my thoughtlessness in not having written before. I will bring you up to date now, but before you read on, please sit down. You are not to read any further unless you are sitting down, okay?

Well, then, I am getting along pretty well now. The skull fracture and the concussion I got when I jumped out the window of my dormitory when it caught on fire shortly after my arrival here is pretty well healed now. I only spent two weeks in the hospital and now I can see almost normally and only get those sick headaches once a day. Fortunately, the fire in the dormitory, and my jump, was witnessed by an attendant at the gas station near the dorm, and he was the one who called the Fire Department and the ambulance. He also visited me in the hospital and since I had nowhere to live because of the burnt-out dormitory, he was kind enough to invite me to share his apartment with him. It's really a basement room, but it it's kind of cute. He is a very fine boy, and we have fallen deeply in love and are planning to get married. We haven't set the exact date yet, but it will be before my pregnancy begins to show.

Yes, Mother and Dad, I am pregnant. I know how much you are looking forward to being grandparents and I know you will welcome the baby and give it the same love and devotion and tender care you gave me when I was a child. The reason for the delay in our marriage is that my boyfriend has a minor infection which prevents us from passing our premarital blood tests and I carelessly caught it from him. I know that you will welcome him into our family with open arms. He is kind and, although not well educated, he is ambitious.

Now that I have brought you up to date, I want to tell you that there was no dormitory fire, I did not have a concussion or skull fracture, I was not in the hospital, I am not pregnant, I am not engaged, I am not infected, and there is no boyfriend. However, I am getting a "D" in American History and an "F" in Chemistry, and I want you to see those marks in their proper perspective.

Your loving daughter,

Sharon

Fig. 15.2. An Example of the Commitment and Consistency Principle...from Cialdini (1993)

obey authority figures far more than they should, an authoritative salesperson sells more. The power of authority has been demonstrated compellingly by Stanley Milgram (1974) and Philip Zimbardo (1974) in their learning and prison experiment studies. Both studies showed that, even in America, where independence is valued highly, simple symbols of authority, such as the wearing of a white coat, are enough to elicit extraordinary obedience. In sales, testimonials from authority figures for the salesperson's products—even if the domain in which these authority figures are expert is quite removed from the buyer's goals—go a long way in achieving sales for industrial products. *Scarcity* is the idea that we want what is hard to get. Suggesting that a car is in limited production (it may be for a good reason) is often enough to get customers to pay higher prices.

These and allied influence tactics are so masterful that there is considerable consensus that salespeople can be taught, and often naturally are exceptionally good at, writing.

15.4.1.2 *Following Good Reading?*

By their nature, these influence tactics make themselves available for corrupt use. Recognizing the power of these tactics and their potential for abuse, Cialdini (1999) has argued that while the failure to use good influence tactics is inept (a bungler of influence), the illicit use of influence tactics (a smuggler of influence) in the long run backfires. The lack of trust, between buyers and seller or between co-workers, creates work inefficiencies and, from time to time, makes it hard to recover from crises. He consequently advocates the use of legitimate, normatively appropriate use of influence tactics.

What exactly is a legitimate use of influence tactics? If a salesperson has poor listening skills and responds to explicitly stated customer needs rather than implicit customer needs (Rackham 1988), this does not seem to violate the norm of legitimacy. It would simply be writing after poor reading—for example, a well-crafted research paper that says nothing new. It is another way to bungle influence. So, learning to read what is implied but not made explicit (Rackham 1988) or learning to read not just verbal but also non-verbal cues (Leigh and Summers 2002, Wood 2006) are important reading skills, the lack of which can compromise effective selling.

What if the salesperson accurately reads an implied or non-verbal cue indicating the customer wants his or her hedonic needs satisfied? And responds to this with a smart influence tactic? Would this not be classified in the Cialdini frame of good and bad use of influence tactics as a sleuth (good cop) of influence? It would. Since leisure time in the United States is devoted largely to watching television, a hedonistic pursuit that is for the most part devoid of learning and antagonistic to social interactions (Kubey and Csikszentmihalyi 1990), and not to conversations/visits, reading, or sports (Robinson and Godbey 1999), good influence as currently practiced is the selling of hedonism. It is not the selling of learning or social engagement. Salesperson sleuths who are currently highly valued, it appears, work to counter consumer wellbeing!

Table 15.2. The Measurement of Action Identification...from Vallacher and Wegner 1989

Instructions: Below you will find several different behaviors listed. After each behavior will be two choices of different ways in which the behavior might be identified. Here is an example: Attending class: a) sitting in a chair, b) looking at the blackboard. Your task is to choose the identification, a) or b), that best describes the behavior for you.

1) Making a list:
   a) *Getting organized*
   b) Writing things down
2) Joining the army:
   a) *Helping the Nation's defense*
   b) Signing up
3) Reading:
   a) Following lines of print
   b) *Gaining knowledge*
4) Washing clothes:
   a) *Removing odors from clothes*
   b) Putting clothes into the machine
5) Picking an apple:
   a) *Getting something to eat*
   b) Pulling an apple off a branch
6) Cleaning the house:
   a) *Showing one's cleanliness*
   b) Vacuuming the floor
7) Paying the rent:
   a) *Maintaining a place to live*
   b) Writing a check
8) Chopping down a tree:
   a) *Wielding an axe*
   b) Getting firewood
9) Measuring a room for carpeting:
   a) *Getting ready to remodel*
   b) Using a yardstick
10) Painting a room:
    a) Applying brush strokes
    b) *Making the room look fresh*
11) Caring for houseplants:
    a) Watering plants
    b) *Making the room look nice*
12) Locking a door:
    a) Putting a key in the lock
    b) *Securing the house*
13) Voting:
    a) *Influencing the election*
    b) Marking a ballot
14) Climbing a tree:
    a) *Getting a good view*
    b) Holding on to branches
15) Filling out a personality test
    a) Answering questions
    b) *Revealing what you are like*
16) Tooth brushing:
    a) *Preventing tooth decay*
    b) Moving a brush around in one's mouth
17) Taking a test:
    a) Answering questions
    b) *Showing one's knowledge*
18) Greeting someone:
    a) Saying hello
    b) *Showing friendliness*
19) Resisting temptation:
    a) Saying "no"
    b) *Showing moral courage*
20) Eating:
    a) *Getting nutrition*
    b) Chewing and swallowing
21) Growing a garden:
    a) Planting seeds
    b) *Getting fresh vegetables*
22) Traveling by car:
    a) Following a map
    b) *Seeing the countryside*
23) Having a cavity filled:
    a) *Protecting your teeth*
    b) Going to the dentist
24) Talking to a child:
    a) *Teaching a child something*
    b) Using simple words
25) Pushing a doorbell
    a) Moving a finger
    b) *Seeing if someone's home*

Why do consumers demand what runs counter to their wellbeing? One explanation is that American consumers think about their choices more as actions than as goals (Vallacher and Wegner 2000). While choosing to spend an evening watching three news channels rather than inviting friends and conversing (about the news) over a carefully designed and prepared dinner menu, the goal of ease versus social connectedness is simply not thought about. In their theory of action identification, Vallacher and Wegner suggest that actions can be identified at a lower level, in terms of little beyond the action itself, or at a higher level, in terms of cherished goals. They suggest that higher order identification coexists with better mental health. The measures they have developed to identify individual differences in identifying actions are shown in Table 15.2. Similar to the inability to link actions to larger, life-defining goals is the inability to link the present with the future. Zimbardo and Boyd (2008) have studied differences in individuals' time perspectives, and have identified a present time perspective defined by hedonistic pursuits

---

Table 15.3. The Measurement of Present (Hedonistic) and Future Time Orientations ... from Zimbardo and Boyd 1999

Instructions: Please read each item and, as honestly as you can, answer the following question: "How characteristic or true is this of you?" (*1 = very uncharacteristic, 2 = uncharacteristic, 3 = neutral, 4 = characteristic, 5 = very characteristic*).

Present Hedonistic Sample Items
1) I try to live my life as fully as possible, one day at a time.
2) Ideally, I would live each day as if it were my last.
3) I make decisions on the spur of the moment.
4) It is important to put excitement in my life.
5) I feel that it's more important to enjoy what you're doing than to get work done on time.
6) Taking risks keeps my life from becoming boring.
7) It is more important for me to enjoy life's journey than to focus only on the destination.
8) I often follow my heart more than my head.
9) I prefer friends who are spontaneous rather than predictable.
10) I like my close relationships to be passionate.

Future Time Sample Items
11) I believe that a person's day should be planned ahead each morning.
12) When I want to achieve something, I set goals and consider specific means for reaching those goals.
13) Meeting tomorrow's deadlines and doing other necessary work comes before tonight's play.
14) It upsets me to be late for appointments.
15) I meet my obligations to friends and authorities on time.
16) Before making a decision, I weigh the costs against the benefits.
17) I complete projects on time by making steady progress.
18) I make lists of things to do.
19) I am able to resist temptations when I know that there is work to be done.
20) I keep working at difficult, uninteresting tasks if they will help me get ahead.

that is distinct and separate from a future-oriented time perspective. Without a future-oriented time perspective, people with a present-oriented, hedonistic frame of mind make choices that disregard important, future consequences. For example, they may gain too much weight through hedonistic consumption and later develop diseases such as hypertension and diabetes (Boyd and Zimbardo 2005). The measures they have developed to identify individual differences in a future and a present hedonistic orientation are shown in Table 15.3.

These two perspectives suggest that the inability to consider abstract goals, or distant goals, prevents consumers from explicitly, verbally asking salespeople for non-hedonistic offerings. Despite this inability, if offered products by sleuthing, persuasive salespeople that connect them socially or enhance their learning they might accept these offers. If they do, their future wellbeing is likely to be enhanced. Quite possibly their current wellbeing might be enhanced too. Likewise for industrial buyers: those with abstract or distant goals will ask their B2B salespeople explicitly and verbally for offerings that are not band-aid fixes. Those who lack these goals, despite their asking inabilities, will benefit from offerings that solve longer-term problems, enhancing organizational learning, and people connectedness.

15.5 SUMMARIZING THE ARGUMENT

The core thesis of the chapter can be summarized as follows:

1. Consumers often pursue hedonistic goals. Industrial buyers often pursue quick-fix solutions.
2. Salespeople who cater to the overt needs of these buyers may make a sale, but are likely to fail to enhance the wellbeing of these consumers/industrial buyers.
3. Sleuth salespeople, by definition smart at influence and persuasion, who in addition are good at reading beyond the obvious, are likely to be able to convince these buyers to buy counter to their stated needs.
4. These salespeople may be able to cater to learning and social connectedness needs, long-term problem-solving, and development needs, and as a result enhance consumer wellbeing.
5. In the aggregate this should lead to a more positive correlation between buying (materialism) and subjective wellbeing (happiness).
6. This increase in correlation implies that consumers and B2B buyers can buy less and stay at the same level of wellbeing (an economic buffer), or buy somewhat less and increase wellbeing (a clearer case of buying smarter).

15.6 Implications of the Argument

If the argument is accepted, it has considerable implications for the practice and study of personal selling and sales management.

1. Salespeople move from being seen as consultants (who do a great deal of talking) to being seen as counselors (who do a great deal of listening).
2. Responsible consumption—e.g. the absence of addictions like reckless credit card debt and the presence of environmentally friendly behaviors—becomes part of the sales job.
3. Relationship selling effectiveness is not judged by loyalty alone: long-term customer happiness or wellbeing is part of the metric.
4. While conducting research on sales management, there is a need to make stronger and more direct links with research on consumer behavior.
5. Selling is seen more than it has been as a cognitively demanding job. The prestige of working in sales is greater.

15.7 Extending the Argument

I would like to introduce two added complexities, both of which concern improved reading by salespeople. One relates to how the salesperson's own goals may influence his or her reading abilities. The other relates to unconscious goals that consumer and B2B buyers may have: are these unconscious goals more likely to be hedonistic and harmful to long-term wellbeing, or are they more likely to be related to learning and relatedness needs?

15.7.1 The Salesperson's Own Goals

Like their customers, salespeople may differ in their goal focus. Some may focus on hedonistic goals, prompting a short-term achievement emphasis. Others may focus on the goal of social connectedness or learning. Research that compares a performance or proving goal orientation with a learning goal orientation, among salespeople, is an example of an evaluation of this difference (e.g. Sujan, Weitz, and Kumar 1994, VandeWalle, Brown, Cron, and Slocum 1999). Does the salesperson's own goal focus alter her or his response to customers who explicitly communicate a disproportionate interest in short-term accomplishments or more generally in hedonism? It appears likely that salespeople who are focused on learning will be more likely to look beyond the hedonistic ask and consider the subjective wellbeing consequences for the customer (or industrial buyer) that follow the satisfaction of this ask. Likewise, salespeople who are more focused on relatedness are more likely to look beyond the hedonistic ask. For selling wellbeing, salespeople who themselves are hedonistically inclined are less suitable. Research contrasting the effect of not just learning and proving goals but also relatedness and proving goals, not just on the salesperson's behavior but also on the customers' long-term wellbeing, promises to suggest important ways in which personal selling can be improved.

Salesperson performance evaluation, as sales management theory has developed, has moved from using sales as the primary basis for this evaluation to using customer satisfaction and, further into its development, to using customer loyalty (Weitz and Bradford 1999). Based on the argument that customer loyalty, more so than customer satisfaction or buying, depends on delivering wellbeing, performance differences between salespeople with a learning or knowledge developmental goal orientation and salespeople with a proving or performance goal orientation should be found to be even larger with this criterion. Although it has been previously shown that a learning orientation enables salespeople to perform better (e.g. Sujan et al. 1994), it has not been pointed out that this improvement in performance could be as a result of improving the customer's subjective wellbeing. Similarly, performance differences between a relatedness and a proving orientation should be found to be larger with customer loyalty as the criterion, and should be explained by differences in customers' long-term wellbeing.

15.7.2 Reading Non-Conscious Goals

Recently research in psychology has begun to suggest that people, customers included, often do not know their own goals (Wilson 2002). They may learn about them when they observe that their behavior is not consistent with the goals they state. To illustrate, most customers would acknowledge that they would prefer being pampered in contrast to being treated no differently from every other customer, in a restaurant, hotel, or on board an aircraft. In fact, they would in all likelihood express delight at such pampering: a bowl with warm water and lemon to wash their hands at the table, water with a single cube of ice in a glass while other passengers attempt to fit their bags in an overhead bin and squeeze into their seats, and flowers and high-fidelity background music as a greeting when they walk into their hotel room. If some customers chose to leave the lemon water bowl untouched and walk to a rest room to wash their hands, abandon their first-class meal to sit with a person they recognize in economy class, and abandon their super-comfortable hotel room to exchange a few words with the bartender, it should be clear to their service providers—and to the customers themselves—that goals other than pampering have priority. Their behavior, more than their words, reveal their goals. Salespeople and service providers who recognize the contradiction, and understand that sometimes consumers themselves do not know what they want, can steer these customers towards the fulfillment of relationship and learning goals. For example, instead of seating a customer at a table by a picture window with a stunning view and giving him a complementary glass of a rare wine, the restaurant could invite him in into the kitchen to ask him if he would like to co-create with the chef a new vegetarian recipe. Should it turn out that greater loyalty follows the participative production than the pampered consumption option, it would reveal to the service provider—and possibly to the customer—what the customer really wants.

Again, it seems likely that salespeople and service providers who have learning and/ or relationship development/maintenance goals are better at spotting unconscious goals than salespeople and service providers who have performance or proving goals.

This conclusion is based on the assumption that unconscious goals are skewed towards learning and relationship development, not towards hedonism. Is this really the case? Current research on unconscious goals claims that they are adaptive, not destructive. It argues that the older, Freudian view that underneath our consciousness are self-destructive goals is not valid (Wilson 2002). The assumption that unconscious consumer goals are skewed towards learning and relationship development, because these goals foster wellbeing more than hedonistic goals do, would be consistent with the suggestion that unconscious goals are adaptive.

If consumers know, even if only unconsciously, that asking for hedonistic products and services is maladaptive, why would they, so prevalently, continue to ask for hedonism? Marketers' offering of hedonism is easier to understand. If marketers only offered learning and relationship products and services, consumers might achieve wellbeing with less and marketers' goals of short-term profit might be compromised. Consumers' over-willingness to oblige marketers with their goals of achieving short-term profits at the cost of their own wellbeing is much harder to understand. A recognition of the extreme power of the situation, illustrated by the experiments conducted by Milgram (1974) and the Stanford Prison experiment conducted by Zimbardo (Zimbardo 1974, Zimbardo, Musen, Stanford Instructional Television Network, and Insight Media 2004), allows an understanding of this paradox. The constant bombardment of messages advocating hedonism that surround the consumer could be the cause of their suppressing their unconscious, adaptive goals and pursuing the goals that salespeople, advertisers, and retail displays advocate.

Wilson (2002) suggests that although a greater willingness to go with one's unconscious, not to suppress these desires, will often prove to be adaptive, people tend to lean towards suppressing their unconscious. In other words, he suggests that controlling the unconscious is seen as good when in fact it is not. This is quite a provocative observation, because psychological control has been identified as an important contributor to human wellbeing (Taylor 1989). Could it be that while perceived control feels good, like a good mood does, at times it does interfere with psychological wellbeing by blocking the pursuit of more adaptive goals? Clearly, this is a question that requires investigation and greater understanding.

The adaptive value of unconscious goals is based on the assumption that they are rooted in learning and social connectedness goals. This is more likely to be true for some people than for others. It is likely to be truer for people with a future time orientation than it is for people with a present time orientation. It is likely to be truer for people who readily identify their actions than it is for people who do not readily identify their actions. While attempting to clarify the question of whether or not controlling one's unconscious desires is maladaptive, it is important to separate out, on the basis of these and other individual differences, those who are more or less inclined to have an adaptive unconscious.

With salespeople too, for those who have a future time orientation and/or a high level of action identification, there is a greater likelihood that their unconscious is driven, adaptively, by learning and relationship goals. Consider this example. A new car salesperson, five days after delivering a car to a customer, receives a phone call from him asking her to take the car back. The customer says that the new car, during a long drive to another town, unexpectedly stopped. The AAA tow truck driver diagnosed the problem to be a malfunctioning computer. Management policy, since the car in five days moves from being new to used (market values of a used car are considerably lower than that of a new car), is to replace the defective part, not the whole car. If this new car salesperson is future time-oriented and able to identify actions, her unconsciousness desire is likely to be to find a way to take the car back and replace it with a new one. If she is present time-oriented and unable to identify actions, her unconscious desire is likely to be far more rooted in the fact that the sales transaction was completed five days ago and the customer moved from a buyer to an owner.

The future-oriented, action-identifying salesperson should find it significantly harder to adhere to management policy. It may result in this salesperson behaving in ways that angers management, going to bat for the customer with management rather than protecting the organization, and while this may serve the customer well it may result in the salesperson's getting fired, then or soon afterwards. This would apparently suggest that the learning and relationship focus of salespeople is maladaptive, even if it is adaptive for customers. Not so, if one takes a long view or identifies the firing more broadly. The fired salesperson would leave with a reputation of integrity rare among car salespeople, and she may get great customer testimonials, all of which in the long run would serve to ensure greater career success than would keeping one's job while acting against one's better judgement.

All in all, research on the unconscious raises a large number of questions that have the potential to clarify what enables salespeople to better read their customers and, as a consequence, better enhance their subjective wellbeing.

15.8 SUMMARIZING THE BROADER ARGUMENT

I have suggested that salespeople can build better relationships with their customers, both consumers and industrial buyers, by going beyond their stated needs. The needs both types of customers are prone to state relate to hedonistic goals or short-term quick fixes of problems. The underlying needs of customers are to improve their relationships with other people and to learn and grow as individuals. These needs are often unstated, either because customers subscribe to the prevalent hedonistic/quick fix norm or because they are unaware of their own needs, and salespeople are left with very little by which to identify their customers' true needs. Research on unconscious goals suggests that a contradiction between stated needs and behavior is a cue that can be used to gauge true needs. Research that argues that relationship management skills are more important for selling success than closing skills suggests that relationship-oriented salespeople are likely to be better at identifying underlying, non-hedonistic needs. Augmenting this research is the identification in psychology of individual differences in a future versus present time orientation, and focusing on the action alone versus identifying the underlying purpose of the action. Those high in action identification and with a future time horizon are more likely, it seems, to read unstated, unaware underlying goals and cater to them.

15.9 RESEARCHING THIS ARGUMENT

At its core, my argument has been that effective salespeople make their customers happy in the long run. Prior to evaluating customer happiness and correlating it with salesperson characteristics such as action identification, it may be instructive to compare salespeople working for organizations with a more happy culture with salespeople working for organizations with a less happy culture. A stringent test would be to pick Fortune Magazine's best 100 companies to work for and compare salespeople working for one of the companies ranked from 1 to 25 with salespeople working for one of the companies ranked from 76 to 100 (Fortune 2009). Illustratively, General Mills with 1,200 salespeople in the U.S. (SellingPower 2008) is ranked 99 in the best companies to work for and Edward Jones with 10,532 salespeople in the U.S. (SellingPower 2008) is ranked 2. Are salespeople who work for Edward Jones in general less hedonistic in their personal pursuits, more inclined towards action identification, and more future-oriented? Or, making the test more stringent, does a comparison of salespeople working for Whole Foods

Market (ranked 22) with those working for Marriott International (ranked 78) reveal these differences? Alternatively, rather than picking organizational happiness in general as a basis for comparison, a more specific criterion such as avoiding or engaging in corporate layoffs could be used. Aflac has never had a corporate layoff. Its salespeople could be compared with salespeople in a company that has had a modest amount of layoffs and with salespeople in a company that has had severe layoffs. Is there a systematic increase in hedonistic values and a present rather than a future orientation? The potential benefit of such a starting point for investigating the relationship between customer happiness and salesperson effectiveness is that the cause of the problem is less likely to be misattributed to aberrant individual salespeople! Ignoring the corporate context in which salespeople work may lead to this misattribution.

If it turns out that companies judged by how happy their employees are or how little they resort to layoffs are better at fostering an emphasis on selling wellbeing, it would strengthen the argument made in this chapter that hiring, training, and supervising salespeople based on (1) an interest in pursuing learning and related-ness rather than performance goals, (2) possessing the proclivity to identify actions and be future-oriented, (3) a skill at guessing unstated needs, and (4) trusting one's own instincts is superior. Of course, such a focus is not as yet the convention— although learning goals and learning organizations have, arguably, been considered superior by some. It would require a significant change in the way job interviews are conducted and it would require a shift away from hiring from "higher-IQ" colleges and universities to colleges and universities known for other strengths, such as making their students happy.

15.10 In Conclusion

If the purpose of selling is to enhance the personal happiness of customers, not short-lived but long-term happiness, then guileful salespeople who persuasively close the sale of hedonistic or quick-fix products do not do an economy good. Illustrating this is a statement by Prime Minister Jigme Thinley of Bhutan, a tiny country in the Himalayan mountains north of India: "Greed, insatiable human greed, is the cause of human catastrophe in the world." Under a new constitution, the government of this nation is not judged by the economic benefits it provides but by its pursuit of gross national happiness. Illustratively, one yardstick is how much time a person spends with his or her family—a relatedness goal. Another is how frequently an individual feels jealous (a minus) and how frequently an individual feels generous (a plus)—both constitute learning greater self-regulation

(Mydans 2009). At least one country has defined national goals away from hedonism towards relatedness and learning, and sees this as a route to improving the wellbeing of its constituents. The thesis that personal selling, a highly prevalent and impactful method in the United States for communicating to consumers and industrial buyers, is good when relatedness and learning goals are catered to has been adopted in at least one culture.

Within the US, this thesis has been advocated in the popular press. Spencer Johnson and Larry Wilson (1986) advocate selling with the purpose of making customers feel pleased; in effect, they advocate that salespeople be high on action identification and cater to customers' personal happiness. They say this leads to invaluable referrals. That is, they recognize the long-term benefits in terms of customer loyalty but suggest that in addition there are short-term benefits. Salespeople who make their customers happy make themselves happy by easing the work they have to do in generating high-probability leads.

The alternative view—that not all selling is relationship- or learning-driven, that there are plenty of situations in which hedonism ought to be the goal—is not easily discounted. The alternative view does not suggest that promoting customer happiness ought not to be an important goal of selling; rather, it suggests that views expressed in this chapter ought to have limited application. This may indeed be true, but the more the limits to this application, the more likely is it that developed countries like the United States will continue to find a large separation between economic and psychological growth.

REFERENCES

BELK, R. W. (1985). "Materialism: Trait Aspects of Living in the Material World," *Journal of Consumer Research* 12.3, 265–80.

BOYD, J. N., and P. G. ZIMBARDO (2005). "Time Perspective, Health, and Risk Taking," in A. Strathman and J. Joireman (eds.), *Understanding Behavior in the Context of Time: Theory, Research, and Application*, Mahwah, NJ: Erlbaum.

CHRISTOPHER, C. (2008). "A Hedonist's Reckoning," *Financial Times* (31 October): 7. This article can also be found at: http://us.ft.com/ftgateway/superpage.ft?news_id=fto103120 081426409516

CIALDINI, R. B. (1993). *Influence: Science and Practice*, 3rd edn, New York: HarperCollins.

——(1999). "Of Tricks and Tumors: Some Little-Recognized Costs of Dishonest Use of Effective Social Influence," *Psychology & Marketing* 16.2, 91–8.

CRON, W. L., and T. E. DeCARLO (2006). *Dalrymple's Sales Management: Concepts and Cases*, 9th edn, New York: Wiley.

CSIKSZENTMIHALYI, M., and E. ROCHBERG-HALTON (1981). *The Meaning of Things: Domestic Symbols and the Self*. Cambridge: Cambridge University Press.

DIENER, E. (2000). "Subjective Well-Being: The Science of Happiness and a Proposal for a National Index," *American Psychologist* 55.1, 34–43.

FORTUNE (2009). "100 Best Companies to Work For," available at http://money.cnn.com/magazines/fortune/bestcompanies/2009/

JOHNSON, S., and L. WILSON (1986). *The One Minute Sales Person*. Glasgow: Collins.

KASSER, T. (2002). *The High Price of Materialism*. Cambridge, MA: MIT Press.

KUBEY, R. W., and M. CSIKSZENTMIHALYI (1990). *Television and the Quality of Life: How Viewing Shapes Everyday Experience*. Hillsdale, NJ: Erlbaum.

LEIGH, T. W., and J. O. SUMMERS (2002). "An Initial Evaluation of Industrial Buyers' Impressions of Salespersons' Nonverbal Cues," *Journal of Personal Selling & Sales Management* 22.1, 41–53.

MAYER, D., and H. M. GREENBERG (2006). "What Makes a Good Salesman," *Harvard Business Review* 84.7–8, 164.

MILGRAM, S. (1974). *Obedience to Authority: An Experimental View*, New York: Harper & Row.

MYDANS, S. (2009). "Recalculating Happiness in a Himalayan Kingdom," *New York Times* 48 (May 7), A8.

MYERS, D. G. (2000). "The Funds, Friends, and Faith of Happy People," *American Psychologist* 55.1, 56–67.

RACKHAM, N. (1988). *Spin Selling: Situation, Problem, Implication, Need-Payoff*. New York: McGraw-Hill.

RICHINS, M. L., and S. DAWSON (1992). "A Consumer Values Orientation for Materialism and Its Measurement: Scale Development and Validation," *Journal of Consumer Research* 19.3, 303–16.

ROBINSON, J. P., and G. GODBEY (1999). *Time for Life: The Surprising Ways Americans Use Their Time*, 2nd edn, University Park, PA: Pennsylvania State University Press.

SCHANK, R. C., and R. P. ABELSON (1977). *Scripts, Plans, Goals, and Understanding: An Inquiry into Human Knowledge Structures*. Hillsdale, NJ: Erlbaum.

SELLINGPOWER (2008). "America's 500 Largest Sales Forces," in *Selling Power*, Fredricksburg, VA: Personal Selling Power, 51–68.

SNYDER, M., and K. G. DEBONO (1985). "Appeals to Image and Claims About Quality: Understanding the Psychology of Advertising," *Journal of Personality & Social Psychology* 49.3, 586–97.

SUJAN, H., B. A. WEITZ, and N. KUMAR (1994). "Learning, Orientation, Working Smart, and Effective Selling," *Journal of Marketing* 58.3, 39–52.

TAYLOR, S. E. (1989). *Positive Illusions: Creative Self-Deception and the Healthy Mind*, New York: Basic Books.

U.S. CENSUS BUREAU (2000). "Census 2000 Summary," available at http://factfinder.census.gov/servlet/QTTable?_bm=y&-geo_id=01000US&-qr_name=DEC_2000_SF3_U_QTP27&-ds_name=DEC_2000_SF3_U&-_lang=en&-redoLog=false&-_sse=on

VALLACHER, R. R., and D. M. WEGNER (1989). "Levels of Personal Agency: Individual Variation in Action Identification," *Journal of Personality and Social Psychology* 57 (October), 660–71.

———(2000). "What Do People Think They Are Doing? Action Identification and Human Behavior," in E. Tory Higgins and Arie W. Kruglanski (eds.), *Motivational Science: Social and Personality Perspectives*, New York: Psychology Press, 215–28.

VANDEWALLE, D., S. P. BROWN, W. L. CRON, and J. W. SLOCUM (1999). "The Influence of Goal Orientation and Self-Regulation Tactics on Sales Performance: A Longitudinal Field Test," *Journal of Applied Psychology* 84.2, 249.

WEITZ, B. A., and K. D. BRADFORD (1999). "Personal Selling and Sales Management: A Relationship Marketing Perspective," *Academy of Marketing Science Journal*, 27.2, 241–54.

——H. SUJAN, and M. SUJAN (1986). "Knowledge, Motivation, and Adaptive Behavior: A Framework for Improving Selling Effectiveness," *Journal of Marketing* 50.4, 174–91.

WILSON, T. D. (2002). *Strangers to Ourselves: Discovering the Adaptive Unconscious*. Cambridge, MA: Belknap Press of Harvard University Press.

WOOD, J. A. (2006). "Nlp Revisited: Nonverbal Communications and Signals of Trustworthiness," *Journal of Personal Selling & Sales Management* 26.2, 197.

ZIMBARDO, P. G. (1974). "On 'Obedience to Authority,'" *American Psychologist* 29.7, 566–7.

——and J. N. BOYD (1999). "Putting Time in Perspective: A Valid, Reliable Individual Difference Metric," *Journal of Personality & Social Psychology*, 77 (December), 1271–88.

————(2008). *The Time Paradox: The New Psychology of Time That Will Change Your Life*, New York: Free Press.

——K. MUSEN, STANFORD INSTRUCTIONAL TELEVISION NETWORK, and INSIGHT MEDIA (2004). *Quiet Rage: The Stanford Prison Study*, Palo Alto, CA: Stanford Instructional Television Network.

ZOLTNERS, A. A., P. SINHA, and S. E. LORIMER (2008). "Sales Force Effectiveness: A Framework for Researchers and Practitioners," *Journal of Personal Selling & Sales Management* 28.2, 115–31.

CHAPTER 16

SALES TECHNOLOGY

GARY K. HUNTER

16.1 INTRODUCTION

Business-to-business (B2B) exchange has long been a fundamental driver of economic growth and a focal point of marketing and sales scholarship. As an economic catalyst, great importance rests in efficient and effective networks among business sellers and their customers. Spanning boundaries between sellers and buyers, according to the US Bureau of Labor Statistics, in the United States alone, over 16 million people—more than 11% of those employed—worked in 'sales or related' jobs in 2008. Of course, global expenditures are multiples of these US-based figures. Not only do sales force investments constitute a healthy portion of economic spending, exceeding US$ 800 billion, sales costs are among the most dominant line items for the firm, representing as much as 40 per cent of revenues (Zoltners, Sinha, and Lorimer 2009). These realities signal the high priority that executives place upon the sales function.

While the term 'marketing' conjures up notions of advertising for the layperson, in aggregate US companies invest almost three times as much in their sales forces as they do on advertising (Zoltners, Sinha, and Lorimer 2009). While a significant portion of those expenditures represent compensation, much is spent on information technology (IT) tools (hardware, software, and systems) and the training and support they need. For example, estimates of 2008 spending on customer relationship management (CRM) software (which includes sales, customer service, and marketing applications) exceeded $US12 billion. Yet publications centred on sales research in premier marketing journals have declined significantly over the past two decades (Williams and Plouffe 2007). With the rapid pace and ongoing diffusion of complex and costly technologies and their accompanying transformational effects on sales strategy, process, and people, more research on IT and the sales function is warranted.

There is continuing debate in both the academic literature and business practice over what or how this domain of inquiry should be referenced. How those differences are resolved remains open for the research and discourse that will follow in the years ahead. For clarification, this chapter uses the term "sales technology" as an umbrella term under which the interrelationships among sales strategy, sales processes, salespeople, and information technology are explored. More formally stated, "sales technology" (ST) refers to information technologies that can facilitate or enable the performance of sales tasks (Hunter and Perreault 2007).

ST includes sales-based CRM and sales force automation (SFA) applications. This use is consistent with other scholarly contributions to the present-day resurgence of this stream of research (Ingram, LaForge, and Leigh 2002, LaPlaca 2005, Schillewaert, Ahearne, Frambach, and Moenaert 2005, Hunter and Perreault 2006, Jelinek, Ahearne, Mathieu, and Schillewaert 2006, Bush, Bush, Orr, and Rocco 2007, Hunter and Perreault 2007, Mathieu, Ahearne, and Taylor 2007, Ahearne, Jones, Rapp, and Mathieu 2008, Rapp, Agnihotri, and Forbes 2008).

Of course, ST management has gone far beyond buying the latest technological innovation and putting it on laptops for sales reps to use. Many firms have organized ST departments, appointed ST general managers, developed ST training programs, formed alliances with ST software vendors, and hired reps with different skills than those sought in contexts better characterized as "low-tech," transaction-based selling. Simply put, ST is having a dramatic impact on personal selling and sales management.

This chapter reviews the current literature on ST and discusses some opportunities for future research. The chapter highlights issues related to the dynamic nature of ST and its pervasive influence on the firm, and argues that the topic warrants more attention from both scholars and managers.

16.2 Defining Sales Technology and its Relationship to CRM and SFA Technologies

This section discusses ST relationship with to two relevant concepts used in both marketing scholarship and practice—namely, sales force automation (SFA) and customer relationship management (CRM).

16.2.1 Defining Sales Technology

"Sales technology" refers to information technologies that can facilitate or enable the performance of sales tasks (Hunter and Perreault 2007). To elaborate, essential work refers to "all the tasks that a company must perform to meet the needs of its customers and prospects" (Zoltners, Sinha, and Zoltners 2001). As such, sales tasks are the essential work expected from direct and indirect sales forces. These tasks include interest creation, pre-purchase information sharing, proposing solutions, cooperative or competitive inter-firm negotiations, and post-purchase relationship management. Information technology can facilitate (make easier) or enable (make possible or practical) many of these sales tasks.

Inevitably, ST affects sales tasks in different ways, including some that may result in sustainable competitive advantage. Thus, it is not surprising that sales organizations continue to invest in and explore new ways to leverage sales technology. It is worth noting that SFA and CRM software represent only a portion of a firm's ST portfolio. A firm's ST portfolio is defined here, as implied elsewhere, as all the information technologies associated with implementing, evaluating, and controlling a firm's selling effort. As such, ST includes mobile hardware technologies, "office suite" software, and the innovations that will inevitably follow an economic activity of such notable magnitude and influence. To elaborate, the domain of ST includes laptops, cellphones, PDA devices, word processing, spreadsheet, graphics, and database applications.

16.2.2 ST, SFA, and CRM technology

Figure 16.1 proposes a conceptualization of the relationships among three relevant domains that intersect IT with the sales function: ST, CRM, and SFA technologies. The figure is adapted from a previously published discussion (Hunter and Perreault 2007).

Despite the explicit references in early and widely cited research on CRM as a strategy or framework for business (Winer 2001), some research on CRM and relationship marketing excludes any reference to the sales function or to salespeople. This shortcoming could occur as a failure by authors either to realize or to acknowledge a role for the sales function in CRM. Some clarification in semantics may be necessary. This shortcoming may relate to the transformation of salespeople, in some industries, from roles focused on acquisition (hunters) to new roles which center more on account retention, maintenance, and business relationship management (farmers). Another alternative is that the absence of "salespeople" in recent "CRM" or relationship marketing research may result from the CRM literature's principle focus on the business-to-customer (B2C) financial services industry and an adaptation of that industry's jargon. Ironically, much of the pioneering work on relationship marketing, the basis for the CRM literature, had more focus on B2B sales contexts (Dwyer, Schurr, and Oh 1987, Sheth, Parvatiyar,

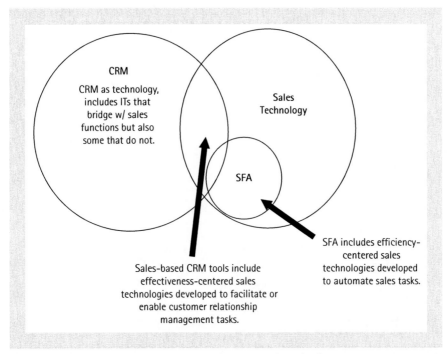

Fig. 16.1. The relationships among sales technology (ST), CRM, & SFA domains

and Roberto 1994, Parvatiyar and Sheth 2000). That is in stark contrast to managing a business relationship with a key account, as is done by B2B salespeople working with business customers.

In any case, if salespeople played no role in CRM or relationship marketing, the relationship between ST and CRM technology would best be depicted by a Venn diagram representing their mutual exclusiveness. On the other hand, in "pro-sales" research, CRM technology is referenced as if CRM applications were used exclusively by salespeople. If that were the case, the CRM technology domain would subsume the ST domain. Yet CRM technologies neither consume sales technologies nor vice versa. Instead, these two domains of technology overlap, and here's why.

16.2.3 Relationship Marketing, Customer Relationship Management, and ST

Indeed, salespeople often play a critical role in managing customer relationships (Weitz and Bradford 1999). Such sales roles occur when the sales force is employed in the firm's go-to-market strategy and charged with responsibility for achieving long-term outcomes with (key) customer accounts. The inter-firm exchanges

pursued through such buyer–seller relationships include both personal and economic dimensions whose relative importance is contingent upon several factors.
These differences in the nature of buyer–seller relationships also alter the type of ST
needed and the ultimate usefulness of any given technology.

In any case, salespeople are so prevalently involved in relationship marketing
efforts that ST vendors routinely target sales organizations with ST solutions
intended to improve the efficiency (e.g. administrative performance) and effectiveness (e.g. relationship-building performance) of the sales process. Over the past
decade, such ST tools have become both increasingly sophisticated. Getting beyond
common SFA era applications—which primarily yielded returns through efficiency
(e.g. accounts and contact management)—innovative ST applications now offer
improvement in sales effectiveness (e.g. analytics and forecasting). For example,
new analytical functionality helps salespeople develop better market knowledge
upon which they can customize better solutions for their business customers
(Ahearne, Hughes, and Schillewaert 2007, Hunter and Perreault 2007).

Collectively, changes in strategy and technology catalyzed new opportunities for
competitive advantage through superior sales force differentiation strategies (Hunter
and Perreault 2007). Concurrently, CRM emerged as both a strategy and technology
industry with a range of definitions and accompanying ambiguity (Plouffe, Williams,
and Leigh 2004, Payne and Frow 2005). In the information industry, CRM is the term
used to describe "methodologies, software, and usually Internet capabilities that help
an enterprise manage customer relationships in an organized way" (Xu, Yen, Lin, and
Chou 2002). Strategically, CRM builds on the rich foundations of scholarship on
relationship marketing (Gummesson 2008). As such, it is far more than a technology,
and, in addition to supply chain management (SCM) and product development
management, can be considered as one of three core processes that constitute the
domain of marketing (Srivastava, Shervani, and Fahey 1999). In an effort to coalesce
CRM research around a common definition, recent research states that:

CRM relates to strategy, the management of the dual creation of value, the intelligent use of
data and technology, the acquisition of customer knowledge and the diffusion of this
knowledge to the appropriate stakeholders, the development of appropriate (long-term)
relationships with specific customers and/or customer groups, and the integration of
processes across the many areas of the firm and across the network of firms that collaborate
to generate customer value. (Boulding, Staelin, Ehret, and Johnston 2005: 157)

Thus, in essence, most scholars would agree that CRM is an organization-wide
strategy centering on customers in which technologies play an important role
(Landry, Arnold, and Arndt 2005). Whether one quibbles over definitions or not,
the undeniable reality of CRM is that salespeople are typically involved in the
strategy (relationship marketing). Moreover, salespeople use IT (sales-based CRM
and others) to help identify, develop, propose, or carry out relational objectives.
These evolutionary changes make the interrelationships between salespeople,

information technology, and sales processes central to any CRM strategy that involves the sales function as a go-to-market participant. CRM strategy can be decomposed into stages ranging from imitation to maintenance to termination (Reinartz, Krafft, and Hoyer 2004). Recent research found that ST tools have different effects on different stages constituting a customer relationship that occurs through different mediation mechanisms (Moutot and Bascoul 2008).

Such strategies include person-to-person interactions centered on resolving the inevitable conflicts of interests that exist between sellers and buyers. This relationship marketing evolution is evidenced by many firms referring to salespeople with titles such as "relationship managers," "account managers," or "customer business development (CBD) representatives." It is worth noting that these title changes often reflect real changes in the roles salespeople perform. Also, the types of sellers represent products ranging from goods to services to experiences, and so on.

Most notably, the nature of selling shifted from mainly "pushing products" (such as goods or services) that optimize returns on transactions (transactional selling) to proposing integrative solutions that help build long-term mutually beneficial business relationships (relational selling). Concurrently, there has been a shift stressing the use of high-tech, knowledge-leveraging innovations over low-tech, persuasive selling tactics.

Thus, many CRM software solutions are designed for use by "salespeople" and can be referred to as sales-based CRM technologies (Hunter and Perreault 2007). Some CRM technologies are sales technologies, yet others are intended as solutions which facilitate, enable, or automate tasks assigned to marketing or customer service roles. Still others help organizations, who from an evolutionary economics perspective should employ excellent process thinking skills to avoid the doom of selection-on-selection market processes (Dickson, Lassar, Hunter, and Chakravorti 2009). Moreover, this process thinking should occur *before* deciding between purchasing commercially available ST and developing proprietary applications customized to support idiosyncratic sales processes.

16.2.4 Technology "Automates" Tasks

Many consider SFA technologies as forerunners to CRM technologies, leading many ST experts to consider the CRM technology industry as an outgrowth of the SFA industry (Chen and Popovich 2003). Yet "automation" is an old term, and thus has an established literature that intersects many social and natural science disciplines. Many claim Del S. Harder of the Ford Motor Company first used the term in 1946, more than a half-century ago. Harder defined automation as a "new word denoting both automatic operation and the process of making things automatic" (Diebold 1952). Generally, the term "automation" refers to this established meaning in both the extant social sciences literature and long-standing business practice.

In general, today, social scientists define automation as "the execution by a machine agent (usually a computer) of a function that was previously carried out by a human" (Parasuraman and Riley 1997). Consistent with this widely held understanding of automation, some sales scholarship adopts the notion for SFA by noting that "automation typically focuses on facilitating tasks that salespeople previously handled in other ways" (Hunter, Perreault, and Armstrong 1998). Additionally, seminal social science research notes the "ironies of automation" that have befuddled researchers and industries for years by three realities associated with automating (using a technology to complete an existing task). Specifically, it is ironic that in automating tasks, one (a) does not necessarily remove its difficulties, (b) may introduce new difficulties, and (c) may induce a need for even greater technological ingenuity to resolve newly created difficulties (Bainbridge 1983).

Understandably, sales scholars may misuse the term "automation" as many SFA vendors use the term to refer to ST tools which never had the potential to displace a salesperson's completion of an existing task. Yet it is not used with a universal meaning in either industry or academic research. In sales research, the rationale for SFA is that "some sales tasks can be done more quickly, cheaply, or effectively through the application of information technology" (Hunter et al. 1998). The idea behind SFA is that by doing administrative tasks more quickly, one improves the ratio of time spent selling to time spent on non-selling tasks.

Indeed, a contact management application simply automates the task of managing contacts. On the other hand, an analytical sales-based CRM application that estimates marketing mix outcomes subject to inputs and interpretations by the salesperson enables use of more sophisticated algorithms which form the basis of solutions customized to the customers' markets. Thus, in a relationship marketing context, the technology enables the salesperson to develop and propose integrative solutions that help build better relationships with her customers (Hunter and Perreault 2007).

16.2.5 Some Firms "Make" Their Own ST Tools

Yet technology can facilitate or enable "selling" tasks—and both SFA and sales organizations realized that soon after the automation era began. For example, multinational enterprise (MNE) sellers faced classic "make or buy" alternatives associated with investments in ST. By the early 1990s, firms like P&G, who had significant enough economies of scale to "make" proprietary ST solutions, organized internal "sales technology" departments. These ST departments worked across key account teams of the global sales organizations to find new ways to employ information technology to improve the efficiency of administrative tasks and the overall effectiveness of their relationship marketing efforts. Software prototypes were developed by studying "best practices" across key account sales teams. The ST department then developed software prototypes to demonstrate its intended functionality. IT specialists then worked to ensure computer programmers developed software consistent with the specifications and desires of the sales force managers. Subsequently, or perhaps concurrently, SFA vendors worked to develop technology solutions for similar purposes. Other similar processes for developing proprietary ST applications are still being used in the consumer packaged goods industries, among others.

16.2.6 Sales Technology Goes Beyond Automating Tasks

Simply put, these evolutions in both academic ideals and practical use reflect efforts to use technology in ways that go beyond the concept of "automation." Clearly, many technological innovations, particularly during more recent years, were developed to *enable new* tasks (Hunter et al. 1998)—and not just to automate existing (old) tasks. Thus, the use of the term "sales automation" captures neither the intent nor their true capability. To elaborate, the intent is not to displace a person's performance of a task with a technology. Likewise, some ST innovations are designed to add organizational capability by centering on ways to make salespeople more effective by enabling the performance of new tasks, and are not limited to automating existing tasks.

16.3 A STRATEGIC PERSPECTIVE ON SALES TECHNOLOGY AND COMPETITIVE ADVANTAGE

This section discusses a strategic conceptualization of ST from the perspective of the selling firm.

16.3.1 Sales Technology and Competitive Advantage: "Lengthening the Spear"

In the military sense, technology is the application of science to war. However, even before the expansion of science in early modern times, man coupled deduction with intuition to produce weapons. The idea that drove the Macedonians to lengthen the spear was impelled by the same spirit that produced the nuclear weapon: the desire to gain advantage over one's opponent. (Greiss 1984: 14)

The annals of military history evidence the importance of technological superiority, and chronicle the natural pursuit of competitive advantage through achieving it.

While the stakes of ignoring technology in warfare far exceed those associated with a similar ignorance in business (sales) practice, technological superiority plays a role in deciding the eventual winners and losers in economic competition.

Yet, while most recognize the importance of ST, many sales managers continue to struggle with how best to use technology to improve the efficiency and effectiveness of their sales efforts. This is reasonable, as ST is both a complex and costly consideration for which no universal solution exists. Specially, contingency theory suggests that use of a technology varies across contexts.

Nonetheless, just as modern salespeople customize and tailor solutions to meet the differing needs of business customers (Tuli, Kohli, and Bharadwaj 2007), so too must sales managers customize their ST portfolios. That customization spawns new ST training programs and needs for ST support. Beyond decisions about ideal portfolios, salespeople themselves must decide which technologies to employ, in what manner they will employ them, and to what extent ST use is helpful to achieving their desired objectives. Managers need better understanding of the contingent factors associated with ST and its interrelationships with sales strategy, sales processes, and salespeople across a much broader range of sales contexts.

16.3.2 ST as a Replacement for a Sales Force: Fully Automating Sales Tasks

Some organizations use a portfolio of technologies to connect their selling function, or elements of it, to its buying organizations. In these cases, there is no reliance on person-to-person communications between buyers and sellers, as a technology interface conducts exchanges—as is the case with online reverse auctions (Jap 2003). Such uses of information technology represent a strategic decision to "automate" fully the sales role by displacing salespeople with technology. For some accounts, this is both viable and ideal strategy, as the costs of such systems may be less than the people-dependent alternative. With people-dependent solutions, managers should consider value added from staffing, supporting, and equipping the sales force with a prospective portfolio of ST tools. Moving along the continuum between a fully automated sales force and one that performs independent of ST, a seller may either automate some tasks across all accounts (full task automation) or automate selected tasks across selected accounts (selected task automation).

16.3.3 ST as an Aid to Adding Value in Collaborative Relationships

Value remains a dominant strategic concern in assessing whether automated sales systems are better alternatives than those which integrate technology with salespeople and sales processes. Sales managers should consider whether salespeople can add value to exchange processes beyond the capabilities of a technology-only (fully automated) buyer–seller boundary. Simply put, when salespeople add no value beyond an automated process, automation makes sense.

In essence, human intelligence or "insight" represents a principal ingredient of value that salespeople afford. That value is delivered within new sales roles in which salespeople need to be embedded in both their firms' and their customers' organizations (Bradford et al. 2010). The current era may be best characterized as one in which B2B salespeople add value to exchanges by transitioning from experts to advisers in collaborative relationships (Sheth and Sobel 2002). Buyers expect solutions to combine goods and services tailored to their specific needs (Tuli et al. 2007). The provision of successful integrative solutions by the salesperson to the buying organization can be improved through the salesperson's use of analytical ST applications (Hunter and Perreault 2007). In this context, salespeople must establish trust through value and loyalty in the relationship exchanges (Sirdeshmukh, Singh, and Sabol 2002) with business buyers—and when buyers agree to the salesperson's proposals, the value provided in those solutions are tested over time.

ST can help salespeople provide better solutions, and the extant research proposes mechanisms through which that may occur. In fact, the extant ST research centers on the antecedents and consequences of ST use.

16.3.4 Sales Technologies Used by Salespeople as a Means for Competitive Advantage

The customer-relating, or customer-linking, capability associated with effective outside-in processes (Day 1994) should be a focal point for firms who seek competitive advantage through integrating ST. Selling firms need to align performance metrics, incentives, structures, and processes to improve their customer relating capability. Yet, instead of considering sales processes first, as proposed in the ST literature (Hunter and Perreault 2007), most firms react to market pressures and think first about information technology (Day 2003). This is suboptimal and costly.

When firms seek to integrate ST with sales processes and salespeople to pursue their sales strategy (Zablah, Bellenger, and Johnston 2004), IT does not displace salespeople, but instead supports salespeople in their performance of assigned sales tasks. Importantly, firms should assess the costs and benefits of ST solutions. By projecting the potential of individual or a portfolio of sales technologies, sales executives can implement STs that go beyond facilitating essential tasks (automation) to enabling accomplishment of new tasks (Hunter 1999, Hunter and Perreault 2006, 2007).

Process thinking skill refers to one's ability to think broadly, deeply, and creatively about selecting, configuring, and implementing superior processes and the ability to lead the implementation (Dickson et al. 2009). Technology can have the opposite of its intended effects if it is applied to poorly designed processes—as it can amplify and accelerate adverse effects. Thus, after applying excellent process thinking skills, managers should consider (a) whether IT solutions already exist, (b) which combinations of ST and salespeople best accomplish the essential work at hand, (c) whether partnering with an ST vendor is desirable, and (d) the potential merit of outsourcing the development of ST tools. In essence, the objective is to design solutions that combine sales-services and product offerings (goods or services) to develop solutions tailored to each business buyer's strategy. When such sales-services are notably unique from those offered by competitor(s), the sales strategy of differentiation is referred to as a "sales-service differentiation strategy" (Hunter and Perreault 2007).

16.3.5 ST from a Sales Management Perspective

At an aggregate level, from a sales management perspective, the impact of technology has been a double-edged sword. On the one hand, the development of information technologies has automated many tasks that previously were handled, at least primarily, by a salesperson. Today, these tasks may be managed through an online marketplace or handled by a customer service call center, each differentiated by the value they afford. For example, the skills needed by call center reps may be significantly different from the analytical demands placed upon a sales team dedicated to a key account.

Thus, for many key account relationships, information technology enables salespeople to do things that in the past were slow, difficult, or impossible to accomplish. For example, salespeople in such roles often use sophisticated demand forecasting algorithms (akin to those found in the marketing science literature) made possible through technology applications that simplify inputs and interpreting outputs. Even a decade or so ago, few sales managers would imagine a sales force comprising individuals who could both estimate such sophisticated models and, in turn, communicate their forecasts well enough to persuade buyers to adopt and implement the integrative solutions represented as outputs of such analytical, technology-dependent sales processes.

16.3.6 The Pervasive Effects of ST Throughout Determinants of Sales Performance

Meta-analytic studies on salesperson performance and satisfaction (Churchill, Ford, Hartley, and Walker 1985, Brown and Peterson 1993) pre-date much of the research on ST. Thus, little is understood about the pervasive effects of ST on salespeople, sales processes, salesperson performance and satisfaction. Yet it makes sense to use proven frameworks to better understand ST, as here. Specifically, there is growing consensus that sales performance is determined by five categories of variables: (1) role, (2) aptitude, (3) skill level, (4) motivation, and (5) personal, organizational, and environmental factors (Hutt and Walker 2006).

Several factors affect the capacity of ST to yield returns on investment, including salesperson skills and abilities, sales organization objectives, the nature of the buyer–seller relationship, the fit between ST and sales tasks, and ST competitive intensity. Thus, each sales industry, organization, role, and even salesperson has different needs for the types of ST most suited to its needs. As such, there exists substantial variance in types of ST adopted, the extent of use by salespeople within an organization, the final acceptance of ST types by salespeople, and the types of returns they afford. So, it is well understood, following Stephen Roach's findings, that investments in ITs do not necessarily lead to improvements in productivity—which has been dubbed the IT productivity paradox (Lucas 1999). Similarly, investments in ST yield variable returns that are difficult to predict prior to implementation or to ascertain in post-implementation phases. This also helps explain why the manner in which salespeople use a sales technology portfolio matters in relation to antecedents, mediation mechanisms, and ultimate outcomes (Hunter and Perreault 2007).

Essentially, the extant research has not fully explained how ST affects sales performance and satisfaction across conditions, industries, salesperson characteristics, sales processes, and so on. Moreover, these issues have not been resolved in practice, as most sales executives report dissatisfaction with their investments in ST investments. There is simply far more heterogeneity in sales processes, strategies, tactics, organizational designs, salesperson characteristics, and STs that have not been adequately addressed by the extant literature.

16.4 Equipping, Training, Supporting, and Motivating Salespeople to Adopt STs

This section discusses the ST industry and how its offerings, or proprietary ST innovations, influence sales management decisions on how best to equip, train, and support their sales forces with ST tools. Additionally, this section discusses how STs may influence the salesperson motivation.

16.4.1 The ST Industry

Forrester Research estimates that 2010 worldwide CRM spending will exceed $US11 billion (Band et al. 2008). Additionally, firms spend three times the costs of CRM software on the integration, support, and maintenance that accompanies it (Ang and Buttle 2006). Commercial software products that are designed as "one size fits all" standardizations of sales processes may only help sales forces meet the competitive imperatives associated with the aforementioned escalations in their customers' escalating expectations for ST use. Some commercial products can be customized for firm-specific applications, but the nature of software development is to gain economies of scale by selling similar solutions to multiple buyers. Thus, to get a truly customer ST solution, some firms develop proprietary applications. The actual size of the ST market is likely a multiple of the above estimates.

16.4.2 Interfirm and Intrafirm (Cross-functional) STs

The impact of ST on selling has been more far-reaching than the simple effects associated with a firm's decision to adopt new commercial software. For example, Electronic Data Interchange (EDI), Enterprise Resource Planning (ERP), Electronic Markets (EMs), Online Marketplaces, Local Access Networks (LANs), and Advanced Planning and Scheduling (APS) may be more hardware-intensive than they are software-dependent. Such technologies may have less to do with *directly* influencing the ways and means salespeople accomplish their tasks. They are also underrepresented in the extant literature, and relevant to strategic ST decision-making concerns related to automation decisions.

These information technology infrastructures serve as necessary support for salespeople in managing relationships with key accounts that often generate multi-million- (or even billion-)dollar annual revenue streams. Such accounts are often represented by an account team of salespeople who negotiate collaborative deals with buying centers. While a fundamental understanding of major factors in the procurement process is essential for key account salespeople (Hunter, Bunn, and Perreault 2006), interfirm STs can improve the efficiency and effectiveness of the exchange process.

In view of the scope and capacity of interfirm technologies to create economic worth, it is not surprising that this field is dynamic and continues to spawn needs for more academic research and better management understanding. Firms and scholars continue their quest to find new ways to employ ITs to improve supply chain management capabilities (Wu, Yeniyurt, Kim, and Cavusgil 2006). For example, private EDI systems are being displaced by Internet Electronic Markets (EMs) to reduce distribution costs (Yao, Dresner, and Palmer 2009). As information sharing has been shown to improve a B2B salesperson's ability to develop better relationships with customer accounts (Hunter and Perreault 2007), ERP systems may improve the efficiency through which such information sharing occurs (Bendoly, Rosenzweig, and Stratman 2009). Some sharing becomes automated, while other information sharing is conducted primarily through social discourse.

Among other functions, some STs integrate sales force functionality across individual applications (e.g. APS software often includes a contact management application). Others may provide operational linkages (e.g. Extranets can link users across firms). Finally, some provide the information inputs required for analytical sales processes (e.g. UPC scanners generate retailer POP data that is often used by manufacturers' key account teams). There are well-documented cost advantages of a coordinated sales forecasting and production planning process over the obsolete silo-based approach through the reductions in the so-called "bullwhip effect" in supply chains (Lee, Padmanabhan, and Wang 1997). ST systems may be used to automate and improve such cross-functional coordination tasks.

16.4.3 An Ever-Expanding Set of ST Choices for Sales Organizations

The wide range of information technology solutions—and differentiated offerings from ST providers—add complexity to ST purchase decisions and scholarship. In either the "make" or "buy" conditions, ST solutions are often very expensive. The logic of ST is that salespeople can employ IT to more efficiently or effectively meet their business customers' needs. While the logic is simple, ST garners scholarly and managerial attention as a complex, costly, and strategically important business concern (Hunter and Perreault 2007). ST research needs both broader and deeper, theoretically and empirically driven insights across a range of selling contexts, as the extant literature focuses primarily on consumer goods and pharmaceutical industries. And there are stark differences both within and across industries that are driven, in part, by role assignments. Variation in contexts alters the essential work demanded and therefore alters the nature and usefulness of different ST solutions.

16.4.4 Extensive Costs of ST Portfolios

ST software implementations often require investments in hardware, training, and support which are even more costly for proprietary applications than for commercial offerings. While sales managers arm salespeople with SFA and CRM software applications, there is a host of other commonly used software programs used by sales organizations. These include spreadsheet (Excel), presentation (PowerPoint), word processing, database (Access), and statistical estimation (SPSS) applications. Additionally, hardware STs go well beyond a "PC for every rep", as the hardware infrastructure (e.g. servers) needed by enterprise applications can be quite extensive. Finally, today's salespeople are mobile warriors with technologies ranging from telecommunications devices like cell phones and personal digital assistants (e.g. BlackBerrys or Palms) to home office equipment such as laser printers and facsimile machines (Hunter 1999).

16.4.5 Motivating Salespeople to Use ST: Effective Training, Post-Adoption Support, and Buyer Encouragement

The adoption issue has primarily been reduced to the factors Rogers highlighted as those which accelerate the adoption of innovations (Hunter 1999). The technology acceptance model (Davis 1989) and its successor (Venkatesh and Davis 2000) draws on Rogers' logic and frames consistently with the theory of reasoned action (TRA). These models have been widely used in both sales (Jones, Sundaram, and Wynne 2002, Avlonitis and Panagopoulos 2005, Robinson, Marshall, and Stamps 2005a, 2005b) and non-sales settings (Legris, Ingham, and Collerette 2003). The technology acceptance model (TAM) proposes that determinants of technology acceptance (usage) fall into two major categories: (1) perceived ease of use and (2) usefulness. These models, among others, focus on predicting usage, and while they can explain as much as 40 per cent of an information system's use (Legris et al. 2003), essentially they are silent on the consequences of use (Ahearne, Weinstein, and Srinivasan 2004).

Perhaps the most apparent means through which a sales manager can increase usefulness is through the selection or design of technologies comprising the firm's ST portfolio. To increase ease of use, sales managers should offer effective training (especially during the initial phases of an ST implementation) and effective ST support (during post-implementation phases). Additionally, sales managers should consider different customer expectations when assigning accounts to salespeople or sales teams.

"Training effectiveness" refers to the extent to which salespeople consider their ST training to have been effective (Hunter 1999)—and could be conducted either internally or externally to the sales organization. While larger organizations often have internal ST training and support, outsourcing is often used by smaller firms. While effective training can occur through either means, it is one of the most widely used methods for making ST easier to use. Training methods vary from classroom instruction to self-help menus on software products (Hunter 1999). Moreover, training effectiveness is a key driver to motivating information technology adoption in sales settings (Hunter et al. 1998, Ahearne, Jelinek, and Rapp 2005) that generalizes to other non-sales settings (Forman and Lippert 2005, Lippert and Forman 2005, Lippert 2007).

Once STs have been implemented, sales managers need to provide enough support to uphold usage levels (Hunter and Perreault 2006, 2007). As new ST innovations are considered, the training and support they require should be part of the sales manager's ST portfolio procurement decisions. The range and variation in innovations with what is dubbed the ongoing 'CRM 2.0' surge in sales technologies demonstrates that technology will continue to evolve favoring dynamic ST portfolio assessments. Assessment cycles may even accelerate as innovations like software as a service (SaaS) reduce switching costs for enterprise and salesperson adoption.

Finally, beyond training and support, the customers' IT expectations provide a strong social influence for salespeople to use ST, and has been found to increase different types of ST use (Hunter and Perreault 2007). Customers do not offer homogeneous encouragement to salespeople to use ST tools as their expectations vary. However, if a sales force can effectively increase their customers' IT expectations, that should, in turn, influence negatively their satisfaction levels with other (competing) sales organizations. As such, customer IT expectations hasten innovation diffusion across industries. When buyers confront important procurement decisions that stimulate consideration of alternative suppliers (Hunter, Bunn, and Perreault 2006), salespeople who fail to respond may retard significantly the continued development of business relationships.

Despite the influences employed, salespeople do not simply embrace and integrate new ST into their routines for several reasons. For example, some ST solutions evoke adverse psychological responses, such as reduced capacity to cope with or commit to using new ST innovations (Panagopoulos and Hunter 2009). Such psychological barriers help explain why sales managers and sales scholarship has primarily centered on motivating salespeople to adopt new technologies (Schillewaert et al. 2005, Cho and Chang 2008). However, the continued focus on adoption prompted leading ST scholars to call for research that goes beyond adoption (Ahearne, Jelinek, and Rapp 2005).

16.5 SALES TECHNOLOGY TO PERFORMANCE RELATIONSHIPS

The overwhelming majority of the extant research focuses on the antecedents and consequences of ST (including SFA or CRM) use. This practice assumes implicitly that all types of use have equivalent interrelationships with variables of importance. That seems implausible, and marks one of the most significant contributions of the recently proposed multiple dimensions of technology use (Hunter and Perreault 2007). Additionally, individual usage may cluster to form different categories of users (Lapierre and Medeiros 2006).

Generally, while most scholars propose and test direct and indirect effects (through mediators and moderators) of ST on sales performance—referred to as the "technology to performance relationship" or chain (Hunter 1999, Rapp et al. 2008). Several empirical papers support a range of antecedents and consequences of ST use—including both direct and indirect effects on aggregate and different aspects of quantitative and subjective measures of performance. It is worth noting that salesperson performance also has multiple dimensions (Behrman and Perreault 1982, 1984). Thus a more detailed perspective of the technology to performance relationship would include multiple dimensions of both ST use and salesperson performance. The number of dimensions included is a function of the research design and the study's objectives.

16.5.1 Sales Technology Use: Conceptualization

Conceptualizing and defining ST use has been a focal area of inquiry in the extant ST literature, perhaps rightfully so. Most scholars agree that different technologies, different uses of ST, and different fits between those specific ST and assigned tasks will have differential effects on performance. In fact, sound theoretical grounding mandates clarity in construct definition and explains why studies must seek better clarity in conceptualizing ST and how it is being used.

16.5.2 Sales Technology Use: Measurement

Over time, the literature shifted from focusing on individual technologies (e.g. cellphones) towards aggregate measures of ST use. When the salesperson is the study's unit of analysis, the most common way to measure use has been to employ an aggregate measure of the salesperson's use of the firm's portfolio of ST tools. When the firm has been the study's unit of analysis, the focus has been on total investment in firm's ST portfolio.

A significant shift in measure employs an intermediate aggregation of use by proposing the underlying dimensions of use based on learning theory (Hunter and Perreault 2007). Specifically, there are three different categories of use—(1) accessing, (2) analyzing and better understanding information, and (3) communicating information—that have established measures and known differential effects on salespeople, processes, and strategy (Hunter and Perreault 2007).

Different categories of use have different interrelationships and effect sizes with the antecedents and consequences of a one-dimensional measure of use (Hunter

1999). More work is needed to test how these different categories of use influence sales processes, tasks, and outcomes across industries, contexts, nationalities, and other contingent factors.

Without clarity in definitions, the burgeoning ST literature is unlikely to achieve the theoretical richness it needs to sustain itself as a scholarly pursuit. As has been discussed, ST is broader than SFA and inconsistent with the consensus definitions of CRM technology, so the terms should not be used interchangeably.

The current trend of a number of ST researchers and visionaries is to use the term "sales technology" to refer to the portfolio of tools made available to salespeople (Buehrer, Senecal, and Pullins 2005, Honeycutt 2005, Robinson, Marshall, and Stamps 2005a, 2005b, Tanner and Shipp 2005, Hunter and Perreault 2007, Ahearne et al. 2008, Rapp, Agnihotri, and Forbes 2008, Tanner et al. 2008). These scholars typically refer to SFA technology (e.g. contact management) as those systems primarily centered on the provision of returns on efficiency (Hunter, Perreault, and Armstrong 1998, Ingram, LaForge, and Leigh 2002), while sales-based CRM technologies are software applications centered on providing returns on customer relationship effectiveness (Hunter and Perreault 2007, Rapp et al. 2008). Other ST tools exist, so SFA and sales-based CRM software applications do not define an exhaustive set representing the domain of sales technology. Moreover, the domain is dynamic and the tools that constitute the domain will change as new ST innovations are used by sales organizations. Ambiguity in terminology is common, and even acceptable, for the industrial press, as it is not based on the scientific method. As sales scholars begin to use terms with consistency, the industrial press may follow, but in the meantime, better clarity is needed to help ST research advance.

16.6 SALES TECHNOLOGY, PRODUCTIVITY, AND PERFORMANCE

This section discusses some of the different approaches used to research sales technology's influence on productivity and performance.

16.6.1 Firm-Level Perspectives on IT and Productivity

At one extreme, the relationship between technology and performance can be addressed through an aggregate modeling of organizational inputs and out-puts—the "black box" approach. In the late 1980s, studies conducted by Stephen Roach, the chief economist at Morgan Stanley, found that firm spending on technology had no relationship to firm productivity—a finding later dubbed the "Roach productivity paradox." While some studies supported Roach's findings (Powell and Dent-Micallef 1997), other studies have reported a positive relationship between technology spending and productivity, contradicting Roach's findings (Sharda, Barr, and McDonnell 1988).

There has been debate and some creative proposals about the proper dependent variable in the technology–performance relationship. For example, Tobin's q ratio is useful as a forward-looking, capital market-based measure of the potential impact of information technology investments (Bharadwaj, Bharadwaj, and Konsynski 1999). Some scholars suggest that contradictions in findings about value may stem from use of different theoretical perspectives—ranging from theories of production and competitive strategy to theories of consumer behavior (Hitt and Brynjolfsson 1996). Generally, these studies use the firm as the unit of analysis and estimate relationships between firm spending and productivity—which is measured as a ratio of firm outputs to inputs.

16.6.2 Individual Sales Technologies and How to Optimize Their Use

In contrast to the black box approach, which treats all technology applications as equals, some scholars have placed more focus on how workers can optimize individual technology tools across multiple business disciplines. For example, marketing scholars have placed a special emphasis on the usage and impact of specific information technology tools.

Among others, Collins and his colleagues published an insightful and forward-looking series of articles on microcomputer applications in personal selling and sales management (Collins 1984a, 1984b, 1988, 1989a, 1989b, Martin and Collins 1991, Honeycutt, McCarty, and Howe 1993). These articles evaluate normative uses and potential benefits of individual technologies ranging from spreadsheets to contact management software. In a similar vein, a wide variety of individual technologies were proposed to fit into a classification system (Wedell and Hempeck 1987).

This forward-looking work on individual technologies made important contributions by informing both scholars and prospective users about the functionality of specific technology tools, stimulating attention to their potential benefits, and prompting adoption in several organizations.

16.6.3 Asking Salespeople What Works Best

Another major domain of research on the impact of information technology relies on user evaluations as a surrogate for IT (especially management information system, MIS) success. One reason to move to this approach is that a financial investment in a particular technology does not necessarily ensure that it is used, or used as intended, by members of the organization.

There has been substantial research on factors that influence the level (and validity) of user evaluations and debate about the advantages and limitations of this approach. For example, Hunter (1999) found that salespeople's reliance on ST did not parallel the estimated value those technologies provided to the selling process. Since asking salespeople to evaluate STs assumes they know which STs add value and in what ways, Hunter's (1999) evidence contradicts the validity of such naïve estimation. However, a seminal contribution from research on user evaluations is the tenet that evaluations result from the corresponding fit between task needs and information system or IT functionality (Goodhue and Thompson 1995).

Goodhue's task–technology fit theory—and the related validation of a task–technology fit instrument (Goodhue 1998)—provide a useful framework for assessing the ability of an organization's MIS to meet the needs of its managers. It also directs attention to several important considerations ignored in the "black box" approach, making the approaches complementary to better understanding. First, it stresses the conceptual distinction between tasks that need to be performed by some individual, and differentiates them from the technology itself. His framework also directly incorporates the human factor in evaluating technologies, and highlights the distinction between discretionary and compulsory use of technology. As such, it calls for consideration of factors, such as social norms and experience, that impact use. It also calls for consideration of how a user's expectations about outcomes motivate her use.

16.6.4 Relationship-Forging Tasks and Other Mediators of ST Effects on Sales Performance

Relationship-forging tasks (Hunter and Perreault 2007) represent the key mechanisms that salespeople, or boundary spanners in general, perform to forge or merge their organizational boundaries with an external organization's boundaries. As such, they build on the rich literature on working harder versus working smarter (Sujan, Barton, and Kumar 1994) as new ways for salespeople to practice smart selling behaviors. It is important to note that relationship-forging tasks (RFTs) influence a salesperson's ability to build effective relationships with customers—irrespective of one's use of information technologies (Hunter and Perreault 2007). However, sales reps can use ST to help accomplish some RFTs. This section focuses on the extant literature on relationship-forging tasks (RFTs) and suggests that this is only a partial set of such tasks.

Two RFTs, the underlying logic for their effects, and their strong explanatory power for relationship-building performance are: sharing market expertise and proposing integrative solutions (Hunter and Perreault 2007). "Sharing market expertise" refers to the extent to which salespeople develop and share their knowledge of the product market both with their associates and with their customers. "Proposing integrative solutions" refers to the extent to which salespeople propose recommendations that are mutually beneficial to the selling firm, the buying firm, and the buying firm's customers.

More RFTs should be conceptualized and proposed in future research by ST scholars as they consider different effects in across sales contexts. For example, another RFT, coordinating activities, has been proposed, but warrants additional research (Hunter 1999). "Coordinating activities" refers to the extent to which salespeople coordinate the activities of members of the selling firm with those of members of the buying firm. Such coordination places the salesperson in the role of advocating solutions to her associates in an effort to better provide solutions that meet business customers' objectives.

Some RFTs may be automated while others are not. For example, EDI could be used to automate the ordering process for frequently purchased goods. More research into the boundary conditions associated with decisions concerning task automation decisions is warranted.

16.7 Conclusion

This chapter goes beyond an understanding of how sales technology, sales strategy, sales processes, and salespeople interact and how they can be used as a means for achieving sustainable competitive advantage. Beyond automating or facilitating accomplishment of an existing technology to process relationship, ST may enable new tasks, thereby suggesting changes in organizational design. The perspective presented here discusses how ST research has evolved from its focus on optimizing the functionality of specific technologies towards a better understanding of how different sales strategies, processes, and salespeople can be integrated. The current B2B context centers on relationship marketing strategies and ST plays an important role in helping salespeople build better relationships with buying organizations (Hunter and Perreault 2007).

It is worth noting that sales managers control both investments in technology and design of work processes. That is, one need not limit the consideration of sales technologies to those that impact existing work processes (e.g. automation technologies). Instead, managers and scholars should consider the potential of redesigning work processes which incorporate ST in ways that optimize returns on both effectiveness and efficiency. A behavioral process modeling approach that begins with the desired outcomes and works in reverse to identify tasks (mediators) and their determinants has been proposed (Hunter and Perreault 2007).

ST may lead to new sales structures or vice versa. For example, there may be some advantage to functionally specialized roles in which individuals assume responsibility for integrating technology across multiple sales teams. Activities such as specialized marketing research inquiries that identify integrative solutions across accounts could be among the responsibilities of the ST specialists. Of course, identification of those integrative solutions is a prerequisite activity to proposing integrative solutions (Hunter and Perreault 2007). While some ST specialists could identify integrative solutions, another member of the sales team might propose the solution to customer accounts. Such specialization in work processes could capitalize on the aptitude and attitudes of various members of an organization—assigning skilled technology specialists to technology-intensive roles while employing people with strong interpersonal communication skills in traditional selling roles.

New sales strategy and structure will alter the skills and abilities required of sales leaders and salespeople (Ingram et al. 2002). Alternatively, of course, an individual may be assigned the entire set of activities constituting a new technology-intensive sales process. Some organizations may view persuasive selling skills and ST analytical skills as separable across individuals, while others may seek individuals who possess both types of skills and aptitudes. On the other hand, other cultures may dictate otherwise. Favoring functionally specialized over more "generalist" sales designs may include consideration of ST and its use by occupants of assigned sales roles. In any case, the structural design decision may well be driven by institutional conditions.

Institutional conditions, such as an organizational culture, may influence ST decisions. For example, an organization with a strong customer-centric culture may design sales processes starting with the customer interface and working back to other functions supporting the sales effort (e.g. accounting, logistics, marketing, and finance). Less customer-centric cultures, on the other hand, may use salespeople as implementers of a centralized strategy, thus relegating salespeople to roles as communicators of marketing strategy. This is a very limited use human potential—and thus affords access to a much larger labor pool.

Thus, while the extant ST literature provides a starting point for better understanding one of the most pervasive and dominant catalysts of change in modern sales organizations, it is merely a starting point. Many issues and concerns related to sales technology and its effects have not been addressed by the extant literature. Sales managers need better insights from academic research to help guide costly and complex decisions in this area—and thus the research domain is relevant to marketing practice.

For academics interested in making their research relevant to practice, as the ST imperative spreads across industries, so too should it become more germane to sales, marketing, and management research. While recent research demonstrates the validity of cross-sectional studies in this area, it also points towards conditions where better insights might be gained through longitudinal designs (Rindfleisch, Malter, Ganesan, and Moorman 2008). Sales scholars are uniquely positioned to add value to the efficiency and effectiveness of sales operations through advancing better understanding of ST, its antecedents, and consequences across various combinations of technologies, processes, salespeople, and strategies.

REFERENCES

AHEARNE, M., D. E. HUGHES, and N. SCHILLEWAERT (2007). "Why Sales Reps Should Welcome Information Technology: Measuring the Impact of CRM-Based IT on Sales Effectiveness," *International Journal of Research in Marketing* 24, 336–49.

——R. JELINEK, and A. RAPP (2005). "Moving Beyond the Direct Effect of SFA Adoption on Salesperson Performance: Training and Support as Key Moderating Factors," *Industrial Marketing Management* 34, 379–88.

——E. JONES, A. RAPP, and J. MATHIEU (2008). "High Touch through High Tech: The Impact of Salesperson Technology Usage on Sales Performance via Mediating Mechanisms," *Management Science* 54, 671–85.

——L. WEINSTEIN, and N. SRINIVASAN (2004). "Effect of Technology on Sales Performance: Progressing from Technology Acceptance to Technology Usage and Consequence," *Journal of Personal Selling & Sales Management* 24, 297–310.

ANG, L., and F. BUTTLE (2006). "CRM Software Applications and Business Performance," *Journal of Database Marketing & Customer Strategy Management* 14, 4–16.

AVLONITIS, G. J., and N. G. PANAGOPOULOS (2005). "Antecedents and Consequences of CRM Technology Acceptance in the Sales Force," *Industrial Marketing Management* 34, 355–68.

BAINBRIDGE, L. (1983). "Ironies of Automation," *Automatica* 19, 775–80.

BAND, W., C. GLIEDMAN, P. MARSTON, S. VITTAL, B. D. TEMKIN, and S. C. LEAVER (2008). "Topic Overview: Customer Relationship Management," in *For Business Process & Applications Professionals*, Cambridge, MA: Forrester Research Inc. March 25, 2008.

BEHRMAN, D. N., and W. D. PERREAULT, Jr. (1982). "Measuring the Performance of Industrial Salespersons," *Journal of Business Research* 10, 355–70.

————(1984). "A Role Stress Model of the Performance and Satisfaction of Industrial Salespeople," *Journal of Marketing* 48, 9–21.

BENDOLY, E., E. D. ROSENZWEIG, and J. K. STRATMAN (2009). "The Efficient Use of Enterprise Information for Strategic Advantage: A Data Envelopment Analysis," *Journal of Operations Management* 27, 310–23.

BHARADWAJ, A., S. BHARADWAJ, and B. KONSYNSKI (1999). "Information Technology Effects on Firm Performance as Measured by Tobin's Q," *Management Science* 45.7, 1008–24.

BOULDING, W., R. STAELIN, M. EHRET, and W. J. JOHNSTON (2005). "A Customer Relationship Management Roadmap: What is Known, Potential Pitfalls, and Where to Go," *Journal of Marketing* 69, 155–66.

BRADFORD, K., S. BROWN, S. GANESAN, G. K. HUNTER, V. ONYEMAH, R. PALMATIER, D. ROUZIES, R. SPIRO, H. SUJAN, and B. WEITZ (2010). "The Embedded Sales Force: Connecting Buying and Selling Organizations," *Marketing Letters* 21(3), 239–53.

BROWN, S. P., and R. A. PETERSON (1993). "Antecedents and Consequences of Salesperson Job Satisfaction: Meta-Analysis and Assessment of Causal Effects," *Journal of Marketing Research* 30, 63–77.

BUEHRER, R. E., S. SENECAL, and E. B. PULLINS (2005). "Sales Force Technology Usage— Reasons, Barriers, and Support: An Exploratory Investigation," *Industrial Marketing Management* 34, 389–98.

BUREAU OF LABOR STATISTICS, *Occupational Outlook Handbook*, 2008–9 edn., Washington, DC: Bureau of Labour Statistics.

BUSH, A. J., V. D. BUSH, L. M. ORR, and R. A. ROCCO (2007). "Sales Technology: Help or Hindrance to Ethical Behaviors and Productivity?", *Journal of Business Research* 60, 1198–1205.

CHEN, I. J., and K. POPOVICH (2003). "Understanding Customer Relationship Management (CRM)," *Business Process Management Journal* 9, 672–88.

CHO, S. D., and D. R. CHANG (2008). "Salesperson's Innovation Resistance and Job Satisfaction in Intra-Organizational Diffusion of Sales Force Automation Technologies: The Case of South Korea," *Industrial Marketing Management* 37, 841–7.

CHURCHILL, G. A., Jr., N. M. FORD, S. W. HARTLEY, and O. C. WALKER, Jr. (1985). "The Determinants of Salesperson Performance: A Meta-Analysis," *Journal of Marketing Research* 22, 103–18.

COLLINS, R. H. (1984a). "Portable Computers: Applications to Increase Salesforce Productivity," *Journal of Personal Selling & Sales Management* 4.2, 75–80.

——(1984b). "Artificial Intelligence in Personal Selling," *Journal of Personal Selling & Sales Management* 4.1, 58–66.

——(1988). "Microcomputer Applications: The Perfect Travelling Companion," *Journal of Personal Selling & Sales Management* 8, 67–70.

——(1989a). "Microcomputer Applications: Mastering Inquiries and Sales Leads," *Journal of Personal Selling & Sales Management* 9.2, 73–6.

——(1989b). "Unleash the Power of Desktop Presentations," *Journal of Personal Selling & Sales Management* 9.1, 70–5.

DAVIS, F. D. (1989). "Perceived Usefulness, Perceived Ease of Use, and User Acceptance of Information Technology," *MIS Quarterly* 13.3, 319–40.

DAY, G. S. (1994). "The Capabilities of Market-Driven Organizations," *Journal of Marketing* 58.4, 37–52.

——(2003). "Creating a Superior Customer-Relating Capability," *MIT Sloan Management Review* 44, 77–82.

DICKSON, P. R., W. M. LASSAR, G. K. HUNTER, and S. CHAKRAVORTI (2009). "The Pursuit of Excellence in Process Thinking and Customer Relationship Management," *Journal of Personal Selling & Sales Management* 29, 111–24.

DIEBOLD, J. (1952). *Automation: The Advent of the Automatic Factory*, New York: Van Nostrand.

DWYER, F. R., P. H. SCHURR, and S. OH (1987). "Developing Buyer–Seller Relationships," *Journal of Marketing* 51, 11–27.

FORMAN, H., and S. K. LIPPERT (2005). "Toward the Development of an Integrated Model of Technology Internalization within the Supply Chain Context," *International Journal of Logistics Management* 16, 4–27.

GOODHUE, D. L. (1998). "Development and Measurement Validity of a Task–Technology Fit Instrument for User Evaluations of Information System," *Decision Science* 29(1), 105–38.

——and R. L. THOMPSON (1995). "Task–Technology Fit and Individual Performance," *MIS Quarterly* 19, 213–36.

GREISS, T. E. (1984). *Ancient & Medieval Warfare*, Wayne, NJ: Avery.

GUMMESSON, E. (2008). *Total Relationship Marketing: Marketing Management, Relationship Strategy and CRM Approaches for the Network Economy*, Oxford: Butterworth-Heinemann.

HITT, L. M., and E. BRYNJOLFSSON (1996). "Productivity, Business Profitability, and Consumer Surplus: Three Different Measures of Information Technology Value," *MIS Quarterly* 20, 121–42.

HONEYCUTT, E. D., Jr. (2005). "Technology Improves Sales Performance—Doesn't It? An Introduction to the Special Issue on Selling and Sales Technology," *Industrial Marketing Management* 34, 301–4.

——T. McCARTY, and V. HOWE (1993). "Sales Technology Applications—Self-Paced Video Enhanced Training: A Case Study," *Journal of Personal Selling & Sales Management* 13, 73.

HUNTER, G. K. (1999). "Sales Technology, Relationship-Forging Tasks, and Sales Performance in Business Markets," doctoral dissertation, University of North Carolina at Chapel Hill.

——M. D. BUNN, and W. D. PERREAULT, Jr. (2006). "Interrelationships among Key Aspects of the Organizational Procurement Process," *International Journal of Research in Marketing* 23, 155–70.

——and W. D. PERREAULT, Jr. (2006). "Sales Technology Orientation, Information Effectiveness, and Sales Performance," *Journal of Personal Selling & Sales Management* 29.2, 111–24.

————(2007). "Making Sales Technology Effective," *Journal of Marketing* 71, 16–34.

————and G. M. ARMSTRONG (1998). "Sales Technology, Selling Smart, and Sales Performance in Business Markets," in *AMA Summer Educators Proceedings: Enhancing Knowledge Development in Marketing*.

HUTT, M. D., and B. A. WALKER (2006). "A Network Perspective of Account Manager Performance," *Journal of Business & Industrial Marketing* 21, 466–73.

INGRAM, T. N., R. W. LaFORGE, and T. W. LEIGH (2002). "Selling in the New Millennium: A Joint Agenda," *Industrial Marketing Management* 31, 559–67.

JAP, S. D. (2003). "An Exploratory Study of the Introduction of Online Reverse Auctions," *Journal of Marketing* 67.3, 96–107.

JELINEK, R., M. AHEARNE, J. MATHIEU, and N. SCHILLEWAERT (2006). "A Longitudinal Examinations of Individual, Organizational, and Contextual Factors on Sales Technlogy Adoption and Job Performance," *Journal of Marketing Theory & Practice* 14, 7–23.

JONES, E., S. SUNDARAM, and C. WYNNE (2002). "Factors Leading to Sales Force Automation Use: A Longitudinal Analysis," *Journal of Personal Selling & Sales Management* 22, 145–56.

LANDRY, T. D., T. J. ARNOLD, and A. ARNDT (2005). "A Compendium of Sales-Related Literature in Customer Relationship Management: Processes and Technologies with Managerial Implications," *Journal of Personal Selling & Sales Management* 25, 231–51.

LAPIERRE, J., and R. MEDEIROS (2006). "Information and Communication Technology Usage Patterns: A Case Study," *Journal of Strategic Marketing* 14, 229–44.

LAPLACA, P. J. (2005). "Letter from the Editor," Special Issue on Selling and Sales Technology, *Industrial Marketing Management* 34.4, 299.

LEE, H. L., V. PADMANABHAN, and S. WANG (1997). "The Bullwhip Effect in Supply Chains," *Sloan Management Review* 38, 93–102.

LEGRIS, P., J. INGHAM, and P. COLLERETTE (2003). "Why Do People Use Information Technology? A Critical Review of the Technology Acceptance Model," *Information & Management* 40, 191–204.

LIPPERT, S. K. (2007). "Investigating Postadoption Utilization: An Examination into the Role of Interorganizational and Technology Trust," *IEEE Transactions on Engineering Management* 54, 468–84.

——and H. FORMAN (2005). "Utilization of Information Technology: Examining Cognitive and Experiential Factors of Post-Adoption Behavior," *IEEE Transactions on Engineering Management* 52, 363–81.

LUCAS, H. C. (1999). *Information Technology and the Productivity Paradox: Assessing the Value of Investing in It*, New York: Oxford University Press.

MARTIN, W. S., and B. H. COLLINS (1991). "Sales Technology Applications—Interactive Video Technology in Sales Training: A Case Study," *Journal of Personal Selling & Sales Management* 11, 61.

MATHIEU, J., M. AHEARNE, and S. R. TAYLOR (2007). "A Longitudinal Cross-Level Model of Leader and Salesperson Influences on Sales Force Technology Use and Performance," *Journal of Applied Psychology* 92, 528–37.

MOUTOT, J.-M., and G. BASCOUL (2008). "Effects of Sales Force Automation on Sales Force Activities and Customer Relationship Management Processes," *Journal of Personal Selling & Sales Management* 28, 167–84.

PANAGOPOULOS, N. G., and G. K. HUNTER (2009). "Managing Sales Technology-Related Change Mechanisms: A Commitment and Coping Perspective," in C. White and K. Reynolds (eds.), *American Marketing Association Winter Educators' Proceedings: Excellence in Marketing Research—Striving for Impact*, Tampa, Fla: American Marketing Association.

PARASURAMAN, R., and RILEY, V. (1997). "Humans and Automation: Use, Misuse, Disuse, Abuse," *Human Factors* 39, 230–53.

PARVATIYAR, A., and J. N. SHETH (2000). "The Domain and Conceptual Foundations of Relationship Marketing," in *Handbook of Relationship Marketing*, Thousand Oaks, CA: Sage.

PAYNE, A., and P. FROW (2005). "A Strategic Framework for Customer Relationship Management," *Journal of Marketing* 69, 167–76.

PLOUFFE, C. R., B. C. WILLIAMS, and T. W. LEIGH (2004). "Who's On First? Stakeholder Differences in Customer Relationship Management and the Elusive Notion Of 'Shared Understanding'," *Journal of Personal Selling & Sales Management* 24, 323–38.

POWELL, T. C., and A. DENT-MICALLEF (1997). "Information Technology as Competitive Advantage: The Role of Human, Business, and Technology Resources," *Strategic Management Journal* 18, 375–405.

RAPP, A., R. AGNIHOTRI, and L. P. FORBES (2008). "The Sales Force Technology–Performance Chain: The Role of Adaptive Selling and Effort," *Journal of Personal Selling & Sales Management* 28, 335–50.

REINARTZ, W., M. KRAFFT, and W. D. HOYER (2004). "The Customer Relationship Management Process: Its Measurement and Impact on Performance," *Journal of Marketing Research* 41, 293–305.

RINDFLEISCH, A., A. J. MALTER, S. GANESAN, and C. MOORMAN (2008). "Cross-Sectional Versus Longitudinal Survey Research: Concepts, Findings, and Guidelines," *Journal of Marketing Research* 45, 261–79.

ROBINSON, L., Jr., G. W. MARSHALL, and M. B. STAMPS (2005a). "An Empirical Investigation of Technology Acceptance in a Field Sales Force Setting," *Industrial Marketing Management* 34, 407–15.

——————(2005b). "Sales Force Use of Technology: Antecedents to Technology Acceptance," *Journal of Business Research* 58, 1623–31.

SCHILLEWAERT, N., M. J. AHEARNE, R. T. FRAMBACH, and R. K. MOENAERT (2005). "The Adoption of Information Technology in the Sales Force," *Industrial Marketing Management* 34, 323–36.

SHARDA, R., S. H. BARR, and J. C. McDONNELL (1988). "Decision Support System Effectiveness: A Review and an Emperical Test," *Management Science* 34, 139–59.

SHETH, J. N., A. PARVATIYAR, and C. ROBERTO (1994). *Relationship Marketing: Theory, Methods and Applications*, Buffalo, NY: Center for Relationship Marketing.

——and A. SOBEL (2002). *Clients for Life: How Great Professionals Develop Breakthrough Relationships*, New York: Simon & Schuster.

SIRDESHMUKH, D., J. SINGH, and B. SABOL, (2002). "Consumer Trust, Value, and Loyalty in Relational Exchanges," *Journal of Marketing* 66, 15–37.

SRIVASTAVA, R. K., T. A. SHERVANI, and L. FAHEY (1999). "Marketing, Business Processes, and Shareholder Value: An Organizationally Embedded View of Marketing Activities and the Discipline of Marketing," *Journal of Marketing* 63, 168–79.

SUJAN, H., A. W. BARTON, and N. KUMAR (1994). "Learning Orientation, Working Smart, and Effective Selling," *Journal of Marketing* 58, 39–52.

TANNER, J. F., Jr., C. FOURNIER, J. A. WISE, S. HOLLET, and J. POUJOL (2008). "Executives' Perspectives of the Changing Role of the Sales Profession: Views from France, the United States, and Mexico," *Journal of Business & Industrial Marketing* 23, 193–202.

——and S. SHIPP (2005). "Sales Technology within the Salesperson's Relationships: A Research Agenda," *Industrial Marketing Management* 34, 305–12.

TULI, K. R., A. K. KOHLI, and S. G. BHARADWAJ (2007). "Rethinking Customer Solutions: From Product Bundles to Relational Processes," *Journal of Marketing* 71, 1–17.

VENKATESH, V., and F. D. DAVIS (2000). "A Theoretical Extension of the Technology Acceptance Model: Four Longitudinal Field Studies," *Management Science* 46, 186–204.

WEDELL, A., and D. HEMPECK (1987). "Sales Force Automation—Here and Now," *Journal of Personal Selling & Sales Management* 7, 11–16.

WEITZ, B. A., and K. D. BRADFORD (1999). "Personal Selling and Sales Management: A Relationship Marketing Perspective," *Journal of the Academy of Marketing Science* 27, 241–54.

WILLIAMS, B. C., and C. R. PLOUFFE (2007). "Assessing the Evolution of Sales Knowledge: A 20-Year Content Analysis," *Industrial Marketing Management* 36, 408–19.

WINER, R. S. (2001). "A Framework for Customer Relationship Management," *California Management Review* 43, 89–105.

WU, F., S. YENIYURT, D. KIM, and S. T. CAVUSGIL (2006). "The Impact of Information Technology on Supply Chain Capabilities and Firm Performance: A Resource-Based View," *Industrial Marketing Management* 35, 493–504.

Xu, Y., D. C. Yen, B. Lin, and D. C. Chou (2002). "Adopting Customer Relationship Management Technology," *Industrial Management and Data Systems* 102, 442–52.

Yao, Y., M. Dresner, and J. Palmer (2009). "Private Network EDI vs. Internet Electronic Markets: A Direct Comparison of Fulfillment Performance," *Management Science* 55, 843–52.

Zablah, A. R., D. N. Bellenger, and W. J. Johnston (2004). "Customer Relationship Management Implementation Gaps," *Journal of Personal Selling & Sales Management* 24, 279–95.

Zoltners, A. A., P. Sinha, and S. E. Lorimer (2009). *Building a Winning Sales Force: Powerful Strategies for Driving High Performance*, New York: AMACOM.

————and G. A. Zoltners (2001). *The Complete Guide to Accelerating Sales Force Performance*, New York: AMACOM.

PART IV

THE ORGANIZATION AND SALES RELATIONSHIPS

CHAPTER 17

ORGANIZATIONAL COMMITMENT TO SALES

WESLEY J. JOHNSTON[*]
LINDA D. PETERS[*]

[T]imes have changed. The focus (of marketing) is shifting away from tangibles and toward intangibles, such as skills, information, and knowledge, and toward interactivity and connectivity and ongoing relationships. (Vargo and Lusch 2004: 15)

We all compete for business. Competition demands that one constantly prepare, practice, and sharpen skill sets. It requires us to develop a systematic approach to each new business relationship. But how many sales people consistently do this? (Schell 2003: v)

---

[*] This chapter draws upon material originally published as:

Linda D. Peters, Jule B. Gassenheimer, and Wesley J. Johnston, "Marketing and the Structuration of Organisational Learning," *Marketing Theory* 9.3 (2009), 341–68.

Linda D. Peters and Wesley J. Johnston, "Network Formation, Collaboration, and Collective Learning: An Exploration of Absorptive Capacity from a Network Perspective," *Journal of Business Market Management* 3.1 (2009): 29–50.

17.1 THE ROLE OF SALES IN THE ORGANIZATION

The role of marketing in the organization has changed, and with it the role of sales as a means of service provision and value creation in organizations. The evolution of a new dominant logic for marketing, originally put forward by Vargo and Lusch in 2004, highlights the evolution of the word "service." This they termed the service-dominant (SD) logic of marketing. In their more recent articles, Vargo and Lusch (2008a, 2008b) acknowledge the subtle but critical shift from the use of the term "services" (reflecting a special type of intangible output) to the singular term "service" (reflecting the process of using one's resources for the benefit of another). This shift is in fact not new: in 1922 Kitson noted that a qualitative change had occurred in the use of the word "service" from something gratuitous which was given in addition to the commodity, and as an added extra, to something regarded as a real part of the commodity, or indeed as the commodity itself. Kitson exhorted the seller to "saturate himself with the idea [of service], concentrating earnestly upon the needs of the buyer and seeking honestly to fulfil them" (p. 419).

Vargo and Lusch (2004, 2008b) brought the work of Kitson to the forefront of marketing by calling for a shift in perspective that focused not on the provision of goods and services to fulfil buyer needs, but rather on intangible resources that produce effect. This revised perspective expands the view of service by emphasizing the connectivity between individuals and organizations through the co-creation of value and relationships (see also Lusch, Vargo, and O'Brien 2007). They argued that the collection of unique benefits the organization promises to deliver to the customer ("value propositions") stem not only from the knowledge and mental competencies of the firm but also from market-oriented feedback and organizational learning. In fact, service co-creation with customers need not be face-to-face, and can in fact be enhanced in some instances through the use of automated and interactive sales technologies (Sheth and Sharma 2008). Lusch and Vargo (2006: 283) recognized that "organizations exist to integrate and transform micro-specialized competencies into complex services that are demanded in the marketplace." In this chapter we examine important aspects of these integration and transformation processes, and identify the support organizations need to provide to enhance their sales efforts. It is the provision of such support to the sales function, and the way in which organizations address the changing needs of the market through their integration and transformation processes in relation to sales activities, that we see as the defining features of an organization's commitment to sales.

In Figure 17.1, we see several macro-trends in sales force management that impact the way in which organizations may support the role and functions of the sales forces. In particular, three main trends are affecting the way in which organizations view, utilize, and support marketing and, as a consequence, their sales efforts. First, the perception of the role of marketing as a translator of value to

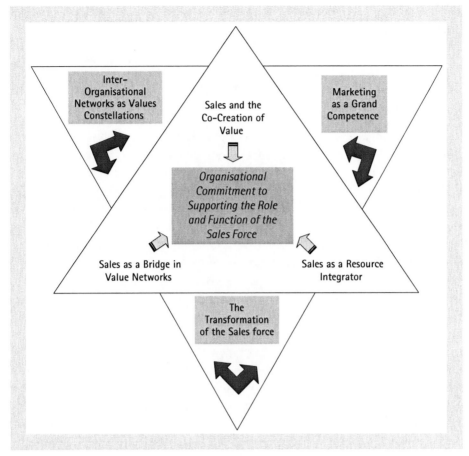

Fig. 17.1. Trends in Sales Force Management

and from the external market is changing to one which sees it as a core (or grand) competence of the firm whose primary obligation is to facilitate value co-creation. Second, the venue of value creation is often now value configurations—economic and social actors within networks interacting and exchanging across and through networks. Third, sales forces are generating more sales with fewer sales people, and therefore the "transformation of the sales force" has been predicted.

These key trends form the basis for our discussion in this section of the chapter, where we begin by addressing the central role marketing plays in enhancing organizational capabilities within business networks. In section 17.2, we go on to discuss the ways in which these three macro-trends then impact organizational commitment to sales—in particular, the role of the sales function in the co-creation of value with customers. In section 17.3 we then look in more detail at the role of sales in facilitating innovation and organizational learning—in particular its role as a resource integrator and a bridge between partners in business network relationships.

17.1.1 The Role of Marketing: Marketing as a Grand Competence

Vargo and Lusch (2004) state that the key organizational capabilities of interest to marketers—those core competencies that enhance the value propositions of the firm—include the coordination of cross-functional, intra-, and inter-organizational network partners so as to gain competitive advantage by performing specialized marketing functions. This is a more recent development of the work of Juttner and Wehrli (1994), who chart the move from: (1) marketing as an "outside-in, short-term and reactive" function in the firm to (2) marketing as a transformer in the process of building and exploiting competencies, through to (3) marketing as the dynamic and ongoing interactions which over time lead to collective learning processes and create marketing as what they term a "grand competence" of the firm. Grand competence differs from competitive competence in that "grand competence does not bestow a specific, time-limited competitive advantage but encompasses the capability of creating renewed competitive advantages" (Juttner and Wehrli 1994: 48), which is dynamic in nature. In discussing the development of competitive advantage, Juttner and Wehrli critique the "inside-out" competence perspective (developing internal competences which are unique to the firm) versus the "outside-in" marketing perspective (focusing on customer needs and market conditions). They point out that in viewing these two perspectives as separate, there is a danger of developing internal competences that do not relate to superior customer value. They proposed to integrate the two perspectives through marketing as a translator of market needs to the firm and of value propositions to the marketplace, and marketing as a grand competence that embeds short-term reactions to customer needs within long-term internal organizational competencies.

However, marketing faces two main obstacles in gaining influence and enacting its role as a grand competence of the firm. The first is the failure of marketing professionals to accept accountability and to appropriately justify their expenditures in terms of direct return on investment. As Verhoef and Leeflang (2009) point out, many marketers do not measure the effect of their actions, and as a consequence, many marketing actions have no effect on sales, sales promotions have no persistent influence on sales at either the brand or the category sales level, and new products suffer from low success rates.

The other is the lack of innovation (Verhoef and Leeflang 2009) from marketing departments. By this they mean the degree to which such departments contribute to the development of new products within the firm. They argue that marketing should use its position as a translator of value to and from the marketplace in a more adequate and effective way to regain its value within the firm. These two obstacles undermine the role of marketing within the firm, and the extent to which organizational commitment to the sales function is forthcoming. In particular, the importance of the sales force in establishing relationships and informing innovation may not be recognized or rewarded by the organization.

Predating the SD logic of Vargo and Lusch, Juttner and Wehrli (1994) recognized that exchanges were just as important to marketing strategies as the competencies that resulted because exchanges incorporated the collective memories of the people in the organization and were therefore idiosyncratic and a potential source of differentiation. This would imply that learning, both individual and collective, is an important feature of sales force competency. In Figure 17.2 we see how marketing as a translator of value to and from the marketplace links the externalization of competitive advantage in the marketplace (value to external markets) with the establishment of more permanent and longer-term competitive advantage (value to the firm). We also see how marketing is a dynamic process in which resources may be acquired and competences developed, along with the creation of value for both the firm and the customer.

The importance of learning as a necessary activity of the sales force is discussed by Chonko, Dubinsky, Jones, and Roberts (2003), who state that: "In the absences of learning, sales organisations and sales personnel are destined to repeat past practices and behaviour—irrespective of their effectiveness." To support such

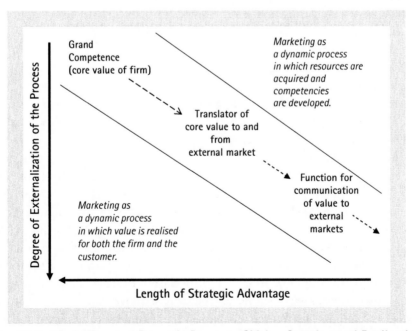

Fig. 17.2. Marketing as a Dynamic Process of Value Creation and Realization

learning, Rangarajan, Chonko, Jones, and Roberts (2004) suggest that organizations need to be ready for change. Marketing, therefore, may support the sales activities of the firm by serving as a grand competence which merges the long-term development of internal competencies with short-term external market dynamics. It thus serves as a transformer between the external environment and the value related core competences of the firm. Here marketing requires long term memory and organizational learning capabilities regarding operational excellence of the firm and how it relates to customer value (Juttner and Wehrli 1994).

As organizations focus on their core competencies and outsource some necessary knowledge and skills to the network, this transformation will become a vital part of what we consider to be marketing (Vargo and Lusch 2004). In developing these core competences, there are implications for the support sales may need from the organization—in particular, establishing routines and practices which facilitate learning and innovation in sales personnel. This is because sales personnel are on the front line of organizations, and are therefore in the best position to facilitate organizational change by implementing the firm's strategies and learning about changing customer preferences and needs (Chonko et al. 2003). As Chonko et al. point out, in sales organizations relationships become structured, and some individual learning and shared understanding among groups becomes institutionalized. Thus, organizational structures, systems, routines, and practices embed the learning of individual sales personnel and allow organizations to maintain their knowledge as individuals enter and leave the organization. Initiatives such as customer relationship management (CRM) and sales force automation (SFA) represent a logical culmination of learning, and help to provide the structures, systems, routines, and practices needed to embed individual learning in the organization. Pullig, Maxham, and Hair (2002) contend that the greatest potential for SFA systems is the sharing of contact information and increased coordination across the firm's various customer service functions. They state that organizations that utilize SFA systems to form superior market-sensing and customer-linking capabilities are in a position to inform and guide the internal processes of the firm that are responsible for creating customer value.

In defining SD logic, Lusch and Vargo (2006) focus upon the relationship between service (as a process, not an output) and a good as a vehicle for service provision. Their definition of service as "the application of specialized competencies (knowledge and skills), through deeds, processes, and performances for the benefit of another entity or the entity itself" (p. 283) is reflected in Figure 17.3. Here the logical transformation of marketing from an undeveloped managerial function through to the primary and most fundamental grand competence of the firm is a reflection of marketing's role in and contribution to organizational learning, and the value propositions that may result from this learning.

As a grand competence, marketing facilitates organizational learning by focusing organizational efforts on enhancing customer knowledge, competitive strategy,

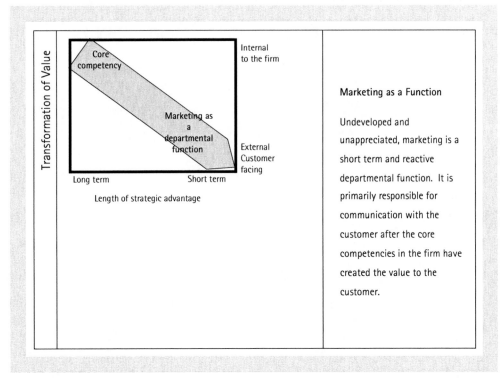

Marketing as a Function

Undeveloped and unappreciated, marketing is a short term and reactive departmental function. It is primarily responsible for communication with the customer after the core competencies in the firm have created the value to the customer.

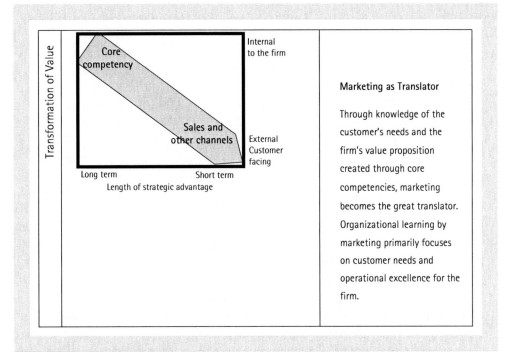

Marketing as Translator

Through knowledge of the customer's needs and the firm's value proposition created through core competencies, marketing becomes the great translator. Organizational learning by marketing primarily focuses on customer needs and operational excellence for the firm.

Fig. 17.3. The Development of Marketing's Contribution to the Value Propositions of the Firm. Continued on next page

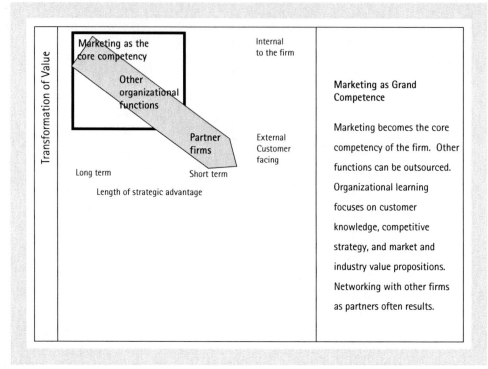

Fig. 17.3. Continued

and market and industry value propositions. This implies that the role of marketing goes beyond that of simply connecting the firm to the marketplace—a role that is now often dispersed throughout the organization and therefore does not act as a distinctive contribution of marketing alone (Verhoef and Leeflang 2009).

17.1.2 Inter-organizational Networks as Value Constellations

Often, in order to engage in value co-creation effectively, networking with other firms that are willing to partner is key (cf. Schembri 2006). Marketing researchers (e.g. Slater and Narver 1995, Glazer 1991) have called for a market-oriented approach, where an organization's knowledge of the customer provides the ability to create value for the market as well as develop an ongoing learning process within the organization. This process allows organizations to work more effectively with a network of participants both inside and outside the firm (Crossan, Lane, and White 1999, Morgan 2004). Learning how organizations may support and influence sales teams (as opposed to individual sales personnel) is posited as a key requirement for sales organizations (Rangarajan et al. 2004). We recognize, as do Vargo and Lusch (2008b), that SD logic has much to offer in understanding value creation in business-to-business networks, where the economic actors (rather than producers and consumers) interact, and these economic actors originate from both the supply network and the customer network (Cova and Salle 2008). Thus, the members of sales teams may detect changes in the business environment, gather knowledge about customers, and improve members' collective understanding of business situations (Rangarajan et al. 2004). However, the interaction of these economic actors raises issues in relation to the role of sales in the organization, the importance and focus of marketing as a competence in the firm, and how the sales efforts relate to value co-creation, innovation, and learning.

For example, Lusch and Vargo (2006) and Vargo and Lusch (2008b) view both the firm and the customer as resource integrators, and call for the refinement and elaboration of this resource integration concept in their ninth foundation premise of SD logic. In particular, they highlight the need for a more explicit connection to the interactivity and networking literature, and the recognition that "the venue of value creation is the value configurations—economic and social actors within networks interacting and exchanging across and through networks" (Vargo and Lusch 2008a: 5). Such interdependence between network members means that network interactions form the key to developing resources that can be transformed into valuable network capabilities (Ford and Hakansson 2006). These interdependencies exists not only in buying but also in selling activities, as the exchange patterns between buying centres and selling centres in the sales force management literature illustrate (Hutt, Johnston, and Ronchetto 1985).

17.1.3 The Transformation of the Sales Force

Three powerful forces have changed the optimal sales force forever: skyrocketing cost per sales call, the web, and key account management (KAM). This leads to "the collapse of the middle," also known as "the death of the sales force" (McMahon 2000). Basically, sales forces are generating more sales with fewer salespeople. They are doing this by increasing the amount of sales through low-end technological channels (Internet, call center, etc.) and high-end key account programs while cutting the traditional, geographically deployed sales force—hence the collapse of the middle portion of the sales channels. A number of companies have cut the direct sales force by 40 percent. The trend started in the pharmaceutical industry and has spread to other industries and sales forces (Lubkeman et al. 2009). When the typical salesperson is making social calls without any sales objectives, there is no value added for the customer. Customers are busy and would prefer more efficient use of their time. Some suppliers got ahead of the trend and began to analyze the buying patterns of their customers. They then moved the routine recurring purchases to the call center for handling, and left problem-solving and new product introductions to the sales force. As time went by, customers began to implement supplier management programs and eProcurement websites to make buying more efficient and eliminate the wasted time spent with socially oriented sales people. The economics of different sales channels is also driving this change. The cost of sales calls can average between $150 and $200 (Keenan 2000) and for technical suppliers can be over $400 (http://www.allbusiness.com). With the call center being able to handle a sales call for $25–65 and the Internet for $5 and less, the trend toward more efficient sales efforts is strong (http://www.jvminc.com/). If the individual salesperson can add sufficient value to the customer interaction, they remain in the equation. When the cost of the sales force exceeds the value they add, downsizing is imminent. Key account management is eating away at the traditional sales force on the other side of the customer relationship. Since 80 percent of many suppliers' business is tied up in 20 percent of the customer base, key account programs make sense as well. In a key account program, team selling is usually the approach. Although this is more expensive than the single salesperson, the improvement in the supplier–customer relationship is worth the additional expense. Key account programs often lead to strategic alliances and long term relationships. "Salespeople" disappear and key account managers take their place. Key account managers have a different attitude than the traditional "hunter, qualifier, closer." They are more like "farmers" with respect to their sales skills. While closing urgency is still part of their approach, key account managers are more interested in bonding and rapport building. They are also effective in communicating to all levels of the customer firm and organizing resources in their own firms to support the customer relationship.

In this first section we have identified three key macro-trends which are impacting the role and function of the sales force. These trends—marketing as a grand competence of the firm, networks as value constellations, and the transformation of the sales force—lead to a new role for sales within the organization and the need for a fresh look at how that role may be supported by the organization—in particular, how the sales function relates to value co-creation with network partners and customers, and the role of sales in facilitating a learning organization. We summarize the key points of this section:

- There is a need to understand marketing as a grand competence of the firm which facilitates organizational learning by enhancing customer knowledge, competitive strategy, and market and industry value propositions. In developing these core competences, there are implications for the support sales may need from the organization, in particular, establishing routines and practices which facilitate learning and innovation in sales personnel.
- In order to engage in value co-creation effectively, networking with other firms that are willing to partner is often required. Learning how organizations may support and influence sales teams (as opposed to individual sales personnel) is seen as a key requirement for sales organizations.

- The transformation of the sales force has come about because sales forces are generating more sales with fewer sales people. They are doing this by increasing the amount of sales through low-end technological channels and high-end key account programs while cutting the traditional, geographically deployed sales force.

We may conclude from these key trends that the role and function of the sales force has significantly changed. In particular, the focus of sales force activities is increasingly one of value co-creation and the facilitation of innovation. We now explore these issues further. In section 17.2 we examine how the sales function might operate as a participant in value co-creation, and the role of the customer in this process. In section 17.3 we look at the role of sales in facilitating innovation and learning in the organization.

17.2 THE SALES FUNCTION AND VALUE CO-CREATION

In sales force activities, new and broader skills are required and the old sales skill paradigms are breaking down. The new skills required combine the "hunter" skills of prospecting, qualifying, and closing with the "farmer" skills of relationship building and consultative sales. This may have implications for the development of market orientation in firms and the role of the sales force in facilitating this. Typically, market orientation has as its focus external stakeholders such as customers and competitors. Lings (2004) points out that, while evidence does exist to suggest that an external market orientation improves performance in the context of service suppliers, there are increasing calls for research to examine the impact of internal orientations on business performance. Such calls echo the desire to extend the notion of value co-creation by consumers and marketers (as extolled in SD logic) to include the notion of *meaning* in "value-in-exchange" and in "value-in-use" (Penaloza and Venkatesh 2006). We examine two key aspects of this shift: value as a result of co-creation (thus engaging resources that are both internal and external to the firm in creating value), and the role of the customer in this value co-creation process.

17.2.1 Value Co-creation

For over a quarter of a century seminal articles in the leading marketing journals have stressed the strategic importance and the multi-level nature of managing knowledge. They have brought organizational learning activities to the forefront in helping to form value propositions based on input from the marketplace (cf. Glazer 1991, Kohli and Jaworski 1990, Slater and Narver 1995, Sujan, Weitz, and Kumar 1994). Vargo and Lusch (2008a) state in their fourth foundation premise that knowledge is the fundamental source of competitive advantage, and that in the terminology of SD logic knowledge and skills represent "operant resources." In fact Kohli and Jaworski (1990) defined market orientation as the organization-wide generation of market intelligence which concerns both existing and potential customer needs, and exogenous factors likely to influence these needs such as disseminating intelligence throughout the organization and responding accordingly on an organization-wide basis.

Where the knowledge management literature has fallen short has been the absence of a service logic that explains the integration of knowledge throughout the value network. This new approach to value creation, where customers co-create value through their interactions with the organization, requires organizations to *manage* knowledge within organizations and between organizational network partners. Organizations and their networks, therefore, must learn what customers value and how that value can be created. Organizations must also transfer knowledge to others in their network of partners so that they too understand customer value. The knowledge gained and transferred is an operant resource that is fundamental to competitive advantage and performance. Vargo and Lusch (2004) define an operant resource as a resource that is often invisible and intangible (such as core competencies or organizational processes) that are then employed through knowledge management to produce effects. As the notion of value creation has shifted from a supply-side provision of value involving a passive customer to the facilitation and co-creation of customer-perceived value, knowledge management thinking must also experience a similar shift in focus.

Traditionally, knowledge management was a centralized function in that management controlled the transfer of knowledge by distributing tasks and resources and then monitoring the execution of those tasks and the use of those resources (Bonifacio, Bouquet, and Traverso 2002). This process assumes that knowledge is separate from the subjectivity of the people that produced it. This assumption mirrors the traditional "marketing as exchange" paradigm which views value as something firms provide to customers (usually through the provision of goods and/or services) and ignores the social nature and intrinsic subjectivity of knowledge gained through the interaction and individuality of customers (cf. Bonifacio, Bouquet, and Traverso 2002). The SD logic notion of *service* as the fundamental basis of exchange recognizes the subjectivity of knowledge, and advocates a shift to a process of mutual service provision (Vargo and Lusch 2008b). It is explicitly stated in their first foundation premise: "The application of specialized skill(s) and knowledge is the fundamental basis of exchange" (Vargo and Lusch 2008a).

A recent shift in the knowledge management literatures recognizes the role of subjectivity by acknowledging that information only becomes knowledge when put into a logical and understandable context that can be verified and recalled from experience (cf. Gunnlaugsdottir 2003). The insights of Polanyi (1958) a half-century ago established a foundation for this school of thought. He stated that processes of tacit integration—by which tacit knowledge (the hidden experiences and skills we possess) and the human cognitive processes we engage in are combined—are the root of what we know and what we do. Providing a managerial perspective, Schlegelmilch and Penz (2002: 6) define knowledge as "the tangible creations of human intellect which include technical expertise, problem-solving capability, creativity and managerial skills which are embodied in the employees of the organization." Arising from these views are two key themes that capture the new perspective of knowledge management. First, knowledge cannot be wholly objectified because the experience, expertise, values, and interpretive meanings are held in the mind of the knower and are the tangible creation of human intellect (see Ballantyne and Varey 2006). Secondly, knowledge is contextual: it is a logical and understandable form of problem solving or task completion where knowledge is embedded in the context of a specific system, for a specific purpose, and is thus a specific asset (Glazer 1991).

These themes represent a shift in the dominant logic of knowledge management from the managerial control of some "thing" (such as information) to the development of subjective and contextual intellectual capital. This shift acknowledges the importance of knowledge management in creating value for firms, their stakeholders, and their customers (Vargo and Lusch 2004). Whereas much of the literature on knowledge management focuses on the management of data and information through information storage, dissemination, and access, SD logic shifts the focus to knowledgeable workers and managerial decision-making. As Foote, Weiss, Matson, and Wenger (2002) point out, knowledgeable workers now must make decisions in unpredictable situations outside the bounds of rules-based processes. This may be particularly true of sales personnel, and the trend in forming cross-functional sales teams makes such decision-making especially complex. The ability to integrate information to foster consistency in team decision-making and assist sales teams in discovering new ways to satisfy customers' needs remains a critical focus of team learning endeavours (Rangarajan et al. 2004). Hanvanich, Sivakumar, and Hult (2006) also bring to the forefront the importance of learning when confronted by turbulent environments. These studies all agree that decisions must be adapted to situations and customer relationships managed in ways that benefit the organization and its stakeholders.

Fiol and Lyles (1985: 811) define organizational learning as "[t]he process of improving actions through better knowledge and understanding . . . the development of insights, knowledge and associations between past actions, the effectiveness of those actions and future actions." Fiol and Lyles take a cyclical view—in which organizational learning is a change process of knowledge development, use, reflection, and modification—thus viewing knowledge management as a process of learning and change. Recently, marketing researchers have recognized the importance of organizational learning, especially in the context of competing in the marketing environment. Of particular interest are the works by Hunt and Morgan (1995), Mouzas, Henneberg, and Naude (2008), and Kandemir, Yaprak, and Cavusgil (2006). These articles position organizational learning within a business network where alliances and multilateral interactions are used along with intangible, higher-order resources to enhance company performance and to capture competitive advantage.

Slater and Narver (1995) contend that marketing and sales act as a prime source of both information about, and understanding of, the market and benefits through individual learning (see also Kandemir, Yaprak, and Cavusgil 2006, Mouzas, Henneberg, and Naude 2008). The actions of marketers and salesforce personnel influence information and knowledge generation across all levels of the organization, and provide unique insights into the interrelationships that span these levels as well as interrelationships outside the organization. This interplay between the organization and its environment is what Staber and Sydow (2002) termed "reflexivity," and implies that the organization is constructed in the process of interpreting and acting on environments. Becoming sensitized to this reflexive process is an important feature of sales force learning, as sales personnel with high contextual understanding will be better able to comprehend what learning is needed, how they learn, and the process used to acquire it (Artis and Harris 2007). An example of this is seen in Box 17.1, where forming learning partnerships is seen as a key to developing a contextual understanding of the application of a particular technology in the creation of value. Hence, organizations need to incorporate learning into their overall sales strategy and support it through the allocation of budgetary, time, and financial resources and by measuring, incentivizing, and rewarding learning activities and outcomes (Artis and Harris 2007).

17.2.2 The Role of the Customer in Value Co-creation

We have seen an increase in the importance of feedback from the customer as a contributor to future value propositions, thus allowing firms to extend their involvement with the consumer both pre- and post-exchange (Ballantyne and Varey 2008). Value networks should ultimately take a market-oriented approach and connect marketers to consumers through the dual nature of value creation (cf. Penaloza and Venkatesh 2006). While the 2007 American Marketing Association marketing definition suggests marketing's function is in fact value creation, Vargo and Lusch (2004) argue that in order to take a market-oriented approach, value

Box 17.1. Forming Learning Partnerships

Collaboration for learning can cut across several dimensions of the value chain, and may involve a non-commercial partner as the catalyst for learning. For example, the US Department of Energy has sponsored a five-year demonstration and validation project designed to show practical applications of hydrogen energy technology. Three related industries have come together to share costs with the Department of Energy. Chevron Texaco (fuel supplier), Hyundai Motor Co (OEM), and UTC Fuel Cells (component supplier) will investigate the issue and jointly build an understanding of the key applications for the technology. Thus, opportunities seem to exist during the project for further networking and learning on related issues.

This intervention by the US Department of Energy to facilitate collaborations showing the practical applications of hydrogen energy technology is primarily aimed at forming learning partnerships which will question revered industry level wisdom by finding new ways to serve the market. At the firm level, the problem definition and commercial objectives of the firm should reflect this change in market understanding achieved at the industry level. At the group level, preferred solutions should give way to new and innovative approaches, and individuals should gain new experience which should alter the understanding of the issues to be addressed. This ripple effect should not be simply one-way (industry to individual): ripples of innovation may also travel upward, where individual innovation and understanding translates into industry-level redefinitions of market needs.

In the automobile industry manufacturers need to react to market demands quickly and more flexibly, to innovate continuously, and to meet increasingly demanding consumer expectations. Collaboration will help the industry (including whole networks of manufacturers, component suppliers, and service providers) understand how to create value faster, undertake more agile processes, implement continuous innovation utilizing both emerging vehicle technologies and new ideas, and respond to ever-increasing customer expectations.

should be defined and determined by the customer rather than by the organization. The organization does however create value propositions through marketplace knowledge and the process of learning what the customer values. Organizations, based on their knowledge of the customer, offer value propositions that are only promises of something that they believe are meaningful and desirable. The customer's participation through feedback and the organization's involved learning help turn value propositions into value. Borrowing from the work of Schembri (2006), we go one step further and argue that the co-creation of value propositions is insufficient. To create true value that is beneficial to all, the customer, the organization, and the organizational network partners must all recognize the same reality in terms of value. Vargo and Lusch (2008a) recognize in their tenth foundation premise that value co-creation is in fact phenomenological and experiential. The implication for sales force activities is that while sales personnel may develop close ties with their customers (e.g. in key account management), sharing their under-standing of these customers and their value desires may not be forthcoming, and may require closer integration with other functions within the organization (John-ston and Marshall 2009).

Penaloza and Venkatesh (2006) recognize the need to address perception and meaning creation in consumers as a paradox. This perspective argues that market-ers and sales personnel attribute to the consumer characteristics that they them-selves understand and identify with (thus using themselves as a template to comprehend the consumer). In support of this scenario, many organizations have lost sight of the true nature of value and exchange for consumers because of the indirect exchange of skills in vertical marketing systems and the distance that may exist between many organizational members and their ultimate customer. As the concept of market orientation prescribes, linking internal perceptions of organizational purpose and action to marketplace realities places the operant resources created by knowledgeable individuals once again squarely at the heart of the value proposition creation process. Thus markets are viewed, not as the arena of exchange, but as a process of social construction that marketers and consumers engage in (Penaloza and Venkatesh 2006). In the social construction of value, salespeople who have highly developed cognitive skills are able to provide more elaborate, distinctive, and hypothetical scripts and to anticipate customer needs, and are thus more effective (Chonko et al. 2003). They may also be more effective in translating those insights into important organizational capabilities (Johnston and Marshall 2009). Thus, as boundary spanners, the sales force may help integrate market sensing and customer information into the organization through their ability to construct and contextualize meaning and not simply act as information providers.

Gunnlaugsdottir (2003) states that knowledge can be either internal or external to the organization, and that a key concern is the difficulty of making internalized knowledge explicit. As sales personnel are generally separated from managers, they may become more autonomous in their learning and may assimilate information from sources other than their own organization (Chonko et al. 2003). Thus, organizational support is needed to help support autonomous learning and to tap into the variety of information sources that sales personnel may have contact with. As Morgan (2004) observes, organizations become learning organizations only when the learning process is applied to practical situations and thus allows the organization to develop enhanced capabilities in which knowing is related to doing. Vargo and Lusch (2004) view the translation of learning processes into organizational capabilities as a defining feature of marketing as an operant re-source. We have already seen how, at the individual level, knowledge of market-place realities helps enhance the development of organizational value propositions. However, in order for this to actually take place this same knowledge must be embedded within wider social practices (Giddens 1984). Organizations that empower their workforces and engage in organizational memory activities (i.e. the storage and retrieval of information) tend to be more successful at learning from previous mistakes than those who exercise empowerment alone and who thus tend to wait for market forces to push them into action (Chonko et al. 2003). Crossan, Lane, and White (1999) refer to this process of embedding knowledge into social practices as "strategic renewal." This is where individuals, groups, and organizations engage in processes which allow the refining and developing of intuitive insights and interpreting those insights by the individuals to be shared with others in groups, who themselves, through conversations and dialogue, interpret and integrate a shared understanding. This then becomes institutionalized in the routines, rules, and practices of the organization.

As individuals sanction these routines, rules, and practices, they do so by drawing on norms or standards of morality, and thus maintain or modify social structures through what Giddens (1984) termed "legitimation." We define legitimation as the rules and norms that help us know "what we should do and how to do it in this organization" (Staber and Sydow 2002). Thus, individuals affect social practices through their collective sharing and interpretation of knowledge and their perceptions of organizational purpose and action. However, these same individuals draw upon the rules and resources of the organization's wider social practices, shared behaviors, and norms to establish a common culture from which they develop and offer value propositions. These social practices should involve creating customer, competitor, and inter-functional coordination if they are to enhance market orientation (Narver and Slater 1990). There is thus a need for both marketing and sales to manage network relationships (i.e. to be simultaneously competitive and collaborative) on the one hand, and to lead the effort of designing and building cross-functional business processes on the other (Vargo and Lusch 2004). Cross-functional boundary-spanning sales teams provide better customer value because individual salespeople do not possess all the knowledge or influence needed to implement complex programs involving the selling and buying organizations (Rangarajan et al. 2004), and thus teams provide a pooled intelligence. The importance of internal partnering in sales management is recognized as a vital aspect of the support the sales function needs from the organization. As Johnston and Marshall (2009) state, internal and external organizational processes are often in conflict. For example, the sales force may seek to maximize all sales, while other functions such as the accounts department may wish to select only those with superior credit ratings.

Argote, McEvily, and Reagans (2003) postulate that organizational relationships influence knowledge management outcomes by providing members with the opportunity to learn from each other. Thus, organizational support for sales activities may include the development of shared values, which then encourages the adoption of beliefs and behaviours that support organizational learning and customer value co-creation (Pullig, Maxham, and Hair 2002). We may summarize the key points of this section:

- Organizational decisions must be adapted to situations and customer relationships managed in ways that benefit the organization and its stakeholders.
- Organizational learning should be understood within a business network context, where alliances and multilateral interactions are used along with intangible, higher-order resources to enhance company performance and to capture competitive advantage.
- Markets are viewed, not as the arena of exchange, but as a process of social construction that marketers and consumers engage in. In the social construction of value, salespeople who have highly developed cognitive skills through the sharing of knowledge in the organization are more effective.
- Strategic renewal, where individuals, groups, and organizations engage in processes which allow the refining and developing of intuitive insights, is an important feature of sales force activities. As the interpretation of insights by the sales force is then shared with others, this then becomes institutionalized in the routines, rules, and practices of the organization.

Thus we see that in the co-creation of value and the increasing role of the customer in such value creation processes, organizational support for the sales force may well need to focus more on the development and appropriate rules, routines and practices that take into account the needs and interests of a wider stakeholder group. This marks a distinct change from the incentivization of individual sales personnel to achieve unit or revenue sales targets. It also encourages the development of innovation and learning practices, which we now discuss in section 17.3.

17.3 THE ROLE OF SALES IN FACILITATING INNOVATION AND A LEARNING ORGANIZATION

17.3.1 The Sales Function as Resource Integrator

As we have noted before, Lusch and Vargo (2006) and Vargo and Lusch (2008b) view both the firm and the customer as resource integrators, and have called for the refinement and elaboration of this resource integration concept in their ninth foundation premise of SD logic. The notion of resource integration implies that knowledge is more than just learning. Knowledge is learning the right things, and those things are acquired through sharing (Cohen and Levinthal 1990). This requires marketplace feedback and adjustments to organizational knowledge. Thus organizational learning is developed through the links between the value proposition offered by the firm, value as determined by the customer, and feedback from the customer that results in the co-creation of the value process. This process contributes to updated knowledge and leads to organizational learning (cf. Fiol and Lyles 1985; Crossan et al. 1999), and represents a fundamental shift in the way the sales force is viewed. The classic view of the sales force as a means of communicating value to the market, termed "the new marketing myopia," is shifting to one of relational selling and value co-creation where providing differentiated services and consultative selling to customers is a primary role of the sales force (Hunter and Perreault 2007). Thus knowledge management and marketing activities are related.

Schlegelmilch and Penz (2002) discuss four stages in the knowledge management value chain as a means of understanding the relationship between knowledge management and marketing activities. The first stage, knowledge creation, works by establishing interactions between individuals and organizations and by creating lateral connections among functional units. This process facilitates the transformation of information into knowledge. When taking a strategic perspective of the knowledge network, the best results evolve when activities are closely aligned with the organization's strategic priorities (Buchel and Raub 2002). Consequently, marketing should lead the effort in designing and building cross-functional business processes, and should be placed at the core of the firm's strategic planning (Vargo and Lusch 2004). Organisational support for the adoption of sales force support initiatives, such as SFA, is critical. Such support includes interfunctional coordination, facilitative leadership, and an organic firm structure (which is more decentralized and exhibits extensive lateral communication across functional areas: Pullig et al. 2002). Organizational support also needs to move beyond the simple aim of motivating sales force personnel to use technology to supporting relationship-forging tasks which help link technology use to sales force performance (Hunter and Perreault 2007). Such relationship-forging tasks include the sharing of market knowledge with customers and proposing integrative solutions that are beneficial to both the buying and selling organizations. Thus, the role of sales in building relationships with customers may include activities such as trust building, setting reasonable customer expectations, educating customers on product/service use, and assisting in service provision and complaint handling (Johnston and Marshall 2009).

The second stage, knowledge storage, refers to knowledge that is made explicit and distributable in raw materials, products and services, business practices and processes, and the organizational culture. Thus, knowledge and skills can be transferred directly through education or training, or indirectly as tangible products (which can be viewed as embodied knowledge: Vargo and Lusch 2004). As such, new definitions of marketing and sales move away from defining products as "vessels of value" to be offered to consumers, and move towards a view of products as transmitters of operant resources to be utilized by consumers in creating value. Encouraging consultative selling activities and facilitating the ability of the sales force to educate customers in how they can create value (both value in use and value in exchange) for themselves from the value propositions of the firm is, therefore, an important way in which organizations may support their sales personnel.

The third stage, knowledge distribution, relates to knowledge that may be exchanged between source and receiver. The aim of this exchange is to integrate the new marketing knowledge into organizational memory for future use. Buchel and Raub (2002) refer to this as the creation of a network context where knowledge networks form a parallel structure that exists alongside the more traditional boundaries of functional departments, product groups, or business units. Clearly, salesforce automation and CRM technologies could be used to support such knowledge sharing.

Finally, the fourth stage, knowledge application, focuses upon the objective of applying knowledge—the objective generally being to leverage the knowledge network so that individual network members will actively transfer their knowledge to the wider organization (Buchel and Raub 2002). Here, the use of SFA and CRM to go beyond information dissemination to support creativity and problem solving would be an important organizational commitment to the sales force. In addition, sales force organization may need to reflect customer rather than product groupings, and may involve alliances with others (such as team selling, multilevel selling, and co-marketing activities), if it is to make the most of the knowledge acquired and shared and thus leverage it for strategic advantage (Johnston and Marshall 2009).

However, transferring knowledge from individuals to the wider organization presents both conceptual and practical challenges. Berends, Boersma, and Weggeman (2003) point out that a central point of debate is how the concept of learning (often associated with knowledge, cognition and mental activities) can best be applied to organizations. While individuals play an important role in organizational learning as the agents or instruments of learning, there is little evidence to suggest that organizational learning processes are similar to individual learning processes. Building theories of organizational learning solely from theories of individual learning creates difficulties when trying to capture the social nature of organizational learning (cf. Berends et al. 2003). This social aspect of organizational learning presents us with a paradox. The paradox is that collective learning, by definition, encompasses both divergence and convergence of the meanings that people assign to their surroundings. Fiol (1994) states that even if individuals disagree about their interpretive pictures (or communication content), they may still converge around a framework that is broad enough to encompass those differences. As seen through the Venn diagram in Figure 17.4, meaning and framing overlap.

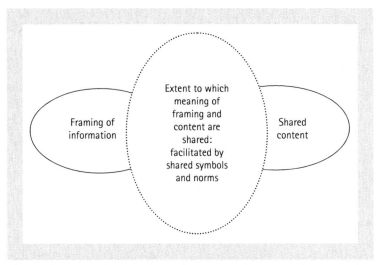

Fig. 17.4. Process of Organizational Learning in a Network taken from Johnston, Peters, and Gassenheimer (2006)

Giddens (1984) would describe this as the interpretive scheme, and would see its role as helping individuals to share in a common stock of knowledge without the need to assume that those individuals have common meanings and values which are somehow—at the level of the organization—identical and replicable across space and time (Boland 1996). For sales force learning to occur, a consensus on the meaning of information and its implications for the business must exist (Rangarajan et al. 2004). Polanyi (1958) placed consciousness partly outside the mind, in the world of intentions and in the observable activities that we can share with others. Thus, collective learning is an action in which individuals perform intentional actions not in isolation, but as embedded actors in active systems of social relations. Such embeddedness reflects the views of both Polanyi (1958) and Granovetter (1973) that actors draw upon interpersonal relations both inside and outside the sphere of economic behavior in forming preferences, desires, and actions (see also Rizza 2006). Polanyi (1958) identified two non-economic regulation mechanisms: reciprocity (in which resources are shared because of common obligations) and redistribution (in which resources are allocated on the principle of authority and power). These two regulatory institutions, reciprocity and redistribution, characterize a hybrid approach to embeddedness which does not see economic phenomena simply entrenched in social networks, but which highlights the historical and time-dependent nature of economic system development. Thus, embeddedness is a result of the interweaving of economic and non-economic institutions. Polanyi (1958) would contend that it is through this interweaving that individuals actively integrate and build up a world of meaning (Hodgkin

1992). Given that role perceptions on the part of sales personnel may affect their performance in many ways (e.g. feelings of ambiguity or conflict), the way in which organizations support the sales function through reciprocity and the redistribution of resources has important implications for sales force effectiveness (Johnston and Marshall 2009).

Argote, McEvily, and Reagans (2003) recognize that the framing of organizational knowledge (i.e. how knowledge is embedded in an organization's memory through rules and routines) helps us to understand how embedded knowledge affects organizational performance outcomes. For example, organizational actions have marketplace consequences that may be experienced at both micro and macro levels. As noted by Pozzebon (2004: 263),

Actions carried out in the name of organizations are driven by individuals. When these actions become a constituent element in the relations between an organization and external bodies, they move onto an even higher level of social process. The consequences of this process for the organization are social in origin but may be interpreted in some circumstances by individual actors primarily in terms of their own personal values or priorities.

Therefore, any gaps in what the sales organization has learned and what it should do presents a challenge. Individual sales personnel need to synchronize institutional learning (which tends to exploit past learning) with new learning that reflects changes in the environment (Chonko et al. 2003). However, from the outset organizational and individual recognition of the need for learning may be divergent, and so organizations must take steps to bridge this gap. Organizational support for such learning may include the incorporation of customers in the innovation process, management recognition of the value for public reinforcement of appropriate rules and practices, appropriate alignment of the organizational and sales force structures, rewards and sanctions that reinforce desired behaviors, and the provision of training and support for sales personnel. In Box 17.2 we see an example of organizational support for learning, where suppliers who are not normally connected to the automotive industry become key partners in the innovation process.

17.3.2 Innovation and the Role of Sales as a Bridge in Network Structures

Argote, McEvily, and Reagans (2003) suggest that one important line of work emerging is on the structural configuration of a set of relationships. They state that the properties of an organization's internal social network as well as its network to other firms affect learning and knowledge transfer. For example, do certain network positions enable differential advantages or liabilities relative to other positions in the network?

Box 17.2. Customers as Co-creators

Consumers, now more than ever, see their car as an extension of their lives and, more importantly, expect to be connected to that life when driving. What this means for the car manufacturer can only be understood in collaboration with suppliers to the other parts of the consumer's life—their office, their entertainment, and their sources of daily information. Such collaborations with companies outside the core automotive industry reflects the need identified by von Hipple (1986) for input from what he termed "lead users." Such lead users will be actively innovating to solve problems present at the leading edge of a trend, and may therefore bring unique and competitively advantageous knowledge (know what, how, and why) to the collaboration. Integration of this knowledge into existing network competences may be an issue. However, as Lilien et al. (2002) discovered, where lead user input facilitated breakthrough ideas, the product development teams involved made explicit efforts to integrate, or "fit," the new knowledge in order to facilitate its support and acceptance within the network firm concerned. Thus the teams attempted to "frame" this new knowledge in ways which would enhance its fit with current understanding and result in a better shared understanding between parties.

Toyota is perhaps, along with Honda, the most active company in collaborations to learn. The knowledge sharing between Toyota and its suppliers was noted several years ago by Dyer and Singh (1998), in particular the placement of Toyota employees within the supplier's firm. They contrasted this with the more arm's-length relationships developed by GM with its supplier network, where innovation and knowledge is considered proprietary and therefore often withheld from supply chain partners. This is a prime example of the difference between a relational view (Toyota) and a resource-based view (GM) of collaborative advantage, according to Dyer and Singh (1998). While GM may attempt to protect rather than share valuable proprietary know-how to prevent knowledge spill-over that might erode or eliminate its competitive advantage, Toyota would systematically share valuable know-how with alliance partners in return for access to the stock of valuable knowledge residing within those partners.

Researchers such as Burt (1992) have argued that network linkages enable and constrain the flexibility, autonomy, and consequently the effectiveness of organizational members. He suggests that individuals seek to enhance their power within a network by forging ties with two or more unconnected others, thus creating indirect ties between the people with whom they are linked. This enables them to broker the relationship between these otherwise unconnected network members. It also widens and diversifies the pool of available information and may thus enhance opportunities for innovation. Sales force personnel are frequently found in network positions that act as bridging mechanisms, connecting customers and stakeholders who are external to the firm with resource providers within the firm. While this role may bring satisfaction and a sense of importance to the sales function, it may also make sales personnel susceptible to role conflict, role ambiguity, and inaccurate role perceptions as they receive demands from customers and other organizations with diverse and perhaps competing goals (Johnston and Marshall

2009). Another important role for the sales force as boundary spanners is to protect the organization from information overload by filtering, interpreting, and channelling relevant information to appropriate functional departmental areas of the firm (Rangarajan et al. 2004). This characterizes the power of the sales function in many organizations.

In addition to the notion of network structure as the presence or absence of ties, the strength of these ties are important structural features of a network. Granovetter (1973) defined tie strength as characterizing the closeness and interaction frequency of a relationship between two parties in a network. Depending on the degree of interdependence, such ties may be more or less dense, complex, or reciprocal. Strong ties may provide timely access to information, and those with whom they are strongly tied are more motivated to share information with these parties. By contrast, those with whom they are weakly tied are likely to travel in different circles from one another, thereby opening up access to new information. Features of a network such as connection strength, direction, and time frame shape the interdependence among network members and influence the learning processes in networks.

Reagans and McEvily (2003: 240) point out that researchers have inferred the association between networks and knowledge transfer by observing the association between network structure (or its surrogate, strength of network ties) and network performance rather than examining the effect of networks on knowledge transfer directly. In particular, they focus on the role of cohesion (the extent to which a relationship is surrounded by strong third party connections) and range (the extent to which network connections span institutional, organizational, or social boundaries) as facilitators of knowledge assimilation and transfer in networks. In addition, the strategic alliance literature, using network theories, has attempted to explain the learning synergies that can arise from sharing insights within a network (cf. Morgan 2004). Morgan (2004) and Barrett, Cappleman, Shoib, and Walsham (2004) stress the importance of understanding how these networks function optimally.

A key component in network functionality is social capital, and the interactions that are sometimes perceived to threaten existing power structures. Social capital is defined as the actual and potential resources which are embedded within, available through, and derived from a network of relationships (Nahapiet and Ghoshal 1998). Defined more broadly, social capital is "the aspects of a social context, such as social ties, trusting relations, and value systems, that facilitate actions of individuals located within that context" (Tsai and Ghoshal 1998: 465). As such, social capital serves as the moral fibre of social exchange and establishes paths for knowledge transfer as well as reciprocal learning (cf. Thibaut and Kelley 1959). Not only do orders flow down and information flow up, but there is the possibility of lateral communication and grass-roots development of ideas and practices. Chonko et al. (2003) suggest that such communication is an important aspect of organizational learning from the sales force, and suggest that organizations need to examine the barriers to such communication and sharing.

The way in which individuals utilize power in such interactions through the ability to allocate material and human resources is a process which Giddens (1984) terms the creation, reinforcement or change of structures of *domination*. Domination is characterized by the way in which control over resources is available to actors, and by the way in which they use facilities to mobilize available resources (Staber and Sydow 2002). This would support the view of Rangarajan et al. (2004) that the manner in which individuals process information and the choice of information to process are important characteristics of sales team members in the boundary-spanning role. We can see domination processes unfold when we examine network structures over time. In terms of network structure and knowledge, Soda, Usai, and Zaheer (2004) note that aspects of network structure, such as the benefits of structural holes (where different parts of the network are largely disconnected but bridged by a few key individuals) as opposed to closure (where dense and mutually interconnected network ties exist between most or all network members), may be time-dependent. They found that while the value of social capital in a dense network persisted over time (and indeed may take time to become established), the benefit of a network full of structural holes diminished over time. Thus actions on the part of the sales force to develop relationships with customers may help to create dense network structures, while their wider discrete exchanges in the overall market may help to identify important gaps or structural holes which the firm may wish to fill. In the immediate period, structural holes may provide access to rich sources of new information and arbitrage value. They may also be more economical, in that they require fewer resources to maintain redundant ties. However, over time those benefits diminish, and thus knowledge would be less accessible in such a network as time passes. This then places pressure upon the sales force to balance the enhancement of existing customer relationships with the acquisition and development of new customer relationships.

At the level of the individual within networks, McFadyen and Cannella (2004) explored the role of interpersonal relationship strength and number of relationships in building social capital. They found that a quadratic relationship existed for both the number and strength of interpersonal relationships with knowledge creation. While interpersonal relationships did enhance knowledge creation up to a point, because of the resources involved in building and maintaining such relationships as they increased in number, returns on knowledge creation diminished. Again, while strong interpersonal relationships were seen as beneficial in knowledge creation, as the strength of these relationships increased through repeated interactions, the knowledge stock between the relationship partners became too similar and thus inhibited further knowledge creation. It is conceivable that while this research focused on the level of the individual, such dynamics might also been present at the network level as well. Organizational guidance in customer relationship development is therefore vital to the sales force so that resources may be best targeted. Understanding which customers represent long-term value and should thus be invested in is another way in which the organization needs to support its sales force. We may summarize the key points of this section thus:

- The classic view of the sales force as a means of communicating value to the market, termed "the new marketing myopia," is shifting to one of relational selling and value co-creation where providing differentiated services and consultative selling to customers is a primary role of the sales force.
- For sales force learning to occur, a consensus on the meaning of information and its implications for the business must exist. Thus, collective learning is an action in which individuals perform intentional actions not in isolation, but as embedded actors in active systems of social relations.
- Sales force personnel are frequently found in network positions that act as bridging mechanisms, connecting customers and stakeholders who are external to the firm with resource providers within the firm.
- An important role for the sales force is to protect the organization from information overload by filtering, interpreting, and channelling relevant information to appropriate functional departmental areas of the firm. This characterizes the power of the sales function in many organizations.

17.4 CONCLUSIONS

We began this discussion with the observation that there has been a marked shift in the relationship between marketing and value creation, one often involving a network of participants both inside and outside the firm itself. As a result of this shift, a new dominant logic for marketing has evolved, one which sees the role of both marketing and sales as that of developing core competencies and positioning them as value propositions that offer potential competitive advantage to the firm. Building from this new perspective, we examined how organizational knowledge, serving as a basis for SD logic, can be applied to the creation of competitively superior value propositions and to the important function of integrating knowledge throughout the value network.

We drew links between the value proposition offered by the firm, value as determined by the customer, and feedback from the process of customer value co-creation to inform further actions on the part of the firm—thus allowing organizations to learn. We also explored how network structures and partnerships enable and constrain learning practices, and how social practices are translated into new value propositions through the creation, storage, dissemination, and application of knowledge within such networks. In particular, we discussed how the position that an individual held within their network might determine the knowledge, processes, and resources that they had access to, and how they then utilized these resources. In order to identify and support those individuals in critical network positions, such as the sales force, marketing should lead the effort in designing and building cross-functional business processes, and be placed at the core of the firm's strategic planning. This implies a need for the marketing to focus on the management of network relationships that takes into account the structural features of the network as a whole, as well as the needs and features of the individuals involved.

In addition, we examined the ways in which learning practices influence and are influenced by knowledgeable individuals through the collective sharing of knowledge and experience, and sought to explain how these social practices are translated into new value propositions through the linking of internal perceptions of organizational purpose and action to marketplace realities. An important role for marketing, and in particular the sales function, as a process of social construction (engaging both firms and consumers) could be to identify and address the unacknowledged preconditions and unintended consequences of corporate action and thus expand the bounds of knowledgeability in the network. For both marketing and sales managers, this implies the need for a much broader understanding of the context of network relationships and knowledge sharing, rather than a focus on actions and activities alone.

Finally, we recognized the embeddedness of learning practices. These practices are undertaken within a structured social context that is both enabling and constraining, and carried out by knowledgeable individuals. Given that translating learning processes into organizational capabilities is a defining feature of marketing, according to SD logic (Vargo and Lusch 2004), then helping to establish norms and rules that embed knowledge within wider social practices within the organization and the collective network may be understood as another key responsibility of marketing, and an important way in which it may support its sales efforts.

17.4.1 Managerial Implications

Value creation is a concept that marketing is rethinking, and this is a challenge. In SD logic, profits provide feedback to the firm about the success of the value propositions offered to customers. Several important questions arise in relation to value co-creation, profitability, and the role of the sales force:

- How should sales and marketing define what is profitable, and what timeframe for measuring profitability would be appropriate?
- How is value now related to value later? What are the implications of this "value time gap" for the sales function?
- Are the profits from value in exchange related to the profits from value-in-use, and if so, how?

• What are the mechanisms that allow value co-creation?

The managerial implications of these questions include revisiting the way in which the sales function is supported in many organizations. If value is now a function of co-creation activities, and if profitability is not simply an economic end product of the sales function but a potentially long-term process of innovation and extended value creation, then organizational support for sales needs to rethink its focus. Traditional performance measures (e.g. sales contact efficiency, conversion efficiency, and repeat orders) simply do not capture the new role of the sales function as a facilitator of value co-creation with customers.

In addition, there is the whole question of evaluating the changes in marketing and sales productivity associated with knowledge management and organizational learning processes.

• What is the role of the sales force in understanding and translating profits into useful organization learning?
• How might organizational learning needs, and the SD logic, change the job of the sales force?
• What impact do different knowledge management and organizational learning processes have on sales productivity?
• How might the makeup of sales teams (or networks) affect sales outcomes?
• Are culturally and experientially homogeneous selling teams better suited for certain tasks (e.g. new product development) than others (e.g. product adaptation), or will diversity in such groups have a more positive impact upon performance?

The managerial implications of these questions includes a new appreciation of the sales role as one of knowledge facilitator and learning enhancer in the organization as a whole. This goes beyond the notion of information collection and dissemination, where the sales force is an observer of marketplace dynamics. As a key network member and a bridge between network participants, the building of social capital is an important feature of sales force activities, and one which needs recognition and support from the organization.

References

American Marketing Association, http://www.marketingpower.com/content2653039. php, accessed May 2008.

Argote, L., B. McEvily, and R. Reagans (2003). "Managing Knowledge in Organizations: An Integrative Framework and Review of Emerging Themes," *Management Science* 49: 571–82.

Artis, A. B., and E. G. Harris (2007). "Self-Directed Learning and Sales Force Performance: an Integrated Framework," *Journal of Personal Selling & Sales Management* 27, 9–24.

BALLANTYNE, D., and R. J. VAREY (2006). "Creating Value-in-Use Through Marketing Interaction: The Exchange Logic of Relating, Communication and Knowing," *Marketing Theory* 6: 335–48.

————(2008). "The Service-Dominant Logic and the Future of Marketing," *Journal of the Academy of Marketing Science* 36, 11–14.

BARRETT, M., S. CAPPLEMAN, I. SHOIB, and G. WALSHAM (2004). "Learning in Knowledge Communities: Managing Technology and Context," *European Management Journal* 22: 1–11.

BERENDS, H., K. BOERSMA, and M. WEGGEMAN (2003). "The Structuration of Organizational Learning," *Human Relations* 56.9: 1035–56.

BOLAND, R. J. (1996). "Why Shared Meanings Have No Place in Structuration Theory: A Reply to Scaperns and Macintosh," *Accounting, Organizations and Society* 21.7–8: 691–7.

BONIFACIO, M., P. BOUQUET, and P. TRAVERSO (2002). "Enabling Distributed Knowledge Management: Managerial and Technological Implications," *Informatik/Informatique* 1: 23–9.

BUCHEL, B., and S. RAUB (2002). "Building Knowledge-Creating Value Networks," *European Management Journal* 20.6: 587–96.

BURT, R. S. (1992). *Structural Holes: The Social Structure of Competition*, Cambridge, MA: Harvard University Press.

CHONKO, L. B., A. J. DUBINSKY, E. JONES, and J. A. ROBERTS (2003). "Organisational and Individual Learning in the Sales Force: An Agenda for Sales Research," *Journal of Business Research* 56, 935–46.

COHEN, W. M., and D. A. LEVINTHAL (1990). "Absorptive Capacity: A New Perspective on Learning and Innovation," *Administrative Science Quarterly* 35, 128–52.

COVA, B., and R. SALLE (2008). "Marketing Solutions in Accordance with the S-D Logic: Co-creating Value with Customer Network Actors," *Industrial Marketing Management* 37, 270–77.

CROSSAN, M. M., H. W. LANE, and R. E. WHITE (1999). "An Organizational Learning Framework: From Intuition to Institution," *Academy of Management Review* 243: 522–37.

DYER, J. H., and H. SINGH (1998). "The Relational View: Cooperative Strategy and Sources of Interorganisational Competitive Advantage," *Academy of Management Review* 23.4: 660–79.

FIOL, C. M. (1994). "Consensus, Diversity, and Learning in Organizations," *Organization Science* 5: 403–20.

——and M. A. LYLES (1985). "Organizational Learning," *Academy of Management Review* 10, 803–13.

FOOTE, N., L. WEISS, E. MATSON, and E. WENGER (2002). "Leveraging Group Knowledge for High-Performance Decision-Making," *Organizational Dynamics* 31.3: 280–95.

FORD, D., and H. HAKANSSON (2006). "The Idea of Business Interaction," *IMP Journal* 11: 4–27.

GIDDENS, A. (1984). *The Constitution of Society: Outline of the Theory of Structuration*. Chicago: Polity Press.

GLAZER, R. (1991). "Marketing in an Information-Intensive Environment: Strategic Implications of Knowledge as an Asset," *Journal of Marketing* 55: 10–19.

GRANOVETTER, M. (1973). "The Strength of Weak Ties," *American Journal of Sociology* 78, 1360–80.

GUNNLAUGSDOTTIR, J. (2003). "Seek and You Will Find, Share and You Will Benefit: Organizing Knowledge Using Groupware Systems," *International Journal of Information Management* 23, 363–80.

HANVANICH, S., K. SIVAKUMAR, and G. T. HULT (2006). "The Relationship of Learning and Memory with Organizational Performance: The Moderating Role of Turbulence," *Journal of the Academy of Marketing Science* 34: 600–612.

HODGKIN, R. A. (1992). "Michael Polanyi on the Activity of Knowing," *Oxford Review of Education* 183: 253–68.

HUNT, S. D., and R. M. MORGAN (1995). "The Comparative Advantage Theory of Competition," *Journal of Marketing* 58: 1–15.

HUNTER, G. K., and W. D. PERREAULT, Jr. (2007). "Making Sales Technology Effective," *Journal of Marketing* 71, 16–34.

HUTT, M. D., W. J. JOHNSTON, and J. R. RONCHETTO, Jr. (1985). "Selling Centres and Buying Centres: Formulating Strategic Exchange Patterns," *Journal of Personal Selling & Sales Management* 5.1, 33–40.

JOHNSTON, M. W., and G. W. MARSHALL (2009). *Churchill/Ford/Walker's Sales Force Management*, New York: McGraw-Hill.

JOHNSTON, W. J., L. D. PETERS, and J. B. GASSENHEIMER (2006). "Questions about Network Dynamics: Characteristics, Structures, and Interactions," *Journal of Business Research* 59, 945–54.

JUTTNER, U., and H. P. WEHRLI (1994). "Competitive Advantage: Merging Marketing and the Competence-Based Perspective," *Journal of Business and Industrial Marketing* 9.4: 42–53.

KANDEMIR, D., A. YAPRAK, and S. T. CAVUSGIL (2006). "Alliance Orientation Conceptualization, Measurement and Impact on Market Performance," *Journal of the Academy of Marketing Science* 34: 324–40.

KEENAN, B. (2000). "Cost-per-Call Data Deserve Scrutiny," *Industry Week* (January).

KITSON, H. D. (1922). "The Growth of the 'Service Idea' in Selling," *Journal of Political Economy* 30.3, 417–19.

KOHLI, A., and B. JAWORSKI (1990). "Market Orientation: The Construct, Research Propositions, and Managerial Implications," *Journal of Marketing* 54: 1–18.

LILIEN, G. L., P. D. MORRISON, K. S. SEARLS, M. SONNACK, and E. VON HIPPEL (2002). "Performance Assessment of the Lead User: Idea-Generation Process for New Product Development," *Management Science* 48.8: 1042–59.

LINGS, I. N. (2004). "Internal Market Orientation, Construct and Consequences," *Journal of Business Research* 57, 405–13.

LUBKEMAN, M., A. PRALLE, M. TSUSADA, S. DURANTON, J. HARSAAE, and J. IZARET (2009). "Collateral Damage: Function Focus, Responses for Marketing and Sales in the Global Downturn," Boston Consulting Group (February).

LUSCH, R., and S. VARGO (2006). "Service-Dominant Logic: Reactions, Reflections and Refinements," *Marketing Theory* 6.3: 281–8.

————and M. O'BRIEN (2007). "Competing through Service: Insights from Service-Dominant Logic," *Journal of Retailing* 83.1: 5–18.

MCFADYEN, M. A., and A. A. CANNELLA (2004). "Social Capital and Knowledge Creation: Diminishing Returns of the Number and Strength of Exchange Relationships," *Academy of Management Journal* 47, 735–46.

MCMAHON, D. (2000). "The Death of the Sales Force," Graziadio Business Report 3(2): accessed online 13 July 2009 at: http://gbr.pepperdine.edu/002/

MORGAN, R. E. (2004). "Market-Based Organizational Learning: Theoretical Reflections and Conceptual Insights," *Journal of Marketing Management* 20, 67–103.

MOUZAS, S., S. HENNEBERG, and P. NAUDE (2008). "Developing Network Insights," *Industrial Marketing Management* 37: 167–80.

NAHAPIET, J., and S. GHOSHAL (1998). "Social Capital, Intellectual Capital, and the Organisational Advantage," *Academy of Management Review* 23.2, 242–66.

NARVER, J. C., and S. SLATER (1990). "The Effects of a Marketing Orientation on Business Profitability," *Journal of Marketing* 54, 20–35.

PENALOZA, L., and A. VENKATESH (2006). "Further Evolving the New Dominant Logic of Marketing: From Services to the Social Construction of Markets," *Marketing Theory* 6: 299–316.

POLANYI, M. (1958). *Personal Knowledge*. London: Routledge & Kegan Paul.

POZZEBON, M. (2004). "The Influence of a Structurationist View on Strategic Management Research," *Journal of Management Studies* 41: 247–72.

PULLIG, C., J. G. MAXHAM III, and J. F. HAIR, Jr. (2002). "Salesforce Automation Systems: An Exploratory Examination of Organisational Factors Associated with Effective Implementation and Salesforce Productivity," *Journal of Business Research* 55, 401–15.

RANGARAJAN, D., L. B. CHONKO, E. JONES, and J. A. ROBERTS (2004). "Organisational Variables, Sales Force Perceptions of Readiness for Change, Learning, and Performance Among Boundary-Spanning Teams: A Conceptual Framework and Propositions for Research," *Industrial Marketing Management* 33, 289–305.

REAGANS, R., and B. McEVILY (2003). "Network Structure and Knowledge Transfer: The Effects of Cohesion and Range", *Administrative Science Quarterly* 48, 240–67.

RIZZA, R. (2006). "The Relationship between Economics and Sociology: The Contribution of Economic Sociology, Setting out from the Problem of Embeddedness," *International Review of Sociology* 16.1: 31–48.

SCHELL, M. (2003). *Buyer-Approved Selling*, Vancouver, BC: Marketshare.

SCHEMBRI, S. (2006). "Rationalizing Service Logic, or Understanding Services as Experience?" *Marketing Theory* 6: 381–92.

SCHLEGELMILCH, B. B., and E. PENZ (2002). "Knowledge Management in Marketing," *Marketing Review* 3, 5–19.

SHETH, J., and A. SHARMA (2008). "The Impact of the Product to Service Shift in Industrial Markets and the Evolution of the Sales Organization," *Industrial Marketing Management* 37, 260–69.

SLATER, S. F., and J. C. NARVER (1995). "Market Orientation and the Learning Organization," *Journal of Marketing* 59: 63–74.

SODA, G., A. USAI, and A. ZAHEER (2004). "Network Memory: The Influence of Past and Current Networks on Performance," *Academy of Management Journal* 47.6: 893–906.

STABER, U., and J. SYDOW (2002). "Organizational Adaptive Capacity: A Structuration Perspective," *Journal of Management Inquiry* 11.4: 408–24.

SUJAN H., B. WEITZ, and N. KUMAR (1994). "Learning Orientation, Working Smart, and Effective Selling," *Journal of Marketing* 58.3: 39–52.

THIBAUT, J. W., and H. H. KELLEY (1959). *The Social Psychology of Groups*, New York: Wiley.

TSAI, W., and S. GHOSHAL (1998). "Social Capital and Value Creation: The Role of Intrafirm Networks," *Academy of Management Journal* 41.4: 464–76.

VARGO, S. L., and R. F. LUSCH (2004). "Evolving to a New Dominant Logic for Marketing," *Journal of Marketing* 68: 1–17.

————(2008a). "Service-Dominant Logic: Continuing the Evolution," *Journal of the Academy of Marketing Science* 36, 1–10.

VARGO, S. L., and R. F. LUSCH (2008b). "From Goods to Service(s): Divergences and Convergences of Logics," *Industrial Marketing Management* 37, 254–9.

VERHOEF, P., and P. LEEFLANG (2009). "Understanding the Marketing Department's Influence Within the Firm," *Journal of Marketing* 73: 14–37.

VON HIPPLE, E. (1986). "Lead Users: A Source of Novel Product Concepts," *Management Science* 32.7: 791–805.

replaceable by an alternate channel because the sales force is lacking in strategic contribution. In Anderson and Trinkle's view (p. 191), the decision to employ a sales force or an alternate channel is a strategic decision that should involve the inputs of "*all* senior managers".

Despite these emerging perspectives that the selling function is a strategic resource and capability of the firm, the dominant view in the sales literature is that the selling function is an element of the marketing mix that is primarily tactical in nature (Viswanathan and Olson 1992, Slater and Olson 2000). Our purpose is to examine the strategic role of the selling function in terms of the resource-based view (RBV) on the firm. We feel that the RBV and its extension to a Dynamic Capability model (DCM) provide fundamental theoretical perspectives within which both strategic selling function research and practice can be enhanced. Hence, we first explore the resource-based theory of the firm to examine the bases on which the sales function may operate as a strategic resource or capability. Drawing on this and marketing literature, we present a Strategic Selling Framework (SSFF), which identifies some of the key selling function resources and capabilities that may impact an organization's ability to enjoy a sustainable competitive advantage. The framework also includes organizational context and capabilities that have the potential to amplify the impact of selling resources/capabilities on sustainable competitive advantage.

18.2 THEORETICAL PERSPECTIVES

As noted, our belief is that selling function[1] resources and capabilities are increasing in their importance in progressive firms. The pace and scope of environmental change stresses the firm's need to identify new revenue streams; to be entrepreneurial; to build and manage customer relationships; and to work closely with customers and channel partners to create mutual value. There are several reasons why the RBV and the DCM are well suited for building a conceptual framework for examining the strategic role of the sales function. First, the RBV and DCM stress change and evolution as an organizational fact of life, and hence elevate the resource and capability dialogue to higher-order, enterprise-level competencies and processes that facilitate organizational learning and marketplace adaptation. These change-oriented processes are fundamental to the emerging strategic entrepreneurship, relationship development, and customer management roles of the selling function in the firm. Second, these perspectives appear to be most relevant to defining a framework to guide future empirical research eliciting executives' models of intangible assets and business processes that underlie external learning,

internal coordination, and knowledge application. These are the very skills, resources, and processes that best fit the nature of the emerging selling function
priorities described. Third, these two perspectives should provide theoretical
propositions to guide the development of theory-driven empirical research
concerning the effect of specific resources and capabilities on variations in resulting
firm performance.

18.2.1 The Resource-Based View of the Firm

The core tenet of RBV is that resource and capability heterogeneity between firms
may provide potential competitive advantages that serve as catalysts for variations
in firm returns (Penrose 1959). The RBV theory includes considerable dialogue
concerning the nature and effect of resources and capabilities that enable sustainable competitive advantage and above-normal returns. In particular, the relative
impact of mere resource possession versus resource exploitation on firm performance has been stressed (Mahoney and Pandian 1992). This issue is important
because: (1) it distinguishes the impact of heterogeneity in resource possession
from that of intelligent resource deployment to produce market-valued goods and
services; and (2) it establishes a role for creativity and entrepreneurship, and other
managerial organizing skills and competences, in driving sustainable competitive
advantage and firm results. In short, managers matter when they are able to
identify and exploit a firm's specialized resources to fit customer values.

In our view, three issues are critical. First, the mere possession of resources, such
as a large sales force, does not provide much competitive advantage; rather, it is the
business processes and systems (e.g. customer solution design or customer relationship management routines) that are employed to convert these assets into
saleable products and services that matter (Rubin 1973, Wernerfelt 1984). It is these
business processes that are imperfectly mobile, valuable, and non-substitutable,
and hence provide sustainable competitive advantage (Barney 1991).

Second, distinctive competencies revolve around management's capability to
rationalize or exploit their allocation to fit value-creating and profit-generating
applications (Prahalad and Hamel 1990). In other words, management's creativity
and competence in leveraging, combining, transforming both resources and people
matters (Newbert 2007). These operant resources (Vargo and Lusch 2004) must be
critically examined in defining the role of the selling function in the firm.

Third, this emphasis on business processes and management capabilities has led
to the recognition of the role of "organizing" capabilities and contexts as drivers of
competitive advantage and performance (Newbert 2007). Hence, such issues as
how to define and facilitate appropriate inter-function cooperation, how to develop
and retain human and social capital, how to define and enable a results-driven

culture, and how to motivate and reward productivity are recognized as core competences (Barney 1997).

A thorough review of the RBV literature by Newbert (2007) concluded that RBV research, while extensive theoretically, is only at its nascent stage empirically. Newbert classifies the extant research into four general categories: resources, capabilities, organizing contexts, and dynamic capabilities. **Resources** are the simplest independent predictors of a firm's sustainable competitive advantage (SCA); they are the heterogeneous and rare stock of assets, tangible or intangible, that the firm possesses at a given point in time. It is important to note that resources would include such market-based or reputational assets as entrepreneurial, market, and innovation orientation. The possession of such resources, if rare and inimitable, is an antecedent of SCA and above normal returns (Barney 1991).

Capabilities provide the firm with the ability to deploy resources by allocating and integrating them to create and support valued products and services or other organizationally productive purposes. Recent research has emphasized a variety of capabilities, processes, or routines that enable management to exploit the latent value of its firm's resources and market-based assets, including core competencies (Fiol 1991), combinative capabilities (Kogut and Zander 1992), transformational competencies (Lado, Boyd, and Wright 1992), and organizational capabilities (Russo and Fouts 1997). These theories provide a basis for understanding the roles of leaders in firms.

Organizing processes and contexts were proposed by Barney (1997) to recognize the value of organizational structure in enabling the exploitation of the full potential of resources to create valued products and services. He argued that organizational capabilities included such firm-level aspects as its general orientation to the market (e.g. market, entrepreneurial, or innovation orientation), its generic strategy (cost leadership, product innovation, differentiation, or customer intimacy strategy), and its implementation model (centralization policy, control systems, and incentive structure). In short, the organization of the firm is considered to be the firm-level orientation, strategy, or context that encourages an overall and systematic approach to the utilization of resources and capabilities (Newbert 2007).

Since the RBV model stresses relatively stable or evolutionary markets, a dynamic capabilities model has been proposed (Teece, Pisano, and Shuen 1997, Teece 2007). A **dynamic capability** is the firm's "ability to integrate, build, and reconfigure internal and external competencies to address rapidly changing environments" (Teece, Pisano, and Shuen 1997: 510). It is important to note that the scholarly work based on the RBV largely emphasizes the *direct* effects of specific resources and capabilities on either firm-level performance or competitive advantage. Empirical studies of predictor variables or moderating contexts that fit either the organizing or dynamic capabilities models are to date rare.

In light of the extant theoretical and empirical research, several observations are offered. First, the specific lists of resources and capabilities described, while broadly defined, hint at the potential relevance and significance of the selling function. Newbert (2007) notes the following resource categories: innovation, customer-related, service climate, knowledge/experience, and price. Under capabilities, he includes: market orientation, information acquisition, customer relationship building, client retention, negotiation, and pricing. Under "organizing" processes and contexts, Newbert includes integration, quality strategy, innovation strategy, growth strategy, cost reduction strategy, and diversification as moderators of the direct effects of resources and reputation assets on firm level performance. The relevance of these resources, capabilities, and organizational context factors to the strategic role of the sales function is intriguing.

Clearly, the conceptual and operational definitions of the aforementioned resources and capabilities as predictors of competitive advantage must be explored for their strategic content relevance for the selling function. For example, when benchmarking marketing capabilities, Vorhies and Morgan (2005) operationalize sales force capabilities as effective sales force training, planning and control systems, selling skills, management skills, and sales support relative to major competitors. This raises the question whether a capability is the sum of its tactical components. The authors acknowledged that there was little relevant literature on marketing and presumably sales capabilities, and so relied on a number of field interviews of marketing managers. Secondly, the existing sales and marketing literature should be re-examined in light of these RBV constructs and their impact on firm performance. For example, market orientation and innovation capacity have been investigated in a variety of marketing studies (Kohli and Jaworski 1990, Slater and Narver 1995). These studies provide the grist for developing a clearer conceptual picture of the strategic role of the sales function from a RBV. They might also provide a basis for prioritizing an otherwise overwhelming specification problem in building and testing models of how resources and capabilities directly and indirectly impact firm performance.

Newbert's (2007) review of the empirical work notes a general lack of studies focused on dynamic capabilities. The paucity of dynamic capabilities research is likely due to the recentness of its emergence to fit hyper-competitive market contexts. Hence, we turn to a brief review of the most recent DCM framework for its relevancy for defining the strategic role of the sales function.

18.2.2 The Dynamic Capabilities View of the Firm

Contemporary to Barney's (1997) "organizing" view of resources and capabilities, Teece, Pisano, and Shuen (1997) proposed the dynamic capabilities model. DCM has been advanced as a more general (and quite complex) model with focus on the evolutionary adaptability of the firm (Teece 2007). As Eisenhardt and Martin (2000: 1107) indicate, dynamic capabilities are the "organizational and strategic routines by which firms achieve new resource configurations as markets emerge, collide, split, or die."

The DCM places its emphasis on management's purposeful decisions to adapt the firm and its resources and capabilities in order to provide strategic options to pursue anticipated marketplace opportunities (Helfat and Peteraf 2003). In the first place, the DCM emphasizes management's capability to *sense* and *shape* opportunities and threats in fast moving "opaque" environments. Hence, higher-order entrepreneurial skills that involve scanning, learning, interpreting, and creating ideas, concepts, and products to fit emerging opportunities are critical. One view is that individual skills and know-how (creativity, problem framing, frame busting, customer need assessment, and practical wisdom), most often learned through experience, are critical. Nevertheless, leaders who embody such capabilities and skills would still need to be able to persuade others in their firms of the need to move in the direction of their preferred strategic choices.

An alternate view is that these skills are organizational in nature, such as information acquisition and sharing, competitor assessment, change-oriented culture, and scientific testing processes and routines. Among these capabilities, Teece (2007) includes: processes for market segmentation, identifying customer needs, and the ability to innovate; processes for relating to suppliers and alliance partners and their innovation initiatives; and processes for relating to outside sources of new ideas and technologies.

The capacity to *seize* opportunities is also critical in the DCM framework. Essentially, seizing involves higher-order skills and know-how in managing the business development or commercialization process. However, it is complicated by the problem of properly timing full-scale investments in new products or services. Thus, knowledge of how markets and technologies typically evolve and how networks or ecosystems work is critical. Interestingly, Teece (2007) argues that there is often a role within the firm for "promoters" whose task is to defeat the naysayers. He also indicates that business success in seizing opportunities is more dependent on organizational than on technological innovations. From our point of view, this may mean that senior sales executives with market and customer knowledge play a key role in seizing processes. With their greater customer and market orientation (Homburg and Jensen 2007), these managers may be advantaged in estimating revenue streams, especially when finance models are fuzzy. More importantly, they may personally accept the responsibility of delivering against a revenue target that is opaque. Hence, it appears that the leadership and motivational skills of key senior executives may matter greatly in determining whether opportunities in rapidly changing markets are realized.

The third dynamic capability identified by Teece (2007) is that of *reconfiguration*. One of the core concepts of the strategy and organizational behavior literatures emphasize the need for "fit." "Fit" may refer to the relationship of one asset to another, or of strategy to structure, or of strategy to process. In a rapidly changing environment, there is a need for continuous or at least semi-continuous realignment within an organization. Reconfiguration is about an organization's ability to recombine organizational assets and structures as the organization grows and as new markets emerge and technologies change. Examples of complementary innovations are ubiquitous. In the enterprise software industry, for instance, new business applications may be especially valuable if they can be somehow integrated into a single tightly integrated program suite. High-energy, rechargeable batteries have been critical to the growth of laptop computers and cell phones. Consider also the difficulties the automobile industry and General Motors in particular is experiencing in incorporating battery innovations into automobiles. Success requires more than just the simple slapping together of technologies. Reconfiguration has everything to do with the framing of new opportunities in order to achieve sustainability in an organization's competitive advantage.

With this understanding of both the RBV and the DCM, we turn towards developing a framework for thinking about the strategic role of the selling function.

18.3 A STRATEGIC SELLING FUNCTION FRAMEWORK

Our goal in our Strategic Sales Function Framework is to use the RBV and DCM as the key to unlock the "black box" relating the selling function to firm-level performance. Our framework is grounded in the core RBV/DCM resources and capabilities relevant to the selling function that are likely to drive SCA and firm performance. We will first present an overview of our framework and then draw on the sales/marketing and strategy literatures to identify concepts of key selling function resources and capabilities and "organizing" contexts and capabilities.

Our Strategic Sales Function Framework is presented in Figure 18.1. The framework modifies Barney's (1991) conceptual framework to reflect recent research concerning the RBV (Newbert 2007) and the DCM (Teece 2007). To reflect the RBV (Barney 1991), our framework posits a *direct* effect of sales function resources (e.g. human, social, and cultural capital) and capabilities (e.g. new customer acquisition, retention, and relationship growth) on sustainable competitive advantage (SCA) and an indirect effect, through the mediation of SCA, on firm financial performance. Resources and capabilities are presumed to drive SCA and superior performance only if they are rare, inimitable, valuable, and non-substitutable.

We also posit a *direct and moderating* effect for a novel set of "organizing" processes and contexts relevant to the selling function's influence on SCA. In addition to directly influencing competitive advantage, in other words, the

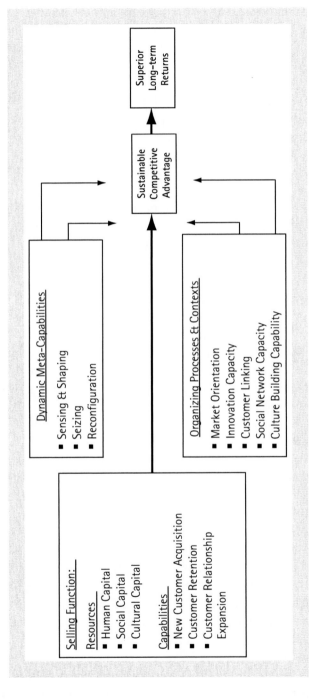

Fig. 18.1. Strategic Selling Function Framework (SSFF)

organizational context within which a resource exists or a capability is executed will serve to amplify or mute the direct effects of the resources and capabilities on a firm's competitive advantage. This is consistent with RBV and with Mahoney and Pandian's (1992) view that it is not the mere possession of resources or assets that matter; rather, managers that are better able to rationalize the allocation of these resources to valuable uses leverage their firm's resources, and hence their firm's financial returns. Our literature review identified the following organizational capabilities and context factors as potentially relevant to the selling function, though we do not claim that this list is exhaustive: market orientation (Morgan, Vorhies, and Mason 2009);[2] innovation capacity (Hurley and Hult 1998); customer linking (Day 1994); social networking capabilities (Gu, Hung, and Tse 2008); and culture-building routines (Homburg and Pflesser 2000). As indicated, this is not at all an exhaustive list (Newbert (2007) lists ten different organizational context factors that have been empirically investigated), but within the limits of this presentation are processes and contexts that are felt likely to have an important impact on selling function resources and capabilities.

Finally, the DCM is incorporated in our sales function strategic framework on the logic that the selling function may play a strategic role in volatile markets, but that the impact of selling functions and capabilities will be moderated by the dynamic meta-capabilities of *sensing and shaping, seizing,* and *reconfiguration.* As customers are often the first to perceive the potential of a new technology, the selling function has the potential to play a vital role in the process of evaluating new technologies. However, the ability of the sales function to effect real change and therefore for an organization to take advantage of new technology will depend on the organization's dynamic meta-capabilities. Accordingly, the Strategic Selling Function Framework (SSFF) proposes that dynamic meta-capabilities will moderate the impact of selling function resources/capabilities on SCA. This reflects the view that these meta-level management capabilities matter in terms of positioning the firm's resource and asset base to the requirements of marketplace conditions, both current and future. In fact, while we do not pursue the moderating role of environmental changes, it is clear that Teece (2007) would posit greater effects for these meta-capabilities as the rate of marketplace change accelerates or becomes more volatile.

In light of this Strategic Selling Function Framework, we revisited the sales/ marketing and strategy literatures for specific insights concerning how the selling function's strategic role might be conceptually and empirically cast in terms of the RBV and DCM models. We develop in some detail the conceptual definitions of the various selling function resources and capabilities, management capabilities, and dynamic meta-capabilities reflected in our SSFF. We seek to identify gaps in the sales/marketing literature from the framework's perspectives. Finally, we provide where possible practical illustrations of these sales function concepts informed by our reading of the business press and our personal experiences.

18.3.1 Resources and Capabilities Relevant to the Strategic Sales Function

According to the RBV, the key to competitive advantage is the uniqueness of each company's resources, and profitability is achieved through exploiting differences in a firm's portfolio of resources. We therefore begin our presentation of the SSFF with a discussion of selling resources from which the potential for competitive advantage may be derived.

The differences between the terms resources, capabilities, and competencies are subtle at best (Barney 1997); nevertheless, it is useful for our discussion to make a distinction between resources and capabilities, since empirical support for the basic RBV proposition differs between the two terms (Newbert 2007). Here we use the term "resources" to describe the productive assets owned or employed by a firm (i.e. firm-specific assets) that can lead to competitive advantage. By contrast, "capabilities" refers to the processes by which a firm deploys resources for a desired end result (Grant 2007). As the above suggests, one would expect capabilities to be more closely aligned with strategic advantage than resources, and indeed this describes the state of empirical research to date. Nonetheless, resources remain the most fundamental element of firm-level analysis, and we begin at this point. Specifically, we feel that there are three selling function resources that are likely to have an important influence on a firm's ability to garner a strategic advantage vis-à-vis direct competitors; human capital, social capital, and cultural capital.

18.3.1.1 *Human Capital*

We are using the term "human capital" here in a broad sense to include the number, selling approach, effort, expertise, and reputation of people involved in the selling function. More specifically, human capital would include such specific factors as the relative size of the sales force, selling approach expertise, knowledge of the sales force, and the sales force's reputation among its customers with respect to being trustworthy, dependable, and likeable. In essence, these resources reflect the current stock of the firm's prior investments to clearly define the role of the sales function in relating to its customers and appropriately conducting its business in a fashion that advances mutual supplier and customer interests. These human capital elements may be rare, inimitable, valuable, and non-substitutable in the sense described by Barney (1991).

The sustainable competitive advantage of Pfizer in pharmaceuticals was for years attributed to the superior position they had established in terms of sales force size. Pfizer believed that scale mattered in leveraging product sales through reach and frequency of contact with doctors and influencers. Industry research also reported that Pfizer's sales force ranked at the top among competitors in terms of doctors' and influencers' regard for its expertise, trustworthiness, and service. Pfizer leveraged this sales resource for years through joint ventures with pharmaceutical firms less able to field a strong sales force. Often they subsequently acquired these firms for their product pipelines, further leveraging their sales force resources. However, with the advent of managed care initiatives, the value of this direct sales force was judged to be diminished and Pfizer's performance flagged relative to firms that had stressed innovation as their core strategy.

Human capital resources are rare and inimitable for several reasons. Building a business model that incorporates the employment of sales force scale effects is difficult. The investments, both in capital and time, required to hire, train, develop, reward, and retain human talent is daunting. The roiling Wall Street marketplace in 2009 had firms acquiring the human capital of other firms, such as experienced mortgage advisers and brokers. These resource acquisitions often come with surprises. For example, Bank of America's acquisition of Merrill Lynch was motivated in part by Merrill's positive brand equity and its real estate and broker assets. The broker asset base was built over a long and storied history. One of Bank of America's first initiatives was to retain the brokers by quickly putting in place a now controversial bonus reward program.

18.3.1.2 *Social Capital*

"Social capital" refers to the goodwill that is derived from the structure and content of an individual or group's social relations and that has the potential to result in a competitive advantage to the firm (Adler and Kwon 2002). The literature suggests that social capital can be drawn either from "bonding," based on common norms and attitudes developed through frequent interaction (Coleman 1988), or by "bridging," which focuses on spanning structural holes in a network, resulting in distinctive solutions in response to opportunities (Burt 1997).

In the selling function, social capital is reflected in both the external and internal social networks that the sales function builds, manages, and maintains on behalf of the firm. External networks directly link sales personnel and customers, such as lead users and strategic customers, who exert influence in relevant external networks or customer communities. External networks also include referral and alliance networks. Internal relationships with other organizational members influence the relative delivery of value to key customers. So, salespeople may work with the supply chain for delivery of services, with engineering and product development to provide customized solutions, and possibly with customer service to implement customer solutions. Moreover, social relationships among a firm's sales force itself, through fostering a good work climate, influence the productivity of the sales unit. These social networks are most often face-to-face; hence, successful firms must invest heavily in social exchanges in an attempt to build the social bonds that drive value delivery. However, social media applications now receive attention as alternate ways to build social capital (Carter 2009).

Edward Jones is widely regarded for its human capital model of high selectivity in its hiring and screening processes, rigor in its training and development approach, and its talent-based relationship model of selecting and managing its customers. In fact, they brag about their "not.com" strategic positioning as they drive their customer business through their independent representatives. Edward Jones also invests heavily in and acknowledges the significance of social capital as a key resource in its business model. Accordingly, Edward Jones brokers are positioned in neighborhood-based offices, where they personally staff, equip, and own their businesses. They build relationships with local referral partners such as accountants and lawyers, with whom they may share customers and common business interests. They also form networks with other Edward Jones brokers because of their shared interests as partners in the privately owned firm. Edward Jones brokers mentor new recruits, they offload customers to new brokers, and they invest time in Edward Jones business management processes. Literally, social capital fuels Edward Jones brokers' success.

18.3.1.3 *Cultural Capital*

Cultural capital refers to the underlying belief system that guides behavior. The unique and historical values, beliefs, attitudes, routines of behavior, and patterns of thought that guide employee actions and customer relationships constitute a firm's cultural capital. With respect to the selling function, cultural capital might include general beliefs and attitudes held by people involved in the selling function regarding enthusiasm, aggressive behavior, ethics, entrepreneurial behavior, and identification with the organization. Homburg and Pflesser (2000), in their study of marketing orientation from a cultural perspective, observe that a marketing orientation culture influences financial performance indirectly through creating superior customer value. We posit a similar role for cultural capital in the Strategic Selling Function Framework. Importantly, Homburg and Pflesser (2000) propose that there are levels of cultural analysis, which include shared basic values, norms, artifacts (e.g. stories, arrangements, rituals, and language), and behaviors.

In the sense described above, cultural capital is a stock construct. That is, it is an important historical characteristic of the firm that is deeply embedded in the firm's essence. We found little explicit research concerning the effect of a firm's cultural capital on its strategic choices or its ability to realize future business trajectories. However, the cultural aspects of mergers and acquisitions are commonly viewed in the consulting world and business press as a critical determinant of the likelihood that a corporate merger is to be successful. For example, Oracle is given considerable credit for its cultural capital due to its successful track record of being able to acquire and integrate software companies (e.g. PeopleSoft and Siebel) and leverage its customer base for incremental sales. Similarly, Cisco Systems has apparently created a success culture of acquisition, in both the B2B and B2C spaces, to achieve its aggressive growth targets. On the other hand, Hewlett Packard's modestly successful acquisition of Compaq has been partially blamed on the constraints imposed by its HP Way culture of innovation and engineering leadership.

Similarly, Xerox still struggles to return to growth and profitability after seeking to change its sales culture to one of enterprise solutions.

18.3.2 Capabilities Relevant to the Strategic Sales Function

As was mentioned earlier, capabilities are defined as processes for deploying resources for desired end results (Helfat and Lieberman 2002). The selling literature is quite extensive with respect to processes for organizing, controlling, and managing the sales force, but these are more organizational in nature and not directly related to creating a sustainable competitive advantage. Likewise, there is considerable research on factors that can drive individual salesperson performance. While these factors and their impact on individual results can be aggregated to the sales force level, this is not the same as a strategic selling capability which goes beyond the individual to the selling function as a whole.

Beginning with a focus on the desired end result of creating a competitive advantage, we proffer three capabilities fundamental to the selling function: new customer acquisition, customer retention, and customer relationship expansion. These capabilities are consistent with the traditional buyer–seller relationship model of building awareness and exploring relationships with new buyers, expansion of relationships with existing buyers, and commitment to the relationship (Dwyer, Schurr, and Oh 1987). Likewise, it is consistent with the customer lifetime value (CLV) model of marketing and its key metrics of customer acquisition, retention, and profit expansion (Gupta and Lehmann 2005). An important contribution from the CLV perspective is that the results from these three capabilities are interrelated in the sense that the new customer acquisition process will influence a firm's ability to retain customers and increase the profit contributions of individual customers. Accordingly, it may be best to think of these selling function capabilities as a portfolio of capabilities, as is suggested in the RBV literature.

18.3.2.1 *New Customer Acquisition Capability*

An important element in the success of the selling function in most companies is the ability to successfully and profitably acquire a sufficient number of new customers. Indeed, this is the lifeblood of the selling process in some organizations. Clearly a number of resources are required in new customer acquisition. For instance, a firm must have enough salespeople to have time to devote to prospecting in addition to servicing existing customers. Salespeople must have sufficient product and market knowledge to build the trust needed for prospects to even explore new relationships. New customer referrals, for instance, are often initiated from current personal relationships. Likewise, there needs to be a culture within the selling function supporting the value and necessity of prospecting.

Successful new customer acquisition requires more than just resources: processes for coordinating and bringing resources to bear on the prospecting are also needed. Examples of such processes include a process for profiling prospects so that a sufficient return on time invested in prospecting is realized. For instance, Allnet Communications Services, a small long-distance phone company, has developed a prospect-scoring system which includes targeting small- to medium-sized businesses with a target level of billings in order to avoid head-to-head competition with AT&T and Sprint. Likewise a process for building a prospect list is needed. This process may include encouraging and generating referrals from current customers or acquaintances, Internet, direct mail, and trade shows. How these prospects lists are generated, prioritized, communicated to the selling function, and results measured will drive a firm's success in acquiring new customers. Other influential processes may include hiring, control, and evaluation processes focused on new customer acquisition. Analyzing these processes within the framework of a new customer acquisition capability is likely to be critical in developing this capability in a manner that is superior to competition and has the potential to lead to competitive advantage.

18.3.2.2 *Customer Retention Capability*

Customer defection is to some degree inevitable, but CLV analysis of customer defection rates has shown that it is often the most important factor driving a company's customer lifetime profitability metric (Gupta and Lehmann 2005) and must be strategically managed.

As with new customer acquisition, quality of resources will have an important role in a firm's success in building a competitive advantage through a competitively superior customer retention capability. Particularly important to gaining and sustaining organizational commitment to a business relationship are processes associated with creating value, meeting expectations, and building trust (De Wulf, Oderkerken-Schroeder, and Iacobucci 2001). ChemStation International, an industrial cleaning company, has built its business model around superior customer retention and is currently the only national player in the industry. ChemStation sells soap for industrial use, formulating soap for a variety of different uses (e.g. dirty dishes, engine grease, glossy paint finishes) all requiring special formulas so that each client's product is unique. What has given ChemStation a competitive advantage, however, is its proprietary scheduling software for monitoring tank levels in order to help its manufacturing facilities know when to produce specific soap formulas and when the company's tanker trucks need to deliver the product. Soap is not an integral product to any of ChemStation's customers, so its customer value is making it easier to do business with ChemStation than with any of its competitors. Because ChemStation is so efficient in its scheduling processes, it is also able to save customers as much as 40 percent on their soap bills. As a result, its customer defection rate is less than half the industry average. Notice that in the case of ChemStation, product and software innovation combine to play a role in elevating the company's selling effort to exceed industry standards with respect to its customer retention capability.

In a recent study comparing suppliers' and customers' perspectives with respect to successful customer solutions Tuli, Kohli, and Bharadwaj (2007) noted that customers identified four specific processes: requirements definition, solution customization and integration, solution deployment, and post-deployment support. Notice that solution deployment and post-deployment support occur following the identification of a solution. It is notable that in this study only 4 per cent of suppliers mentioned either of these processes as being important to the success of a customer solution-selling situation, yet customers noted that these processes are critical to customer satisfaction and retention.

18.3.2.3 *Customer Relationship Expansion Capability*

Relationship expansion refers to the continual increase in benefits obtained by exchange partners and to their increasing dependence (Dwyer, Schurr, and Oh 1987). From a selling perspective, relationship expansion would include two types of selling: cross-selling and up-selling. Cross-selling involves selling additional products and services to an account in addition to what they already purchase. Up-selling is closely related to cross-selling, but relates to selling larger systems or products in addition to the ones already being sold to a particular customer. GE Medical Systems, for instance, sells a large array of products to hospitals and other acute care facilities. The products they sell include MRI machines, CT scanners, and x-ray imaging devices among others. So a customer that has already purchased a CT scanner from GE Medical is also a good candidate for an MRI machine. Taking relationship expansion one step further, GE Medical is now able to design the imaging rooms for hospitals as well as train imaging personnel. These added capabilities lead to a deeper relationship between GE Medical and its customers, based on deeper and broader customer relationships.

In some selling situations, the processes for relationship expansion may be fairly straightforward. In others it is much more complex, and involves an expansion in social networks in order to expand the relationship. Consider the processes utilized by a large IT company when delivering consulting, systems integration, and outsourcing solutions to its strategic clients. An important process for sustaining strategic relationships is its Competency-Driven Strategic Account Management (CDSAM) program. Key elements of the process are a jointly developed relationship vision and establishing a multilayered relationship between the tops of the two organizations on down. Another element of the program is that once required competences have been identified, dedicated competency teams are developed for linking with customer teams to solve customer problems. The number of employees focused on a single strategic customer may be well over 200.

We have argued that selling function resources and capabilities will have an impact on a firm's competitive advantage and ultimately on its financial performance. A number of selling function resources and capabilities have been identified that have a high potential to achieve this advantage.

18.3.3 Organizing Contexts and Capabilities and the Strategic Sales Function

In the discussion above, resources and capabilities have been proposed to have direct effects on the firm's future choices and trajectory possibilities, and hence on its SCA and firm-level performance. However, Barney (1997) notes that these direct effects will be moderated by organizational-level capabilities that enable management to exploit the full potential of resources and capabilities so as to be leveraged into value-added products and services that drive SCA and superior performance. Newbert (2007: 124) concurs with this perspective, and notes that "firm-level orientation, strategy, or context encourages a general and unified approach to the utilization of its resources." Thus, a firm such as Pfizer might leverage its large, well-trusted sales organization as a market asset by using its capability to identify underdeveloped, innovative pharmaceuticals firms for strategic partnership or outright acquisitions. Or Schwab may leverage its sales force resource by leveraging its culture of customer orientation to attract customer investments.

Accordingly, the Strategic Selling Function Framework lists five organizing processes and contexts that have a high potential to amplify selling function resources and capabilities as well as having a direct influence on sustainable competitive advantage: market orientation, innovation capacity, customer linking, social network capacity, and cultural building capability. Each of these organization level processes and contexts are discussed in this section.

18.3.3.1 *Market Orientation*

Kohli and Jaworski (1990) define market orientation (MO) as the organization-wide generation, dissemination, and responsiveness to market intelligence pertaining to current and future customer needs. They have stressed that top management emphasis on MO, willingness to risk its consequences, interdepartmental dynamics (conflict and connectedness), and organizational systems (structure and rewards) are critical antecedents to MO. MO has also been viewed as a firm-level cultural orientation that stresses "trust, openness, keeping promises, respect, collaboration, and viewing the market as the raison d'etre" (Gebhardt, Carpenter, and Sherry 2006). From either perspective, MO is clearly an important organization-level process or context, and is treated as such in the SSFF.

Empirically, the direct effects of market orientation on firm performance are robust. It has been found that MO directly affects firm performance regardless of industry or company strategy (Kirca, Jayachandran, and Bearden 2005). The potential for MO to also have a moderating influence on selling function capabilities is suggested by the significant interaction of MO with marketing mix capabilities (Morgan, Vohries, and Mason 2009). It is interesting to note that Morgan and Mason (2009) defined and operationalized marketing capability in terms of a firm's performance of various marketing activities vis-à-vis that of direct competitors. Selling capability was included in this marketing capability measure, but the measures were principally tactical (e.g. training, selling skills, management skills, and selling support). Hence, it would appear that considerable opportunity exists for RBV-based conceptualization of the strategic selling function role within a firm.

18.3.3.2 *Innovation Capacity*

The capacity to innovate, as first defined by Burns and Stalker (1961), refers to the ability of an organization to adopt or implement new ideas, processes, or products successfully. The innovativeness of a firm's culture is expected to act in concert with various structural properties of the company as a whole to affect the innovative capacity of the organization. Hurley and Hult (1998) have demonstrated that firms that have a greater capacity to innovate, as measured by number of new ideas adopted by an organization, are able to develop a competitive advantage and achieve higher levels of performance.

An organization's capacity to innovate is also likely to enhance or retard the impact of selling function resources and capabilities on SCA. Increasingly the role of the sales force in terms both of generating new customers and of growing the business with existing customers relies on providing solutions to customer problems (Tuli et al. 2007). However, the solutions required are often not off-the-shelf products or services, but innovative new or customized services. Accordingly, success will depend increasingly on non-selling capabilities.

18.3.3.3 *Customer Linking*

Considered as one of the key processes by which an organization defines its internal capabilities to the external environment, "customer linking" refers to the organization's capacity to create durable relationships with customers (Day 1994). Customer linking has become more critical as firms are pressed to relate more closely to their core customers by developing shared business goals, end-market strategies, business and information systems, and mutual performance metrics. The P&G–WalMart collaborative partnership presents a highly evolved form of collaborative enterprise (Sebenius and Knebel 2007). In these complex relationships, the role of the sales function evolves from market-based transactions to enterprise-to-enterprise relationships. Traditional salesperson tactical management of transactional contacts, selling approaches, and follow-up processes with buyers or category managers are executed within a larger, often strategic customer relationship. The customer relationship is frequently managed strategically by senior executives directly involved in customer relationship processes (Workman, Homburg, and Gruner 1998). Often, these senior manager roles are formal, as the collaborative relationship operates as an SBU (strategic business unit). Hence, the selling function may be incorporated as part of a strategically centered revenue and risk management capability of the firm.

Interestingly, Day (1994: 45) concludes that the sales function adopts a "different—possibly subordinate—role in a collaborative relationship." Our view is that the roles that Day (1994) specifies for the sales force, in particular anticipating customer needs, coordinating cross-functionally on the customer's behalf, managing customer responsiveness and service, coordinating the development of joint business systems, and working with customers on mutually advantageous business objectives, plans, and metrics, *elevates*, rather than depreciates, the strategic role of the selling function in the firm. Furthermore, as Anderson and Narus (1991) and Chrzanowski and Leigh (1998) indicate, the fact that customers must be strategically selected for their collaboration potential and payback, as well as the need to develop complex go-to-market strategies that involve multi-function teams, B2B eCommerce solutions, and multi-channel communication opportunities, suggests that the selling function should be considered part of the combinative or organizational capability of the firm (Barney 1997).

18.3.3.4 *Social Network Capacity*

To our knowledge, academic research on social networks as a source of competitive advantage in sales and marketing is limited. However, a recent study of the effects of *Guanxi*, or the "use of durable social connections and networks a firm uses to exchange favors for organizational purposes" (Gu, Hung, and Tse 2008: 12), examines the distinctions between social network relational exchange and a Guanxi network model in driving firm-level performance. This article provides empirical evidence that the Guanxi networks of senior managers affect channel capability, or the firm's ability to manage its channel to ensure that its products are delivered to its target markets efficiently, and responsive capability, or the firm's ability to scan and respond to market changes. However, the effects of Guanxi on firm-level performance are moderated by competitive intensity: it shows positive effects under less competitive conditions, and reduced or negative effects as competition intensifies. Further research is needed, since social networks are prominent in Western societies, while the Guanxi model governs exchange in China. However, what struck us as relevant to the strategic role of the sales function is the emphasis on the social networks and relational management capabilities of senior executives in driving firm-level capabilities relevant to external ties to customers, partners, and the government. Hence, we suggest that academic research should attend to the strategic role of senior officers from an external and internal social capital perspective.

18.3.3.5 *Culture Building Capability*

Homburg and Pflesser (2000) explicitly develop organizational culture, in a market-oriented firm examining basically the following logic: values → norms → artifacts → behaviors → market performance. This perspective on culture is important because it suggests that a *culture building capability* is critical in moderating or amplifying the effect of cultural resources on firm-level performance. In other words, management must be able to translate the cultural assets of the firm into an effective set of values, norms, artifacts, and behaviors that fit the firm's intended strategic direction. This cultural change process is apparently richer and more complex than that which the information-processing view offers. Gebhardt et al. (2006) report that the process of cultural change that is so critical in changing markets requires top management focus to initiate the change process and form a coalition to lead the transformation process. Beyond that, a consensus has to be developed around new values and norms, shared language and meaning, processes for selecting and indoctrinating employees, and dispersion of powers and rewards.

18.3.4 Dynamic Capabilities and the Strategic Sales Function

The previous section on organizational processes and contexts proposes that a number of organization-level factors will amplify the impact of selling function resources and capabilities on SCA in addition to having a direct impact. However, in fast-moving business environments characterized by global competition and by dispersion in geographical and organizational sources of innovation and manufacturing, the Strategic Selling Function Framework proposes that an additional set of organization-level factors comes into play. Accordingly, the dynamic capabilities model (DCM) stresses a higher-order set of knowledge meta-capabilities that focus on managing change and discontinuities. These capabilities can be developed to create, extend, upgrade, and keep relevant an organization's unique selling resources and capabilities. Based on Teece (2007), the SSFF specifies three dynamic meta-capabilities: (1) sensing and shaping opportunities and threats, (2) seizing opportunities, and (3) reconfiguring the organization's assets.

DCM is proposed both to enhance the impact of selling capabilities and to have a direct influence on SCA, with the focus being on sustaining advantages over time. DCM is so novel that its concepts have not been substantially articulated in managerial terms or extensively tested empirically. However, a recent article by Harreld et al. (2007) reviews IBM's attempt to interpret its business processes in terms relevant to the dynamic capabilities model. Hence, our discussion here will generally examine the three meta-capabilities and what Teece (2007) refers to as "micro-foundations" of each meta-capability that are considered most relevant to the selling function.

18.3.4.1 *Sensing and Shaping*

Some emerging marketplace trajectories are relatively easy to discern. Digitization and compression of information in information and communications technology for instance. However, many, if not most, emerging trajectories are hard to discern. Sensing new opportunities is about scanning, creation, learning, and interpretive activities. Notably, investment in research and development is usually a necessary complement to this activity, but it is not strictly the same thing. Organizations and individuals are likely to differ in their ability to sense and discern new business opportunities due either to heterogeneity in access to existing information or to the development of new knowledge that creates opportunities. Shaping may follow from sensing of opportunities, in that those organizational actions with respect to opportunities, along with actions of customers, suppliers, and governments, can change the nature of the opportunity and the manner in which competition unfolds.

Teece (2007) describes some of the organizational foundations for successful sensing and shaping of opportunities. To identify and shape opportunities, an organization must constantly scan, search, and explore across technologies and markets. Additionally, success often requires understanding latent demand, the structural evolution of industries and markets, and supplier and competitor responses. This requires that information must be filtered and must flow to those capable of making sense of it. Activities such as hypothesis development, hypothesis "testing," and synthesis about the meaning of information are critical. The rigorous assembly of data and facts is needed to test hypotheses. Accordingly, a more decentralized organization with greater local autonomy is more likely to be successful in this filtering, interpreting, and acting on information. As noted in Teece, Pisano, and Shuen (1997), these types of decentralized organizations are less likely to be blindsided by market and technological developments.

Past success and well-established routines and processes may serve as an impediment to seizing and shaping opportunities. Henderson (1994) notes, for instance, that General Motors and IBM have at times been prisoners of their deeply ingrained assumptions, information filters, and problem-solving strategies. Collectively, these processes and approaches constitute their "world views." As a result, solutions that once contributed to their past success become strategic straitjackets.

Why might opportunity sensing and shaping moderate the influence of selling function resources/capabilities on SCA? One of the key sources of new opportunities is changes in customer needs, problems, and values. Teece (2007) argues that customers are often the first to perceive the potential for new technology. If customer insights can be obtained and interpreted by a supplier, a supplier will be more likely to be successful. Indeed, a consistent finding from empirical studies is that the chances that an innovation will be successful commercially are significantly correlated with the developer's understanding of user/customer needs (Freeman 1974). As the customer-facing function of an organization, the selling function is most likely to obtain the critical information and interpret its meaning. Whether this gets transmitted to the individuals setting an organization's strategic direction and future offerings, however, may depend on the organization's sensing and shaping capability.

18.3.4.2 *Seizing Opportunities*

After a new market or technology opportunity has been identified, the opportunity must be addressed through new products, processes, or services. In addition, investments in development and commercialization processes are almost always required. This involves more, however, than simply new process and product innovations, as discussed earlier with respect to innovation capacity. In addition to selecting just when, where, and how much to invest, the organization must also select and create a particular business model that defines its commercialization strategy and investment priorities. The function of the business model is to articulate the value proposition, select the appropriate technologies and features and to identify target market segments, financial terms (e.g. sales vs. leasing), bundled solutions, joint venture vs. licensing vs. go-it-alone, etc. (Chesbrough and Rosenbloom 2002). Nevertheless, the academic literature has not devoted much attention to the importance of business models. The capacity of an organization to create, adjust, hone, and replace business models is fundamental to the dynamic capability of seizing an opportunity.

Obviously, top management must be intimately involved in business model development. Designing a new business model requires creativity, insight, and a good deal of customer, competitor, and supplier information and intelligence. Accordingly, there is a significant tacit component, usually associated with entrepreneurship. At the same time it takes detailed factual information, including a deep understanding of customer needs and willingness to pay, procurement and sales cycles, supply and distribution costs, and competitive positioning and responses (Teece 2007). So processes and resources must be utilized in developing a seizing capacity, and the selling function is likely to play an integral role in customer and market information gathering and dissemination processes.

It is also important to recognize that management decision-making processes are also critical to seizing new opportunities. Bureaucratic procedures are useful for many purposes in hierarchically organized enterprises, but formal processes may also work against taking advantage of new business opportunities. Committee decision-making structures frequently tend towards balancing and compromise. As a consequence, there is a strong possibility that "program persistence bias" and an "anti-cannibalization bias" may work against innovation. As a result, one should not be surprised if an organization can sense a new opportunity but fail to invest in it. In a similar manner, customer-facing selling capabilities may not result in fully realized long-run competitive advantages if an organization is unable to seize new market opportunities. Similarly, dynamic capabilities are likely to be related to an organization's ability to change and improve selling function capabilities.

18.3.4.3 *Reconfiguration*

A key to sustained competitive advantage is the ability to reconfigure and recombine organizational assets and structures as the organization grows and as markets and technologies change. Reconfiguration is needed to maintain an organization's ability to successfully evolve and to escape destructive path dependencies because success is likely to breed some level of routine for operational efficiency. This works fine until there is some disruptive change in the competitive environment, because over time hierarchies and rules and routines begin to unnecessarily constrain interactions and behaviors. In such situations, organizations will tend to frame new opportunities within the framework of current assets, established problem-solving heuristics, and business models.

What sorts of organizational structures are most conducive to reconfiguration? As was discussed earlier, organizations are unlikely to be continuously responsive to customers and new technologies in highly centralized organizations. With decentralized decision-making, however, different managers are privy to different information, and control different decisions without the necessity of a "roll-up" of information to a single central decision-maker. Accordingly, one widely adopted organization structure as organizations grow is that of a multi-divisional form with a relative abandonment of functional structures (Williamson 1975). Studies have shown that decentralization along product and market lines has led to high organizational performance in a variety of industries when innovation was diffusing (Armour and Teece 1978). There is also some evidence that human resource practices may also influence performance in these fluid conditions. Techniques such as de-layering, teamwork, and flexible task responsibilities have also been shown to improve performance (Jantunen 2005).

In summary, the dynamic capabilities of sensing and shaping, seizing, and reconfiguring are organizational-level capabilities that are expected to directly influence long-run SCA under the right conditions. Dynamic capabilities are about organizational change. Changing organizational routines is costly, so generally change should not be embraced instantaneously. Shifts in the market and in technologies, however, will necessitate that an organization develop the capacity to change, and this is at the heart of an organization's dynamic capabilities. As Teece (2007) indicates, customers are often among the first to perceive potential applications for new technologies and/or business process innovations. Furthermore, customers are frequently unable to carry initial ideas to application. Accordingly, the selling function is likely to be at the forefront of market-based change, but whether an organization takes advantage of these opportunities is not strictly the purview of the selling function. This is why dynamic capabilities are expected to moderate the relationship between selling function resources and capabilities and SCA.

There is little empirical research concerning the DCM in the marketing and sales literature. However, the cultural transformation model provides a useful perspective (Gebhardt, Carpenter, and Sherry 2006: 53). They note that "market-oriented firms are learning organizations." To adapt successfully over time, these organizations must create higher-order processes for creating cultural change to fit rapidly changing markets. These higher-order schemas guide management thinking concerning the firm's future trajectory. More important, Gebhardt, Carpenter, and Sherry (2006: 53) argue, is the emergence of a set of "elite insurgents" who lead the development of a consensus for organizational direction and change. Thus, this model of organizational change offers a basis for exploring the involvement of key executives in the organizational learning and change process.

A case interpretation of the application of the DCM at IBM is presented by Harreld, O'Reilly, and Tushman (2007). As part of this change management process, IBM reframed its Strategic Insight model to emphasize four disciplines: strategic intent ("become an on-demand company"), market insight (become a strategic solutions provider), innovation focus (actively create and experiment), and business design (target customer selection, value proposition leadership, value capture), open scope of innovation to partners, and sustainability model. They also built a Strategic Execution model to identify critical tasks and processes, restructure the firm for change, manage human resources, and build a less risk-averse culture. The dynamic aspects of the new structure are captured in a series of team sensing and sharing structures and forums (technology team, strategy team, strategic leadership forum, corporate investment fund) and seizing business processes (deep dives, IV & T winning plays, and emerging business opportunities). Hence, while the evidence is not available that this DCM-based thinking is in fact driving the enhanced performance at IBM, it is apparent that DCM ideas are starting to permeate IBM and its business practices.

18.4 SUMMARY AND CONCLUSIONS

This chapter draws on the resource-based view (RBV) and dynamic capabilities model (DCM) literatures to sketch an outline of the Strategic Selling Function Framework (SSFF). The ambition of the SSFF is to extend the current perspective as to the strategic role of the sales force. Accordingly, the potential role of the selling function in creating a sustainable competitive advantage (SCA) for an organization is at the heart of this framework.

A framework, like a model, abstracts from reality. The SSFF endeavors to identify relevant variables and their interrelationships. It should be recognized that a framework, unlike a model, is agnostic as to the particular form of the theoretical relationships that may exist. The SSFF can help managers delineate relevant strategic considerations and the priorities they should adopt to appreciate the strategic role of the selling function and to enhance organizational performance. The framework can also help sales and marketing scholars understand the foundations of long-run competitive advantage, and how sales force research can contribute to the strategy literature.

Two aspects of the SSFF are felt to be of particular importance to the practice of sales management. First, attention should be devoted to the three selling capabilities listed in the framework. Capabilities for obtaining new customers, relationship expansion, and retaining customers are critical to the success of any organization and should be thought of as a portfolio of capabilities. That is, the three capabilities should be considered and evaluated as a whole due to their interrelatedness. Also, the relative importance of these three capabilities within the business model of a firm will differ, with some emphasizing new customer acquisition to the relative exclusion of retention, while in other business models relationship retention and expansion are paramount. Mapping out the components of each of these capabilities is critical to fully understanding the strategic role of the selling function and to identifying opportunities for enhancing performance.

Second, the SSFF identifies key aspects of the organization itself that are critical to making sure that the organization fully benefits from its selling capabilities. It is frequently the case that there is a barrier, a wall if you will, between the inside organization and the more outward-focused selling function. This framework highlights the interdependencies that exist at a strategic level between the inside and outside. The framework suggests that such fundamental factors as an organization's information processing, innovation capability, social networks, and culture will amplify or retard the strategic impact of the sales force. Certainly, the issue is larger than simply a need for financial resources.

The SSFF may also serve to guide strategic selling and management research. First, it suggests three selling capabilities—acquiring new customers, relationship expansion and retention—as critical areas of research. Very little attention has been devoted to any of these three selling function capabilities, so identifying appropriate resources and practices for enhancing each of them would be important to elevating scholarly research in sales to the strategic level. Likewise, there is a need to identify the nature of the interplay between these three capabilities and organizational performance.

A second area of research is in the interplay between selling capabilities and the organizational factors identified in the framework. In the scholarly community there is some feeling that selling and sales management research is becoming increasingly isolated from the larger marketing community and, perhaps, relegated to specialized journals and books. The SSFF provides a basis for connection to the marketing literature in closely relating the three selling capabilities to Customer

Lifetime Value (CLV) metric. Additionally, the interactions of these selling capabilities with the larger organizational context and DCM meta-capabilities provide an opportunity to link with the marketing organization and business strategy literature. This affords selling and sales management scholars the opportunity both to draw from a larger research base and to contribute to this literature. We hope this Framework provides the impetus for such a development.

NOTES

1. Personal selling is usually distinguished from other elements of the promotion or communications mix as consisting of "verbal communication between a salesperson (or team) and one or more prospective purchasers with the objective of making or influencing a sale" (Cravens and Piercy 2009). We are similarly construing the term "selling function" though more broadly defining the function to include any personal contact focused on facilitating exchange between organizations. Accordingly, the selling function is not limited to face-to-face contact via an outside, dedicated sales force, but would also encompass telemarketing and selling efforts as well as certain aspects of internet selling involving personal customer contact. Selling function would also include the efforts of outside agents, consultants, and value-added resellers as they also facilitate exchange in a personal manner.

2. It should be noted that Morgan, Vorhies and Mason (2009), investigate market orientation as a resource or capability of the firm in their analysis. Consistent with this we consider market orientation (MO) a firm level or organizational process while our model considers resources and capabilities from the perspective of the selling function. As a result, MO is considered an organizational capability or context factor for purposes of focusing on the selling function.

REFERENCES

ADLER, P. S., and S. W. KWON (2002). "Social Capital: Prospects for a New Concept," *Academy of Management Review* 27, 17–40.

ANDERSON, E., and B. TRINKLE (2005). *Outsourcing the Sales Function: The Real Costs of Field Sales,* Mason, OH: Thomson South-Western.

ANDERSON, J. C., and J. A. NARUS (1991). "Partnering as a Focused Market Strategy," *California Management Review* 33, 95–113.

ARMOUR, H., and D. TEECE (1978). "Organizational Structure and Economic Performance: A Test of the Multidivisional Hypothesis," *Bell Journal of Economics* 9, 106–22.

BARNEY, J. B. (1991). "Firm Resources and Sustained Competitive Advantage," *Journal of Management* 17, 99–120.

——(1997). *Gaining and Sustaining Competitive Advantage,* Reading, MA: Addison-Wesley.

BURNS, T., and G. M. STALKER (1961). *The Management of Innovation,* London: Tavistock.

Burt, R. S. (1997). "The Contingent Value of Social Capital," *Administrative Science Quarterly* 42, 339–65.

Capron, L., and J. Hulland (1999). "Redeployment of Brands, Sales Forces and General Marketing Management Expertise Following Horizontal Acquisitions: A Resource-Based View," *Journal of Marketing* 63, 41–54.

Carter, S. (2009). *The New Language of Marketing 2.0: How to Use Angles to Energize your Market*, Boston, MA: Pearson Education.

Chesbrough, H., and R. Rosenbloom (2002). "The Role of the Business Model in Capturing Value from Innovation: Evidence from Xerox Corporation's Technology," *Industrial and Corporate Change* 11, 529–55.

Chrzanowski, K., and T. W. Leigh (1998). "Customer Relationship Strategy and Customer-Focused Teams," in R. LaForge and T. Ingram (eds.), *New Horizons in Sales Force Strategy and Management*, Westport, CT: Greenwood, 51–79.

Coleman, J. S. (1988). "Social Capital in the Creation of Human Capital," *American Journal of Sociology* 94, 95–120.

Cravens, D. W., and N. F. Piercy (2009). *Strategic Marketing* (9th edn), Burr Ridge, IL: McGraw-Hill/Irwin.

Day, G. S. (1994). "The Capabilities of Market-Driven Organizations," *Journal of Marketing* 58, 37–52.

De Wulf, K., G. Oderkerken-Schroeder, and D. Iacobucci (2001). "Investments in Consumer Relationships: A Cross-Country and Cross-Industry Exploration," *Journal of Marketing* 65, 35–50.

Dickie, J. (2004). "Increasing Sales Effectiveness by Blending CMM and CRM," in *Defying the Limits: The CRM Project*, vol. 5, San Francisco, CA: Montgomery Research, 58–60.

Dwyer, F. R., P. Schurr, and S. Oh (1987). "Developing Buyer–Seller Relationships," *Journal of Marketing* 51, 11–27.

Eisenhardt, K. M., and J. A. Martin (2000). "Dynamic Capabilities: What Are They?" *Strategic Management Journal* 21, 1105–21.

Fiol, C. M. (1991). "Managing Culture as a Competitive Resource: An Identity-Based View of Sustainable Competitive Advantage," *Journal of Management* 17, 191–211.

Freeman, C. (1974). *The Economics of Industrial Innovation*, Harmondsworth: Penguin.

Gebhardt, G. F., G. S. Carpenter, and J. F. Sherry, Jr. (2006). "Creating a Market Orientation: A Longitudinal, Multifirm, Grounded Analysis of Cultural Transformation," *Journal of Marketing* 70, 37–55.

Gerstner, L. V. (2002). *Who Says Elephants Can't Dance?* New York: Harper Business.

Grant, R. (2007). *Contemporary Strategy Analysis*, Malden, MA: Blackwell.

Gu, F. F., K. Hung, and D. K. Tse (2008). "When Does Guanxi Matter? Issues of Capitalization and Its Dark Side," *Journal of Marketing* 72, 12–28.

Gupta, S., and D. Lehmann (2005). *Managing Customers As Investments*, Upper Saddle River, NJ: Pearson Education.

Harreld, J. B., C. A. O'Reilly III, and M. L. Tushman (2007). "Dynamic Capabilities at IBM: Driving Strategy into Action," *California Management Review* 49, 21–43.

Helfat, C., and M. B. Lieberman (2002). "The Birth of Capabilities: Market Entry and the Importance of Pre-History," *Industrial and Corporate Change* 11, 725–60.

——and M. A. Peteraf (2003). "The Dynamic Resource-based View: Capability Lifecycles," *Strategic Management Journal* 24.10, 997–1010.

HENDERSON, R. (1994). "The Evolution of Integrative Capability: Innovation in Cardiovascular Drug Discovery," *Industrial and Corporate Change* 3.3, 607–30.

HOMBURG, C., and O. JENSEN (2007). "The Thought Worlds of Marketing and Sales: Which Differences Make a Difference?" *Journal of Marketing* 71, 124–42.

——and C. PFLESSER (2000). "A Multi-Layer Model of Market-Oriented Organizational Culture: Measurement Issues and Performance Outcomes," *Journal of Marketing Research* 37, 449–62.

HUNTER, G. K., and W. D. PERREAULT, Jr. (2007). "Making Sales Technology Effective," *Journal of Marketing* 71, 16–34.

HURLEY, R. F., and T. M. HULT (1998). "Innovation, Market Orientation, and Organizational Learning: An Integration and Empirical Examination," *Journal of Marketing* 62, 42–54.

JANTUNEN, A. (May 2005). "New HRM Practices and Knowledge Utilization," paper presented to the 5th International Workshop on Human Resource Management, Seville, Spain.

KIRCA, A., S. JAYACHANDRAN, and W. BEARDEN (2005). "Market Orientation: A Meta-analytic Review and Assessment of Its Antecedents and Impact on Performance," *Journal of Marketing* 69, 24–41.

KOGUT, B., and U. ZANDER (1992). "Knowledge of the Firm, Combinative Capabilities and the Replication of Technology," *Organization Science* 3, 383–97.

KOHLI, A., and B. J. JAWORSKI (1990). "Market Orientation: The Construct, Research Propositions and Managerial Implications," *Journal of Marketing* 54, 1–18.

LADO, A. A., N. G. BOYD, and P. WRIGHT (1992). "A Competency Based Model of Sustainable Competitive Advantage: An Integrative Framework," *Journal of Management* 18, 77–91.

LEIGH, T. W., and G. W. MARSHALL (2001). "Research Priorities in Sales Strategy and Performance," *Journal of Personal Selling & Sales Management* 21, 83–93.

MAHONEY, J. T., and J. R. PANDIAN (1992). "The Resource-Based View Within the Conversation of Strategic Management," *Strategic Management Journal* 13, 363–80.

MORGAN, N. A., D. W. VORHIES, and C. MASON (2009). "Market Orientation, Marketing Capabilities and Firm Performance," *Strategic Management Journal* 30; available online at: http://www3.interscience.wiley.com/cgi-bin/fulltext/122262517/PDFSTART.

NEWBERT, S. L. (2007). "Empirical Research on the Resource-Based View of the Firm: An Assessment and Suggestions for Future Research," *Strategic Management Journal* 28, 121–46.

PENROSE, E. (1959). *The Theory of the Growth of the Firm*, Oxford: Blackwell.

PRAHALAD, C. K., and G. HAMEL (1990). "The Core Competence of the Corporation," *Harvard Business Review* 68, 79–81.

RUBIN, P. H. (1973). "The Expansion of Firms," *Journal of Political Economy* 81, 936–49.

RUSSO, M. V., and P. A. FOUTS (1997). "A Resource-Based Perspective on Corporate Environmental Performance and Profitability," *Academy of Management Journal* 40, 534–59.

SEBENIUS, J., and E. KNEBEL (2007). *Negotiating the P & G Relationship With Walmart (A)*, Harvard Business School Cases; available online at: http://harvardbusinessonline.hbsp.harvard.edu/b01/en/common/item_detail.jhtml?id=907011&referral=2342

SLATER, S. F., and J. C. NARVER (1995). "Market Orientation and the Learning Organization," *Journal of Marketing* 59, 63–74.

——and E. M. OLSON (2000). "Strategy Type and Performance: The Influence of Sales Force Management," *Strategic Management Journal* 21, 813–29.

SMITH, J. B., and D. W. BARCLAY (1997). "The Effects of Organizational Differences and Trust on the Effectiveness of Selling Partner Relationships," *Journal of Macromarketing* 61, 3–22.

SRIVASTAVA, R. K., T. SHERVANI, and L. FAHEY (1999). "Marketing, Business Processes, and Shareholder Value: An Organizationally Embedded View of Marketing Activities and the Discipline of Marketing," *Journal of Marketing* 63, 168–79.

TEECE, D. J. (2007). "Explicating Dynamic Capabilities: The Nature and Microfoundations of (Sustainable) Enterprise Performance," *Strategic Management Journal* 28, 1319–50.

——G. PISANO, and A. SHUEN (1997). "Dynamic Capabilities and Strategic Management," *Strategic Management Journal* 18, 509–35.

TULI, K. R., A. K. KOHLI, and S. G. BHARADWAJ (2007). "Rethinking Customer Solutions: From Product Bundles to Relational Processes," *Journal of Marketing* 71, 1–17.

VANCE, A. (2008). "A Page from an Old Playbook," *New York Times*, 29 December, p. B1.

VARGO, S., and R. F. LUSCH (2004). "Evolving to a New Dominant Logic for Marketing," *Journal of Marketing* 68, 1–17.

VISWANATHAN, M., and E. OLSON (1992). "The Implementation of Business Strategies: Implications for the Sales Management Function," *Journal of Personal Selling & Sales Management* 12, 45–58.

VORHIES, D. W., and N. A. MORGAN (2005). "Benchmarking Marketing Capabilities for Sustainable Competitive Advantage," *Journal of Marketing* 69, 80–94.

WERNERFELT, B. (1984). "A Resource-Based View of the Firm," *Strategic Management Journal* 5, 171–80.

WILLIAMSON, O. E. (1975). *Markets and Hierarchies*, New York: Free Press.

WORKMAN, J. P., C. HOMBURG, and K. GRUNER (1998). "Marketing Organization: An Integrative Framework of Dimensions and Determinants," *Journal of Marketing* 62, 21–41.

CHAPTER 19

SALES FORCE AGILITY, STRATEGIC THINKING, AND VALUE PROPOSITIONS

LARRY B. CHONKO

ELI JONES

19.1 INTRODUCTION: SALES FORCE AGILITY, STRATEGIC THINKING AND VALUE PROPOSITIONS

For decades, business leaders and academics have advocated the wisdom of strong strategic commitments that guide firms toward achievement of ambitious objectives. However, "sticking to the knitting" has been posited to lead to a form of inertia, particularly in the face of marketplace disruptions (Doz and Kosonen 2008). Thinking strategically evokes thoughts of seeing far into the future. Thinking strategically suggests making decisions and holding firm to commitments, having an unwavering devotion to planned resource allocation, and having every salesperson acting in a single-minded fashion in accord with the organization's strategic plan. However, today's rapidly changing business environment challenges salespeople to be agile, as long-standing customer relationship development demands more flexibility from companies and their salespeople. Hewlett Packard is an example of one firm seeking to provide its sales force with improved agility capabilities (Tam 2006). Just as firms are expected to act quickly and offer new value to customers or risk losing them, salespeople are challenged to proffer new value propositions.

A value proposition is a clear and succinct collection of factual statements about tangible results that a customer derives from a product/service. Strategically, proven value propositions are essential for sales success. However, as customers' needs for value change, sales forces must cope with the possibility of customers requesting modification of existing strategic value propositions. This chapter presents a framework for understanding decision-making about value propositions under circumstances in which there is a need for sales force agility. In a world ruled by strategy, a sales force must be dynamic, demonstrating the agility required to realize that yesterday's value propositions may be inappropriate today and tomorrow. At the same time, sales forces cannot forget the strategic thinking that has fostered success even when customers continuously change their way of thinking. Consider the following in relation to communicating value:

A salesperson was asked during the 30-second elevator ride, "So what do you do?" To which he responded, "I sell office furniture and equipment to small and medium-size businesses." The sales manager accompanying the salesperson added, "We provide office solutions to small and medium-size businesses ... solutions that enable employees and owners to convey a quality image while reducing workers' compensation claims due to medical injuries on the job."

• Which value proposition communicates the company's true value offering?
• Which value proposition provides the most degrees of freedom so that salespeople can be most flexible in satisfying their customers' changing needs?

Agility has only recently found its way into the sales literature (Chonko and Jones 2005). Agility means being flexible and nimble, quick to respond, and quick to consider change that departs from past choices. It means that salespeople and sales organizations are willing to consider new evidence, change direction, and consider adjustments to strategy, offering new value propositions in light of new or anticipated customer developments. Agile salespeople act with speed to market by offering new value propositions designed to retain customers. The great paradox in today's selling environment is that salespeople are expected to be both flexible and steadfast in their strategic thinking.

Figure 19.1 presents a framework for understanding the sales force's need for agility in the consideration of offering new value propositions that may break

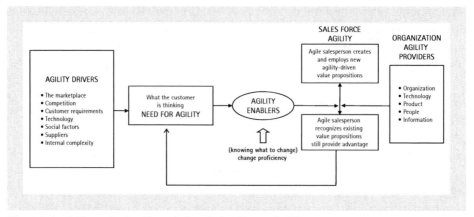

Fig. 19.1. A Domain for Examining Sales Force Agility

strategic precedent when salespeople confront new customer needs. In Figure 19.1, *agility drivers* serve as the foundation for knowledge of the business environment (Chonko and Jones 2005) and impose pressures on salespeople. Changes that occur among the agility drivers may be catalysts for salespeople to consider new value propositions to maintain advantage in the marketplace (Zhang and Sharifi 2000). Uncertainties and pressures stemming from changes in the agility drivers may lead customers to change their way of thinking. Based on knowledge of agility drivers, agile salespeople must ascertain if customers needs and wants have changed. Thus, the need for anticipatory agility is invoked.

When customers change, salesperson change proficiency—the ability to exploit value to take advantage of change as opportunity allows—is required. Both salesperson knowledge of what to change (translated to new value propositions) and salesperson change proficiency—the ability to make the change—are necessary to formulate value propositions targeted to changes in what the customer is thinking. When customer thinking changes, the salesperson faces the decision: when to maintain commitment to current strategic value and when to consider departing from those strategies in the face of marketplace changes.

Finally (see Figure 19.1), sales force agility is intertwined with company strategy that can be described by a variety of an organization's *agility providers*. These agility providers, the essence of the organization's strategy, can enhance or detract from the salesperson's ability to be agile. The salesperson's response to and ultimate performance of that response will further impact what the customer is thinking.

Sales force agility has three components: (1) improved organization and management practice, (2) human capabilities, skills, and motivations, and (3) tools, such as technology (Chonko and Jones 2005). The combination of these three components distinguishes agility from adaptive selling, "the altering of sales behaviors during the customer interaction or across customer interactions based on perceived information about the nature of the selling situation" (Weitz, Sujan, and Sujan 1986: 2). Adaptive behavior has been shown to have positive impacts on desired sales outcomes (e.g. Franke and Park 2006). Agile salespeople have a broad knowledge base, also characteristic of adaptive salespeople (Morgan and Stoltman, 1990). However, agility specifically calls for change proficiency, including rapid response through reduced reaction time (Gutmann and Graves 1995), improved ability to anticipate (Goldman, Nagel, and Preiss 1995), the integration and positioning of resources to effectively respond to change (Global Logistics Research Team 1995), continuous market place scanning (Van Oyen, Gel, and Hopp 2001), autonomy in decision-making (Zhang and Sharifi 2000), and willingness and ability to make strategic commitments about positioning, competitive strategy, and sales strategy (Kass, Probot, and LaSalle 2006).

19.2 AGILITY AND STRATEGY

Knowledge about external and internal events (agility drivers) and circumstances is the foundation for both sales force strategy and agility. Salespeople need knowledge that is accurate, timely, relevant, and content-valid (Garstka 2000). Yet salesperson judgment cannot be driven solely by the need for speed. Salespeople, and their firms, must develop strategic change proficiency and value proposition alternatives so that intelligent choice-making occurs quickly in the face of customer change.

In enduring customer relationships, the path to value fulfillment is continuous and changing. Salespeople must deliver response to customer change frequently. Figure 19.2 depicts the challenges that firms and salespeople face in seeking to be agile in the face of changing marketplace conditions, identified as transition points. At the same time, salespeople must seek to remain consistent with strategy. For example, a customer may seek a service upgrade. This shift sets in motion potential changes in value propositions offered by salespeople. If a change in service levels is warranted, the salesperson who adapts, who keeps up, will continue to succeed. But the agile salesperson who can anticipate the change and stay ahead of some change (transition points) might be more successful.

One consequence of increased customer pressure for value fulfillment is an increase in the number of transitions between a salesperson and a customer, as shown in Figure 19.2. Each transition requires a decision. When salespeople employ their firm's strategic approach, they invest in the firm's planning and the firm's traditional value propositions. When salespeople are asked by customers to engage in changed need/want fulfillment, salespeople may find themselves in conflict with the firm's plan, which generally favors stability over change. The firm's strategic

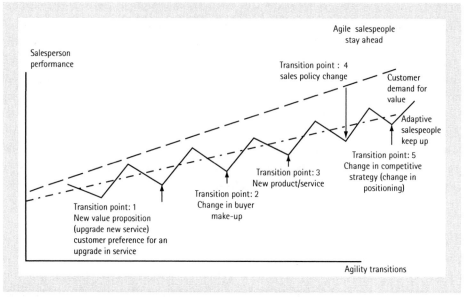

Fig. 19.2. Why Salespeople Must Be Agile

infrastructure (agility providers) may be capable of supporting short-term value fulfillment. But if it is not positioned to do so in the long term, problems of continuously providing customer value can arise. Regardless of the firm's strategy, the customer has signaled that the selling firm must give serious consideration to what their offerings are really worth to the customer. For the salesperson, this situation could cause conflict, as he or she balances his or her commitment to the sales organization and to the customer.

The commitment literature may allow some understanding of the challenges of blending agility thinking and strategic thinking. On the seller's side, commitment to an organization involves an individual/firm that is bound by past strategies and, through their actions, maintains a belief set that sustains activities and involvement. Such commitment is what can drive people/firms to continue to do what they do. Side bet theory and cognitive dissonance theory support this, asserting that people/firms will behave in consistent ways to avoid losing previously earned investments and to reduce internal conflict.

Commitment to a relationship might explain an individual's business relationships and his/her motivation to stay in those relationships. Individual customers can become committed to a relationship based on exchanges of rewards and costs with the salesperson and/or the firm. On the buyer's side, part of the customer's reward thought process may include whether salespeople proffer new value propositions designed to solidify the buyer's commitment to the relationships. We might seek further explanation by exploring other aspects of commitment. For example, affective commitment reflects the emotional attachment a buyer might have to a relationship (Meyer and Herscovitch 2001) and helps maintain a relationship due to favorable attitudes, emotions, and perceptions that might arise when salespeople offer innovative value propositions. Further, continuous commitment involves a buyer recognizing the costs of leaving a relationship. A buyer might foresee high costs associated with leaving a relationship if a salesperson continuously offers new value propositions. Furthermore, new value propositions could deepen the buyer–seller relationship as the customer and salesperson *co-create* the value offered by the selling firm.

Enduring customer relationships require salespeople to go beyond the adding or deleting of value through the simple addition or subtraction of features and benefits without really seeing the larger value they bring to the customer (Anderson, Narus, and van Rossum 2006). Salespeople must assess the deeper impact of the value they offer customers. Agile salespeople recognize that the greatest value often lies outside the bounds of what they are selling. The value can be intrinsic or extrinsic, economic or non-economic, as shown in Table 19.1. A key problem faced by salespeople is to anticipate meaningful value in customer situations in which the *capabilities* of the selling firm are invoked to address customer challenges that might require unique solutions. For example, value may materialize in the reputation of the firm. Cisco is known for constant innovation and quality products. The cost of switching from a Cisco product may be high because of Cisco's reputation as a leader in technology solutions.

Value propositions proffered by agile salespeople may be rooted in other intangibles such as the nature of the relationship, the responsiveness of the company, the flexibility of the company, or its performance in meeting commitments.

Table 19.1. Components of Prospect/Customer-Perceived Value

	Economic	Noneconomic
Intrinsic (Product)	Performance	Brand name
	Reliability	Styling
	Technology	Packaging
	Price	Appearance
	Maintenance	
	Durability	
Extrinsic (Seller)	Operator training	Reputation
	Maintenance training	Reliability
	Warranty	Responsiveness
	Parts availability	Salesperson relationship
	Postpurchase costs	Service

Source: Adapted from N. Tzokas and M. Saren (2000), "Value Transformation in Relationship Marketing," http://www.relationshipmarketing.com

Adapted from the Strategy-Structure-Performance (SSP) model by Chandler (1962). SSP suggests that firms adopt different strategies at different stages in their life cycle in order to meet growth and profit objectives.

Indeed, for the agile salesperson, creation of value propositions means paying attention to the sometimes implicit needs, wants, and preferences of each member of a customer firm that is affected by the buying decision. Each has different needs or wants that change over time, seemingly instantaneously in some cases.

Salespeople cannot forget that an individual customer's demands are unique and specific to that customer. Thus, value focus, as identified in Figure 19.3, is a constant quest for superior effort and performance in delivering what really makes a difference to customers over time. A value focus leads to salespeople developing value commitments which are clear, unique, and relevant to customers. Value commitment leads to the crafting of value propositions that are targeted to specific and changing needs of customers. This requires an ability to be more than adaptive; it requires the ability to *anticipate* customers' needs (i.e. agility selling). The salesperson's ability to offer targeted value is enhanced by an agile firm's agility providers. Strategically, intensifying communication of the same value across different customer contexts may appear to offer the promise of increased sales potential. And, in cases where there is consistency in demand for value across customers, this can be the case. Thus, firms typically segment markets in some way. However, according to Christenson and Raynor (2003), segmentation attributes do not define the real reasons why customers buy. The real reasons are rooted in functional, emotional, and social dimensions of problems that require unique value propositions targeted to offer unique customer solutions.

When rapid change occurs, capturing new potential requires agility to develop new value propositions in anticipation of customers' changing needs. Ideally,

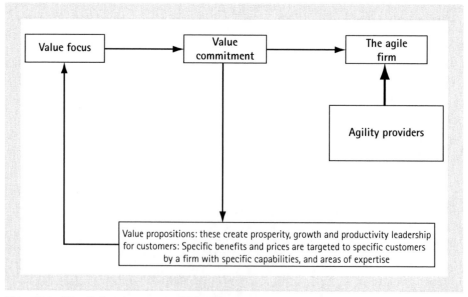

Fig. 19.3. The Salesperson as a Value Creator

meeting changes can be accomplished in harmony with the supporting agility providers involved in delivering value. Value to a customer may lie in past abilities to provide value—the makings of a value proposition. However, change can involve disrupting the firm's usual ways of doing business. The need for agility requires salespeople who are capable of analyzing and managing demand-side risks on implementing new value propositions.

19.3 WHAT THE CUSTOMER IS THINKING

As noted in Figure 19.1, key for salespeople is assessment of the need for agility to cope with changes in what the customer is thinking (Michel, Brown, and Gallan 2008). The degree of turbulence among the agility drivers and the more immediate and/or sophisticated the sales requirements, as dictated by what the customer is thinking, determine the degree to which agility is needed. The answer to the customer's seemingly constant question, "Why should I buy from this firm?" can be a moving target in a turbulent market environment. Salespeople cannot presume that yesterday's answers and solutions are applicable today.

Agile sales strategy requires that changes in agility drivers (see Figure 19.1) be viewed as opportunities. However, in order to do so, salespeople must be prepared to cope with what the customer is thinking. Change in customer thinking might manifest itself in one of four types of change that may occur among the agility drivers (Sharifi, Colquhoun, Barclay, and Dann 2001):

Anticipated change can be reasonably well predicted and tends to lead to few problems for salespeople unless it is large-scale. Agile salespeople have a contingency plan to manage anticipated change such as the implementation of a new software product to facilitate communications. Process-oriented situations like parts ordering are changes that can be anticipated by examining customer growth projections.

Created change may be organized by the salesperson, often in response to anticipated change. Such created changes are usually undertaken within the organization's capabilities to support the change process. If the rate of change accelerates, change proficiency becomes a key element of sales force capability. A salesperson can create change by providing new information that might drive account penetration strategies. For example, engineering a new product might focus on feature A versus feature B. However, a salesperson with deeper customer insights might suggest an equally or more viable feature C.

Unpredicted change can cause major problems and disconnects. The ability to respond quickly and purposefully is essential for salespeople to maintain competitive advantage with customers. This type of change is classified as "within normal expectations" of an agile salesperson's conceptualization of change. A customer might employ the Web to leverage capabilities not anticipated. For example, at the time streaming video technology started, few foresaw all its applications including those found on YouTube.

Unprecedented change is similar to unpredicted changes, but lie outside the salesperson's "normal expectations." An ad agency customer might decide to change its method of promotion, opting to work exclusively through the Web, and departing from traditional promotional approaches. The recent downturn in home construction sales, and the mortgage situation represent a chaotic situation for salespeople in these industries, and will likely foster innovative coping strategies and new value propositions.

The first two types of change are those for which the salesperson can engage in what might be called anticipatory agility. Agile salespeople position themselves to anticipate these types of change and to consider new value propositions in advance of the change occurring. Sales opportunities and threats that deal more with unprecedented change and unpredicted change evoke reactive agility, salespeople making adjustments to value propositions after change has occurred. For all types of change, increasing competitive pressures and customer demands and the emergence of new performance criteria call for agility. The more quickly and effectively a salesperson anticipates change before the face-to-face interaction with the customer, the better able will the salesperson be to maintain relationships in turbulent business environments.

Assessing the need for agility in response to changes in what the customer is thinking encompasses consideration of three elements: the salesperson, the customer lifecycle, and the salesperson's mosaic of relationships. How the **salesperson** has coped with past change, his/her ability to proactively capture marketplace and customer needs, and ability to take advantage of unexpected opportunities all are relevant to agility capability.

At any time within the **customer lifecycle**, the salesperson must be alert for changes in what the customer is thinking that can lead to abandonment, attrition, or churn. Early in the cycle, prospects may simply abandon the salesperson. Early in the customer lifecycle, when salespeople make sales, they convert prospects to customers. But customer attrition still presents a problem. Further through the customer lifecycle, tasks shift to retention of customers and developing loyalty among them. At latter stages of the lifecycle, churn represents a problem for salespeople. The agile salesperson knows who to contact in the prospect/customer organization at any time in the customer lifecycle to provide the best response to changes in the way the customer is thinking.

Enhancing the need for agility is the fact that salespeople operate within a **mosaic of relationships** ranging from transactional relationships to collaborative relationships. For salespeople who deal mostly with transactional relationships, the emphasis is on the timely exchange of products for prices. For salespeople who engage in collaborative relationships, the salesperson and customer form strong social, economic, service, and technical ties over time. The relationships mosaic reflects the strategies to be pursued across the set of relationships, the agile salesperson electing to span the mosaic rather than treating all customers alike or having a narrow range of relationship types. As relationships grow in sophistication from single transaction towards partnering solutions, agile salespeople create and implement strategies to build and maintain different relationships. Creating models for specific customers requires broad knowledge that focuses on understanding of the customer, and current industry issues and trends.

19.4 CHANGE PROFICIENCY

Agile salespeople reflect the ability of the firm (as manifested by the agility providers discussed later in this chapter) to focus facilities, resources, and staff. Firms have traditionally competed on low price or high quality; many of today's customers want products/services that are priced competitively—not necessarily the lowest-priced. Thus, it is critical for salespeople to understand the value-adding criteria that can be incorporated in new value propositions. For example, some customers place high value on after-sales technical support and product use training. Salespeople must develop change capabilities regarding value propositions that are customized to the specific needs of a customer at a specific point in time (Eisenhardt and Martin 2000, Winter 2003).

Salespeople must view the value proposition from the perspective of an array of economic, social, and sustainable components. It is a salesperson's ability to be agile that allows him/her to blend new values and value propositions with changing customers' preferences and the selling firm's strategic posture. Without the salesperson's change initiative capability, the firm faces the prospect of the end of a customer lifecycle.

Assessing the need for agility is like the identification of problems—the difference between an existing state and an aspired to or desired state. To the extent that the disparity is based on value, salespeople must navigate these value gaps by proffering new value propositions. Change proficiency, an agility enabler identified in Figure 19.1, is the competency that allows salespeople to apply knowledge (the second agility enabler) effectively, knowing what to change and how to manage successful change. Dove (1996) offers a gauge of change proficiency which progresses through five stages.

Accidental change proficiency, the lowest level of change proficiency, is not a competency. With accidental change, salespeople lack any change process knowledge, even though occasional change manages to occur. For salespeople at the accidental stage, change processes are ad hoc, with many false starts and restarts. Speed is not considered critical. Costs and deadlines are not predictable. Surprising results occur. Undesirable reactions from customers occur. Salespeople at this level of change proficiency work overtime, make multiple solution attempts, operate according to the fad of the day, fight many fires, and expedite. Adaptive salespeople are prone to perform better in this stage of change proficiency.

Repeatable change proficiency for salespeople is based on conceptual knowledge that is anecdotal. "Lessons learned" from past change activities seem to dominate, even though little was actually learned from these experiences. Salespeople that are viewed as "successful" in effecting change are branded as specialists, and are often consulted on the basis of prior successes and ability to repeat successes in relatively quick time frames. Repeatable change competencies include activities such as developing value propositions that are customized for each customer or the efficiency of cost reductions for a customer as a result of accepting the salesperson's value propositions, the replacement of defective products or solving an unforeseen problem, and accommodating specific customer preferences for some aspect of the selling firm's market offering.

Agile salespeople improve their agility to **defined change proficiency** when they begin to develop preemptive capabilities. A salesperson in the defined stage begins to recognize the formal change process with documented procedures. The field of successful practitioners of change is broadened as a process rather than as anecdotal as in the repeatable stage. Metrics for the change processes are identified, but predictability is elusive. Change procedures for salespeople at this stage are rigid and based on studied experience and analysis.

Managed change proficiency allows agile salespeople to manage opportunities such as customers dramatically increasing order sizes, or to handle changes in buying center members' roles as seamless events. Managed change involves salespeople reassembling existing resources in such a way as to proffer new value propositions to customers. The salesperson has an evolving knowledge base of change process fundamentals, and appreciation for the value provided by others is evident. Rigid adherence to sales procedures is loosened and predictability of outcomes is the norm.

Finally, agile salespeople advance to a stage in which change is a non-event. **Mastered change proficiency** is characterized by a principle-based appreciation for agility. The salesperson understands that process alone is not sufficient. Conscious creation and manipulation of business models occur. Change loses its event status and takes on a fluid motion for the salesperson. The mastered competency allows agile salespeople to eliminate or add sales practices with relative ease. These latter two change competencies represent more than just a sharpening of sales skills. They require that salespeople actually develop a strategic posture aimed at providing superior value to customers over time while understanding the selling firm's strategies more broadly.

The opportunity to achieve success in a turbulent marketplace resides in staying connected with customers. It requires salespeople to continuously evaluate value propositions on an absolute and relative basis. A salesperson with high change proficiency has knowledge of procedures, people, practices, and processes. This salesperson also has knowledge management strategies—what knowledge to acquire, when to acquire it, why it is needed, and how to value it. High change proficiency implies that the salesperson can implement fast, low-cost predictable solutions and is flexible in doing so. A salesperson who possesses effective change management capabilities has much tacit knowledge, uses multiple knowledge repositories, and has built knowledge relationships in the organization. However, even though speed of change is considered important, rapid change at any cost is not viable. Agility enablers require a balance of these competencies and strategies.

19.5 REVIEW THE FIRM'S STRATEGY

The crux of the strategy–agility challenge is shown in Figure 19.4. Generally, a firm's strategy is stable, requiring adjustment only in the face of major marketplace changes. The strategy is dictated by the customers it serves. For salespeople to break through the formal barriers, they must learn how to unfreeze the system—to get the organization to consider moving away from its comfort zone and examine the consequence of no change versus change. The task is one of influencing management to be open to diverging views. Facilitating the development of new/improved value propositions involves developing new competencies, new products, or new processes with a better fit with changing customer circumstances. The challenge is to convince the organization that the new direction is not one of a change of culture, purpose, etc. Rather, it is one of expanding the values that can be offered to customers and simultaneously expanding the selling firm's capabilities to offer new value in the future.

As indicated in Figure 19.4, an *organization's purpose, values, and management tenets* are stable over time, reinforcing the tendency for exploitation within a stable *strategy* framework. But salespeople always face choices. Exploitation-driven value propositions are those that require small changes and little deviation from current customer circumstances. Thus, *resource* allocation decisions and firm *structure* issues are relatively minor. Arguably, retail salespeople fall into this category.

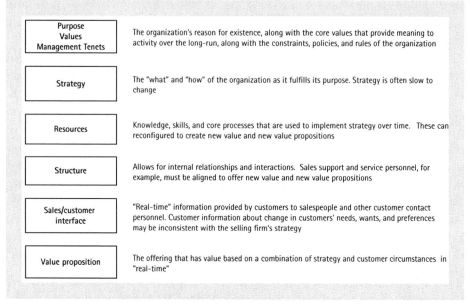

Purpose Values Management Tenets	The organization's reason for existence, along with the core values that provide meaning to activity over the long-run, along with the constraints, policies, and rules of the organization
Strategy	The "what" and "how" of the organization as it fulfills its purpose. Strategy is often slow to change
Resources	Knowledge, skills, and core processes that are used to implement strategy over time. These can reconfigured to create new value and new value propositions
Structure	Allows for internal relationships and interactions. Sales support and service personnel, for example, must be aligned to offer new value and new value propositions
Sales/customer interface	"Real-time" information provided by customers to salespeople and other customer contact personnel. Customer information about change in customers' needs, wants, and preferences may be inconsistent with the selling firm's strategy
Value proposition	The offering that has value based on a combination of strategy and customer circumstances in "real-time"

Fig. 19.4. The Strategy–Agility Challenge

Consumers still want the highest-quality product at the best price, distributed to them as conveniently as possible. Thus, the core value proposition remains relatively stable over time.

At the *sales–customer interface,* exploitation-based *value propositions* may be more easily proffered by salespeople in firms with rigid structures, reliance on routinization, and steadfast loyalty to strategic plans (Ancona, Goodman, Lawrence, and Tushman 2001). Exploitation value propositions are proffered in circumstances when salespeople can leverage existing knowledge related to customers and capitalize on opportunities brought about by small changes in customer demands. Salesperson awareness of such changes allows them to refine value propositions to meet changing needs. As salespeople gain deeper knowledge of customers, they are in a position to cultivate existing value and deploy existing value propositions in order to continue to conduct business with customers.

For example, a focus on products can lead to a slow obsolescence as salespeople cling to what they know: product features and benefits as a source of value propositions. Firms often seek to use a differentiation strategy in which they may offer unique products/services. However, this view limits firms to the basics of the products services they offer. Today's economy is about information, and there are many other values, and therefore value propositions, that a firm can offer to its customers. As set out in Figure 19.4, agility is about understanding the selling firm's strategy, capabilities, and structure, and being nimble enough to mold the selling organization to fit the customers' changing needs and preferences. Real-time information is critical, whether changes in customer needs, wants, and preferences are incremental or large.

Agile organizations allow salespeople to engage in experimental learning that might offer some freedom from the shackles of "strategic thinking." Exploration-driven value propositions are associated with less structured organizations that engage in improvisation, and allow for some autonomy among employees (Garcia, Calantone, and Levine 2003). When customers sense that they need something new, salespeople can embark on exploration. Salespeople may be required to diverge from existing knowledge and value propositions to capitalize on prior unexploited opportunities. With exploration-driven value propositions, suggested changes are more pronounced. In both cases, changes in value propositions address changed needs of customers and offer something of substantive value to customers.

Salespeople must realize that exploration-based and exploitation-based value propositions are closely linked (Rothaermel and Deeds 2004). Since long-run intelligence requires some exploration, the tendency to increase exploitation leads to potentially self-destructive change processes. Salespeople who exploit old value propositions without exploring new ones may find themselves offering obsolete marketplace responses.

Learning also can become a liability, because it could cause companies and salespeople to stretch beyond their comfort zone, particularly in highly competitive markets (Voss and Voss 2008). Turbulent markets require more rapid change than slowly changing ones. Firms in more stable markets put less at risk when they do not offer new value propositions. However, in turbulent markets, new value propositions are essential to survival. Salespeople are in a "poised to deploy" position when faced with changing customer demands, and their companies must be in a "willing to consider deployment change" posture under these circumstances. Being agile requires that firms embrace the possibility of a "strategic plan" that might have as short as a six-month life. Many examples can be found in financial services today (Goldman Sachs, Lehman Brothers, etc.). Salespeople who are successful recognize the importance of working in a value proposition network defined by the firm—the context within which the firm identifies and responds to customers' needs, solves problems, reacts to competitors, and seeks profit.

19.6 AGILITY PROVIDERS

Change proficiency is a salesperson competency that can be hindered or supported by the firm's culture as manifested through the agility providers. Change proficiency must be developed and championed by both the firm and its salespeople as a worthwhile pursuit in the face of customer change. Salespeople today must antici-pate customers' wants and needs by focusing more on their customers' strategies, and the impact of changes in agility drivers on their customers.

New value propositions driven by customer change must fit new customer challenges. Key considerations in providing new value include aligning the selling firms' and their customers' business strategies, and having a deeper understanding of relevant customer needs, competitive pressures, and the overall economic climate. To assist salespeople, the selling firm must create an agility-driven infra-structure (the agility providers) to enhance the sales force's ability to provide new value. Google, for example, continues to reinvent itself in anticipation of con-sumers' needs. This desire for continuous change is deeply embedded in the company's corporate culture and its knowledge workers. Agility, as a form of intellectual capital, can impact a firm's dynamic capabilities, defined as organiza-tional and strategic routines in which new value propositions are created in response to market place changes. Agility may focus on integrating, reconfiguring, gaining, or releasing resources in response to change. Agility may even create change (Eisenhardt and Martin 2000).

As salespeople transition between strategy and agility, a firm's support infra-structure must also make this transition. Thus, tools must support salesperson agility, but so too must attitudes of support personnel. When details of customer fulfillment change quickly, everyone must know what every one else is doing. Sales force agility development does rely on infrastructure. For example, if, by being agile, salespeople offer continuous improvement in meeting changing customer needs, the firm's infrastructure must also change to eliminate incompatibilities between strategy needs and agility needs.

The salesperson's approach to customers is based on knowledge, an organization-al and personal asset that is difficult to imitate. Knowledge shapes the firm's capabilities (Eisenhardt and Martin 2000, Zollo and Winter 2002) and is also instrumental in shaping the salesperson's capabilities (Chonko and Jones 2005). Customers rely on the salesperson's new knowledge and the knowledge in the organization's agility providers and their ability to integrate and organize knowl-edge and resources to the benefit of customers. Reconfiguring a firm's knowledge resources is never easy, but is necessary as customer problems change and the firm's marketing strategy changes. When agility providers are insufficient, improvements are needed. Internal adjustments may be needed if the resources available from the agility providers are judged insufficient for customer purposes. Similarly, when salesperson knowledge or change proficiency is inadequate, improvement is needed.

Knowledge exists at different levels of relevance and success—hence the need for agile capabilities. Salespeople must constantly integrate new knowledge and exist-ing knowledge to avoid obsolescence. The evolution of a firm's strategy and a sales force's knowledge and change proficiency are guided by the integration of knowl-edge and resources embodied in the agility providers and driven by what the customer is thinking. Such integration can allow the firm to adapt its strategies to marketplace changes (Zahra, Neubaum, and Larraneta 2007).

The basic element of strategy is how a firm will achieve returns. There are, to simplify, two approaches to strategy. One is achieving lower costs than competitors. A second is achieving higher perceived quality and being able to charge premium prices (Hambrick and Fredrickson 2001). In this context, and in the context of creating value positions, the firm must value the knowledge and the change proficiency of its sales force. These firms that value creativity and innovation would be expected to be more supportive of their sales forces being able to create value in real time. 3M, for example, embraces experimentation and innovation not just in R&D but throughout the company, and certainly in its field sales force.

It is a task of the agile salesperson to assemble resources from the organization's agility providers in such a way that they are aligned with the nature of the customer's problem if value is to be created. For example, simple problems require less knowledge and change proficiency skills, and probably demand fewer resources from the firm's agility provider mix. More complex customer problems will require greater levels of sales force knowledge and change proficiencies as well as more resources from the firm's agility provider mix. Further, if customers exist in stable environments, resource configuration may not need to be reconsidered as often. However, salespeople will have to modify their knowledge, improve change proficiencies, and maintain real-time knowledge of the selling firm's agility provider capabilities.

A goal of strategy is to fully understand the market environment via knowledge and the ability to anticipate actions of customers and competitors. This ability, in essence, represents a value that can be offered to customers, and in some ways represents a source of competitive advantage (Greenwald and Kahn 2005). Traditional strategy analysis is still critical. Porter's five forces model (i.e. supplier power, buyer power, threats of substitutes, degree of rivalry, and barriers to entry), for example, offers a sound foundation for evaluation of marketplace circumstances. However, advantage and sustainability can often be found in information networks that enable a firm and its sales force to extend capabilities through being agile in the marketplace.

19.7 CONCLUSION

Value propositions proffered as a result of sales force agility are entrenched in risk management. The purpose of sales force agility is to be both reactive and proactive in anticipation and in response to decision situations that include uncertainty. In the longer term, agility capabilities increase options that lower risk as salespeople become more knowledgeable and change proficient. Agility expands the options for the sales force when unpredictable events occur. Agility can reduce the cost of responses, the time of responses, the predictability of responses, and the range of responses (Chonko and Jones 2005). It does so through the sales force's interface with the firm's infrastructure and business processes that are structured for response agility.

Borrowing from the work of Dove (2004, 2005) several factors that stem from human and organizational behaviors must be managed in order to create an agile sales force.

19.7.1 Increasing Pace of Change

Salespeople and their firms must upgrade their knowledge and the ability to make application of that knowledge if they are to maintain competitive advantage in the marketplace. Both must be willing to consider changing the legacy that led to past successes as dictated by current and future marketplace realities. Decreasing customer lifecycles and increasing changing customer needs, wants, and preferences only magnify the situation.

19.7.2 Increasing Complexities of the Marketplace

Agility requires improved alignment between sales force activities and organization infrastructure, the agility providers. The complexities introduced by global competition have tested sales force capacity for marketplace analysis. Having sales forces overloaded with changes in customer requirements and information contributes to the increased complexity. Thus, it is difficult to produce the results of any change strategy no matter how small.

19.7.3 Increasing Competition/Globalization

Businesses are outsourcing, merging, appearing, and disappearing. There is more interconnectedness among business operations both within and outside the firm. With these changes come different value propositions, different perceptions of risk, and different customer perceptions. They must also be driven by the need for improved response capability, improved knowledge, and improved change proficiency.

19.7.4 Human Behavior

Interconnectedness impacts individual behavior and priorities. The impact is felt in the individual salesperson's daily activities. Salesperson perceptions of proper customer-focused behavior may be prejudiced by past successes, but they must be influenced by current and future customer needs, wants, and preferences.

19.7.5 Organization Behavior

Firms are collections of individuals. Their collective behavior differs from individual behavior. Strategy is deployed collectively, but implemented individually. Thus, salespeople, as decision-makers offering value propositions, are likely to find themselves in disagreement with policies and procedures of the firm that may have been crafted under different market circumstances. Their priorities may not be the same as the collective priorities of the firm. The risks in the field, particularly when in personal contact with a customer who is expressing changed needs, are often different than those assumed by those who are further removed from the customer. Thus, a firm's strategy and the individual salesperson's viewpoint about customer change may not be aligned. They must be made so if the salesperson and the firm are to be change proficient.

Agility is key to the creation of timely value propositions in response to marketplace change. Agility must be made manifest through the entire organization across different processes, functions, and departments. Indeed, *agility* itself is a value proposition. As sales forces and firms make the transition to agility, a critical analysis of the firm's business model is necessary to determine the dimensions of agility that are most critical for success.

Salespeople are positioned to receive signals from their customers. In addition, salespeople are probably the best positioned to evaluate customer signals in a specific context. The importance of context highlights the crucial role of the salesperson in receiving information and evaluating it from the perspective of current value being provided versus the value needed at that time. Customers provide information from the perspective of their own specific set of circumstances, so it cannot be summarily ignored. Highly effective organizations are faster at deriving meaning from signals and using it to their advantage (Haeckel 2001). Listening to the sales force and enabling the salespeople to experiment are hallmarks of agility selling.

It has been noted that a firm's innovative performance is due, in part, to human capabilities (Hitt, Bierman, Shimizu, and Kochar 2001). Salespeople, as talented individuals, can play a role in building a firm's capabilities. They have much tacit knowledge and excellent sales skills through which they can build capabilities (Almeida, Song, and Grant 2002).

The salesperson may be the champion of decision-making in the face of change, as he/she is closest to customers. The champion must win the approval of those who control firm strategy and priorities, and those who control resources. Thus, when a salesperson seeks to change value propositions in the face of customer change, that individual must champion the need for change through the proper firm entities . . . quickly. From a customer perspective, the salesperson must demonstrate that the new value proposition provides improved value for the customer. The selling firm will ultimately benefit as a result of providing the new value. The old adage "The only thing constant is change" also must apply to value propositions.

References

ALMEIDA, P., J. SONG, and R. GRANT (2002). "Are Firms Superior to Alliances and Markets? An Empirical Test of Cross-Border Knowledge Building," *Organization Science* 13, 147–61.

ANCONA, D. G., P. S. GOODMAN, B. S. LAWRENCE, and M. L. TUSHMAN (2001). "Time: A New Research Lens," *Academy of Management Review* 26.4, 645–63.

ANDERSON, J. C., J. A. NARUS, and W. VAN ROSSUM (2006). "Customer Value Propositions in Business Markets," *Harvard Business Review* 84 (March), 90–99.

CHANDLER, A. D., Jr. (1962). *Strategy and Structure: Chapters in the History of American Industrial Enterprise*, Cambridge, MA: MIT Press.

CHONKO, L. B., and E. JONES (2005). "The Need for Speed: Agility Selling," *Journal of Personal Selling & Sales Management* (Fall), 371–82.

CHRISTENSON, C. M., and M. E. RAYNOR (2003). *The Innovator's Solution*, Boston, MA: Harvard Business School Press.

DOVE, R. (1996). "The Voice of Industry Speaks on Agility Priorities," *Automotive Production* 108.3, 16–18.

——(2004). *Frameworks for Analyzing and Developing Agile Security Strategies*, Santa Fe, NM: The Agility Forum.

——(2005). "Agile Enterprise Cornerstones: Knowledge, Values, and Response Ability," in *Business Agility and Information Technology Diffusion*, Boston, MA: Springer, 313–30.

DOZ, Y., and M. KOSONEN (2008). "The Dynamics of Strategic Agility: Nokia's Rollercoaster Experience," *California Management Review* 5.3, 95–118.

EISENHARDT, K. M., and J. A. MARTIN (2000). "Dynamic Capabilities: What Are They?" *Strategic Management Journal* 21, Special Issue, 1105–21.

FRANKE, G. R., and J. E. PARK (2006). "Salesperson Adaptive Selling Behavior and Customer Orientation: A Meta-Analysis," *Journal of Marketing Research* 47 (November), 693–702.

GARCIA, R., R. J. CALANTONE, and R. LEVINE (2003). "The Role of Knowledge in Resource Allocation to Exploitation Versus Exploration in Technologically Oriented Organizations," *Decision Sciences* 34.2, 323–50.

GARSTKA, J. (2000). "Network Centric Warfare: An Overview of Emerging Theory" (Alexandria Virginia, Military Operations Research Society), December, retrieved from: www.mors.org/publications/phalanx/decoo/feature.htm

GLOBAL LOGISTICS RESEARCH TEAM (1995). *World Class Logistics: The Challenge of Managing Continuous Change*, Oak Brook, IL: Council of Logistics Management.

GOLDMAN, S. L., R. N. NAGEL, and K. PREISS (1995). *Agile Competitors and Virtual Organizations: Strategies for Enriching the Customers*, New York: Van Nostrand.

GREENWALD, B., and J. KAHN (2005). "All Strategy Is Local," *Harvard Business Review* 83 (September), 94–104.

back to Porter's (1985) "value chain," and in particular, the internal coordination required to serve effectively and satisfy external customers.

Consider the day-to-day functioning of a typical organization which manufactures goods for sale into either business-to-business or business-to-consumer markets in the following vignette:

The Sales Manager's Tale: A New Major Customer Places an Order

After much time and effort, the Sales Manager of a manufacturing company has secured an order from an important new customer, one likely to purchase a significant amount of product in the future. To satisfy this new customer, however, the Sales Manager depends on virtually every other department in the organization. Let's see why.

The product to be supplied will only require minor modifications to an existing product. But is it likely that R&D will drop what they are currently working on to make these changes? No, it is not. They may even have strong reservations about doing this, as it would require them to test the new product, ensure that could be manufactured efficiently, and at an acceptable standard cost. Moreover, this will need to be done to a strict timetable, as the customer requires these products by a fixed date.

The Sales Manager therefore needs to work closely with the R&D Manager, to convince them of the importance of the new account, and to increase the priority of this customer's product, to the detriment of other current projects. However, the R&D Manager is a good friend of the Sales Manager; they have worked together for a long time, and trust each other's competence. The R&D Manager understands the importance of this customer to the organization and has agreed to prioritize this project. Can the Sales Manager feel confident that the order will be filled by the due date? Sadly not, as there are other managers who need to be approached to deliver this order on time.

Are there, for example, sufficient raw materials on hand to manufacture these new products? If not, the Sales Manager will need the Purchasing Manager to raise some purchase requisitions. If new packaging is required, this will also need to be sourced and then a commercial quantity of the packaging ordered. There are a few things in the Sales Manager's favor in getting the Purchasing Manager to do these things. First, the Sales Manager is very well regarded by the General Manager, because of an excellent track record of securing large customers, and the Purchasing Manager is aware of this. Also, the Purchasing Manager is new to the organization, and has noticed that the General Manager places great importance on departments within the organization working more closely with each other. Clear signs of this are the frequent cross-functional job rotations, and the use of joint incentives and rewards for separate departments that are working on joint projects.

The next priority is to liaise with the Marketing Manager to ensure that the designs for the new packaging meet the customer's requirements. Further, the customer has requested some point-of-sale materials and leaflets to promote the new products. As there is an opportunity to develop further promotions with this client in the future, the Marketing Manager is happy to provide this expertise within the time frame available.

The Sales Manager now is confident the promotional and raw materials are in hand, and that R&D can modify the product to the required technical specifications. However, the Sales Manager isn't able to breathe easy yet. His department need to liaise with the Production Manager to schedule this order into their production runs. This manager is very busy, and has two production shifts running per day, with all machines fully deployed. There is already a backlog of products to manufacture for existing orders and for stock, and the Production Manager isn't exactly excited about this new order, as it will affect the smooth operation of the factory. Machines will need to be redeployed, and extra staff will be required, perhaps at overtime rates. All of this will disrupt the Production Manager's normal work.

However, the Sales Manager has managed to convince the Production Manager to schedule this new order into a production run. One reason for this was that the Sales Manager pointed out to the Production Manager that if this new client is secured on a long-term basis, it will lead to large, ongoing orders. This will help the Production Manager justify their capital expenditure request for two new machines. Can the Sales Manager now get a good night's sleep? No, not yet at least! There are other things to consider.

The company has a policy for all new accounts: a strict 30-day requirement applies for accounts receivable. However, the new customer is a large, highly reputable organization that is likely to place large orders for at least the next 12 months. Also, they are unlikely to default on their account. They have requested 90 days, though the Sales Manager knows that this is against company policy. The Sales Manager now needs to talk to the Finance Manager! The Finance Manager recognizes the opportunity that this new client represents for the organization as a whole, and agrees to waive the usual rules relating to the new customer.

The Sales Manager has to do far more than simply prospecting, qualifying, targeting, convincing, and finally securing an order from a high-potential customer. When the order comes in, it will automatically be filled without any further action by the Sales Manager. The Sales Manager will need to take considerable time, apply some fairly sophisticated techniques of argument and persuasion, and exercise various forms of power and influence to get the order filled, and to meet his own personal and departmental objectives. This is why cross-functional relationships are vital within organizations, and why Sales Managers require a good understanding of them, to allow them to better achieve their own personal and professional goals.

20.2 The Origins and Importance of Cross-Functional Relationships

20.2.1 Functional Interdependence

As the Sales Manager's Tale above illustrates, managers and departments within organizations are often highly interdependent. This can be in a linear fashion, i.e. where one manager provides inputs to a downstream manager, e.g. the Production Manager depends on the Purchasing Manager to ensure that adequate, timely stocks of raw materials are available for production runs. Interdependence can also be reciprocal where one manager provides inputs for the other manager and vice versa. Sales Managers and Marketing Managers, for example, have this form of interdependence. Sales rely on Marketing for marketing research reports, customer satisfaction survey results, and advertising and sales support materials to be used in the field by the sales force. Conversely, Marketing relies on Sales for information from key customers, ideas for new products, and for information on competitive activity. Sales and Marketing Managers therefore need to recognize their interdependence, and forge effective CFRs with those interdependent managers.

One way to think about cross-functional interdependence is in terms of "internal marketing" (e.g. Ballantyne 1997, Grönroos 1981). Gummesson (1991) has suggested, for example, that interactions between departments and their managers can be thought of as supplier–customer relationships within an internal market. Indeed, George (1990) argues that effective *internal* exchanges between managers and their departments is a prerequisite for successful exchanges with *external* markets, i.e. the organization's customers.

One can also conceptualize CFRs as part of an organization's "market orientation" (see Kohli and Jaworski 1990, Narver and Slater 1990), i.e. an organization's disposition to continuously deliver superior value to their customers. Narver and Slater (1990) argue that market orientation requires a customer orientation, a competitor orientation, and, importantly, *inter-functional coordination*. As we will see later in this chapter, this internal cross-functional coordination is strongly influenced by the effectiveness (or otherwise) of an organization's CFRs.

20.2.2 Cross-Functional Relationships

CFRs are important for any organization which has separate, specialized departments under the control of different managers. There is a large body of evidence on the importance of these CFRs. Effective CFRs have performance implications not only for individual departments and their managers but also for interdependent managers and their departments, and for the organization as a whole. Better cross-functional coordination is known to significantly improve service delivery to external customers (e.g. George 1990, Lovelock 2000). Also, effective Marketing/R&D CFRs are vital for organizations seeking to develop successful new products (e.g. Massey and Kyriazis 2007, Souder 1981, 1988). This is important, as many organizations recognize that much of their future income, and indeed their survival, hinges on their ability to continue to develop new products. Similarly, effective Marketing/Information Technology CFRs are vital to good customer relationship management (e.g. Winer 2001).

As mentioned previously, until recently Sales/Marketing CFRs have not attracted much attention in the academic literature. This is surprising, as it is now widely recognized that the Sales/Marketing CFR is one of the most important relationships within organizations, particularly those with a strong focus on customer satisfaction. Sales/Marketing CFRs are vital to the efficient operation of an organization, because Sales implement Marketing's strategies at an operational, day-to-day level (Strahle, Spiro, and Acito 1996). In this following section we review the key outcomes of Sales/Marketing CFRs, and demonstrate their importance within organizations.

20.3 PERFORMANCE OUTCOMES

The relevant performance outcomes of Sales/Marketing CFRs can be broadly classified into "task" outcomes, and "psychosocial" outcomes. We define and review these two types of outcome, and also reveal the links between them. Sales Managers and Marketing Managers have a shared responsibility within organizations to work together effectively to achieve the task/performance outcomes that will satisfy the organization's stakeholders.

20.3.1 Metrics

The key measures or metrics of an organization's sales performance come in various forms. First, there are the "hard" measures, such as the overall quantity of goods sold, and there may be targets set for these by "stock-keeping unit" (SKU), by product/brand and by category. The performance of the Sales Department, the Marketing Department, their managers, and the organization's salespeople will be judged against these targets and this is a relatively straightforward thing to do.

A similar "hard" measure might be market share. Again, it is likely that organizations will have set targets for market share, by SKU, by product/brand, and by category, and again, performance will be judged against these targets. "Softer" measures also exist, such as measures of "customer satisfaction," and an important aspect of the new service-dominant logic to marketing (see Vargo and Lusch 2004) is that customers and their satisfaction are at the core of value creation. Accordingly, many organizations routinely track customer satisfaction, and use this as a key metric of their market performance.

What is the link between Sales/Marketing CFRs and these outcome variables? If you had already begun to suspect that the link is not as direct as we might like, you are correct. Many things can contribute to achieving sales targets, market share, and customer satisfaction, including the organization's advertising and sales promotions, and whether they are trade- or consumer-targeted. They may also have experienced production or quality control problems, inability to source raw materials, or may simply have run out of stock. External events can also affect performance, e.g. competitors' advertising and sales promotions, or new product launches.

So what exactly is the role of Sales/Marketing CFRs in this? How do we assess the contribution of these CFRs to these performance outcomes? Until recently, most of the evidence of the importance of effective CFRs to these hard performance outcomes was indirect. Good evidence exists, for example, from other CFRs that the more effective they are, the better the task outcomes from joint project work. Some of the most compelling evidence on this comes from studies of the effectiveness of Marketing/R&D CFRs during new product development (NPD) projects. Souder (1988) studied both industrial and consumer goods organizations and found strong evidence that when Marketing/R&D CFRs were "harmonious," most of the NPD projects were either partially or fully successful. In contrast, where there was severe disharmony in the CFR, most of these projects were considered to be failures.

More recently, however, empirical evidence has for the first time established a link between the "effectiveness of Sales–Marketing relations," "superior value creation," and "market performance" (Guenzi and Troilo 2007). Similarly, Le Meunier-FitzHugh and Piercy (2007b) and Homburg and Jensen (2007) found strong links between improved collaboration between Sales and Marketing and superior business performance. Hence, whilst the importance of effective Sales/Marketing CFRs are intuitively obvious, we now finally have some relatively "hard" evidence that they are an important determinant of organizational performance.

20.3.2 Psychosocial Outcomes

Now that a direct link between the effectiveness of Sales/Marketing CFRs and "hard" performance measures has been established, we should review the evidence regarding the "soft" measures of Sales/Marketing effectiveness, as we can be fairly confident that this will lead to performance on the "hard" measures. "Psychosocial" measures are those which have psychological or social components, e.g. the extent to which managers perceive their CFRs to be effective, and the levels of dysfunctional conflict in these CFRs (see Ruekert and Walker 1987a).

One interesting aspect of the literature on these psychosocial outcomes is the view that Sales/Marketing CFRs are usually ineffective, and fraught with conflict. Early qualitative work (e.g. Cespedes 1993) and anecdotal accounts (e.g. Carpenter 1992), for example, suggest that this CFR is problematic, and Dewsnap and Jobber's (2000) summary of the literature notes that it is characterized by negative outcomes—a lack of cohesion, distrust, and dissatisfaction. Recent small-sample empirical work (e.g. Kotler, Rackham, and Krishnaswamy 2006), and exploratory work (e.g. Biemans and Brenčič 2007, Guenzi and Troilo 2006) supports this view.

There is, however, no definitive evidence about whether Sales/Marketing CFRs problems are endemic, and some studies suggest that Sales/Marketing CFRs may be more effective and harmonious than is generally believed (e.g. Dawes and Massey 2005, Massey and Dawes 2007a, 2007b).

20.3.3 The Perceived Effectiveness of Sales/Marketing Relationships

One variable that has been used to assess the quality of Sales/Marketing CFRs is "perceived relationship effectiveness" (PRE) (e.g. Massey and Dawes 2006, 2007a). This variable relates to how worthwhile, equitable, productive, and satisfying a manager perceives their working relationship to be with the other manager. This is a useful psychosocial outcome, variable for various reasons. First, a number of important existing studies of working relationships have also focused on subjective outcomes (e.g. Anderson and Narus 1990, Smith and Barclay 1999). Secondly, objective, "hard" measures of effectiveness (e.g. sales volume) may not accurately reflect the quality of a relationship due to confounding factors such as long sales cycles (Smith and Barclay 1997). Last, as noted above, positive perceptions about the effectiveness of CFRs are known to be associated with improvements in hard outcomes.

Little hard data exists on PRE in Sales/Marketing CFRs, though the results of these few studies are generally quite encouraging (Dawes and Massey 2006, Massey and Dawes 2007a, 2007b). Their results reveal that on average PRE is quite high, however within their samples there were a significant number of ineffective Sales/Marketing CFRs. So, whilst there is not universal harmony in this CFR, and there are definitely organizations in which Sales and Marketing are at war, a good proportion of organizations seem to enjoy quite high levels of PRE in Sales/Marketing CFRs. In summary, the jury is still out on whether these relationships are as ineffective as is commonly assumed. However, there is evidence to show that improvements in this CFR are beneficial. We will return to this point below when we reveal the evidence on the psychosocial variable "conflict" between Sales Managers and Marketing Managers.

20.3.4 Conflict in Sales/Marketing Relationships

There is some debate as to whether conflict between Sales and Marketing functions is detrimental or beneficial to efficiency and business performance. Some deeper insights can be found in the notion that there are at least two distinct types of conflict in CFRs: *dysfunctional conflict*, which results in negative outcomes and poor performance, and *functional conflict*, which results in more positive outcomes in terms of efficiency driven by healthy competition and an open exchange of ideas and views (e.g. Menon, Bharadwaj, and Howell 1996, Song, Xie, and Dyer 2000). As Barclay (1991: 145) noted, "Conflict can have constructive or destructive outcomes depending on its management, and an emphasis on managing conflict requires a discriminating understanding of its causes." However, the distinction between functional and dysfunctional conflict may be considered simplistic if viewed as two ends of a continuum. The two concepts should be treated as separate variables that incorporate the full range of consequences outlined in the organizational behavior literature from which they originated (e.g. Jehn and Mannix 2001). Below, we review the theory and evidence for the prevalence of these two forms of conflict in Sales/Marketing CFRs.

20.3.4.1 *Dysfunctional Conflict*

Dysfunctional conflict is known to be a powerful variable within relationships such as CFRs, and is associated with a range of negative outcomes including the distortion and withholding of information to the detriment of others within the organization, hostility, and distrust during interactions (Thomas 1992, Zillman 1988), opportunistic behavior (Barclay 1991), information gatekeeping (Jaworski and Kohli 1993), and the creation of obstacles to decision-making (Ruekert and Walker 1987b). Dysfunctional conflict is also believed to reduce team performance and member satisfaction, because the associated tension and antagonism can distract people from their task performance (De Dreu and Weingart 2003). Dysfunctional conflict is generally unhealthy, and associated with dysfunctional behaviors, dissatisfaction, and poor individual and/or group performance. It is therefore an important outcome variable to investigate when diagnosing Sales/Marketing CFRs

There are many reasons cited for the lack of cooperation between Sales and Marketing, including that they have developed strong group identities, very different philosophies, and that staff often have different educational backgrounds (Griffin and Hauser 1996, Lorge 1999, Dewsnap and Jobber 2000). This has led to the development of two very different cultures and working practices in the two groups (Beverland, Steel, and Dapiran 2006). Homburg and Jensen (2007) suggest that sales and marketing exhibit two different "thought worlds" based on alternative orientations and competences, but that these different perspectives are necessary to perform their individual functions effectively. Major problems arise when Sales and Marketing departments become independent "silos" with poor cross-functional communications (Dewsnap and Jobber 2000, Olsen, Cravens, and Slater 2001, Rouzies et al. 2005, Le Meunier-FitzHugh and Piercy 2007a). Sales and Marketing functions may also find themselves in competition for resources and/or have differing perspectives on how to achieve their objectives, which may lead to dysfunctional conflict (Anderson, Dubinsky, and Mehta 1999, Olsen, Cravens, and Slater 2001, Kotler, Rackham, and Krishnaswamy 2006).

A number of dysfunctional activities have been observed in the Sales/Marketing CFRs, e.g. working at cross-purposes, being obstructive, and not appreciating each other's roles in achieving marketing objectives. It may be too easy, for example, for the marketing department to ignore immediate concerns in the market place and focus on long-term objectives such as creating brand value or launching new products; and for the sales department to become focused on achieving short-term sales objectives (Cespedes 1995, Lorge 1999). In addition, Sales repeatedly complain that support tools provided by Marketing are inadequate, and Marketing frequently accuses Sales of misunderstanding or misusing Marketing collateral. As a result, some scholars suggest that reducing dysfunctional conflict created by interdepartmental competition for scarce resources should be an objective of senior managers (e.g. Kotler, Rackham, and Krishnaswamy 2006).

Dysfunctional conflict between Sales and Marketing may result in customers observing inconsistencies in their interactions with the organization, resulting in damage to their relationship with the organization. This can lead to a reduction of performance. Further, Song et al. (2000) found that the increasing cross-functional conflict led to a greater chance that the departmental managers concerned would withdraw from the relationship rather than collaborate. Dysfunctional conflict can therefore lead to distrust that is detrimental to both cross-functional collaboration and efficient performance (Colletti and Chonko 1997, Dewsnap and Jobber 2002, Dawes and Massey 2005, Biemans and Brenčič 2007).

Although there is some evidence to indicate that dysfunctional conflict exists in Sales/Marketing CFRs, it may not necessarily be endemic or inevitable. Two quantitative studies, Dawes and Massey (2005) and Le Meunier-FitzHugh and Piercy (2007b), for example, found that dysfunctional conflict was low between Sales and Marketing functions. So things may not be as bad as is often believed, which is good news for both Sales Managers and Marketing Managers, as they do not inevitably have to be in conflict. As there are only a few large-scale studies examining dysfunctional conflict in Sales/Marketing CFRs, more research is required to answer this question. However, as things currently stand there is a positive message in these results—do not immediately assume that there has to be dysfunctional conflict in this CFR, but instead treat each situation as it comes. Also, if there is dysfunctional conflict in this the Sales/Marketing CFR, take proactive steps to resolve this.

20.3.4.2 *Functional Conflict*

Much of the existing literature on relationships such as CFRs has taken a rather simplistic view of conflict: that it is always bad, and that management needs to reduce it wherever possible. It is now increasingly recognized, however, that conflict can also have a functional form ("functional conflict")—in other words, it can be beneficial to CFRs and to the organization as a whole (see Amason 1996 for a good review of functional conflict). Functional conflict is important as it involves consultative interactions, and useful give-and-take. Where functional conflict is present, people feel free to express their opinions, and to challenge others' ideas, beliefs, and assumptions, and people respect others' viewpoints even when they disagree (e.g. Baron 1991, Cosier 1978, Schwenk 1989, Tjosvold 1985). Functional conflict can be considered an antidote to "groupthink" (De Dreu 1997), where feelings of solidarity and loyalty to a decision-making group override the imperative to logically and realistically evaluate all options (Filley 1970).

Few studies exist in the marketing literature examining functional conflict. The first major study was by Menon, Bharadwaj, and Howell (1996), which examined functional and dysfunctional conflict in Marketing CFRs, and reported quite high levels of functional conflict. Similarly, Massey and Dawes (2007a) found high levels of functional conflict in Sales/Marketing CFR, and again these results give Sales Managers and Marketing Managers some basis to believe that they are not inevitably going to be involved in dysfunctional and ineffective relationships with each other. This is important because, where functional conflict is present, "individual departments exhibit not only a willingness to consider new ideas and changes suggested by other departments but also to volunteer information and ideas to others within the organization" (Menon, Bharadwaj, and Howell 1996: 303). It may be that functional conflict may help to reduce "silo" mentalities, and feelings of group loyalty that may prevent the consideration of other possible options, and "even if there are disagreements, discussions focus on issues rather than on people" (Massey and Dawes 2007b: 1122). Challenging others' ideas and beliefs may result in positive exchanges, and has been linked to innovation and sales success as parties consider alternatives and challenge their assumptions, thereby improving the quality of their decision-making (Menon, Bharadwaj, and Howell 1996).

There are compelling arguments for maintaining some tension between Sales and Marketing. Sales activities require different skills and personal attributes than Marketing activities, and the different perspectives of the two groups may be necessary to maintain efficient/optimum performance (Shapiro 2002, Homburg and Jensen 2007). Sales and Marketing staff will need to maintain the ability to freely discuss solutions and consider each others' perspective and information. This will help to establish open communication and greater collaboration.

20.4 Factors Influencing the Effectiveness of Sales and Marketing CFRs

Various factors can influence the effectiveness of CFRs, and these fall into two broad categories. There are the formal, structural/bureaucratic influences such as "formalization" and "centralization," and the physical structure and location issues that may facilitate or obstruct CFRs. Further, there is the key factor of senior managers' attitudes towards coordination. We will now review these influences.

20.4.1 Structural/Bureaucratic Factors

The internal workings of functionally specialized organizations are complex. With the division of labor, functional specialists tend to be located within their own separate departments, entailing the need to coordinate the activities of those departments (see the opening vignette of this chapter, The Sales Manager's Tale). The most frequently employed method for this involves "organizational structure" or "bureaucracy," as senior management need to actively encourage cross-functional integration by implementing appropriate structures (Ayers, Dahlstrom, and Skinner 1997; see the seminal work of Max Weber 1947[1924]). The key features of Weber's bureaucracy for CFRs are "centralization" (of decision-making), and "formalization" (of policies, rules, and procedures when performing one's job). Formalization helps coordinate an organization's activities by reducing variability in behavior, in order to predict and control those behaviors (Mintzberg 1979). Formalization reduces confusion because staff know what they are expected to do, and it therefore helps to coordinate effort (Thompson 1967).

Centralization is the extent to which decisions are made at higher levels in an organization's hierarchy (Aiken and Hage 1968). A key issue facing top management is to trade off control against greater adaptability from decentralization (McCann and Galbraith 1981). Routine tasks such as normal production runs require only "mechanistic" structures, i.e. high formalization and centralization. However, in situations of high task uncertainty, or where creativity and innovation are required (e.g. NPD projects), more "organic", less formalized and centralized structures are appropriate (Burns and Stalker 1961, Olsen, Walker, and Ruekert 1995).

Whilst there is no hard evidence on the effects of Weber's (1947[1924]) structural/ bureaucratic variables in Sales/Marketing CFRs, evidence from other Marketing CFRs can provide insights. Massey and Kyriazis's (2007) study of Marketing/R&D CFRs during new product development, for example, found that formalization enhanced cross-functional integration because it was positively associated with increased communication between these managers. Given that cross-functional integration is increased through effective communication, formalization may be useful to help integrate Sales and Marketing. The opposite was found for centralization: higher centralization appears to suppress cross-functional communication, and would therefore act as a barrier to Sales/Marketing integration.

20.4.2 Location and Physical Structure of Sales and Marketing

It has been suggested that the location and physical structure of Sales and Marketing may affect their ability to work collaboratively, meet organizational goals more effectively, and reduce conflict (e.g. Germain, Droge, and Daugherty 1994). Le Meunier-FitzHugh and Piercy (2008) discovered that Sales and Marketing may be found in a number of different locations—within a single office, in two separate offices in one building, or in separate buildings/continents. There does not seem to be a standard way of physically structuring Sales and Marketing functions.

It has been proposed that closer physical proximity of the Sales and Marketing functions may lead to an increased perception of achieved integration and lower conflict of interests (Dewsnap and Jobber 2000). Further, creating structural links between Sales and Marketing, for example by placing a senior manager in charge of both Sales and Marketing functions, may help to improve communications and help to align activities (Rouzies et al. 2005, Matthyssens and Johnston 2006, Oliva 2006). However, recently Dawes and Massey (2005) found that changing the physical structure had no effect on Sales/Marketing CFRs and had little impact on collaboration between Sales and Marketing. Further, no correlation was found between a particular structure for Sales and Marketing and superior performance (Le Meunier-FitzHugh and Piercy 2008). Changing location or physical structure to alter working practices or implement organizational changes may create new challenges and problems for the organization to overcome (Bartlett and Ghoshal 2000, Hammer 2001, Homburg, Workman, and Jensen 2000) and is therefore unlikely to be effective on its own.

Sales and Marketing perform very different functions that may benefit from a particular configuration, and research suggests that there is little difference in interfunctional conflict or collaboration in organizations operating as two separate Sales and Marketing departments or as a single joint department (Le Meunier-FitzHugh and Piercy 2008). The existing physical structure and location of Sales and Marketing departments is likely to be based on historical and cultural factors as well as industry norms, and will probably be effective for that organization and industry. However, there are many reasons why these two groups should develop the mechanisms and processes to improve their ability to collaborate to the benefit of the organization and its business performance (Shapiro 2002, Le Meunier-FitzHugh and Piercy 2007b). The location and physical structure of Sales and Marketing does not appear to have a significant of impact on the effective operation of their functions.

20.4.3 Senior Management Attitudes

Studies of Marketing/R&D CFRs stress the value of working together to achieve common goals to the benefit of both departments (e.g. Lucas and Busch 1988, Krohmer, Homburg, and Workman 2002) and the creation of common goals is one function of senior management (Viswanathan and Olsen 1992). The Sales Manager's Tale also illustrates this idea through the General Manager's use of job rotation and joint incentives and rewards, which demonstrates explicit top management support for cross-functional integration. Senior managers who have bought into the concept of creating internal collaboration will be able to share a vision of how the culture of the organization operates. They are also in a position to create processes that help to build and establish a shared vision that can lead to staff achieving more than they thought they could (Senge 1990). Managers should be seen to take responsibility for the complex relationship between Sales and Marketing, as the staff may not prioritize collaboration if they do not (Holden 1999). Management involvement in creating positive CFRs will encourage staff to "buy into" working on a more collaborative basis (Athens 2002).

One of the key factors in Sales/Marketing CFRs is that Sales' targets are often short-term, while Marketing's targets may be focused on the longer term (Webster 1997). However, senior managers may have difficulty in balancing the costs and benefits of short-term and long-term financial performance (Gupta, Raj, and Wilemon 1985, Webster 1997). Sales and Marketing are frequently set different goals by senior management that may mean that they are working at cross-purposes (Lorge 1999, Piercy 2006, Rouzies et al. 2005, Strahle et al. 1996). It has been suggested that joint planning may provide a basis for aligned objectives. If targets are set jointly, then the overall direction and individual contributions to achieving objectives may become explicit (Le Meunier-FitzHugh and Piercy 2007a, 2007b). Managers may be able to clarify overlapping activities and those that are mutually dependent, especially where there is potential for role ambiguity (Menon, Bharadwaj, and Howell 1996). Senior management should be focused on aligning values and objectives, facilitating a better understanding of Sales and Marketing roles, and fostering CFRs (Schmonsees 2006).

If senior managers are not focused on, or do not understand, the issues involved in creating improved CFRs, then there is little chance that they can be addressed effectively. To achieve greater collaboration between Sales and Marketing, senior managers have to acknowledge the need to improve the interface, understand the existing relationships, and be able to create clear strategies to facilitate improvement—for example by sharing objectives, supporting joint planning, aligning activities, and communicating the importance of collaboration (Le Meunier-FitzHugh and Piercy 2009). Sales and Marketing groups should be given clear and specific direction on what has to be achieved, and an understanding of how the other's role contributes to achieving the organization's objectives.

A number of coordination mechanisms are available to managers who wish to improve the Sales and Marketing CFR, and these will be reviewed in the next section.

20.5 COORDINATION MECHANISMS

Two types of coordination mechanism may be employed to improve Sales and Marketing CFRs: lateral linkage devices such as cross-functional job rotation, joint incentives, and rewards, and managerial use of influence tactics. In this section we consider how effective these coordination mechanisms may be in Sales/Marketing CFRs.

20.5.1 Lateral Linkage Devices

As already established, organizations structured along functional lines into separate departments require effective CFRs to become a cohesive whole, where each unit contributes to organizational goals and satisfies external customers. To improve collaboration, management often employ "lateral linkage devices" (see Olsen et al. 1995). A wide variety of these devices are advocated in the literature. For example, joint incentives and rewards (Saghafi, Gupta, and Sheth 1990, Souder and Chakrabati 1978), the use of "integrators," i.e. persons specifically responsible for facilitating cross-functional cooperation (Lawrence and Lorsch 1967b, Souder 1977), cross-functional teams (Lawrence and Lorsch 1967a), job rotation and personnel movement across functional boundaries (Griffin and Hauser 1996), periodic clarification of roles, and relocation of personnel to improve interpersonal communication flows (Allen and Fustfeld 1975). In the Sales Manager's Tale, the General Manager uses two of these lateral linkage devices (job rotation and joint incentives and rewards) to help integrate departments within the organization.

Whilst some of these devices were found to be effective in other contexts, e.g. Marketing/R&D CFRs, there is little evidence as to their effects in Sales/Marketing CFRs. Theory suggests that it may be due to characteristics of the organization, e.g. goods versus services organizations, consumer versus business-to-business organizations. Massey and Dawes (2001), however, found no differences between B2C and B2B organizations in the perceived effectiveness of any linkage device. However, their results did suggest that, for organizations selling into both types of market, joint incentives and rewards, using cross-functional teams, using "facilitators," and exchanging documents were more effective than in organizations which sold only into one of these types of market. These results are therefore consistent with organizational theory, i.e. that complex organizations require greater efforts to cross-functionally reintegrate. Similarly, goods producers used more integration methods than service providers, and this makes sense given that goods producers are typically more complex than service providers. It may therefore be important for goods producers to bear this in mind, and consider using a range of lateral linkage devices, rather than just one.

Beyond these findings for complex organizations, there is still the issue of why the effectiveness of these devices is the same in less complex organizations. One possible explanation is that it may not matter what method is used—what is important is that senior management are seen to be taking an active interest in attempting to integrate the two departments (e.g. Cass and Zimmer 1975). By doing this, senior management are demonstrating the importance they attach to improving cross-functional integration, and in these circumstances even "weaker" linkage devices may be more effective than might otherwise be expected. In the Sales Manager's Tale the Purchasing Manager is clearly aware of the importance the General Manager places on cross-functional integration, and thus quickly agrees to the Sales Manager's requests.

A key implication of these findings is that when seeking to increase Sales/Marketing cooperation, senior management must be explicitly seen to support the CFR, though the choice of linkage device used seems relatively unimportant. Also, if greater Sales/Marketing integration is required in more complex organizations, senior management may need to make greater efforts and use more linkage devices.

20.5.2 Managerial Use of Influence Tactics

In the previous section we reviewed various types of lateral linkage devices that may be useful in building or sustaining effective Sales/Marketing CFRs. In this section we examine a special form of informal managerial communication—influence tactics. As we have established, Sales and Marketing are highly interdependent but, at the same time, have different issues, priorities, and time frames. Consequently, Sales Managers and Marketing Managers may not always agree on what needs to be done in a given situation, or how it might best be achieved.

In such situations managers therefore need to try and convince other managers that their ideas, plans, or approaches are the best way to proceed. This is where influence tactics fit in. "Influence tactics" are attempts by one manager (the "agent") to secure compliance or cooperation from another manager (the "target") (Yukl 2002). It is well known that a manager's effectiveness is determined partly by his or her level of informal influence, so it is in the interests of managers to understand the nature of these tactics, and how they might be usefully employed in Sales/Marketing CFRs.

The type of influence tactics that can be used differ widely, though they can be broadly categorized into two groups: hard/coercive and soft/non-coercive. The hard/coercive tactics involve promises of rewards for compliance, or threats of punishment for non-compliance (e.g. threats or legalistic pleas). The second type, soft/non-coercive tactics, appeal to the target's values, emotions, morality, or altruism, or debts owed to the person making the request (e.g. rational persuasion or consultation). We will begin with a discussion of these tactics first, before we move onto the hard/coercive tactics.

In CFRs between managers on the same level in an organization's hierarchy (such as Sales Managers and Marketing Managers), non-coercive tactics are far more likely to be used than coercive tactics (Yukl and Falbe 1990). There are a wide range of non-coercive tactics, including *rational persuasion* (in which a manager uses explanations, logical arguments, and factual evidence to demonstrate that a request is feasible and relevant) and *consultation* (inviting the other manager to plan how to carry out a request, or implement a change). *Collaboration* involves the agent offering to provide resources or assistance to the target to carry out the request, and involves a joint effort to achieve the objective. *Ingratiation* is where the agent gives compliments, does unsolicited favors, and acts in a friendly or respectful way. Also, *inspirational appeals* seek a target's compliance or cooperation by appealing to the target's emotions or needs, values, hopes, and ideals.

The second broad category of tactics is the hard/coercive type. These include the use of threats where the agent makes it clear that they will take actions which will be adverse to the target if they fail to perform the desired action. Also, there are legalistic pleas where an agent cites either legalistic, contractual, or informal agreements that require or suggest that the target perform a certain action (Frazier and Summers 1984). These are used less frequently in Sales and Marketing CFRs. Both coercive and non-coercive tactics are all considered to be effective in achieving the compliance or cooperation of another manager. However, the soft/non-coercive tactics should be used first in any attempt to secure another manager's cooperation, rather than resorting immediately to coercive tactics, especially as these managers are interdependent and rely on each other to get their jobs done. It is therefore unwise to begin an influence attempt with a coercive tactic, as they have been found to be negatively correlated with interpersonal trust and also with the perceived effectiveness of the CFRs (Dawes and Massey 2006).

The Sales Manager's Tale provides an example of the successful use of a non-coercive influence tactic (rational persuasion), when the Sales Manager convinces the Production Manager to schedule the new order into production on the basis that these large ongoing orders will strengthen the Production Manager's case for a capital expenditure request to justify the purchase of two new machines. In summary, Sales Managers should carefully consider the means by which they attempt to influence Marketing Managers. A short-term strategy of getting the job done no matter what the cost to the relationship is almost certainly the wrong approach. CFRs are vital to an organization's effective operations, and should not be damaged through the capricious use of coercive tactics. CFRs require nurturing, and it is important for Sales Managers to have a range of soft, socially acceptable influence tactics at their disposal, for use in their CFRs with Marketing Managers. This section has reviewed the importance of influence tactics, which are just one specialized form of communication. In the next section we shall consider other, more general forms of communication.

20.6 COMMUNICATION BETWEEN SALES AND MARKETING FUNCTIONS

One of the greatest barriers to effective CFRs is poor communication, and hence a discussion about communication types and level is essential to any review of CFRs (e.g. Fisher, Maltz, and Jaworski 1997, Griffin and Hauser 1996, Rouzies et al. 2005, Yandle and Blythe 2000). Improvements in communication are associated with a better understanding of each other's perspectives, and are important to establishing mutual appreciation of each other's roles. Improvements in inter-departmental communication can also enhance strategy formulation and reduce dysfunctional conflict.

A key issue, therefore, is what forms of communication exist between these two managers, and what their effects are. Early approaches to communication in CFRs emphasized the quantity, or frequency, of communication between managers. An assumption behind this approach is that the greater the quantity/frequency of communications, the more effective the CFR. A more realistic approach to understanding communication in Sales/Marketing CFRs is to recognize that "communication" has multiple forms. There are, for example, *formal* communications such as memoranda and reports, and *informal* communication such as impromptu conversations at the coffee machine. As noted earlier, often the formal side of the organization is less important than the informal. As early as 1938 Chester Barnard noted in *The Functions of the Executive*:

You can't understand an organization or how it works from its organizational chart, its charter, rules and regulations . . . Learning the organization ropes in most organizations is chiefly learning who's who, what's what, why's why of its informal society . . . In fact, informal organization is so [taken for granted] . . . that we are unaware of it, seeing only a part of the specific interactions involved. (Barnard 1938: 12)

The key point to remember is that whilst formal communications have an important role in coordination and integration, they may be less powerful than informal communications, as these seem more helpful to managers in fostering effective CFRs. As anyone who has worked in an organization knows, a casual chat with a key manager will often reveal more about what is going on than a formal exchange, such as a question asked during a formal meeting.

Turning now to the effectiveness of *frequent* communications between managers as an integrating tool, one should be cautious in assuming that mere frequency is sufficient. What evidence exists on this suggests in fact that high-frequency communications between peer managers can actually damage the CFR. Dawes and Massey (2005) found that greater communication frequency between Sales Managers and Marketing Managers was strongly associated with an increase in dysfunctional conflict between those two managers. It is not difficult to see why. If one manager sends multiple e-mails, memos, telephones many times a day, or leaves multiple voicemails and the like to another manager, the manager receiving those communications would rightly feel under siege, as though they are being closely monitored, or badgered by the sender. There is an inherent danger in simply increasing frequency of communication, as it may overload the recipients and may possibly lead to acrimony (Rouzies et al. 2005). Neither do frequent communications appear to have a direct effect on the perceived effectiveness of the Sales/Marketing CFR (Dawes and Massey 2006).

This then begs the question: what forms of communication appear to be best at integrating Sales and Marketing and improving this CFR? It is suggested that "bidirectional communication" (i.e. two-way communication), and "communication quality" may be the two forms of communication that are most effective in CFRs. Communication "quality" is the extent to which the receiver of the communications perceives the content of the communication to be credible, understandable, relevant, and useful for the task at hand (e.g. Souder 1988, Menon et al. 1996). It is not difficult to see why these two forms of communication are likely to be effective. Bidirectional communication, for example, signals a collaborative relationship where each party responds to the other's messages. This allows them to clarify issues, and iron out problems in joint work. Accordingly, bidirectional communication has been found to significantly decrease dysfunctional conflict in Sales/Marketing CFRs, increase functional conflict, and increase the perceived effectiveness of the CFR (Dawes and Massey 2005, Massey and Dawes 2006). Similarly, the quality of communication between managers appears to be important, as it has been found to decrease dysfunctional conflict, and increase both functional conflict and the effectiveness of the Sales/Marketing CFR.

This review of interdepartmental communications raises the following points. First, do not overemphasize formal communications. These are useful and important, but it is likely that informal communication has an equal if not greater influence on building effective Sales/Marketing CFRs. Second, one should not fall into the "mere frequency" fallacy—that what needs to be done to improve CFRs is to communicate more. The reverse in fact seems to be true, i.e. high-frequency communication actually works against the building of effective CFRs. Following on from this, when we do communicate, make sure that what we say is important, relevant, credible, and useful. The receiver is interested in information that helps them in their job, and not in communication for communication's sake. If we demonstrate our competence and credibility to another manager via high-quality communications, that manager may then start to trust in us. Third, managers need to build reciprocal communications with other interdependent managers. An effective Sales/Marketing CFR is more likely to develop when the two managers freely exchange ideas and information and provide feedback to each other on issues of importance. Good communications can also lead to a greater understanding of each other's roles and may eventually lead to trust and respect. The next section will consider the role of trust in the intra-functional relationship as well as in the inter-organizational relationship between suppliers and their customers.

20.7 The Role of Trust

This section will review what is known about interpersonal trust and its effects in Sales/Marketing CFRs, as well as the role of inter-organizational trust and how this may be influenced by Sales/Marketing CFRs. As Golembiewski and McConkie (1975) noted, there is probably no other single variable so important in influencing interpersonal and group behavior.

20.7.1 Types of Interpersonal Trust

Interpersonal trust is particularly important in CFRs because, as we have noted earlier, managers are often highly interdependent, and poor CFRs can therefore have adverse effects on other managers, their departments, and the organization itself. Usually organizations try to reduce the risks of non-performance by peer managers, and to control CFRs, by using formal policies and procedures. The problem is that, whilst these formal bureaucratic measures are legitimate tools for senior managers to use, they tend to be relatively ineffective and weak impersonal substitutes for interpersonal trust to manage CFRs and processes within organizations (Agyris 1994, Sitkin and Roth 1993).

Many of an organization's key activities are potentially affected by the presence (or absence) of interpersonal trust. Trust within CFRs can have wide-ranging positive outcomes, such as improving organizational decision-making (Schwenk 1990, Williams, 2001), and overall organization performance (Song, Xie, and Dyer

1997), while low trust is associated with reduced cooperation and coordination on strategic issues (Ruekert and Walker 1987a). Trust can also help motivate groups towards joint efforts and better performance (e.g. Dirks 1999), and when it is absent, it can adversely affect team performance (e.g. Porter and Lilly 1996). Trust between departmental managers can also improve cross-functional coordination, and this can in turn markedly improve service delivery to external customers (e.g. George 1990, Lovelock 2000). Interpersonal trust is therefore important in Sales/Marketing CFRs, given the extent to which these two functions must interact on day-to-day issues, and because Sales implement Marketing's strategies at the operational level (Strahle, Spiro, and Acito 1996).

Various types of trust are identified in the literature, though a well-established body of work suggests that there are two main forms. One is the rational, task-related form of trust, and relates to the extent to which the other person in the CFR is competent and reliable in doing their job. This form of trust is known as *cognition-based trust*. Other studies refer to this form of trust as credibility (e.g. Moorman, Zaltman, and Deshpandé 1992). If this form of trust exists in Sales/Marketing CFRs, the two managers trust each other because there is good evidence, from previous occasions in which they have worked together, that the other manager is competent, reliable, and dependable. Consequently, where this form of trust is low or absent, it will be associated with low relationship effectiveness (Massey and Dawes 2007a).

The other form of trust is *affect-based trust*, and this form is where emotional bonds have formed between managers in the CFR. In this case, a manager is trusted because they exhibit genuine care and concern for the other person in the CFR. Relationships low in affect-based trust will not enjoy the benefits of the voluntary assistance provided by the other manager in that CFR. This form of trust helps the relationship in ways that are over and above the normal work-related assistance and support provided under conditions of cognition-based trust. As such, a CFR in which this form of trust exists can provide extra performance benefits than a CFR in which only cognition-based trust exists, as managers will actively look for opportunities to meet that peer manager's needs (McAllister 1995). The Sales Manager's Tale provides a number of examples of how trust can affect CFRs. Cognition-based trust exists between the R&D Manager and the Sales Manager, because they have worked well together before, and affect-based trust has emerged, because they like each other, and try to help each other achieve personal and work-related goals.

In summary, whilst there is an important role for formal coordination to improve Sales/Marketing CFRs, this is by no means the only mechanism through which improved CFRs and better coordination is achieved. It is likely that informal factors such as interpersonal trust are equally powerful, if not more powerful than the formal factors. It is therefore useful for senior managers to understand this, and to consider means by which these forms of trust might be fostered.

20.7.2 Inter-Organizational Trust

In an uncertain world and an increasingly complex market environment, interpersonal and inter-organizational trust are becoming crucial to successful business relationships and superior performance (Lane 2002). Interpersonal trust has been considered in the previous section, but it is also important to consider inter-organizational trust, as it is a critical coordination mechanism for successful trade (Bradach and Eccles 1989). Sato (2002) characterizes inter-organizational trust between trading organizations as consisting of contractually based trust, goodwill trust, and competence-based trust. Goodwill trust may be similar to affect-based trust in sentiment, and competence-based trust may be akin to cognition-based trust. The types of trust outlined by Sato (2002) are important in other exchange relations relevant to Sales Managers, but it should be noted that almost all trust will begin with interpersonal trust being established between individuals.

Once communication is established between, for example, the salesperson and the customer, trading agreements may be made and trust established based on the belief that each organization will honor its agreements to their mutual advantage (contractually based trust) (Sato 2002). Over time, the customer begins to trust in the ability of the organization to deliver what has been agreed and builds an understanding of its way of working, which becomes competence-based trust. In addition, the customer builds a relationship with customer-facing individuals within the organization and recognizes the individual's contribution to transactions (Sato 2002). As the relationships develop between individuals within both companies, goodwill trust may become established. Goodwill trust is the belief that their business is important to the corresponding organization and that they also wish to invest in the relationship (Sato 2002). The customer may then invest more with the supplier, thereby exposing themselves to greater risk. It is goodwill trust and competence-based trust that lack of collaboration between Sales and Marketing may damage.

As trust develops between organizations, there may be an increase in interdependence, and as time goes on there is a tendency to create shared resources and increased social capital (Rousseau, Sitkin, Burt, and Camerer 1998). Social capital has been described as the benefits and resources created through networked connections between organizations, groups, and individuals (Tsai and Ghoshal 1998, Koka and Prescott 2002). Customers and organizations (suppliers) may develop social capital as they exchange resources and search for solutions to satisfy consumers. Social capital may also be developed intra-organizationally, through personal relationships between members of the Sales and Marketing teams when they collaborate to create solutions to marketing issues.

Trust is a fragile commodity (Lane 2002) and is built up over an extended period, but it may be permanently damaged by individual incidents or others' actions: for example, promises (e.g. support for sales promotions or customized offers) made by Sales staff are not carried through by the organization, or Marketing collateral is not understood and conveyed by sales staff. Sales staff aim to build trust with their customers, but customers may stop relying on the organization and may even question its reputation if its trust in the organization as represented by Sales and Marketing function is compromised. Damaged trust between organization and customer may result in falling sales as customers replace the organization's offer with those of its competitors.

20.8. CONCLUSIONS

The CFR between Sales and Marketing is complex and vital to creating a successful sales/market-oriented organization. This chapter has reviewed the available literature and highlighted some of the current thinking about this intra-organizational relationship. It is established early in the chapter that effective CFRs between Sales and Marketing are essential in the creation of improved performance, in terms both of metrics and of psychosocial outcomes, although it is only recently that this interface has attracted attention from academics and practitioners.

The chapter identifies the levels and types of conflict found in Sales/Marketing CFR based on studies in the UK, US, Europe, and Australia. The Sales and Marketing interface demonstrates both dysfunctional and functional conflict, and managers should be aware of how these types of conflict operate. It was found that functional conflict is required to retain a necessary tension between the two groups, challenge their assumptions, and helps to develop creativity. However, the growth of dysfunctional conflict should be avoided, and senior managers should be aware of strategies and techniques that may be employed to improve the CFR.

A number of factors may be considered to influence the effectiveness of the Sales/Marketing CFR. Structural and bureaucratic factors were considered, and it was found that formalization helped to promote CFRs in the Marketing/R&D interface by reducing confusion, because staff know what they are expected to do and this helps coordinate effort. However, centralization, where decisions are made at higher levels in an organization's hierarchy and disseminated, may reduce the amount of cross-functional communication. Location (Sales and Marketing in one office or geographically distant) and physical structure (separated or joint departments), on the other hand, were found to have little impact on the operation of the Sales/Marketing CFR—although there is some evidence to indicate that placing a senior manager in charge of both functions may lead to a perception that integration is improved.

Senior management's attitudes towards improving CFRs emerged as a key factor: managers should take responsibility for the complex relationship between Sales and Marketing, and give staff clear guidance on what is expected from them, or they may not prioritize collaboration. This may not be as easy as it first appears: senior managers may experience difficulty in balancing the imperatives of short-term and long-term objectives. To overcome this problem, it has been suggested that joint planning with Sales Managers and Marketing Managers may provide an effective basis for aligning objectives. If targets are set jointly, then the overall direction and individual contributions to achieving objectives may become explicit, and the understanding of each other's roles should be improved. Senior managers should be able to clarify overlapping activities and remove role ambiguity.

A number of tools and techniques may be used by managers and senior managers to improve the sales and marketing CFR. Studies of other CFRs have outlined a number of lateral linkage devices that may be effectively employed by managers. The conclusion was drawn that complex organizations require greater efforts to cross-functionally relate and may need to employ a greater number of lateral linkage devices, but that the choice of linkage device used seems relatively unimportant as long as the senior management are seen to explicitly support CFRs.

Influence tactics may be used between managers when they do not agree on what needs to be done in a given situation or how it might best be achieved. They will then need to try and convince other managers that their ideas or plans will succeed and gain their "buy-in." It is well known that a manager's effectiveness is determined partly by their level of informal influence, so it is in the interest of managers to understand the nature of these tactics, and how they might be usefully employed in Sales/Marketing CFRs. Two types of tactics were reviewed: hard/coercive tactics (e.g. threats or legalistic pleas) and soft/non-coercive tactics (e.g. rational persuasion or consultation). Both are considered to be effective in achieving the cooperation of another manager, but it is recommended that soft/non-coercive tactics should be used in the sales and marketing CFR before resorting to coercive tactics, especially as these managers are interdependent and rely on each other to get their jobs done. CFRs require nurturing, and it is important for Sales Managers to have a range of soft, socially acceptable influence tactics at their disposal, for use in their CFRs with Marketing Managers.

Existing literature highlights that effective communications are essential to the operation of any CFR, but that there is an inherent danger in simply increasing frequency of communication, as it may overload the recipients and may possibly lead to acrimony. Further, communications should be important, relevant, credible, and useful to the recipients. Communication should be bidirectional, thereby building reciprocal communications with other interdependent managers. An effective Sales/Marketing CFR is more likely to develop when the two managers freely exchange ideas and information and provide feedback to each other on issues of importance. There are, for example, formal communications such as memoranda and reports, and informal communication such as impromptu conversations at the coffee machine. Often the formal communication side is less important than the informal, as this is likely to build into personal relationships and trust.

Trust is the last element of the Sales/Marketing CFR to be reviewed in the chapter. Trust is critical to successful CFRs and can have wide ranging positive outcomes, such as improving organizational decision-making and information flows. When trust is absent, it can adversely affect team and business performance. Cognition-based trust (that the other party is competent and reliable) between departmental managers can improve cross-functional coordination, and this can, in turn, markedly improve service delivery to external customers. The other form of trust is affect-based trust, where emotional bonds have formed between managers in the CFR. This form of trust can also provide extra performance benefits as managers will actively look for opportunities to meet the corresponding manager's needs. Improvements in inter-personal trust positively affect CFRs, but they also affect the organizational trust between suppliers and buyers. The development of contractually based trust, goodwill trust and competence-based trust may be supported or destroyed by effective CFRs, and demonstrates why CFRs are so important to improving customer satisfaction and business performance, as CFRs are based on trust.

In response to the increasing complexity of the sales environment and the growing demands of customers, Sales Managers, and Marketing Managers should aim to find a common understanding, and to improve their CFR as a basis of developing solutions for customers. Improving collaboration between Sales and Marketing may be assisted by senior managers developing strategies to help manage any dysfunctional conflict in the Sales/Marketing CFR, employ lateral linkage devices to facilitate integration, and engage in joint decision-making processes, so that Sales Managers and Marketing Managers are aware of each other's perspectives and can establish clear lines of communication. Sales Managers and Marketing Managers should be aware of their role in achieving organizational and departmental objectives and aim to establish good communication practices and trust in their relationship. Improved collaboration between Sales and Marketing through more effective CFRs can lead to superior profit levels and greater customer satisfaction.

References

Agyris, C. A. (1994). "Litigation Mentality and Organizational Learning," in S. B. Sitkin and R. J. Bies (eds.), *The Legalistic Organization*, Thousand Oaks, CA: Sage.

Aiken, M., and J. Hage (1968). "Organizational Interdependence and Intra-organizational Structure," *American Sociological Review* 33, 912–30.

ALLEN, T. J., and A. R. FUSTFELD (1975). "Research Laboratory Architecture and the Structuring of Communications," *R&D Management* 5.2, 153–64.

AMASON, A. C. (1996). "Distinguishing the Effects of Functional and Dysfunctional Conflict on Strategic Decision Making: Resolving a Paradox for Top Management Teams," *Academy of Management Journal* 39.2, 123–48.

ANDERSON, J. C., and J. A. NARUS (1990). "A Model of Distributor Firm and Manufacturer Firm Working Partnerships," *Journal of Marketing* 54 (January), 42–58.

ANDERSON, R. E., A. J. DUBINSKY, and R. MEHTA (1999). "Sales Managers: Marketing's Best Example of the Peter Principle," *Business Horizons* 42.1, 19–26.

ARTHUR, L. B. (2002). "Guided Selling: Merging Marketing and Sales," available at: http://www.okc.marketingpower.com/contenet-printer-Friendly.php?&Item_ID=15696 (accessed 28 July 2005).

ATHENS, D. (2002). "Integration Between Marketing and Sales," available at: http://www.marketingpower.com/live/contenet-printer-friendly.php?&Item_ID=16836 (accessed 19 March 2002).

AYERS, D., R. DAHLSTROM, and S. J. SKINNER (1997). "An Exploratory Investigation of Organizational Antecedents to New Product Success," *Journal of Marketing Research* 34 (February), 107–16.

BALLANTYNE, D. (1997). "Internal Networks for Internal Marketing," *Journal of Marketing Management* 13, 343–66.

BARCLAY, D. W. (1991). "Interdepartmental Conflict in Organizational Buying: The Impact of Organizational Context," *Journal of Marketing Research* 22 (May), 145–59.

BARON, R. (1991). "Positive Effects of Conflict: A Cognitive Perspective," *Employee Response and Rights Journal* 4.1, 25–36.

BARNARD, C. (1938). *The Functions of the Executive*, Cambridge, MA: Harvard University Press.

BARTLETT, C. A., and S. GHOSHAL (2000). "Matrix Management: Not a Structure, a Frame of Mind," *Harvard Business Review* 68 (July/August), 138–45.

BEVERLAND, M., M. STEEL, and G. P. DAPIRAN (2006). "Cultural Frames That Drive Sales and Marketing Apart: An Exploratory Study," *Journal of Business and Industrial Marketing* 21.6, 386–94.

BIEMANS, W. G., and M. M. BRENČIČ (2007). "Designing the Marketing–Sales Interface in B2B Firms", *European Journal of Marketing* 41.3–4, 257–73.

BRADACH, J. L., and R. G. ECCLES (1989). "Price, Authority and Trust: From Ideal Types to Plural Forms," *Annual Review of Sociology* 15, 97–118.

BURNS, T., and G. M. STALKER (1961). *The Management of Innovation*, London: Tavistock.

BUTLER, S. L., and E. STROUT (2003). "Happy Together," *Sales & Marketing Management* 155.4, 51.

CARPENTER, P. (1992). "Bridging the Gap Between Marketing and Sales," *Sales & Marketing Management* (March), 29–31.

CASS, E. L., and F. G. ZIMMER (eds.) (1975). "The Hawthorne Studies: A Synopsis," in *Man and Work in Society*, New York: Van Nostrand Reinhold, 278–306.

CESPEDES, F. V. (1993). "Coordinating Sales and Marketing in Consumer Goods Firms," *Journal of Consumer Marketing* 10.2, 37–55.

—— (1994). "Industrial Marketing: Managing New Requirements," *Sloan Management Review* (Spring), 45–60.

—— (1995). *Concurrent Marketing Integrating Product, Sales and Service*, Boston, MA: Harvard Business School Press.

COLLETTI, J. A., and L. B. CHONKO (1997). "Change Management Initiatives: Moving Sales Organizations to High Performance," *Journal of Personal Selling & Sales Management* 17 (Spring), 1–30.

COSIER, R. A. (1978). "The Effects of Three Potential Aids for Making Strategic Decisions on Predictions Accuracy," *Organizational Behavior and Human Performance* 22, 295–306.

DAWES, P. L., and G. R. MASSEY (2005). "Antecedents of Conflict in Marketing's Cross-Functional Relationship with Sales," *European Journal of Marketing* 39.11–12, 1327–44.

—— —— (2006). "A Study of Relationship Effectiveness between Marketing and Sales Managers in Business Markets," *Journal of Business and Industrial Marketing* 21.6, 346–60.

DE DREU, C. K. W. (1997). "Productive Conflict: The Importance of Conflict Management and Conflict Issues," in C. K. W. De Dreu and E. Van De Vliert (eds.), *Using Conflict in Organisations*, London: Sage, 9–22.

—— and L. R. WEINGART (2003). "Task Versus Relationship Conflict, Team Performance, and Team Member Satisfaction: A Meta Analysis," *Journal of Applied Psychology* 88.4, 741–9.

DEWSNAP, B., and D. JOBBER (2000). "The Sales–Marketing Interface in Consumer Packaged-Goods Companies: A Conceptual Framework," *Journal of Personal Selling & Sales Management* 20 (Spring), 109–19.

—— —— (2002). "A Social Psychological Model of Relations between Marketing and Sales," *European Journal of Marketing* 36.7–8, 874–94.

DIRKS, K. T. (1999). "The Effects of Interpersonal Trust on Work Group Performance," *Journal of Applied Psychology* 84.3, 445–55.

FILLEY, A. (1970). "Committee Management: Guidelines from Social Science Research," *California Management Review* 13 (Fall), 13–21.

FISHER, R. J., E. MALTZ, and B. J. JAWORSKI (1997). "Enhancing Communication Between Marketing and Engineering: The Moderating Role of Relative Functional Identification," *Journal of Marketing* 61 (July), 54–70.

FRAZIER, G. L., and J. O. SUMMERS (1984). "Interfirm Influence Strategies and their Application within Distribution Channels," *Journal of Marketing* 48 (Summer), 43–55.

GEORGE, W. R. (1990). "Internal Marketing and Organizational Behavior: A Partnership in Developing Customer-Conscious Employees at Every Level," *Journal of Business Research* 20, 63–70.

GERMAIN, R., C. DROGE, and P. J. DAUGHERTY (1994). "The Effects of Just-in-Time Selling on Organisational Structure: An Empirical Investigation," *Journal of Marketing Research* 31 (November), 471–83.

GOLEMBIEWSKI, R. T., and M. MCCONKIE (1975). "The Centrality of Interpersonal Trust in Group Processes," in C. L. Cooper (ed.), *Theories of Group Process*, New York: Wiley, 131–85.

GRIFFIN, A., and J. R. HAUSER (1996). "Integrating R&D and Marketing: A Review and Analysis of the Literature," *Journal of Product Innovation Management* 13, 191–215.

GRÖNROOS, C. (1981). "Internal Marketing: An Integral Part of Marketing Theory," in J. H. Donnelly and W. R. George (eds.), *Marketing of Services*, Chicago: American Marketing Association, 236–8.

GUENZI, P., and G. TROILO (2006). "Developing Marketing Capabilities for Customer Value Creation Through Marketing–Sales Integration," *Industrial Marketing Management* 35.8, 974–88.

GUENZI, P., and G. TROILO (2007). "The Joint Contribution of Marketing and Sales to the Creation of Superior Customer Value," *Journal of Business Research* 60, 98–107.

GUMMESSON, E. (1991). "Marketing Orientation Revisited: The Crucial Role of the Part-Time Marketer," *European Journal of Marketing* 25.2, 60–75.

GUPTA, K. A., S. P. RAJ, and D. WILEMON (1985). "The R&D–Marketing Interface in High-Technology Firms," *Journal of Innovation Management* 12, 12–24.

HAMMER, M. (2001). *The Agenda: What Every Business Must Do To Dominate the Decade*, New York: Three Rivers Press.

HOLDEN, J. (1999). *World Class Selling*, New York: Wiley.

HOMBURG, C., and O. JENSEN (2007). "The Thought Worlds of Marketing and Sales: Which Differences Make a Difference?" *Journal of Marketing* 71 (July), 124–42.

——J. P. WORKMAN, Jr., and O. JENSON (2000). "Fundamental Changes in Marketing Organization: The Movement Toward a Customer-Focused Organizational Structure," *Journal of the Academy of Marketing Science* 28.4, 459–78.

————and H. KROHMER (1999). "Marketing's Influence Within the Firm," *Journal of Marketing* 63 (April), 1–17.

JAWORSKI, B. J., and A. K. KOHLI (1993). "Market Orientation: Antecedents and Consequences," *Journal of Marketing* 57.2, 53–70.

JEHN, K. A., and E. A. MANNIX (2001). "The Dynamic Nature of Conflict: A Longitudinal Study of Intragroup Conflict and Group Performance," *Academy of Management Journal* 44.2, 238–51.

KOHLI, A. K., and B. J. JAWORSKI (1990). "Market Orientation: The Construct, Research Propositions, and Managerial Implications," *Journal of Marketing* 54 (April), 1–18.

KOKA, R. B., and J. PRESCOTT (2002). "Strategic Alliances as Social Capital: A Multidimensional View," *Strategic Management Journal* 23, 795–816.

KOTLER, P., N. RACKHAM, and S. KRISHNASWAMY (2006). "Ending the War between Sales and Marketing," *Harvard Business Review* (July–August), 68–78.

KROHMER, H., C. HOMBURG, and J. P. WORKMAN (2002). "Should Marketing Be Cross-Functional? Conceptual Development and International Empirical Evidence," *Journal of Business Research* 55, 451–65.

LANE, C. (2002). "Introduction: Theories and Issues in the Study of Trust," in C. Lane and R. Bachmann (eds.), *Trust Within and Between Organizations*, Oxford: Oxford University Press, 1–30.

LAWRENCE, P. R., and J. W. LORSCH (1967a). *Organization and Environment*, Homewood, IL: Irwin-Dorsey.

————(1967b). "New Management Job: The Integrator," *Harvard Business Review* (November–December), 142–51.

LE MEUNIER-FITZHUGH, K., and N. F. PIERCY (2007a). "Exploring Collaboration Between Sales and Marketing," *European Journal of Marketing* 41.7–8, 939–55.

————(2007b). "Does Collaboration Between Sales and Marketing Affect Business Performance?" *Journal of Personal Selling & Sales Management* 27.3, 207–20.

————(2008). "The Importance of Organisational Structure for Collaboration Between Sales and Marketing," *Journal of General Management* 34.1, 19–36.

————(2009). "Drivers of Sales and Marketing Collaboration in Business-to-Business Selling Organisations," *Journal of Marketing Management* 25.5–5, 611–33.

LIM, J.-S., and D. A. REID (1992). "Vital Cross-Functional Linkages with Marketing," *Industrial Marketing Management* 21, 159–65.

Lorge, S. (1999). "Marketers Are From Mars, Salespeople Are From Venus," *Sales & Marketing Management* 151.4, 27–33.

Lovelock, C. (2000). "Functional Integration in Services," in T. A. Schwartz and D. Iaccobucci (eds.), *Handbook of Services Marketing and Management*, Thousand Oaks, CA: Sage, 421–37.

Lucas, G. H., and A. J. Bush (1988). "The Marketing–R&D Interface: Do Personality Factors Have an Impact?" *Journal of Product Innovation Management* 5, 257–68.

McAllister, D. J. (1995). "Affect- and Cognition-Based Trust as Foundations for Interpersonal Cooperation in Organizations," *Academy of Management Journal* 38.1, 24–59.

McCann, J., and J. R. Galbraith (1981). "Interdepartmental Relations," in P. C. Nystrom and W. H. Starbuck (eds.), *Handbook of Organizational Design*, vol. 2, *Remodelling Organizations and their Environment*, Oxford: Oxford University Press, 60–84.

Massey, G., and P. L. Dawes (2001). "Integrating Marketing and Sales: The Frequency and Effectiveness of Methods Used in Australia and the United Kingdom," *ANZMAC 2001 Conference*, Massey University, Auckland, NZ.

—————— (2007a). "Personal Characteristics, Trust, Conflict, and Effectiveness in Marketing/Sales Working Relationships," *European Journal of Marketing* 41.9–10, 1117–45.

—————— (2007b). "The Antecedents and Consequence of Functional and Dysfunctional Conflict between Marketing Managers and Sales Managers," *Industrial Marketing Management* 36, 1118–29.

——and E. Kyriazis (2007). "Interpersonal Trust between Marketing and R&D during New Product Development Projects," *European Journal of Marketing* 41.9–10, 1146–72.

Matthyssens, P., and W. J. Johnston (2006). "Marketing and Sales: Optimization of a Neglected Relationship," *Journal of Business & Industrial Marketing* 21.6, 338–45.

Menon, A., S. G. Bharadwaj, and R. Howell (1996). "The Quality and Effectiveness of Marketing Strategy: Effects of Functional and Dysfunctional Conflict in Intraorganizational Relationships," *Journal of the Academy of Marketing Science* 24.4, 299–313.

Mintzberg, H. (1979). *The Structuring of Organizations*, Englewood Cliffs, NJ: Prentice Hall.

Moorman, C., G. Zaltman, and R. Deshpandé (1992). "Relationships between Providers and Users of Market Research: The Dynamics of Trust Within and Between Organizations," *Journal of Marketing Research* 29 (August), 314–28.

Murray, J. A., A. O'Driscoll, and A. Torres (2002). "Discovering Diversity in Marketing Practice," *European Journal of Marketing* 36.3, 373–90.

Narver, J. C., and S. F. Slater (1990). "The Effect of a Market Orientation on Business Profitability," *Journal of Marketing* 54 (October), 20–35.

Oliva, R. A. (2006). "Three Key Linkages: Improving the Connections Between Marketing and Sales," *Journal of Business & Industrial Marketing* 21.6, 395–8.

Olsen, E. M., D. W. Cravens, and S. F. Slater (2001). "Competitiveness and Sales Management: A Marriage of Strategies," *Business Horizons* 44 (March–April), 25–30.

——O. C. Walker, Jr., and R. W. Ruekert (1995). "Organizing for Effective New Product Development: The Moderating Role of Product Innovativeness," *Journal of Marketing* 59 (January), 48–62.

Piercy, N. F. (1986). "The Role and Function of the Chief Marketing Executive and the Marketing Department: A Study of Medium-Sized Companies in the UK," *Journal of Marketing Management* 1.3, 265–98.

Piercy, N. F. (2006). "The Strategic Sales Organization," *Marketing Review* 6.1, 3–28.

PONDY, L. R. (1967). "Organizational Conflict: Concepts and Models," *Administrative Science Quarterly* 12, 296–320.

PORTER, M. E. (1985). *Competitive Advantage*, New York: Free Press.

PORTER, T. W., and B. S. LILLY (1996). "The Effects of Conflict, Trust, and Task Commitment on Project Team Performance," *International Journal of Conflict Management* 7.4, 361–76.

PUGH, D., D. HICKSON, C. R. HININGS, and C. TURNER (1968). "Dimensions of Organizational Structure," *Administrative Science Quarterly* 13 (June), 65–105.

ROUSSEAU, D. M., S. B. SITKIN, R. S. BURT, and C. CAMERER (1998). "Not So Different After All: A Cross-Discipline View of Trust," *Academy of Management Review* 23.3: 383–404.

ROUZIES, D., E. ANDERSON, A. K. KOHLI, R. E. MICHAELS, B. A. WEITZ, and A. A. ZOLTNERS (2005). "Sales and Marketing Integration: A Proposed Framework," *Journal of Personal Selling & Sales Management* 15.2, 113–22.

RUEKERT, R. W., and O. C. WALKER (1987a). "Marketing's Interaction with Other Functional Units: A Conceptual Framework and Empirical Evidence," *Journal of Marketing* 51 (January), 1–19.

————— (1987b). "Interactions between Marketing and R&D Departments in Implementing Different Business Strategies," *Strategic Management Journal* 8 (May–June), 233–48.

SAGHAFI, M. M., A. K. GUPTA, and J. N. SHETH (1990). "Marketing/R&D Interfaces in the Telecommunications Industry," *Industrial Marketing Management* 19, 87–94.

SATO, M. (2002). "Does Trust Improve Business Performance?" in C. Lane and R. Bachmann (eds.), *Trust Within and Between Organizations*, Oxford: Oxford University Press, 88–117.

SCHMONSEES, R. J. (2006). *Escaping the Black Hole: Minimizing the Damage from Marketing–Sales Disconnect*, Mason, OH: Thomson South-Western.

SCHWENK, C. R. (1989). "A Meta-analysis on the Comparative Effectiveness of Devil's Advocacy and Dialectical Enquiry," *Strategic Management Journal* 10 (May–June), 303–6.

————— (1990). "Conflict in Organizational Decision Making: An Exploratory Study," *Management Science* 36.4, 436–48.

SCLATER, I. (2005). "Sales 4 Marketing?" *The Marketer* 14 (June), 9–21.

SENGE, P. M. (1990). "The Leader's New Work: Building Learning Organizations," *Sloan Management Review* 31 (Fall), 7–23.

SHAPIRO, B. (2002). "Want a Happy Customer? Coordinate Sales and Marketing," Boston: Harvard Business School; available at: http://hbswk.hbs.edu/pubitem.jhtml?id=3154&sid=0&pid=0&t=customer (accessed April 6, 2006).

SITKIN, S. B., and N. L. ROTH (1993). "Explaining the Limited Effectiveness of Legalistic Remedies for Trust/Distrust," *Organisation Science* 4, 367–92.

SMITH, B. J., and D. W. BARCLAY (1997). "The Effects of Organizational Differences and Trust on the Effectiveness of Selling Partner Relationships," *Journal of Marketing* 61 (January), 3–21.

————— (1999). "Selling Partner Relationships: The Role of Interdependence and Relative Influence," *Journal of Personal Selling & Sales Management* 19 (Fall), 21–40.

SONG, M., J. XIE, and B. DYER (1997). "Antecedents and Consequences of Marketing Managers' Conflict Handling Behaviours in Cross-Functional Integration: A Five-Country Comparative Study and Strategic Implications," Cambridge, MA: Marketing Science Institute.

————————(2000). "Antecedent and Consequences of Conflict-Handling Behaviours," *Journal of Marketing* 64, 50–66.

Souder, W. E. (1977). "An Exploratory Study of the Coordinating Mechanisms Between R&D and Marketing as an Influence on the Innovation Process," *National Science Foundation*, Final Report 75-17195, Washington, DC, August 26.

————(1981). "Disharmony Between R&D and Marketing," *Industrial Marketing Management* 10, 67–73.

————(1988). "Managing Relations Between R&D and Marketing in the New Product Development Process," *Journal of Product Innovation Management* 5 (March), 6–19.

————and A. K. Chakrabati (1978). "The R&D/Marketing Interface: Results from an Empirical Study of Innovation Projects," *IEEE Transactions on Engineering Management* EM-25.4, 88–93.

Strahle, W. M., R. L. Spiro, and F. Acito (1996). "Marketing and Sales: Strategic Alignment and Functional Implementation," *Journal of Personal Selling & Sales Management* 16 (Winter), 1–20.

Thomas, K. (1992). "Conflict and Negotiation Processes in Organizations," in M. D. Dunnette and L. M. Hough (eds.), *Handbook of Industrial and Organizational Psychology*, 2nd edn, vol. 3, Palo Alto, CA: Consulting Psychological Press, 651–717.

Thompson, J. D. (1967). *Organizations in Action*, New York: McGraw-Hill.

Tjosvold, D. (1985). "Implications of Controversy Research in Management," *Journal of Management* 11 (Fall–Winter), 21–37.

Tsai, W., and S. Ghoshal (1998). "Social Capital and Value Creation: The Role of Interfirm Networks," *Academy of Management Journal* 41, 464–77.

Van de Ven, A. (1976). "On the Nature, Formation, and Maintenance of Relations among Organizations," *Academy of Management Review* 4 (October), 24–36.

Vargo, S. L., and R. F. Lusch (2004). "Evolving to a New Dominant Logic for Marketing," *Journal of Marketing* 68 (January), 1–17.

Viswanathan, M., and E. M. Olsen (1992). "The Implementation of Business Strategies: Implications for the Sales Function," *Journal of Personal Selling & Sales Management* 21.1, 45–57.

Watkins, H. (2003). "Getting Sales and Marketing on the Same Team," available at: http://www.btobonline.com/cgi-bin/article.pl?id=10844 (accessed 22 April 2004).

Weber, M. (1947[1924]). *The Theory of Social and Economic Organization*, trans. A. H. Henderson and T. Parsons, New York: Free Press.

Webster, F. E., Jr. (1997). "The Future Role of Marketing in the Organisation," in D. R. Lehmann and K. E. Jocz (eds.), *Reflections on the Futures of Marketing*, Cambridge, MA: Marketing Science Institute.

Williams, K. Y., and C. A. O'Reilly (1998). "Demography and Diversity in Organizations: 40 Years of Research," *Research in Organizational Behaviour* 20, 77–140.

Williams, M. (2001). "In Whom We Trust: Group Membership as an Affective Context for Trust Development," *Academy of Management Review* 26.3, 377–96.

Winer, R. S. (2001). "A Framework for Customer Relationship Management," *California Management Review* 43.4, 89–105.

Workman, J. P., Jr., C. Homburg, and K. Gruner (1998). "Marketing Organization: An Integrative Framework of Dimensions and Determinants," *Journal of Marketing* 62 (July), 21–41.

YANDLE, J., and J. BLYTHE (2000). "Intra-departmental Conflict between Sales and Marketing: An Exploratory Study," *Journal of Selling & Major Account Management* 2.3, 13–31.

YUKL, G. (2002). *Leadership in Organizations*, Upper Saddle River, NJ: Prentice Hall.

——and C. M. FALBE (1990). "Influence Tactics and Objectives in Upward, Downward, and Lateral Influence Attempts," *Journal of Applied Psychology* 75.2, 132–40.

ZILLMAN, D. (1988). "Cognition–Excitation Interdependencies and Aggressive Behavior," *Aggressive Behavior* 14, 51–64.

....

CHAPTER 21

MARKETING:

THE ANCHOR FOR SALES

....

NOEL CAPON

21.1 INTRODUCTION

....

The activities conducted by the firm's sales force and marketing are inextricably linked. A well-thought-through market strategy[1] is useless unless it leads to a well-designed and executed sales strategy. A hard-working, highly motivated sales force will not achieve its potential unless its actions are guided by a market strategy that is well tuned to environmental realities. In a very real sense, marketing is the architect, and the sales force is the builder.

At a fundamental level, marketing is responsible for attracting, retaining, and growing customers; if it succeeds in this effort the firm makes profits, survives and grows, and enhances shareholder value. To accomplish these tasks, marketing's job to is identify and access the firm's market and other environments and to formulate a strategy to win in the marketplace. In order for the firm to win, marketing must succeed in two very different integration tasks.

External integration is well known to marketing students. Perhaps the most widely cited domain is the core set of implementation actions often called "the marketing" mix or "the 4Ps and an S"—product, price, place (distribution), promotion, and service. The external integration job is to ensure that the firm delivers this total package of benefits and values at the time and place that the customer wishes to buy.

Internal integration is less well known as a task of marketing. It focuses on the resources that the firm requires to succeed in its external integration. Marketing must pull together the firm's various functions so that the firm can execute on the core set of implementation actions. Operations, human resources, research and development, information systems, finance, technical service, customer service, and the sales force must all work together with the same mission of serving customers.

External integration is necessary to win in the marketplace, but the firm can only succeed with superb internal integration. The sales force has a critical role to play in both the external and internal integration tasks. However, the sales force can only do a superb job if it understands what marketing is trying to do. In my career, I have found all too frequently that sales managers, even senior sales managers, often have only a hazy idea about marketing's real *raison d'être*. Hence, in this concluding chapter, we focus on marketing's role and the critical tasks that it must accomplish. In a sense, we could retitle this chapter: "What every sales manager must know about marketing."

In this chapter, we identify the core role of marketing in the firm. In particular, we identify six marketing imperatives—the tasks that marketing must accomplish—and four marketing principles that act as guidelines for making marketing decisions. We then move to lay out the elements of a market strategy. The market strategy is a crucial output from marketing's efforts, and the sales strategy should implement the market strategy. Hence the sales force must understand how the firm constructs a market strategy, so it can creatively work within that framework to design and implement an effective sales strategy.

For the sales force to be effective, sales managers must know what marketing is trying to accomplish, for they have an important role in helping marketing be successful. They can also play a useful role in making sure that marketing is in fact doing what it is supposed to be doing. By the same token, successful marketing helps the sales force succeed. Indeed, if marketing is doing the wrong things or doing the right things but poorly, then the sales force is fighting competition in the marketplace with one hand tied behind its back. The goal of this chapter is to make sales managers more familiar with marketing, and by doing so to improve the performance of both these critical firm functions.

21.2 MARKETING: THE ANCHOR FOR SALES

integrate to bring together parts to form a whole (*Shorter Oxford English Dictionary*)

In a marketing book I wrote several years ago (Capon with Hulbert 2007), I explained why I had included a chapter on sales management. Now, in a volume focused on the sales force, I need to explain why I am contributing a chapter on marketing. The foregoing chapters in this volume delve deeply into an increasingly important area for business organizations—creating, directing, and managing sales force efforts. But organizations that heed the wisdom of my co-contributors will improve their performance if, and only if, they get their marketing right.

As I indicated in the introduction, in addressing the firm's markets, marketing is the architect, and the sales force is the builder. Absent an architect, if you ask a builder to build a house you will get a house, but it probably won't please you that well. Architects bring to house construction a set of skills and experience that builders cannot hope to replicate. It's the same in our world: a well-created, directed, and managed sales force will make sales, but unless the approach to the market has been well designed, the firm's sales performance will fall well short of what is possible. The purpose of this chapter is to put the preceding chapters and the sales force efforts in context in terms of the way that the firm addresses its markets.

Firms achieve success in many ways, but fundamental to all successful firms is their ability to provide value to customers. Because of their role as functions operating at the organizational boundary, especially their interfaces with customers, marketing and sales have a special part to play in designing and delivering customer value. Traditionally, marketing's role has been to undertake the research necessary to gain insight into what customers require, and to design value propositions that take into account these needs and required benefits. Correspondingly, the sales role was to execute on the offer the firm makes to implement this value proposition and to persuade customers of that value. Today, these roles are shifting as firm revenues are increasingly concentrated with fewer customers. Deep insight into these customers by the sales force and account managers at the domestic and global level is giving them a greater role both in securing insight into customer needs and in the design function. Regardless, marketing and sales together are both critical players in gaining customer insight, and designing and delivering value to customers.

The fundamental business model (Figure 21.1) shows that the firm's long-run goal is to enhance shareholder value. It achieves this goal by being profitable today and promising profits in the future. Profitability success allows the firm to survive and grow; survival and growth in turn lead to success in enhancing shareholder value. But to be successful in making profits, the firm must attract, retain, and grow customers. It is only by being successful with customers that the firm can hope to earn profits. Indeed, if the firm is unsuccessful in acquiring, retaining, and growing customers ultimately it will fail. General Motors and Chrysler did not really enter bankruptcy because they had a finance problem; they did so because they had a customer problem.

At this point in the argument, customer value becomes critical. The only way to attract, retain, and grow customers is by delivering them value. By delivering value,

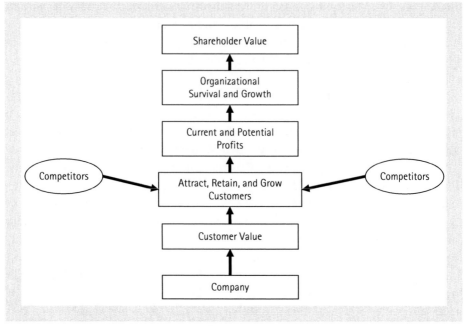

Fig. 21.1. The Fundamental Business Model

the firm is successful with customers and good things happen. There is just one problem; some other guys—competitors—are trying to do the same thing. If the firm does a better job than its competitors in attracting, retaining, and growing customers, it will enhance shareholder value. If competitors do a better job, ultimately the firm will fail and go out of business. This calculus is very simple yet very powerful. The firm does not enhance shareholder value directly; rather, enhanced shareholder value is the reward for delivering superior customer value. Of course, delivering customer value is the responsibility of the entire organization, but marketing and sales have especially critical, different, but related roles to play in ensuring that this occurs.

But how should the firm design and deliver customer value? We lay out a series of specific steps as the marketing imperatives in the next section. Suffice it to say here that, speaking broadly, the firm has many diverse but limited resources. If we believe that the core responsibility of the firm's managers, as agents for the owners—the shareholders—is to deliver them value by delivering value to customers, then the firm as a whole should devote its efforts toward that goal. The broad approach that management must take is to integrate the entire set of the firm's resources so that the "whole" that they form provides greater value to customers than the offers of competitors.

We do not have the space in this chapter to discuss deeply how to ensure that the firm dedicates its resources to delivering customer value. Suffice it to say that successful firms embrace a corporate purpose in which serving customers is the central goal. Management understands at a visceral level that enhancing shareholder value is not the core purpose, but rather is the reward for successfully delivering customer value. Only by focusing centrally on the delivery of customer value does the firm fulfill its core responsibility of delivering shareholder value.

We can say that organizations that "get it" operate with an external orientation in which marketing is everybody's business. After all, if the firm is unsuccessful in attracting, retaining, and growing customers, nobody gets a paycheck! Externally oriented firms look outward and condition their decisions on environmental realities. By contrast, internally oriented firms focus on specific internal functions and take their eyes off the customer ball. A firm may have an operations orientation, a finance orientation, or a technology orientation in which one particular function is ascendant and customers take second place.[2]

But an external orientation and a visceral understanding that delivering customer value should be central does not just happen—there are too many other organizational pressures. This viewpoint must be driven from the top of the organization. If the CEO truly believes in the customer-driven corporate purpose, communicates that belief broadly and frequently, and puts in place organizational structures, human resources, processes, and systems—especially measurement and reward systems—to support that purpose, then good things will happen. If this does not occur and priorities other than customer value are ascendant, management will neither be acting as a faithful steward of the owners' assets nor maximizing the owners' returns. As a not-unrelated matter for readers of this volume, when top management takes its eye off the customer ball, life can be very difficult for marketing and sales.[3]

21.3 MARKETING IMPERATIVES AND PRINCIPLES

21.3.1 The Marketing Imperatives

Regardless of the level of support that marketing receives from top management, its core focus is to ensure that the firm delivers value to customers—not just value, but more value than its competitors. However, it is one thing to assert that focus, quite another to act on that focus successfully. The firm will do a better job of customer value delivery if it adheres to six fundamental marketing imperatives that I discuss here. These imperatives function as a sort of job description for the marketing

Six Marketing Imperatives

    1. Determine and recommend which markets to address
    2. Identify and target market segments
    3. Set strategic direction and positioning
    4. Design the marketing offer
    5. Secure support from other functions
    6. Monitor and control execution and performance

Four Marketing Principles

    1. Selectivity and concentration
    2. Customer value
    3. Differential advantage
    4. Integration

Fig. 21.2. Six Marketing Imperatives and Four Marketing Principles

function. In the next section, we lay out four marketing principles that guide decisions within the six imperatives (Figure 21.2).

21.3.1.1 *Imperative 1: Determine and Recommend Which Markets to Address*

The firm must decide where to invest—to compete or not compete—in various markets. It must also decide how much to invest. In particular, the firm must answer critical questions about its business and market portfolio:

- In which new businesses and markets should the firm invest—people, time, and dollars?
- From which businesses and markets should the firm withdraw?
- Which current businesses and markets should continue to receive investment?
- How much investment should these various businesses and markets receive?

The decisions comprising Imperative 1 are crucial, for they define where the firm is going to play. To be made well, they require deep understanding of the firm's customer, competitor, complementer, and general environments (PESTLE: political, economic, sociocultural, technological, legal/regulatory, environmental (physical)). The sales force can play an important role for this imperative by feeding information into marketing. Of course, marketing rarely makes these decisions, but it should play a key role in advising top management. There are two important yet conceptually different areas: identify potential opportunities and make the case to top management; and make sure that marketing's views are represented in corporate decisions like mergers, acquisitions, and divestitures. Much research shows that over 60 per cent of acquisitions fail; better marketing input might lead to more favorable results.

21.3.1.2 *Imperative 2: Identify and Target Market Segments*

In any B2B (business-to-business) or B2C (business-to-consumer) market, customers have a diverse set of needs. A single offer directed at the overall market may satisfy some customers, but typically many customers would be dissatisfied. This marketing imperative states that marketing must identify specific market segments—groups of customers with similar needs that value similar benefits, with similar levels of priority. Any segment so defined differs from the other segments. Once the firm has defined the market segments, it must decide which ones to target.

Note that this imperative comprises two very different tasks and two very different skill sets. The first identify task requires some combination of creativity and analytic skill; marketing must secure and analyze data that allows it to map the chosen markets (Imperative 1) into a set of segments. The second target task requires a decision-making skill set. Given the set of segments that marketing has identified, the firm must select—target—some segment for effort and affirmatively reject others.

21.3.1.3 *Imperative 3: Set Strategic Direction and Positioning*

The firm must decide how to compete in the market segments it has targeted. For each target segment, marketing must formulate a market-segment strategy comprising performance objectives, strategic focus, and positioning. Performance objectives guide the firm's future strategic decisions for these segments; strategic focus states generally where the firm will place its efforts; and positioning defines how the firm will persuade customers to buy (or recommend) the firm's products rather than those of competitors. Marketing must make these decisions for each segment, and then integrate its various decisions across the set of segments it has decided to target. Together with identifying target segments, these elements constitute the core market strategy triumvirate of segmentation, targeting, and positioning (STP).

Other key considerations in setting strategic direction concern branding and lifecycle strategy. In recent years, many writers have shown that brands have enormous value for the firm. Branding decisions are often critical for delivering customer value and ultimately bring value to shareholders. Lifecycle strategy concerns the evolution of markets, and helps the firm to decide how to approach markets at different developmental stages like introduction, growth, maturity, and decline.

21.3.1.4 *Imperative 4: Design the Marketing Offer*

Imperative 4 focuses on the effective design of the market offer; it flows directly from the strategic decisions the firm makes in Imperative 3. The market offer is the total benefit and value package the firm provides its customers; essentially, it is the implementation of the value proposition. Tools for designing marketing offers are the best known part of marketing. The marketing mix elements—product, price, promotion, place, and service (a.k.a. the 4Ps and an S)—constitute the basic building blocks of the firm's offer to the market. As a key element in *promotion*, the sales force strategy forms an important element of implementing the market offer.

21.3.1.5 *Imperative 5: Secure Support from Other Functions*

Imperative 5 states that the firm's functions—like finance, human resources, operations, R&D, and sales—must work together to ensure that the firm makes the *right* marketing offer to customers. Marketing requires two very different types of support:

- **Support for design.** Marketing must encourage the different functions to design and deliver what customers require, regardless of current economic, operational, and technical feasibility. Securing this type of support requires significant strength, for many organizational members may say that the firm cannot, at the present time, do what is necessary. Marketing must continue to make the argument for meeting customer requirements, and press for assigning corporate priorities to serve key customer needs.
- **Support for implementation.** This support assumes the design is agreed upon and fixed. Marketing must secure organizational buy-in so that the firm delivers what marketing and sales promise and what customers require. This is a quite different challenge. Marketing has to ensure that other functions agree to perform in areas where they are already capable, and then make sure they do so. Of course, marketing must ensure that the sales force buys into its design.

21.3.1.6 *Imperative 6: Monitor and Control Execution and Performance*

The final marketing imperative focuses on monitoring and control—letting the firm know whether it is on track and achieving the desired results. All things being equal, if the firm is successful, it should keep on truckin'. If results are not reaching expectations, it must make changes. Essentially, marketing should continually answer three questions and act accordingly:

- Are the firm's various functions and departments implementing the marketing offer as planned?
- Is the firm's market and financial performance reaching planned objectives?
- Based on the current environment, are the firm's objectives, strategies, and implementation plans on track, or should it make changes?

The key issue for this principle is steering control. The firm should not wait for some long period to occur before it recognizes that a problem exists. Rather, it should monitor continually and take the appropriate action when it is clear that an unexpected trend is occurring.

21.4 THE MARKETING PRINCIPLES

The marketing imperatives state what the firms should do, but, in and of themselves, they do not provide guidance on how to make decisions within each imperative. That is a job for the four marketing principles. These principles form the basis for marketing decision-making. They act as guidelines for implementing the six imperatives. The firm should continually ask: Is this decision consistent with the marketing principles? They are:

21.4.1 Principle 1: Selectivity and Concentration

The Principle of Selectivity and Concentration provides guidance on how the firm should allocate its resources. It comprises two core elements:

- **Selectivity.** Carefully choose targets for the firm's efforts.
- **Concentration.** Concentrate the firm's resources against those targets.

The alternative is for the firm to spread its resources in many different areas. This principle especially provides advice to firms making decisions related to marketing imperatives 1 and 2: determine and recommend which markets to address, and identify and target market segments.

21.4.2 Principle 2: Customer Value

As we noted earlier, the firm's success depends on providing value to customers. The Principle of Customer Value is central to marketing's role. Customer and competitor insight should drive the design of customer value and implementation of marketing offers. Delivery of customer value should direct the firm's product and investment decisions—and its performance evaluation. The firm develops, produces, and delivers products and services, but customers perceive value *only* in the benefits that these products and services provide.

21.4.3 Principle 3: Differential Advantage

The Principle of Differential Advantage is closely related to the Principle of Customer Value but goes one stage further. Differential advantage is similar to having a competitive advantage, a unique selling proposition (USP), or an edge.[4] The Principle of Differential Advantage asserts not only that the firm should deliver value to customers, but that the value should be such that customers cannot get it, or believe they cannot get it, elsewhere. Differential advantage lies at the heart of every successful market strategy.

21.4.4 Principle 4: Integration

Successful integration is critical for all marketing efforts; it has two dimensions:

- **The customer.** The firm must carefully integrate and coordinate all design and execution elements it offers to customers. For example, poor advertising can ruin an excellent product or service; delayed promotional materials or an ill-trained sales force can doom a product launch.
- **The firm.** To achieve integration at the customer level, the firm must integrate and coordinate all of its functional activities. This is often very difficult. Different functions or departments often squabble over priorities, and senior management may send ambiguous messages. All too often, individual departments focus on defending their turf at the expense of delivering customer value. In addition, there must be integration up and down the managerial hierarchy so that lower-level decisions reflect the priorities set by senior management. Finally, the firm may have to integrate across business units; this is especially critical in the area of strategic (key) and global account management, where important customers increasingly want to deal with a single supplier interface.

Marketing and sales have special integration issues. At a process level, senior sales management should be involved in the market planning process and not merely recipients of what marketing decides. Parenthetically, it is a lack of process that gives rise to negative stereotypes about marketing and sales. Further, as noted, marketing develops strategy by market segment. Because sales forces are typically organized differently, sales has an important integration job to implement the market strategy.

21.4.5 Marketing Imperatives and Principles

In the preceding discussion, we laid out the core job of marketing as six marketing imperatives. We also presented four marketing principles that act as guidelines for making decisions contained in the imperatives. The sales force should have a very clear understanding of these marketing roles and the basis on which marketing people should make decisions.

What is perhaps more acutely relevant to the sales force is the design of the market strategy. The market strategy forms the basis for developing the sales strategy. The sales strategy is really the implementation phase of the market strategy; hence sales management is critical to implementing the market strategy. Sales managers should play a role in designing the market strategy so that they can develop more effective sales strategies. In the market strategy development process, sales management should have a seat at the table. Only by ensuring sales' participation in strategy formulation can marketing hope to get the sort of cooperation it requires to achieve its performance objectives.

21.5 A COMPLETE MARKET STRATEGY

We now move to laying out the elements of a market strategy—that it to say, the manner in which the firm decides to address customers in its chosen markets. We assume that the firm has already acted on marketing's recommendations from Imperative 1: determine and recommend which markets to address. We also assume that the firm has completed its segmentation analysis and has decided to address one or more market segments. The task at hand is to be successful in those market segments.

By definition, the needs and required benefits for customers in one segment are different from those of customers in another segment. Because the firm must deliver different values to customers in different segments, the basic unit of market strategy is the market segment strategy. For a firm that targets several market segments, its market strategy must combine several interrelated market segment strategies. First, we lay out the market segment strategy, then discuss integrating the several market segment strategies into a unified market strategy. Figure 21.3 shows the four pillars of a market segment strategy and how they relate to one another:

- **Performance objectives.** Stated as results the firm seeks, including both strategic objectives and operational objectives.
- **Strategic focus.** The broad direction of the strategy.

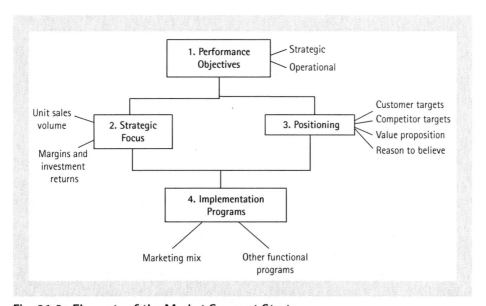

Fig. 21.3. Elements of the Market Segment Strategy

- **Positioning.** How the firm wants customers to view its offer so they select the firm rather than competitors. Components of positioning are customer targets, competitor targets, the value proposition, and the reasons to believe.
- **Implementation programs.** How the firm should implement the market strategy, including the marketing mix and supporting functional programs.

21.5.1 Performance Objectives

Before the firm figures out what it will do, it must know where it is headed. Performance objectives articulate the firm's goals for the market segment. They state clearly and simply what the firm is trying to achieve, broken down into two related components: strategic objectives and operational objectives.

- **Strategic objectives.** These objectives establish the type of results the firm intends to achieve; they are qualitative and directional. Strategic objectives are not concerned with numbers but declare, in general terms, how the firm will measure its success. The three broad categories of strategic objectives are growth and market share, profitability, and cash flow. Each is attractive, but they often conflict. For example, many firms set growth and market share as key strategic objectives, but then have to spend on fixed assets, working capital, and marketing expenses. This spending negatively affects short-term cash flow and profitability.

    Because they conflict, the firm must make trade-offs among its strategic objectives. It must set explicit priorities—primary and secondary—for various stages of the market or product lifecycle. The firm must resist the tendency to demand increased growth, market share, profit, and cash flow, all at the same time. The conditions for achieving on all dimensions simultaneously are very rare. If the firm is well positioned in a growth market, growth and market share are likely strategic objectives; in maturity and decline, profits and cash flow may be more appropriate (see also Slywotsky and Shapiro 1993: 97–107).

- Operational objectives. While strategic objectives are qualitative, establishing the general direction the firm wants to take, operational objectives are quantitative and time-dependent. They provide the numbers to attach to the strategic objectives. What types of numbers? The firm creates operational objectives to answer the following questions: How much is required, and when? Operational objectives should specify how much growth, market share, profit, or cash flow the firm should earn during a specific time frame.

    The firm uses operational objectives to evaluate performance. They should be SMART—specific, measurable, achievable, realistic, and timely. Operational objectives should also be challenging but not out of reach and demotivating. Early in the market segment strategy development process, the firm should establish tentative short-term and long-term operational objectives. As it develops its strategy and implementation programs, it should continually assess the budgetary implications. The firm should also revisit its operational objectives, ultimately freezing on them as finite expectations and targets.

- **Performance objectives.** Sometimes managers do not distinguish between strategic and operational objectives. Far too often, they state objectives in terms of profits: "Our profit target for 20XY is $45 million." In principle, setting a $45 million target is not wrong, but the problem is in not asking (yet alone answering) two basic questions. How will achieving this profit objective affect the firm's overall objectives? and How shall we get there?

  Improving short-term profits is not that difficult. Just cut spending on new products, advertising, sales promotion, and salaries; raise prices; and tighten credit terms. The firm will quickly increase profits, but in time it will lose market share and profitability. To avoid such results, the firm must articulate the trade-offs among the various possible strategic objectives. Early on, managers from all functional areas should agree on appropriate strategic objectives for the firm's long-term health; only then should numbers be added to form the operational objectives. Of course, ultimately these performance objectives will become sales targets and quotas.

21.5.2 Strategic Focus

Now that the firm has established performance objectives for its market segment strategy, it must decide where to allocate resources. The strategic focus does exactly that. Figure 21.4 illustrates the firm's options using a means/ends tree: management can assess, and choose among, the various alternatives for improving profits and return on investment (ROI). The tree has two main branches. Branch A focuses on increasing unit sales volume; branch B focuses on improving margins and investment returns. The firm must select among the branches and sub-branches to create a focus that best helps achieve its strategic and operational performance objectives.

- **Increase unit sales volume.** The firm has four sub-options. Two focus on the current revenue base; two focus on new revenues:

  - **Increase customer retention.** A firm's customer base is like a leaky bucket. Some customers defect to competitors, no matter how hard the firm tries to retain them. Plugging holes by deploying approaches to reduce customer defection helps the firm retain customers longer and grow faster.
  - **Increase customer use.** The firm can encourage customers to increase repeat purchases and/or buy the firm's other products. In B2C markets, it can sell its products in larger containers; speed up obsolescence by introducing new versions—like cars and software; find new product uses—like Arm & Hammer's baking soda for toothpaste, cleaning agent, cat litter, deodorizer, and

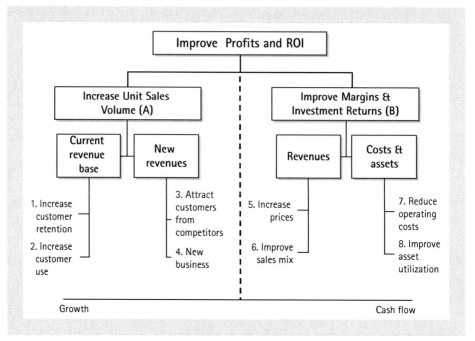

Fig. 21.4. Strategic Focus: *Developing Alternatives*

even cattle feed; and provide price incentives for purchasing large quantities. In B2B markets, many firms' sales forces work with customers to engineer new product applications. Alcoa helps auto firms reduce weight and increase gas mileage by replacing steel with aluminum. A powerful alternative is helping customers grow their businesses like the Intel Inside campaign. Other growth approaches include distributor training, joint promotions, advertising and promotion allowances, guarantees and warranties, and spiffs—cash incentives for retailer and distributor salespeople.

- **Attract customers from competitors.** The firm can add two types of customer—previous customers that defected to competitors and customers that purchase exclusively from competitors. These are quite different customer types. The first type previously had a relationship with the firm: the challenge is to win back these customers. The second has never had a relationship: the challenge is to switch them from competitors.
- **Secure new business.** Non-users have never purchased this type of product—from the firm or its competitors. In the previous options, customers already had product experience, and the firm's challenge was to beat competitors. Here, the firm has a double selling task. First, it must convince non-users to buy this type of product. Second, it must convince them to purchase from the firm.

Each of these sub-options has important implications for the sales force, requiring different knowledge, skills, and abilities (KSAs) and maybe different people.

- **Improve margins and investment returns.** Figure 21.4 shows that, holding unit sales constant, the firm has four sub-options. Two focus on increasing the firm's revenues; two focus on lowering costs and assets:
  - **Increase prices.** This option is straightforward: The firm increases revenues by raising prices—increasing list price, cutting discounts, reducing trade allowances, and/or tightening credit terms.
  - **Improve the sales mix.** The firm sells more of its higher-profit products and less of its lower-profit products. Gillette has pursued this strategy for many years by successively introducing more expensive multi-blade shaving systems.
  - **Reduce operating costs.** The firm has many options for reducing its operating costs—related and/or unrelated to marketing. Potential marketing-related cost reductions include the sales force, promotion and advertising, administration and training, and new product development. The firm may also be able to reduce operating costs by outsourcing, insourcing, and re-engineering work processes.
  - **Improve asset utilization.** Generally speaking, the firm has little asset investment in marketing—the closest are accounts receivable and finished goods inventories. Marketing can reduce accounts receivable by implementing stiffer credit terms and insisting on faster payments. Supply-chain improvements can reduce the firm's inventory investment. In the Wal-Mart–P&G relationship, marketing plays a major role in getting retail store transaction data into the P&G system. This helps reduce inventory throughout the supply chain and benefits not only P&G but also its suppliers and Wal-Mart.
- **Increase unit sales volume or improve margins and investment returns.** The big question is: How should the firm trade off among the various alternatives? After all, many are in conflict. Targeting a competitor's customers may be a viable option for increasing unit sales, but this will not be successful if the firm simultaneously cuts advertising and selling expenses.

  The answer is straightforward. The firm's choice of one alternative over another should closely parallel its primary strategic objective. If its primary strategic objective is growth, the firm should focus on alternatives that increase unit sales volume. If its primary strategic objective is increasing cash flow, it should select alternatives that improve margins and investment returns. If the primary strategic objective is improving profits, the firm should mix and match—select some alternatives from each branch. One thing is clear: the firm cannot pursue too many alternatives simultaneously without losing focus. The crucial issue for the firm is to closely integrate its strategic focus with its performance objectives.

21.5.3 Positioning

For many marketers, positioning is the heart of the market segment strategy. The firm seeks to create a unique and favorable image for its product in customers' minds. Clarity is key; confusion is the enemy of positioning. We emphasize the distinction between *targeting* a market segment and *positioning* in a market segment. The firm has already made the targeting decision; it selected one or more target segments from those it formed. Now we are focusing on developing a strategy to compete successfully in one of the target segments. Positioning requires the firm to make four key decisions within the segment: select customer targets, frame competitor targets, design the value proposition, and articulate the reasons to believe. It is absolutely critical that the sales force be very clear about the firm's positioning in the various segments it targets.

We discuss these decisions sequentially, but they are highly interrelated. Typically, the firm goes back and forth making these decisions until they form a coherent and integrated whole. Figure 21.5 breaks down the process by illustrating considerations in selecting customer targets, framing competitor targets, and designing the value proposition:

- **Selecting customer targets.** Customer targets are where the firm places the bulk of its marketing effort. If you don't target the right customers, your

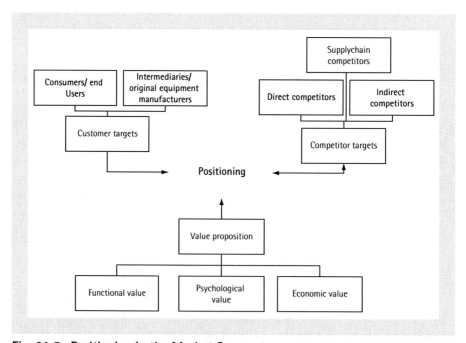

Fig. 21.5. Positioning in the Market Segment

chances of success will be slim. Three issues are important when targeting customers:

- **Structure of the distribution and influence systems.** The firm must identify the appropriate distribution and influence system for its products and services—possibly comprising multiple levels—to reach end user customers. Note that some customer targets might be outside the flow of goods and services, like architects for building products.
- **Targeting levels within the distribution and influence system.** The firm must decide at which level(s) in its distribution and influence system organizations should receive the most marketing effort—for example, wholesalers, retailers, end users, or other entities.
- **Targeting specific individuals or types of individual.** The firm must identify what specific persons or types of person it should target for effort at the chosen distribution and influence levels.

- **Framing competitor targets.** The firm decides which competitors to compete against. Competitor targets can be current and/or potential competitors, direct and/or indirect competitors, and/or supply chain competitors. The choice of competitor target depends on the firm's strength in the market segment. For small competitors, choosing the right targets is vital—large and strong firms can be less delicate. A relatively small soft drinks firm like Schweppes has less leeway than Coca-Cola. Key issues are:

  - **Categories of competitors.** The firm can place competitors in one of two categories—competitors to avoid and competitors the firm is quite happy, and chooses, to face. This partition helps the firm design its value proposition (next section) and guide the sales force.
  - **Customer perceptions.** Competitive targeting shapes customers' perceptions of the firm's offer. The positioning alternatives in Figure 21.6 suggest four potential competitors for 7-Up. The choice among them has important implications for 7-Up's market opportunities.
  - **Subtlety in competitor targeting.** The most effective competitor targeting may not be obvious. Who benefits from designating major accounting firms as the Big 3?—Number 3! The Big 3's competitor target is number 4. Visa advertises that many restaurants around the world accept its card, but relatively few accept AmEx. Visa wants customers to believe that AmEx is a direct competitor. But Visa's real competitor target is MasterCard.

- **Designing the value proposition.** A well-designed value proposition provides a convincing answer to a deceptively simple question: "Why should target customers prefer the firm's offer to those of competitors?" Positioning is the heart of the strategy—the value proposition is the heart of positioning. The firm bases its value proposition on functional, psychological, and economic value and

Claim	Type of Competition	Opportunity Implications	Customer Implications
"7-up tastes better than Sprite"	Comparison with individual direct competitor	One lemon-lime soda must substitute for another	Compare us
"7-up, the best-tasting lemon-lime soda"	Product form superiority	The whole lemon-lime product form	The best choice when drinking lemon-lime
"7-up, the uncola"	Out of product form	The cola product form	The alternative to drinking cola
"7-up, the real thing, the only one," etc.	Implied or claimed uniqueness	All beverages?	There's no other drink quite like it

Fig. 21.6. Example of Competitive Framing

related benefits—it shows how to gain customers and beat competitors. Other terms are "key buying incentive," "differentiated core benefit," "core strategy," and "unique selling proposition," but "value proposition" best captures the critical concept. Some examples of clear and effective value propositions are:

- Federal Express delivers on time—when it absolutely, positively has to get there overnight
- Apple's MacIntosh computers—it just works
- iTunes—Largest legal digital music library—it's easy to use
- HSBC—Global reach, local understanding
- Wal-Mart—Always low prices—Always

The firm's value proposition should be closely integrated with the principles of customer value and differential advantage. It should always:

- focus on satisfying important customer needs,
- attempt to meet these needs better than competitors and, where possible,
- offer values and benefits that are difficult for competitors to imitate.

In particular, the value proposition should follow the **BUSCH** system; it should be believable, unique, sustainable, compelling, and honest.[5] The *value proposition* plays two separate but related roles:

- **Externally.** Value proposition is the firm's major competitive weapon for attracting, retaining, and growing its target customers. *Value proposition* defines why the firm's benefits and values—functional, psychological, and/or econom-ic—are superior to competition in the target segment.

- **Internally.** Value proposition defines the firm's implementation task. It pro-vides the organizing framework for implementing and integrating all of its activities. Of course, it is also critical for the sales force to be very clear about what the firm is offering.

The firm must develop a value proposition for each target customer type. Con-sumer goods manufacturers often target both consumers and retailers, so they must develop two value propositions:

- **Consumers.** The value proposition typically focuses on specific consumer benefits and values. Detergent manufacturers such as Lever Brothers and P&G offer functional benefits like clean clothes, stain removal, and whiter whites. They also offer psychological benefits like caring for the family and the ability to demonstrate being a good parent.
- **Retailers.** The value proposition typically focuses on economic benefits like potential profits, promotional support, or functional benefits like ease of doing business, one-stop shopping, expertise, and product delivery.

Value propositions for separate customer targets are not independent but must be tightly integrated. Suppose the firm communicates its value proposition for con-sumers with heavy advertising and promotion. Its advertising spending weakens the economic value proposition the firm can offer to retailers. By contrast, private-label manufacturers offer retailers a strong economic value proposition based on low price by avoiding the heavy advertising and promotion incurred by brand-building manufacturers.

- **Articulating the reasons to believe.** Stating the firm's intentions in the value proposition is one thing; convincing target customers it will deliver on its promises is quite another. As the sales force well knows, the "reasons to believe" statement supports the firm's value proposition with compelling facts to make its claims believable—like scientific evidence, independent testing data, testi-monials, the firm's competencies and/or prior performance, and/or informa-tion on product attributes. Examples of possible reasons-to-believe statements include:
  - **Cisco.** Cisco has technical expertise in routers and many successful installa-tions worldwide.
  - **P&G—detergents.** P&G's long experience in detergents and a huge commit-ment to R&D.
  - **Citibank.** Citibank's vast network of branches around the world.
  - **J&J—Tylenol.** Clinical evidence of superior pain relief.

21.5.4 Developing Positioning Statements

Positioning is not what you to do a product—positioning is what you do to the mind of the prospect. (Reis and Trout 1993)

A compelling positioning statement is vital for guiding and coordinating the firm's marketing efforts. But developing the positioning statement is a complex, difficult, and time-consuming task. Many individuals may be involved. A senior Unilever marketing executive alleged that it often takes longer to develop product positioning than to develop the product! When P&G developed Whitestrips, it held off on expensive TV ads and store testing. It undertook a six-month online advertising and sales campaign while it assessed consumer interest and refined its positioning.

The positioning statement must clearly distinguish the firm's offer from competitors' offers: It should:

Convince	[customer target]
In the context of other alternatives	[competitor target]
That they will receive these benefits	[value proposition]
Because we have these capabilities/features	[reasons to believe]

Figure 21.7 shows an example of a positioning statement for Cemex, the Mexican cement producer.

Task	Focus	Positioning Item
Convince	Builders and contractors	Customer Target
In the context of other alternatives	Traditional cement producers	Competitor or Targets
That they will receive these benefits	Consistent delivery within 30 minutes of Cemex receiving an order (versus the 3-hour standard)	Value Proposition
Because we have these capabilities	A global positioning satellite system on each truck, and computer software that combines truck positions with plant output and customer orders to calculate optimal destinations and make en route redirections.	Reason to Believe

Fig. 21.7. Positioning Statement: *Cemex Example*

Positioning statements should be distinct, compelling, authentic, persuasive, and sustainable (DCAPS). Creativity in positioning can be crucial. Guinness Stout traditionally served a limited market of largely older men and women. In the early 2000s, Guinness repositioned its product as a friendly beverage for younger consumers. It also leveraged its brand heritage by offering the Guinness experience at more than 2,000 Irish pubs worldwide. Sales increased dramatically. Positioning is especially important for new products. Unilever and P&G "get it," but many firms launch new products with ineffective positioning. Many firms waste millions of dollars in ineffective advertising campaigns because of poorly developed positioning, and sales forces fail because marketing is ineffective in communicating its positioning statements. Positioning statements are not advertising messages, but DCAPS positioning provides excellent guidance for creative personnel at advertising agencies.

21.5.5 Implementation Programs

Strategic focus and positioning specify the firm's approach to achieve its performance objectives. Two types of implementation programs describe specific actions the firm must take to execute its approach (Figure 21.8). Marketing and associated functions like the sales force are responsible for implementing the marketing mix. Personnel from functions like finance and manufacturing implement other functional programs. Integrating the marketing mix and other functional programs is critical for optimizing the firm's effort. Top executive support is crucial for superb implementation.

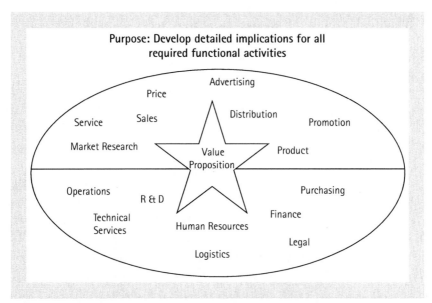

Fig. 21.8. Developing Implementation Programs: *Marketing and Other Functional Areas*

Marketing Mix Element	Steubenware
Product	Extremely high quality—Steuben destroys products with imperfections
Advertising	High-quality shelter magazines like *Good Housekeeping*
Sales promotion	Brochure material and display racks are high quality
Selling strategy	Focuses on product quality
Distribution	Few retail outlets, but high quality — specialty and upscale department stores
Service	High-quality pre- and post-sale service
Price	High price — reflecting high image

Fig. 21.9. Marketing Mix for Steubenware

- **Implementing the marketing mix.** Each element in the marketing mix must support the value proposition, and each element must also support the others. Figure 21.9 shows how the Steubenware marketing mix elements support one another for high-quality glass crystal in the gift segment. We assume that the value proposition revolves around psychological value, assurance that recipients will love Steubenware gifts.
- **Implementing the firm's functional programs.** Today's competition is so intense that the entire firm must work together as a competitive weapon by aligning all functional areas to support the value proposition. A leading US business periodical faced a difficult crisis when competition challenged its 50-year market dominance. The firm pulled together a cross-functional team of advertising, sales, operations, finance, marketing, editorial, publishing, fulfillment, and circulation executives to develop and implement a new market strategy. This approach successfully reinforced the periodical's leadership position and produced its best-ever financial result.

Domino's Pizza provides functional support for its value proposition—delivering hot pizza quickly. Domino's selects locations with easy access to many homes; its customer database saves time taking orders and making deliveries; and R&D produced technology to cook pizza en route to the customer. Disney designs theme parks to implement its value proposition—the fantasy. A lot happens behind the scenes. The customer never sees Mickey in the bathroom or two Dumbos at the same time; even street sweepers are scripted. Disney simplified its ticket book to one price, and installed an easy pass system to minimize the hassle of waiting in lines.

If one or more functional areas cannot provide support, the firm must revisit its value proposition. Going forward without full support is the cardinal marketing sin—making promises to customers the firm cannot fulfill. Customers do not care which individual or department is at fault. They expect and want the benefits and values the firm promised. They rightly believe the firm should fix the problem.

21.5.6 Managing Multi-segment Strategies

We just showed how to construct a strategy for addressing a target market segment. When the firm targets several segments, it must develop several market segment strategies. Each segment strategy requires its own strategic focus and positioning—customer targets, competitor targets, value proposition, and reasons to believe. The firm must make sure that each segment strategy is distinct. Pottery Barn Kids' positioning is distinct from Pottery Barn, but Pottery Barn is not well distinguished from its downmarket chain, West Elm.

When the firm targets multiple segments, it faces three possible situations in implementation:

- **Independence.** Individual segment strategies and their implementation programs are unrelated.
- **Positive synergies.** The firm enjoys positive synergies from implementation programs for individual segments. There are cost efficiencies from using the

Marketing Mix Element	Potential Negative Synergies	Approaches to addressing
Product	Increased production costs, delivery delays, increased inventory carrying costs	Modular design, just-in-time (JIT) assembly
Advertising	Exposure to different appeals	Ensure that appeals do not conflict
Sales force	Salespeople ineffective in multiple segments	Extra training or develop specialized sales forces
Pricing	Trans-shipment (diversion)	Manage price differentials; consider differentiating elements like brand and package
Distribution	Alienate existing intermediaries	Secure financial-service package for existing intermediaries; consider different brand, package
Service	Alienate customers not receiving premium service package	Try to ensure perceived equity, physical separation where possible

Fig. 21.10. Managing Multi-segment Strategy: *Possible Issues*

same sales force and similar distribution channels and/or sharing brand equity.

• **Negative synergies.** The firm suffers negative synergy by targeting an additional segment. New products may confuse the sales force—extending a brand may confuse customers. Almaden is a strong brand of popularly priced wine, but a $100 bottle of Almaden would probably not do well.

The firm's individual market segment strategies and implementation plans must be well integrated to form a coherent market strategy. Because of increasing complexity in customer need profiles, multiple-segment issues are especially intriguing and challenging. Figure 21.10 identifies the sorts of problems that may arise and potential solutions the firm may explore.

21.6 CONCLUSION

Marketing is the anchor of sales. Marketing decisions should form the broad parameters for sales force decisions and actions. In a very real sense, marketing is the architect and sales is the builder. The sales force will do a far better job if marketing has done a good job. It follows that sales managers should have an unambiguous view of what marketing is supposed to do, the sorts of decisions they should make, and the principles it should use to guide its decision-making. Sales should not be shy to push marketing to live up to its responsibilities and to challenge marketing's data and assumptions.

Sales managers should be engaged with marketing so they ensure that marketing decisions reflect the market understanding that only a sales force can provide. When sales has a deep understanding of marketing, the results can be a joy to behold. After all, marketing and sales are in the competitive battle together. The purpose of this chapter is to provide sales managers with a snapshot view of the marketing function. The success of this effort will lie in the level of marketing and sales collaboration that you are able to achieve.

NOTES

1. We use the term "market strategy" rather than "marketing strategy"—many functional areas, not just marketing, should help develop and implement the strategy.
2. Peter Drucker famously stated: "Because it is [the purpose of a business] to create a customer, [the] business enterprise has two—and only these two—basic functions, marketing and innovation" (Drucker 1954: 37–8).

3. As an imperfect gauge to their own firm's customer focus, readers may care to apply the C4I: Capon's Customer-Centric CEO Index: http://www.axcesscapon.com/en/the-c4i-capon's-customer-centric-ceo-index.
4. Differential advantage is similar to monopolistic competition—firms earn a return greater than the going interest rate.
5. Thanks to Mary Murphy for this acronym.

REFERENCES

CAPON, N., with J. M. HULBERT (2007). *Managing Marketing in the 21st Century*, Bronxville, NY: Wessex.

DRUCKER, P. F. (1954). *The Practice of Management*, New York: Harper & Row.

REIS, A., and A. TROUT (1993). *Positioning: The Battle for Your Mind*, New York: McGraw-Hill.

SLYWOTSKY, A. J., and B. P. SHAPIRO (1993). "Leveraging to Beat the Odds: The New Marketing Mind-Set," *Harvard Business Review* 71 (September–October): 97–107.

INDEX